Understanding
Social Inequality

THIRD EDITION

Understanding
Social Inequality

Intersections of Class, Age, Gender, Ethnicity, and Race in Canada

Julie McMullin
& Josh Curtis

OXFORD
UNIVERSITY PRESS

OXFORD
UNIVERSITY PRESS

Oxford University Press is a department of the University of Oxford.
It furthers the University's objective of excellence in research, scholarship,
and education by publishing worldwide. Oxford is a registered trade mark of
Oxford University Press in the UK and in certain other countries.

Published in Canada by
Oxford University Press
8 Sampson Mews, Suite 204,
Don Mills, Ontario M3C 0H5 Canada

www.oupcanada.com

Library and Archives Canada Cataloguing in Publication
McMullin, Julie Ann, 1965-, author
Understanding social inequality : intersections of class,
age, gender, ethnicity, and race in Canada / Julie McMullin &
Josh Curtis. — Third edition.
Includes bibliographical references and index.
ISBN 978-0-19-901092-9 (paperback)
1. Equality—Canada—Textbooks. 2. Social classes—Canada—
Textbooks. 3. Canada—Social conditions—1991-—Textbooks.
I. Curtis, Josh, author II. Title.

HN110.Z9S6 2016c   305.0971   C2016-904353-3

Cover image: © iStock/naqiewei

Oxford University Press is committed to our environment.
Wherever possible, our books are printed on paper which comes from
responsible sources.

Printed and bound in the United States of America

1 2 3 4 — 20 19 18 17

Contents

Part I

1 • Introduction

2 • Class and Inequality

3 • Gender and Inequality

4 • Race, Ethnicity, and Inequality

5 • Age and Inequality

12 • CAGE(s) and the State

13 • Conclusion: Equality, Politics, Platforms, and Policy Issues

Preface

When I was five years old, I decided that I wanted to visit a friend who lived quite a distance away. When I asked my mother and father if I could go to Susan's house, they said no. When I asked why, they said, "Because we said so." At this point I became aware of the fact that I was young and that being young didn't seem fair. I remember this incident because when my parents couldn't give me a good reason for not visiting my friend, I decided to run away from home. Luckily, as I was hitchhiking down the street with my hand open wide (my version of the one-thumb-up pose), a friendly woman picked me up and told me she'd take me home. I couldn't remember where I lived, so the woman drove me up and down many streets until we found one that I recognized as my own.

When I was 16 years old, I worked as a waitress, but I was paid less per hour than my 18-year-old friend. This too seemed unfair.

When I was 8, my younger brothers and I were playing outside on a very hot day. My mother took off my brothers' shirts for relief from the heat. When I started to take off my shirt, my mother told me that girls must keep their shirts on. "Why?" I asked. "Because," she said. I couldn't understand this at all; my brothers and I looked the same. I thought to myself that being a girl wasn't fair.

When I went to university, I discovered I was a member of the working class. My professors told me that capitalists employed workers at relatively low wages to ensure high levels of profit for themselves. They told me about the social and cultural disadvantages of being from a working-class background. Gradually my university experience began to make some sense. I couldn't figure out why my grades were only average despite my considerable effort. Part of it was that I didn't know how to play the game—that is, how to ask my professors for help, how to use a big library, how to study effectively—and no one I knew could coach me. This seemed unfair.

It wasn't until I was in my late twenties that I discovered I was white. This awareness came as I was reading Patricia Hill Collins's book, *Black Feminist Thought* (1990). Of course, at some level I knew I was white, but I wasn't fully aware of the privileges associated with the colour of my skin until then. This too seemed unfair.

Structures of inequality in Canada are organized along age, class, gender, ethnic, and racial lines. The preceding stories, as trivial as they may seem, show some of the ways in which this occurs. They show that inequality involves power, the ability of individuals or groups to impose their will, with or without resistance, on others. They show that ideology is an important dimension of inequality; that societal beliefs about what is appropriate for people to do on the basis of their sex, class, race, or age create advantage for some and disadvantage for others. The stories show that inequality is about the distribution of material, cultural, and social resources. And they show that the meaning people attribute to sex, class, race, and age is shaped by experience. These are some of the complex issues that I will consider throughout this book.

Acknowledgments

As I wrote the first and second editions of this book, I often reflected upon my life as an academic and thought about how privileged I am. Part of what makes my life so privileged is that I am surrounded by wonderful colleagues, family, and friends to whom I owe much gratitude for the help and support that they have graciously given me. When I was having trouble when I first began to write this book, James Teevan, Michael Gardiner, Edward Grabb, Victor Marshall, and Ingrid Connidis read my proposal and provided me with valuable feedback. To Ed I am especially grateful because he suggested that I send my proposal to Megan Mueller, then acquisitions editor for Oxford University Press. Megan liked my proposal and pursued the book project with vigour. Although Megan persuaded me to write this manuscript much more like a textbook than I had originally intended, I thank her for her welcome and very positive encouragement along the way.

In writing the first edition of this book and in revising it for the second edition, I was fortunate to work with very talented research assistants. Thanks go to Katherine Pendakis and Erin Demaiter (first edition) and to Catherine Gordon, Jennifer Silcox, and Juyan Wang (second edition), who did literature and data searches, tracked down references, and combed the Internet for stories that could be used in the boxed inserts. I am particularly indebted to Tammy Duerden Comeau, who also worked as a research assistant on both editions of the book. Tammy saved my sanity by agreeing to co-author chapters 10, 11, and 12 with me for the first edition and helped me revise them for the second. Finally, Emily Jovic deserves a very special thank you for her work on the second edition of this book. Emily's industry and resourcefulness helped to make this book what it is, and I will be forever grateful for her help.

For this third edition of the book, I took on a co-author, Josh Curtis. Josh worked on updating the data, included a new cross-national perspective, and added his own voice to the book through the new boxed inserts that appear here. Thank you, Josh.

Parts of this book have been adapted from some of my previously published work. Chapter 5 is a revised version of my article "Diversity and the State of Sociological Aging Theory," which appeared in volume 40 of the *Gerontologist*, and bits of chapter 9 were taken from "Social Class and Inequality," which appeared as chapter 14 in *Sociology: A Canadian Perspective*, edited by Lorne Tepperman and Jim Curtis and published by Oxford University Press.

As I was writing this book and working on both of its subsequent editions, Ingrid Connidis, Lorraine Davies, and I shared many moments of joy, sadness, anger, and frustration owing to both our work and our personal lives. It is impossible to imagine my life without having Ingrid and Lorraine to celebrate the good times with and to lean on when the times are tough. What an honour it is to have them as friends, collaborators, and colleagues.

I am very fortunate to have a wonderful family. My brothers, my sisters-in-law, my father-in-law, my nieces and nephews all serve as important diversions from my work. Emma and Scott are the loves of my life, and without them my work, and this book, would be for naught. Thank you both.

— Julie McMullin

I am grateful to Julie McMullin for the opportunity to collaborate with her on the third edition of this book. Although Julie might not know this, collaborating with her has been on my mind since I decided to become a sociologist. Before pursuing graduate studies at the University of Toronto, I made a phone call to Ed Grabb—a long-time family friend— to ask his advice about mentors, sociology departments, and universities in Canada. Knowing that I was keen to pursue research in social inequality and political sociology, he immediately mentioned Julie (along with several other important Canadian researchers, including Bob Andersen, John Myles, Lorne Tepperman, Bob Brym, Harvey Krahn, Neil Guppy, and Doug Baer, all of whom have influenced my research along the way). After weeks of deliberation, lost sleep, and of course more phone calls to Ed, I decided that Toronto would be the best fit.

Having taken Ed's advice to heart, over the next several years I followed the research of every Canadian sociologist he mentioned. When I finished my dissertation and the opportunity to study at Western with Julie presented itself, the decision was an easy one. I have enjoyed talking and writing about inequality in Canada with Julie. I am honoured to co-author this textbook with her, and I look forward to many more years of research and collaboration. Thank you, Julie!

— Josh Curtis

PART I

The first objective of Part I is to discuss and assess theories of class, age, gender, ethnicity, and "race" that have been used to explain inequality. Of course, it would be impossible to discuss all of the theories; instead, the first part of this book considers theories that have made influential contributions to our understanding of class, age, gender, ethnicity, and race in relation to inequality, especially in Canada. Further, theories that consider the structural nature of these factors are prioritized. However, because structures do not exist outside of the individual interaction that creates them, some symbolic-interactionist perspectives are discussed. In particular, some very good work has been done on gender and race from a symbolic-interactionist perspective, and it would be remiss to ignore it.

The second objective of Part I is to examine human agency and its relationship to social structure and human agency. Although most of the work on social inequality is at the macro, structural level, sociologists recognize that for social life to be better understood, assessments of the intersection between individual agency and social structures are required. However, there is very little agreement regarding the specific relationship between agency and structure.

The third objective of Part I is to integrate ideas from the various perspectives on class, age, gender, ethnicity, race, and human agency into a cohesive conceptual framework. The aim of this exercise is to provide an organizational tool that will enable us to explore social inequality without giving a priori emphasis to any of class, age, gender, ethnicity, or race. In doing so, we will be able to examine how structures of inequality are produced and reproduced through human agency and interaction.

1

Introduction

This is a book about social inequality, and it begins by describing the life of a woman I (McMullin) know. Anna was born to white, English-speaking parents of British descent in 1915, just after the First World War began. She grew up on a farm in Ontario with her mother, father, and two brothers. Although it was only a small farm, Anna's father and mother worked hard and were able to provide their family with the essentials of life. Anna graduated from high school, which was unusual for a rural girl in that day, and although she had the opportunity to go on to teachers' college, as her mother had done, she decided to marry John Warner, a local man who was seven years her senior. She married well. John's family members were well-to-do small-business owners, and with their help, Anna and John began their marriage in the late 1930s in relative financial stability. They moved to town and had two daughters, one in 1941 and the other in 1943.

Anna was always a homemaker, and John never had a stable job. His older brother, who was married and childless, inherited their father's business and John worked for him occasionally. John also bought houses, restored them, and sold them for a profit. Money was tight in the Warner household, but no one seemed to want for anything. There was food on the table, they had paid for the house in full when they bought it, and they had a few good clothes.

In 1970, John died suddenly in a car accident. He was 62 and Anna was 55. John's estate consisted of some savings and his house. His will stipulated that Anna could draw $200 per month from his estate until she either remarried or died, at which time the estate would be divided equally among her daughters. Suddenly, Anna was poor. Her income was well below the qualifying cut-off for social assistance, but she refused to apply for it and was too young for the old age pension. The will stipulated that she could not sell John's house. Aside from a brief stint in business college, Anna had no training, no work experience, and no marketable skills. Besides, at 55 she was unlikely to find work. Her daughter hired her to babysit her grandchildren, and for the next 10 years she made do with the clothes she already owned, shopping at yard sales, and eating anything that she could buy for next to nothing in the grocery store—old bread, dinted canned food, and so on. After 10 years Anna turned 65 and began receiving Old Age Security. Though she was still poor, she was no longer destitute. Five years later her sister-in-law, the widow of John's childless brother who had inherited the family business, died, leaving Anna one-third of her quite large estate. Suddenly, at age 70, Anna was better off financially than she had ever been before.

Throughout most of Anna's life she lived in a house with sturdy walls, running water, hot water, a toilet, and electricity, and she had enough food and nutrition. She never directly experienced a war fought on Canadian soil, genocide, or acts of terrorism. Anna lived in a country where human rights were respected, public gatherings were permitted, and things like freedom of speech and moving across borders were taken for granted. During her life she saw the birth of universal health care and took advantage of elementary and high school education that was provided without cost to all children.

Although this book is primarily about social inequality in Canada, it is important to recognize Canada's relative wealth and advantage compared with other countries of the world. Anna's life, while disadvantaged in some ways within the context of Canada, was privileged in many other ways because she was lucky enough to be born in one of the most prosperous countries in the world. In this edition of *Understanding Social Inequality*, we explore Canada's advantage in this regard by situating it in relation to other countries, such as Rwanda and China. We do this primarily through discussions in boxed inserts that describe what it is like to live in countries where the necessities of life and liberty are not taken for granted. In these boxes, we also situate the Canadian experience in relation to experience in other privileged European countries and the United States.

A central aim of this book is to develop a conceptual framework that will help explain the ebb and flow of poverty that Anna

experienced throughout her life. We often think of the conditions of inequality, such as poverty or homelessness (see Box 1.1), as inescapable fixed states, and indeed there is ample evidence that for many this is true (see 1.5 million people experiencing persistent poverty in Box. 1.2). However, the description of Anna's life demonstrates that, for others, experiences of inequality may be more complex, involving multiple transitions in and out of relative states of deprivation (see Cooke 2005; L. Davies, McMullin, and Avison 2001; Leisering and Leibfried 1999). And for those who live outside of Canada, poverty can sometimes be extreme (see Box 1.3).

As Box 1.2 shows, 7.6 million Canadians experienced poverty for at least one year between 1997 and 2001. Yet, in any given year, that number is lower. To understand inequality in this way requires a definition that considers durable patterns of advantage and disadvantage, the capacity of individuals to act toward change, and time. Unfortunately, the data in Box 1.2 comes from the previous edition of this book and could not be easily updated with current Canadian statistics. This is because Canada has witnessed profound cuts to social research under the Harper government. Programs such as the Canadian Policy Research Network (CPRN) and the National Council of Welfare (1969–2012), which served as an advisory group to the federal minister responsible for the welfare of Canadians, lost federal funding in 2012 (only requiring $1 million per year to operate). Statistics Canada's mandatory long-form census survey was also abolished for the 2011 Canadian Census. This has led to the underrepresentation of data on First Nations people, new immigrants, and lower-income Canadians. These budget cuts were puzzling given other national trends in data collection—most other governments celebrate such data collection, understanding that smart social planning needs robust data and analytics. This

HIGHLIGHT

Box 1.1 Measuring Poverty

Low income cut-offs (LICOs)—more commonly known as Canada's "unofficial" poverty lines—are established by Statistics Canada using data from the Family Expenditure Survey (now known as the Survey of Household Spending). Measures of low income were first introduced in Canada in 1968 based on family expenditure patterns. Overall, Canadian trends indicated that families spent nearly 50 per cent of their total income on food, shelter, and clothing. Currently, and somewhat arbitrarily, it is commonly believed that if families spend 70 per cent or more of their income (i.e., 20 per cent above the national average 50 per cent) on these basic necessities of life they would be living in "strained circumstances." LICOs indicate the level of income at which a family may be living in economic hardship because it spends a greater proportion of its income on the necessities of food, shelter, and clothing than does the average family of a similar size.

As the table below shows, separate cut-offs are determined for seven sizes of family—from unattached individuals to families of seven or more persons—and for five sizes of communities—from rural areas (a one-person LICO cut-off is $16,038) to urban areas with a population of 500,000+ (a one-person LICO cut-off is $23,298).

Statistics Canada does not refer to the LICOs as poverty lines, although it concedes that LICOs identify "those who are substantially worse off than the average." And, in the absence of official poverty lines, many analysts use LICOs to study the economic security of Canadian families and to report on important trends over time.

Statistics Canada's After-Tax Low-Income Cut-offs (1992 Base) for 2011

Size of Family Unit	Community Size				
	Rural areas outside CMA or CA[1]	Census Agglomeration (CA)		Census Metropolitan Area (CMA)	
		Less than 30,000 inhabitants[2]	30,000 to 99,999 inhabitants	100,000 to 499,999 inhabitants	500,000 inhabitants or more
	Current Dollars 2011				
1 person	16,038	18,246	19,941	20,065	23,298
2 persons	19,966	22,714	24,824	24,978	29,004
3 persons	24,545	27,924	30,517	30,707	35,657
4 persons	29,802	33,905	37,053	37,283	43,292
5 persons	33,800	38,454	42,025	42,285	49,102
6 persons	38,122	43,370	47,398	47,692	55,378
7 or more persons	42,443	48,285	52,770	53,097	61,656

1. Can include some small population centres.
2. Includes population centres with less than 10,000 inhabitants.

Source: Statistics Canada (2013). Income Research Paper Series (75F0002M). www.statcan.gc.ca/pub/75f0002m/2012002/tbl/tbl02-eng.htm

HIGHLIGHT

Box 1.2 Persistence of Poverty

Many people and families move in and out of poverty. Some stay in poverty for only a short period of time while others experience deep and persistent poverty. For children, chronic poverty has a significant effect on both their short-term and long-term developmental outcomes.

Approximately 7.6 million people or 30.7 per cent of the population experienced poverty for at least one year from 1996 through 2001.

Just over 2 million people lived in poverty for only one year. Nearly 1.5 million people lived in poverty for all six years.

Persistent Poverty

Almost 400,000 children lived in poverty for all six years between 1996 and 2001.

About 13 per cent of people with less than a high school education lived in poverty for all six years. Less than 2 per cent of people with university degrees lived in poverty for all six years.

Transitions in and out of Poverty

The one age group that stands apart is youth aged 18 through 24. This group has a high poverty rate in any given year but often tends to be poor for only one or two years at a time. They have the highest rate of moving into or out of poverty, almost double that of people aged 25 to 54.

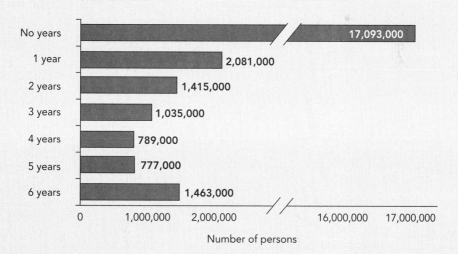

Number of Years in Poverty[a]

[a] Excludes persons whose status was not known in each of the six years.

Source: National Council of Welfare (2006a).

Global perspectives

Box 1.3 The World Bank Initiative for Reducing Global Poverty

The World Bank Group (WBG) was created in 1944 and was intended to help rebuild post–Second World War Europe. Since then it has grown into an international organization with the core goal being to reduce global poverty and inequality. To do this, the WBG offers zero- to low-interest loans so that middle-income and low-income countries can invest in areas such as education, health care, national infrastructure, the environment, and public and private sector development. Today, the WBG works closely with nearly 145 countries around the world to lessen poverty and to invest in and grow their economies. The World Bank Group's lending commitments have sharply increased in recent decades. For example, in 1981 $12.29 billion was invested in poverty-reducing initiatives around the world. Today, however, this group has invested in 12,414 projects around the world, and in 2015 alone $42.49 billion was loaned to countries in need.

The State of Global Poverty

Although groups like the World Bank are more common today than they were in the past, levels of global poverty are still very high. For example, in the developing world almost 17 per cent—or 1.91 billion—of people lived on less than $1.25 per day in 2011 (World Bank 2015). While this number has dropped from 1.93 billion people in 1981, it has been only a modest decline. According to GRID-Arendal, a research institute concerned with poverty and the environment, at the global level poverty has fallen from 52 per cent in 1981 to only about 26 per cent in 2005. However, as the map opposite shows, there are noticeable regional differences today. For example, poverty in sub-Saharan Africa has remained around 50 per cent since the 1980s, making it one of the most economically unequal countries today. East Asia, however, has seen a noticeable

was the first instance of many where sources from which data could be drawn in earlier book editions were eliminated. Fortunately, when the Trudeau-led Liberal government was elected in 2015, the mandatory long-form census was restored.

The nature and character of poverty are different depending on where in the world one lives. As Box 1.3 shows, in 2011 over 1 billion people in the world lived on less than $1.25 per day. Although the percentage of people who live in poverty has declined considerably, the World Bank's dream to eliminate poverty remains elusive, particularly in South Asia and sub-Saharan Africa.

Defining Social Inequality

Sociologists argue that innate personality flaws do not cause inequality. People are not poor because they are lazy or because they lack motivation, ambition, or intellect. They are poor because opportunities are distributed differentially in society on the basis of things such as class, age, gender, ethnicity, and "race." Sociologists are interested in why social inequality exists, what factors contribute to social inequality, how and through which processes it is maintained, and what changes need to be made to create a more equal society. A unifying assumption in much of the contemporary sociological work on social reduction in poverty. In 1981, 80 per cent of people living in East Asia lived in poverty, but the figure dropped to only 7.2 per cent in 2012 (www. worldbank.org). To provide more context about poverty and income inequality around the world, we turn to the following map, which graphically classifies countries by gross national income (GNI) per capita.

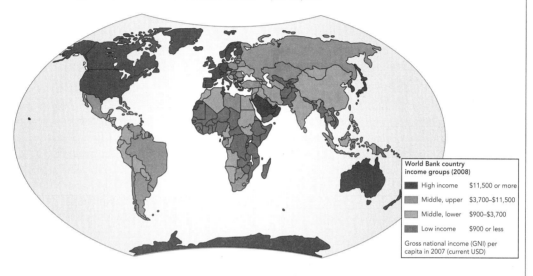

Global Poverty Map

Source: Hugo Ahlenius, UNEP/GRID-Arendal, data from: World Bank. 2008. World Bank list of economies (country classification). http://go.worldbank.org/K2CKM78CC0.

inequality is that it is a social problem. Few sociologists would argue that we need higher rates of poverty; more hungry, malnourished people in the world; or more disparity in wealth and power between the rich and the poor. Indeed, many sociologists search for ways in which problems of inequality can be alleviated, and in doing so, they specify policies and programs that would help to eradicate it. This line of inquiry is as old as the discipline itself, for Karl Marx and Max Weber both considered these important issues (see Grabb 2007 for a detailed account).

At a very basic level, inequality is a condition or situation that is not equal. This suggests that *inequality* does not simply refer to differences among individuals but rather reflects differences that matter, differences that result in unfairness and disadvantage for some and privilege for others. In Canada, class, age, gender, race, and ethnicity are differences that matter; hair colour or texture do not. **Social inequality**, as it is usually defined, refers to relatively long-lasting differences among individuals or groups of people that have implications for individual lives, especially "for the rights or opportunities they exercise and the rewards or privileges they enjoy" (Grabb 2007: 1; see also Pampel 1998). So, for example, compared with people from the middle and upper classes, people who are a part of the working class do not have the same educational opportunities and tend to have worse health. Women and members of racial

HIGHLIGHT

Box 1.4 The State of Canadian Homelessness

Homelessness emerged as a social problem—even a crisis—in Canada during the 1990s. Communities across Canada have struggled to respond as rates of homelessness have steadily risen. Declining wages (a minimum wage that has not kept pace with inflation), reduced benefits (weak pension and social assistance programs), and a dwindling supply of affordable housing have placed increasing numbers of Canadians at risk. According to 2014 research from the Canadian Alliance to End Homelessness (CAEH), a large responsibility for this problem rests on the federal government and its lack of investment in affordable housing. As the figure to the right shows, from 1993 to 2013 social housing spending and support dropped to $2.054 billion from $2.8 billion. In terms of GDP per capita, the amount of spending has declined from $115 per person in 1989 to about $60 per person in 2013.

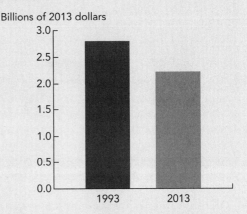

Billions of 2013 dollars

Federal Government Spending on Affordable Housing, 1993 and 2013

Source: Gaetz et al. (2014).

and ethnic-minority groups tend to work in bad jobs, while good jobs are reserved for men and members of privileged racial and ethnic groups. And, compared with middle-aged adults, older and younger people suffer longer bouts of unemployment and earn less money. In these examples, class, gender, race, ethnicity, and age are social structures of inequality that result in outcomes that matter. These **structures of inequality** are patterns of advantage and disadvantage that are durable (Tilly 1998) but penetrable.

At an individual level, the experience of inequality refers to the meaning that is attached to unequal life conditions as well as to the things that people do to manage or penetrate the structures of inequality. These issues reflect human agency or the capacity of individuals to interpret their situation and act to change it. However, the experience of inequality is at odds with the experience of privilege by which those in positions of power act to maintain their advantage and reproduce the structures of inequality (see Box 1.4). Furthermore, the experience of inequality must be examined within the context of social time. For our purposes, *social time* refers to issues of generation and the life course. The experience of inequality in this context is understood as a dynamic process that evolves throughout one's life and is influenced by the generation in which one is born.

In short, the perspective developed in this book suggests that to understand social inequality we need a framework that integrates social structure, human agency, and social time. Hence it is important to define each of these terms carefully and to discuss the assumptions made about them in this book.

In 2013, government spending to counterbalance homelessness was in the billions, yet

- 235,000 Canadians experience homelessness in any given year;
- 150,000 Canadians a year use a homeless shelter at some point;
- 50,000 Canadians are part of the "hidden homeless" each night—staying with friends or relatives on a temporary basis.

Ending Homelessness in Canada

In *The State of Homelessness in Canada*, Gaetz et al. (2014) argue that the Canadian government must target three areas in order to help reduce the homelessness crisis in Canada:

- **Eliminate chronic homelessness in Canada.** More than 20,000 chronically and episodically homeless Canadians will obtain and maintain housing with necessary supports.
- **Shorten the average time people experience homelessness to less than two weeks.** Our emergency services will no longer provide long-term housing but will return to their original mandate—to help people through a short-term crisis. Homelessness in Canada will become a rare, brief, and one-time experience.
- **Bring all three levels of government—as well as Aboriginal governments—to the table to support local plans to end homelessness,** develop coordinated local homelessness systems of care, and ensure that housing investment matches unique local priorities and support (Gaetz et al. 2014: 9).

Source: Gaetz et al. (2014).

Defining Social Structure

If we acknowledge the assumptions that sociologists make about social structures in their work, we can understand better why certain research questions are asked in the first place and we can interpret research in context. **Social structure** generally refers to relatively long-lasting patterned relationships among the elements of society (Abercrombie, Hill, and Turner 2000). Although this broad definition holds true regardless of one's sociological perspective, there is little agreement in sociology about what precisely social structures are and even less agreement about their relationship to individuals. In general, however, there are two dominant views of social structure; one has its intellectual roots in structural functionalism, the other in **critical theory**.

Following the work of Talcott Parsons, structural functionalists conceive of society as an all-encompassing social structure that may be decomposed into several specialized substructures. Examples of these substructures are the economic, the political, and the educational systems of society. From this point of view, the elements of social structures include social institutions (e.g., work organizations and political institutions) and patterns of social roles (Parsons 1951). Roles are the building blocks of institutions, and institutions are, in turn, the building blocks of society (Parsons 1951; Riley 1971). Structural functionalists tend to overemphasize the degree to which individuals conform to the values and norms established in the social structure and the degree to which society is based on consensus (Layder 1994). Furthermore, structural functionalism de-emphasizes the possibility of conflict in society or the possibility that individual choices are constrained by the forces of social structures.

Stratification approaches to the study of inequality tend to make assumptions about social structures that are in line with structural-functionalist thought (see Grabb 2007: 98–102). According to stratification theory, individuals can be ranked hierarchically according to socially desirable characteristics such as income, education, occupation, status, or prestige. This hierarchical procedure groups individuals together in discrete categories or social strata (J.H. Turner 1988). Because social structures are thought to comprise patterns of social roles that are acted out by individuals, much of this work focuses on the characteristics of individuals rather than on relationships among people. This led Tilly (1998: 34) to suggest, "Instead of reducing social behaviour to individual decision-making, social scientists urgently need to study the relational constraints within which all individual action takes place." The idea of "relational constraints" points to the importance of adopting a more critical view of social structures when studying inequality.

Critical approaches to studies of inequality and social structures are sometimes informed by Marxist sociology; they assume that social relations, especially class relations, are the fundamental elements of the social structure. Of course there are many definitions of *social class*, the details of which will be discussed in chapter 2. Put simply, however, *class relations* refer to the relative rights and powers that people have in production processes (Wright 1997). The structural significance of class relations is the manner in which they produce durable and patterned systems of inequality; central to this process is the conflict embedded in class relations. According to these approaches, inequality results largely from class structures, and thus explanations of inequality are reduced to issues of economic subordination. Yet, to understand inequality better, the structures of age, gender, ethnicity, and race must also be considered.

Structures of Inequality

In studies of inequality, scholars make different assumptions about which social structures are important. Some emphasize class, social gerontologists focus on age, feminist researchers concentrate on gender relations, and still others consider race or ethnic relations as the central element of social inequality. This is not to say that there has been no overlap. Many have considered at least two of these dimensions, but few have examined each of them in relation to the others. This book begins with the assumption that researchers should consider all of these factors and that neglecting one or more of them may distort descriptions and explanations of social inequality. Consider, for example, the following discussion of age, social inequality, and social policy.

The importance of age relations in the analysis of social inequality is crucial, particularly in light of population aging. The fact that Canada's population is aging is well known. At the beginning of this century, 5 per cent of the Canadian population was aged 65 and over; by 2014, this had more than doubled, to 17.3 per cent (www.ciaworldfactbook.com). Beaujot, McQuillan, and Ravanera (2007) predict that by 2051 the proportion of the population aged 65 and over will be 26.4 per cent. The proportion of the population aged 75 and over is growing even faster. By 2051 it is expected to reach 14.7 per cent, more than double the 2006 figure of 6.3 per cent (Beaujot, McQuillan, and Ravanera 2007). Although demographic predictions about the aging of the population vary depending on the assumptions made about future immigration, mortality rates, and fertility rates, most people agree that, barring disaster or unforeseen circumstances, the trend is real and significant.

The economic strain that an aging population may impose on Canada cannot be ignored. However, the crisis ideology that often frames political and media discussions of this topic serves to create a sense of urgency about Canada's financial problems while downplaying the economic needs of disadvantaged people. Thus, the emphasis is placed on Canada's fiscal well-being rather than on that of the over 3 million Canadians who are poor (Citizens for Public Justice 2012).

These discussions also create an environment of competition over the distribution of limited resources between younger and older adults. Although debates over generational equity have been slow to evolve in Canada (V.W. Marshall, Cook, and J.G. Marshall 1993), with health care and pension reform at the anterior of the political agenda, politicians started to make proposals in the 1990s that fuelled such debates. For instance, in 1994 Lloyd Axworthy, then human resources minister of Canada, suggested that a portion of the money spent on Old Age Security should be redirected toward job retraining for young working-aged people (*Globe and Mail*, 9 March 1994, cited in Myles and Street 1995). Indeed, poverty is an important issue among the working population. Figure 1.1 shows how income inequality has risen for single working-aged working adults from 1981 to 2011. In 2011, about 40 per cent of people under 65 were living below the LICO compared with only 19 per cent in 1981. As Figure 1.2 shows, the poverty rate for lone-parent families is drastically higher than for couples with no children and two-parent families with children. Yet one might ask why these monies could not also be redirected toward older people who are economically disadvantaged.

Part of the problem with policy directives like the ones mentioned above is that the population is categorized into the old and the young without taking gender, class, race, ethnicity, or further age distinctions into account. Close examinations of poverty rates do not support the simple bifurcation of the population according to age. For instance, in 2010 there were 2,114,950 men (about 8.4 per cent) and 2,224,030 women (about 8.5 per cent) between 55 and 64 living in poverty (almost 5 per cent more women than men). This gender difference was more pronounced among those aged 75 and over, for whom the poverty rate for women was almost 25 per cent higher (Statistics Canada 2011a). Being a single parent also differentially affects the poverty rate for men and women. In 2010, there were 2,834,695 women and 646,335 men lone parents living under the poverty line (about 23 per cent more likely for women) (Statistics Canada 2011).

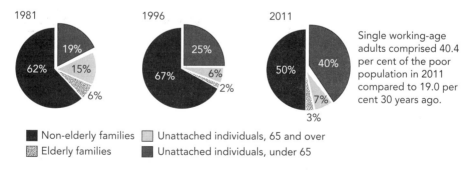

Single working-age adults comprised 40.4 per cent of the poor population in 2011 compared to 19.0 per cent 30 years ago.

■ Non-elderly families ▨ Unattached individuals, 65 and over
▨ Elderly families ■ Unattached individuals, under 65

Figure 1.1 Percentage Distribution of Poor Households, 1981–2011

Source: Citizens for Public Justice, *Poverty Trends Highlights, Canada 2013* (Ottawa: CPJ), 4. Statistics Canada, Table 202-0804. Persons in low income, by economic family type, annual.

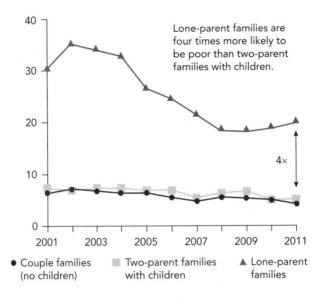

Figure 1.2 Poverty Rate among Working-Age Families, by Type, 2001–2011

Source: Citizens for Public Justice, *Poverty Trends Highlights, Canada 2013* (Ottawa: CPJ). Statistics Canada, Table 202-0804. Persons in low income, by economic family type, annual.

Poverty rates vary by occupation (which is often used as a measure of social class) among those under age 65. Persons employed in managerial and professional occupations have lower poverties rates than those employed in service industries (Statistics Canada 2011). Poverty rates also vary considerably across Canada. Map 1.1 displays three measures of poverty: the **low income cut-off** (LICO)—the level at which a family spends 63.9 per cent or more of its income on food, shelter, and clothing—the **low-income measure** (LIM)—a relative measure of low income that is set at 50 per cent of the adjusted mean household income—and the **market-based measure** (MBM)—an absolute measure of poverty that shows the level at which a household does not have the necessary income to purchase goods or essential services. Indeed, we must keep in mind that the "average" Canadian who falls below these cut-off points lives 33 per cent below these income thresholds. This means, for example, that the average single person below the LICO

in Toronto earns only $6,371.31 per year. It is important to keep in mind that full-time workers who earn minimum wage (e.g., $10.25 in Ontario in 2011) fall $1,361 below the poverty line each month.

These figures provide useful information about economic inequality in Canada, but they are limiting because they do not take more than two factors into account at the same time. This narrow type of analysis, which is typical of the analyses conducted by governments, is thus also somewhat misleading. One of the key assumptions that the analysis in this book makes clear is that class, age, gender, ethnicity, and race must each be considered in studies of inequality. Scholars have attempted to integrate two or three of these factors with varying success. The challenge here is to give equal theoretical weight to each of these factors in order to understand social inequality. To do this we will argue that a framework must evolve that considers at least three interconnected processes of social life: production, reproduction,

Remember that the average poor household in Canada relies on an income that is 33 per cent below the poverty line.

Low income measures only capture material dimensions of poverty; poverty also manifests itself in other ways including social exclusion, diminished well-being, and stress.

Poverty rates and lines in select communities in Canada, 2011

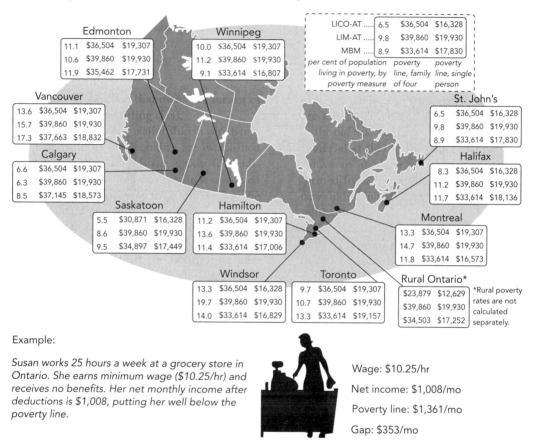

Edmonton

11.1	$36,504	$19,307
10.6	$39,860	$19,930
11.9	$35,462	$17,731

Winnipeg

10.0	$36,504	$19,307
11.2	$39,860	$19,930
9.1	$33,614	$16,807

LICO-AT	6.5	$36,504	$16,328
LIM-AT	9.8	$39,860	$19,930
MBM	8.9	$33,614	$17,830

per cent of population living in poverty, by poverty measure / poverty line, family of four / poverty line, single person

Vancouver

13.6	$36,504	$19,307
15.7	$39,860	$19,930
17.3	$37,663	$18,832

St. John's

6.5	$36,504	$16,328
9.8	$39,860	$19,930
8.9	$33,614	$17,830

Calgary

6.6	$36,504	$19,307
6.3	$39,860	$19,930
8.5	$37,145	$18,573

Halifax

8.3	$36,504	$16,328
11.2	$39,860	$19,930
11.7	$33,614	$18,136

Saskatoon

5.5	$30,871	$16,328
8.6	$39,860	$19,930
9.5	$34,897	$17,449

Hamilton

11.2	$36,504	$19,307
13.6	$39,860	$19,930
11.4	$33,614	$17,006

Montreal

13.3	$36,504	$19,307
14.7	$39,860	$19,930
11.8	$33,614	$16,573

Windsor

13.3	$36,504	$16,328
19.7	$39,860	$19,930
14.0	$33,614	$16,829

Toronto

9.7	$36,504	$19,307
10.7	$39,860	$19,930
13.3	$33,614	$19,157

Rural Ontario*

	$23,879	$12,629
	$39,860	$19,930
	$34,503	$17,252

*Rural poverty rates are not calculated separately.

Example:

Susan works 25 hours a week at a grocery store in Ontario. She earns minimum wage ($10.25/hr) and receives no benefits. Her net monthly income after deductions is $1,008, putting her well below the poverty line.

Wage: $10.25/hr

Net income: $1,008/mo

Poverty line: $1,361/mo

Gap: $353/mo

Map 1.1 Provincial Variation in LICO, LIM, and MBM Measures in 2011

Source: Citizens for Public Justice (2013). Statistics Canada, Table 202-0804. Persons in low income, by economic family type, annual.

and distribution—processes that are central to the survival of individuals and societies. In chapter 2, we define these processes, and in chapter 7, we elaborate upon how they are structured by the power relations that are assumed to exist among class, age, gender, and ethnic and race relations.

Class, age, gender, ethnicity, and race are conceptualized here as sets of **social relations** that are characterized by power and that are fundamental structures or organizing features of social life (Calasanti 1996; Calasanti and Slevin 2006). Power relations, which are essential to Weberian approaches to inequality, are determined by the ability of individuals in social relationships to impose their will on others regardless of resistance (Weber [1922] 1978). Conceptualizing class, age, gender, ethnicity, and race as social relations characterized by power suggests that conflict is present more often than consensus in these sets of relations (McMullin and Marshall 1999: 308–9). Indeed, a relational understanding of class, age, gender, ethnicity, and race requires an emphasis on "structured forms of power, organization, direction, and regulation that exist in modern societies and through which ruling groups maintain and reproduce their dominant positions" (Layder 1994: 159; see also D.E. Smith 1987). These structured forms of power are established and reproduced through daily experiences as individuals and groups interact with one another (Grabb 2007; McMullin 2000; D.E. Smith 1987).

These views of social structures and power fall more in line with critical approaches to social inequality than with those found in stratification theory or structural-functionalist approaches. It is generally assumed that social relations are composed of social structures and that conflict and power are fundamental characteristics of these relations. This does not mean that social relationships are in a state of constant conflict or that people engage in daily power struggles. It does suggest, however, that the possibility of conflict and power struggles in these relations is omnipresent. In chapters 2 to 5, we expand on these ideas by providing an overview of the principal theories of social class, gender, race and ethnicity, and age.

Chapter 2 considers sociological debates about the conceptualization of social class. It begins with a discussion of Karl Marx's and Max Weber's theories of social class. It then considers the elaboration and extension of these classics by leading neo-Marxist and neo-Weberian thinkers and briefly discusses stratification approaches to social class. Chapter 2

concludes with a working definition of *social class* that will be used in this book.

Chapter 3 explores the relationship between gender and social inequality. It discusses various feminist approaches to social inequality, including radical feminism and socialist feminism. In particular, this chapter considers how the combination of patriarchy and capitalism leads to gender inequality. The chapter moves on to examine the pervasiveness of gender inequality in daily life; it concludes with a discussion of the approach to gender that will be used in this book.

Chapter 4 examines conceptualizations of race and ethnicity in relation to inequality. Beginning with the contentious debate about whether the term *race* should be used at all, chapter 4 outlines and contrasts various points of view about this issue. It considers the relationship between the concepts of race and ethnicity, although the emphasis is more on the former than the latter. The chapter also examines some theoretical work that has considered the experience of everyday racism. It concludes with a discussion of how race and ethnicity will be conceptualized in this book.

Chapter 5 considers various approaches to the study of age relations and the conceptualization and social construction of age. This chapter discusses how age is a structure of inequality in society and considers the stratification approaches and political economy approaches to age relations in this regard. Chapter 5 concludes with a working definition of *age relations* that will be used in the conceptual framework presented in chapter 7.

Human Agency: Connecting Individuals to Social Structures

Too often, research and theory on inequality concentrate either on structure or on individuals rather than combining the two. The framework in this book highlights the importance of agency and its relationship with social structures. *Agency* expresses the idea that individuals do not passively conform to the circumstances of their lives. Rather, they are active participants in social relationships. They sometimes rebel and sometimes choose to follow the crowd, and so on. In this regard, we make two related assumptions about social life. First, "social structures do not stand outside of the human, social behaviour that produces them, yet, they nevertheless take on properties that transcend the behaviour of those who construct it"; and second, "while these properties of durability constrain and limit the agency of the individual they never do so completely" (McMullin and Marshall 2001: 114). In this light, although we assume that analyses of social inequality cannot be reduced to issues of individual motivation, ambition, and the like, individuals nonetheless make choices and decisions that influence their lot in life.

In chapter 6, we discuss how actors are conceptualized in this book by drawing on key works in several different theoretical traditions. In particular, we argue that we need to clarify and specify what is meant by *structuration theory* (Giddens 1984) by focusing on how individuals and structures are connected to one another. Thus, we place emphasis on how individuals negotiate real social structures, the mechanisms through which they do so, the constraints placed on individual negotiation by social structures, and how social structures gradually change or are reproduced through individual negotiations.

Lives in Time and Place

As noted above, *social time* refers to life course and generation issues. The life-course perspective allows us to examine how individuals manage social change and how past experiences affect their ability to cope. It also considers transitions and trajectories involving school, work, parenthood, retraining, job exit and re-entry, and retirement, as well as the timing of these, all of which influence inequality. *Generation* refers to the idea that people are born into groups that have meaningful significance because of the social-political culture of a given time in a given place. For instance, individuals who were born between 1910 and 1915 were coming of age during the Depression and their lives have been similarly shaped by that experience. But the effects of the Depression were experienced differently in farming communities in southern Ontario than they were in Vancouver, Montreal, or Toronto.

Although theories of social inequality have been slow to recognize the importance of spatial inequality (Lobao, Hooks, and Tickamyer 2007; Tickamyer 2000), patterns of social inequality clearly vary regionally in Canada. Higher rates of low income are found in the Maritime provinces, in northern Ontario, and in central Saskatchewan than is true in most of southern Ontario and much of Alberta. Inequality also varies drastically around the world. Map 1.2 shows comparative data on income inequality as well as the number of billionaires and their net worth as a percentage of their countries' GDP. As shown, the United States and China are among the most unequal and have the most billionaires whose salaries occupy the highest GDP percentage in their country. Europeans tend to be the most egalitarian and believe that a fair society should have few income gaps between occupations. The United States and China support equality of opportunity: as long as people can move up the class ladder, income gaps are seen as fair and just. This wide variation in inequality also results from structural and political factors that will be discussed throughout this book. For now, suffice it to say that where one is born and where one subsequently lives influences life chances and the likelihood of experiencing outcomes of social inequality.

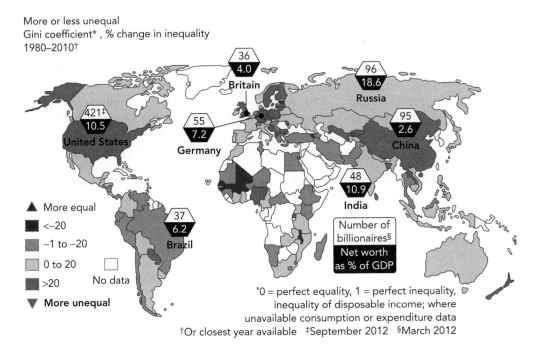

More or less unequal
Gini coefficient* , % change in inequality
1980–2010†

▲ More equal
■ <−20
■ −1 to −20
■ 0 to 20
■ >20   □ No data
▼ More unequal

Number of billionaires§
Net worth as % of GDP

*0 = perfect equality, 1 = perfect inequality,
inequality of disposable income; where
unavailable consumption or expenditure data
†Or closest year available ‡September 2012 §March 2012

Map 1.2 Cross-National Differences in Income Inequality, 2010

Source: *The Economist*, www.economist.com/node/21564414

In chapter 7, we discuss the life-course perspective and the concept of generations and integrate these perspectives into a conceptual framework of inequality that also considers the intersections between agency and structure. We revisit Anna's life and show how the conceptual framework developed in Part I of this book is a useful tool in explaining the ebbs and flows of social inequality she experienced.

The second part of this book considers empirical research on social inequality in various domains. In sociological research, studies of social inequality often consider the gap in earnings, income, and assets between advantaged and disadvantaged groups of people

(Albrecht 2007; L. Casper, McLanahan, and Garfinkel 1994; Grabb 2007; Langton and Pfeffer 1994; Martin and Robinson, 2007; Morris, Bernhardt, and Handcock 1994). To restrict analyses of social inequality to economic issues is limiting because inequality encompasses all differences between people that become embedded in the social structure and that influence social relations (Grabb 2007). Hence, among the other issues that are important to consider when examining social inequality are education, health, and unpaid labour.

Chapters 8 to 12 examine the ways in which the factors considered in the conceptual framework developed in Part I influence outcomes of inequality in families (chapter 8), labour markets (chapter 9), schools (chapter 10), health (chapter 11), and states (chapter 12). These chapters show how class, age, gender, ethnicity, and race affect outcomes of inequality through the processes of production, distribution, and reproduction. Each chapter concludes with policy implications and directions for further research.

Chapter 8 examines inequality in families. In particular it considers how the processes of reproduction are organized in such a way as to assign the unpaid labour responsibility of housework and caring disproportionately to women and, when these tasks are paid for, to women in ethnic and racial minorities. The relationship between these issues and the processes of production and distribution are also explored. Finally, this chapter considers the power imbalances in families and the violence that occurs there.

Chapter 9 outlines aspects of inequality in labour markets. It considers changes in Canada's class structure, the polarization of income, and issues related to skill and alienation in the workplace. Each of these points, and related issues that classify jobs as good or bad, are examined. Chapter 9 also examines how the social organization of production processes and the relationship between production, distribution, and reproduction lead to inequality in various working conditions and in the intrinsic and extrinsic rewards of paid work.

Chapter 10 considers educational attainment in Canada. In particular, it examines the barriers to education and how they are influenced by social class, race, ethnicity, gender, and age. It also examines the influence that each of these factors has historically had on educational attainment, how they affect educational attainment today, and the relationship between these factors and the returns on education achieved through labour markets.

Chapter 11 considers inequality in health in Canada. It critiques current theoretical perspectives that focus too little on how health experiences are structured by class, age, gender, ethnicity, and race. It moves on to consider the relationships between class, age, gender, ethnicity, and race and each of mortality, morbidity, mental health, lifestyle behaviour, and access to and use of health care services.

The state is ubiquitous; it weaves through all aspects of our lives and determines who is a deserving recipient of state benefits. The "deservingness" of Canadians revolves around the concept of citizenship, the central topic of chapter 12. Chapter 12 discusses unemployment insurance, parental benefits and maternity leave, social welfare, pensions, and Old Age Security and shows how they reproduce existing inequalities and shore up long-standing advantages for privileged groups. Chapter 12 also considers the role that the state plays in social regulation and how the law works to the advantage of some and the disadvantage of others.

Chapter 13 begins by summarizing the main points and findings of this book. Next, it discusses the ways in which research and policy would be improved by adopting an inclusive and integrated approach to inequality, such as the one outlined here. For instance, feminist scholars have long argued that much social policy, although seemingly gender-neutral, is not, and that this has harmful effects for women. We argue that the same can be said for age, ethnicity, and class and that when the four are considered together, the effects are particularly troublesome. The same is true of research. We argue that to understand social inequality, we must understand better how the bases of inequality are connected and how actors negotiate these structures in day-to-day life. Until we do so, our assessments of inequality will remain both biased and inaccurate.

⠿ Questions for Critical Thought

1. Some people argue that social welfare recipients are lazy, that they don't want to work, and that governments should not contribute to the "cycle of poverty" by providing these people with monetary assistance. These arguments focus on individual attributes in explanations of poverty. Discuss the alternative structural explanation of poverty.
2. What are the structural factors that contributed to the ebb and flow of poverty in Anna's life? How did agency affect the ebb and flow of poverty in her life? What role does social time play in explaining Anna's relative advantages and disadvantages throughout her life?
3. Is it possible to understand and explain poverty in Canada by considering only social class? Why or why not? Do you think other socio-demographic characteristics better explain poverty and inequality?
4. What are the advantages and disadvantages to stratification approaches to social inequality?
5. What have you learned about poverty in Canada? Is it possible to work for minimum wage and also live above the poverty line? Were you surprised to learn how little many Canadians live on?
6. Map 1.2 shows data on cross-national income inequality. What does this data tell you about the relationship between income inequality and the state? As this data shows, Canada is far from the most equal society in the world. Does this surprise you? Why or why not?

⠿ Glossary

Critical approaches, critical theory Approaches to the study of social inequality that (1) assume that social relations are the essential elements of social structures and that (2) assume that social relations are characterized more by conflict than by consensus. Commentators sometimes reserve the term *critical theory* to refer to the work of scholars associated with the Frankfurt school of sociology. These theorists, however, have strong intellectual roots in Marxist and Weberian thought and were certainly not the first to think "critically" about social life.

Low-income cut-off (LICO) The level at which a family spends 63.9 per cent or more of its income on food, shelter, and clothing.

Low-income measure (LIM) A relative measure of low income that is set at 50 per cent of the adjusted mean household income. It is categorized by the number of persons in each household.

Market-based measure (MBM) An absolute measure of poverty that shows the level at which a household does not have the necessary income to purchase goods or essential services—healthy diet, clothing, shelter, personal care, etc.

Social inequality The existence of advantages and disadvantages in many aspects of social life, including income, education, health, opportunities for paid work, and unpaid work responsibilities. The study of social inequality involves an examination of the factors that contribute to meaningful differences in the rights, resources, and privileges of individuals and groups of people.

Social relations Fundamental elements of the social structure. The term does not refer to interpersonal relations. Rather, social relations are structural and reflect power differences among groups of people. Examples of structured sets of social relations are class, age, gender, and ethnic and race relations.

Social structure A well-established pattern of social organization among the elements of society. Sociologists disagree over which elements of society are of most concern.

Stratification An approach to the study of social inequality that ranks individuals in a hierarchy on the basis of socially desirable characteristics such as income, status, wealth, or occupation. These approaches often draw on structural-functionalist thought and assume that social roles are the principal elements of the social structure.

Structures of inequality Durable patterns of social organization that influence social inequality.

▦ Recommended Reading

Davies, Lorraine, Julie Ann McMullin, and William R. Avison. 2001. *Social Policy, Gender Inequality and Poverty*. Ottawa: Status of Women Canada. A study that uses both qualitative and quantitative data to examine how the social policy changes in Ontario in the mid-1990s affected poverty among women.

Grabb, Edward G., and Neil L. Guppy, eds. 2009. *Social Inequality in Canada: Patterns, Problems, and Policies*. 5th edn. Scarborough, ON: Pearson Education Canada. This is *the* information source on various aspects of social inequality in Canada.

Leisering, Lutz, and Stephan Leibfried. 1999. *Time and Poverty in Western Welfare Studies*. Cambridge: Cambridge University Press. One of the very few books that take a life-course approach to poverty and emphasize agency in the transitions onto and off of social assistance.

National Council of Welfare. 2000. *Poverty Profile: A Report*. Ottawa: Minister of Works and Government Services Canada. An excellent source book with lots of data on and information about poverty in Canada.

Piketty, Thomas. 2013. *Capital in the Twenty-First Century*. Cambridge, MA: Harvard University Press. This book focuses on wealth and income inequality in Europe and the United States since the eighteenth century.

Ross, David P., Katherine J. Scott, and Peter J. Smith. 2000. *The Canadian Fact Book on Poverty*. Ottawa: Canadian Council on Social Development. This book provides a comprehensive overview of poverty in Canada.

▦ Relevant Websites

Make Poverty History
www.makepovertyhistory.ca

**The Make Poverty History campaign, symbolized by a white bracelet, started in the United Kingdom and aims to increase awareness of absolute poverty and pressure governments into taking action toward relief. The Canadian chapter calls for urgent and meaningful policy change in four areas: more and better foreign aid, trade justice, cancelling the debts owed by poor countries, and the elimination of child poverty in Canada.

Campaign 2000—End Child and Family Poverty in Canada
www.campaign2000.ca

**Founded in 1991, Campaign 2000 is a cross-Canada movement to eliminate child poverty in Canada. This organization aims to build awareness and support for the 1989 House of Commons resolution to end child poverty by the year 2000. Nearly a decade past the deadline, this group continues to lobby all parties in the federal and provincial governments to enhance social policies relating to child care, social housing, community services, and labour market supports.

Raising the Roof—Long-Term Solutions for Canada's Homeless
www.raising theroof.org

** Raising the Roof provides national leadership on long-term solutions to homelessness through partnership and collaboration with diverse stakeholders, investment in local communities, and public education.

2

Class and Inequality

When I look back on my childhood I wonder how I survived at all.... People everywhere brag and whimper about the woes of their early years, but nothing can compare with the Irish version: the poverty; the shiftless loquacious alcoholic father; the pious defeated mother moaning by the fire; pompous priests; bullying schoolmasters; the English and the terrible things they did to us for eight hundred long years.
— Frank McCourt, *Angela's Ashes*[*]

Introduction

The quotation that opens this chapter is from *Angela's Ashes* (1996), Frank McCourt's touching and funny yet disturbing memoir. Indeed, as one reads this book one wonders how Frank did survive his childhood. He did not have enough clothes to keep him warm, proper shoes for his feet, enough food, or much of a roof over his head. The neighbourhoods where he lived were decrepit and unsanitary. Frank's father was an alcoholic who couldn't hold down a job; his mother

was chronically depressed and thought it improper for women to work. In reading this book, one also wonders why Frank's parents didn't do something to change their lives—if only Mr McCourt had stopped drinking and held down a job, and if only Mrs McCourt had gotten a job instead of "moaning by the fire." But to blame the McCourts' poverty on an individual's alcoholism or mental health ignores the complex reality of the social structures in which the McCourts were embedded. Class, gender, and ethnic structures in Ireland during McCourt's childhood (the 1930s) were pervasive. English imperialism over Ireland produced and reproduced economic and other hardships for the Irish. Advanced education was essentially unavailable to the poor, women, and minorities. Labour laws did little to protect workers, and as a result, the conditions of the "working man" were deplorable. And, on top of it all, because Frank's parents came of age during the Depression, paid work was hard to come by.

The conditions of Frank McCourt's childhood may be explained by his class position, which, in turn, negatively affected his

---

*McCourt, Frank. 1996. *Angela's Ashes: A Memoir*. New York: Touchstone.

family relations, education, and health. The McCourt family was in a state of constant conflict. Frank's mother and father either fought or did not speak to one another, and the children were often ignored and neglected. Education, beyond the state-required minimum, was unattainable. The children had various health difficulties, the most severe of which culminated in the death of Frank's baby sister.

Although the effects of the McCourts' class position are evident, a more complex question is, what accounts for their lower-class position? Is it because they had no money and little food? Is it because Mr McCourt rarely had a job and when he did it was a bad one? Is it because his family had too little power or authority to impose their will on others? Is it because Mr and Mrs McCourt were poorly educated? Sociologists who study social class and inequality often ask questions like these. Each of the causes mentioned above likely contributed to the economic hardship experienced by the McCourt family. As we will show throughout this book, understanding inequality in Canada is not a straightforward task and is often the result of interrelated economic, social, and biological factors.

There is considerable disagreement among sociologists over how to conceptualize social class, how many classes there are, the extent to which class conflict exists, and how classes are formed. These points of contention stem from the analysis of social class that was put forth by Karl Marx and then critiqued and expanded upon by Max Weber. Volumes have been written about these issues since, and it is certainly beyond the scope of this chapter to engage in all of these debates. Instead, the ensuing discussion will focus on the question of how to conceptualize social class and will venture into other areas of debate only if they are important to the argument being presented.

Marx and Marxism

Marx: Class as a Productive Social Relation

In the *Communist Manifesto*, Marx ([1848] 1983: 203–4) wrote,

> The history of all hitherto existing society is the history of class struggles. Freeman and slave, patrician and plebeian, lord and serf, guild-master and journeyman, in a word, oppressor and oppressed.... Our epoch, the epoch of the bourgeoisie, possesses, however, this distinctive feature: It has simplified class antagonisms. Society as a whole is more and more splitting up into two great hostile camps, into two great classes directly facing each other—bourgeoisie and proletariat.

In these few lines Marx emphasizes the importance of class and class conflict in his work and implies that a distinctive feature of capitalism is the division of society into two central classes. But what is left unsaid here and in much of Marx's work is a precise definition of *class*, of what distinguishes capitalists from workers, and whether the polarization of the classes assumes that the **petite bourgeoisie** and others in the middle classes will become extinct. Ambiguity around these issues has led to various interpretations of who belongs to what class, how many classes there are, and what distinguishes the middle class from the others (Poulantzas 1975; Wright 1985).

Marx began what appears to be a systematic analysis of social classes in the last chapter of volume 3 of *Capital* ([1893–4] 1956: 178–9) but wrote only a few paragraphs before the project was interrupted. In the first two paragraphs Marx writes that the three classes of modern capitalist society are the owners of **labour power**, the owners of capital, and the landowners, but he suggests that this is the pure form of class distinction. "Intermediate and transitional strata obscure the class boundaries" even in the case of England, where the "economic structure of modern society is indisputably the most highly and classically developed" (178). However, Marx dismisses strata distinctions as immaterial to his analysis because of the tendency of capitalism to transform labour into wage-labour, the means of production into capital, and landed property into a form that corresponds with the capitalist mode of production.

In the next paragraph of this last chapter of *Capital* ([1893–94] 1956: 178), Marx suggests that the answer to what constitutes a class can be determined by answering the question "What constitutes wage-labourers, capitalists and landlords as the three great social classes?" For Marx, the answer to this question does not come from examining differences in income or social status. Rather, the key is the means by which people earn income, through their labour power, capital, or landed property. In the concluding paragraph, Marx's analysis breaks off just as he suggests that this distinction is not complete.

On the basis of the scattered references to class throughout Marx's work, researchers generally agree that, in principle, Marx believed that society is divided into classes that are defined by their relationship to the principal means of production in society (Giddens 1971; Zeitlin 1990). Put simply, in capitalism those who own the means of the production (the **bourgeoisie**) exploit labourers (the **proletariat**), who have no choice but to sell their labour power to—or to work for—the bourgeoisie in order to survive. The emphasis in Marx's work, then, is on relationships between those who appropriate the labour of others to make a profit and those who need to sell their labour power to earn a living. Hence, Marx is not so concerned with how resources are distributed within capitalism and instead emphasizes the relationships among people who engage in economic systems of production. In this regard, the most distinctive element of Marx's theory of class is the notion of exploitation. For Marx, classes are defined by the social relations that connect people to resources associated with the means of production. These resources define the class structure and shape economic life chances.

According to Giddens (1971: 37), Marx developed a dichotomous conception of two antagonistic classes; these classes "are constituted by the relationship of groupings of individuals to the ownership of private property in the means of production." Marx recognized that, historically, class societies were more complex than this theoretical dichotomy revealed (Giddens 1971; Zeitlin 1990). He was also aware that in bourgeois society, classes were divided into strata and that there were individuals who were located at the margins of the class system, such as lumpenproletariat and a reserve army of labour (Giddens 1971).

Erik Olin Wright (1999: 5) identifies two themes from Marx's work on social class that help us define what is meant by *class* in Marxist sociology:

1. *Social class is based in productive relations.* That is, individuals who engage in production processes have various rights and powers over the resources that are used in production processes.

2. *Social class is conceptualized in relational terms.* Unequal access to the rights and powers associated with productive resources (which by definition is relational) is thought of as class relations. Ownership of the tools that are required in production processes is a necessary but not sufficient condition for being a member of the bourgeoisie. Thus, the issue is not simply that capitalists own machines, but that

they "deploy those machines in a production process, hire owners of labor power to use them, and appropriate the profits from the use of those machines. A collector of machines is not, by virtue of owning those machines, a capitalist."

The preceding discussion focuses on two limitations to Marx's conceptualization of the class structure. Implementing a "classical" conception of social class in modern society is difficult. For example, we show that there is a great deal of uncertainty in Marx's work about how many classes there are (although most agree that Marx believed that as capitalism developed, society would become polarized into two central classes: the *bourgeoisie* and the *proletariat*). We also discuss how we should conceptualize social classes that do not always fall neatly into either the "capitalist" or "working-class" categories. Indeed, these are two crucial issues for present-day Marxists.

Neo-Marxism: Issues of Exploitation, Authority, and Credentials

More than two decades ago, Alfred A. Hunter (1981: 12) observed that "contemporary Marxism is a growing and several-headed beast which defies simple, summary description." This observation still applies today. Some rather orthodox Marxists who believe that Marx got it right stray very little from his ideas and theories (Braverman 1974; Rinehart 2006). Others, while maintaining the basic premises of Marx's work, elaborate, modify, and extend his theories with the belief that social life, the economy, and the nature of work have changed too much since Marx's time to leave his theories unchanged (Poulantzas 1975; Wright 1997). Into this latter category falls the work of Erik Olin Wright.

Although many neo-Marxists have rethought Marx's ideas of social class, we will focus on Wright's class analysis because it has arguably been the most influential neo-Marxist approach to class issues, at least in North American sociology. Shortly after completing his doctoral dissertation in 1976, Wright began his international research on class structure and class consciousness. Since that time he has written an impressive amount of work on Marxist conceptualizations of social class and has rethought his original ideas of class several times.

Exploitation is a central dimension of Wright's latest approach to class analysis. He argues that the following principles form the basis of class exploitation:

a. The inverse interdependence principle: The material welfare of one group of people causally depends upon the material deprivations of another.
b. The exclusion principle: The inverse interdependence in (a) depends upon the exclusion of the exploited from access to certain productive resources, usually backed by property rights.
c. The appropriation principle: Exclusion generates material advantage to exploiters because it enables them to appropriate the labor effort of the exploited. (Wright 1997: 10; Wright 1999: 11)

According to Wright, if the first of these two conditions is met, "non-exploitative economic oppression" occurs but is not technically a situation of class exploitation per se. Exploitation exists only when all three principles are operating simultaneously.

Let's consider these principles by way of example. Consider gender and social inequality in relation to (a) and (b) above. In Canada, men's material advantage (e.g., better jobs, higher salaries) is causally dependent upon women's material deprivations. This is largely because women are excluded from having access to certain productive resources primarily owing to their caregiving responsibility within families. This idea will become clearer in chapters 3 and 9. But the point here is that this is not class exploitation but rather, in Wright's terms, "non-exploitative economic oppression."

According to Wright, exclusions in (b) through ownership and the appropriation of labour are conditions of class-based exploitation. Consider, for instance, the owner of an auto parts manufacturing company. This person owns the factory or the infrastructure that is required to make the auto parts—the building, the machinery, and so on. In order for this owner to make a high income, the business needs to have a significant profit margin. To make a profit (that profit being the owner's material welfare), the owner of the company must pay those who work in the firm less (material deprivation) than they would make if the profits of the company were split equally among the workers. This is legitimized because the workers do not own the factory and have no property rights in this regard. In other words, owners take the work of those who work at their firm for their own benefit (appropriation) in order to make a profit. The result is class exploitation.

Note the relational component in each of these exploitation principles. Explicit in these statements is the idea that class exploitation involves social interaction and that this interaction is structured by sets of productive social relations that serve to bind exploiter and exploited together (Wright 1997: 12). Following Marx, Wright's conceptualization of class exploitation also highlights the presence in class relations of inherent conflict. Put simply, a profit-driven capitalist system requires that owners want workers to work longer, harder, and for less than the workers would freely choose to. Hence, class conflict results not simply over wage levels, but also over how much "work effort" is expected (Wright 1997: 18).

Turning back to the example of the auto parts manufacturing company owner and workers, it could be that if the owner reduced his profit margins, auto parts workers could work for half a year and make the wages that they currently make. But owners want to make as much money as possible in a profit-driven capitalist system, so they require a worker to work for the entire year earning the half-year salary.

Rising income inequality in Canada can be partly traced, at least in part, to steep declines in large-scale manufacturing. From 1980 to 2010 the percentage of the Canadian labour force employed in the manufacturing sector dropped from a fifth to a tenth of our population. This decrease coincided with low rates of unionization, which meant lower wages in the manufacturing sector that remained. Today, the likelihood of unions forming in new manufacturing sectors is small (Brady 2005; Tope and Jacobs 2009) because the **power resources** of the working class are low (Korpi 1983). This not only perpetuates, but likely increases the wage gap between low- and high-skilled workers (McCall 2001). In short, what has resulted is a shrinking of the middle class, at least in terms of income.

Canada's manufacturing sector once provided people with "good" working-class jobs, competitive wages, and greater job security. These jobs have since been replaced by lower-paying non-salaried service sector work (Andersen and McIvor 2013). As demonstrated in Box 2.1, Canada is not the only country that has felt the negative effects of declines in the manufacturing industry. The United States has arguably been more greatly affected.

To deal with the problem of "middle classes," Wright (1997) integrates two key concepts, authority and skill, into his ideas of exploitation. For Wright, authority involves domination and is one axis upon which employees in capitalist

Global perspective

Box 2.1 Manufacturing Jobs Have Taken a Hit in Today's Economy

OECD Picture

According to the US Bureau of Labor Statistics, manufacturing employment in the United States prospered in 1979, employing more than 19.6 million Americans. Many of these jobs paid well, were unionized, and had decent benefit programs. However, between 2001 and 2010 the American economy shed 33 per cent of its manufacturing jobs, meaning that almost 5.8 million people lost their jobs. The vast majority of other OECD (Organisation for Economic Co-operation and Development) countries have also recorded major job losses, although for the most part, they have been less adversely affected than the United States. The United Kingdom and Sweden reported similar losses (35% and 32% respectively), whereas Germany lost only 11 per cent of its manufacturing jobs, Australia 20 per cent, and Canada 29 per cent (Pilat et al. 2006).

Few countries have been hit harder by this decline than the United States. Michigan, for example, was once a manufacturing hub in the US. Because of this prosperous industry, it was once the eleventh richest state (it is now only the thirty-fourth richest). Today, the average wage in the Michigan manufacturing sector is only half of what it was (above $10.50 per hour) only a decade ago (www.marketwatch.com).

Sources: Barry D. Wood. (August 20, 2013) "The new normal in Michigan factories is lower pay." *Marketwatch.com*; Pilat et al. 2006. www.marketwatch.com/story/the-new-normal-in-michigan-factories-is-lower-pay-2013-08-20; and Pilat et al. 2006.

systems are differentiated. If owners of capital relinquish control over the production process to managers or supervisors, then people in these positions have various degrees of authority and are able to dominate their subordinates in the workplace. Furthermore, managers and supervisors earn wages that are higher than the costs of producing and reproducing their labour power. Managers and supervisors are in contradictory class locations because (1) they earn higher wages than what makes sense under the logic of capitalism, (2) they help to exploit the workers they manage, and (3) the capitalists for whom they work exploit them (Wright 1997: 20–1).

The second axis of class differentiation in Wright's scheme is skill. As is the case with authority, there is an emphasis here on the wage. Because certain skills or credentials are scarce resources in certain labour markets, people who possess them are able to command a wage that is higher than the costs of producing and reproducing their labour power. Furthermore, when workers have control over knowledge or skill sets, their labour is hard to monitor or control (Wright 1997: 22–3).

In the end, Wright comes up with a class typology that is outlined in Figure 2.1. Here we see that people are cross-classified according to their relation to the means of production, their relation to scarce skills, and their relation to authority. Also included in this scheme is the number of employees. This latter classification category refers to the number of people under the authority of each particular class location. For example, managers tend to have many employees over whom they have authority and dominance, whereas non-managers have authority over no one. Owners are separated from employees in this scheme. Owners are differentiated from one another only on the basis of whether they have employees and, if so, how many. Hence, owners who have only a few employees are thought to be different from both those who have many and those who have none. Employees, on the other hand, are differentiated

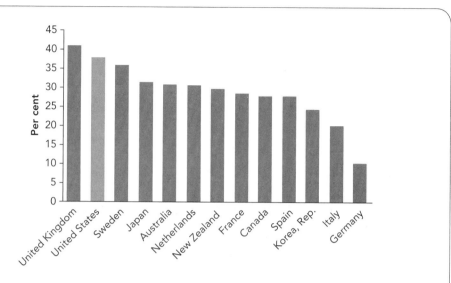

Sources: *International Comparisons of Annual Labor Force Statistics, 1970–2012*. U.S. Bureau of Labor Statistics, International Labor Comparisons. www.bls.gov/fls/flscomparelf/lfcompendium.pdf; www.innovationfiles.org /how-americas-manufacturing-job-loss-outpaces-other-leading-industrialized-countries/

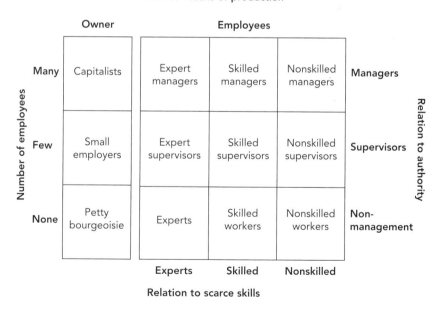

Figure 2.1 Wright's Class Typology

Source: Wright (1997: 25).

on the basis of skills, authority, and the number of employees "beneath" them. Expert managers, then, have high levels of authority and high levels of skill and tend to supervise many employees. They stand in most stark contrast to non-skilled workers, who have no authority and no skill and who supervise no other employees.

In this typology, the cells do not represent classes as such; rather, they refer to class locations within the capitalist class structure. The distinction here is a subtle but important one that allows Wright to cover all his bases. Unlike an earlier version of this framework, in which he refers to the various groupings in this model as classes (Wright 1985), in his most recent work Wright makes it clear that these cells represent class locations within an overriding framework of class relations.[1] In doing this, Wright can stay true to a Marxist version of class relations in which exploitation is at the core while at the same time identifying contradictory places within class relations that individuals occupy.

Again, let's turn back to the auto parts manufacturing company's owner and workers. The owner would fall in either the "capitalists" or the "small employers" cell of Wright's framework, while the worker could fall into any of the "employees" categories. Auto parts manufacturing companies have many employees, and occupations range from "expert managers" (head of the information technology department) to "non-skilled workers" (assembly-line workers). These workers are differentiated in terms of their class location: some have more authority and control in the workplace than others. But, according to Wright, regardless of the specific cell in which an employee is located, an exploitative, class-based relationship exists between that employee and the employer.

Wallace Clement and John Myles also take a Marxist approach to the study of social class. Through their work on Eric Olin Wright's Comparative Project on Class Structure and Class Consciousness, Clement and Myles (1994) developed a four-category class-classification scheme. As Table 2.1 shows, the capitalist-executive class controls both the labour power of others and the means of production. The "old" middle class—the petite bourgeoisie in Marxist terminology and in Wright's classification—commands the means of production but not the labour power of others (e.g., a local butcher owns her shop and employs one or two people). The "new" middle class controls the labour power of others but not the means of production. The advantage of this approach lies in its parsimony. It accurately explains the relations of ruling in Canada while at the same time eliminating the unnecessary and often tedious class-location distinctions of Wright's approach. And, although academically these distinctions are important, precise class categorizations matter little for those facing economic hardship. Box 2.2 tells the story of Canadian Eric Schuppert and his fall from Canada's middle class. It is stories like this that remind us that *actual people* live in, and fall out of, the class structure that social researchers theorize. Eric's life story reminds us of the importance of social class to inequality and also foreshadows the relationship between age and inequality that will be discussed in chapter 5.

Table 2.1 Clement and Myles's Class Typology

	Command Labour Power of Others	
Command Means of Production	Yes	No
Yes	Capital-executive	Old middle class
No	New middle class	Working class

Source: Clement, Wallace, and John Miles. 1994. *Relations of Ruling: Class and Gender in Postindustrial Societies*. Montreal: McGill-Queen's University Press, p. 61. Reprinted by permission of McGill-Queen's University Press.

HIGHLIGHT

Box 2.2 From Middle Class to Minimum Wage. With No Way Back

by Michael Valpy

Eric Schuppert's realization that he had left the middle class did not occur in 2008, when his $75,000-a-year salary with full benefits, pension and five weeks' paid vacation vanished along with his job as a public-service manager for the municipality of Caledon.

It did not occur when, at age 46, he had to borrow money from his parents to meet his monthly living costs. It did not occur when he was forced to sell his house in nearby Alliston.

It did not even occur when he found himself behind a counter at his local Tim Hortons—"Standing there in that crappy uniform with that dinky little hat on serving my friends coffee"—at the minimum wage of $10.25 an hour, taking direction from kids 20 years younger.

It occurred when the fear came to him that he would never be back to where he had been, that he was looking at a slammed-shut door to anything that resembled progress.

And with that fear, Schuppert, now 51 and working in Toronto as a night-shift college porter earning $30,000 a year, became part of a new phenomenon in Canada that social scientists haven't previously encountered: he self-deselected from the middle class.

Middle class is a state of mind, an emotional state, a feeling of optimism, a feeling of belonging to the great swath of Canadian society that has been resolutely marching forward in the sunshine for decades. It is an important element of social cohesion.

Eric Schuppert's narrative, to be sure, is about income and struggling to earn enough money to survive. But primarily it's about a place in society and his links to the connecting points of middle-class existence.

He's a soft-spoken, thoughtful, well-read man. He tells his story without complaints, and yet a listener can hear very clearly the pain he's experienced over the past five years.

He'd worked 22 years for Caledon, population 50,000, rising up the ladder from manager of aquatics

to a senior recreation position to manager of customer services with a staff of 10. His job included being in charge of the municipal cafeteria, overseeing the municipality's office supplies and managing the public reception services.

On the day he was fired—"restructured" in the language of the municipality's human resources department—he asked his boss, the chief administration officer, if he'd done anything wrong and was told no, the municipality just figured they could do his job better and cheaper without him.

"It wasn't a fun day," says Schuppert. "But you can't let something like that ruin 22 years associated with a wonderful community."

The CAO sent out an email to the staff saying he was leaving "to pursue other opportunities."

It was a bad time in the fall of 2008 to be out of a job.

Initially Schuppert says he felt marginalized but not hurt—an interesting word he chooses: without a job, he felt pushed to the sidelines of life.

In the first six months after being restructured, he sent out about 100 resumés and got three interviews, none of which led to anything. By August 2009, he had run out of money and needed financial help from his parents. He realized at the same time he was going to have to take whatever job he could find and not wait for something commensurate with his skills and experience.

Within a week he had a job at a Tim Hortons outlet a five-minute walk from his house in Alliston, just north of Toronto. When his friends and neighbours came in, "I could see the click in their eyes when they recognized me, and then they moved on pretty quickly."

In addition to standing for an eight-hour shift taking orders, Schuppert had to move boxes around. He has a bad back. The work gave him constant pain. He lasted a month and then quit.

The local McDonald's offered him a job. He asked if there was a chance to move into management, was

continued

told yes, and was then assigned to be the overnight cleaner starting at midnight. He declined.

At this point he started to cut off his social connections.

He went to work for Swiss Chalet, again asking for an opportunity to move into management. He was told yes. He worked for nine months, was given periodic management training but never got beyond minimum wage.

"George saved me from full-blown depression," Schuppert says. George was his dog, arthritic and going blind, and Schuppert loved and cared for him.

He'd saved for 20 years to buy his house. His house was part of who he was in his community, in his circle of friends. His house was where he once gave parties and cooked dinners until he could no longer afford to do either. The For Sale sign stood on the street in front of his house for eight months, proclaiming his downward journey.

Schuppert found an apartment in the Beach where he could take George for long, healthy walks. He kept looking for a job. He was turned down for a City of Toronto posting that involved working on its 311 municipal service, which irritated him, because he had led the project to design the service at Caledon.

And then he got the college porter's job.

The college staff, he says, are wonderful. The students he enjoys. He likes the opportunity to help people. He's provided with dinner. "I'm underutilized but there's dick-all elsewhere."

There's also the night shift. "I didn't realize just how lost you are. I live at home alone. I get up in the morning and everyone else has gone to work. By the time I get home, it's 11 o'clock and everyone else is in bed. I spend the whole day alone and that's depressing."

There's the fear—the fear that's made him say he's no longer middle class. "I still don't see anything more than $30,000 a year in my future. That's not a lot of money for a single person in Toronto. My biggest fear now is that I'm going to wind up on the street. I've just got to get back to trying to find jobs. If I don't I'm going to be well on the path to the working poor. I think progress has passed me by."

There's what Eric Schuppert identifies as the middle class things that are gone.

"I used to go out for dinner.

"I used to throw dinner parties at home. I love to cook.

"I used to have parties all the time.

"Dating. How can I take someone out at 14 bucks an hour?

"I don't get to see concerts and events any more. I used to see live music all the time.

"I have lost the ability to buy new clothes of some quality. I did get used to wearing a jacket and tie for 10 years and looking sharp. It is definitely a status thing."

All things that middle class people do in middle class society.

"No house."

Middle class people own houses, or at least a condo.

"I'm wondering if I'll ever have a meaningful job using my skills and experience again."

Middle class people have meaningful work.

George died two months ago. Schuppert is now looking for a smaller apartment "down the chain."

Source: Michael Valpy. (December 13 2013). "From Middle Class to Minimum Wage With No Way Back." *The Star.* Reprinted courtesy of the Atkinson Foundation. www.thestar.com/news/atkinsonseries/2013/12/13/the_incredible _disappearing_middle_class.bb.html

Weber and the Neo-Weberians

Weber: Class, Power, and Distribution

Some scholars argue that Max Weber's assessment of social class is in fundamental opposition to that of Marx (Parsons 1929; J. Turner and Beeghley 1981). Others suggest that it is more likely that Weber attempted to develop Marx's thought—agreeing with some of his points, disagreeing with others, and elaborating upon his ideas in a way that corresponded to recent developments in the capitalist system (Zeitlin 1990). Indeed, some of the concepts that are central to Marx's analysis—class consciousness, class conflict, and class interest—are found in

Weber's writing as well (Zeitlin 1990). Weber also agrees with Marx regarding the importance of property ownership in the assessment of class (Giddens 1971; Zeitlin 1990).

For Weber, classes are groups of people who share a common class situation. In *Economy and Society*, Weber defines *class situation* as the

> typical chances of material provision, external position, and personal destiny in life which depend on the degree and nature of the power, or lack of power, to dispose of goods or qualifications for employment and the ways in which, within a given economic order, such goods or qualifications for employment can be utilised as a source of income or revenue. ([1922] 1978: 57)

Weber argues that there are three types of classes: property classes, income classes, and social classes. A *property class* is one in which differences in property ownership determine the class situation. An *income class* is one in which "the chances of utilising goods or services on the market determines the class situation" (Weber [1922] 1978: 57). A *social class* is a combination of the class situations created by property and income, and one where mobility between the social classes is a typical occurrence either within an individual lifetime or over successive generations.

Weber identifies four main social classes: (1) classes privileged by property or education; (2) propertyless intellectuals, technicians, commercial workers, and officials who are possibly different from one another socially, depending on the cost of their training; (3) the petite bourgeoisie; and (4) the working class as a whole. Although these social-class distinctions are similar to those proposed by Marx (except in the emphasis on education and on the cost of training), Weber employs a different method in assigning groups of individuals to each class. For Weber, classes are comprised of people who have similar command over economic resources and who have in common a causal component

of their life chances (see the definition of class situation above). Marx, on the other hand, is mainly concerned with the social relations of production.

Parties and **status groups** are other pillars of social power according to Weber. By *parties*, Weber means voluntary associations that organize for the collective pursuit of interests, such as political parties or lobbying groups. A *status group* consists of a number of individuals who share a common status situation. Although members of a particular class may not be aware of their common situation, members of a status group usually are (Giddens 1971; Grabb 2007). Classes, status groups, and parties sometimes overlap, but not always. Thus, each is analytically distinct and central to any class analysis (Weber [1922] 1978; see also Giddens 1971; Grabb 2007).

Weber's assessment of status groups and parties and the analytical importance that he attaches to these multiple bases of **power** point to the fundamental difference between his analysis of class and Marx's. According to Weber, although status groups and parties are analytically distinct from classes, they are central to class analysis (Giddens 1971; Grabb 2007). For Weber ([1922] 1978), *status situations*, although related to class situations, are distinct from them and refer to the social status, prestige, and esteem that are associated with a social position. Unlike Marx, who believed that power is held by those who own the means of production, Weber felt that certain people in high-status groups derive power by virtue of their social position rather than through economic control.

The analytical importance that Weber attaches to the concept of power is evident in the preceding discussion. Unlike Marx, who believed that power relations are structural and cannot be separated from class relations, Weber ([1922] 1978: 38) defines *power* as "every possibility within a social relationship of imposing one's own will, even against opposition, without regard to the basis of this possibility." Weber clarifies this broad definition of power by introducing the concept of **domination**. Domination exists in social relationships when one person (or group) comes to expect that their orders will be followed by the other person (or group) (Weber [1922] 1978: 38–9).

Domination is a specific power relation in which "regular patterns of inequality are established whereby the subordinate group (or individual) accepts that position in a sustained arrangement, obeying the commands of the dominant group (or individual)" (Grabb 2007: 56). Weber states that although relations of domination are usually at work in associations or in cases where an individual has an executive staff, other non-economic situations are also characteristic of relations of domination. One of the examples Weber gives is that the head of the household exercises domination over the members of the household "even though he does not have an executive staff" (Weber [1922] 1978: 39).

Although Weber recognized that subordinate groups or persons accept domination for a host of reasons, his analysis focuses on three pure types of legitimate domination, or *authority*. *Traditional authority* is a dominating relationship based on the acceptance that those in charge should be in charge because of traditional right. Individuals might also be in dominant relationships based on *legal authority*, in which case subordinates accept the legal right of those in charge. Finally, *charismatic authority* refers to the situation in which leaders have control of others because of the leaders' appeal or charm (Weber [1922] 1978).

Three themes in Weber's concept of class separate his work from that of Marx. First, Weber's insistence that classes, class situations, parties, and status groups must all be considered if we are to understand the class structures of societies differs significantly from Marx's view. Second, and related to the first, is Weber's emphasis on power. Marx felt that power was derived from an economic base and was largely structural. Weber, on the other hand, saw power as multi-faceted, derivable from many sources, and with both structural and individual dimensions. And third, rather than adopting the social-relational approach to class in Marxist sociology, Weber focuses far more on distributional issues. For Weber, people's ability to gain access to scarce resources such as income and education is central to any analysis of class. Indeed, these three central themes of Weber's work lie at the heart of its appeal.

Neo-Weberian Approaches: Frank Parkin

In the tradition of Weber, power is a central component of Frank Parkin's approach to class analysis. But Parkin takes a rather different view of power than Weber, and indeed suggests that Weber's definition is unhelpful (Parkin 1979). Instead, Parkin discusses power in relation to the idea of social closure. *Social closure*, as discussed by Weber, refers to processes through which collectivities restrict access to resources and opportunities to those inside the group. According to Parkin, classes should be defined not in relation to the means of production, but rather in relation to their modes of social closure.

Parkin argues that the classes of the bourgeoisie are formed and continue through two means of social closure, one involving property and the other involving credentials. The issue for property ownership is that the exclusionary powers of certain groups determine the basis of whether individuals own property that can be used in production processes. The legal, exclusionary property rights that come with this ownership are critical for class analysis to the extent that they have "important consequences for the life chances and social condition of the excluded" (Parkin 1979: 53). The crucial issue in this exclusionary process of social closure is not exploitation, but whether property owners can legally exclude people from making a living. Hence, the role of the state in legitimizing social closure is central to Parkin's framework.

The second means through which social closure is invoked is *credentialism*, which is the "inflated use of educational certificates as a means of monitoring entry to key positions in the division of labour" (Parkin 1979: 54). Credentialism allows high-status occupations to limit entrance to their ranks by making the credentials for entrance into the occupation increasingly onerous. Professional occupations thereby limit the supply of their labour, thus heightening its value and status. Credentialism also masks variations in skill among the members of a professional group and in that way protects the least skilled among them from the sanctions that might otherwise come their way (less pay, demotion, firing). As is the case with exclusion on the basis of capital ownership, the state is important in legitimizing the exclusionary practices of credentialism. States legitimize exclusionary strategies by issuing professional licences only to members of professional organizations who have achieved the credentials required by the professional organization.

Recall that Parkin argues that social classes should be defined in relation to the modes of social closure. The two central modes of closure for Parkin are exclusion on the basis of property and exclusion on the basis of credentials. Both modes of closure use exclusionary rules to confer rights and privileges on some while denying those rights and privileges to others. Hence, according to Parkin, "the dominant class under modern capitalism can be thought of as comprising those who possess or control productive capital and those who possess a legal monopoly of professional services" (1979: 58).

That said of the dominant classes, the question that remains is, how does Parkin deal with subordinate class boundaries? If exclusionary practices are power tactics that dominant classes use to maintain social closure,

then, for Parkin, *usurpation strategies* are countervailing uses of power mobilized by subordinate classes to gain access to scarce resources or to achieve "distributive justice" (1979: 75). Members of subordinate classes have no legal property rights and have limited credentials. However, subordinate classes vary in the extent to which they can activate usurpation strategies. For instance, if a group of workers is unionized, those workers have considerably more usurpation power by which to achieve distributive justice than do workers who are not unionized (Parkin 1979). The middle classes, for Parkin, consist of persons who tend not to have legal property rights but who do have certain credentials. There is also variation among semi-professionals in the power they have to encroach on the privileges of professional groups. Such power depends, in large part, upon how successful a semi-professional group has been in gaining legitimate authority in the eyes of the state and of group members' clients. Semi-professionals are not, however, completely aligned with the "working class," for they use usurpation strategies to gain privilege and exclusionary strategies to maintain the privilege they already have. Parkin (1979) refers to this as a *dual-closure strategy*.

Several well-founded criticisms are levied against Parkin for his emphasis on the legal bases of power to the neglect of other dimensions of power (see Grabb 2007). But what is particularly problematic about Parkin's approach is his use of the term *power* to refer to the strategies that subordinate classes use for gaining access to scarce resources and privileges. This lies at the heart of Parkin's argument regarding class boundaries. Notably, Parkin sees usurpation as a mechanism of closure that is less powerful than exclusion, but does it really make sense to discuss this as an issue of power? We think not. Power is held by dominant groups in society and is structural in form. Individuals may draw on the power they have by virtue of being a member of a dominant group in order to get what they want. However, as Parkin points out, power is much more than the ability of an individual to exercise his or her will over someone else. To be sure, subordinate groups act; they struggle to get higher wages, more prestige, or more status—they mobilize themselves and lobby to achieve these goals. But do they use power in doing so? No. At best, to gain distributive justice, they use mechanisms such as resistance, influence, or persuasion.

The idea that subordinate groups do not hold real power is worth pursuing here. Parkin is certainly not the only scholar who argues that subordinate groups or individuals have power (see Giddens 1979). More radical thinkers such as Wright (1997) argue that workers have power because they control their labour and can therefore use that control to struggle for their interests. Yet although it is true that, collectively, workers can generate opposition to capital because they control their labour, to suggest that they are in a position of power as a result is misplaced. Further, although it is also true that a worker could choose not to work, the alternative to working for a wage is rather bleak in contemporary capitalism. Is this then a true choice that confers power upon the labourer? Imagine this rather extreme analogy: A man is being held at gunpoint in a secluded area by another man, who is demanding that the first man hand over his wallet. The victim in this case has two choices—he can either hand over the wallet or not. Suppose he chooses not to and is shot. The victim acted, he made a choice, and he used his agency, but did he use power in this situation? No. This analogy demonstrates that clear distinctions need to be made between power and agency, and this is true even in situations that are far less extreme.

Ironically, though, the strength of Parkin's approach lies in this criticism of his concept of power. In Parkin's model, the importance of human action, both collective and individual, is evident. Hence, his model effectively considers the intersection of individual action and social structure, and on this score it is an improvement over most theoretical and empirical accounts of social inequality.

Neo-Weberian Approaches: John Goldthorpe

The class schema of John Goldthorpe and his colleagues (see also Erickson, Goldthorpe, and Portocarero 1979; Goldthorpe 1980; Erikson and Goldthorpe 1992) is widely used in comparative class analysis. Following Weber's classic theory, this conceptualization of class takes into account differences in life chances (i.e., "experiences of affluence or hardship, of economic security or insecurity, of prospects of continuing material advance, or of unyielding material constraints" [Erikson and Goldthorpe 1992: 236]), and it groups classes based on their command over economic resources.

This conceptualization of class differentiates the positions people hold within labour markets and production units, but it also acknowledges differences in employment relations (Erikson and Goldthorpe 1992: 37). In this regard, one distinction is based on employment positions that are regulated by *labour contracts* compared with those based on *service* relationships. Differences in employment relations are given close attention in Goldthorpe's famous book *The Constant Flux*:

> Employment relationships regulated by a labour contract entail a relatively short-term and specific exchange of money for effort. Employees supply more-or-less discrete amounts of labour, under the supervision of the employer or of the employer's agents, in return for wages which are calculated on a "piece" or time basis. In contrast, employment relationships within a bureaucratic context involve a longer-term and generally more diffuse exchange. Employees render service to their employing organization

in return for "compensation" which takes the form not only of reward for work done, through a salary and various perquisites, but also comprises important prospective elements—for example, salary increments on an established scale, assurances of security both in employment and, through pensions rights, after retirement, and, above all, well-defined career opportunities. (Erikson and Goldthorpe 1992: 41–2)

Goldthorpe's schema is heavily organized by employment relationships related to service and labour contracts. Classes are also organized by skill level, specialized knowledge, expertise, and job reward. Those who belong to the "service class" are often trusted more by their employers and are given greater workplace autonomy. Lower- and working-class occupations are more often closely regulated, non-salaried, and have more precarious contractual obligations.

Table 2.2 displays three versions of Goldthorpe's class concept. As this table shows, some class groups can be aggregated together to produce more simplified versions. Class "I" is comprised of high-grade professionals, technicians, and managers. Class "II" represents lower-grade workers in these positions. For example, an economics professor at the Richard Ivey Business School in London, Ontario, would belong to Class "I," whereas a grade 9 math teacher at London Central Secondary would belong to Class "II." Employees in Class "III," or the "routine non-manual" class, are distinct from higher service sector employees because they tend to be paid hourly wages instead of salaries and are often non-unionized. Examples include administrative staff, commerce, and secretarial workers. Class "IV" includes self-employed and small-scale business owners (petite bourgeoisie). In some categorizations, farm owners are included in this class, but as

Table 2.2 The Goldthorpe Class Schema

11-Class (Maximally Disaggregated) Version	7-Class Version	4-Class Version
I Upper service class	**I** Upper service class	**I+II** Service class
II Lower service class	**II** Lower service class	
IIIa Routine non-manual employees, higher grade	**III** Routine non-manual	**III+V** Intermediate class
IIIb Routine non-manual employees, higher grade		
IVa Small proprietors with employees	**IV** Petty-bourgeoisie	**IV** Petty-bourgeoisie
IVb Small proprietors without employees		
IVc Farmers and other self-employed workers in primary production		
V Lower grade technicians and supervisors of manual workers	**V** Technicians and supervisors	**III+V** Intermediate class
VI Skilled manual workers	**VI** Skilled manual	**VI+VII** Manual class
VIIa Semi- and unskilled manual workers (not in agriculture)	**VII** Non-skilled manual	
VIIb Semi- and unskilled manual workers in agriculture		

Source: From Richard Breen, (2005), "Foundation of a neo-Weberian class analysis", Erick Olin Wright (ed.), *Approaches to Class Analysis*. New York: Cambridge University Press, p. 41.

Table 2.2 shows, they could represent a distinct class in and of themselves. The remaining classes make up the lower, most unequal segment of Goldthorpe's class schema. Class "V" (lower-level routine non-manual workers), Class "VI" (skilled manual workers), and Class "VII" (unskilled manual workers) engage primarily in labour contracts with their employer, earn lower wages, and are much more precarious in their employment positions than the ones mentioned above. Examples include cashiers or custodians (Class "V"), pipefitters or master mechanics (Class "VI"), and construction labourers and lawn maintenance workers (Class "VIII").

Neo-Weberian Approaches: Edward Grabb

In Edward Grabb's work on social inequality and social class, power is of central importance. According to Grabb (2007: 211), power is the "differential capacity to command resources, which gives rise to structured asymmetric relations of domination and subordination among social actors." In an elaborate scheme of power, domination, and social inequality, Grabb (2007: 211) suggests that there are three means of power—control of material resources, control of people, and control of ideas—that correspond primarily with economic structures, political structures, and ideological structures respectively (see Figure 2.2). These structures of power are crossed by class and non-class bases of inequality that represent the "human content" of power relations. Hence, like Parkin, Grabb should be commended for rightly emphasizing the dualism between structure and human agency.

Grabb defines *class* on the basis of ownership, education, and occupation. For Grabb, these factors represent a synthesis of the key concepts in class analysis discussed by other influential class analysts, such as Wright and Parkin. *Ownership* includes ownership of property but also material possessions and income. *Education* comprises credentials and knowledge. *Occupation* involves distinctions such as manual versus non-manual labour but also includes issues of skill. Grabb (2007: 214–15) suggests that although classes should not be considered in static terms because they vary over time and space (i.e., historically and across different regions and countries), there tend to be three main class categories in modern capitalist systems: an upper class, a heterogeneous central category, and a working class. Like Wright and Parkin, Grabb defines the working class as those who do not own capital, have no special skills or credentials, and sell their labour to make a living. The upper class consists mostly of the capital owners, although persons with significant political or ideological power fall into this category as well. The middle class is a diverse group that may or may not have limited ownership but that is distinguishable from the working class mostly on the basis of credentials.

According to Grabb, the means of power (economic, political, and ideological) are differentially distributed along class lines. Of course, people in the upper classes control the means of material production or the economic structure by virtue of their ownership of the means of production. The middle classes may have some economic power depending on whether their incomes are sufficient to purchase desirable consumer goods and to the extent that their occupation confers upon them a certain amount of authority or autonomy. And the working classes tend not to have economic power at all. In Grabb's scheme, class also crosses political and ideological structures of power. Hence, those in the upper class, by virtue of their capital, high levels of education, and good occupations, tend to

The Major Means of Powers, Structures of Domination, and Bases for Social Inequality

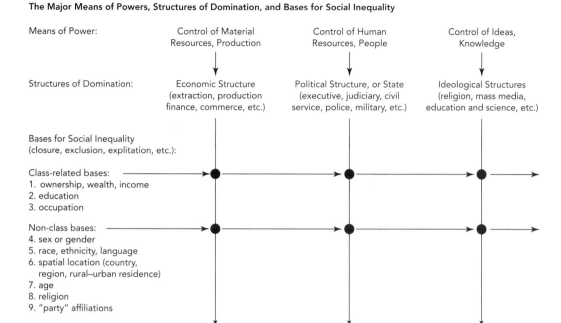

Figure 2.2 Grabb's Conceptual Framework

Source: Grabb, Edward. 2007. *Theories of Social Inequality*. 5th edn. (Toronto: Thomson Nelson) p. 212.

control political and ideological institutions such as the judiciary and educational systems. Those in the working class tend not to have ideological or political power, and those in the middle class vary in the extent to which they hold such power, again on the basis of class-related factors.

Assuming that social inequality is a multi-faceted phenomenon that involves many bases of inequality (as most researchers and theorists now acknowledge), then both Grabb's and Parkin's work represents significant conceptual contributions to understanding inequality. Why? Because the emphasis in both frameworks is on power, not class. The inherent problem with theories of inequality that begin with class is that other bases of inequality, such as gender, "race," ethnicity, and age, carry less theoretical significance. Notably, in both Grabb's and

Parkin's work, class takes a certain primacy, but there is nonetheless room for conceptual development in each approach across the other significant bases of social inequality.

One minor point in Grabb's framework needs to be addressed: the underlying tendency in his approach toward a reification of the structures of power. According to Grabb, the organizations and collectivities that compose the power structures operate in complex ways, and "together they largely determine the nature and extent of inequality in society, what the social bases for inequality will be and how much they will matter" (2007: 213). Thus, although Grabb discusses a "dualistic view of power," it is unclear whether or how people act within power structures to either resist or maintain them (see chapter 6 for an in-depth discussion of agency).

The Death of Social Class? Economic Prosperity and Globalization

Following the Second World War, many OECD economies made significant economic gains—their economies prospered, wages increased, and income inequality lowered to levels not seen for many years. According to Ronald Inglehart (1987), economic security stemming from sustained economic growth had reduced the importance of economic issues and class conflict. This was the foundation for Inglehart's **postmaterialist thesis**. Inglehart argues that people in modern industrial society no longer concern themselves with social class issues or material concerns. He argues that most people—including those in the working class—have become "affluent enough" and no longer worry about poverty, inequality, and economic well-being. Building on this argument, others have made even more extreme claims, suggesting the "Death of Class" (Clark and Lipset 1991; Pakulski and Waters 1996a, 1996b). The argument is simple: social class identity has become of little importance for values and behaviours, and as a result, people's attention has drifted elsewhere.

For other researchers, globalization is the cause of waning class relations. The quite recent insurgence of globalization in sociological discourse is interesting because *globalization* is "a new word for an old process": "the integration of the global economy that began in earnest with the launch of the European colonial era five centuries ago" (Ellwood 2001: 12). However, the recent accelerated pace of globalization has been fuelled by rapid technological change, an unprecedented number of free trade agreements, and the powerful rise of multinational corporations; this has led to heightened concerns over the impact of globalization on nation-states and individuals (Ellwood 2001).

According to Ulrich Beck, *globalization* refers to the convergence of economic, political, cultural, and social changes emergent in the "second modernity" (Beck 2000; Beck, Bonss, and Lau 2003). A key aspect of these changes is that boundaries that were rigid and fixed in the first modernity now prove to be malleable (Beck, Bonss, and Lau 2003). The globalization of labour is evident in, for instance, the "social despatialization of work and production" (Beck 2000: 73). Individualization, gender revolution, underemployment, and global risks lead, within the context of globalization, to a "new kind of society" that is organized according to the rules of a "new kind of capitalism" and a "new kind of economy" (Beck 1999: 2). All of this, in turn, means that risks in employment or other aspects of social life are extending their reach to groups that have previously been sheltered from them (Beck 1999).

There may be some merit to Beck's argument. Fears over job losses in Canada and the United States as a result of globalization are reaching beyond the manufacturing sector to semi-skilled work (Villarreal and Fergusson 2014). But, for Beck and others, the rise in global economic capitalism means that social class, which has traditionally been assessed according to national boundaries, is dead, or at least of less significance today than in the past (Beck 1992; Beck and Beck-Gernsheim 2002; see also Pakulski and Waters 1996a; Kingston 2001).

Although it is true that, with increases in globalization, risk is being distributed to other classes and groups (see Beck 1992), alienation and exploitation are still organizational features of capitalism and the working class is still at *heightened* risk of unemployment and poverty, pointing to the continued importance and relevance of social class (Goldthorpe 2002).

Our discussion above has outlined a conceptual framework for understanding social class—that is, how many there are, the sources of class conflict, and how they are formed. This discussion begs the question of whether class structures are comparable across modern societies. Is belonging to the working class in Canada the same as belonging to the working class in the United States? What about in much more equal countries like Norway, Denmark, or Sweden? In fact, research shows that class structures are remarkably similar (in terms of distributions) across the developed world. However, just because the composition of social classes is similar does not mean workers in all countries share similar work experiences, enjoy the same comfortable wages, and have similar levels of job security. Throughout Part II of this book, we will show that class inequality varies according to national context and that oftentimes politics and the state play crucial roles in its development.

As an example, an auto worker in Sweden or Denmark has much greater economic opportunity (higher wages, more benefits, and greater job security) than auto workers in other parts of the world. This is because early class struggle and class politics in Scandinavian countries set a benchmark for greater equality. Recall Box 2.1 and its discussion of low-wage factory work in Michigan. Though the size of the working class may be similar in comparative perspective, the opportunities and resources available to workers are not.

The story becomes even more complicated when we think of class comparisons between the *developed* and the *developing* world. Do social classes exist in countries like Rwanda or China, and if so, are they comparable to the class structures in Canada, the United States, and other industrialized countries? That income inequality is so much higher in the developing world makes the nature of social classes much different. Box 2.3 discusses economic inequality, economic growth, and income differences in South Africa.

Global perspective

Box 2.3 Income Inequality, Economic Growth, and Social Class in South Africa

Poverty and Economic Inequality

According to standard measures of poverty, nearly 47 per cent of South Africans were considered poor in 2013. In 1994, this figure was 45.6 per cent, suggesting that unlike what was reported by the World Bank in chapter 1, poverty may be growing in South Africa rather than declining. Other measures of economic inequality are also jarring: South Africa's national unemployment rate is 25.4 per cent, and its GINI coefficient is 0.69, making the country one of the most unequal in the world.

According to Haroon Bhorat, a lack of economic growth in South Africa is responsible for stagnant income inequality in many of South Africa's most impoverished regions. According to Bhorat (2013), it will be very difficult for South Africa's economy to grow because the only sectors that are prosperous are those that are highly organized (through unions) and that employ workers who are well educated and skilled. As a result, very little growth occurs in poorer regions making it difficult for income and wealth to be spread equally.

To address income inequality more successfully, economic growth needs to be more inclusive regarding smaller enterprises, rural areas, and the young and jobless. This is no simple task. South Africa has among the most unequal income distributions in the world: approximately 60 per cent of the population earns less than US$7,000 per year, whereas only 2.2 per cent of the population has an income exceeding about US$50,000. The number of people living on less than $1 a day doubled to four million in 2006 (Klein 2007). According to Leo Zeilig, South African poverty is rooted in a historic relationship of exploitation within a larger capitalist system. The resistance of industrial development under colonialism and the reliance on single-commodity export economies have combined to produce debt crises, collapses of infrastructure, widespread poverty, and significant cross-class income difference across South Africa's large population.

Sources: Bhorat (2013); Klein (2007); Zeilig (2002).

A Note on Stratification Approaches

It would be remiss to discuss social inequality without paying heed to social stratification research. Indeed, stratification approaches to social inequality have been very influential, particularly in American sociology. As noted in chapter 1, stratification approaches conceptualize inequality as a hierarchal order (Davis and Moore 1945), in which individuals are grouped into strata on the basis of their income, education, occupation, prestige, or status. Inequality, then, tends to be conceptualized at the level of individual difference rather than in relational terms or on the basis of class structures (Grabb 2007: 112–13; Tilly 1998: 27–31). Traditionally, stratification approaches have assumed that the rank ordering of people into socially defined strata is a universal and functionally necessary dimension of society (Davis and Moore 1945). In other words, some ordering of people according to their worth, variously defined, is required for the smooth functioning of society. Certain positions in society are more valued than others because of the high level of skill attached to them.

Only a few people can attain the skill required to fulfill these positions, and the appropriate training for such attainment requires significant time. People who choose to invest the time in such training deserve higher-status positions in society and the resultant rewards attached to these positions. Furthermore, there is general agreement among the members of society that such stratification systems are acceptable (Davis and Moore 1945).

Nonetheless, there are two common underlying assumptions in contemporary stratification research that set it apart from the Marxist or Weberian approaches to inequality discussed in this chapter. The first is the tendency to overemphasize the extent to which society operates on the basis of consensus. The second, related to the first, is the underemphasis in stratification research on issues of power and exploitation (see Grabb 2007 for an extensive discussion of these issues). These are the crucial problematic assumptions of stratification research that scholars have taken issue with for decades and that are highlighted by Melvin Tumin's 1953 response to Davis and Moore's 1945 seminal article "Some Principles of Stratification" (see Table 2.3).

Table 2.3 Some Principles of Stratification

Davis, K., and W.E. Moore. 1945. "Some Principles of Stratification." *American Sociological Review* 10: 242–9.	Tumin, M. 1953. "Some Principles of Stratification: A Critical Analysis." *American Sociological Review* 18: 378–94.
(1) Within any society, certain positions are functionally more important than others and require special skills for their operation.	(1) There is no clear understanding of what is meant by "functionally important"; rather, judgments are usually arbitrary, based upon the dispensability and replaceability of a particular division of skills in the population.
(2) There is a limited number of individuals who have the particular talent to be trained in the skills required for the functionally more important positions.	(2) The range of talent within any society is not known within stratified systems, as there are obstacles to the exploration of available talent. This is true of societies where the opportunity to discover talent is dependent upon the resources of the parent generation. In addition, the unequal distribution of rewards of the parent generation results in the unequal distribution of motivation in the succeeding generation.

(3) A period of training is necessary for the conversion of talent into skill, during which period sacrifices are made.

(3) The two sacrifices are said to be a loss of earning power and the cost of training. However, the latter is usually assumed by parents, and the former becomes inconsequential as those with training acquire much higher wages than their untrained counterparts once they are employed.

(4) In order that an individual may be persuaded to endure these sacrifices, positions must contain inherent value in the form of privileged access to scarce rewards.

(4) There are an assortment of alternative motivational mechanisms that could be institutionalized and used effectively, such as the "joy of work" inherent in a position.

(5) These scarce goods consist of rights and advantages attached to or built into the positions and can be organized into those things which contribute to (a) sustenance; (b) humour and diversion; (c) self-respect and ego expansion.

(5) There are alternative rewards that could be used, but Davis and Moore's analysis does not allow for this.

(6) The consequence of differential access to rewards is the differential of the prestige and esteem which various strata acquire. This, along with rights and privileges, constitutes institutionalized inequality, or social stratification.

(6) There has been no demonstration that it is unavoidable that differential prestige and esteem shall accrue to positions that command differential rewards in power and prestige.

(7) Therefore, social inequality in the amounts of scarce goods and in the amounts of prestige and esteem individuals receive is functional and inevitable.

(7) The only things that must be distributed unequally are the power and property necessary to accomplish particular tasks. If in this differential, power and property are deemed merely to correspond to the differential responsibilities, and to be resources rather than rewards, then it is not necessary that differential prestige and esteem follow.

The identification of problematic assumptions in stratification research has not, however, led to its demise. Such research remains influential in studies of inequality and informs much empirical research on the subject. Grimes (1991: 212) argues that many researchers apply stratification measures to the study of class inequality either because they remain committed to certain aspects of functionalist thought or because stratification measures are often used in large surveys. It is important to clarify that stratification researchers do not suggest they are studying class and that class researchers, though they sometimes do stratification research, make the distinction between the class and stratification. The point that Grimes makes is nonetheless an important one that stems, perhaps, from a more general observation that researchers whose primary interest lies outside of class and stratification analysis tend to confound the two approaches. This propensity is most likely a result of the significant overlap among the various social factors that are examined in these approaches. For instance, occupation, defined in various ways, tends to be at the core of research on social inequality regardless of theoretical perspective. Further, there is a general concern in all conceptual frameworks over the distribution of scarce resources such as income, education, and skill. Hence, the tendency to use stratification measures as indicators of inequality likely stems from the continued use of traditional measurements in survey research and from the fact that the indicators of social inequality are quite similar, regardless of theoretical perspective.

Conceptualizing Social Class in a Framework of Inequality

The preceding discussion highlights several issues central to the conceptualization of social class—power, exploitation, oppression, property ownership, education, and so on. All of these approaches contribute in one way or another to the working definition of *social class* presented here. In this section we draw on approaches discussed above to develop a concept of social class that is compatible with the view that gender, age, ethnic, and race relations are equally important structural dimensions of inequality.

One way to approach our understanding of social inequality is to consider how social processes are shaped by structured sets of social relations such as class, age, gender, ethnicity, and race. Three such processes that are critical for individual and societal survival are production, distribution, and reproduction. According to Marx, *processes of production* are the ways by which raw materials are converted into useful and valuable objects (Allahar 1995). *Processes of distribution* are the ways in which material resources change hands in society (Acker 1988, 1989; Weber [1922] 1978). Distributive processes include wage, state, personal, and marital transfers (Acker 1988). The term *processes of reproduction* refers to the ways in which life is maintained both daily and from one generation to the next; these processes include "how food, clothing, and shelter are made available for immediate consumption, the ways in which the care and socialization of children are provided, the care of the infirm and elderly, and the social organization of sexuality" (Laslett and Brenner 1987: 382).[2] The mere fact of these social processes does not necessarily imply an outcome of social inequality, but understanding the historical

context and the nature of the social relations that structure these processes is fundamental to understanding and explaining social inequality (McMullin 2000).

A central problem in traditional class analysis is that it has focused far too much on production to the neglect of reproduction and, to a lesser extent, distribution. Yet class relations are social relations that extend beyond the arena of production; Marxist approaches that conceptualize social class simply as a relation of production are too restrictive. This is true, in part, because traditional class analysis excludes far too many people who are not directly linked to production processes, such as homemakers and retired individuals. Notably, scholars have tried to reconcile this problem by attributing to homemakers the social class of their husbands and by assigning a class to retired persons based on their pre-retirement status. However, none of these approaches is satisfactory because they do not capture important distributive and status differences between housewives and their husbands or between a retired auto worker and her employed counterpart (see Acker 1988; Estes 1999).

How then do we conceptualize social class in such a framework? At the outset, it is important to point out that there are many indicators of social class—occupation, education, status, income, wealth, ownership—all of which tell us something about class-based inequality. However, these indicators cannot fully capture the view of social class presented in this book. Instead, as we suggested above, a relational understanding of social class is necessary. Such an understanding follows a long tradition in Marxist sociology that suggests that class is not merely an economic matter. Rather, social class manifests itself when people from various classes interact with one another. On the shop floor, employers and employees interact with one another in production processes, and it is through that interaction that social class is produced and reproduced (Reiter 1996). In schoolyards, working-class children interact with middle-class children, and their social class is realized in relation to the other (Willis 1977). In other words, class awareness is highest when people feel that they share common interests and experience with people from their social class. Marx believed that this awareness would lead to the idea of a "class for itself" or to the organized and active pursuit of class-based economic interests (see also Wright 1985).

Second, material oppression is a primary organizing principle of social class in this framework. This view stands in contrast to Marxist approaches that focus on exploitation (see Wright 1997). Modifying Wright's account of "non-exploitive economic oppression,"[3] material oppression occurs if (1) the material welfare of one group of people depends upon the material deprivations of another and (2) the material deprivations of the oppressed group depend upon the exclusion of the oppressed group from access to productive resources, backed by *ownership of the means of production, occupation, or some combination of the two* (italics indicate modification to Wright's principles).

Much research and theoretical effort has been devoted to trying to establish elaborate and conclusive typologies or categorizations of social class. Although this work is valuable, we do not plan to add to that dialogue here. For the purposes of this book, we assume that, in Canada and other Western societies, three broad classes can be distinguished from one another on the basis of ownership of the means of production and occupation. Of course, there will be important variation within these classes with respect to income, status, power, relative oppression, and so on.

Members of the upper class own the means for production and/or control the work process. Hence, company presidents and CEOs are part of the upper class not necessarily because they own

the means of production (although most have a stake in it) but because they are ultimately in control of how work gets done. Working and middle classes are distinguished from one another largely on the basis of occupational characteristics. Working-class jobs are highly oppressive, and workers have very little control over the work process. Assembly-line workers are part of the working class because (1) the material welfare of one group (their employers) depends on the material deprivation of the workers; (2) their material deprivation depends upon their exclusion from access to productive resources (note that these first two points are the conditions of material oppression listed above); and (3) they have little say about how they do their work. Middle-class jobs may be characterized by similar levels of oppression but more control over the work process, as is the case in many middle-management positions. Alternatively, middle-class jobs may not be oppressive in the preceding sense, but individuals employed in these jobs have relatively little control over how they do their work. This is true for nurses, elementary and high school teachers, social workers, and other similar-status service occupations. There is also evidence that earnings inequality has risen for many people in the middle class. As Banting and Myles (2014) show, in Canada, average incomes have been stagnant since the 1980s, and the earnings power and savings of young people have fallen. Similar patterns hold across many other OECD countries as well, with no significant policy response from the state (OECD 2011).

At first glance, the self-employed and professionals seem not to fall anywhere in this schema. Members of each group tend to have control over their work, and their material well-being seems not to rely on the material welfare of another group. Nonetheless, the self-employed are thought to fall into this middling category because their ability to make a living is often contingent upon whether large global conglomerates actively seek to monopolize their markets.

It is difficult to think of professionals (e.g., physicians, professors, or lawyers) as an oppressed group, and for the most part, they also control their work processes. How then do they fall into the middle? Professionals are not part of the upper class because their access to productive resources is restricted. Professionals tend not have the exploitive capabilities of the upper class, and productive resources are generally outside of their reach. Thus, professionals fall between the upper- and working-class groups.

One important issue missing from the preceding discussion is the effect of social class on identity formation and everyday interaction, issues that are of particular concern to scholars such as Anthony Giddens and Pierre Bourdieu.

These are issues that will be discussed in chapter 6. For now, it is important to recognize that the conceptualizations of class presented here do not take into account how class identities and inequalities are produced and reproduced through daily interaction. Indeed, the view of social class presented in this chapter does not stray very far from more established structural approaches. However, as the next chapters show (see especially chapter 7), the subtle differences in the conceptualization of social class presented here merge nicely with conceptualizations of gender, ethnicity, race, and age to form an integrated and coherent framework of structural social inequality. With that in mind, we now turn to a discussion of gender relations.

▓ Notes

1. Wright has vacillated on this issue since his earliest work. In the late 1970s he referred to these groups as *class locations*; then, in his 1985 publication *Classes*, he called them *classes*. In *Class Counts* (1997), however, he makes it quite clear that these are class locations but not classes as such.
2. This view of reproduction is generally held by socialist feminist scholars and should not

be confused with reproduction in the Marxist sense of the term.
3. Recall that Wright argues that if appropriation of labour power does not exist, neither does exploitation. He suggests, however, that if the inverse interdependence and exclusion principles are fulfilled, "non-exploitive economic oppression" occurs.

▓ Questions for Critical Thought

1. Some researchers have argued that social class is becoming insignificant to issues of inequality in contemporary Western nations. Do you agree or disagree with this view? Why?
2. How does Wright's view of social class differ from that of Karl Marx? Is Marx's approach to social class useful in present-day Canadian society? In what ways?
3. What are the chief differences between Marxist accounts and Weberian accounts of social class? Which view of social class is more helpful for understanding class-based inequality in Canada?
4. Compare and contrast Wright's view of social class with Grabb's. Which is more helpful for understanding class-based inequality in Canada?

5. What are the advantages of defining *class* in terms of material oppression as opposed to exploitation? What are the disadvantages?
6. Do class structures exist in developing nations? If yes, do you think they are comparable to their Western counterparts?
7. Do you agree that social classes have become less meaningful in contemporary Western

nations? Have economic prosperity and globalization muted class differences and the importance of economic issues?
8. Which class schema—either Wright's or Goldthorpe's—do you think best captures the class structure in modern society?

⠿ Glossary

Bourgeoisie The class that owns the means of production; the ruling class.

Domination A power relationship in which regular patterns of inequality are established whereby the subordinate group (or individual) accepts that position in a sustained arrangement, obeying the commands of the dominant group (or individual).

Exploitation At the heart of Marxist sociology, *exploitation* refers to the situation under capitalism in which the bourgeoisie take advantage of the proletariat. Class-based exploitation occurs when the bourgeoisie appropriate the labour effort of the proletariat to create their own material advantage.

Labour power Marx argues that *labour* is work and *labour power* is the capacity to work. According to this view, the only "real" power that the proletariat has under capitalism is the power to choose whether to work.

Parties Voluntary associations, such as political parties or lobbying groups, that organize for the pursuit of collective interest. The term is common in Weberian scholarship.

Petite bourgeoisie In Marxist sociology, those who own the products of their labour and who do not exploit the labour power of

others. Members of the petite bourgeoisie are self-employed and are also referred to as the *old middle class*.

Postmaterialist thesis The belief that people's values in modern societies have transformed from materialist and economic to new individual values of autonomy and self-expression.

Power In Marxist sociology, *power* is essentially a social relationship that has a material base. Those who own the means of production have the power to exploit workers through the appropriation of their labour efforts. In Weberian sociology, where the term is more broadly defined, *power* can mean an individual's or group's capacity to impose their will on others.

Power resources Characteristics that provide workers with the ability to punish or reward other workers.

Proletariat The working class, the members of which sell their labour power to the owners of the means of production in exchange for a wage.

Status groups Organized groups comprising people who have similar social-status situations.

⠿ Recommended Reading

Clement, Wallace, and John Myles. 1994. *Relations of Ruling: Class and Gender in Postindustrial Societies*. Montreal and

Kingston: McGill-Queen's University Press. Applies Wright's conceptualization of social class in an analysis of class and gender inequality. Although it is concerned primarily with Canada, there are also comparisons with the United States, Norway, Sweden, and Finland.

Erickson, Robert, and John Goldthorpe. 1992. *The Constant Flux: A Study of Class Mobility in Industrial Societies.* Oxford: Oxford University Press. This study of social mobility within the developing class structures of modern industrial societies is based on a unique data set constructed by the authors.

Grabb, Edward. 2007. *Theories of Social Inequality.* 5th edn. Toronto: Thomson Nelson. An excellent overview and analysis of classical and contemporary theories of social inequality.

Goldthorpe, John. 1980. *Social Mobility and Class Structure in Modern Britain.* Oxford: Oxford University Press. Reviews some of the long-standing debates over social class and the structure of social-class mobility in Britain.

Kingston, Paul. 2001. *The Classless Society.* Stanford, CA: Stanford University Press. This book challenges the long-standing tradition of class analysis, arguing that "classes" in modern society no longer share distinct, life-defining experiences.

McCourt, Frank. 1996. *Angela's Ashes: A Memoir.* New York: Touchstone. An autobiography that tells a heart-wrenching story of what it is like to grow up poor.

Wright, Eric Olin. 1997. *Class Counts: Comparative Studies in Class Analysis.* Cambridge: Cambridge University Press. A comprehensive book that outlines Eric Olin Wright's ideas on social class.

Wright, Eric Olin. 2005. *Approaches to Class Analysis.* Cambridge: Cambridge University Press. This book provides an excellent overview of competing theories from both a classical and contemporary perspective.

▦ Relevant Websites

Eric Olin Wright's home page
www.ssc.wisc.edu/~wright

**In addition to a cv and descriptions of research projects and course syllabi, this unique website offers users PDF links to Wright's books, recent articles, and unpublished versions of manuscripts and interviews. Going beyond the typical academic website, Wright's home page facilitates learning by granting users access to his work.

Canadian Centre for Policy Alternatives— Growing Gap
www.growinggap.ca/

**The GrowingGap.ca is an initiative of the Canadian Centre for Policy Alternatives' Inequality Project, a national project to increase public awareness about the alarming spread of income and wealth inequality in Canada.

GrowingGap.ca is an informative website about "the growing gap between the rich and the rest of us." This group envisions a Canada where no one is left behind and is hopeful that this can be achieved.

Harry Ganzeboom's web page for deriving occupational status
www.harryganzeboom.nl/ISCO08/index.htm

** This online resource outlines how different classifications of Goldthorpe's class schema can be coded using the isco (International Standard Classification of Occupations) occupational classification. This resource includes theoretical discussion, syntax modules, and question/answer pages to help students and researchers understand the logic behind creating an aggregated class measure from over 1,500 individual occupations.

3

Gender and Inequality

Introduction

In 1998 I (McMullin) met Beth, a 64-year-old mother of seven children, who agreed to be a part of my three-generation family study. One of the things we asked the study participants was how they had managed to combine employment, domestic labour, and child care when their children were young. Beth had married when she was 18 years old and had seven children in the next eight years. Although it was not what she would have preferred, her husband John insisted that she work for pay. Beth was also responsible for all of the housework and child care when their children were young. Indeed, John, who worked the day shift in a manufacturing company, spent most of his free time with his friends at the pub.

To manage her family responsibilities in combination with her factory job, Beth worked the night shift. When she was pregnant with her seventh child, she would arrive home from work at 8:00 a.m., get the three oldest children ready for school, and spend the rest of the day caring for her two preschool-age children:

> I would come home [from the factory] and get the kids off to school and then tend to the younger kids. And do what had to

be done [housework]. And the older kids would come home for lunch…. I'd look after them [the two youngest children] through the day and just sleep when I could get them down together. When they got up, I got up…. The younger kids went to bed at 7 o'clock at night, I'd lay down from 7 to 10 before going back to work…. I didn't have the energy to even think that it wasn't fair.

Gender affects almost every aspect of social life and is often the basis of differential access to resources and power in Canada and in most other countries. Usually, although not always, men as a group benefit from gender patterns. Beth's situation is somewhat extreme because she had both a large family and an absent husband. However, the fact that she was responsible for unpaid work in the home and needed to combine that responsibility with paid labour is a typical experience for women. Indeed, research on families and unpaid labour shows that women are disproportionately responsible for household labour, child care, and emotion management in families and for caring for older relatives (see chapter 8).

Beth's story also demonstrates gendered disadvantage in labour markets. In fact, industries, labour markets, occupations, and jobs are segregated on the basis of gender (see chapter 9). Compared with women, men tend to be concentrated in industries, labour markets, occupations, and jobs that are characterized by higher salaries, more benefits, greater autonomy, and higher status. Women are sometimes subjected to discrimination and sexual harassment in their workplaces (Welsh 1999; Welsh et al. 2006), and they often encounter the "glass ceiling," or invisible barriers to promotion, in their careers (see Krahn, Lowe, and Hughes 2007 for an overview). At the same time, when men are employed in occupations that are typically seen as female, they are often given a ride on the "glass escalator" and promoted early and often (Williams 1992). As Box 3.1 shows, the glass ceiling is a global phenomenon.

One of our goals in writing this book is to show that inequality is experienced differently depending on where in the world you live. Map 3.1 shows that women across the globe are exposed to different levels of inequality. This map displays the "Gender Inequality Index" which is based on labour force participation, educational attainment, political representation, and reproductive health. Darker shades reflect greater levels of inequality. As this map shows, Canada does relatively well from a comparative, gender-inequality perspective. As we will explore in Part II of this book, we are far from achieving complete gender equality in Canada and much can be learned about reducing gender inequality from countries around the world.

Global perspective

Box 3.1 China's Political Glass Ceiling: Women's Exclusion from High-Level Politics

During the 1950s, Chairman Mao Zedong famously stated, "Women hold up half the sky." He used this rhetoric to promote gender equality in China during a time in which significant economic, social, and political gender disparities existed. Indeed, for Mao, a major initiative of the socialist revolution in China was to liberate women and to raise their status as equal members of Chinese society. Mao later appointed China's first female vice premier, Wu Guixian, who held the position for one year during the Cultural Revolution.

However, gender equality in Chinese politics has been slow moving. According to Fubing Su (2006), while women make up 20 per cent of lower-level party members, they only account for 10 per cent of provincial-level Chinese politics elites. This distinction is important because it implies that women are still strongly underrepresented in positions of power with decision-making responsibilities. In other words, as much as Chinese women have gradually gained political rights, they are playing only peripheral roles. Men continue to dominate the top levels of leadership in the Chinese government. For example, the Politburo Standing Committee, the highest body of the party, has had only two female members (elected in 2015) since its establishment.

Women in rural areas are even worse off than women in urban areas. Women's participation in rural governance remains limited. Representation of women in local governments remains low, and women villagers' political aspirations and sense of empowerment are similarly limited; those who make their way into government bodies or villager committees are often delegated only to lower-level positions, such as marginal portfolios (e.g., family planning), which only reinforces and institutionalizes gendered social roles, thus reproducing women's lower and limited status in the social and political structure.

Sources: Su (2006: 143–63); Lotus Yuen. (Jun 6, 2013). "China's Glass Ceiling: Women Still Excluded from High-Level Politics." *The Atlantic*.

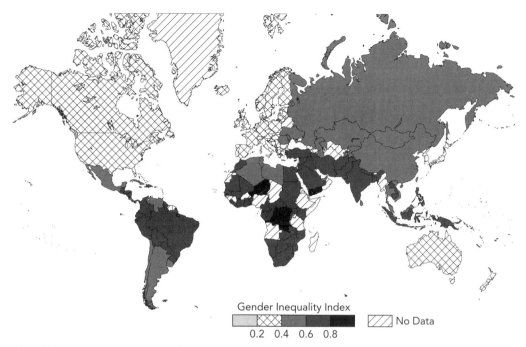

Gender Inequality Index

0.2 0.4 0.6 0.8   No Data

Map 3.1 Gender Inequality Index

Source: © Reproduced by the permission of the The Economist Intelligence Unit, www.citylab.com/work/2012/01/
how-economic-development-helps-worlds-women/907/

Explanations of Gender-Based Inequality

Scholars disagree about how to explain gendered inequality, and they emphasize different factors in understanding the role that gender plays in individuals' lives. Unlike social class, gender relations were not generally studied before the 1970s. Although there were before that time various statements about sex differences (see, for example, Parsons 1942), these were not generally framed in relation to inequality. Research over the past few decades has evolved so that gender relations are now widely recognized as a ubiquitous pillar of inequality. Yet, as with social class, there is much disagreement in the literature over

how gender should be conceptualized and what lies at the root of gender-based inequality.

Before we turn to various conceptualizations and explanations of gender-based inequality, the distinction between sex, gender, and sexual orientation must be addressed. The term **gender** was introduced in sociology as a way of avoiding biological essentialist views that were associated with the term **sex**. Essentialist perspectives reinforced beliefs that biological differences between men and women determine their disparate positions in society. *Gender*, on the other hand, was used to express the view that there is nothing innate about men or women that makes one sex more suitable for performing a particular task than another. *Gender*, then, refers to the social construction of difference that is largely organized around biological sex. This view of gender is widely held in sociology and in feminism (Nicholson 1994). Inequalities also exist based on **sexual orientation**, an issue we discuss in greater detail below.

One significant point that feminist sociologists identified in their critique of sex research is that it is difficult, if not impossible, to address structural aspects of gender through empirical research. Framing their argument in a more general critique of positivist science that privileges hegemonic knowledge, feminists argued that multivariate, empirical models can take our understanding of gender only so far because the interpretation of these models tends to be reduced to individual difference (D. Smith 1987). Most sociologists now dismiss arguments that treat such differences as innate. Yet there remains a tendency to interpret these sex and gender differences as individual characteristics rather than as structural features of social life.

Structural accounts of gender inequality generally address how various social institutions such as states, families, and labour markets are "gendered." In other words, feminist researchers have shown that women and men have different experiences and opportunities in most institutions. For example, labour markets are structured such that women have fewer opportunities for promotion than men, and this, in turn, is related to women's primary responsibility for domestic labour within families. Although studies that consider the gendered nature of social structures have advanced our understanding of gender inequality, they fall short of assessing the full nature of gender inequality because they tend not to treat gender itself as a social structure (Risman 1998). To suggest that gender is a social structure is to see gender as a central organizing feature of social life. What we do, who we are, how we interact with others, our opportunities and constraints, our advantages and disadvantages are all patterned by gender (Chafetz 1990; Lorber 1994). Patterns of gender, in turn,

are made manifest through human interaction (West and Zimmerman 1987) in our productive, reproductive, and distributive activities. In similar ways, sexual orientation is also a central organizing feature of social life that structures inequality in its various forms.

In summary then, although the conceptualization of gender may at first seem straightforward—there are women and there are men—the seeming simplicity of this exercise adds to its complexity. Gender relations are historically variable, cultural, ideological, biological, sexual, political, and material (see K. Marshall 2000). Gender involves identity, power, exploitation, and oppression. The debate among feminist scholars and others about which of these matters lie at the heart of gendered inequality is long-standing and ongoing. Many of these debates consider sexual orientation as well. Though more accepted in today's society, people who do not hold a **heterosexual** orientation face disadvantage and inequality, especially when it comes to the workplace and organizations (Acker 2006a).

Social Relations of Reproduction: Patriarchy as a System of Domination

Whereas the social relations of production are an essential element of social-class analysis, assessments of gender inequality are often grounded in the relations of social reproduction and sexuality. **Radical feminists**, for instance, generally assume that gender inequality is a function of men's control of women's reproduction and sexuality (Firestone 1971; O'Brien 1981). This produces an inherently unequal gendered power relationship that determines the sexual division of labour, is perpetuated by the nuclear family, and makes women economically dependent upon men. Hence, radical feminists suggest that gender inequality is distinct from other forms of oppression, that sex-based inequality is the original and most basic form of oppression, and that the dominance of women by men is universal (Firestone 1971; Millett 1969; O'Brien 1981).

According to Shulamith Firestone (1971), women's subordinate position in relation to men is rooted in the human *biological family*. Biological families are characterized by four universal features: (1) women's biological capacity to reproduce made them dependent on men for their survival; (2) children take a long time to become independent compared with the young of other species; (3) bonds between mothers and children are universal, and these bonds determine the psychology of all women and children; and (4) the reproductive biological capacity of women led to the first categorical division of labour. According to Firestone (1971), these characteristics of biological families and the sexes led to a power imbalance between men and women that needs to be overcome. She argues that if women are to be emancipated, there must be a revolution in which women gain control over their reproduction in much the same way as a working-class revolution would lead to the control of the means of production. She argues that to free "women from the tyranny of their reproductive biology," natural reproduction must be replaced by the use of new reproductive technologies.

In *The Politics of Reproduction*, Mary O'Brien (1981) also argues that the root of women's oppression lies in their biology, but unlike Firestone, she suggests that the reproduction process is dialectical and has changed throughout history. Men need to control reproduction because, unlike women, they are "alienated from their seed of reproduction" through the act of sexual intercourse. To compensate for this alienation, men seek to control women through patriarchal order.

Although radical feminists differ in their explanations of how and why men have come to control reproduction, they agree that it is, in part, through this process that gendered subjectivities—defined as psyches, personalities, or levels of self-conscious awareness—are born (Firestone 1971; O'Brien 1981). Furthermore, gendered ideologies of love, sexuality, and motherhood perpetuate gender inequality by keeping women unaware of their subordinate status (Burton 1985). For instance, Firestone (1971) argues that the joy of giving birth is a patriarchal myth. Instead, she says, pregnancy is barbaric and natural childbirth is "at best necessary and tolerable" and at worst "like shitting a pumpkin."

Explanations of gender inequality have benefited from radical feminist thought, in particular the importance it places on the relations of reproduction, gendered ideology, power, and control. However, radical feminist thought has been criticized on several counts. For our purposes, the most important criticism is that it treats the system of male dominance or **patriarchy** as a "universal, trans-historical and trans-cultural phenomenon; women were everywhere oppressed by men in more or less the same ways" (Acker 1989: 235). Conceptualizing patriarchy in this way tends to reduce male oppression of women to biological essentialism and is limiting because it does not consider historical or contemporary variations in women's situations (Acker 1989; Fox 1988). Moreover, this view of patriarchy leads to assessments of men as having an "innate desire for power" (Fox 1988: 165).

Building from the criticism above, Box 3.2 provides examples of communities around the world that are based either on **matriarchal systems of order** or on societies with strong foundations of gender equality. Most of the examples are of small, usually tribal, groups within the developing world. Nonetheless, this evidence implies that patriarchal authority structures are not universal or inherent to human society.

Global perspective

Box 3.2 Matriarchal Communities and Gender Equality

China

Lugu Lake, an area deep in southwest China, is a place known as *the Kingdom of Women*—the Mosuo, one of the world's last matrilineal societies. Mosuo women do not marry. They practise "walking marriages," an alternative system whereby women can choose and change partners as they wish. Property is exclusively handed down through the female line. In fact, the Mosuo do not have words for "father" or "husband."

Central African Republic and Democratic Republic of Congo

Men in the Aka tribe located in Africa's Congo Basin have been described as the "best dads in the world." Couples share hunting, food preparation, and social and leisure activities. When women hunt, men cook, and are known to play with their children at least five times as often as men in other societies. In 2003, the Aka were proclaimed one of the Masterpieces of the Oral and Intangible Heritage of Humanity by UNESCO.

Iceland

Female-friendly laws in Iceland have made it one of the most gender-equal societies in the world.

"I guess men will have to get used to the idea that women are not for sale," said prime minister Johanna Sigurdardottir, the world's first openly lesbian head of state. Impressively, over 40 women hold political seats under Prime Minister Sigurdardottir, one of the highest rates of female representation around the world.

The campaign for women's rights began on 24 October 1975, known as "women's day off." Almost 90 per cent of the country's women refused to work, cook, and perform domestic and household duties.

India

The Indian state of Meghalaya boasts one of the world's few surviving matrilineal systems where women, rather than men, own land and property. The youngest daughter in the family inherits all the property and acts as caretaker of aging parents and unmarried siblings.

Rwanda

What country has the highest percentage of women parliamentarians in the world? Rwanda. After the genocide in the early 1990s, legislation required that 30 per cent of the parliamentary seats be held by women. The country has far surpassed that quota. And by way of comparison, in 2015, 64 per cent of Rwanda's parliamentarians were women, compared to Canada's 26 per cent. Worldwide, 21.9 per cent of elected seats are held by women.

Sources: Christian Koach. (March 5, 2015). "Where women rule the world: Matriarchal communities from Albania to China." *Metro.co.uk*; Jennifer Ditchburn. (Nov. 6, 2015). "'Because it's 2015': Trudeau forms Canada's 1st gender-balanced cabinet." *CBC News*; Jane Dudman. (July 1, 2014). "Lessons from Rwanda's female-run institutions." *The Guardian*.

Another problem with radical feminist thought is its rather limited focus on the procreative aspect of social reproduction. Missing in these accounts is an assessment of social reproduction as a material relation that includes "the activities and attitudes, behaviours and emotions, responsibilities and relationships directly involved in the maintenance of life on a daily basis, and intergenerationally" (Laslett and Brenner 1987: 382). Social reproduction is work, and how social reproductive labour is divided is critical to social organization. Finally, in its emphasis on social reproduction, radical feminist thought tends to neglect the relationship between gender and the processes of production.

Sexual Orientation and Heterosexism

Sexuality and sexual orientation have become noticeable sources of inequality in modern society (Acker 2006b). For example, Acker (2006b: 445) argues that "heterosexualism is assumed in many organizing processes and in the interactions necessary to these processes.... [and] homosexuality is disruptive of organizing processes because it flouts the assumptions of heterosexuality." In other words, many hold the opinion that **homosexuality** disrupts the status quo in organizations. As a result, those who identify as homosexual often face numerous inequalities in politics, the workplace, and

schools. In some countries homosexuality is still illegal. In many more parts of the world, same-sex marriage is illegal. In these places, governments do not recognize policy benefits to domestic partners of the same sex. These inequalities stem from **heteronormative ideology**: the belief that heterosexuality is the dominant sexual orientation in our society and that **LGBT** sexual identification is an abnormal expression.

Although heteronormative ideologies are still common, tolerance (but not integration and full acceptance) toward homosexuality has risen in many societies. In 2005, for example, nearly 50 per cent of Canadians approved of gay marriage. Although this number may seem low, only 10 per cent of Canadians were supportive of it in 1987, which marks a 40 per cent

HIGHLIGHT

Box 3.3 An Historic Evolution of Same-Sex Marriage in Canada

It was only in 2005, when it enacted Bill C-38, that Canada became the fourth country to legalize same-sex marriage. At that time, only the Netherlands, Belgium, and Spain had government policy that legalized gay marriage. Bill C-38 marked Canada as one of the world pioneers in same-sex equality. The passing of this bill, however, would not have been possible without decades of political support and activism.

We now list a rough history of the evolution of same-sex marriage in Canada, adapted from www.cbc.ca/news/canada/timeline-same-sex-rights-in-canada-1.114751:

1967 Pierre Trudeau proposes amendments to the Criminal Code that would reduce the laws against homosexuality. Trudeau famously pronounces that the state had "no right or duty to creep into the bedrooms of the nation."

1969 These amendments by Trudeau finally pass into the Criminal Code, thus decriminalizing homosexuality in Canada.

1977 Sexual orientation is included by Quebec in its Human Rights Code.

1980 Read by MP Pat Carney, Bill C-242 is brought into the House of Commons. This bill proposes that discrimination on grounds of sexual orientation would be prohibited in Canada. This bill did not pass.

1992 The federal court lifts the country's ban on homosexuals in the military.

1992 Justice Minister Kim Campbell introduces Bill C-108. This legislation seeks to add sexual orientation to the Canadian Human Rights Act.

1995 A Supreme Court ruling allows Jim Egan and Jack Nesbit the right to claim an Old Age Security (OAS) spousal pension.

2002 A Canadian court rules in favour of recognizing same-sex marriages as a legal marital union under the law. This marks the first of such rulings in Canada.

2005 Bill C-38 receives royal assent and becomes officially formalized in Canadian law. On 20 July 2005, same-sex Canadian couples are legally able to marry in Canada.

increase in tolerance over this time period. Box 3.3 traces the evolution of same-sex marriage in Canada. As its legal status evolved, so too did public opinion in Canada.

Compared with the United States, Canada is often regarded as "kinder" and more tolerant. Yet, attitudes toward gay marriage in the United States are markedly similar to those in Canada: American acceptance of gay marriage stands at 48 per cent, an increase of only 27 per cent in the early 1990s. However, other countries are still intolerant, to varying degrees, of sexual diversity and homosexuality. Figure 3.1 shows country differences in the acceptance of homosexuality. Here we see that Canada is one of the most accepting countries of homosexuality (only Spain and Germany are more tolerant). Religion helps explain some of the cross-national variation in attitudes. As this figure also shows, some parts of Asia, the Middle East, and Africa are still highly intolerant. Unfortunately, prejudice sometimes manifests itself in extreme forms. For example, in Africa, homosexuality is illegal in 37 of 54 countries, and in some of these countries it is punishable by death.

New research suggests that cross-national differences in tolerance toward homosexuality can be explained by rising postmaterialism, spurred by increasing economic prosperity in developed societies. According to Inglehart (1990), economic development is a major contributor to the shift to more liberal values in modern society. This would explain, at least in part, why Asian, Middle Eastern, and African societies display much less tolerance toward homosexuality than more developed nations. According to the postmaterialist thesis, prosperity in modern societies allows people to shift their attention toward social issues and self-expression (Andersen and Fetner 2008). This theory, however, does not explain why such variation exists among more developed countries.

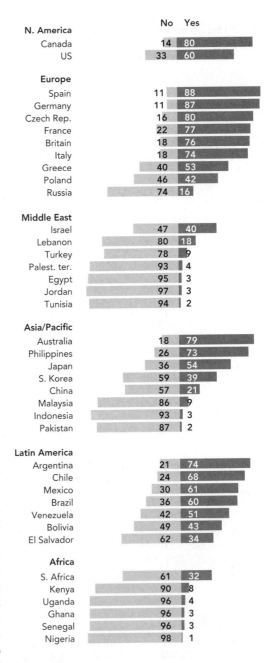

Figure 3.1 Should Society Accept Homosexuality?

Source: "The Global Divide on Homosexuality" Pew Research Center, Washington, DC (June, 2013). www.pewglobal.org/2013/06/04/the-global-divide-on-homosexuality/

Social Relations of Production and Reproduction: Capitalism and Patriarchy as Intersecting Systems of Domination

Socialist-feminist accounts of gender inequality consider the relations of production and reproduction in their work. Influenced by Marxism, **socialist feminism** has united the relations of production and reproduction by linking the systems of patriarchy and capitalism in an integrated theory (Young 1981). **Dual-system theorists**, for instance, suggest that patriarchy and capitalism are two distinct systems that intersect in relation to the oppression of women. Heidi Hartmann developed one of the most prominent and most debated dual-systems theories in her paper "The Unhappy Marriage of Marxism and Feminism: Towards a More Progressive Union." Hartmann (1981: 14) defines patriarchy as "a set of social relations between men, which have a material base and which, though hierarchical, establish or create inter-dependence and solidarity among men that enable them to dominate women." The material base of patriarchy, she suggests, is the control of women's labour power by men. Men control women by restricting their economic and sexual activity. Women, according to Hartmann (1981), work for men by raising their children and doing their housework. These social relations are perpetuated ideologically through the systems of patriarchy and capitalism, in part by equating male characteristics with capitalist values and female characteristics with social reproduction (Hartmann 1981: 28).

According to Hartmann (1981: 24), capitalism and patriarchy are systems with competing interests that adjust to and reinforce one another. Capitalism is not an "all-powerful"

system of inequality; rather, it is responsive and flexible to contradictions that stem from patriarchy. This is the crux of Hartmann's argument, and to illustrate this point she relies on a historical analysis of women's labour power and the development of the family wage in the nineteenth-century United States. During this time, working-class men, women, and children were working in factories; this kept the supply of labour large and wages low. Wages were based on what would be required for individual, not family, subsistence. Hence, many members in working-class families were required to work in factories for their very survival. Male workers and unions opposed women's factory work, recognizing, first, that the excess supply of labour lowered wages, and second, that if women worked for pay, there was no one left to tend to the home. According to Hartmann (1981: 21), rather than organizing the labour of women and children, a tactic that would have solved the first problem, working-class men fought for the family wage, a solution that would allow them to maintain patriarchal power in the home as well as to obtain higher wages. Hence, "family wages may be understood as a resolution of the conflict over women's labour power which was occurring between patriarchal and capitalist interests" (Hartmann 1981: 22).

According to Hartmann, although women's labour-force participation has increased dramatically since the Second World War, this does not signify the emancipation of women, as Marxist scholars might argue. Rather, the family wage is still institutionalized in capitalism because men continue to be primarily responsible for earning a living, women remain primarily responsible for maintaining families, and women earn lower wages in labour markets than men do (Hartmann 1981: 25). Hence, Marxist analyses of women's oppression are flawed because they do not fully acknowledge the strength of patriarchy in maintaining a system of disadvantage for women. Box 3.4 addresses gender inequality in the labour market, specifically the **gender wage gap**. As this

HIGHLIGHT

Box 3.4 Women's Day in Canada: Much to Celebrate, Much More Work to Do

by Emanuela Heyninck

International Women's Day gives us an opportunity to celebrate the many achievements on the journey to gender equality. It also gives us pause to assess where we are in that journey. We are reminded daily that millions of women in developing countries struggle for personal and economic freedom, including the freedom to learn, work, and participate.

Compared with their situation, women in Canada are doing well. Our young men and women may wonder whether the theme for this year's International Women's Day, Inspiring Change, applies to us. When they look around, they see that men and women are attending colleges and universities at equal rates. In some professions, women make up more than half of the graduating classes. Men and women are participating in equal numbers in the work force. In Ontario, we have human rights, pay equity and employment standards laws, in addition to many other services and community organizations that protect the rights of women and continue to advocate for the full integration of women in all areas of public and private life. What, they may ask, needs to change in Canada?

The gender wage gap is one indicator of the fact that progress to economic equality has plateaued. While there are many ways to measure the gap, a common statistic—comparing full-time/full-year average wages—puts the gender gap at 26 per cent. This means that for every $1 earned by a male worker, a female worker tis earning only $0.74. In the last decade this figure has barely moved. For women of colour and Aboriginal women, the gap is even wider. Royal Bank has estimated that if the gender wage gap were addressed and women and men in Canada received the same economic opportunities, women would have $168-billion more in disposable income.

The poor representation of women in leadership roles is another indicator. Despite the overwhelming evidence that demonstrates without doubt that companies with more diverse boards are more profitable, women make up only about 16 per cent of corporate board seats.

Business structures and practices have not caught up to modern day realities because stereotypes about women and work persist.

Many employers continue to make assumptions about women and their roles as caregivers, consciously or unconsciously overlooking them for advancement and training opportunities or by not considering them for more lucrative projects.

Women have been told to take the initiative by negotiating their pay, but numerous studies show that women who attempt to negotiate for better salaries either don't receive them or are viewed negatively by their managers and co-workers.

Finally, "women's work"—and the so-called "soft skills" that women are respected for—are still being undervalued and under-compensated.

We need to be inspired. We also need to take action—to make use of the laws, strategies and tools that have been developed so that a real and substantive culture shift about women at work becomes the new standard.

Culture shift is never easy. It requires introspection and change at both the organizational and individual level. It takes strong leadership and men and women working together to come up with new ways of doing things. Where gender workplace equality is concerned, it means restructuring our business and compensation practices to mirror the realities of today's world.

By acting to change our own culture to ensure that women are fully integrated into the economic and social fabric of our country, we inspire other jurisdictions and populations and economies to aim for our successes.

Source: Emanuela Heyninck. (March 08, 2014). "'Women's Day in Canada: Much to celebrate, much more work to do." *The Globe and Mail*. www.theglobeandmail.com/globe-debate/womens-day-in-canada-much-to-celebrate-much-more-work-to-do/article17370856/

box shows, Canadian women are doing comparatively well, but more ground still needs to be gained in order from women to reach earnings parity.

Responding to Heidi Hartmann's article and other dual-system approaches, some feminists argue that it is a mistake to treat patriarchy and capitalism as separate systems of oppression (Young 1981). This is largely because dual-system theories tend to relegate patriarchy to one level of analysis—usually the ideological, which organizes women's unpaid work—and capitalism to another, the material, which organizes women's paid work (Hartmann 1981; Young 1981). Although Hartmann avoids this specific problem by giving patriarchy a material base, it is unclear how the analytic separation between patriarchy and capitalism can be maintained. Others, most notably Sylvia Walby, suggest that dual-system theorizing is appropriate but that it must be further developed, conceptualizing patriarchy as a multidimensional structure.

In several publications in the late 1980s and early 1990s, Walby developed a theory of patriarchy that attempted to correct the shortcomings of the concept by defining patriarchy as "a system of social structures and practices in which men dominate, oppress, and exploit women" (1989: 214). According to Walby (1989, 1990, 2011), considering the social-structural nature of patriarchy corrects the problems of biological essentialism and the idea that all individual men dominate all individual women.

In order to understand the structural nature of patriarchy, Walby (1989: 214) argues that it should be considered at different levels of analysis. Most abstractly, patriarchy is a system of social relations that exists alongside capitalism and racism. At the next level are six patriarchal structures: the patriarchal mode of production (household production), patriarchal relations in paid work, patriarchal states, male violence, patriarchal relations in sexuality, and patriarchal culture. Finally, in each of the patriarchal structures, patriarchal practices establish or reinforce systems of

patriarchy (Walby 1989, 1990). Walby argues that these patriarchal structures are not sites of oppression but rather are defined "in terms of the social relations in each structure" (1989: 220); these structures "represent the most significant constellations of social relations which structure gender relations." This statement leads to some difficulty in understanding Walby's work because she does not define what is meant by "constellations of social relations."

Further on in both her 1989 article and her 1990 book, *Theorizing Patriarchy*, Walby suggests there are characteristics of gender relations that are crucial in every patriarchal structure. In paid employment, these characteristics are a sex-segregated labour force, sex-based wage discrimination, and the fact that women engage in the paid labour force at lower rates than men; in household production, the domestic division of labour, reproductive capabilities, and household compositions more generally are the key features of gender relations. What remains unclear is how "constellations of social relations" shape these features of gender relations and what these social relations are.

Nonetheless, Walby, in identifying six structures of patriarchy, addresses another of the central criticisms of the concept, namely, the tendency among those who use it to locate women's oppression in one or possibly two domains of social life (Acker 1989; Fox 1989). As shown above, radical feminists most often discuss patriarchy in relation to women's domestic responsibilities, their reproductive capacity, or "compulsory" heterosexuality (Firestone 1971; O'Brien 1981; Rich 1980). The problem with such approaches is that they fail to acknowledge that the oppression of women occurs outside the home as well, most notably, for Walby, in paid labour, culture, and the state. Furthermore, variations in women's experiences, both historically and cross-culturally, are difficult to capture if assessments are limited to one domain. Hence, Walby (1990) suggests—and rightly so—that she rescues patriarchy from one of its essential pitfalls by considering six structures of the oppression of women.

In her work, Walby (1989, 1990, 1997) is concerned primarily with patriarchy and capitalism, although she does acknowledge that these systems vary by other dimensions as well, such as "race" and age. Hence, she favours a dual- or plural-system theoretical approach and conceptualizes patriarchy as a system of oppression that is separate from capitalism, racism, and agism. In dual-system theories, the roots of patriarchy are generally thought to be located within the reproductive sphere of the family, whereas the roots of the political-economic system are located in the mode of production (Hartmann 1981). Walby (1989, 1990) argues that patriarchy infiltrates both, and that over time women's oppression and inequality have come to be based less on "private" patriarchy and more on "public" patriarchy. Private patriarchy is centred on the home and is distinguished by the exclusion of women from public roles and by men's appropriation of women's domestic labour. Public patriarchy, on the other hand, is centred on the economic and political spheres of social life and is characterized by the segregation of women into less powerful positions than men (Walby 1989, 1990). Table 3.1 outlines each of the six patriarchal structures as well as their fit in the public/private realm.

Walby concludes *Theorizing Patriarchy* (1990: 243) by stating bluntly that patriarchy is an essential concept for understanding gender inequality. Interestingly enough, Walby is less inclined to use the term *patriarchy* in her 1997 book, *Gender Transformations*, favouring instead the term *gender relations*. Yet her theoretical premises have changed only slightly, and she continues to insist on a separate-system approach.

Combining the Relations of Production and Distribution

Taking issue with both dual-system theory and the concept of patriarchy, Joan Acker (1988, 2000, 2006a, 2000b) sets out to develop a single-system theory of social relations that places equal emphasis on gender and social class. According to Acker, this requires "broadening class" and "the economic" (2000: 59). She argues that one way to do this is to consider in conceptualizing class both the social relations of distribution and the social relations of production, an idea that she introduced in her 1988 article "Class, Gender, and the Relations of Distribution."

The relations of distribution "are sequences of linked actions through which people share the necessities of survival" (Acker 1988: 478). According to Acker, the fact that there has

Table 3.1 Private and Public Patriarchy

Form of Patriarchy	Private	Public
Dominant structure	Household production	Employment/state
Wider patriarchal structures	Employment	Household production
	State	Sexuality
	Sexuality	Violence
	Violence	Culture
	Culture	
Period	C19th	C20th
Mode of expropriation	Individual	Collective
Patriarchal strategy	Exclusionary	Segregationist

Source: Walby, S. 1990. *Theorizing Patriarchy*. Oxford: Basil Blackwell, p. 24.

always been a sexual division of labour suggests that in all known societies the relations of distribution are influenced by gender and take on a gendered meaning. Gender relations of distribution in capitalist society are rooted in history and are transformed (like the relations of production) as the means of production change.

Acker suggests that the wage, which is rooted in the relations of production, is the essential component of distribution in capitalist society. The wage has developed historically as a gendered phenomenon because women have always been paid less than men and gendered job segregation is typical. Thus, "the wage and the work contexts within which it is earned are gendered in ways that re-create women's relative disadvantage" (Acker 1988: 483).

Personal relations, marital relations, and state relations are the gendered processes through which distribution occurs. According to Acker, *personal relations of distribution* are held together by emotional bonds, usually between blood relatives, and are dependent upon the wage. As a result of both the sex-based division of labour and the ideology of the family wage, gender serves to organize the personal relations of distribution. In its simplest form, this system requires that at least part of the male wage be distributed to women, who then redistribute it to the dependants in their families. The personal relations of distribution often extend beyond the household. In instances where economic hardships are typical, women often maintain extensive kinship networks in which survival is ensured through the allocation of resources between households. Among the economically advantaged, gender-based personal relations of distribution also occur, thereby helping to ensure the stability and reproduction of class (Acker 1988).

Marital relations are the central component of distribution for married women who do not work for pay and are thus dependent upon their husbands for their wage. According to Acker,

unwaged housewives are connected to the production process through their husband's wages. Although they share common standards of living with their husband, they do not assume the same class, because their situations, experiences, and activities are different. Unwaged wives have little control over their economic situation, although Acker suggests that this control likely varies by the men's and women's class.

State relations of distribution are the final type of distribution arrangement that Acker considers. State relations of distribution are based on laws and governmental policies that have historically been developed in gendered ways. Policies and laws established to alleviate the financial burden of the working class when the market fails are based on gendered ideologies supporting the "male breadwinner/ dependent housewife" ideal. This renders some groups of women—those who remain unmarried, single mothers, poor working women— particularly disadvantaged. Women are further disadvantaged by the gendered nature of entitlement regulations, because many social security programs are based on the labour-force experiences of men. As Figure 3.2 shows, however, there is often a disconnection between state policy towards gender equality and its actual implementation.

For Acker (1988: 495), the culmination of these gendered relations shapes social class. Conceptualizing class in this way allows unwaged persons to be included in the class structure. Thus, to fully understand the links between gender and class, divisions must be changed. One way to do this is to see class as rooted in relations of distribution (as well as in relations of production) that necessarily embed gender, both as ideology and as material inequality (Acker 1988: 496).

Besides "broadening class" and "the economic" (Acker 2000: 57), Acker draws on the work of E.P. Thompson (1963) and Dorothy Smith (1987) to argue that class should be conceptualized as social relations that take into

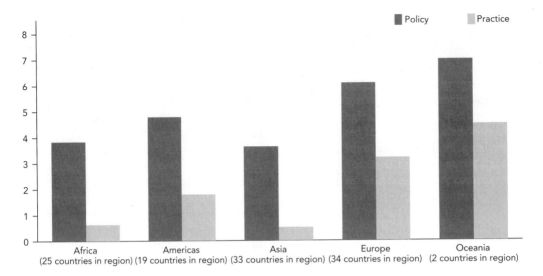

Figure 3.2 Equal Pay for Equal Work: A Comparative Perspective on Gender Wage Inequality

Source: International Labour Organisation. © Economist Intelligence Unit Limited 2010.

account the "processes that produce contradiction, conflict, and different life experiences" (Acker 1988: 496) and that are understood from the "standpoints of a multiplicity of women" (Acker 2000: 59). This view stands in contrast to those that argue for categorical conceptualizations of class; instead it emphasizes the things people do to manage their day-to-day lives. Furthermore, when class is understood from the standpoint of women, activities that may seem irrelevant in traditional class analysis, such as housework, become subjects worthy of analysis.

Finally, Acker (2000) argues that to understand fully the intersections between gender and class, scholars must understand that each mutually constitutes the other. In other words, the experience of being a woman or a man is fundamentally shaped by her or his social class, but class experience is also fundamentally shaped by one's gender. Acker points out that this applies to intersections between class, race, and gender as well; and, although underdeveloped in Acker's work, this mutually constitutive nature of gender, race, and class has been taken up by multicultural feminist scholars,

notably Evelyn Nakano Glenn and Patricia Hill Collins. What is missing in feminist scholarship, however, is a systematic assessment of the relationships between age relations and gender, class, ethnicity, or race (Calasanti and Slevin 2006; McMullin 1995, 2000).

"Doing Gender": Issues of Agency and Identity

Also missing in the preceding discussion is an assessment of how gender is produced and reproduced, or socially constructed, in daily interaction and of how **gendered identities** are formed. Candace West and Don Zimmerman's seminal article "Doing Gender" (1987) deals with these issues. As Table 3.2 shows, West and Zimmerman argue that to understand gender, a distinction needs to be made between sex, sex category, and gender. *Sex* refers to the biological criteria that are widely accepted in society to signify whether one is a man or a woman. *Sex category* is defined as the "socially required identificatory displays" that help to determine whether

Table 3.2 Sex, Sex Categorization, and Gender

	Definition	Example of Agnes: A transsexual, raised as a boy who developed a female identity at age 17
Sex	Biological criteria: genitalia at birth (i.e., penis or vagina) or chromosomal typing (i.e., XX or XY).	Agnes had a penis. She thought it was a mistake and had sex reassignment surgery (several years after she developed a female identity) to correct it.
Sex categorization	Socially required identification that determine one's membership in a sex category (i.e., style of hair or dress; mannerisms, etc.).	At age 17 Agnes began looking like a woman by dressing "appropriately," wearing makeup, etc.
Gender	Configurations of behaviour and activities involved in "being" a woman or man.	Agnes began acting like a woman by learning appropriate and inappropriate gendered behaviours. This behaviour was learned, in part, through interactions with her fiancé, who would comment on whether other women were acting appropriately. For instance, she learned that it was "offensive," for a woman to sunbathe on her front lawn because "it put her on display to other men."

Source: West and Zimmerman (1987) "Doing Gender." *Gender and Society* 1: 125–51.

one is a man or a woman (see Table 3.2 for examples). *Gender* is "the activity of managing situated conduct in light of normative conceptions of attitudes and activities appropriate for one's sex category" (West and Zimmerman 1987: 127).

According to West and Zimmerman, if we are to understand the social significance of gender, consideration needs to be given to both sex category and gender. Sex is less important, because we rarely scrutinize individuals' genitals or chromosomes. Rather, sex is assumed on the basis of sex categorization. Yet "socially required identificatory displays" in and of themselves are not sufficient explanations of gender. Rather, we must understand that individuals "do gender," and it is through doing gender that sex categorization is reproduced:

> Doing gender involves a complex of socially guided perceptual, interactional, and micropolitical activities that cast particular pursuits as expressions of masculine and feminine "natures." ... Gender is an emergent feature of social situations: both as an outcome of and a rationale for various

social arrangements and as a means of legitimating one of the most fundamental divisions of society. (West and Zimmerman 1987: 126)

Unlike the preceding discussions, in which gender inequality is largely considered a structural issue, West and Zimmerman draw on **symbolic interactionism**, arguing that gender inequality is realized and socially constructed through our daily activities in interaction with others. It is through social interaction that we develop gendered identities (masculinity and femininity) that come to be seen as "natural."

Although West and Zimmerman make occasional references to social structures in their work, the relationship between gender (as an activity) and the social structure remains ambiguous. This is, in part, because they never define what they mean by "social structure." Early in the article they seem to suggest that gender is a social structure when they note that Agnes's situation (see Table 3.2) "demonstrates how gender is created through interaction and at the same time structures interaction" (West and Zimmerman

1987: 131) and that "doing gender" is institutional in character (137). But in their concluding discussion of gender, power, and social change, they state that "if we do gender appropriately, we simultaneously sustain, reproduce, and render legitimate the institutional arrangements that are based on sex category" (146). Hence, rather than gender being a structure in itself, West and Zimmerman argue (147) that

> doing gender furnishes the interactional scaffolding of social structure.... Gender is a powerful ideological device, which produces, reproduces, and legitimates the choices and limits that are predicated on sex category. An understanding of how gender is produced in social situations will afford clarification of the interactional scaffolding of social structure and the social control processes that sustain it.

Here, doing gender seems to reflect the interactional activities that are temporarily attached to an evolving social structure based on sex category.

In short, West and Zimmerman seem to vacillate between an approach that conceptualizes gender as a social structure and one that

locates it as part of what Goffman (1983) has referred to as the "interaction order." It is likely that West and Zimmerman intended to develop a conceptualization of gender that encompassed both structural and interactional components. However, their lack of clarity about what social structure is and about the relationship between structural and interactional orders leaves the reader rather confused about their assessment of gender. Nonetheless, their article is one of the few conceptual papers on gender that explicitly consider agency and interaction (see McMahon 1995 for an excellent example of this approach with respect to motherhood).

Bringing It All Together

In an effort to incorporate macro and micro assessments of gender, Barbara Risman develops an instructive conceptual framework that treats gender itself as a social structure. As Figure 3.3 shows, Risman argues that to conceptualize gender as a structure in its own right, one must consider three levels of analysis. At the individual level, socialization processes and identity formation are at issue. The interactional level of analysis considers cultural, taken-

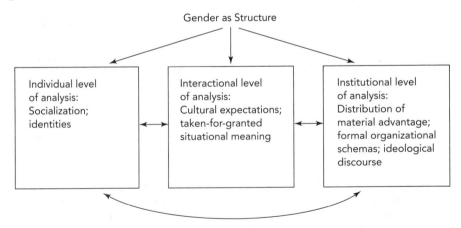

Figure 3.3 Risman's Structure Framework

Source: Risman (1998: 29). Copyright © 1998. Reprinted by permission of Yale University Press.

for-granted expectations about behaviour, whereas the institutional level of analysis considers processes of distribution, organizational rules, and ideological discourse. For a full understanding of the structural nature of gender, Risman (1998: 26–9) argues, the relationship between all three levels of analysis must be considered: "Gender itself must be considered a structural property of society.... Gender is deeply embedded as a basis for stratification, differentiating opportunities, and constraints" (28). The idea that gender is a structural property of society aligns well with the conceptual development of gender presented in this book. Yet, because Risman does not discuss gender in relational terms, the gender structure seems, in her argument, somewhat unconnected from individual experience. This idea is developed further in the next section.

Conceptualizing Gender in a Theory of Inequality

An essential task for the present analysis is to develop gender as a concept that can be well integrated with class, ethnic, race, and age relations. Some argue that, to accomplish this, the gendered division of labour must be at the core of the analysis (Chafetz 1990; Young 1981). Indeed, our emphasis on the processes of production, reproduction, and distribution suggests that we are sympathetic to such calls. However, it is a mistake to place the "gendered" division of labour at the forefront of such work: the division of labour in society, in families, and at work is organized simultaneously around the structures of gender, class, race, ethnicity, and age. What we need to ask, rather, is how labour and distribution processes are racialized, gendered, class-based, and age-based (with the exception of age, see also Acker [2006a, 2006b]. In other words, we need to know how these fundamental processes of social life are structured by the intersections of class, gender, age, race, and ethnic relations. Focusing on the practices of everyday life—on the things that people do—rather than on categories of people is important for understanding social inequality (Lorber 2006; Ray 2006).

A relational understanding of gender assumes that it is through our interactions with others that the structure of gender is realized. This view is similar to West and Zimmerman's view of gender in its emphasis on interaction. As West and Zimmerman point out, the structure of gender is not something that acts upon people. Rather, as individuals engage in interactive processes of production, reproduction, and distribution, they reinforce and sometimes modify existing masculine and feminine identities and structures. Structure does not exist outside of the individuals who produce it. However, unlike in West and Zimmerman's view of gender as an activity, in this analysis gender as a structured social relation is conceptualized as a "deep" social structure (Sewell 1992). Deep social structures underlie all of the activities of everyday life, and they are often invisible. In other words, a deep social structure such as gender is so pervasive in its influence that it is often "unconscious" and reflects "taken-for-granted mental assumptions or modes of procedure that actors normally apply without being aware that they are applying them" (Sewell 1992: 22). These taken-for-granted mental assumptions reflect the formal and informal cultural rules of behaviour (Sewell 1992) that influence the actions of women and men and frame society's assumptions and beliefs about compulsory heterosexuality (Rich 1980). It is important that assumptions about gendered behaviour are not thought to emerge from biological sex differences. Rather, these gendered structures refer to socially constructed differences that reinforce inequality on the basis of one's membership in a particular sex category (Gerson and Peiss 1985; Glenn 2000; Tilly 1998).

As is the case in most structural accounts of gender (see especially Acker's and Walby's, discussed above), a relational understanding of gender focuses on how oppression is implicated in relations among women, among men, and between women and men. Hence, like social class, oppression is an organizing feature of gender relations. For gender relations, however, material oppression is extended to include all types of oppression. Oppression occurs if (1) the welfare of one group of people depends upon the deprivations of another, and (2) the deprivations of the oppressed group depend upon the exclusion of that group from access to resources, rewards, and privileges. In this sense, gendered oppression can be both material and non-material and it can take place in various settings, including families, labour markets, states, and the education and health systems.

Charles Tilly (1998) argues that exploitation and opportunity hoarding are two mechanisms through which categorical inequality is produced. These mechanisms are especially helpful in explaining the relationship between oppression and structured gender relations. Unlike Wright's view of exploitation (see chapter 2), Tilly's definition does not depend on the appropriation of labour but rather sees exploitation as a mechanism "which operates when powerful, connected people command resources from which they draw significantly increased returns by coordinating the effort of outsiders whom they exclude from the full value added by that effort" (1998: 10).

Opportunity hoarding is a second mechanism through which categorical inequality is produced. Tilly (1998: 10) defines *opportunity hoarding* as a mechanism that "operates when members of a categorically bounded network acquire access to a resource that is valuable, renewable, subject to monopoly, supportive of network activities, and enhanced by the network's modus operandi."

Although these definitions are abstract, if we consider housework as a concrete example, we can see how gendered oppression is produced through exploitation and opportunity hoarding. When applied to the situation of housework, the assumption of power in Tilly's definition of exploitation suggests that men have the power and resources to have women do their housework for them. Power, in this instance, stems from many sources, including the ideological and cultural schemas that guide gendered behaviour. In twenty-first-century Western civilizations, our ideology and culture suggest that housework is, for the most part, women's work and responsibility. These ideologies combine with the material advantages that most men have over most women to create a situation in which men can exploit the unpaid labour of women. Men, then, benefit from increased returns on their material advantages by coordinating the unpaid work efforts of women, "whom they exclude from the full value added by that effort" (Tilly 1998: 10).

In the case of housework, opportunity hoarding works to men's advantage in dyadic relationships in which women have more material resources. In these situations, women are still generally responsible for the housework and men tend not to labour for their wives (L. Davies and McAlpine 1998). This happens because men are members of a *categorically bounded network* (Tilly 1998) who have access to unearned resources (i.e., to traditional authority) simply by virtue of their group membership. Recent work on the important connections between hegemonic masculinities and capitalism also points to the significance of opportunity hoarding but notably neglects the problems that older men may face within the context of hegemonic masculinities (Calasanti 2004; Calasanti and Slevin 2006).

According to Tilly (1998), categorical inequality is maintained through emulation and adaptation. That is, we learn from our interaction in social relations in one place, such as the family, and transpose that knowledge to another one, such as labour markets, and adapt accordingly. Continuing with the example of gendered oppression in unpaid work, the experiences of women labouring for men in the home may be transposed to other settings, thereby reinforcing and reproducing gendered oppression. Consider, for instance, a secretary getting her boss a cup of coffee or the segregation of women in undervalued nurturing-type jobs, such as nursing or elementary school education. Both examples reproduce a structure of gender relations that privileges men at work and at home.

While the concepts of exploitation, opportunity hoarding, emulation, and adaptation account nicely for the depth of structured gender relations, they shed very little light on how the structure of gender relations has changed or on how it continues to evolve. The challenge, then, is to tie the insights gained from "doing gender" to more structural accounts of gender relations so that social change and the significance of human agency are accounted for (see Gerson and Peiss 1985). Structure and agency will be discussed in chapter 6, but before that, the structures of race, ethnicity, and age will be examined.

▓ Questions for Critical Thought

1. What is the difference between "sex" and "gender"? What do sociologists means when they say that sex is socially constructed?
2. Do you believe that we still live in a patriarchal society? Do you think the examples of *matriarchal* societies discussed in this chapter may become more prominent in the future?
3. Have gender roles and norms become less rigid in modern societies? Choose an activity you regularly engage in. Does that activity reflect the idea of "doing gender"? Try to think of a social activity that is not gendered. Now, show how gender may influence that activity.
4. How was Beth's life shaped by gender? Discuss the processes of production and reproduction in this regard.

5. What is "opportunity hoarding"? Can you think of examples in which both men and women engage in this practice?
6. Do you think men entering traditionally female-dominated positions in the labour market is a bad thing? Is it possible that making these jobs "gender neutral" will have an advantageous outcome for both genders? Or, will men be the main beneficiaries?
7. Will we ever live in a society in which homosexuality is completely normalized? What about in the less developed world?
8. Are you surprised that attitudes toward gay marriage are similar in Canada and the United States? Why do you think it is that people are less accepting of *gay marriage* than they are of *homosexual behaviour*?

▓ Glossary

Dual-system theorists Socialist feminists who consider patriarchy and capitalism simultaneously as they interact with one another. The problem with dual-system theory is that it does not acknowledge how capitalism and patriarchy mutually constitute one another.

Gender The social construction of difference that is largely organized around biological sex.

Gendered identities The feelings, meanings, and subjective experiences attached to a particular gender. Such meanings are developed as we interact with others and are shaped by dominant gender ideologies.

Gender wage gap The total difference between male and female earnings expressed as a percentage of what men earn.

Heterosexual Sexual attraction to people of the opposite sex.

Heteronormative ideology The belief that heterosexuality is the dominant sexual orientation.

Homosexuality Sexual attraction to people of the same sex.

LGBT An acronym referring to the "lesbian, gay, bisexual, and transgendered" community.

Matriarchal systems of order A form of authority and social organization in which women exert power over men in the family, society, community, or the state.

Patriarchy As discussed by Weber, a form of traditional authority that reflects the relations between men and the power men have had over women, children, and often slaves. Feminists consider patriarchy a system of inequality in which men dominate women.

Radical feminism A branch of feminism that places emphasis on the relations of reproduction and the disadvantages that women face as a result of how reproduction is organized in society. Traditionally, this branch of feminism has tended to reduce explanations of women's inequality to their capacity to give birth.

Sex Refers to the biological differences between men and women that reinforce socially constructed differences that lead to disparate positions in society for men and women.

Socialist feminism A branch of feminism that explains gender inequality by considering simultaneously gender relations and class relations or patriarchy and capitalism.

Symbolic interactionism A sociological approach that bases its understanding of social phenomena on daily interpersonal interactions. One important criticism of this approach is that it emphasizes individual behaviour to the neglect of social-structural issues.

▦ Recommended Reading

Acker, Joan. 1988. "Class, Gender, and the Relations of Distribution." *Signs* 13, 8: 473–97. A seminal article that tackles the complexities of integrating gender and class into a single system of inequality.

Acker, Joan. 2006. *Class Questions, Feminist Answers*. Lanham, MD: Rowman & Littlefield. In this book, Joan Acker further develops her theories on the mutual constitution of class and gender.

Fox, Bonnie J. 1988. "Conceptualizing 'Patriarchy.'" *Canadian Review of Sociology and Anthropology* 25: 163–83. This article provides a good overview of the debates in feminism about the problems with the concept of "patriarchy."

Marshall, Barbara L. 2000. *Configuring Gender: Explorations in Theory and Politics*. Peterborough, ON: Broadview Press. In this book, Marshall explores the concept of "gender," how it has changed, and how it has been used politically in various contexts.

Nelson, Claudia, and Michelle H. Martin, eds. 2004. *Sexual Pedagogies: Sex Education in Britain, Australia, and America, 1879-2000*. New York and Basingstoke: Palgrave Macmillan. This book explores how sex education has changed in recent decades in modern society.

Risman, Barbara J. 1998. *Gender Vertigo: American Families in Transition.* New Haven, CT: Yale University Press. Barbara Risman is an American feminist scholar. *Gender Vertigo* provides an accessible account of how gender structures inequality within American families while acknowledging the importance of agency.

Walby, Sylvia. 2011. *The Future of Feminism.* Cambridge: Polity Press. Sylvia Walby is an ardent supporter of the "patriarchy" concept. In her latest book, she outlines how gender inequality has been addressed and work still lies ahead.

West, Candace, and Don Zimmerman, 1987. "Doing Gender." *Gender and Society* 1: 125–51. This is perhaps the most widely cited theoretical article on gender. Using a symbolic-interactionist perspective, it is a theoretical account of how gender is reproduced in everyday life.

⠿ Relevant Websites

Status of Women Canada
www.swc-cfc.gc.ca

**This website is run by the government of Canada and provides much statistical information, many reports, and funding opportunities for research about women and social inequality.

United Nations Population Fund: Promoting Gender Equality
www.unfpa.org/gender/index.htm

**This website focuses on gender equality across the globe. It includes information on gender and development, gender and health, and gender and violence against women.

Gender Equality and Development
www.oecd.org/dac/gender-development/

** This is an international forum where experts from development co-operation agencies meet to define common approaches in support of gender equality and women's empowerment.

The International Gay and Lesbian Human Rights Commission
http://iglhrc.org

** The International Gay and Lesbian Human Rights Commission (IGLHRC) is a leading international organization dedicated to human-rights advocacy on behalf of people who experience discrimination or abuse on the basis of their actual or perceived sexual orientation, gender identity, or expression.

The World Bank
www.worldbank.org/mdgs/gender.html

** The World Bank has established a program to promote gender equality and empower women. It is part of their *Millennium Development Goals.* This web resource outlines their gender-equality strategy and their current progress in reducing gender inequality.

4

Race, Ethnicity, and Inequality

Introduction

The following quotation is from the end of an influential book by Michael Omi and Howard Winant, *Racial Formation in the United States* (1994: 158–9):

> In the US, race is present in every institution, every relationship, every individual. This is the case not only for the way society is organized—spatially, culturally, in terms of stratification, etc.—but also for our perceptions and understandings of personal experience. Thus as we watch the videotape of Rodney King being beaten, compare real estate prices in different neighborhoods, select a radio channel to enjoy while we drive to work, size up a potential client, customer, neighbor, or teacher, stand in line at the unemployment office or carry out a thousand other normal tasks, we are compelled to think racially, to use the racial categories and meaning systems into which we have been socialized.

Although there are notable differences between the historical processes of racial formation and racism in Canada and the United States, it is nonetheless clear that racial issues of social inequality are omnipresent in Canada as well. In Canada, we need only be reminded of Darrell Night, a First Nations man who was dumped by the police on the outskirts of Saskatoon on a freezing February night in 2000, and of the numerous other instances of police brutality and racialization in justice and policing that have occurred across Canada. We need only remember how Native children were taken from their homes, placed in residential schools, and often abused in the last century. We need only remember Oka and Caledonia, and the injustice that Native Canadians still face over land rights.

Of course, the history and magnitude of white privilege and racism in Canada extends beyond the First Nations/white racial dichotomy. During the early twentieth century, Chinese immigrants were required to pay an exorbitant $500 "head tax" for entry to Canada; according to one government spokesperson, this tax "so effectually restricted the inflow from China that it ceased to be a cause for alarm" (Craig 1968, cited in Knowles 1992: 48). During the Second World War, nearly 25,000 Japanese Canadians were systematically moved to internment camps simply because of their ancestry. Japanese Canadians have since received compensation and a formal apology from the federal government for the injustices they suffered, and in 2006 the Canadian Government recognized that Chinese head taxes were discriminatory. Although these events appear to be part of a distant past, the racialized persons and their families who were affected by these events still suffer the social, economic, and health effects of the original injustice (Ujimoto 1994).

Those are some examples of the blatant racism that has occurred in Canada. Unfortunately, ethnic and racial inequality is still widespread in Canada, though it exists in much more subtle forms. Racial and ethnic inequalities in schools, families, labour markets, and health systems— and in the state—will be discussed in the second part of this book. The purpose of this chapter is to assess several approaches to race that have been proposed in the sociological literature, as well as the relationship between ethnicity and race. We will also discuss how racial and ethnic inequality varies cross-nationally, paying close attention to how Canada's minority groups fare compared with others across the globe. The chapter will conclude with a discussion of the conceptualization of race that will be used in this book.

Thus far in this discussion we have taken as given the concept of "race." Some sociologists argue that using the concept of "race" without being critical of it is misleading, analytically incorrect, and politically dangerous (Loveman 1999; Miles and Torres 2000; Satzewich 1998). They argue that if scholars use the concept of "race" without problematizing it, race becomes reified. Sociologists use the term **reification** to refer to processes in which abstract concepts become real. Usually, processes of reification involve a generally held acceptance of a particular concept as immutable and somehow grounded in nature. Although most sociologists now accept that the character of race varies historically and temporally and that it has no biological basis, the problem is that these are not universally held views. By using the concept of race, it is argued, sociologists reinforce and reproduce commonly held assumptions about the "nature" of race. Hence, scholars who see reification as a problem argue that race as a category of sociological analysis should be abandoned entirely. Debates about this issue are rampant and contentious. It is to these debates that we now turn.

Abandoning the Concept of Race

The dangers of reifying race, combined with ambiguities about the concept itself, have led some to argue that the concept should not be used at all in social-scientific analysis (Loveman 1999; Miles and Torres 2000; Satzewich 1998). Arguments of this sort emerged in the social sciences in the early twentieth century, when scholars such as Max Weber, W.E.B. Du Bois, and Franz Boas rejected biological assessments of race (Omi and Winant 1994). In his controversial and bold book *Man's Most Dangerous Myth: A Fallacy of Race* (see Reynolds 1992), Ashley Montagu was perhaps the first physical anthropologist to adopt this view. Montagu argued against the use of mainstream classifications of race that relied on biological or physiological criteria. Since then, social scientists have disputed the scientific "evidence" that suggests that *Homo sapiens* can be neatly divided and classified into different racial categories on the basis of some physical characteristic (by phenotype, e.g., skin colour) or genetic difference (by genotype—e.g., identification of a "race" gene). Historical research outlining how the meaning of race has changed over time and place (Miles 1989) adds support to the idea that race categories are fluid. Most sociologists who study race are persuaded by these arguments and view race as a **social construction** rather than a biological essence. Notably, however, there is still a tendency among physical and developmental psychologists either to endorse the existence of a biologically grounded race concept or to be ambivalent about it (Reynolds 1992). Outside of academia, it is generally believed that clearly demarcated races do exist. The persistence of these beliefs combined with the limited academic endorsement of biological race is one of the central reasons that critics of the term call for it to be abandoned (Miles and Torres 2000; Satzewich 1998).

A second argument against the use of the concept of race reflects the complexity and ambiguity associated with the term (Hugenberg and Bodenhausen 2004). If we accept, for instance, that physical characteristics and biological differences cannot accurately classify races of people, then what can? Country of birth? Nationality? Mother tongue? Some combination of these things? Does the colour of one's skin matter at all? Further confusion arises when one considers the relationship between race and **ethnicity**. Is race different from ethnicity? If so, how?

Notably, scholars who condemn the use of the race concept in the social sciences do not dispute that white privilege, racism, and inequality on the basis of what many refer to as race exists. And, indeed, arguments that call for us to abandon race in our scholarship are meritorious. However, just as using the concept of race is risky business, so too is abandoning it. This is especially true in an era in which academic work is increasingly subjected to scrutiny by politicians, members of the media, and the public and in which the potential exists for a conservative misinterpretation of race as insignificant (Omi and Winant 1994). In fact, others argue that because race is real in its consequences, it should not be abandoned as a category of sociological analysis (Bonilla-Silva 1997; Fleras and Elliott 2007; Omi and Winant 1994). Indeed, Omi and Winant go so far as to say that it is only

by noticing race [that] we can begin to challenge racism, with its ever-more-absurd reduction of human experience to an essence attributed to all without regard for historical or social context. By noticing race we can challenge the state, the institutions of civil society, and ourselves as individuals to combat the legacy of inequality and injustice inherited from the past. By noticing race we can develop the political insight and mobilization necessary to make the US [and Canada] a more racially just and egalitarian society. (1994: 159)

Race is *not* rooted in biology. It is *not* a natural category of distinction. Race *is* socially constructed. And the social construction of race *does* matter. Although the use of the term *race* is unfashionable, we are convinced by Omi and Winant's argument and hence we use the term here. The challenge lies in conceptualizing race in a way that (1) does not disregard the complex social processes that lead to racialized outcomes of inequality (e.g., differences in income or occupational status) and (2) does not lead to a legitimation of the "essence" of race by either academics or non-academics (see Miles and Torres 2000).

Conceptualizing Race/ Ethnicity and Racism/ Ethnicism

Although the preceding discussion has focused on race, both race and ethnicity have historically been significant structures of inequality in Canadian society (see Kalbach and Kalbach 2000) and across the globe (Blakemore and Boneham 1994; Breen and Jonsson 2005). Not surprisingly, in light of some of the questions posed above, there is in the empirical literature on race and ethnicity considerable conceptual confusion between the two terms. Indeed, one cannot understand race without understanding ethnicity, and yet distinguishing between them is complex.

Ethnicity: Issues of Culture and Identity

There is a decided emphasis in ethnic studies on culture, **ideology**, and descent as determinants of ethnic group and ethnic identity. Such accounts probably stem, at least in part, from Weber's assessment of ethnicity in *Economy and Society* ([1922] 1978). For Weber, ethnicity is socially constructed because beliefs about group differences serve to exclude individuals from certain associations while including them in others. Actual group differences need not have considerable social consequences. The social consequences of group differences emerge only when people begin to believe that those differences are significant. For Weber, ethnicity is constructed around several dimensions, including differences in language, customs, religion, ancestry, and physical characteristics. Again, however, these various differences have social significance only when they serve as the basis for labelling people as members of one ethnic group or another (Weber [1922] 1978). Weber argues that the reason for this labelling is not to identify groups of people with a common ancestry or nation. Rather, it is to exclude some groups from the rights and privileges that other groups enjoy. Social exclusion is thus a crucial concept in Weberian scholarship on ethnic-based inequality.

Similarly, Allahar and Côté (1998: 72) rely on social exclusion, or what they refer to as an "in-group/out-group dynamic," in their definition of ethnicity. In their view, ethnic-group identification and membership involve both subjective and objective assessments about whether the following characteristics apply to an individual or group:

a. a common history with a set of shared values and customs, language, style of dress, food, music, and other cultural attributes

b. a myth of common descent

c. national or territorial claims to sovereignty

d. an assumed inherited racial marker such as skin colour, hair texture, or facial features

e. some degree of economic or occupational specialization (Allahar and Côté 1998: 72)

Using one or more of these criteria, most Canadians engage in subjective assessments about whether they belong to a particular ethnic group and about which ethnic group others belong to. We often interpret each other's names and physical characteristics and ask questions such as "Are you Italian?" "What am I?" or assign some sort of ethnic identity (Scottish, Greek, Italian) to ourselves and others. Researchers also examine ethnicity on the basis of these self-assessments. Figure 4.1 provides a description of the racial and ethnic composition of Canada's population. According to this figure, in 2031 Canada's visible-minority population will rise to approximately 30.6 per cent (Statistics Canada 2010).

Studies of ethnicity tend to be concerned with assimilation (the extent to which ethnic groups are integrated into communities), cultural pluralism (the extent to which ethnic groups have maintained their ethnic identity), and whether certain ethnic groups are socially or economically disadvantaged compared with other ethnic groups (see Kalbach and Kalbach 2000; Satzewich 1998). Although all of these issues are related, the focus in this book is on the last. Some research shows that ethnic minorities in Canada experience less social and economic inequality than ethnic-minority groups in other countries. One reason may be because Canada has extremely high levels of immigration (See Table 4.1), which coincides with greater social and economic support among ethnic communities and groups.

It is hard to imagine Canadian society without ethnic diversity. Indeed, as Box 4.1 shows,

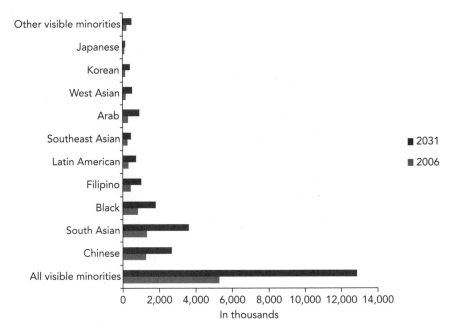

Figure 4.1 Visible-Minority Groups in Canada, 2006, 2031

Source: Statistics Canada. Projections of the Diversity of the Canadian Population. Catalogue no. 91-551-X. www5.statcan.gc.ca/olc-cel/olc.action?ObjId=91-5511X&ObjType=2&lang=en&limit=0

Canada's immigrant and visible-minority population is growing rapidly, especially in major immigrant-receiving provinces like Ontario.

Canada is not the only country that receives large populations of immigrations. Box 4.2 paints a global picture of immigration.

Many view Canada as an exemplar of how governments should incorporate ethnic populations and new immigrant groups into their society. According to the OECD (see Figure 4.2 below), Canada ranks sixth among all OECD nations in overall immigrant well-being. Each bar in Figure 4.2 represents an OECD nation, with the dark grey bar representing Canada and the medium grey bar representing the average OECD country scores. As this figure shows, Canada's efforts are not perfect. In only four measures is it among the top five countries for immigrant well-being, and in one case—skill matching—it is far below the average.

Other evidence suggests that Canada's ethnic populations may not be doing as well as previously thought. For example, it has often been reported that ethnic-minority groups in Canada experience less perceived discrimination and social exclusion, and that most fare better in the labour market than ethnic minorities in other societies (including the United States and many parts of Europe). However, according to the Bureau of Labour Statistics, *highly skilled* immigrant workers with university degrees do much better in the US than in Canada.

Somewhat surprisingly, ethnic and racial exclusion and income inequality are particularly strong in Sweden and many other Scandinavian countries. This surprises many, because Sweden is revered for its progressive stance on reducing inequality and social exclusion. As Box 4.3 shows, that understanding of inequality is often much more complicated than it appears. Despite boasting a lower than average **GINI**

Table 4.1 Immigration to Canada, 2000 to 2013

Category	2000	2001	2002	2003	2004	2005	2006	2007	2008	2009	2010	2011	2012	2013
Family class	60,613	66,785	62,290	65,120	62,272	63,374	70,515	66,240	65,583	65,207	60,224	56,449	65,010	79,684
Economic immigrants	136,282	155,716	137,863	121,046	133,746	156,313	138,248	131,244	149,067	153,491	186,915	156,118	160,821	148,181
Refugees	30,091	27,917	25,110	25,983	32,686	35,774	32,499	27,954	21,859	22,850	24,697	27,873	23,099	24,049
Other immigrants	460	206	3,782	9,196	7,115	6,779	10,375	11,312	10,733	10,623	8,845	8,305	8,960	7,039
Category not stated	0	1	0	1	0	2	2	1	2	1	7	3	5	0
Gender not stated	10	12	4	3	4	1	1	2	1	0	0	1	0	0
Grand total	227,456	250,637	229,049	221,349	235,823	262,243	251,640	236,753	247,245	252,172	280,688	248,749	257,895	258,953

Source: Statistics Canada. March 2010. Projections of the Diversity of the Canadian Population. Catalogue no. 91-551-X.www.cic.gc.ca/english/resources/statistics/facts2013/permanent/01.asp

HIGHLIGHT

Box 4.1 2011 National Household Survey Highlights: Immigration in Canada

Proportion of Foreign-Born Highest in Ontario

- According to 2011 data from the National Household Survey (NHS), there were 3,611,365 immigrants living in Ontario (28.5 per cent of the total population). This was the highest proportion among all Canadian provinces and territories. British Columbia was second highest at 27.6 per cent. In 1961 immigrants accounted for 21.7 per cent of Ontario's population.
- Ontario accounted for 53.3 per cent of Canada's immigrant population (6.8 million) in 2011.
- Between 2006 and 2011, Ontario's immigrant population increased by 6.3 per cent.
- Ontario attracts 43.1 per cent of the 1.2 million newcomers who arrived in Canada during the 2006 to 2011 period.

Recent Immigrants Mainly from Asia

- Between 2006 and 2011, 63.1 per cent of Ontario immigrants arrived from Asia and the Middle East, making them Ontario's largest source of immigrants.
- European immigrants made up the second-largest group (12.0 per cent), down from 14.6 per cent during the previous five years.
- Immigration rates increased for immigrants from Africa, the Caribbean, Central and South America between 2006 and 2011—20.4 per cent in 2011 versus 18.2 per cent in 2006.
- The United Kingdom and the Russian Federation led all European countries in Canadian immigration.

Toronto Is Canada's Major Immigrant Gateway

- The NHS survey estimated that there were 2,537,410 (comprising 70.3 per cent of Ontario's and 37.4 per cent of Canada's overall immigrant populations) foreign-born individuals in Toronto in 2011. This was the largest number of any census metropolitan area.
- The foreign-born population grew by 9.4 per cent in Toronto between 2006 and 2011 compared with 8.1 per cent for the Canadian-born population.
- Toronto's foreign-born population accounted for 46 per cent of its total population in 2011, unchanged from 2006.

More Than Three-Quarters of New Immigrants to Ontario Settled in the Toronto Census Metropolitan Area

- Between 2006 and 2011, an estimated 381,745, or 76.2 per cent, chose to settle in Toronto. These recent immigrants made up about 7 per cent of Toronto's total population in 2011.
- The top two source countries for recent immigrants to Toronto were India and China.
- Between 2006 and 2011, immigrants from India (59,670 or 15.6 per cent) outnumbered immigrants from China (46,255 or 12.1 per cent) settling in Toronto.

Source: Summarized from Statistics Canada, 2011 National Household Survey. www.fin.gov.on.ca/en/economy/demographics/census/nhshi11-1.html

coefficient, Sweden has witnessed the largest increase of income inequality among the developed world over the past 25 years (OECD 2015). This increase has coincided with greater ethnic and racial tension.

Notably, certain characteristics that are usually associated with race, such as skin colour, are included as one component of ethnicity in Allahar and Côté's definition. Indeed, in sociological research, race is often subsumed under

Global perspective

Box 4.2 Rates of Immigration in Cross-National Perspective

Recent estimates suggest that 230 million people around the world are living outside the country they were born in. Not surprisingly, immigration often flows from poorer regions to rich ones: in the world's 18 richest countries, immigrants constitute 16 per cent of the population (Clark 2014). If one includes descendants of recent immigrants (i.e., second, third, and higher generations), the percentage is significantly larger, since immigrants generally have more children than the average native-born citizen.

According to Clark (2014):

Policymakers in rich countries have tended to treat immigration as a challenge, but a surmountable one. Previous eras of mass migration produced good outcomes, for immigrants and settlement countries alike. The vast pool of immigrants that arrived in the United States prior to 1914—a group that included Christian Arabs, Greeks, Hungarians, Italians, Japanese, Jews from the Russian Empire, and Scandinavians—assimilated rapidly and contributed to an economic boom. Similarly, since World War II, Australia, Canada, and New Zealand have successfully absorbed large numbers of immigrants from varied countries and backgrounds.

In other words, although immigrants faced many challenges—for example, social, cultural,

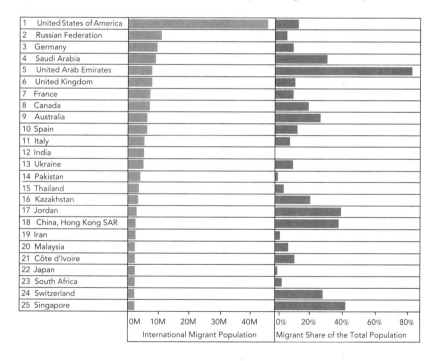

International Migrant Population and Migrant Share of Total Population— Top 25 Countries of Destination, 2013

Source: Migration Policy Institute tabulation of data from the United Nations, Department of Economic and Social Affairs (2013). Trends in International Migrant Stock: The 2013 revision (United Nations database, POP/DB/MIG/Stock/Rev.2013).

continued

and economic integration into the host society—for the most part, at least from an historical perspective, most had considerable success when integrating and contributing to their host society. However, as Clark notes, "it would be a mistake to assume that those experiences will be repeated for all immigrants." For example, recent research shows that immigrants to the United States and Europe have faced numerous difficulties in recent years. As Clark suggests, "policymakers would be wise to take those risks into account. Rather than focus on policies for integrating new immigrants, they should concentrate on avoiding selection policies that threaten to create near-permanent ethnic or religious underclasses."

Many countries around the world have taken in large numbers of immigrants. For example, according the Migration Policy Institute (mpi), in 2013, the United States was the top destination for immigrants with just over 45,785,000 people living as US residents. By comparison, Canada (ranked eighth) had 7,284,000, China (ranked eighteenth) had 2,805,000, and South Africa (ranked twenty-third) had 2,399,000 in 2013. In terms of immigrants' share of the total population (i.e., as a percentage), in 2013 the United States, Canada, China, and South Africa had 14.3, 20.7, 38.9, and 4.5 per cent respectively.

Sources: Gregory Clark. (August 26, 2014). "The American Dream Is an Illusion," Foreign Affairs; www.migrationpolicy.org/programs/data-hub/international-migration-statistics

Housing
Immigrants living in a suitably sized dwelling, %, 2009

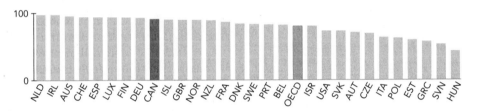

Income
Annual equivalized disposable income, USD, 2008

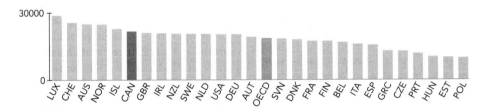

Health
Foreign-born adults in good health, %, 2009
Income

Education
Mean reading score of native-born children of immigrants, points, PISA 2009

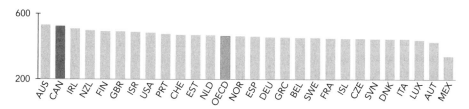

Employment
Employment rate of the foreign-born population (15-64), %, 2009–10

Skill matching
Highly educated immigrants (15-64) in highly skilled jobs, % of highly educated immigrant employees, 2009–10

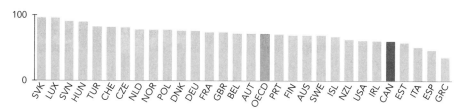

Naturalization
Naturalization rate, % of foreign population, 2010

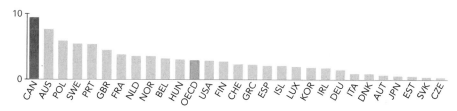

Figure 4.2 OECD Comparison in Immigrant Well-Being

Source: OECD. (2012) Indicators of Immigrant Integration 2012: Settling In, OECD Publishing, Paris. www.cic.gc.ca/english/resources/statistics/facts2013/permanent/01.asp

Global perspective

Box 4.3 Why Sweden Has Riots: The Fault-Line in Polly Toynbee's Perfect Society

by Johan Norberg

"All of them should have been very happy," Robert A. Heinlein begins his 1942 novel *Beyond This Horizon*. The material problem has been solved on this future earth, poverty and disease have been eradicated, work is optional. And yet parts of the citizenry are not enthusiastic. Some are bored, others are preparing a revolt. Why should that be, in such a utopian world?

A similar puzzlement has been the dominant reaction from commentators after riots broke out and cars and buildings were burned in heavily immigrant-populated suburbs of Stockholm in late May. *Sweden?* Since the standard interpretation is that violence is the only weapon the marginalised have against an oppressive socioeconomic system, it is more difficult to explain it when it takes place in "the most successful society the world has ever known," as Polly Toynbee once called it.

But it hasn't stopped some from trying. If all you have is two terms of sociology studies, everything looks like a justified grievance. Leftists abroad have blamed the rioting on the liberalization that has taken place in Sweden in recent years, and the supposed increase in inequality and poverty. The country's big social democratic daily, *Aftonbladet*, tried to point to the effects of austerity (in a country

where it has not been implemented) and claimed that the kids in the suburb of Husby rioted because "the health care centre, the post office, the midwives" centre and the youth centre have been wound up."

In fact, there are three youth centres in Husby. Its old health care centre closed, but a new one took its place. The midwives moved, but just one station away on the metro. You can find postal services 14 minutes from the centre, on foot. Where I live, you need to walk for 12 minutes. One shivers at the thought of what I could have been like had I lived another two minutes away. Would I also spend Friday nights torching nursery schools?

The Swedish poverty rate may very well be too high, but at 1.2 per cent, no European country has a lower one. The average in the European Union is 8.8 per cent. If poverty is the cause of riots, almost every city on the continent should have been burned down before Stockholm's turn came, including most of those in Norway and Switzerland.

But inequality has increased, you say. Yes, since the extremely egalitarian mid-1980s (the last time Stockholm saw large-scale youth riots, by the way). But since 2005, when Toynbee proclaimed Sweden the egalitarian utopia, it has barely moved.

---

the broad rubric of ethnicity (Anthias 1992; Loveman 1999). For instance, Anthias (1992: 421) argues that race categories "belong to the more encompassing category of ethnic collectivity" because race is only one of many ways in which exclusion is perpetuated on the basis of one's ethos or origin (either socially constructed or real). Similarly, Loveman (1999: 895) argues against the separation of race and ethnicity as categories of analysis because she questions whether there is anything "unique about the

operation or consequences of 'race.'" Omi and Winant (1994), on the other hand, argue that processes and consequences of racial formation are very different from processes and consequences of ethnic formation. For example, the social construction of "Native" or "black" in Canada and the United States—rooted in processes of geocide and slavery—is very different from the ethnic formation of and **discrimination** experienced by Irish immigrants in North America in the nineteenth century. What is

My country is the most equal in Europe save for Slovenia. Of course, some might argue that you need equality at Slovenia's level to maintain social harmony. That's unless you had heard of the series of mass protests — sometimes violent — which have rocked Slovenian cities since last November, resulting in the fall of the government.

Low poverty and inequality, generous welfare benefits, and schools, universities and health care for free. A society in which you are not poor just because you don't work.

All of them should have been very happy.

In fact, there is serious inequality in Sweden, but the divide is not so much between the rich and the poor as between those with jobs and those without. And frequently this is an ethnic divide. As the author Fredrik Segerfeldt points out in a new study, Sweden has the largest employment gap between natives and foreign-born of all the rich countries where data is available. Only 6.4 per cent of native Swedes are unemployed, but almost 16 per cent of the immigrants are. In Stockholm, as in Paris, this problem is concentrated in the suburbs. In Husby, where the riots started, 38 per cent of those under 26 neither study nor work.

So what's to blame? The aspect of the Swedish social model that the government has not dared to touch: strong employment protection. By law, the last person to be hired must be the first person to be sacked. And if you employ someone longer than six months, the contract is automatically made permanent. A system intended to protect the workers has condemned the young to a succession of short-term contracts. Sweden's high de facto minimum wage—around 70 per cent of the average wage—renders unemployed those whose skills are worth less than that. Sweden has the fewest low-wage, entry-level jobs in Europe. Just 2.5 per cent of Swedish jobs are on this level, compared with a European average of 17 per cent.

Those with poor education, experience or language skills have found that Sweden is not such a utopia after all. If you never get your first job, you never get the skills and experiences that would give you the second and third job. All that labour "protection" has created a society of insiders and outsiders. Sweden has generously welcomed immigrants into its borders. But there is another border—around its jobs market—and it is heavily fortified.

The result? Young men with nothing to do and nothing to lose, standing on the outside, looking in, with a sense of worthlessness, humiliation and boredom. It's not the first time that such a situation has ended in violence. When this happens in Sweden it shocks the left, because it shows that money isn't everything. A government can supply you with goods and services, but not with self-worth and the respect of others. A government can fulfil all your material needs, but it can't give you the sense that you accomplished this yourself.

Source: Johan Norberg. (8 June 2015). "Why Sweden Has Riots." *The Spectator*. www.spectator.co.uk/features/8927011/why-sweden-has-riots/

needed, Omi and Winant argue, is a structural approach to race that does not reduce it to issues of ethnicity.

Toward a Structural Account of Race and Racism

In the Marxist tradition, race and ethnicity "are the masks behind which actors conceal their class position both from each other and from themselves" (McAll 1990: 70). Marxist accounts of social inequality examine the role that race and ethnicity play in maintaining class boundaries. According to these perspectives, owners in certain manufacturing industries have traditionally hired immigrant workers at low levels of pay in order to maintain or increase their profit margins. Because these immigrant workers have little choice but to work for low wages, they are considered a threat by the established and higher-paid working class. Race and ethnicity become divisions within the working class.

This process is useful for capitalism because hostilities that would normally be directed toward the owners of the means of production are now contained among the workers themselves (Miles 1989; see also McAll 1990). As Miles (1989: 111) argues, "racism became a relation of production because it was an ideology that shaped decisively the formation and reproduction of the relation between exploiter and exploited: it was one of those representational elements that became historically conducive to the constitution and reproduction of a system of commodity production." The main problem with Marxist approaches to race and ethnicity is that their analysis is reduced to issues of social class; ethnicity and race do not warrant investigation in their own right (Bonilla-Silva 1997). Taking issue with approaches to race that focus on class (or ethnicity or nation), Omi and Winant (1994: 55) define race as "a concept which signifies and symbolizes social conflicts and interests by referring to different types of human bodies."

Racial Formation

According to Omi and Winant (1994: 55), racial formation is a "sociohistorical process by which racial categories are created, inhabited, transformed, and destroyed." The theory of racial formation centres on two related social phenomena: (1) historically situated racial projects and (2) the evolution of **hegemony**. Hegemony, a concept Omi and Winant borrow from the work of Antonio Gramsci, is the achievement and maintenance of rule by both political coercion and ideological consent (Gramsci 1971). Hence, Omi and Winant emphasize the role that political structures play in racial formation, arguing that "race is now a preeminently political phenomenon" (1994: 65) maintained through hegemonic forms of racial rule (67).

According to Gramsci (1971), hegemonic forms of rule evolve in modern societies as the force and coercion necessary for a ruling class

to achieve dominance give way to consent. Consent does not replace coercion in hegemonic forms of rule, but it takes on a more central role in modern systems of domination. Consent is achieved through the assimilation of the crucial interests of subordinate groups with the interests of dominant groups, often to the disadvantage of the dominant groups themselves. It is maintained through an ideological system that is controlled by the ruling group but that subordinate groups accept as legitimate. Such ideological systems are perpetuated in practice through institutions such as the family, religion, education, and the media.

With respect to racial formation in the United States, Omi and Winant note that the use of extreme force in a racial dictatorship through African slavery and the mass murder and expulsion of First Nations peoples gave way to consent in what might now be referred to as a "racial democracy." Crucial to this process were efforts of the subordinate racial groups to usurp, and later embrace, the religious and philosophical ideas of their oppressors. Regarding African slaves, Omi and Winant (1994: 67) write:

> In their language, in their religion with its focus on the Exodus theme and on Jesus's tribulations, in their music with its figuring of suffering, resistance, perseverance, and transcendence, in their interrogation of a political philosophy which sought perpetually to rationalize their bondage in a supposedly "free" society, the slaves incorporated elements of racial rule into their thought and practice, turning them against their original bearers.

Besides hegemony, Omi and Winant argue, racial formation also relies on racial projects. *Racial projects* are processes through which "human bodies and social structures are represented and organized" (Omi and Winant 1994: 56). They link everyday experiences with social structures. In other words, racial projects "connect what race means in a particular discursive practice and the ways in which both social structures and everyday experiences are racially organized, based on meaning" (Omi and Winant 1994: 56). Hence, racial projects occur at both the structural level and as individuals interact with one another. Racial projects are historically situated, and, say Omi and Winant, conventional understandings of race vary accordingly. In other words, what is meant by *race*, *black*, *white*, or *Aboriginal* today is very different from what these words meant 100 years ago. And the meanings of these words are different depending on where one lives (e.g., Canada as opposed to South Africa).

Structural racial projects occur in social, political, and economic domains, and examples of structural racial projects appear in Canada's newspapers nearly daily. For instance, in 2001 the government of British Columbia attempted to resolve Native land claim disputes and other "Native" issues by conducting a survey of its residents to assess their views on these issues. The questions were worded in such a way that the answers would favour right-wing government action. Aboriginal groups and human rights advocates argued that the questions were biased against First Nations peoples. The use of the survey by the BC government and the negative response to it by some groups are examples of politically structured racial projects.

Racial projects also occur at the individual level as people interact with one another. People make assumptions about others on the basis of their race and interact with them accordingly. Box 4.4 provides many examples of interactional racial projects. In it is the story of Crystal Samms, an Aboriginal 15-year-old who recently transferred to a Toronto high school that takes pride in its diversity. One of Crystal's racial projects becomes clear early in the article when she notes, referring to Caribbean classmates, that she is "not racist, but there's a certain race that causes trouble." And the racial projects of others in her class emerge when Crystal recounts

how she was mistaken for Hispanic and how, when she corrected this misconception, her friends stared at her blankly, not knowing how to respond.

These examples of racial projects point to the importance of distinguishing racist racial projects from non-racist racial projects. Omi and Winant argue that "a racial project can be defined as racist if and only if it creates or reproduces structures of domination based on essentialist categories of race" (1994: 71). The BC government's survey can be defined as a racist project because it meets both of these criteria. However, mistaking Crystal for Hispanic does not contribute to creating or reproducing a structure of domination and hence it is not likely "racist." As Omi and Winant (1994: 71) conclude, "to attribute merits, allocate values or resources to, and/or represent individuals or groups on the basis of racial identity should not be considered racist in and of itself."

Paying close attention to the ways in which social structures and individual experiences intersect, Omi and Winant argue that it is through structural and interactional racial projects that race becomes "common sense" (Omi and Winant 1994), conventional (Giddens 1993), or a deep structure (Sewell 1992). Through our experiences with racial projects, we internalize racial classification schema and make assessments about our own racial identity and that of others. For Omi and Winant, then, racial projects connect social structures with individuals and are simultaneously interactional and structural.

Omi and Winant's racial-formation theory has been most strongly criticized for their use of the concept of race (Loveman 1999; Miles and Torres 2000; Satzewich 1998). As noted above, while we are sympathetic to arguments in favour of abandoning "race," we remain convinced of the utility of studying it as a social-structural, relational, and socially constructed concept. Eduardo Bonilla-Silva's comments in defence of

HIGHLIGHT

Box 4.4 Canada's Apartheid Part 2: Crystal's Choice: The Best of Both Worlds

by John Stackhouse

Beneath the west flight path into Toronto's international airport sits a swath of portable classrooms, unheated and dimly lit, and each one resounding with a medley of accents.

On a field that was part of an Indian village before it was plowed by British settlers, converted to subdivisions and finally jammed with apartment blocks full of new immigrants, St Francis Xavier Secondary School in central Mississauga has become the image of a new Canada.

In a Grade 9 portable, a couple of Jamaicans talk about a coming track meet and plans for a weekend party. Italian, Ecuadorean and Chinese kids join in, ignoring their math assignments as they jabber in some of the 16 languages known to the school, and then revert as easily to English.

After a while, the conversations weave through each other so much that any inflection or slang becomes indistinguishable from the next. It seems as though the students and their families have always been here.

Except for one girl. She looks a bit uncomfortable as she sheds her nylon jacket and settles at the back of the classroom, but she knows that even though she is new to the school, her people always have been here.

At 15, Crystal Samms bubbles with the pride and confusion of someone trying to find her way in a foreign land. St Francis Xavier's 1,000 students list 90 countries as their homelands, but she is the only native Canadian among them. "When you speak of Canada, I am Canadian," she says. "This is my country."

Which is why, in Grade 9, she represents the biggest emerging challenge for native Canadians. Once segregated and forgotten on remote reserves, Aboriginal people are fast becoming urban people. But in the ethnic sprawl of Toronto or Vancouver, or even Edmonton, Winnipeg, and Ottawa, they are finding a very new Canada that is not very white, not very homogenous and not very interested in their concerns.

For Crystal, there is an age-old struggle here to preserve her native identity as she grows more distant from her ancestral reserve in Southwestern Ontario. But there is also that new challenge: how to forge an identity as one minority among many.

Inside the main building at St Francis Xavier (which relies on portables to keep up with local population growth), the hallways are a river of colours and torrent of international concerns. There are posters denouncing Third World sweat shops, coffee slaves and sugar slaves, as though the school were preparing for a Naomi Klein convention. By the entrance, there are also sacks and sacks of clothes, toys, and cooking utensils, collected by students as part of a drive to help families in Zambia and Malawi.

Soon after she transferred here in September, 2000, Crystal discovered that most students hang out with kids of their own race or colour. The school is proud of its diversity, even in the face of emerging ethnic gangs. ("I'm not racist, but there's a

his use of the concept of race are telling in this regard:

As long as "reified" blacks in the United States are still lynched by individual whites (as in the recent case in Jasper, Texas) and are 4.3 times more likely than whites to receive the death sentence; insofar as "reified" white Brazilians are 8.5 times more likely than black Brazilians certain race that causes trouble," Crystal says of the Caribbean girls in her class.)

At first, many kids took her for Hispanic, with her lip gloss, long nails and dark hair slicked back into a ponytail. When she told them she was Aboriginal, most of them stared blankly, which angered her more.

Didn't the students understand, she wondered, that there is a Third World just down the highway, a place where she once lived?

"I want them to focus on our world," Crystal says as her teacher interrupts his lesson to listen to her. "This is our land. The Spanish people, their land is in Ecuador. The Jamaican people, their land is in Jamaica. The English, their land is London. Our land is right here and we had it taken away."

By the time math class ends, Crystal has calmed down and turned her attention to another conversation, to find out where the weekend party will be. She also needs to collect her books and hurry to the main building to find her friend Amber. They need to talk about lunch.

While Crystal may have to shout to express her native identity, she also has to cope with the struggle of every teenager, to find herself in a world her parents do not understand. On the reserve, it might have been dictated by elders and traditional mores. But in the city, she has only herself, in an ocean of choices.

As Crystal goes in search of her best friend, she passes through the crowded school atrium, slipping by the taunts of a thuggish Hispanic gang. She hopes to find Amber at the entrance to the cafeteria, which is licensed to Harvey's, but the doorway is blocked by a group of black kids.

Crystal pushes past them too, as if she were at Square One, Mississauga's nearby shopping centrepiece. She's in a hurry, and afraid of no one.

When she was introduced at an assembly as the school's only Aboriginal student, jokers began to call her "Running Water" and ask if she parked her canoe in the school lot. Others showed reverence. "I wish I could be native, it's the coolest culture," she remembers one girl saying to her. "It's so spiritual."

Those who knew anything about natives seemed to get their images from television, from Hollywood stereotypes and shocking nightly news clips, like the ones last year that showed children sniffing gasoline in Sheshatshui. At the time, someone asked Crystal why the Labrador gasoline sniffers did it. She said she didn't know. They weren't her kids. She said she was "disgusted" with the media for focusing on one negative image of native life.

"I had friends come up to me and ask me, 'So what's that all about?'

"I said, 'How am I supposed to know?'

"'You're native.'

"I said, 'Because I'm native, I'm supposed to know all the answers?'

"Then an Italian friend said, 'Is it like that on your reserve?'

"'Like what?'

"'I heard there's lots of drugs and drinking on reserves.'

"I was disgusted. I told her to walk away. Then I said, 'Oh, yeah, I heard Italians are fat and eat a lot of pasta. Is that true?'"

and 5 times more likely than *pardos* to receive a college education; and as long as black Puerto Ricans have little access to political, economic, and social resources, I, a "reified" black-looking Puerto Rican,

will continue to study racial structurations throughout the world. (1999: 905)

Although he agrees with Omi and Winant in their use of the concept of "race," Bonilla-Silva

(1997) is critical of them for not placing enough emphasis on the structural component of race and racism.

Structural Racism

Dissatisfied with Omi and Winant's work, as well as with Marxist and ideological accounts of race and racism, Bonilla-Silva (1997) argues that a structural view of race and racism is necessary. While he recognizes that races are socially constructed, he nonetheless feels that we need to understand that the social relations that emerge through these constructions are real in their consequences. Racial classifications in particular require analysis because they limit the life chances and status of certain racial groups in relation to others.

Bonilla-Silva (1997) develops a conceptual framework of racialized social systems to understand various racial phenomena. He argues that many societies experience a process of racialization as racialized groups oppose one another at all societal levels. Such societies are racialized social systems "in which economic, political, social, and ideological levels are partially structured by the placement of actors in racial categories or races" (Bonilla-Silva 1997: 469) where "races" are socially constructed categories usually identified by phenotypes. The placement of actors in racial categories corresponds with a hierarchy of social relations in which "superior races" have advantages that "subordinate races" do not have. According to Bonilla-Silva (1997: 470), subordinate races are in positions in society that limit their access to valuable resources. These resources are both material (e.g., lower-status occupations) and ideological (e.g., superior races being considered smarter or better looking), and "the totality of these racialized social relations and practices constitutes the racial structure of society." Furthermore, the dynamics of everyday life in racialized social systems "always include[s] a racial component" (473).

Bonilla-Silva argues that in racialized social structures, races come to define their interests collectively, not individually, according to relations between racial groups. Race relations are rooted in power struggles where power is defined as a "racial group's capacity to push for its racial interests in relation to other races" (Bonilla-Silva 1997: 470). Racial power struggles lead to racial "strife," or what Bonilla-Silva refers to as "racial contestation" (1997: 473). Racial contestation is the "struggle of racial groups for systematic changes regarding their position at one or more levels," where "levels" refers to economic, social, political, and ideological domains (473). Hence, it is through the processes of racialization and racial contestation that "a set of social relations and practices based on racial distinctions develops at all societal levels" (474).

The crucial distinction between Bonilla-Silva's perspective and other views of race and racism is his focus on the structural nature of race relations rather than on their ideological character. In his view, although ideology plays a significant role in determining how various races are treated and viewed, the structure of race relations extends to social, political, and economic realms as well. In short, race also has a material base. Race relations are deep structures that are taken for granted and that inform individual interaction every day. Race structures everything.

Despite Bonilla-Silva's view that his approach differs significantly from Omi and Winant's, the two views seem more similar than different. It is true that Omi and Winant focus somewhat more on ideology than Bonilla-Silva, but that does not necessarily mean that their view of race and racism is not structural, as Bonilla-Silva implies. Indeed, Bonilla-Silva recognizes that ideology is one of several structural dimensions of race that need to be acknowledged. Further, by focusing on the structural nature of race and racism, Bonilla-Silva underemphasizes human agency and its relationship to structure in the process of racialization. Hence, one advantage of Omi and Winant's perspective is their conceptualization of racial projects as a link between structure and agency. However, neither of these approaches theorizes the relationship between social structure and agency fully enough for us to understand the everyday experience of racism.

Racism in Everyday Life

In her book *Understanding Everyday Racism*, Philomena Essed (1991) formulates a theory of race and racism that starts with the assumption that to understand the experience of racism, we must consider both macro and micro issues, or the relationship between structure and agency (see chapter 6 for a detailed discussion of structure and agency). On the question of race, Essed uses the term in quotation marks and refers to it as both an ideological and a social construction. Her ideas about the social construction of race are similar to those of Omi and Winant and Bonilla-Silva, but her approach differs in its emphasis on race's ideological construction. According to Essed, race is an ideological construct because the "idea of race has never existed outside of a framework of group interest . . . in which whites rank higher than non-whites" (1991: 43–4).

Essed's view of the structure of race is also very similar to those of both Omi and Winant and Bonilla-Silva. She argues, for instance, that "racism is a system of structural inequalities and a historical process, both created and recreated through routine practices" (1991: 39). In her definition of racism, Essed uses the term *system*, which follows Anthony Giddens's use (see chapter 6) to mean the "reproduced social relations between individuals and groups organized as regular social practices" (Essed 1991: 39). The term *social relations* does not refer to interpersonal relations between two people; rather, it is a structural term that refers to the rights, privileges, and rewards that define relationships among groups. Hence, the term *race relations* highlights the fact that access to resources and political, economic, and social rights varies among racial groups, creating systems of advantage for some and of disadvantage for others.

Essed differs from Omi and Winant and Bonilla-Silva in her emphasis on agency. She argues that, at a micro level, we must pay attention to the intentional and unintentional practices and consequences of human agency. In short, "structures of racism do not exist external to agents—they are made by agents—but specific practices are by definition racist only when they activate existing structural racial inequalities in the system" (Essed 1991: 39).

Racism, for Essed, is at once an ideology, a structure, and a process in which power, **prejudice**, and meaning are central elements. Relying on the work of Hannah Arendt and Steven Lukes, Essed defines power as a process in which certain groups (not individuals) maintain their position of power by drawing on ideologies that suggest there are innate differences between the powerful group and others. Furthermore, power "over other people affects them, through action or inaction, in a manner contrary to their interests, whether or not those who exercise power are aware of the success or consequences of their practices and whether or not the other party is aware of the power being exercised over him or her" (Essed 1991: 41). According to Essed, the idea that inaction is a form of power is especially important in understanding racism. Its importance is particularly evident when individuals from dominant racial groups do not speak out against racism and instead are passively tolerant of it. Say, for example, that you are a part of a privileged racial/ethnic group and that you have just been told a joke by someone who is also part of a privileged racial/ethnic group. This joke makes fun of a racial/ethnic group that is less privileged than your own. You do not find the joke funny and, indeed, feel that it is offensive. But rather than telling the person who told the joke that it is offensive, you say nothing. According to Essed, this inaction on your part reinforces the power your privileged group holds in society: you are reinforcing that power by being passively tolerant of the racism and by not speaking out against it.

According to Essed (1991: 44), racism is a process whereby structures and ideologies are produced and reproduced through prejudice and discrimination. The central components of prejudice are feelings of superiority, perceptions of intrinsic group differences, feelings of "propriety claim" to privileges and resources, and fear or suspicion that the subordinate race may take privileges away from the dominant race. Whereas prejudice is an attitude, discrimination consists of acts of behaviour with "intended or unintended negative or unfavourable consequences for racially or ethnically dominated groups" (Essed 1991: 45).

Finally, Essed argues that meaning is central to understanding the process of everyday racism. From this point of view, the meaning assigned to everyday events and interpersonal interaction is critical to the existence of society. Through processes of socialization, we learn to take the rules and norms of social behaviour for granted, and we attribute meaning to them accordingly. Although individuals engage in heterogeneous activities, there are underlying patterns of uniformity and acceptable modes of behaviour on which we rely in our everyday encounters with others. Hence, everyday racism is defined as a process in which "(a) socialized racist notions are integrated into meanings that make practices immediately definable and manageable, (b) practices with racist implications become in themselves familiar and repetitive, and (c) underlying racial and ethnic relations are actualized and reinforced through these routine or familiar practices in everyday situations" (Essed 1991: 52).

Essed elaborates upon her theory of everyday racism as she recounts the intensive interviews she conducted with well-educated, professional black women who live in the United States and the Netherlands. The story of Rosa N.

is particularly telling. Summarizing the experiences of everyday racism she has experienced as a doctor at a hospital in the Netherlands, Rosa discusses how difficult it is to acknowledge racism in an environment where it is not supposed to be tolerated:

> I can never in my life bring up the subject of racism. That just can't be, because they'll only trip me up. If you want to say anything about racism, you've got to state your case very well. Otherwise . . . they tackle you and lay down a thousand pieces of evidence to prove the opposite, and they make you ridiculous. (Essed 1991: 155)

Hence, the subtle nature of everyday racism exists in part because people of dominant groups are reluctant to acknowledge and address their own racist behaviour.

Essed develops a theoretical framework, shown here in Figure 4.3, that outlines the structure, ideology, and process of everyday racism. Here we see that culture (at the top of the diagram) and structure (at the bottom of the diagram) serve to rationalize and legitimize racial hierarchies (centre column) that are defined by meaning ("definitions of reality" in the diagram), norms and values, and access to resources. Structure and culture influence and are influenced by processes of exclusion and subordination. Examples of exclusion include racial- and ethnic-based labour-market segmentation (see chapter 9), the banning of certain racial minority and ethnic minority groups from organizations such as golf clubs, not recognizing certain credentials, and ignoring racism (e.g., the earlier example of not voicing objections to a racist joke). These forms of exclusion lead to a reproduction of the dominant views of the status quo. Examples of subordination include patronizing as well as other forms of racist behaviour and attitudes; subordination is influenced by tolerance, including a reluctance to take a stand against racism.

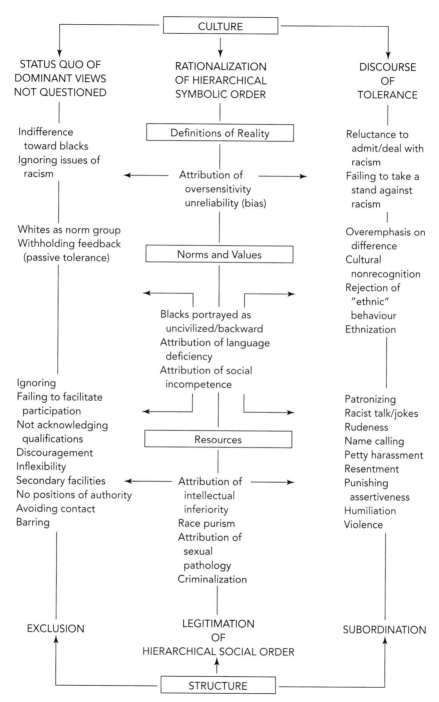

Figure 4.3 The Structure of Everyday Racism

Source: Essed (1991: 279). Copyright © 1991. Reprinted by permission of Sage Publications.

The strength of Essed's approach is its theoretical emphasis on the relationship between structure and agency and its acknowledgement of the intended and unintended consequences of human action, including the decision not to act at all. However, Essed's emphasis on ideology as the structural base on which race relations are organized is unfortunate. As Omi and Winant and Bonilla-Silva point out, race relations have historically had and continue to have a material base, characterized by exploitive labour practices. Although this oversight may be somewhat justified because of Essed's analysis of professional black women, her neglect of the material base of the social structure becomes problematic when one considers other occupational groups.

Conceptualizing Race and Ethnicity in a Theory of Inequality

If we are to understand inequality in Canada, both race and ethnicity must be addressed. Although some argue that race and racism must be given priority to fully appreciate inequality (Dei 1996), the approach taken here is that class, age, gender, ethnicity, and race must all be given equal weight. Some will be critical of such an approach and will question a white woman's right to make such claims. Though we empathize with such views, we agree with Davia Stasiulis, who says, "No one gender, race, or class should have the monopoly on intersectional theorizing" (1999: 391).

Markers of race and ethnicity, such as skin colour, mother tongue, and country of birth, may be identified for the purpose of empirically analyzing various outcomes of inequality. Such markers do not tell us much about the historical processes of racial and ethnic formation (Omi and Winant 1994) or about the everyday experiences of racism (Essed 1991); nevertheless, they are important for descriptive assessments of various outcomes of inequality, such as income, poverty, and perceived discrimination and vulnerability. Indeed, as Table 4.2 shows, such markers indicate that **"visible minorities"** have lower incomes and higher poverty rates and that they perceive

Table 4.2 Objective and Perceived Ethnoracial Inequality in Canada, by Ancestry

	IE Income (mean $)[a]	Poverty Rate (%)[b]	Perceived Discrimination (%)	Perceived Vulnerability (%)	N
Nonvisible minorities (by ancestry)[c]					
Canadian	1,258.7	16.4	10.7	14.3	10,293
French	750.5	16.6	9.1	19.2	592
British	3,386.1	11.8	10.7	15.0	1,744
Northern and Western European	2,238.2	12.5	10.0	11.2	4,356
Russian and Eastern European	405.7	16.2	12.5	16.5	299
Other Southern European	−2,778.6	14.3[d]	14.7	16.8	2,098
Jewish	11,637.7	13.3[d]	20.0	38.7	276
Arab and West Asian	−6,058.4	29.2	18.9	21.2	125

Table 4.2 *Continued*

	IE Income (mean $)[a]	Poverty Rate (%)[b]	Perceived Discrimination (%)	Perceived Vulnerability (%)	N
Latin American	−7,416.6	25.1	24.2	23.8	5,893
Greek	−617.4	16.3[d]	13.6	15.6	291
Italian	1,278.0	12.2[d]	11.5	19.2	207
Portuguese	−5,832.7	12.8[d]	8.9	15.9	568
Other European	9,453.1	12.5	16.2	16.0	4,109
Total nonvisible minorities	**1,895.3**	**14.2**	**10.6**	**16.0**	**30,851**
Visible minorities (all ancestries)					
Chinese	−6,730.2	26.9	33.2	33.6	513
South Asian	−5,815.8	21.7	33.1	38.7	1,424
Black	−10,607.2	31.1	49.6	43.0	2,421
Filipino	−5,063.5	16.4[d]	35.8	48.8	653
Latin American	−10,270.3	29.3	28.6	30.0	362
Southeast Asian	−6,829.3	25.6	34.5	37.7	148
Arab and West Asian	−13,359.4	40.8	29.8	27.0	386
Korean	−17,145.0	40.8[d]	40.5	49.0	209
Japanese	4,079.5	n/a	42.8	34.2	1,892
Other visible minorities	−7,114.5	23.7	33.3	36.8	331
Multiple visible minorities	−4,304.2	n/a	41.5	28.7	283
Total visible minorities	**−7,686.4**	**26.6**	**35.9**	**37.3**	**8,622**
Total					39,473

[a] Individual-equivalent household income, relative to the census metropolitan area (CMA) mean. The individual-equivalent income adjusts household incomes for household size, and is calculated by dividing household income by the square root of household size.

[b] Data on poverty rates are from the 2001 Census Public Use Microdata File, 2.7 per cent sample, for people aged 15 and over, and are based on Statistics Canada's low-income cut-off. In those data, visible minorities are identified only as Black, South Asian, Chinese, and other visible minorities. In this table, "other visible minorities" are further identified as Filipino, Latin American, Southeast Asian, Arab and West Asian, and Korean, based on ancestry.

[c] The origins of the groups in the "nonvisible minorities" category include Arab, West Asian and Latin American, and these also appear in the "visible minorities" group. Those who are considered in the "nonvisible minorities" category described themselves as White in the visible minority question. Those who did not identify any ancestry or visible minority group or did not report household income or perceived inequality were excluded.

[d] Data exclude Maritime provinces.

Source: Statistics Canada. 2003a. Ethnic Diversity Survey 2002. Ottawa: Statistics Canada.

more discrimination against them and more vulnerability than do non-visible minorities. Hence, in Part II of this book, such markers will be used as indicators of race and ethnicity, although it will be noted simultaneously that race and ethnicity are social and ideological constructions that cannot be fully understood by being reduced to variables.

The challenge that remains is to conceptualize race and ethnicity within the theoretical framework of inequality that has slowly been evolving in this book. Recall that the processes of production, reproduction, and distribution are at the core of such a framework. Race and ethnicity, like gender and class, are consequential to these processes (Acker 2000). For instance, racial and ethnic-minority groups face discrimination in production processes, and their positions within production processes are often less autonomous and more alienated than those held by members of dominant groups (Das Gupta 1996). Dominant racial and ethnic groups have exploited and continue to exploit the reproductive labour of subordinate racial groups (Glenn 1992), and processes of reproduction vary considerably among racial groups (Collins 1990). Processes of distribution are also structured by racial and ethnic relations, as is evident in "racially and ethnically neutral" state unemployment insurance policies that model entitlement on the typical employment patterns of white middle-class men.

As was the case with gender and class, a relational understanding of race and ethnicity that focuses on how oppression is implicated in relations among various racial and ethnic-minority groups is necessary for this framework. Although the theories discussed in this chapter do not elaborate upon issues of racial and ethnic oppression, they all mention its importance. Recall that oppression occurs if (1) the welfare of one group of people depends on the deprivations of another and (2) the deprivations of the oppressed group depend upon the exclusion of the oppressed group from access to resources, rewards, and privileges. Racial and ethnic oppression, like gender and class, is both material and non-material and can take place in various settings. Exploitation, opportunity hoarding, emulation, and adaptation, as Tilly (1998) discusses them and as they are discussed in relation to gender in chapter 3, are also important considerations in assessments of race and ethnic relations.

Clearly, ideology is a central concept in assessments of race relations, and although we have discussed ideology in relation to class and gender, we have yet to provide a working definition of the term. This is, in part, because it is used in many diverse ways, making it an elusive concept in sociological theory. At a very basic level, *ideology* refers to the ideas, attitudes and beliefs, and norms and values that are held by members of a particular social group. With respect to race and ethnicity, ideology encompasses, for instance, ideas of racial and ethnic inferiority and attitudes toward inclusion or segregation. In theories of inequality, ideology is important to the extent that ideology serves to reproduce the rewards and privileges of certain groups in relation to others. Hence, when ideology is used to legitimize the inferior position of members of racial and ethnic-minority groups in social hierarchies, it becomes a central issue in studies of inequality. Indeed, recall from chapter 2 that Grabb (2007) considers the control of ideas to be one of three constituent elements of power (the other two are control of material resources and control of people).

The difficulty with integrating the concept of ideology into a theory of inequality is the relative emphasis that the concept is given in the framework of inequality. In Marxism, it is often thought that ideology stems from the economic relations of production and that dominant belief systems exist only to serve the interests of capitalists and of capitalism more broadly. On the other hand, radical feminists, as well as some of the theorists discussed in this chapter, tend to think of ideology as systems of ideas (e.g., patriarchy and racism) in their own right that have little to do with the relations of production. Neither of these approaches is sufficient for a theoretical framework of inequality that assesses the intersection of class, age, gender, ethnicity, and race. Hence, for the purpose of the theoretical framework presented in this book, we view ideology as systems of ideas and beliefs (sexism, racism, agism, individualism, elitism, and so on) that are dialectically intertwined with one another and with the structures of gender, class, age, race, and ethnicity. Hence, as Omi and Winant put it, "ideological beliefs have structural consequences and social structures give rise to beliefs" (1994: 74).

⠿ Questions for Critical Thought

1. Based on your reading of this chapter, how would you define "race" and "ethnicity"? Which concept is most useful for social research? Should researchers abandon "race" as a concept?
2. What are racialized projects? What is Omni and Winant's definition of racialized projects? Think of an example of a racialized project that you have encountered either at work or at school.
3. Assume that two people who have equal qualifications apply for a job. One of these people is black, the other white, and all else is equal. The place of employment has an equal-opportunity hiring policy and the black person is hired. According to Omni and Winant, is this a racial project? Is this racist? Why or why not?
4. We presented evidence that in 2031 Canada's visible-minority population will be nearly 30 per cent. If this number continues to grow, do you think that ethnic and racial inequalities will disappear in Canada? Why or why not?
5. We have discussed some examples of blatant racism that occurred at the hand of the Canadian government (residential schools, Chinese head taxes, and Japanese internment camps). Do you feel that the Canadian government has done enough to repair the lingering damage done by these actions?

⠿ Glossary

Discrimination Prejudicial treatment of a person or group. Although related to prejudice, *discrimination* refers to behaviour rather than to subjective feelings. Discrimination results when individuals or groups carry through with their prejudice and preclude members of other groups from gaining access to resources, rewards, or privileges.

GINI coefficient A measure of statistical dispersion across the income distribution.

Hegemony The dominance of one group over another. *Hegemony* expresses the idea that dominance is achieved and maintained through both ideological and coercive processes.

Ideology Generally held beliefs, ideas, attitudes, or opinions about social life that significantly influence human behaviour. These ideas are not viewed simply as a product of thought but are based on economic and social realities. Some argue that people who hold power in society actively construct a dominant ideology that will allow them to maintain their control (see also *Hegemony*).

Prejudice Feelings of superiority that often result from beliefs in intrinsic differences between racially classified groups.

Reification Social processes through which social phenomena or characteristics become naturalized and thereby considered immutable.

Social construction The process through which meaning is attributed to social rather than to biological or genetic factors. Closely connected to ideas associated with reification. Although much sociological work is socially constructive, the social construction of sex and race is more controversial.

⠿ Recommended Reading

Andersen, Benedict. 1991. *Imagined Communities: Reflections on the Origin and Spread of Nationalism*. Verso. *Imagined Communities* is a landmark in the studies of nationalism and national identities.

Bonilla-Silva, Eduardo. 1997. "Rethinking Racism: Toward a Structural Interpretation." *American Sociological Review* 62: 465–80. This controversial theoretical article acknowledges race as a socially constructed category and works toward developing a structural conceptualization of race with respect to inequality.

Borjas, George J. 1999. *Heaven's Door*. Princeton, NJ: Princeton University Press. This book analyzes immigrants' skills, national origins, welfare use, economic mobility, and impact on the labour market using new data to trace current trends in ethnic segregation.

Essed, Philomena. 1991. *Understanding Everyday Racism: An Interdisciplinary Theory*. Newbury Park, CA: Sage. This research monograph is based on a qualitative study of black women. The quotations and analyses in this book provide valuable insight into the experience of racism.

Fleras, Augie, and Jean Leonard Elliott. 2007. *Unequal Relations: An Introduction to Race, Ethnic, and Aboriginal Dynamics in Canada*. Toronto: Pearson, Prentice Hall. This comprehensive text covers the politics of race, racism, immigration, and multiculturalism and also includes excellent website links and film suggestions relevant to these issues.

Kalbach, Madeline A., and Warren E. Kalbach, eds. 2000. *Perspectives on Ethnicity in Canada*. Toronto: Harcourt Canada. Topics in this collection of articles on race and ethnicity in Canada include ethnic identification, ethnic diversity, and intersections of gender, race, and ethnicity.

Omi, Michael, and Howard Winant. 1994. *Racial Formation in the United States from the 1960s to the 1990s*. 2nd edn. New York: Routledge. This is a very influential book on the formation of race in the United States. The authors argue in favour of using race as an analytic concept.

Satzewich, Vic, ed. 1998. *Racism and Social Inequality in Canada*. Toronto: Thompson Educational. This comprehensive collection of articles on racism in Canada covers both theoretical and empirical issues and includes discussions of education, immigration, and justice.

⠿ Relevant Websites

Canadian Heritage

www.pch.gc.ca

**A federal government website with links to official pages for anti-racism, multiculturalism, diversity, and official languages.

Colour of Poverty

www.colourofpoverty.ca

**This website is sponsored by the Department of Canadian Heritage and contains useful facts about racialized poverty in Canada.

National Anti-Racism Council of Canada

www.narcc.ca

**This is a national community organization that works to eliminate racism in Canada.

OECD

www.oecd.org/migration/integrationindicators/keyindicatorsbycountry/

**The key indicators section allows for quick cross-national comparisons of OECD countries related to immigrant economic inequality.

5

Age and Inequality

Privacy is a privilege not granted to the aged or the young. Sometimes very young children can look at the old, and a look passes between them, conspiratorial, sly and knowing. It's because neither are human to the middling ones, those in their prime, as they say, like beef.
—Margaret Laurence, *The Stone Angel*

Introduction

In the short quotation from *The Stone Angel* that prefaces this chapter, Hagar Shipley, the 90-year-old protagonist of Margaret Laurence's novel, laments that her son and daughter-in-law have not complied with her request to put a lock on her bedroom door. In doing so, she astutely recognizes several issues that will be discussed in this chapter. First, Hagar recognizes that certain privileges in society are distributed on the basis of age. Second, she notes that age distinctions are made between the old, the middle-aged, and the young. And third, she observes a connection between the young and the old because of their relationships to the more privileged "middling ones."

Margaret Laurence's choice of the word *middling* to refer to those who are neither young nor old is interesting. At first one is struck by how much the word "middling" sounds like "meddling"—interfering in other people's lives. The *Oxford English Dictionary* (*OED*) illustrates this use of the word with the following quotation: "A meddling government, a government which tells them what to read, and say, and eat, and drink, and wear." This meddling government bears a striking similarity to Hagar's perceptions of the roles her son and especially her daughter-in-law play in her life. Second—and, in the context of the above quotation, ironically—the word *middling* may refer to "a person who or a thing which is mediocre or second-rate" (*OED*). Hence, Laurence may also use the phrase "middling ones" to express Hager's contempt for those who, because of their age, occupy a more privileged position in society than she does.

The privileges that are distributed on the basis of age relations extend far beyond that of privacy. In Canada in the early twenty-first century, very rarely are young children or teenagers afforded higher levels of status and power than middle-aged adults. Regardless of maturity, dexterity, or intellectual ability, teenagers who live in the developed world must reach a certain chronological age before they can legally drive a car, vote, get married, or drink alcohol. Wage scales are established for teenagers not on the basis of what they do, but by their chronological age. Hence, a 17-year-old working at the same job as a 20-year-old can legally be paid less for doing the same work. All of this suggests that the status and power of younger people lag far behind that of middle-aged or older persons.

Yet, as Hagar Shipley knows, this age-based assessment of status and power is far too simple because it does not account for the decline in status and power older adults experience. How does this happen? In North American culture there is a cult of youth that favours young over old and that suggests that to be young is to be vibrant, beautiful, and happy whereas to be old is to be tired, unattractive, and grim. These cultural views do little to take away from the status and power of middle-aged people. They are, however, especially detrimental for older adults because, combined with the loss of youthful appeal and the resultant difficulties with self-image and self-esteem (Hurd Clarke 2001; McMullin and Cairney 2004), these adults lose the power and status associated with middle-aged activities, such as working for pay and raising families (see Calasanti and Slevin 2001).

Age inequality also exists in the developing world. Oftentimes, inequalities based on age are more severe in less developed countries. Though there are many explanations, one reason is because less developed countries tend not to have progressive welfare states and have higher levels of income inequality. Income inequality often follows people throughout the life course. Thus, living in more unequal conditions for extended periods of time eventually takes its toll. The ensuing discussion will focus

on this theme, as we pay close attention to *how* and *why* age inequality manifests and how it is counterbalanced (either by the state or the individual). In doing so, we discuss both the developed and the developing world.

Explanations of Age-Based Inequality

Age is the fifth dimension of inequality considered in this book, and it may well be the most understudied of the five. This is curious in light of the fact that the Canadian population is aging and that changes to the population age structure have led to considerable discussion of the challenges facing public pension schemes such as the Canada Pension Plan (CPP). Of all the policy platforms in Canada, our pension design has changed the least since its establishment in the late 1950s and early 1960s. It was the only social program in Canada to withstand major retrenchment during our government's shift toward **neoliberalism** in the 1990s. As recently as 2010, Canada's federal and provincial governments discussed *increasing* spending on CPP (Banting and Myles 2013), recognizing the importance of providing for older age groups (even during times when social spending was unpopular).

One reason that the state is paying greater attention to aging populations is because, relative to past generations, our current populations are *much* older. As Table 5.1 shows, in 2015, 16.1 per cent of Canada's population was aged 65 and over (an increase of over 15.3 per cent since 2006), while 21.9 per cent was aged 19 and younger. This figure represents nearly a 15 per cent increase in the number of people aged 65 and over since 1996 and nearly a 2 per cent decrease in the number of persons aged 19 and under since 2001.

Of course, it is not just Canada's population that is getting older. Figure 5.1 displays

Table 5.1 The 2015 Age Distribution in Canada by Gender

	2015					
	Canada	Male	Female	Canada	Male	Female
	Persons (thousands)			% of total each group		
Age group						
Total	35,851.8	17,776.7	18,075.1	100.0	100.0	100.0
0 to 4	1,933.4	990.9	942.5	5.4	5.6	5.2
5 to 9	1,951.8	999.6	952.2	5.4	5.6	5.3
10 to 14	1,864.2	957.5	906.7	5.2	5.4	5.0
15 to 19	2,099.4	1,079.5	1,019.9	5.9	6.1	5.6
20 to 24	2,465.6	1,263.3	1,202.3	6.9	7.1	6.7
25 to 29	2,467.6	1,239.9	1,227.7	6.9	7.0	6.8
30 to 34	2,501.9	1,247.3	1,254.6	7.0	7.0	6.9
35 to 39	2,403.2	1,197.6	1,205.6	6.7	6.7	6.7
40 to 44	2,350.3	1,173.5	1,176.8	6.6	6.6	6.5
45 to 49	2,433.1	1,219.0	1,214.1	6.8	6.9	6.7
50 to 54	2,763.7	1,387.2	1,376.5	7.7	7.8	7.6
55 to 59	2,602.4	1,298.4	1,304.0	7.3	7.3	7.2
60 to 64	2,234.2	1,103.5	1,130.6	6.2	6.2	6.3
65 to 69	1,909.8	931.7	978.1	5.3	5.2	5.4
70 to 74	1,371.4	652.2	719.1	3.8	3.7	4.0
75 to 79	998.5	456.2	542.2	2.8	2.6	3.0
80 to 84	742.9	318.9	424.0	2.1	1.8	2.3
85 to 89	478.3	180.8	297.4	1.3	1.0	1.6
90 and older	280.2	79.7	200.5	0.8	0.4	1.1

Source: Statistics Canada, CANSIM, Table 051-0001. www.statcan.gc.ca/tables-tableaux/sum-som/l01/cst01/demo10a-eng.htm

data from 1950 to 2050 (a statistical projection) and shows that in the developed world—e.g., in Canada, the United States, Sweden, and other Western nations—over 20 per cent of the population will be over age 60 in 2050 (an increase from about 10 per cent today). Less developed countries—e.g., China, Israel, Puerto Rico—and least developed—e.g., Africa and South-Central Asia—show a similar, albeit more muted, pattern.

Although obvious challenges will result from the aging of populations, if we place too much emphasis on older adults and on the elderly, we are liable to ignore the difficulties that face younger adults and to fuel intergenerational equity debates. Indeed, age relations are important in assessments of inequality regardless of chronological age. This is discussed in Box 5.1. Here we show that Chinese employment discrimination based on age has become so widespread that "older" university graduates (above 25 years of age) now face significant employment barriers and discrimination when trying to enter the labour market.

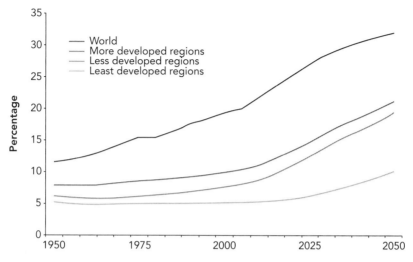

Figure 5.1 Proportion of the Population Aged 60 and Over, 1950–2050

Source: From World Population Ageing 2013, p. 18, by United Nations, Department of Economic and Social Affairs, Population Division. © United Nations 2013. Reprinted with the permission of the United Nations.

Global perspective

Box 5.1 Ageism in China: Why 25-and-Up Is Already Too Old to Hire in Beijing

by Zhang Fan

Last month, this city's Human Resources and Social Security Bureau introduced an administrative circular that stipulates "in principle" municipal government departments should impose age restrictions when hiring graduates settling in Beijing who are not officially residents holding local household registrations.

Those with undergraduate degrees who have moved to Beijing shouldn't be hired if they are older than 24, graduate students should be 28 or younger, and doctoral students, 35 or younger. The uproar came quickly.

On May 3, when interviewed by the Xinhua News Agency, the Beijing Human Resources and Social Security Bureau stated that their policy "has the premise of strictly controlling Beijing's household population growth." It stated that this new policy is not aimed at specific populations.

The system of "household registration" denies certain rights to migrants from other parts of China.

On April 16th, China's Education Ministry issued a paper that "strictly prohibits discrimination in employment." The aim is to protect the legitimate rights and interests of graduates from violations related to gender, household registration or academic qualifications. Nevertheless, Beijing does not seem to be affected. On the contrary, it seems to be putting into practice this new policy of discrimination involving one's age and household registration.

So should graduates who wish to stay on in Beijing be subject to an age threshold? Is it considered to be a reasonable administrative policy attempting to balance population control and social equity?

continued

Zheng Ge, Assistant Professor of Law at the University of Hong Kong, is convinced that in Beijing, where the environmental resources are below China's national average, it is necessary to enforce population control. However, the question is: does the cost of doing this have to be borne by those groups striving to change their own destiny?

Zheng pointed out that although it is recognized that age distinction and exclusion are flawed, it is effective in practice. Despite the age threshold appearing to be arbitrary, compared with gender, ethnicity, or educational degrees, it is relatively fairer. After all, when one knows the existence of an age threshold, one can adjust ones choice by continuous study without the interruption of working in between, or, even choose to study in Shanghai instead of in Beijing.

However, a fair society should provide channels of upward mobility for people who strive hard, Zheng Ge also pointed out. The reason why talent flocks to Beijing is not just because it has superior material conditions such as infrastructure and medical and education facilities, but also because the fierce job competition is actually a sign of an open labor market.

The smaller the place is, the more one relies on *guanxi*, the relationship, explains Zheng. The more interesting posts are often occupied by the relatives of local bigwigs. Older fresh graduates are often people who return to school aspiring to change their fate. The majority of them do not wish to go back to where they originally worked.

The Chinese government, says Zheng, should make efforts to break the local feudal networks so as to create a relatively fair and open nationwide job market. This is how to break the infatuation that the talented have with the Imperial capital.

"Even though differentiating and rejection are necessary management measures, the authorities should nonetheless try their best to reduce the harm to citizen rights when using this kind of method," Zheng asserts. Even though the one-size-fits-all age policy is fairer than gender or ethnicity discrimination, it nevertheless remains as a rigid policy that lacks sensibility to specific conditions. The government should allow employers autonomous decision-making so as to develop a screening mechanism based on merit rather [than] solely on birthplace or age.

Although the native Beijing people are not to be driven away, they should participate in fair competition instead of using household registration as an advantage on the job market.

Zheng Ge puts it bluntly: restricting official residency in fact cannot control the number of people who actually come to live and work in Beijing. The existence of a large number of "North drifting" migrants is an indisputable fact. Not to allow them to settle down in fact increases the government's management cost. Therefore, in the long run, migration should be dispersed, not blocked.

More generally, the current system of household registration solidifies regional disparities between urban and rural areas, and ought to be gradually replaced by a population registration system for security and management purposes.

"With the rapid development of China's process of urbanization, the transition function of the household registration system is gradually subsiding," concludes Zheng Ge. "The corresponding reform is inevitable. Against this backdrop, Beijing's new policy about settlement is going in the wrong direction."

Source: Zhang Fan. (May 22, 2013) "Ageism in China: Why 25-And-Up Is Already Too Old To Hire." Worldcrunch Media.

Age Stratification Theory

Age stratification theory is used by social theorists to improve the understanding of and better explain age-based inequality (e.g., the new phenomenon that being 25 is now "too old" in the Chinese labour market). The development of a formal statement of age stratification theory was foreshadowed in the late 1950s and early 1960s by Leonard Cain and Bernice Neugarten (V.W. Marshall 1995), but it was Matilda White Riley and her colleagues who were responsible for the formalization and subsequent elaborations of the theory. The basic premises of age stratification theory have changed little since its conception, although recent statements of this approach, now referred to as the **aging and society paradigm**, are perhaps clearer and more succinct (Riley, Foner, and Waring 1988; Riley and Riley 1994b).

Riley and her colleagues conceptualized age as both a process and a structure. At the structural level, similar-aged individuals form strata that may be defined on the basis of either chronological age or biological, psychological, or social stages of development (Riley, Johnson, and Foner 1972: 6). **Age strata** differ from one another in size and composition as well as in the relative contributions that each makes to society. Age is also established in the social structure as a "criterion for entering or relinquishing certain roles" (Riley, Johnson, and Foner 1972: 7), and thus it is used as a marker by which age-appropriate behaviour is gauged.

Riley uses the concept of structure without providing a concise definition of the term (Dowd 1987). Functionalist leanings are, however, clearly present in her discussions of social structures. Elements of the social structure are viewed either as social institutions (families, schools, work organizations, and nations; see Riley 1994; Riley and Riley 1994a, 1994b) or as patterns of social roles (Riley, Johnson, and Foner 1972). People (population structure) and roles (role structure) are differentiated by an age structure (Riley, Johnson, and Foner 1972: 6), the elements of which are age strata, age-related acts, age structure of roles, and age-related expectations and sanctions.

The fundamental processes in age stratification theory (Riley, Johnson, and Foner 1972) are cohort flow, individual aging, allocation, and socialization. Figure 5.2 documents how these processes influence the age-related social structures discussed above. In describing this figure, Riley and colleagues suggested that cohort flow is the "essential process underlying the changing size and composition of the age strata [and] consists of the formation of successive cohorts, their modification through migration and the gradual reduction and eventual dissolution of each cohort through the death of individual members" (Riley, Johnson, and Foner 1972: 8).

The aging process is conceptualized as a **biopsychosocial process** (Riley 1994), thus

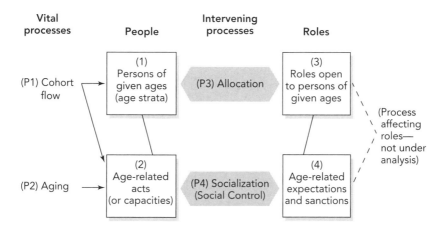

Figure 5.2 Processes Related to Structural Elements: Age Stratification Perspective

Source: Riley, Johnson, and Foner (1972: 9). © 1972 Russell Sage Foundation, 112 East 64th Street, New York, NY 10021. Reprinted with permission.

capturing psychological and biological development as well as the experience of entering and exiting social roles (Riley, Johnson, and Foner 1972). According to this theory, the aging process influences the structure of age-related acts or capacities (see Figure 5.2). Allocation and socialization are the processes that intervene between the social structures relating to people (persons of given ages or age strata and age-related acts or capacities) and those relating to roles (roles open to persons of given ages and age-related expectations and sanctions). **Allocation** is the process by which individuals are continually assigned and reassigned to particular roles; **socialization** is the process of teaching individuals how to perform new life-course roles (Riley, Johnson, and Foner 1972).

To disentangle issues related to aging from those related to cohort succession, Riley and colleagues (1972) developed another conceptual scheme, one that incorporates time. Figure 5.3 presents this scheme and shows that as cohorts

age, they move through time and through age strata (represented by the vertical lines). Thus, differences in age strata reflect a culmination of the effects of individual aging as well as different patterns of cohort composition (Riley, Johnson, and Foner 1972: 11).

The difference between the earlier and later models and theory that Riley developed lies more in clarity than in content. The first model (Figure 5.2) is now considered a synchronic view of the paradigm, while the second model (Figure 5.3) expands the first by enveloping it in social values and the physical environment. The second model is now considered to represent a **diachronic** view of the paradigm. The conceptual clarity of this model is greatly improved; it is reproduced here in Figure 5.4. The vertical axis represents aging, which is conceptualized as changes in individual lives and in the age criteria for entering and leaving roles. The horizontal axis represents time or history and refers to political, economic, and cultural

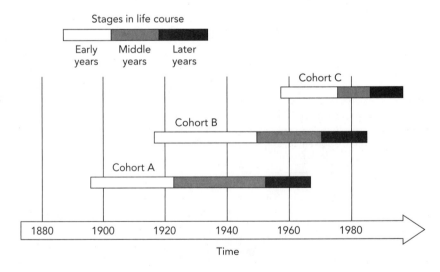

Figure 5.3 Processes of Cohort Formation and Aging Showing Selected Cohorts over Time: Age Stratification Perspective

Source: Riley, Johnson, and Foner (1972: 10). © 1972 Russell Sage Foundation, 112 East 64th Street, New York, NY 10021. Reprinted with permission.

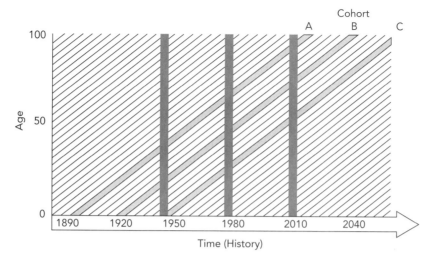

Figure 5.4 The Age-Stratification System: A Schematic View

Source: Riley, M. W., Foner, A., & Waring, J. (1988). Sociology of age. In N. J. Smelser (Ed.), Handbook of sociology (pp. 243-290). Newbury Park, CA: Sage. Copyright © 1988. Reprinted by permission of Sage Publications, Inc.

changes in society over time. The letters A, B, and C, representing **cohorts**, are placed on the diagonal to show the simultaneous processes of cohort flow and aging. The vertical bars represent the people and associated roles that constitute age-related structures, such as families, schools, and work organizations. Finally, the cross-sections show "how many people who are at different stages of their lives and involved in different social roles and institutions, are organized roughly in socially recognized age divisions or strata" (Riley, Foner, and Waring 1988: 244). The addition of age-related structures and the clarity of this model make it different from its predecessors. It does not, however, represent a significant change in the perspective itself: its components and their specification are the same.

Nonetheless, subtle changes in the terminology used to describe the theory came with the elaboration of the model, the change of name to "aging and society paradigm" being not the least of these. In the mid- to late 1980s, the word *dynamism* appeared in association with the model, encompassing both process and

change (Riley 1988). Riley described the evolution of the paradigm when she noted that the "distinction between people and roles led us to focus directly on the central theme of the paradigm: the two dynamisms—changes in lives and in structures" (Riley 1994: 438). Each dynamism is a distinct and separate process, they are interdependent, and both are asynchronous (different in timing) (Riley, Foner, and Waring 1988; Riley and Riley 1994b); as a result, they produce a **structural lag**, as human lives change faster than the social structure (Riley and Riley 1994b).

The models that make up age stratification theory were primarily established to organize a large body of data and to dispel several fallacies that were common in the aging literature before 1972 (some of which persist today). The *life-course fallacy* is the assumption that cross-sectional age differences capture the process of aging. *Cohort centrism* is the error of assuming that other cohorts age in the same way as one's own. *Age reification* treats chronological age as *the* life-course variable and does not take into account other factors that influence aging.

Finally, *reifying historical time* places emphasis on historical change rather than drawing attention to the particular aspects of change that are central to an understanding of variations in age structures or processes (Riley, Foner, and Waring 1988: 248).

By recognizing these misinterpretations, the aging and society paradigm seeks to explain the processes that underlie the movement of age cohorts through time and through age-related social structures. Exploring the asynchrony between individual and structural change, it attempts to resolve issues of conflict related to this structural lag. The theory also strives to understand the interdependence between age cohorts, social structures, and individual aging processes (Bengtson, Parrott, and Burgess 1994).

Age Strata

In age stratification research, the age system of inequality is generally conceptualized in terms of the differences between older, middle-aged, and younger age strata. Although there is some recognition that inequalities arise as age strata are constructed and reformulated through the changes in society and age-related processes (Riley, Foner, and Waring 1988: 268), age tends to be treated in static rather than dynamic terms. Thus, the processes and changes that are captured in the diachronic view of age stratification theory (see Figure 5.4) are generally absent in assessments of social inequality. Instead, there is a tendency to start with the assumption that age strata, with clearly defined roles and consequential rewards and expectations, exist and that they constitute a system of age-based inequality (Foner 1974, 1986; Riley, Foner, and Waring 1988; Riley, Johnson, and Foner 1972). Hence, these theories of inequality are generally framed within the **synchronic** model of age stratification theory (see Figure 5.3) and focus on the process of allocation and on the structure of roles and age-related expectations and sanctions.

Literature on the cultural meanings that individuals attribute to age casts doubt on the assumption that there are clearly defined age norms for different age strata. For instance, Neugarten, Moore, and Lowe (1965) showed long ago that the importance individuals assign to age norms in determining appropriate behaviour is a function of the age of the respondent (see also Elder and Rockwell 1976; Fallo-Mitchell and Ryff 1982). Compared with younger and middle-aged respondents, older adults tend to hold stronger convictions about age norms. Compared with older women, younger women prefer later ages for the onset of family events and earlier ages for educational and occupational events (Fallo-Mitchell and Ryff 1982). Assumptions about widely held age norms are also tenuous in the face of anthropological evidence showing that there are variations in the meanings attributed to age both within a given society and cross-culturally (Fry 1976, 1980, 1985, 1986). For instance, when Christine Fry (1976) asked a group of American adults to sort pictures that depicted people in different life situations into as many age categories as they deemed necessary, the respondents created between 2 and 15 age categories and used more than 100 different terms to describe them. The average number of age categories chosen was between 5 and 6, depending on other variables such as gender or marital status. Indeed, some argue that boundaries between culturally specified age categories are becoming increasingly blurred as active lifestyles, related consumer products, and the promotion of never-ending sex through medicalization (e.g., Viagra) are being marketed to aging baby boomers (Katz and Marshall 2003; B.L. Marshall and Katz 2002).

The preceding findings suggest that there are problems with the underlying assumptions about age strata as used in the age stratification approach. Nonetheless, the usefulness of this conceptualization comes from the idea that age distinctions are fundamental in our society and that they influence patterns of resource distribution for youth, the "middling ones," and the old.

Cohorts

The process of cohort flow is considered in age stratification discussions of inequality. In fact, Riley (1985: 386) goes so far as to suggest that age may predominate over other bases of inequality,[1] largely because cohort differences in education have strengthened the age stratification system. Here, the concept of cohort flow is discussed within the confines of the synchronic model. Historical, time-related issues—such as the experience of the Depression or of the Second World War—are left unmentioned, even though their influences on an individual's life chances have been demonstrated (Easterlin 1987; Elder 1985).

The relative neglect of temporal issues in this approach suggests that the conceptualization of cohort in age stratification theory may be problematic. Riley defines a cohort according to the definition Norman Ryder (1965) proposed in his seminal article "The Cohort as a Concept in the Study of Social Change." For Ryder (1965: 845), a *cohort* is an aggregate of individuals who experienced the same event within the same time interval; birth cohorts are only a special case of this more general definition. Notably, Ryder's conceptualization allows for individuals to be grouped according to any significant event. In practice, however, birth tends to be the event that is assigned the greatest significance. Thus, Riley views cohorts as aggregates of individuals who are born in the same time interval.

However, conceptualizing cohorts in arbitrarily defined single- or five-year age categories reifies chronological age as the basis of inequality and ignores more subjective dimensions of age that may be relevant (V. Marshall 1983; Passuth and Bengtson 1988). By assuming that one-year or five-year age cohorts take on meaningful significance, this approach masks qualitative differences in personal experience that are related to age (V.W. Marshall 1983).

Age Stratification Theory and Inequality

Age stratification theory has been applied to a large gamut of substantive research, including research into inequality in labour markets and families. In fact, in Canada, income inequality based on age has become so widespread that some commentators believe that it has eclipsed gender as a source of stratification (See Box 5.2). The average disposable income of 50- to 54-year-olds is about 65 per cent higher than that of 25- to 29-year-olds. This difference has risen from 47 per cent in the mid-1980s. According to age stratification theory, paid employment and family membership are considered socially valued roles because they function to maintain order in society. Older and younger age strata are relatively disadvantaged because they tend not to take part in the productive roles that are highly valued in modern society. Labour-force entries and exits are allocated by age, both directly through labour laws (see Box 5.3) and indirectly by educational criteria, for job entry, and by perceived age-related performance abilities, for job exit. There are also age differences in the kinds of jobs people hold and in the age distribution of the workforce (see chapter 9 for details). Younger workers are disproportionately employed in "bad jobs" that are poorly paid and have few benefits. Age-related roles and expectations for labour-force participation lead to different

HIGHLIGHT

Box 5.2 Age Passes Gender as Canada's Major Income Gap

Age-based income inequality has become a serious social issue in Canadian society.

New research from the Conference Board of Canada finds that younger workers are making less money relative to older workers regardless of gender and marital status. This report also finds that the income gap between older and younger workers has risen dramatically since the 1980s, leaving Canadians in their twenties to be much worse off today than they were in past generations. For example, in the 1980s the average disposable income of Canadians 50–54 was 47 per cent higher than Canadians 25 to 29. This gap has now increased to 64 per cent only a few decades later (see the figure below).

According to Conference Board vice-president David Stewart-Patterson, this new study was motivated by anecdotal evidence that suggested that Canadian youth were falling behind.

"We all know the stories—all our kids getting really good educations but too many of them are still stuck living in their parents' basements, still in low-end service jobs that don't really take advantage of all the education that we've paid for. . . . Our report provides some pretty persuasive, quantitative evidence that yeah, there really is a systemic pattern here. These aren't just stories of individuals—there really is a pattern that's unfolded over

a prolonged period, a pattern which has some disturbing implications going forward."

One of the reasons age inequality has grown so rapidly is because many employers offer new employees much less pay and reduced pensions for the same job. This trend is even more troubling because as the Baby-Boom generation moves into retirement, Canadians will be relying on a smaller share of the population to drive economic growth. According to Stewart-Patterson, Canada needs average employment incomes to rise once large portions of the baby boom generation retires so that we can pay for increasing health-care costs and a host of other expenses.

"Our generation fought for the principle of equal pay for work of equal value, and yet young people are coming into workplaces today and are being paid less for the same work," David Stewart-Patterson, the report's co-author and a Conference Board vice-president, said in an online video promoting his research.

"Age, rather than gender, is becoming the new divide in our society."

Sources: (Sep 23, 2014) "Younger workers poorer than parents' generation, research says." *CBC News*; Barrie McKenna. (Sept 23, 2014) "Age eclipsing gender as Canada's major income gap, report warns." *The Globe and Mail*.

Income Inequality between Canadian Generations, 1984–2010

Source: Data from Conference Board of Canada. 2014. The Buck Stops Here: Trends in Income Inequality Between Generations.

Global perspective

Box 5.3 Age Laws across the Globe

Denmark

Age discrimination laws were enacted in Denmark in 2004 as an amendment to the existing Danish Anti-Discrimination Act, which prohibited employers from discriminating on the basis of "race," colour, religion or belief, political opinion, sexual orientation, national, social, or ethnic origin, and disability.

According to the law it is illegal to discriminate on the grounds of age in all aspects of recruitment, dismissal, training, and retirement (prior to age 65).

However, Denmark employers can legally ignore this legislation if they can show that there are objective reasons for the age discrimination. However, despite this clause, Danish employers almost always follow the age discrimination legislations.

United States

The Age Discrimination in Employment Act (ADEA) was established 1967 in the United States. It prohibits age discrimination against employees 40 years of age or older. The ADEA is wide-ranging and includes hiring, discharge, and promotion decisions. Compared with other discrimination laws (in Denmark, for example), the US legislation is much narrower in its scope.

The US ADEA prohibits employers from dismissing (or failing to hire) someone because of their age, if they are over 40. A clear shortcoming of this law is that it does not protect workers under 40, especially younger Americans who are particularly at risk of employment and income inequality. Perhaps not surprisingly, then, the United States exhibits very high levels of employment inequality among younger and older workers.

Ireland

Ireland was one of the first EU members to prohibit workplace discrimination based on age. The main body of the legislation is the Employment Equality Act which was established in 1998, followed by the Equality Act of 2004 which was implemented to comply with EU Directive 2000/78 establishing a framework for equal treatment in the labour market.

The Acts prohibit direct and indirect discrimination on nine grounds, including age. Unfortunately, age has very little impact on age discrimination in Ireland, especially for older workers. While it is illegal for employers to ask how old applicants are, Cantillon and Vasquez del Aguila (2011) find that older people are often discriminated against in the hiring process.

Australia

The Age Discrimination Act 2004 (AD Act) is the Australian federal law that prohibits age discrimination. Prior to the AD Act, age discrimination laws were available under state or territory anti-discrimination legislation, which all prohibit discrimination based on a person's age.

The AD Act makes it unlawful to discriminate against a person on the ground of age in the following areas:

- employment and employment-related matters (including the employment of contract workers);
- education;
- access to premises;
- provision of goods, services, and facilities;
- provision of accommodation;
- disposal of land;
- administration of Commonwealth laws and programs; and
- requests for information on which age discrimination might be based.

Australian state and territory anti-discrimination laws operate alongside the AD Act. Thus, a person or group will have to decide whether to bring a complaint under the AD Act or the applicable state or territory law.

Sources: Julian Knight (Sept. 25, 2006) "How age laws work across the globe." *BBC News*; Sara Cantillon and Ernesto Vasquez del Aguila, (2011). "Older people and age discrimination in the Irish labour market." 11(4) *Social Justice*, p. 28-48.

rewards according to age, as well. Thus, compared with labour-force participants, retired workers and young people tend to be less powerful and are economically disadvantaged (see Box 5.2 for a narrative on the experience of inequality in later life). In labour markets, middle-aged and, sometimes, older workers assume more power and tend to make more money than younger workers, especially in well-established firms (Foner 1986; Foner and Schwab 1981; Riley, Foner, and Waring 1988; Riley, Johnson, and Foner 1972). However, when older workers lose their job, they are unemployed longer than younger workers (McMullin and Marshall 2001) and experience age discrimination in their search for employment (McMullin and Berger 2006).

Age stratification discussions of the family have concentrated on the age-graded nature of the family, its changing structure, its functions, and the roles and norms associated with different types of membership in families (Foner 1986). Inequality in families is generally assessed through economic differences and power imbalances between parents and their younger children. In families of procreation, parents have more power and economic control than their children because they assume the socializing and caregiving roles. In some of the worst cases, power imbalances in families cause children to run away from home, quit school, and live on the streets. The emphasis in discussions of later-life families is on whether older parents are neglected by their adult children (Riley, Foner, and Waring 1988). Although these discussions tend not to be framed within the context of power, an imbalance is implied in which the power shifts from parents to children.

In summary, age stratification researchers believe that people and roles are differentiated by an age structure, the elements of which are cohorts, age strata, age-related acts, age structure of roles, and age-related expectations and sanctions (Riley 1994; Riley, Johnson, and Foner

1972). Although this approach has made the theory accessible to large audiences of gerontologists (Dowd 1987), it has led to an oversimplification of the inequalities that are associated with age. Age strata, with their related roles, expectations, and sanctions, are assumed and are considered necessary to the functioning of society. Hence, this approach neglects the conflict that occurs when normative—in this case, age-based—roles are violated.

Disability and Inequality

Theorizing Disability

One of the most prominent social theories of disability is the **social model of disability theory**. Social models of disability argue that a disability is not inherently a part of the person, but instead a function of the interaction between the person and his or her environment. This theory takes the perspective that attitudes and social practices make people "disabled" by making it difficult for them to participate fully in their social and economic environments. This theory contends that social practices—including those at schools and in the workplace—should be reframed to allow for full inclusion of disabled people in every social and economic activity. In summary, the social model of disability emphasizes that the problems faced by disabled individuals are caused by discrimination rather than by physical or mental conditions alone (Oliver 2013; Putnam 2002; World Health Organization 2011).

Poverty, Socio-economic Status, and Disability

Perhaps one of the most overlooked and under-studied patterns of inequality is the association between disability and poverty. According to the World Health Organization (WHO), it is estimated that 1 billion people—15 per cent of the world's population—live with some form of disability (World Health Organization 2011). People with disabilities include those with long-term physical, mental, intellectual, or sensory impairments. These groups often have less education, fewer economic opportunities, and thus higher rates of poverty and economic inequality compared with non-disabled people. In Canada, the literacy gap between disabled and non-disabled students has been used to explain how poverty follows disabled people throughout the life course. Consider, for example, the literacy gap between disabled and non-disabled students by province. The average reading score for students with cognitive and emotional disabilities was 430 (i.e., the mean score across all provinces), compared with the national average, which was 530. In other words, there is a substantial gap in performance between students with reported cognitive and emotional disabilities and those with no disabilities, though students with physical disabilities scored only slightly lower than students without disabilities. These early disparities in academic achievement set the stage for people to experience even greater inequality later in life (Kohen et al. 2006).

In fact, a 2009 OECD study of 21 developed countries concluded that there were much higher rates of poverty among working-aged people with disabilities than among non-disabled working-aged groups. People with disabilities were nearly twice as likely to be unemployed, and more likely to work part-time and to hold low-income positions in the labour market (OECD 2009; World Health Organization 2011). Panel data from the UK from 1991 to 1998 also revealed that low socio-economic status (SES)—i.e., less education and low-paying or unpaid work—was a "selection" factor for disability. Average income and the employment rate fell drastically with the onset of disability, indicating that people were forced to leave the workforce once they became disabled (Jenkins and Rigg 2003).

Cross-national research finds that old age often leads to some form of disability.

For example, older people (those 65 and above) experience disability far more acutely than younger people. This pattern holds cross-nationally, with South Africa (81.4 per cent) and Sri Lanka (77.5) exhibiting the highest proportion of disability among their 65+ age groups. Germany and Canada hold the highest percentage of people under 65 representing people with disabilities (54.3 and 39.8 respectively).

However, it is more common for people of low SES groups to experience disability-associated impairments compared with people from high SES groups. According to Guerra et al. (2008), experiencing inequality throughout the life course increases the likelihood of disability among the elderly. Illiteracy, employment in low-skill occupations, poverty, and hunger each increase the likelihood of disability. In other research (Ramsay et al. 2008), elderly British men from low SES backgrounds were seen to be at a greater risk of developing disabilities associated with "activities of daily living" (ADL) and "instrumental activities of daily living" (IADL). ADL disabilities include not being able to perform simple daily tasks such as feeding and basic mobility, while IADL involves the inability to manage finances and use the telephone. In sum, people with disabilities tend to experience more poverty and have fewer opportunities to escape poverty than people without disabilities (World Health Organization 2011; Thomas 2006).

New research from the World Health Organization (2011) and the Economic and Social Research Council (ESRC) (2013) finds that the relationship between poverty and disability is most acute in low-income countries. This research shows that disabled people comprise one of the largest single groups of excluded and poverty-stricken people in the developing world (ESRC 2013). According to the World Health Organization (2011), the prevalence of disability increases with age and is more pronounced in low-income countries. For low age groups (i.e., ages 45–54) cross-country differences are less pronounced, but they are sharply polarized over the life course (i.e., ages 75+ in). This implies that older people are disproportionately represented in disability populations, but with far greater prevalence in low-income countries (WHO 2010).

The Political Economy of Aging

Between the late 1960s and the early 1980s, social gerontologists and youth theorists began to critique the normative and highly individualistic theories that neglected the importance of social class (V.W. Marshall and Tindale 1978; Tindale and Marshall 1980; Rowntree and Rowntree 1968). Responding to these critiques and to calls for a more radical and critical approach, several scholars from different countries began to assess age from a political-economy perspective: old age in one body of literature (Estes 1979; Estes, Swan, and Gerard 1982; Guillemard 1982, 1983; Myles 1980, 1981, 1984; Phillipson 1982; Townsend 1981; Walker 1981) and youth in another (Côté and Allahar 1994, 2006; Rowntree and Rowntree 1968).

Political-economy theorists seek to explain the relative situation of older and younger individuals by examining the relationship between the economic, political, and ideological structures that these systems of domination construct and reconstruct. Rather than explaining the problems that older people face as a result of their inability to adjust to retirement or aging or that young job seekers face because of a lack of experience, political economists attribute their problems to structural characteristics of the state and the economy and to inequalities in the distribution and allocation of resources and opportunities that these institutions create (Côté and Allahar 1994, 2006; Myles 1989; Phillipson 1982; Walker 1981).

The following are among the topics political-economy scholars have examined in relation to old age and youth:

1. How social policy has structured dependency and limited opportunities in old age and in youth (Côté and Allahar 1994; Phillipson 1982; Townsend 1981; Walker 1981).
2. How the commodification of the needs of older adults benefits capital and creates an "aging enterprise" (Estes 1979, 1991).
3. How old age and youth are dependent on the division of labour in society as well as on the distribution and allocation of resources. Related to this is how the institution of retirement creates a "social death" that serves to define old age (Guillemard 1982, 1983) and how limited job opportunities and other structural factors have created a situation of "arrested adulthood" among youth (Côté 2000).
4. The contradiction between the principles of democratic citizenship and the principles governing the capitalist system of allocation (Côté and Allahar 2006; Myles 1989).

To a greater or lesser extent, these studies consider the socially constructed nature of age and dependency; the influence of ideology in this construction; the influence of state, capital, and labour relations on the construction of age and age relations; and the effects of social policy for the elderly and youth. Although it is beyond the scope of this chapter to discuss the specifics of each of these arguments, it is important to consider the role of the state in political-economy research.

Although the state comprises many institutions (such as those concerned with education, criminal justice, and health care), research focusing on old age from a political-economy perspective generally equates the state with the governing bodies responsible for policies related to **social welfare**. Social welfare in studies of aging most often refers to social security and health benefits (Estes, Linkins, and Binney 1996). The importance of the state in this research stems from the power the state has over resource allocation and distribution because of its relations with capital and labour and its ultimate responsibility for the survival of the economic system (Estes, Linkins, and Binney 1996; Myles 1989, 1995). From the political-economy perspective, the state is thought to represent the interests of the most powerful members of society, and the existing social order is thought to be the result of power struggles in which the state participates (Estes 1991; Estes, Linkins, and Binney 1996). Rather than using consensus models in which the state is considered a "neutral entity, operating in the universal interests of all members of society" (Estes 1991: 22), political-economy scholars generally believe either that the state acts to maintain its own bureaucratic control (Offe and Ronge 1982, cited in Estes 1991) or that power struggles within the state represent class struggles (Myles 1989).

Similarly, and as Côté and Allahar discuss (2006), in studies of youth, the political-economy approach posits that the state serves the interests of capitalism by creating and reinforcing education and labour-market systems in which youth become dependent and alienated. According to this view, youth are, for instance, encouraged to gain further education

not only because it is in their best interests but because it serves the interests of the capitalist economy. In an environment where jobs are scarce, keeping people out of the labour market is seen as a good thing. Youth are then put into a kind of holding pattern in which they are either circling through poorly paid jobs or they are investing prolonged periods of time in the educational system, waiting until they can land a decent job and properly come of age. In fact, there has been a steady increase in the time spent in school among 18- to 24-years-olds (in 2011, 45 per cent were still attending school—a 15 per cent increase since 1990). Though this data does not go beyond 2011, by all accounts the trend has continued. Box 5.4 discusses it in more detail.

Important advances in the study of social inequality and aging have come from the political-economy analysis of state policies regarding retirement and pensions. For instance, Myles (1980, 1984, 1989) shows that income inequality in older age is a function both of the overall levels of inequality in a society and of the way pension systems alter or reproduce that inequality. Although inequalities in

HIGHLIGHT

Box 5.4 Delayed Adulthood and Transitions of Young Adults

The Transition to Adulthood

A notable demographic trend in Canada over the last two decades has been the delayed entry of young people into adulthood. The transition to adulthood is viewed as a period in which youth move though different stages into adult roles. During this transition period, young people make a wide range of choices about where to live and with whom, how to pursue their education, what type of work to do, and whether or not to marry and have children.

According to Rumbant (2004), there are five markers of adult transition:

Left school—has not attended school, college or university either full-time or part-time during the nine-month period between September and May.

Left parental home—is not a child in an economic family or a never-married child in a census family.

Full-time full-year work—has worked full-time for at least 49 weeks during the last year.

Ever in a conjugal union—is married, widowed, separated, or divorced (i.e., ever married) or is currently in a common-law relationship. In the text, this concept is referred to as "ever in a conjugal union."

continued

Has children—has never-married children living in the same household.

According to many large-scale national studies, since the 1970s it has taken longer for each successive generation to finish school, establish financial independence, marry, and have children. Compared with their parents, 25-year-olds today are twice as likely to be students, only half as likely to be married, and twice as likely to be receiving financial assistance from their parents.

Why Is This Transition Delayed?

Many social and economic factors have contributed to the delay in transitions to adulthood. Perhaps the most notable is the need to acquire higher-level education to compete in the labour market. Young adults have a strong economic incentive to continue their schooling beyond secondary completion. People with university degrees have higher earnings and considerably lower unemployment rates than high school graduates. Since the 1990s, the number of jobs requiring a degree doubled, while the number demanding high school education or less has strongly diminished. As a result, prolonged education is necessary to gain the skills needed in today's information- and knowledge-based economy.

Sources: Laurence Steinberg. (Sept 19, 2014) "The Case for Delayed Adulthood." *The New York Times*; www.statcan.gc.ca/pub/11-008-x/2007004/10311-eng.htm

pre-retirement years persist after retirement, an understanding of income inequalities among older people and between the old and the young requires an analysis of public pension structures. Traditionally, public pensions have been based either on pre-retirement incomes or on the idea of a national minimum benefit. In the first instance, pensions perpetuate class-, gender-, and ethnicity-based inequalities in older age by graduating pension incomes according to pre-retirement income. In the second instance, income equality among older people is achieved because the same sum of money is paid to everyone (this is known as *flat-benefit structure*; see Myles 1980, 1984, 1989).

Most Western capitalist nations have pension structures that combine flat and graduated schemes (Myles 1980). In Canada, for instance, the Canada Pension Plan/Quebec Pension Plan (**C/QPP**) represents a graduated scheme in which employees and employers pay into the plan according to the employees' pre-retirement income. However, these plans have an upper contribution limit that renders the pension scheme graduated at the bottom and flat on top (Myles 1980). Old Age Security (**OAS**) is a Canadian pension scheme that traditionally guaranteed a flat, per month benefit to all people aged 65 and over. There are also several provincial and federal programs that, based on income tests, provide income supplements to low-income pensioners.

The interplay of the C/QPP and OAS highlights a contradiction in modern, liberal-democratic states between the rights attached to the ownership of property and the rights afforded to persons in their capacity as citizens (Myles 1984, 1989). According to Myles (1989), the strategies used by different countries to come to terms with this contradiction determine the relative pension benefits of older people and are a reflection of class struggles within the state. Thus, Myles suggests that the quality and quantity of pension benefits are largely a function of the political mobilization of the working class and the election of working-class parties.

As noted earlier, compared with systems of other established welfare states, Canada's public pensions system was only marginally clawed back by political retrenchment efforts in the 1980s and 1990s. This speaks to the resiliency of class mobilization in Canada over this time period. However, as Map 5.1 shows, though Canada has not experienced a significant "claw back" on pension spending, this may be because, by international standards, the Canadian government spends much *less* on pensions than elsewhere around the world. As this map shows, the federal government spends about the same as Mexico, Australia, China, and many parts of Africa on public pensions, at least, as a percentage of spending relative to the gross domestic product (GDP).

Regardless of the specific details of government spending on public pensions in Canada compared with other countries, this brief summary of Myles's work illustrates the power that the state has in determining the economic status of older adults. Few researchers who study aging would dispute this point, although there is some disagreement among

political economists over the precise conceptualization of the state (see Estes 1991; Estes, Linkins, and Binney 1996) and the relative emphasis that should be placed on state relations (Myles 1989) as opposed to the relations of production (Guillemard 1982, 1983) in assessments of inequality. Most would also agree that old age and aging are socially constructed, in part, through these and other state policies.

Crucial to the political-economy perspective is the concept of social class. It is in discussions of social class that the Marxian influence in this perspective is most evident. Like Marx (1969; Marx and Engels [1848] 1970), political-economy researchers emphasize the relations of production in their conceptualization of social class, specifically the relations between those who own the means of production and those who do not (Guillemard 1982, 1983; Myles 1980, 1984, 1989; Phillipson 1982; Townsend 1981; Walker 1981). Thus,

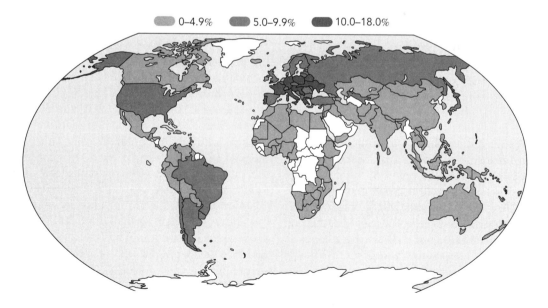

Map 5.1 Pension Spending as a Percentage of GDP (late 2000s)

Source: Pensions Database, Human Development Network Social Protection & Labor (HDNSP) Unit, World Bank, Washington, DC.

according to Guillemard (1982: 228), "the traditional Marxist definition, which analyzes the class structure of the capitalist mode of production by basically contrasting the two antagonistic classes—capitalist and proletarian—must be upheld."

The emphasis on the relations of production in the political-economy approach is paradoxical in the study of old age because many older people are no longer directly engaged in socially defined productive relations (Dowd 1980; Estes 1991; Estes, Swan, and Gerard 1982). One strategy of political economists to deal with this paradox is to use a life-course framework to assess the class relations of older adults according to their pre-retirement social class (Guillemard 1982, 1983; Phillipson 1982; Walker 1981). Aware of life-course processes, these political economists believe that power relations and resources in later life are shaped by people's earlier location within the social structure or by their class position. Missing in these accounts, however, is an analysis of the relationship between age relations and class relations as they structure inequality in later life. As others point out (Kohli 1988; Myles 1980), the economic and social locations of older people result not only from class inequalities in early life but also from unique processes that are structured by age relations.

Estes deals with the contradiction between the Marxist emphasis on productive labour and assessments of the social location of older people by turning to a more Weberian view of class. Drawing on Ehrenreich and Ehrenreich (1979: 11), she suggests that a social class is "characterized by a coherent social and cultural existence; members of a class share a common life style, educational background, kinship networks, consumption patterns, work habits, and beliefs" (Estes 1991: 25). This definition of social class, Estes argues (1991; Estes, Swan, and Gerard 1982), is analytically appropriate for older people because it does not necessarily reflect productive relations and can capture the dynamics involved with aging and social inequality.

Another way of dealing with this paradox is to assume that more than one structure of domination influences social inequality. Myles (1989), who employs this approach, argues that inequality in older age is shaped by two structures of domination in Western capitalist societies. One is based on the productive relations by which power is given to those who control economic resources. The other is based in the polity, where power is maintained by those who control political resources. The interplay between these power sources determines, both in principle and in practice (these do not often converge), the value of old age pensions and hence structures economic inequality in later life.

According to Myles (1989), negotiations between the polity and the economy over old age benefits are framed in contradictions because the principles of democratic politics are inconsistent with the principles of a capitalist economy. Public pension systems represent the compromise between these sets of principles that have been negotiated in the political arena. Thus, Myles argues that income inequality in old age is structured by the state rather than controlled by the market's invisible hand. However, a critical factor determining the extent of pension entitlements is the political mobilization of the working class (defined in Marxist terms), for Myles believes that power struggles within the state are essentially class conflicts.

Notably, income from public pensions is not always sufficient for living. As these data show, older age cohorts in both the developed and the developing world still rely on the market for adequate living (either because they are not eligible for public pensions or because the money provided is not adequate). In the developed world, about 10 per cent of people rely on labour income, while nearly 45 per cent do in the developing world. Though people above the age of 70 are much less likely to work, these data show that many people in both the developed and undeveloped work still do.

The Social Construction of Old Age and Youth

Theorists who study age from a political-economy perspective tend to conceptualize age in terms of **age groups**. From this perspective, central to one's place in the social organization of Western capitalist societies is whether one is old, middle-aged, or young. Political economists are, however, critical of these divisions; they question how a particular chronological age becomes the marker by which one is defined as old or young and how the polity and the economy legitimize old age and prolonged youth by defining them as a problem and then developing solutions to deal with the problem (Côté and Allahar 2006; Estes 1979; Guillemard 1982, 1983; Myles 1989; Phillipson 1982; Walker 1981). *Adolescence*, for instance, is a relatively new term for a period of life that did not exist until quite recently; the prolongation of youth has more to do with a lack of the opportunities typically available to adults than it does with chronological age (Côté 2000; Côté and Allahar 1994). And, some are now advocating that the terms *teenager* and *adolescent* and the corresponding lack of legal rights and citizenship privileges be eliminated entirely.

Estes describes an "aging enterprise" that comprises "programs, organizations, bureaucracies, interest groups, trade associations, providers, industries, and professionals that serve the aged in one capacity or another" (1979: 2). The interests of those who constitute the aging enterprise are realized by making the elderly dependent upon the services they offer. In this way, the aged are processed

and treated as a commodity (Estes 1979; Estes, Swan, and Gerard 1982). The social construction of old age is especially fuelled by the medical profession, which has transformed aged bodies into sick bodies (Katz 1996). Further, this "socially constructed problem, and the remedies invoked on the policy level, are related, first, to the capacity of strategically located interests and classes to define the problem and to press their views into public consciousness and law and, second, to the objective facts of the situation" (Estes, Linkins, and Binney 1996: 349).

The crisis ideology perpetuated by the state and the media regarding social welfare and the aging of the population is another example of how old age becomes socially constructed as a problem (Gee 2000b). The message put across is that with the increasing number of seniors will come a financial burden too large for Canada to bear (the emphasis is usually on the baby-boom generation reaching old age). However, as Myles (1980, 1995) and others have demonstrated, although the structure of state spending, ownership, and control will probably change, it is unlikely that population aging will "break the national bank."

The political-economy approach has advanced the state of theorizing gerontological and youth studies over the last 20 years by examining issues relating to age through a critical lens. Nonetheless, the conceptualization of age by political economists is problematic on several counts. First, although this approach places emphasis on the structural characteristics that frame the aging experience, youth, and older age, age relations themselves are often considered secondary to issues of social class. Second, political economists have been critical, and rightly so, of research that seeks to explain age by "naturalizing" the biological conditions of aging or by providing essentialist kinds of explanations for problems associated with youth (Côté and Allahar 2006). As a result, the tendency in this school of thought has been to understate the significance of the biological aging process. Rather than examining the subtle institutional procedures that discriminate on the basis of age (Charness, Dykstra, and Philips 1995), understating biological aging has the effect of rendering the aging process insignificant. Third, the emphasis on social structure in this approach leads to a neglect of human agency. This serves to depict older people and youth as powerless and exploited without paying attention to the meaning older adults and youth attribute to their experiences and to the strategies that they might use in dealing with some of their difficulties.

Conceptualizing Age in a Theory of Inequality

The way in which age is conceptualized depends a lot on what it is that people want to study. Age strata, biopsychosocial processes, cohorts, and age groups are the four views of age that emerge from the theories discussed above. Age-strata and age stratification research stems from the economic stratification research discussed in chapter 2 and, for similar reasons, is discarded here. More useful in studies of inequality are conceptualizations of age that consider biopsychosocial processes, cohorts, and age groups. The importance of **biopsychosocial processes** and cohorts is discussed in greater detail in the conceptual framework presented in chapter 7. For now, we must consider how age groups are viewed in this approach.

The idea stemming from the political-economy approach that Western societies are loosely organized or structured according to socially constructed age groups is correct as long as we emphasize the social construction of age and recognize that the chronological ages associated with such groupings depend on the specific social context. There are old workers,

middle-aged workers, and young workers, and there are old family members, middle-aged family members, and young family members; the chronological ages associated with age groups at work are different from the chronological ages associated with age groups in families. And, as Box 5.1 showed us, one can be considered an old worker at age 25 depending on the country and occupational context.

According to the political-economy perspective, age groups structure social life in large part because an age structure serves the interests of the dominant social classes (Côté and Allahar 2006; Estes 1999; Myles 1989). Power does not seem to be derived from relations between age groups but rather from relations between classes. Yet to understand age and inequality better, age relations must be conceptualized as oppressive relations in their own right. What then are age relations, and what distinguishes age relations from age groups?

In this book we argue that age is a relational and structural basis of inequality in Canada. On the one hand, it is relational because people define their various positions in society according to their membership in a particular age group as it relates to other age groups. It is relational in a second sense as well, because various rights and privileges are assigned on the basis of age-group location.

A relational understanding of age requires an emphasis on forms of oppression and power that are structured on the basis of membership in age groups. Recall that oppression occurs if (1) the welfare of one group of people depends upon the deprivation of another and (2) the deprivation of the oppressed group depends upon its exclusion from access to resources, rewards, and privileges. In this sense, age-based oppression, like gender-, race-, and ethnicity-based oppression, can be both material and non-material, and it can take place in various settings, including families, labour markets, states, and the education and health systems. An obvious example of age-based oppression for older adults is mandatory retirement, which still exists in some countries, and for younger adults, it is the fact that the minimum wage varies with age.

Besides the differences in economic power that result from material oppression, ideological power also varies on the basis of age (Calasanti and Slevin 2001; Côté and Allahar 2006). Recall that the dominant ideology in North American culture favours youth and suggests that to be young is to be vibrant, beautiful, and happy whereas to be old is to be tired, unattractive, and grim. At the same time, people are judged on the basis of whether they act their age, look their age, and are aging well. Yet there is no linear relationship between age and ideological power, for while it is considered a great compliment to be told you look young if you are old and mature if you are young, an older woman who wears a miniskirt may be scolded for not acting her age (see Calasanti and Slevin 2001) and a mature young man may be criticized for not being one of the boys.

▦ Note

1. Notably, Riley may be overstating the significance of age here. In contrast, Neugarten (1970; Neugarten and Hagestad 1976) has argued that the potential exists for an age-irrelevant society because the cohorts that are currently becoming old are like the young in terms of health, educational attainment, income security, and social values.

▦ Questions for Critical Thought

1. Discuss the social construction of age in the following domains: work, sport, and health. How old does one have to be to be considered old in each of those domains? What factors influence the social construction of age in each domain?
2. Many provinces in Canada require their employees to retire at age 65. Yet the human-rights codes in these same provinces state that it is unlawful to discriminate on the basis of age. Using what you have learned about the social construction of age, do you think that mandatory retirement is discriminatory?
3. Age strata, age groups, and cohorts are related but distinct categories of analysis. Compare and contrast each of these terms in relation to the chronological age markers that are used to demarcate categories within these concepts.
4. Increasingly, consumer products are being developed for older adults. Using a political-economy perspective, apply the "aging enterprise" concept to critically assess this marketing strategy.
5. Drawing on what you know about class, age, gender, ethnicity, and race, discuss why there has been less research on age structures of inequality than on class, gender, ethnicity, and race.
6. Do you think that the state has a responsibility to provide for aging populations? If

not, whose responsibility should it be (e.g., the individual themselves, families, religious organizations)?

7. Based on what you've learned in this chapter, is the Canadian government doing *enough* through its pension platform to provide for the elderly? Where do they sit in terms of spending relative to other countries (either developed or developing)? Does their relative position surprise you?

8. We have shown throughout this chapter that age inequality exists at all stages of life. Reflect on your own life for a moment. Can you think of any adversity that you experienced as a result of your age?

9. Which generations do you think experience the *most* adversity because of their age?

⊞ Glossary

Age group In Canada, adults are often categorized as being old, middle-aged, or young. These are social constructions of age categories that are referred to as "age groups."

Age strata Recognizing that all societies are organized on the basis of age and the associated rites of passage, *age strata* and related terms such as *age set* refer to the stratification of societies along these lines. The assumption is that there are specific sets of roles and responsibilities attached to membership in a particular age stratum and that status varies accordingly.

Aging and society paradigm A modified and more dynamic version of Matilda White Riley's original approach. Known formally as the *age stratification perspective*.

Allocation Processes through which individuals are assigned and reassigned to social roles.

Biopsychosocial processes The intersections of social, psychological, and biological factors that contribute to processes of aging and development.

Cohorts Aggregates of individuals who are born in the same time interval.

Diachronic Changing, in reference to states.

Neoliberalism The philosophy that market exchange is an ethic in itself, capable of acting as a guide for all human action. Its spread has depended upon a reconstitution of state powers such that privatization, finance, and market processes are emphasized. State interventions in the economy are minimized, while the obligations of the state to provide for the welfare of its citizens are diminished.

Social model of disability theory This theory argues that disability is caused by the way society is organized, rather than by a person's impairment or difference.

Social welfare A system, or set of programs, that provides assistance to needy individuals and families. The types and amount of assistance available to individuals and families vary by country, state, and region.

Socialization Processes through which individuals learn how to engage in appropriate social roles. This involves learning and conforming to normative rules of behaviour.

Structural lag The gap between the activities individuals engage in and the ability of structures to adapt to people's behaviour. Recall that in age-stratification theory, *structures* refer to institutions. The idea of structural lag is that institutional arrangements need to be modified to catch up with behaviour. For example, although women's rates of labour-force participation are higher than they have ever been, institutional family and work arrangements have not kept up with these changes. As a result, women (and some men) find it difficult to balance work and family responsibilities.

Synchronic Static, in reference to states.

Recommended Reading

Banting, Keith, and John Myles. 2013. *Inequality and the Fading of Redistributive Politics*. Vancouver: UBC Press. This book points to the failure of public policy to contain surging income inequality. In Canada, government programs are no longer offsetting the growth in inequality generated by the market, and Canadian society has become more unequal.

Binstock, Robert H., and Linda K. George. 2011. *Handbook of Aging and the Social Sciences*, 7th edn. San Diego: Academic Press. This handbook provides extensive reviews and critical evaluations of research on the social aspects of aging.

Calasanti, Toni M., and Kathleen E. Slevin. 2001. *Gender, Social Inequalities, and Aging*. Walnut Creek, CA: Altamira Press. An excellent book that examines the intersections between age and gender as they frame social inequality throughout life and especially in old age. A particularly useful part of this book is its discussion of the body, which is rare in assessments of inequality.

Côté, James E., and Anton L. Allahar. 2006. *Critical Youth Studies: A Canadian Focus*. Toronto: Pearson, Prentice Hall. This book provides a very good overview of issues related to youth, such as education, work, and financial independence. It takes a critical approach and draws on evidence from several disciplines to support its theses.

Estes, C.L. 1999. "The New Political Economy of Aging: Introduction and Critique." Chapter 1 in M. Minkler and C. Estes, eds, *Critical Gerontology*. Amityville, NY: Baywood. In this article, Estes elaborates upon her previous work by including gender in her critical assessment of aging and later life.

Katz, Stephen. 1996. *Disciplining Old Age: The Formation of Gerontological Knowledge*. Charlottesville: University Press of Virginia. A theoretically rich account of the "social, political, organization, and epistemological conditions" that made the study of aging and old age possible.

Myles, John F. 1984. *The Political Economy of Public Pensions*. Boston: Little Brown. A classic Marxist account of how the state and economy intersect in creating situations of relative advantage and disadvantage in later life.

Riley, Matilda White, Anne Foner, and Joan Waring. 1988. "Sociology of Age." pp. 243–90 in N.J. Smelser, ed., *Handbook of Sociology*. Newbury Park, CA: Sage. One of the most comprehensive accounts of how age is conceptualized from a sociological perspective.

Relevant Websites

Youth Canada
www.youth.gc.ca

**This is a portal for government programs relating to youth (Service Canada) as well as information on education, employment, travel, and community events.

MySafeWork.com
www.mysafework.com

**This site is one focus of the charitable foundation Our Youth at Work, which advocates for health, safety, and wellness in the workplace with a focus on young workers.

CARP
http://carp.ca

**Although CARP (formerly the Canadian Association of Retired Persons) is a membership organization, you can check this site out for the latest issues facing older Canadians.

AARP
www.aarp.org

**Search AARP (formerly the American Association for Retired Persons) for research and you will find over 600 links to various publications regarding older adults.

Agediscrimination.info
www.agediscrimination.info/Pages/Home.aspx

** This is a comprehensive resource of statistics and information for employers, employees, researchers, students, journalists, and others interested in age-discrimination issues in the United Kingdom as well as internationally, including the United States, Canada, India, and other countries.

6

Actors and Agency

Introduction

As the preceding chapters show, sociological theories of inequality usually highlight social structures as key explanatory mechanisms of advantage and disadvantage in social life. In chapter 2, for instance, we saw how Frank McCourt's childhood poverty may be understood on the basis of his position in the class structure rather than through individual characteristics of his father or mother. Chapter 3 showed how the structure of gender can explain the various hardships that women, such as Beth, experience. Chapter 4 showed how racial projects structure the everyday experiences of individuals such as Crystal Samms, and chapter 5 outlined how age structures Hagar Shipley's experiences with her family in Margaret Laurence's novel *The Stone Angel*. The preceding chapters also illustrate how structures of class, age, gender, ethnicity, and "race" constrain the choices of individuals who are disadvantaged as a result of these structures. Individuals are poor, for example, not because they are stupid, unambitious, or lazy, but because they have had limited opportunities to be anything other than poor. However, if we were to take these structural explanations to the extreme, there would

be no room in society for the **social mobility** demonstrated by Frank McCourt.

Studies of social mobility are common in sociology. Some of this work characterizes particular countries on the basis of how much opportunity each has for social mobility. These studies often examine patterns of **relative mobility** (also called *social fluidity*) to determine the prevalence of *equality of opportunity* across capitalist societies. Studies of intergenerational mobility examine the characteristics of parents and assess the likelihood that children will attain higher-status occupations or higher levels of education than their parents. According to this research, children are constrained by their parents' education and occupation, but in some countries there is more opportunity for ambitious and able children to do better than their parents (see Box 6.1 for a comparison of social mobility).

In explaining Frank McCourt's situation, then, social mobility researchers might argue that McCourt's ambition and ability led him to move to a country that offered more opportunity than his homeland and that as a result he was able to live a better life than his parents. But there is a tension in sociology, between structural and individual explanations of

Global perspective

Box 6.1 Social Mobility around the World

In a recent article in FG magazine, Gillian Tett writes about growing up in England in the 1980s. There she saw evidence of downward social mobility every day of her life. And the reality was bleak. She noticed that most families either reproduced their class position (i.e., the children of working-class parents became working class themselves) or fell even further down the social class hierarchy (i.e., *downward* class mobility). Moving up the social class structure, she believed, was certainly not the norm.

Tett's own story was one of downward mobility. She described living in a middle-class suburban home with her only link to the upper class being a portrait of a maternal, eighteenth-century, Anglo-French aristocrat ancestor. Tett notes that the picture hung from a central wall in her family home, almost to serve as a reminder of where her family once sat in the social hierarchy. As Tett recalls, "in the intervening centuries, my aristocratic forebears had lost their status and wealth due to drink, gambling and poor decisions. Thus, my only link with royalty was that portrait and the fact that I have the same unusual middle name—Romaine—as the noblewoman in the picture."

Is Tett's story of downward mobility a unique example of a widespread global pattern? This question has become politically charged, causing economists and sociologists to track mobility by looking at social surveys concerned with wealth, employment, and educational attainment over the past few generations. This research typically finds that mobility is generally highest in Scandinavian countries and lowest in places in Latin America, with the United States, the United Kingdom, and Canada falling somewhere between.

Many studies find that more mobile societies—such as Denmark—are also more economically equal. Thus, the commonly reported belief (especially in the United States) that inequality can be justified because mobility is high is simply untrue.

The figure below give some further perspective on cross-national differences in mobility by displaying rates of *income elasticity*. If there was no intergenerational mobility at all (i.e., the intergenerational income elasticity was equal to 1), all poor children would become poor adults and all rich children would become rich adults. In Canada, Finland, Norway, and Denmark,

inequality. How do we explain the lives of those of McCourt's peers who did not do as well as he? The logic in social mobility studies suggests that these children were less ambitious and less able to succeed than McCourt was. Although we do not dismiss the importance of ambition and ability in one's life, such explanations oversimplify the processes through which individuals either challenge or comply with the structural circumstances of their lives.

Unlike proponents of theories that emphasize the social structure over and above the actor, we do not start with the assumption that structure ultimately determines individual action. Individuals are not passive objects

who conform to structural forces in their day-to-day lives. Nor do we start with the assumption that individuals act freely in a world that is untouched by structural pressures. Indeed, the range of options available to individuals varies, and these options are constrained by a host of structural factors, including gender, class, ethnicity, race, and age. The theories of inequality presented in the preceding chapters vary in the extent to which they put emphasis on individuals, social structures, or some combination of the two. Indeed, we see glimpses of actors in even the most structural of these theories. As Marx suggested, "men make their own history." Yet Marx focused not so much on the human

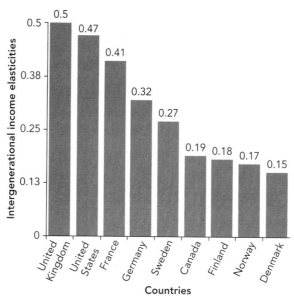

Intergenerational Income Elasticities in Nine Developed Countries

Sources: Miles Corak. (2006) "Do Poor Children Become Poor Adults? Lessons from a Cross-Country Comparison of Generational Earnings Mobility," John Creedy, Guyonne Kalb (ed.) *Dynamics of Inequality and Poverty (Research on Economic Inequality)*, Volume 13, Emerald Group Publishing Limited, p. 143–188. © Emerald Group Publishing Limited all rights reserved.

people are much more likely to belong to *different* income groups (either higher *or* lower) relative to their parents. This movement is much less likely in the United States and the United Kingdom where class reproduction is much more common.

Source: Gillian Tett. (March 7, 2014) "Social mobility: a family affair." Financial Times.

action that was required in doing this as on the idea that while people make their own history, "they do not make it just as they please; they do not make it under circumstances chosen by themselves, but under circumstances directly encountered, given, and transmitted from the past. The tradition of all the dead generations weighs like a nightmare on the brain of the living" (Marx [1852] 1963: 15). The task ahead here is to develop an approach to inequality that considers the intersections between social structures and individual actors. Before considering such intersections, however, we consider what is meant by *actors* and **action** in sociology.

Actors and Human Action

When sociologists discuss actors and **social action**, they are examining social life at the level of the individual. Most of the sociological insight we have regarding individuals comes from the symbolic-interactionist tradition. **Symbolic interactionism** is, however, a diverse field of inquiry, and action is only one small component of it. Although in the symbolic-interactionist tradition, action is related to other individual-level concepts, such as self, identity, and meaning, it must not be confused with them.

The sociological understanding of actors and action stems, in large part, from the work of Max

Weber. In Weber's conceptions of social life and social theory, unlike those of Marx, actors and action were central. Indeed, according to Weber ([1922] 1978), the objective of sociology is to interpret social action through causal explanations. Put simply, actors or agents are individuals who take part in action that is meaningful or intentional. Most of us, then, are actors in the sociological sense, most of the time.

Weber ([1922] 1978) distinguished between action and social action. He considered action to be meaningful human behaviour from the point of view of the actor or actors involved. Action can be internal behaviour, as when individuals justify or rationalize spending money on something that they don't really need, and action can be external behaviour, including decisions to either act or not. Thus, action is implied both in sending flowers to someone on their birthday and in deciding not to send them. Weber also suggests that *action* can refer to the act of having something done to you. For instance, your receiving or not receiving flowers from someone on your birthday is action because this act is subjectively meaningful to you.

Whereas action is behaviour that is individually meaningful, social action according to Weber refers to action that is meaningful only in relation to another person's behaviour. To explain this point, Weber ([1922] 1978: 23) discusses two cyclists who collide with each other. The fact that the cyclists collide is not social action but merely an event. Social action involves the negotiation that transpires after this event, whether it be a fight, an argument, or a peaceful resolution. Notably, and as with action, social action also includes deciding not to act or being acted upon.

Weber ([1922] 1978: 24–6) distinguished four **ideal types** of action and social action: traditional, affectual, instrumental (*zweckrational*), and rational (*wertrational*). *Traditional action* refers to actions that take place because they are habitual and have taken place in the past; *affectual actions* are the things people do to display emotion. The latter two types of action can be categorized as *rational action* and were of most concern to Weber. *Zweckrational*, or *instrumental*, *action* refers to appropriate actions in which individuals engage while deciding how they can attain something and whether it is worth attaining. It also refers to meaningful assessments about what is required to achieve this goal. For example, if a woman decides—by carefully assessing what she is required to do, what she may have to give up, what the consequences of these actions are likely to be, and whether attaining a law degree is worthwhile—that she wants to go to law school, she is acting rationally in the *zweckrational* sense. *Wertrational*, or *value-rational*, *action* refers to action performed to attain a goal rather than the means through which the goal must be attained. The actor does not compare different means to an end or evaluate the consequences of the action but rather acts out of conviction. A mother who is committed to breastfeeding her premature baby and does so against her doctor's orders and without regard for the possible consequences of disregarding the status quo is acting in the *wertrational* sense.

Drawing on Weber, Talcott Parsons (1951) developed a theory of social action in which motivation and values determine action. Parsons believed that people are naturally capable of making choices and that they behave rationally to attain goals. Action is constrained by social systems, but it also conveys the idea that actors make conscious decisions to attain goals (Parsons 1949). Values and motives determine the type of action individuals engage in. Parsons identified three types of action: instrumental, expressive, and moral. *Instrumental action*, which is similar to the rational action of Weber's framework, refers to action that allows people to achieve a particular goal efficiently. *Expressive action*, which is similar to Weber's affective action, is what people do to attain emotional satisfaction. *Moral action*, which is not found in Weber's framework, is behaviour that is concerned with standards of right and wrong (Parsons 1951: 45–51).

While Weber acknowledged that an individual's behaviour could consist of more than one type of action simultaneously, Jürgen Habermas (1984) makes this point central to his theory of action. According to Habermas, there are different kinds of action, and what distinguishes them from one another has nothing to do with the act itself but rather with how agents are oriented to the act. The task for theory is to determine the various ways in which individuals may be compelled to act. In this vein, Habermas identifies five kinds of action: instrumental, strategic, normatively regulated, dramaturgical, and communicative (1984: 273–337). Individuals engage in *instrumental* and *strategic action* when they are striving for success in the physical world (instrumental action) or for success that takes the social context into account (strategic action; for both, see Habermas 1984: 285–6). *Normatively regulated action* occurs when individuals take norms into account before acting. An individual who is concerned about how he or she appears to others and who acts accordingly is acting *dramaturgically*. Finally, *communicative action* aligns with needs for mutual understanding; the term refers to actions people engage in to make themselves understood (Habermas 1984: 333–4).

To illustrate Habermas's views on action, let us consider the act of sitting down in a chair. We cannot classify this act as normatively regulated, instrumental, or dramaturgical unless we know what prompted the individual to sit down. The kind of action that this act reflects depends on whether it was in response to being tired or a reaction to someone saying, "Please sit down." When an employee enters an employer's office and chooses to stand until asked to sit down, the behaviour is normatively regulated action and probably involves

some component of dramaturgical action. If the employee chooses to remain standing after the invitation to sit down, he or she is probably acting strategically as well.

Several key ideas from the work of Parsons, Weber, and Habermas have informed most sociological views on actors and action. First, part of being human is the capacity to make intentional choices. Second, action is not simply the act of doing but also both the act of not doing and having something done to you. Third, there is a rational component to action: people calculate the potential rewards and sanctions of their actions and behave accordingly. Fourth, there is also a non-rational component to action: people act in traditional, normative, and affectual ways without rationalizing their behaviour. Fifth, any particular act may represent more than one kind or type of action. And sixth, people act within a social structure that constrains and orients action. This last point has been most contentious among sociologists and has led many to use the term *agency* in their work.

Agency

In an effort to avoid overly deterministic views of social life in which actors are like puppets being manipulated and constrained by social structures, scholars began using the term *agency*. In contrast to Parsons's theory of action, which emphasizes structure over and above action, the term *agency* stresses the idea that structures are composed of individuals who engage with social structure and can initiate structural change (Barnes 2000: 45–9). It is on this point that the similarities in theories of agency end. Indeed, there is little theoretical consensus over what *agency* means (Barnes 2000: 49) and whether or how it is different from the concept of action. In this section, we will discuss two central views of agency, one put forth by Anthony Giddens and a second developed by Margaret Archer in reaction to Giddens.

Since the mid-1970s, Anthony Giddens has been arguing for a conceptualization of social structure that is inextricably bound to human action, and it is arguably through his work that *agency* has become a fashionable term in sociology. In developing his theory, Giddens, claiming that agency and structure "presuppose one another" (1979: 53), developed a theory of structuration that involves "the duality of structure which relates to the fundamentally recursive character of social life, and expresses the mutual dependence of structure and agency. By the duality of structure I mean that the structural properties of social systems are both the medium and the outcome of the practices that constitute those systems" (Giddens 1979: 69).

As Figure 6.1 shows, for Giddens, agency refers to a continuous flow of conduct by an actor or the activities of an agent and captures the ideas of progress, intentionality, and responsibility in the actions of human beings. Another central feature of agency is the capacity of actors to have acted differently, either by doing something else or by not acting at all. Involved in action are issues relating to its purposive or intentional processes, its human accountability, its unintended consequences, and the unacknowledged conditions under which it takes place.

Clearly, there are many similarities between Giddens's view of agency and the views of action espoused by Weber, Parsons, and Habermas. Indeed, Giddens uses the terms *agency* and *action, agent,* and *actor* interchangeably in his

structuration theory; this has led Margaret Archer to be critical of his work and to theorize the distinctions between action and agency.

Unlike Giddens, who views structure and agency as part of the same thing, Archer favours analytic dualism in her approach to sociology. In other words, she believes that structure is analytically distinct and temporally separate from agency yet "intimately intertwined" with it (1995: 65–75). And, for Archer (1995: 252–3), agency and structure must be separated if we are to understand the processes through which both are transformed over time. This is the crux of Archer's response to Giddens, and it is a point that we return to below. For now, we will focus on Archer's conception of agency, keeping in mind that she makes a distinction between agency and social structure.

According to Archer (1995: 248–9), there is a fundamental difference between action and agency and between human beings, social actors, and social agents. Archer (2000: 261) defines *agents* as "collectivities sharing the same life-chances" and suggests that all persons are agents because all persons occupy a position in relation to the distribution of resources in society. Hence, agents are not individuals but rather groups of individuals who have in common their privilege or disadvantage in society. When Archer refers to an agent, she is referring not to an individual, but rather to a single group of people who share the same life chances. People are born into predetermined structures and are hence "involuntarily situated beings"

Figure 6.1 Action and Agency in Giddens's Framework

Source: Cassell (1993: 92).

(Archer 2000: 262). Thus, according to Archer (2000: 262), "humanity enters society through the maternity ward doors and we immediately acquire the properties of Primary Agents through belonging to particular collectivities and sharing their privileges or lack of them— as males/females; blacks/whites; foreigner/indigenous; middle class/working class."

Social agency, then, refers to relations or interactions between groups and can affect social change and stability. It is "reflective, purposive, promotive, and innovative" (Archer 1995: 249), and it often operates under "unacknowledged conditions of situated action [that] lie beyond the ken of time-and-space-bound agents" (Archer 1995: 250). Finally, "courses of action are produced through the reflexive deliberations of subjects who subjectively determine their practical projects in relation to their objective circumstances" (Archer 2007: 17).

According to Archer (1995, 2000), time links agents with actors and agency with action because we are born agents and grow into mature actors. Individuals have no choice about their agent status or over the social collectivity they are born into. One is either male or female, white or black, middle class or working class, and so on. Choice is, however, implied in Archer's view of social actors. Social actors are "role incumbents" (Archer 2000: 283). Action, which seems to be synonymous with choice in Archer's view, is exercised as individuals decide which roles they will take and which they will reject. Agents vary, however, in the options and opportunities that are available to them, and therefore action is conditioned by agency.

This rather confusing view of agents and agency is Archer's critical response to approaches to inequality that view categorical distinctions (between, for instance, women and men or blacks and whites) as individual characteristics. It is also a critical response to Giddens, who, in Archer's view, does not allow for collective action in his theory. According to Archer,

by conceptualizing agents as collectivities and actors as role incumbents, we eliminate both problems.

Intersections of Agency and Structure

As the preceding discussion shows, there is little agreement in sociology over what is meant by *agency* and *action*. Indeed, the two concepts are often used to mean the same thing. For the time being, then, let us think of the terms *agency* and *action* as interchangeable and as referring to the capacity of humans to make choices and to behave in meaningful, thoughtful ways. That being said, the next issue to consider is the relationship between agency and structure. Approaches to this topic fall into two broad camps. In the first, the "integrated" camp, scholars consider structure and agency to be part of the same thing. In the second, the "analytic dualism" camp, scholars treat structure and agency as separate yet related features of social life.

Integrated Approaches

One of the best-known integrated approaches is described by Peter Berger and Thomas Luckmann in their book *The Social Construction of Reality* (1967). Berger and Luckmann approach the relationship between structure and action in dialectic terms. According to Berger and Luckmann (1967: 18), reality is socially constructed through three dialectical processes in which "subjective meanings become objective facticities." The first of these processes is *externalization*. In this process, individuals create their social worlds through their own actions. Social order is the result of past human activity, and the reproduction of this social order is only possible through this action. The second process, *objectivation*, involves the views about social reality that individuals share. In this process, individuals come to understand that everyday life is ordered and prearranged. The third process is called *internalization*. In this stage, social order is legitimized and reinforced. Elements of socialization are apparent in internalization as individuals learn what is expected of them and behave accordingly. When individuals engage in this process by conforming to the existing social order, they are also reproducing that social order. Reification of the social order occurs when individuals forget that human activity created the social order in the first place.

In Berger and Luckmann's (1967) approach to social life, individuals are treated as active participants. Individuals are able to evaluate the social structure and respond critically to it. However, it is assumed that individuals are on a level playing field in their ability to oppose any aspect of the social order. Furthermore, although this approach recognizes that many actors feel that their choices are limited, the responsibility for perceptions of limited choice lies in the hands of the individual. If individuals perceive that they have no choice, the dialectical processes that create and recreate the social structure disappear and the actor is only acted upon. This analysis underemphasizes the fact that it is in the interests of some individuals or groups to maintain the existing social order and to limit the choices available to others. Hence, by assuming that individuals are on a level playing field and by locating limited choice within the realm of individual responsibility, this approach neglects to consider power relations as fundamental elements in social life and in an explanation of inequality.

Perhaps the best-known integrated approach is Anthony Giddens's structuration theory. According to Giddens, structure is composed of rules and resources that are organized as properties of social systems. Rules are the norms and practices of a society, and resources are bound to power relations. In fact, resources are the bases of power that make up the structures of domination. Social systems are systems of social interaction that reproduce relations between actors or collectivities and have structural properties. The theory of structuration seeks to explain "the ways in which that [social] system, via the application of generative rules and resources, and in the context of unintended outcomes, is produced and reproduced in interaction" (Giddens 1979: 66).

According to Giddens, structure is involved in the production of action, but structure is not thought to place limits on action. Giddens (1979: 71) suggests that "rules and resources are drawn upon by actors in the production of interaction but are thereby also reconstituted through such interaction. Structure is thus the mode in which the relation between moment and totality expresses itself in social reproduction." (See Box 6.2 for a conversation with Anthony Giddens on structuration theory.) Accordingly, the assumption that structure is involved in the production of action stands in opposition to the view that structure places limits on action. However, one might argue that to adhere to the assumption that structure is involved in the production of action is not to oppose the view that structure places limits on action; the distinction is more subtle, and it lies more in language than in philosophy.

In fact, Giddens's discussion of power points to the distinction, not the opposition, between a structure that produces action and one that confines it. Giddens rejects views of power that treat it as a phenomenon of intended action. He also rejects views of power that locate it within the social structure as a medium by which group interests are realized. According to Giddens, Lukes comes closest to the correct consideration of power. Lukes (1974) suggests that

> a person or party who wields power could have acted otherwise, and the person or party over whom power is wielded, the concept implies, would have acted

HIGHLIGHT

Box 6.2 Conversations with Anthony Giddens: Interview Three: Structuration Theory

Christopher Pierson *The relationship between agency and structure and, paralleling that, between voluntarism and determinism is amongst the most ubiquitous and difficult issues in all social theory. In a number of texts in the late 1970s and early 1980s, culminating in the publication of The Constitution of Society in 1984, you developed your own distinctive resolution of this issue under the rubric of the theory of structuration. Perhaps I could begin by asking how you understand the traditional problem of structure and agency in social theory.*

Anthony Giddens It isn't a "traditional problem," at least expressed in these terms. In the past it was usually seen as a dualism between individual and society, or the actor and the social system. Thinking about this traditional question of the relationship between the individual and society lay at the origin of the idea of structuration. I felt these were all unelaborated notions. People would speak of the individual as though it was obvious what "the individual" was and quite often the same was true of "society." I wanted to break them down and give them more substance. The term "structuration" I originally borrowed from French—I don't think it was used in English before I appropriated it. I wanted to place an emphasis on the active flow of social life. We should see social life not just as "society" out there or just the product of "the individual" here, but as a series of ongoing activities and practices that people carry on, which at the same time reproduce larger institutions. That was the original thought and from there I tried to elaborate each of the key terms, precisely by speaking of "agency" and "structure." I put the idea of recurrent social practices at the core of what social sciences are about, rather than either starting with "the individual" or starting with "society."

The Constitution of Society is not necessarily the easiest book. Could you give some indication, in fairly straightforward terms, of how the theory of

structuration resolves the dualism between structure and agency?

This depends on two things really. The first is rethinking the notion of structure. I wanted to get away from the characteristic Anglo-Saxon way of conceptualizing structure, where structure is some given form, even a visible form of some sort. But I also sought to get away from the idea that agency is just contained within the individual. I wanted to see it as more of a flow of people's actions and to connect it with attributes of self-consciousness. Within certain limits, speaking a language shows us something about what the relationship between them might be. In other words, language has structure, language has form, but it isn't visible and it is only "there" in so far as it actually forms part of what people do in their day-to-day use of it. That is what I call the recursive quality of language. I didn't claim that society "is like a language," as the structuralists used to say; but language gives us key clues as to how recursiveness happens. "Society" can be understood as a complex of recurrent practices which form institutions. Those practices depend upon the habits and forms of life which individuals adopt. Individuals don't just "use" these in their activity but these life practices constitute what that activity is.

You talk in some places about structural effects and these being a better way of describing the impact of structure. Are "structural effects" simply a euphemism for some kind of structure which is observable or has some existence other than through these perceived effects?

The structural properties of societies and social systems are real properties, but at the same time they have no physical existence. They are real properties in the sense in which they depend upon the routine qualities of people's actions and they can be very fixed or "hard." I don't want to discard the Durkheimian point that society is a structured phenomenon and that

continued

the structural properties of a group or a society have effects upon the way people act, feel, and think. But when we look at what those structures are, they are obviously not like the physical qualities of the external world. They depend upon regularities of social reproduction. Language has this incredibly fixed form. You can't go against even the most apparently minute rules of the English language without getting very strong reactions from other speakers. But at the same time, language doesn't exist anywhere, or it only exists in its instantiations in writing or speaking. Much the same thing is true for social life in general. That is, society only has form and that form only has effects on people in so far as structure is produced and reproduced in what people do. This to me applies right through from the most trivial glance you might give someone to the most globalized of systems.

Source: Giddens, Anthony, and Christopher Pierson. 1998. *Conversations with Anthony Giddens: Making Sense of Modernity.* Cambridge, UK: Polity Press.

otherwise if power had not been exercised. In speaking thus, one assumes that, although the agents operate within structurally determined limits, they none the less have a certain relative autonomy and could have acted differently. (Cited in Giddens 1979: 91)

However, Giddens (1979: 91) argues that by suggesting that structure places limits on agency, this approach is "unable satisfactorily to deal with structure as implicated in power relations and power relations as implicated in structure." This problem can be alleviated only "if the resources which the existence of domination implies and the exercise of power draws upon are seen to be at the same time structural components of social systems. The exercise of power is not a type of act; rather, power is instantiated in action, as a regular and routine phenomenon." For Giddens, it is important to consider the dialectic between action and structure in discussions of power: "Resources are the media whereby transformative capacity is employed as power in the routine course of social interaction; but they are at the same time structural elements of social systems as systems, reconstituted through their utilisation in social interaction" (1979: 92). Thus, the subtle difference between the view that structure limits action and that structure produces action lies in Giddens's dialectical assumption that one mutually creates the other.

Arguably, a more accurate view of social life lies within the combination of these two approaches. Structure produces action, but the particular action that is produced lies within the realms of structure itself. Only under exceptional circumstances does human agency push structural barriers to the extent that structure itself is changed. Yet agents have a certain relative autonomy and could have acted differently even though they operate within structurally determined limits. This view of social life challenges integrated approaches to social structure by considering agency and structure as distinct yet related social phenomena, as do theorists in the analytic-dualism camp.

Analytic Dualism

Scholars who favour analytic dualism suggest that integrated approaches are problematic because they conflate issues of structure and agency (Archer 1995, 2000; Layder 1994). Analytic dualists argue that agency and structure are distinguishable yet related features of social life (Archer 1995: 65). The task of sociologists, according to analytic dualists, is to examine how structure and agency are related and to analyze the processes and mechanisms that bind them together.

Although Erving Goffman was much more concerned with the interactional order than with the structural order, in his undelivered presidential address to the American Sociological Association, published after his death, he discusses the relationship between the two. In this paper, Goffman (1983) argued that there are social membranes that act like filters to determine which structural influences are let through and whether they are transformed in the process. The relationship between structure and agency, he claims, is fluid or "loosely coupled" (Goffman 1983), and the membranes that connect them will vary depending on the empirical and historical reality that encompasses them. One example Goffman (1983: 11) mentions is "precedence through a door." Door-opening rituals are situated within the interaction order, and "at best they are likely to have only loosely coupled relations to anything by way of social structures that might be associated with them" (11). Indeed, Marilyn Frye (1983) quite convincingly discusses the practice of men opening doors for women as an expression of women's structural oppression in relation to men. But we know from our experiences that this "act" is only loosely coupled with structural realities. There are men who hold doors open for painfully long periods of time for women who are 10 yards away from the door. Yet women also hold doors open for men and some men do not hold doors open for women. A membrane is at work here such that "social structures don't 'determine' culturally standard displays [but] merely help select from the available repertoire of them" (Goffman 1983: 11). Although Goffman does not explain precisely how these membranes work, he does point us to the mutual and reciprocal constitutive processes between the structural and interactional orders.

In a similar vein, Pierre Bourdieu (1977) argues that structure and agency are linked through habitus. *Habitus* refers to relatively stable sets of attitudes and beliefs that social actors hold and that reflect their social circumstances, such as their class background, gender ethnicity, or race. They are "generative principles of distinct and distinctive practices" (Bourdieu 1998: 8) that influence the behaviour of individuals as well as their preferences and choices. Habitus is the mechanism through which the structural circumstances of individual lives play out in the actions of individuals—what and how they eat, what activities they engage in, and how they are engaged in them. Individuals can act only on the basis of what they know, and past experience crucially influences action. Members of different classes or different ethnic or racial groups eat and play differently not because of innate differences between them, but because their habitus informs their behaviour and distinctions get reproduced. Distinctions in behaviour between groups take on a certain value status, and here we see a striking similarity to Goffman's idea of loose coupling. Acts tend to be judged by members of society as good or bad, distinguished or vulgar, and so on. But the very same act can be perceived in many ways depending on the structural circumstances of the actor and of the perceiver. Box 6.3 shows that gender stereotypes still affect some women's behaviour at work. Many women still feel pressured to conform to outdated gender stereotypes. This example implies that habitus is still embodied in individuals as links between social structural circumstances and actions while they simultaneously serve to distinguish between groups of people (Bourdieu 1998).

A central problem in Bourdieu's work on structure and agency is that social change seems unlikely (Sewell 1992). Habitus influences behaviour but in a unidirectional way; it tends to constrain individual actions because people can only act on the basis of what they know and within the limits of their social-structural constraints. This is, in part, because Bourdieu does not engage in a discussion of time, an issue

HIGHLIGHT

Box 6.3 What Does "Acting Like a Man" at Work Even Mean Anymore?

by Julia Oliphant

Why is [it] that male leadership traits have become synonymous with "aggressive," "dominant" and "loud," asks Julia Oliphant, after a survey showed half of women feel they need to "act like men" to get ahead in the workplace.

Friday afternoons often find me at the Tesco Express just down the road from my office. Deeply disappointed by the dregs of the boring biscuit tin, which has been attacked all week, my colleagues and I normally venture out in search of more satisfying treats. Recently, against my better judgement, I opted for a Crispello—marketed as "the women's chocolate bar."

Why? Well, it comes in a resealable bag and has fewer calories. The latter, I was upset to discover, is due to the main ingredient being air, the former I assume is because girls find air too filling? Needless to say, I inhaled the bar (there is no need for resealing, trust me) and felt so unsatisfied, I was compelled to march back to the office munching on a Yorkie and thinking about why women are still viewed so differently to men these days. What is it about women that warrants the existence of such an offensively light chocolate bar? And why is there no such thing for a man, especially as so many modern men watch their figures?

The conundrum easily extends to the workplace. Last month O2 surveyed 2,000 women, 47 per cent of which said they "acted like a man" to get ahead at work. Like it or not, I understood exactly what was implied with the term "acting like a man." Bullish. Aggressive. Dominant. Loud. I also knew why this may be beneficial to women in the workplace, where many outdated ideas about what good "leadership" is still exist.

But how has that come to be? Why is it that "male leadership" equates to bullish, aggressive, dominant, loud? If you think about "female leadership," you don't tend to think those same things. It's more like communicative, nurturing, good listener. But why is [it] that men get to be aggressive and eat proper chocolate bars, but women are stuck with being nurturing and pathetic excuses for edible treats?

Dr Meg Barker, psychologist and author of *Rewriting the Rules*, a guide to love, sex and relationships, says we've been brought up to think like this. "In our culture at present, men are perceived to be more rational, more assertive and more focused, whereas women are generally seen to be more emotional, less able to take risks and better at multitasking. Typical stereotypes of masculinity are therefore considered the necessary attributes to succeed in a work environment," she says.

"There is a human tendency to put people in boxes in order to create simple rules of how to operate. We have a long history of structuring society in a certain way which benefits those in power: men are seen as better in business and women as better in nurturing roles, roles which are less highly valued."

Dr Gary Woods, social psychologist and author of *Unlock Your Confidence* agrees. "In crude, simplistic terms, men and women are expected to act out the shape of their genitals, so men's activities are externalised and women's, internalised. Looking at gender stereotypes in this way only underlines how ridiculous they are."

Girls v. boys

Certainly the ideas society has about what it means to have different "bits and bobs" has [sic] a huge impact on how we are treated, and what is expected of us. As Barker says, "it is tough to know which of the differences that do seem to be present would still be there if we weren't treated so radically different from an early age." Just think back to all your favourite childhood toys.

Anita Sarkeesian, founder of Feminist Frequency, last year discussed the launch of Lego for Girls. Lego, a toy upheld as a promoter of maths, science and engineering, created the female suburb "Heartlake City," where the gals can bake, decorate and hang out at the beauty salon! And just in case you didn't see it, everything is pink. Everything.

There's nothing wrong with "pink" of course, but before the 19th century came along, pink was actually the colour associated with *boys*, while blue was considered a feminine colour. This is a pretty strong piece of evidence indicating that gender is, to some extent, constructed.

Thankfully the contrast between treatment of men and of women is not as stark in the real world as it is in Lego land, but that's not to say we don't have preconceptions of what it means to be a certain sex. It's a fact which has infiltrated every aspect of our lives in the West. "Nine times of out of 10 if I'm ordering an espresso for me and a cappuccino for my boyfriend, it will be served to us the other way round. It's the same story when we order steak and fish, it's the same when we order red and white wine. When the waiter is left to decide between us, I always receive the seemingly "weaker" option," says one 30-year-old London-based consultant, who asked to remain anonymous.

To its credit, the working environment is an increasingly level playing field and there has been a realisation in recent years that typical female stereotypes are valuable assets in the workplace, particularly for managerial positions. Yet, bias towards both genders creeps in.

One woman who works in media (and has asked to remain anonymous) discusses her encounter with prejudice at work. "When my boss' PA is away, I am the one he asks to go get his coffee or book a restaurant, despite my male counterpart often having more time on his hands and even sitting closer to him," she tells me.

Elsewhere, Nana Triay, a 24-year-old teacher, reveals: "When my class are acting up, I find it very telling that my efforts to regain order are largely ignored, but as soon as my male colleague walks in the room and tells them to quieten down, they listen." No wonder then that some women feel a need to adopt an archetypally masculine persona given that traditionally feminine attributes can be culturally undervalued.

Psychologist Elisabeth Ronson was not surprised by the O2 study findings. "Many of my female patients find it very hard to gain the respect of their male and female colleagues. If women take on a masculine persona, they are criticised for being 'unfeminine' but being traditionally feminine can result in less recognition or reward at work."

It works both ways

The issue is that women claiming to act "like a man" not only implies that acting "like a woman" is not as effective in the workplace but also reinforces the notion that being assertive is not something women do. Ambition for women at work is still a dirty word. Being forthright in the office should not be deemed unfeminine. That would allow for easy criticism of women who choose to act this way and encourage the association between assertiveness and masculinity, which is not necessarily the case. Confidence is not about bravado.

It works both ways. Describing a man as "in touch with his feminine side, works to undermine him, as Woods points out. "We are actually describing a more psychologically rounded human being. We should promote all people to appreciate a broader range of attributes," she says.

Divorcing gender from behaviour is the first step to learning to value these characteristics equally. Above all, people should do well at work based on merit; because of what they do, rather than how. If different models of behaviour achieve the same outcome, then we can start to rethink what "good" leadership actually looks like.

"We're all different. Succeeding in the workplace is about being your own person, using your strengths and being aware of your weaknesses. It shouldn't matter whether you're a man or woman," says Ronson.

Gender shouldn't have to matter at work. On some days we all (men and women) might fancy a Yorkie, other days, a Galaxy. But under no circumstances can I imagine either sex ever truly fancying a Crispello.

Source: "What does 'acting like a man' at work even mean anymore?" *The Telegraph.* Julia Oliphant, 11th October 2013 © Telegraph Media Group Limited. www.telegraph.co.uk/women/womens-business/10370413/What-does-acting-like-a-man-at-work-even-mean-anymore.html which is at the heart of Margaret Archer's theory of structure and agency.

The problem of structure and agency is a "vexatious fact of society" according to Archer; neither society nor social interaction can be discussed in isolation from the other, and yet there are properties of both that transcend the other (Archer 1995, 2000). In fact, Archer takes issue with theorists in the integrated tradition, and much of her work serves as a useful critique of these perspectives. Archer elaborates upon her critique by developing a theory that relies on the notions of **morphogenesis** and **morphostasis**. The former means the processes that "elaborate or change a system's given form, state, or structure" (Archer 1995: 166). The latter means "processes in complex system-environmental exchanges which tend to preserve or maintain a system's given form, organization or state." Put simply, Archer is referring here to the transformation and reproduction of social systems or to the processes through which social systems change or remain the same. Hence, unlike Goffman's and Bourdieu's views, one advantage of Archer's theory is that it explicitly considers social change.

According to Archer (1995: 193), problems with both practical theorizing and **realist social ontology** can be overcome by creating bridges between the two. To accomplish this, Archer conceives of three related morphogenetic/static cycles that refer to structures, cultures, and agency (see Figure 6.2). Regarding the structural and cultural morphogenetic/static cycles, at time one (t_1), individuals are faced with structural and cultural conditioning. Between times two (t_2) and three (t_3), social interaction transpires. The result, at time four (t_4), is structural and cultural elaboration. In the morphogenesis of agency, t_1 is characterized by the sociocultural conditioning of groups. Recall that, in Archer's view, agents are groups of people born in similar structural and cultural circumstances. Between t_2 and t_3, group interaction

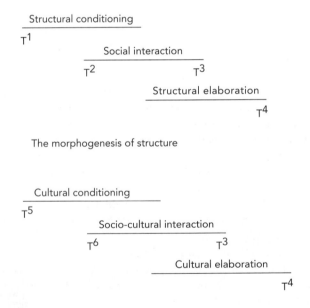

Figure 6.2 Archer's Morphogenesis of Structure and Culture

Source: Archer, Margaret. 1995. *Realist Social Theory: The Morphogenetic Approach.* Cambridge: Cambridge University Press, p. 193. Reprinted by permission of Cambridge University Press.

occurs; it is at t_4 that there is group elaboration. All of these cycles intersect because they have as a common thread social interaction, which is the middle component in each of them.

One important component of Archer's theory is her distinction between corporate agents and primary agents. Corporate agents are more able than primary agents to effect social change because they are born into structural circumstances that better enable them to effect change. In Archer's words, "corporate agents maintain/re-model the socio-cultural system and its institutional parts: primary agents work within it and them" (1995: 265). Social change occurs when the lives of primary and corporate agents are altered by the other group; it is "the resultant of aggregate effects produced by primary agents in conjunction with emergent properties generated by corporate agents and thus does not approximate to what anyone wants" (1995: 265). In other words, for social change to take place, agents with different amounts of power and resources must enter into a state of conflict; change occurs to resolve the conflict. A double morphogenesis is possible whereby "agency leads to structural and cultural elaboration, but is itself elaborated in the process" (Archer 2000: 258). It is important to note that in Archer's view, agents are not actors. Social actors only embrace sets of social roles, and inasmuch as Archer is concerned with large-scale social change, social actors then have very little influence.

For the purpose of research on inequality, Archer's work is dense, complex, and overly complicated. It is unclear, for instance, why Archer feels the need to distinguish agents from actors on the basis of what social circumstances individuals are born to. Individuals are born into lives that vary on continua of advantage and disadvantage. This has much more to do with structure than with agency. Indeed, referring to groups of people who share similar life circumstances as agents who vary in terms of whether they can initiate social change serves only to conflate structures and agency. Ironically, this is the very problem Archer was trying to avoid in her work.

Nonetheless, it is clear from Archer's work (and from Goffman's and Bourdieu's) that there are advantages to analytic dualism. Primary among these is that analytic dualism allows us to study properties of structures and individuals that do not transcend one another. Empirically, this is a very useful strategy. And to the extent that sociologists are concerned with the practicalities of social inequality as much as with abstractions of it, such approaches are worthwhile. However, unlike integrated approaches, these theories usually end up favouring either structure (Archer and Bourdieu) or agency (Goffman). What is required then is a perspective that bridges integrated and analytic dualism approaches, a framework that gives equal theoretical weight to structure and agency while at the same time noting their distinctiveness.

A View in the Middle

William Sewell's (1992) account of structure and agency, which straddles the integrated and analytic-dualist positions, represents the best statement on the relationship between structure and agency. Notably, Sewell wants to retain Giddens's idea of the duality of structure, and he rethinks certain categories that are central to Giddens's structuration theory in this light. Simultaneously, he relies quite heavily on Bourdieu's notion of habitus, specifies nicely what is meant by *agency* and *structure*, and discusses how the two are linked. Hence, his theory is best described as lying somewhere between analytic dualism and integrated approaches.

To begin, Sewell (1992; see also Sewell 2005) takes Giddens to task for the idea that structures are virtual and composed of rules and resources. To do so, he first explains what he means by *rules*. In line with Giddens, Sewell suggests that rules are things that people draw on when they engage in social interaction. They are the taken-for-granted informal schemas that guide individual action. This, of course, stands in opposition to a more common definition of *rules* as being formally stated regulations, such as laws, about how one should behave. To resolve the possible confusion about these two very different views of rules, Sewell suggests using the term *schemas* to refer to "generalizable procedures" that apply to a variety of social interactions. Schemas are generalizable in the sense that individuals draw on them in various contexts. Some examples of schemas are etiquette, aesthetic norms, or the assumptions about how people should act on the basis of categorical distinctions such as "female" and "male." Such "recipes" for behaviour can be applied to both old and new situations, and it is because of their transposability that they may be understood as virtual. Hence, schemas are virtual because they are generalizable and cannot be specifically located in any particular social interaction or in any particular place and time. In other words, they exist but they cannot be empirically specified.

Resources, for Sewell, are of two types, human (Giddens's *authorization*) and non-human (Giddens's *allocation*). Human resources are things such as physical strength, emotional commitments, and knowledge; non-human resources are animate or inanimate objects; and both can be deployed in power relations. Unlike Giddens, Sewell argues that whereas schemas are virtual, resources are actual. Here lies a contradiction between Giddens and Sewell that Sewell must reconcile before moving on. If structures are virtual, then they cannot be composed of both schemas and resources as Sewell has defined them. To solve this conundrum, Sewell argues that we should think of resources as the effect of schemas and of schemas as the effect of resources. This is similar to Bourdieu's idea of habitus, whereby a dialectic

process occurs such that structures are formed through the mutual constitution of schemas and resources.

Having defined *structure*, Sewell goes on to describe how agents intersect with social structures, thereby potentially changing them. According to Sewell (1992: 20), "to be an agent means to be capable of exerting some degree of control over the social relations in which one is integrated, which in turn implies the ability to transform those social relations to some degree." Sewell conceptualizes agency as the human capacity to be intentional, creative, and ambitious, but he suggests that people develop different levels of this capacity depending on the structural circumstances they are faced with.

Because societies are characterized by a "multiplicity of structures" that intersect one another—for example, the class, age, gender, ethnicity, and race structures discussed in this book—social actors are required to draw on a range of schemas and resources in their social interactions with others. This creative capacity allows for the possibility that actors may transpose the schemas that they draw upon from one structure to another. Furthermore, because of the intersection and multiplicity of structures, individuals may attribute different meanings and interpretations to resources and schemas. The various meanings that may be attached to one structure or another by different actors, depending on the array of schemas and resources at their disposal, signify the possibility of social change.

Finally, according to Sewell (1992: 18), there is a certain "unpredictability of resource accumulation" that allows for the transformation of social structures. Because social actors attribute different meanings to structures, have the creative capacity to transpose schema from one to another, and are located across a wide array of structural positions, "the resource consequences of the enactment of cultural schemas is never entirely predictable" (Sewell

1992: 18). What Sewell seems to be referring to here are the unintended consequences of one's actions: "If the enactment of schemas creates unpredictable quantities and qualities of resources, and if the reproduction of schemas depends on their continuing validation by resources, this implies that schemas will in fact be differentially validated when they are put into action and therefore will potentially be subject to modification" (Sewell 1992: 18). Thus, according to Sewell, if the unintended consequences of one's actions affect one's resources, then structural change is likely to occur (see also Archer 1995, 2000).

In short, although Sewell suggests that his approach modifies and expands on Giddens's idea of the duality of structure, he veers away from the heart of this approach by discussing the intersections of structure and agency rather than their presuppositions. In other words, he discusses the unique characteristics of agency, agents, and structures in a way

that Giddens does not, while at the same time recognizing their influences on one another. Furthermore, his approach avoids the problems with Bourdieu's tendency toward structural determinism and Archer's view that agents are only collectivities that share similar structural backgrounds. Although we quibble with some of the specifics of Sewell's approach to structure and agency (more on that in the next chapter), it is, in our minds, the best statement on the topic.

This chapter has examined various sociological meanings of *action* and *agency* as well as theoretical views on the links between agency and structure. In the next chapter, a conceptual framework is developed that specifies how the concepts introduced in the preceding chapters come together. Also clarified in the next chapter is the relationship between structure and agency. In particular, several mechanisms are introduced that link structure and agency in relation to social inequality.

::: Questions for Critical Thought

1. Critically assess the views of action put forth by Weber, Parsons, and Habermas. Evaluate an action that you do every day according to each of these perspectives.

2. Consider the decision that you made to attend university. What role did structure play in that decision? What role did agency play? Which theory of structure and agency best explains your decision-making process?

3. Compare and contrast the theories of structure and agency put forth by Giddens and Sewell. Why is Sewell's theory more

applicable than Giddens's structuration theory to the study of social inequality?

4. Does Sewell's theory improve upon the work of Berger and Luckmann? If so, how? If not, why not?

5. In chapter 3, housework and child care were discussed in relation to the oppression, exploitation, and opportunity hoarding that characterize the structure of gender relations. Continue that discussion by evaluating how Goffman's idea of membranes relates to the negotiation of child care and housework in families.

⠿ Glossary

Action Meaningful human behaviour from the point of view of the actor or actors involved.

Class reproduction Occurs when one's class position is reproduced across generations.

Ideal types Theoretical abstractions of a particular social phenomenon. Observations that are exaggerated and used as a methodological tool to provide insight into the observed phenomena and for assessing variations from the abstraction. Introduced by Weber.

Morphogenesis Processes that elaborate or transform an existing system or structure.

Morphostasis Processes that work at maintaining a system's organizational structure.

Realist social ontology Philosophical assumptions about the realism of unobservable social phenomena. *Realism* is the idea that abstract ideas are real in their consequences. Social structures, for instance, are not directly observable but their social influence is real. *Ontology* refers to the philosophical beliefs about the nature or essence of being.

Relative mobility An estimate of the chance of upward or downward movement for a member of one social class in comparison with a member from another social class.

Social action According to Weber, action that is meaningful only in relation to another person's behaviour.

Social mobility The process of moving between status positions in society. Studies of social mobility sometimes examine country variations in opportunities for occupational or educational mobility. Other social mobility studies examine intergenerational mobility and whether children have surpassed the occupational status or educational attainment of their parents.

Symbolic interactionism An approach to sociological study that situates analysis within interaction. People evaluate and define themselves on the basis of how they think others view them. We imagine ourselves in other social roles, and through role playing we learn appropriate and inappropriate forms of behaviour.

⠿ Recommended Reading

Archer, Margaret. 2000. *Being Human: The Problem of Agency.* Cambridge, UK: Cambridge University Press. In this book, Archer argues that being human depends on one's interaction with the real world in which practice takes primacy over language in the emergence of human self-consciousness, thought, emotionality, and personal identity.

Bourdieu, Pierre. 1998. *Practical Reason: On the Theory of Action.* Stanford, CA: Stanford University Press. A collection of Bourdieu's lectures that covers his key ideas, including that of habitus.

Giddens, Anthony. 1984. *The Constitution of Society: Outline of the Theory of Structuration.* Berkeley: University of California Press. This book develops Giddens's seminal work on structuration theory.

Goffman, Erving. 1983. "The Interaction Order." *American Sociological Review* 48, February: 1–17. This is Goffman's presidential address to the American Sociological Association, published shortly after his death. Notwithstanding the title, this paper considers the relationship between the interaction order and social structures.

Layder, Derek. 1994. *Understanding Social Theory*. Thousand Oaks, CA: Sage. This book focuses on the agency/structure dualism in sociology. It covers theorists ranging from Dorothy Smith to Michel Foucault.

Lawrence, Thomas B., Roy Suddaby, and Bernard Leca. 2009. *Institutional Work: Actors and Agency in Institutional Studies of Organizations*. Cambridge, UK: Cambridge University Press. This compilation explores the conceptual core of institutional work, identifies institutional work strategies, provides exemplars for future empirical research, and embeds the concept within broader sociological debates and ideas.

Sewell, William H.J., Jr. 1992. "A Theory of Structure: Duality, Agency, and Transformation." *American Journal of Sociology* 98: 1–29. In this excellent, clearly written article on agency and structure, Sewell draws heavily on Giddens and Bourdieu to develop his own ideas about the production and reproduction of social life.

⁛ Relevant Websites

Margaret Archer on Reflexivity

http://video.google.co.uk/videoplay?docid=9156562982538374872

**A video of Margaret Archer speaking on reflexivity at the launch of the *Critical Realism Dictionary*.

Theory.org.uk

www.theory.org.uk

**This site of "social theory for fans of popular culture" is also the parent site for social-theorist trading cards, including of Giddens, Goffman, and Foucault. The site contains media and identity resources and serves as well as a link to order Giddens and Foucault action figures.

7

Actors and CAGE(s)

Introduction

The preceding chapters have outlined many of the elements of inequality that are included in the conceptual framework developed in this chapter. The remainder of this book brings these elements together in a coherent whole. As a first step, we begin by acknowledging the general assumptions that guide this approach. These assumptions are informed by several branches of critical theory and are summarized by Connidis and McMullin (2002: 559) as follows:

1. The social structure of Western nations is comprised of interlocking sets of social relations that privilege certain groups of people over others. Key sets of social relations include those that are based on class, gender, age, race, and ethnicity (Acker 1988; Collins 1990; Glenn 1992; McMullin 2000; Tilly 1998).

2. Individuals, though constrained to varying degrees by the social structure, attempt to exert control over their lives. They act with agency (Dannefer 1984; Habermas 1987; Lukes 1974; V.W. Marshall 1995; Weber [1922] 1978).

3. Social life is negotiated through interaction. It is constituted by and constitutive of interaction (Berger and Luckmann 1967; Dannefer 1984; Giddens 1979; V.W. Marshall 1995).

4. Society is more accurately characterized as based on conflicting interests than on consensus. Different placement in the social structure creates conflicting interests and investments in the status quo (Marx [1848] 1983). There is an essential conflict or tension between the constraints placed on individuals by social structure and the desire of individuals to act with agency (Habermas 1987). Such an approach recognizes that conflicts are not episodic and unpredictable but rather are patterned features of relationships (D.H.J. Morgan 1985).[*]

Although theoretical assumptions influence all sociological work, they are often left unacknowledged. Yet to understand theoretical frameworks, the assumptions that guide them must be recognized. These assumptions are listed for readers to keep in mind as they consider the conceptual framework developed here. To develop the framework, this

*Connidis, Ingrid Arnet, and Julie Ann McMullin. 1994. 'Social Support in Older Age: Assessing the Impact of Marital and Parent Status': *Canadian Journal on Aging* 13, 4: 510-27: 559, reproduced with permission.

chapter begins by revisiting the life of Anna (the woman discussed in chapter 1). It then discusses social time and the life-course perspective and in doing so introduces the concept of the *substantive birth cohort*. Next, the concepts discussed in earlier chapters are integrated into the framework throughout this chapter. Finally, this conceptual framework is used to analyze Anna's life.

Figure 7.1 graphically depicts Anna's life. As shown on the far left of the figure and as mentioned in chapter 1, Anna was born to white, English-speaking parents of British descent in 1915, during the First World War. She grew up on a farm in Ontario with her

mother, father, and two brothers. Although it was only a small farm, Anna's father and mother worked hard and were able to provide their family with life's essentials. The arrow at the bottom of Figure 7.1 maps out the timing of some life events and transitions that Anna experienced. Anna graduated from high school, an unusual achievement for rural girls in that day, and although she had the opportunity to go on to teachers' college, as her mother had done before her, she decided to marry John Warner, a local man seven years her senior. She married well. John's family were well-to-do farmers, and with their help, Anna and John began their

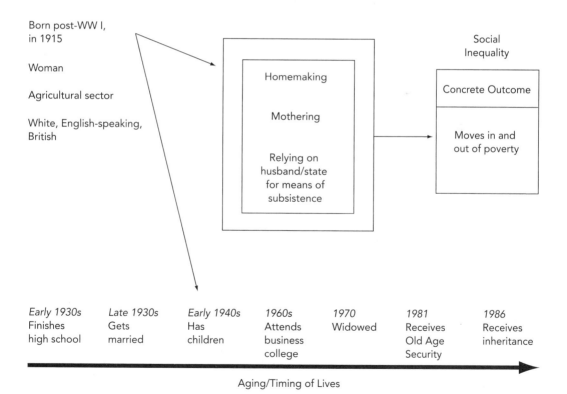

Figure 7.1 Anna's Life

marriage in the late 1930s in relative financial stability. John and Anna moved to town and had two daughters, one in 1941 and the other in 1943.

Located in the centre of Figure 7.1 are the central activities in which Anna engaged to maintain her life and the life of her family. Anna was always a homemaker, and John never had a stable job. His older brother, who was married and childless, inherited their father's farm, and John worked for him occasionally. John also bought houses, restored them, and sold them for a profit. Money was tight in the Warner household, but no one seemed to want for anything. There was food on the table, John had paid for the house in full when he bought it, and the family had a few good clothes.

John died suddenly in 1970, when he was 62 and Anna was 55. His estate comprised some savings and his house. He had stipulated in his will that Anna could draw $200 per month from his estate until she either remarried or died, at which time the estate would be divided equally between her daughters. Suddenly, Anna was poor. Though her income was well below the qualifying cutoff for social security, she refused to apply for it and was too young to receive Old Age Security. The will stipulated that she could not sell the house. Other than a brief stint in business college, Anna had no training, no work experience, and no marketable skill. Besides, at 55 she was unlikely to find work. Her daughter hired her to babysit her grandchildren and for the next 10 years she made do with the clothes she already owned, shopping at yard sales and eating anything she could buy for next to nothing in the grocery store—old bread, food in dinted cans, and so on. After 10 years Anna turned 65 and began receiving the Old Age Pension. She was still

poor but no longer destitute. Five years later Anna's sister-in-law, the wife of John's childless brother who inherited the family business, died and left Anna one-third of her quite large estate. Suddenly, at age 70, Anna was better off financially than she had ever been before.

In chapter 1, we noted that a central aim of this book is to develop an understanding of inequality that can help us explain the ebb and flow of poverty that Anna experienced. In the preceding chapters, class, age, gender, ethnicity, and "race" have been considered mostly as static structures that constrain opportunity. Yet, as was noted in chapter 1, social inequality as it is experienced by individuals is dynamic, and to understand it we need to take social time into account.

Social Time

Structural accounts of gender and of race and ethnicity rarely take social time into account. This is partly because gender, race, and ethnicity are usually considered to be ascribed and static individual characteristics. Yet historical sociology shows us the importance of the social context to variations in gender, racial, and ethnic inequality (Adams 2000; Laslett and Brenner 1987). Moreover, the individual experiences of gender, racial, and ethnic inequality may vary throughout one's life. Social time is, however, considered in studies of social mobility (see chapter 6) that examine whether social class changes across generations. It is also considered in studies of aging that assess the biopsychosocial processes associated with the passage of time. Indeed, Anna's life shows that to understand the structural inequalities faced by individuals throughout their lives, we must address the intersection of individual and historical time. The life-course approach, as outlined by Glenn Elder (1974, 1995), provides useful insight into how issues of time might be considered in an integrated framework.

The Life-Course Perspective

The life-course idea, that people progress through life by taking on different roles and statuses at various ages, is not a new one. Among the earliest depictions of the life course is the seventeenth-century anonymous Dutch painting entitled *The Stairway of Life* (see Figure 7.2). In this picture we see a boy who ascends in his life until he reaches a peak at age 50 and then descends thereafter until his death at age 100. The various roles and statuses this boy takes on are conveyed through his clothes, the objects he holds, and his posture on each step of the stairway. For centuries, until recently, Europeans were given, as gifts to mark life transitions such as birth or marriage, stairways made in various media, which they would hang on the walls in their homes (Dekkers 2000).

The life-course perspective develops the ideas represented by *The Stairway of Life* and theoretically guides research in problem identification and formulation (Elder 1995; Elder and O'Rand 1995). In particular, it has "made time, context, and process more salient dimensions of theory and analysis" (Elder 1995: 104).

Figure 7.2 Anonymous, *The Stairway of Life*, c. 1640

Life-course research conceptualizes social time by recognizing and attempting to understand (1) that individuals begin the dynamic and contextual aging process at birth; (2) that historical time, period, and cohort influence the aging process; (3) that aging is a bio-psychosocial process related to and shaped by social contexts, cultural meanings, and social-structural locations; and (4) that age-related life transitions and trajectories are heterogeneous and are marked by sequences of events and social transitions (Bengtson, Parrott, and Burgess 1994; Elder 1995; Elder and O'Rand 1995; Hagestad 1990; Hagestad and Neugarten 1985; Passuth and Bengtson 1988). Furthermore, in the European tradition, life-course researchers emphasize the influence of the state and social policy in structuring individuals' life courses (Heinz 2001; V.W. Marshall and Mueller 2002).

According to Elder (1994, 1995), two of the central principles of the life-course paradigm are the **timing of lives** and **lives in time and place**. Issues related to the timing of lives include historical time, the social timing of transitions across the life course, the synchrony (or asynchrony) of individual careers, and one's life stage at the point of social change (Elder 1995). Thus, "social timing refers to the incidence, duration, and sequence of roles; and to related age expectations and beliefs" (Elder 1995: 114). Hence, for instance, the era in which people are born (i.e., historical time) influences the average age at which they get married for the first time (social timing of the transition to marriage), which in turn influences the age at which it is socially appropriate for individuals to marry for the first time. For instance, during times of economic recessions and depressions, the average age of first marriage tends to be higher than during times of economic prosperity.

The "lives in time and place" principle refers to the effect of contextual change caused by a particular historical event on individual life trajectories, given that historical changes do not uniformly occur in different places. This is conceptually distinct from other life-course work that either studies birth cohorts in their relevant historical context (as in age-stratification theory—see chapter 5) or examines individual life courses as they are framed and constrained by a social system (see Mayer and Muller 1986). Instead, Elder's research starts with the properties of social change and then moves to an assessment of how this change affects individual life trajectories (Elder 1995), taking into account the age of individuals at the time of the historical event that led to social change. For example, Elder (1974, 1995) suggests that research on the effects of the Depression (with its resultant social changes), once traced through individuals and families, shows that children of the Depression developed individual characteristics such as a "sense of industry and responsibility from the required helpfulness experience of needy households" (Elder 1995: 110).

Figure 7.3, which depicts our conceptual framework, illustrates the influence of the life-course perspective (Elder 1995). The "lives in time and place" principle is located on the far left of the diagram under the umbrella term **substantive birth cohort**. Substantive birth cohorts also represent the geographic location (place), generation, gender, ethnicity, race, and class positions in which people are born through no choice of their own. This concept takes social time into account, which Margaret Archer (see also chapter 6) alludes to when she says, "We are all born into a structural and cultural context which, far from being of our own making, is the unintended resultant of past interaction among the long dead" (1995: 253). The social structures and experiences of gender, ethnicity, race, and class have been discussed in previous chapters, but it is their relationship to

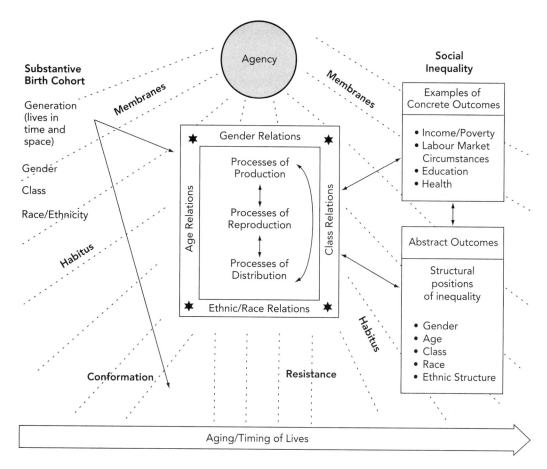

Figure 7.3 The Coalescence of Class, Age, Gender, and Ethnicity

the "generation" concept and to the ideas of social time that requires introduction here.

The term **generation**, as used here, is similar to the "lives in time and place" concept in Elder's life-course perspective. *Generation* is used in various ways in the literature. According to Simon Biggs (2005; 2007), "generation" has two different meanings in everyday society. Some scholars use it to refer to age-based kinship, or biological, locations within families. Hence, four-generation families are those comprising great-grandparents, grandparents, parents, and

grandchildren. Others, however, use the concept of generation to mean time-specific social locations that are similar to social-class locations and that might give rise to group conflict and consciousness (Mannheim [1928] 1952; V.W. Marshall 1983). According to Biggs, this meaning refers to membership in an age group whose members share social and historical qualities and experiences or, as Biggs writes, "the public sphere of age-based cohorts travelling through time together" (2007: 696). It is the latter understanding of *generation* that we use here. Box 7.1

Global perspective

Box 7.1 What Growing Income Inequality Is Costing Canada's Future Generations

by Barrie McKenna

It's been dubbed the Great Gatsby Curve.

Plot countries on a graph. Put income inequality on one axis, mobility between generations on the other.

A sobering picture emerges. The dream of achieving a better life than your parents is more elusive in countries where the gap between rich and poor is larger.

For now, Canada sits comfortably in the middle of the curve among developed countries. It's more equal and traditionally more upwardly mobile than those at the extremes of the scale, including the United States, but it trails countries such as Denmark, Norway and Sweden.

And yet a disquieting trend has taken root as Canada emerges from a decade transformed by powerful forces—some beyond our borders, others closer to home. Globalization, a digital revolution and public austerity programs are reshaping the economy. Good paying factory jobs continue to vanish, and middle-class incomes are getting squeezed. Many of the great equalizers—pensions, public health care and education—are threatened by the fiscal challenges facing governments at all levels.

That leaves a greater share of income, wealth and power in the hands of contemporary Jay Gatsbys.

The challenge for the country is to preserve for future generations all the good things that helped previous generations—especially the massive Baby Boom cohort—thrive and get ahead, argues University of Ottawa economist Miles Corak, one of Canada's leading experts on poverty and mobility.

"We have a sense of being relatively successful in terms of mobility, but it reflects an era that was more equal," he points out.

Today's twenty and thirtysomethings are likely to find it much harder to get ahead than their parents did, he warns. For them, even a middle-class life is increasingly elusive.

Sicco Naets, a 39-year-old manager at an Ottawa high-tech start-up, is emblematic of many post–Baby Boomers, who worry the Canadian dream is passing them by. He and his wife earn "well above" the national average. They have two children, one car, little debt and a modest suburban town home.

And yet Mr. Naets is frustrated and angry that his generation seems to be slipping further behind. He dreams of a larger house for his growing family, but he's fearful moving up will leave him too much debt, too little savings for retirement, or both.

"Compared to my parents, I'm way further ahead from a job point of view, I'm better educated and I'm probably in a higher income bracket. But my standard of living is a lot lower than theirs was," he says.

Stuck in a slow-growth economy after a decade of stagnating incomes for the middle class, experts say Canada is at a crossroads. It can look to countries that have found creative ways to nurture greater equality and mobility, without sacrificing economic growth. Or it can follow the U.S., Britain and other countries down the path of increasingly isolated social extremes.

illustrates the relationship between income inequality and social mobility across generations in Canada.

In his classic article "The Problem of Generations," Karl Mannheim ([1928] 1952) generalizes Marx's conception of class to demonstrate the sociological significance of generations. Mannheim criticizes previous assessments of generations, arguing that those assessments relied too much on chronological

While inequality is significantly less pronounced than in the U.S., Canada is trending in the same direction as its neighbour on several key metrics, including ebbing mobility, a rising share of income in the hands of the top 1 per cent and a swelling gap between what CEOs and workers make.

The country's business elite—the chief executives of the top 100 companies—took home 122 times what the average worker did in 2012, up from a ratio 84-to-one a decade earlier, according to research commissioned by the *Globe and Mail*.

The reality is that perfect equality is both unattainable and undesirable. Nowhere are wealth and income distributed completely evenly across a population. Countries are all unequal, and that's generally a good thing. Inequality creates a powerful incentive to work, to invest and to get ahead. More income is the reward for success, which is spread to others when those at the top invest, start new businesses and hire more workers.

But it's all a question of degree. You can have too much of a good thing.

Former prime minister Paul Martin, 75, figures he's part of the most fortunate generation in Canadian history. He entered the work force in the booming 1960s, at the vanguard of an age group that would only know rising incomes and boundless opportunity.

But Mr. Martin frets that Canada is now drifting towards a society of extremes and a hollow middle—conditions he argues have helped spawn the anti-government Tea Party movement in the United States.

"The ability for succeeding generations to do better than preceding generations is an essential part of the glue that makes a democracy work," says Mr. Martin, who now devotes his energy and part of his wealth to fighting for better aboriginal education. "The gutting of the middle class is more than the canary in the coal mine. It essentially opens your society and your economy to all kinds of fissures."

The major economic transformations of the past couple of decades have certainly been a mixed blessing for the middle class. Rapid globalization and huge advances in technology have depressed wages and marginalized routine work.

They have also made life cheaper, driving down the cost of most household goods, from flat-screen TVs to clothing to furniture. Cheap money has meant people can borrow more to fuel these purchases.

The economic emergence of countries such as China has driven up demand, and prices, for Canada's prized natural resources—fertilizer, oil, metals, canola and the like. And the benefits of the long resource boom have spread wealth across the country.

But the Great Recession ended the party, leaving the world in slow growth mode for a while.

The 1 per cent will be okay. No worries there. But the transition to sluggish growth and government austerity has left many middle-income earners feeling frustrated, financially squeezed and worried about slipping backwards.

This middle-class angst has made inequality fertile ground for politicians, right across the political spectrum, in Canada and elsewhere.

age or on the biological fact that generations reproduce themselves. Hence, past treatments of generations neglected the true sociological importance of generational relations.

According to Mannheim, although it is true that the sociological phenomenon of generations is based on the biological rhythm of birth and death, "were it not for the existence of social interaction between human beings—were there no definable social structure, no history based on a particular sort of continuity, then generations would not exist as a social location phenomenon" (Mannheim [1928] 1952: 290–1).

Thus, Mannheim believed that a generation represents a unique type of social location based on the dynamic interplay between being born in a particular year in a particular place and the socio-political events that occur while a birth cohort comes of age. Generational location is an objective fact similar to that of class position. Hence, all individuals, whether they acknowledge it or not, belong to a particular generational location within a given society (Box 7.2 provides an example by discussing the *entitlement generation*). According to this view of generations, the importance of generation lies not in the fact that one is born in a particular year, but in the sociological relevance of being born at a particular historical time in a given society. It reveals that belonging to the same generation

endow[s] the individuals sharing in them with a common location in the social and historical process, and thereby limit[s]

HIGHLIGHT

Box 7.2 Canada's "Entitlement" Generation

Ken Coates, a professor of history and a former dean at the University of Waterloo, believes that students in Canada have become part of the "entitlement generation." In a *Bright Ideas* blog, Coates writes that Canada's youth are not to blame, however. "[I]t is not your fault . . . the reality is that many young Canadians have been protected from the harsh realities of life. . . . If I wanted to be more direct, I would refer to you as the *Entitlement Generation* and claim you are among the most spoiled generation in history—a criticism of your parents, including me, more than you!"

Coates drew these conclusions after reviewing a compilation survey based on responses from current university students. This survey probed Canadian students about their attitudes about work and their expectations once they graduated. Rather than "hard work" and "dedication to their employers" being a top priority, most students expected to earn high salaries and they valued leisure and vacation time as a priority for accepting employment.

This problem, Coates believes, is further complicated by the fact that higher education no longer necessarily leads to "good jobs" for everyone in our society. If Canada's youth believe that a higher education will immediately lead to an escalator that brings them directly to a six-figure income with flexible job hours and a focus on lifestyle and leisure, many are in for a harsh reality post-graduation.

Coates offers a solution in his 2011 book *Campus Confidential*. He advocates educational streaming and believes that vocational education should be more important than it is now. Students should go to university because they are capable of and interested in engaging in high-level work. Colleges and tech schools—which increasingly offer competitive salaries—offer more practical, job-oriented education for everyone else.

Nevertheless, there is no fast track to success. Whether students pursue college or university degrees, Coates believes that the labour market expectations of Canada's youth must be tempered now more than ever.

Sources: http://talentegg.ca/ideas/tag/entitlement-generation/; Coates and Morrison (2013).

them to a specific range of potential experience, predisposing them for a certain characteristic mode of thought and experience, and a characteristic type of historically relevant action. Any given location, then, excludes a large number of possible modes of thought, experience, feeling, and action, and restricts the range of self-expression open to the individual to certain circumscribed possibilities. (Mannheim [1928] 1952: 291)

The significance of substantive birth cohorts may be illustrated with a simple example. The life choices available to a white English woman born into a working-class family in 1920 are not the same as those available to a white English woman born into a working-class family in 1965. For the first woman, the likelihood of finding work in the manufacturing sector (particularly because she was probably looking for work during the Second World War) is much greater than it is for the second woman, who is likely to find work in the service sector. The Second World War, while significantly influencing the first woman's life, will only indirectly influence the second woman's life. Likewise, the second woman will be influenced by the women's movement in a much different way than the first. Furthermore, the locale in which these women are born (urban versus rural; Maritime versus central regions in Canada) will influence their life experiences and opportunities (Lobao, Hooks, and Tickamyer 2007). This story is even more complicated today. As a result of modern lifestyle and consumption patterns, many working-class people no longer identify as "working class" (Andersen and Curtis 2012; Curtis 2013). Previous cohorts were likely more class aware, because they experienced more class-divisive economic and political conditions compared

with people today. Not only are the relations of production, reproduction, and distribution different, but the way those relations are shaped by gender, age, and racial and ethnic processes is considerably different as well. In turn, all of these processes influence and are influenced by the timing of lives.

The timing-of-lives concept and aging are dimensions of social time (which are represented along the bottom of Figure 7.3), and both are influenced by substantive birth cohorts. The timing-of-lives concept mirrors the life-course perspective's conceptualization of it (see above). Thus, the substantive birth cohort into which one is born shapes the incidence, timing, duration, and sequencing of various life-course events and transitions such as marriage, parenthood, and retirement. For instance, people who were born in the generation that came of age during the Depression were more likely to delay marriage than was the generation that followed them, in part because of the macroeconomic situation in which members of each generation were required to make decisions.

The process of aging, which is also shown along the bottom of Figure 7.3, is the final dimension of social time that is considered in this framework. *Aging* refers to the experiences that come with the passage of time, as well as to the biopsychosocial processes that alter one's body and physical capabilities. The substantive birth cohort into which one is born influences aging processes to the extent that physical decline can be reduced by certain social habits that have changed over time, such as eating, smoking, and exercising. Such processes are also influenced by the generation, gender, ethnicity, race, and class in which one is born, as is evident from the different life expectancies of these various groups at birth.

Social Processes

Located in the centre of Figure 7.3 are the interrelated processes of production, reproduction, and distribution. These three processes constitute the organization and nature of the activities that are required for the survival of individuals and species. Recall from chapter 2 that *processes of production* are the ways by which raw materials are converted into useful and valuable objects; *processes of distribution* are the ways in which material resources change hands in society (Acker 1988, 2000, 2006a; Weber [1922] 1978); *distributive processes* include wage, state, personal, and marital transfers (Acker 1988); and *processes of reproduction* are the ways in which life is maintained both daily and intergenerationally (Laslett and Brenner 1987). Social processes of production, reproduction, and distribution are interrelated. People who have indirect relationships with a particular social process tend to be more directly involved with another. A retired worker, for instance, has no direct relationship with production processes but is indirectly linked to them through the distributive processes by which he or she receives a company pension. A divorced father may not have a direct relationship with the processes of reproduction but may be linked to those processes through the distribution of money to his children and former wife.

Processes of production, distribution, and reproduction become sociologically significant when we recognize that they are carried out by individuals in interaction with other individuals. In other words, it is the social relations of production, distribution, and reproduction that are of primary concern to sociologists. In the literature on social inequality, researchers generally emphasize one set of social relations as it relates to a specific social process. For example, social-class relations are often seen as the root of inequality in production processes, and indeed the terms *social-class relations* and *relations of production* are often used interchangeably. Similarly, gender relations are most often considered at the heart of inequality in processes of reproduction. However, there is ample evidence to suggest that the rewards, privileges, and resources associated with one's relationship with the processes of production, distribution, and reproduction are affected by a complex interplay of class, age, gender, ethnic, and race relations. Class, for instance, does not account for all of the power differentials that occur as a result of production processes (Acker 2006). Hence, it is unacceptable to suggest, as Wright (1997) does, that gender-based worker exploitation is simply a specific kind of class relation; this privileges class in the analysis of inequality and ignores the uniqueness of other forms of disadvantage. What is needed is a theoretical shift in which the relations of production will assume not only class relations but gender, ethnic, racial, and age relations as well.

Social Structure

The existence of the social processes discussed above does not necessarily imply an outcome of social inequality. Rather, understanding how these processes are structured is of fundamental importance to understanding and explaining social inequality (McMullin 2000). Figure 7.3 shows that class, age, gender, race, and ethnic relations frame the interrelated processes of production, reproduction, and distribution. Here, the connections (indicated by the stars in Figure 7.3) of class, age, gender, race, and ethnic relations with the power and rewards associated with one's position within these structures shape the ways in which production, reproduction, and distribution are organized.

As noted in the previous chapters, class, age, gender, and ethnicity or race are conceptualized as sets of social relations characterized by power that are fundamental structures or organizing features of all aspects of social life (Calasanti and Slevin 2006), including the processes of production, distribution, and reproduction (Ng 1993). Embedded in these social relations (or structures) are the taken-for-granted informal schemas (see Sewell 1992 and chapter 6) that guide individual action (e.g., ideas about appropriate behaviour) and various human resources (e.g., physical strength and knowledge) and non-human resources (e.g., money and property). Structures of class, age, gender, ethnicity, and race are formed through the mutual constitution of such schemas and resources (see Sewell 1992 and chapter 6).

Although the processes of class, race, ethnic, age, and gender formation are unique, several interrelated theoretical constructs have been identified in preceding chapters that apply, in varying degrees, to all of them: oppression (see chapters 2 through 5), power (see especially chapter 2), exploitation, and opportunity hoarding (chapter 3 and Tilly 1998). Recall that oppression occurs if (1) the welfare of one group of people depends upon the deprivation of another and (2) the deprivation of the oppressed group depends upon the exclusion of the oppressed group from access to resources, rewards, and privileges. As we have seen in the preceding chapters, in contemporary Canadian society both conditions of oppression apply to class, age, gender, race, and ethnic relations.

Oppressive relations are produced and reproduced through power. Power results from the control that certain groups have over economic, political, and ideological resources (Grabb 2007). It is through these systems of control that certain groups exclude others from gaining access to resources, rewards, and privileges. Thus, certain groups are deprived relative to others through mechanisms of power. Notably, a recursive relationship between power and oppression is actualized in class, age, gender, ethnic, and race relations through which patterns of inequality are produced and reproduced.

This recursive relationship is fostered through two mechanisms of control. First, exploitation produces oppressive relations when individuals and groups control resources (economic, political, ideological) and use those resources to their advantage by mobilizing others' efforts for their own gain (Tilly 1998). Second, oppressive relations are produced and reproduced through the mechanism of opportunity hoarding. Here, members of a particular group obtain a valuable resource that reinforces the group's privilege and status. The group then acts in ways that will ensure the maintenance of its monopoly over that resource (Tilly 1998).

When the disadvantage of certain groups depends on the advantage of others, the oppression that results is relational. It is in this sense that class, age, gender, and race/ethnic relations were discussed above. Relationality takes on a second meaning when it is positioned within a structure and agency framework. Here, a relational understanding of class, age, gender, ethnic, and race relations takes into account the meaning that is attributed to these categories of inequality based on their relative positioning within social hierarchies (Glenn 2000; Stasiulis 1999). Meaning is derived through the assessment of difference, by which "oppositional categories require the suppression of variability within each category and the exaggeration of differences between categories" (Glenn 2000: 10). Hence, even though men and women are physiologically more similar than different (Lorber 1994), small differences are exaggerated and problematized. Men appear genderless, and the inequalities that women face are assigned meanings that are derived from these differences (Glenn 2000).

The graphical depiction of class, age, gender, ethnicity, and race relations surrounding the processes of production, reproduction, and distribution resembles a picture in its frame.

This representation illustrates that these structured sets of social relations are not thought to be causally linked, in any linear sense, to the processes of production, distribution, and reproduction. Rather, they mediate these processes and cannot be separated from them. This approach allows for considerable latitude in assessing both the independent and the combined effects of these sets of relations on the processes of inequality. This suggests, following Wright's (1997) discussion of the connections between gender and class, that some of what is consequential about each of these sets of relations occurs independently of the other sets of relations, and yet an assessment of inequality would be incomplete without one also considering intersecting influences.

However, this does not imply that one can pick and choose among the components of the framework that one deems worthy of study. Rather, the issue of coalescence in this approach suggests that inaccurate assessments of social inequality will result from such strategies. Although one can examine both the independent and interlocking effects of the components of this framework, the processes and sets of relations contained within it must be considered as a whole if we wish to understand the nature of social inequality. To examine one component without the other will present a distorted picture of social reality. It will also miss the fact that social life is mutually constituted by gender, class, race, age, and ethnicity (Glenn 2000). Thus, the coalescence represented in this approach might be visualized as a colourful and tightly woven fabric; the threads may be discernible from one another, but the removal of any one of them distorts the overall pattern.

Interestingly, the first letters of class, age, gender, and ethnicity or race form the word CAGE. A lot of imagery comes to mind when one hears the word CAGE, and much of it is relevant to studies of inequality. We use this acronym to depict images of the social-structural constraints that individuals and groups often face. However, to make too much use of this metaphor would diminish the significance of individual agency in systems of inequality and in everyday life.

Agency and Structure: Actors and CAGE(s)

In the coalescence framework in Figure 7.3, agency flows throughout the diagram in a way that represents its omnipresence in social life. Recall that agency is the ability to exert some control over the social relations in which one is enmeshed (Sewell 1992). Agency includes decisions to act and not to act, and discussions of agency and structure must take into account both the intended and unintended consequences of one's action or non-action. The location of agency at the top of the diagram does not imply that it has a superior status to social structure. Rather, it is meant to capture the idea that agency runs through social structures and that "social structure does not stand outside of the human, social behaviour that produces it, yet it nevertheless takes on properties that transcend the behavior of those who construct it" (McMullin and Marshall 1999: 309)

As argued in chapter 6, this approach favours analytic dualism over enmeshed accounts of the relationship between structure and agency. Recall that analytic dualism suggests that there is something unique about agency and about social structure, even though the two are intricately connected. Notably, the theories presented in chapter 6 were not established primarily as explanations of social inequality but were concerned with explaining the relationship between structure and agency in relation to social change. Although social change is a central topic in the study of inequality, it is not the subject of this book. However, the organizational and conceptual framework developed here will help us to understand social inequality as it exists in Canada in the early part of the twenty-first century. A remaining challenge is to explain the mechanisms that link structure and agency in relation to inequality.

Habitus (Bourdieu 1977) and membranes (Goffman 1983) represent two linking mechanisms that apply generally to daily interactions. Recall that *habitus* is the cumulative embodied experiences that are shaped by structural realities. Individuals rely on their habitus in their daily interaction with others. Recall also that membranes are meant to represent Goffman's idea of the loose coupling of social orders. According to Goffman, *membranes* determine which aspects of the social structure influence an individual's behaviour and which do not. Both habitus and membranes work simultaneously in everyday life as individuals negotiate the social-structural realities of their lives.

Two other mechanisms—conformation and resistance—pertain more specifically to inequality. **Conformation** refers to the processes through which individuals comply with and accept the various schema and resources that structure society. Conformation captures Sewell's (1992) idea of transposability (see chapter 6) and Tilly's (1998) notions of adaptation and emulation. Thus, schemas are learned in one setting and used in others, thereby reinforcing the social structure itself. **Resistance** refers to the processes through which individuals reject and act against established social structures. Resistance can be subtle (a wife ignoring her standards of cleanliness so that her husband will continue to clean the bathroom) or blatant (protesting discrimination on Parliament Hill), and it can be chronic (being an ongoing and active member of the Grey Panthers) or acute (taking part in one activist march). Although

conformation and resistance are set up here as antitheses of one another, no one ever completely conforms or resists. Rather, a complexity of resistance and conformation emerges as individuals negotiate their interests within the various domains of social life. Conformation and resistance are acted out by individuals, but the choice to conform or resist, as well as the specific strategies one uses in these processes, is influenced by the structured sets of social relations described above. Furthermore, tensions, contradictions, and paradoxes result from the complexities of resistance and conformation. Individuals then act to negotiate the ambivalence created by these tensions, contradictions, and paradoxes in everyday life (see Connidis and McMullin 2002).

Structure, Agency, and Anna's Life

The discussions of social time and place, social processes, structure, and agency presented above are necessarily abstract. To demonstrate how they work in real life we turn back to Anna's life and superimpose Figure 7.1 (Anna's life) onto Figure 7.3 (the coalescence framework), the result of which is depicted in Figure 7.4.

The substantive birth cohort in which Anna was born structurally affected her life chances. Even though women's rights and opportunities were expanding during the early twentieth century, women who were born during this time were still not encouraged to be economically self-sufficient, especially if they lived in rural areas as Anna did. Instead, they were expected to marry a man who would be able to provide for them and their families. English common law, by which property was passed on to the eldest son, was still well established in practice in Canada. Hence, Anna, by virtue of the fact that she had been born a girl, had little hope of inheriting any property from her family. The fact that Anna's family worked in agriculture meant that there was little money to spare and that all family members needed to work on the farm and in the home in order to make ends meet. Anna helped her mother with household chores, gathering eggs, gardening, and making meals for her family and the boarders they took in.

Like many other farmers of British descent, Anna's mother and father embraced white, middle-class ideologies of family and work: a woman's place was in the home and good men provided for their families. Anna's parents also embraced the middle-class idea that their children should pursue post-secondary education. For Anna, these two sets of ideals created a tension. Why go to teachers' college if it is not needed to be a wife and a mother? A complexity of resistance and conformation emerged in Anna's life when she was caught between the structure of gender, which suggested that she didn't need post-secondary education in order to fulfill her social role, and middle-class ideals that encouraged higher education. Anna resolved this complexity by completing high school but marrying instead of going on to teachers' college. This complexity was negotiated not only through Anna's actions and the meaning that she attributed to the structures of class and gender, but also through her parents' actions and their understanding of white, middle-class values. Anna did not regret this resolution but rather interpreted it as a "proper" course of events.

Anna became a full-time homemaker and mother who relied for her means of subsistence on the money her husband distributed to her (see centre of Figure 7.4). Indeed, her life progressed in a typical fashion after she completed high school. She was married in her mid-20s, which was considered "on time" for women who were coming of age during the Depression. Anna and John had two children shortly after they married. Their daughters were born "on time," and it was typical for people who came of age during the Depression to have only two children.

The ways in which the processes of distribution, production, and reproduction were organized in Anna's life were a direct result of the gender, age, ethnic, and class relations in which she was enmeshed. Anna and her family of procreation were no longer farmers. John occasionally worked for his older brother in the family business but earned his living mostly by buying and selling property. They had little money, but John did own the house in which his family lived. The Warners tried very hard to achieve the white, middle-class standards that were typical of the times, especially regarding education, the appropriate gendered division of labour in the family, and religious morality. The fact that Anna chose not to rely on social assistance after the death of her husband was linked to the pressures that she felt to continue to maintain these standards. Paid work may have been an option for her, but the structures of gender and age stood in her way.

Clearly, the choices Anna made during young adulthood and through the middle years of her life fell much more toward the conformation end of the conformation–resistance continuum than toward the resistance end. But these choices must also be seen in light of the habitus that Anna developed through her early experiences—a habitus that was shaped by rigid gendered expectations, middle-class ideals of work and family, and the hardships many faced during the Depression. Anna would probably not view the choices she made as choices at all but rather just as "the way things were meant to be." Hence, for Anna,

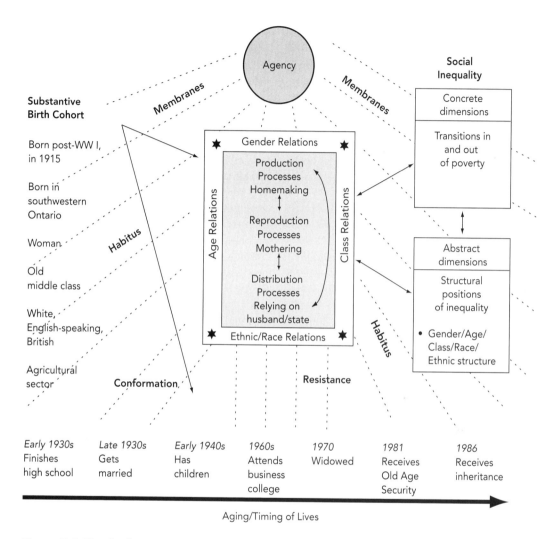

Figure 7.4 The Coalescence of Class, Age, Gender, Ethnicity, and Race in Anna's Life

the membranes that linked social structure and agency during this time were very thin; structural constraints were adhered to, not challenged.

Given the circumstances and habitus of Anna's life, it is difficult to make sense of her decision to go to business college. One possible explanation, however, is linked to her daughters' decisions to pursue post-secondary education (one attended business college and the other went to teachers' college). Perhaps she decided that if her daughters could further their education, she could too, especially since her daughters now needed less of her time. That the decisions and circumstances of others in our social networks influence our choices and life circumstances is an important consideration. This idea is captured by the term *linked lives* (see Elder 1995). Indeed, there are several times at which the circumstances and choices of people close to Anna affected her life and the ebb and flow of her poverty. Her husband decided to invest his wealth rather than leave it to her, so when he died, she became poor. Her brother and sister-in-law did not have children, both died, and, at a time quite late in her life, Anna became rich.

Social Inequality

Recall from chapter 1 that *social inequality* refers to relatively long-lasting differences between individuals or groups of people and that these differences have considerable implications for individual lives, especially "for the rights or opportunities they exercise and the rewards or privileges they enjoy" (Grabb 2007: 1; see also Pampel 1998). Thus, social inequality has both abstract and concrete dimensions. Rights and opportunities are shaped by one's position in structured social hierarchies. As Figure 7.3 shows, the interplay between agency and structure organizes the processes of production, reproduction, and distribution, the combination of which leads to abstract outcomes of inequality. These abstract outcomes are the structural hierarchy of inequality in which categorical differences between sexes, races, ethnic groups, age groups, and classes are reinforced and, in some cases, modified. There is a reciprocal relationship between objectively defined structural positions of inequality and the organization of the processes of production, reproduction, and distribution: the two mutually constitute one another.

The second dimension of social inequality is more concrete, representing the advantages and disadvantages experienced by members of society. Hence, the ways in which the processes of production, reproduction, and distribution are organized shape, in Anna's case, transitions in and out of poverty. More broadly, the organization of production, reproduction, and distribution influences the rewards, privileges, and resources that are accrued in various social domains, such as families, labour markets, states, education, and health. These issues are discussed in Part II of this book.

▓ Questions for Critical Thought

Map the life course of either your mother or your father on the conceptual framework presented in the coalescence framework in Figure 7.3, and consider their paid- and unpaid-labour circumstances.

1. What structural conditions influenced these circumstances in your mother's or father's life?
2. Did your mother or father act with agency in determining these circumstances? What are the choices she or he made that influenced

    paid and unpaid labour? Were these truly choices?
3. What role did your mother's or father's substantive birth cohort play in influencing her or his paid- and unpaid-labour circumstances?

4. What role has aging and the timing of lives played in your mother's or father's paid- and unpaid-labour circumstances?
5. What other factors influenced your mother's or father's paid- and unpaid-labour circumstances? Where do they fit in the framework (i.e., structure, agency, linking mechanism)?

▓ Glossary

Conformation The processes through which individuals comply with and accept the various schemas and resources that structure society.

Generation The subjectively meaningful cohort into which one is born. This concept is similar to the "lives in time and place" concept in Elder's life-course perspective but reflects Mannheim's ideas involving the sociological relevance of being born at a particular historical time in a given society.

Lives in time and place The effects of contextual change, caused by a particular historical event, on individual life trajectories.

Resistance The processes through which individuals reject and act against established social structures.

Substantive birth cohort An umbrella term that includes the ideas captured by "lives in time and place" while also representing the generation, gender, ethnicity, race, and class positions into which people are born through no choice of their own.

Timing of lives An umbrella concept that captures issues relating to social time, the timing of significant transitions (e.g., transition to parenthood), historical time, and the duration and sequencing of life events.

▓ Recommended Reading

Biggs, Simon, and Ariela Lowenstein. 2011. *Generational Intelligence: A Critical Approach to Age Relations*. Abingdon: Routledge and Kegan Paul. Aging populations may lead to increased conflict or solidarity in society and may provoke a profound ambivalence both in public and in the private sphere. In a new approach, Biggs and Lowenstein offer a critical examination of generational intelligence as one way of addressing these issues.

Elder, Glenn H., Jr. 1974. *Children of the Great Depression: Social Change in Life Experience*. Chicago: University of Chicago Press. A classic study of how substantive cohorts and historical time influence inequality and other life experiences.

Elder, Glenn H., Jr, and Angela M. O'Rand. 1995. "Adult Lives in a Changing Society." pp. 452–75 in K. Cook, G. Fine, and J.S. House, eds, *Sociological Perspectives on Social Psychology*. New York: Allyn and Bacon. A clearly written article that lays the foundations of Elder's life-course perspective.

Laslett, Barbara, and Johanna Brenner. 1987. "Gender and Social Reproduction: Historical Perspectives." *Annual Review of Sociology* 15: 381–404. Perhaps the best historical account of the processes of reproduction and the social construction of gender and gender relations.

Mannheim, Karl. [1928] 1952. "The Problem of Generations." In Karl Mannheim, *Essays on the Sociology of Knowledge*, edited by P.

Kecskemeti. London: Routledge and Kegan Paul. In this essay, Mannheim applies Marxist theories of social class to the study of "generations."

Tilly, Charles. 1998. *Durable Inequality*. Berkeley: University of California Press. A comprehensive account of categorical inequality. In this book, Tilly argues that some categories of inequality have more depth than others depending on how and whether various mechanisms, such as opportunity hoarding, are implemented by the dominant group.

PART II

Part II reviews literature on social inequality in five domains of social life: families and domestic labour, paid work, health, education, and states. The conceptual framework presented in Part I is used as an organizational tool for presenting the information in Part II. Although efforts were made to find literature that considered the intersections of class, age, gender, ethnicity, and "race," few if any studies have examined all of these factors simultaneously. And even fewer have explicitly considered the links between structure, agency, and social time and place. As a result, the goals of Part II are modest. It provides a partial picture of various outcomes of inequality as they play out in families, paid work, health, education, and the state in Canada.

Each chapter in Part II begins with an example or case study. Through these examples, the ideas presented in the conceptual framework are most easily observed. Next, an overview of the literature on each domain of social inequality is presented. This will enable the reader to gain an understanding of the structure of social inequality in Canada. It is also important to recognize that inequality in Canada is not the same as inequality elsewhere in the world. And, despite the persistent inequality that exists in Canada, compared with those living in many other places, Canadians are relatively privileged. In the chapters that follow, boxes and figures illustrate inequality in different regions of the world.

8

CAGE(s), Families, and Domestic Labour, and the Processes of Reproduction

Introduction

In 1998 and 1999, I (McMullin) worked on a project that involved collecting life-history interviews with 60 low-income mothers (see L. Davies, McMullin, and Avison 2001). Part of this research examined the extent to which mothers' family responsibilities influenced their poverty. Using life-history analyses, we found that the processes through which women became mothers influenced their experiences of poverty. Mothers faced barriers in continuing their education and in securing gainful employment (see chapter 10). One of the most significant barriers for these mothers was finding suitable and affordable child care, but there were also ideological barriers. One of the mothers in our study told us that she quit high school after she became pregnant because of the attitudes of the teachers and principal. In fact, the principal told her she could not take her physical education class because he feared that someone from the board of education would come to the school and see a "big fat blimp running around the gym" (L. Davies, McMullin, and Avison 2001: 63).

Beginning in early childhood, beliefs about motherhood and family are instilled in us. For some of the study participants, these beliefs acted

as barriers to education and employment. One mother had this to say: "Girls were raised to think they had to grow up and get married and I thought that was the be-all and end-all and the only way that I was ever going to be independent was to be married. It didn't even enter my mind to think well I could go to school and get a job and I don't have to be married." And another said, "I wasn't getting a lot of support or encouragement at home [regarding her schooling]. In fact, I was basically told by my parents that it wasn't as important for me to succeed as it was for my brothers." These ideological beliefs about families and women's roles within them were best summarized by the comments of a third study participant:

I had two or three [career] goals, lawyer, nurse, airline stewardess, but my parents said don't go into that, just get a job, get married, and you know you're going to get married and you're going to have a husband that looks after all that. Like you're so wrapped up in what you want but you're going to get married and you're going to have kids, so there's no sense even setting a goal like that, just do well in school and get yourself a job. . . . So that's what I did.

Such traditional belief systems "place girls on trajectories of low income because they often emphasize the importance of marriage and family at the expense of economic self-sufficiency" (L. Davies, McMullin, and Avison 2001: 63).

Traditional family belief systems, combined with family violence or insidious poverty, made life especially difficult for some of the mothers in our study. In these cases, physical or sexual abuse, neglect, or parental alcoholism in their families of origin often led them to leave home when they were young teenagers. In one study participant's case, the mother helped her daughter leave home when she was 14 so that Mary could escape her mother's abusive partner. Unable to support Mary for very long outside of the home, Mary's mother encouraged her to become pregnant so that she could collect social assistance and mother's allowance. Mary did as her mother said, had a baby when she was 15 years old, and continues to struggle with poverty.

Among the low-income mothers in this study, 87 per cent had received social assistance at least once in their lives, but 60 per cent of these women were not receiving social assistance at the time of the interviews. This allowed us to assess the pathways through which women move from social assistance to economic self-sufficiency. For the mothers in this study, the most common pathway off welfare was a marriage or common-law relationship with an employed man (L. Davies, McMullin, and Avison 2001: 72).

The preceding discussion points to the importance of the intersections between the processes of production, distribution, and reproduction in systems of inequality that were discussed in Part I of this book. It shows that women provide for families and children and that the ideologies that shape this care (reproduction) limit their opportunities for education and paid work (production). As a result, distributive processes vary accordingly, with

women often relying on spouses or the state for their means of subsistence (see the coalescence framework, chapter 7, Figure 7.3, page 143). Furthermore, the findings from the poverty study discussed above suggest that the family is one of the principal domains in which the processes of reproduction, distribution, and production are organized.

Over the last several decades there has been considerable debate among academics and policy-makers regarding the status of families in Canada, the United States, and other advanced industrial societies. Some commentators argue that contemporary families are in a state of crisis. For example, the American sociologist David Popenoe (1993, 2005, 2009) argues that the family is in a state of decline. According to Popenoe, families do not provide functions such as procreation, socialization, caring, economic support, and sexual regulation as effectively as they once did. He argues that families have lost their social power and control over their members, in part because they are smaller and less stable and do not last as long as they used to. In a move toward individualism, American families are less willing to invest time, money, and energy in family life.

For Popenoe, who uses statistics about American families from the 1960s until the 2000s to support his claims, the most significant trends since the 1960s have been the following: (1) considerable fertility decline; (2) "marital role erosion," with more women working for pay and fewer taking full responsibility for the care of their children; (3) increases in divorce rates, stepfamilies, and lone-parent families; and (4) increases in singlehood and non-family living. As a result of these trends, Popenoe concludes that families are in a state of decline. Family members are less bound to one another because women are more economically self-sufficient than they used to be. Families are less willing and able to carry out their traditional functions (see above), and they have transferred their power to other institutions such as schools and states. According to Popenoe, families are also in a state of decline because family values are eroding. Family identification, loyalty, mutual assistance, and concern for the perpetuation of family have given way to values of self-fulfillment and egalitarianism. The consequences of such decline are alarming to Popenoe because the family is the most fundamental unit of society and "breaking up the nucleus of anything is a serious matter" (Popenoe 1993: 539). He considers the most serious consequence of family decline to be that fewer children are living in nuclear families, and he believes that children cannot become successful adults without proper socialization within families (Popenoe 2005). In his most recent work, Popenoe (2009) expands on his theory that the erosion of nuclear families and the increase in the number of "non-traditional" families (e.g., as a result of divorce, single parenthood, and stepfamilies) are redefining the ways we live together and raise our children. These changes, he argues, come with great cost—especially when families lack a strong "father figure" (Popenoe 2009).

The American trends that Popenoe uses in support of his argument are indisputable and are similar to trends seen in Canada (see K.L. Johnson, Lero, and Rooney 2001: 17–19). In 1961, the **fertility rate** in Canada was 3.85; by 2014, it had fallen to 1.59 (www.ciafactbook.com). More Canadian women and mothers are working for pay now than ever before (see chapter 9). Canadian divorce rates are higher now than they were 30 years ago, and there are fewer nuclear families than in the past. Higher proportions of Canadians are remaining single, getting married much later in life, or living in "non-traditional" families, such as same-sex unions (Gee 2000a), and more men are heading single-parent families (see Box 8.1). Common-law unions continue to rise (16.7 per cent in 2011 versus 5.6 per cent in 1981—see Figure 8.1 below), and although they are typically associated with a younger demographic, common-law relationships among those over age 60 are increasing as well (Agrell 2007). This is because, at least in part, people today feel less pressure to marry, as stigma toward non-traditional partnerships has declined.

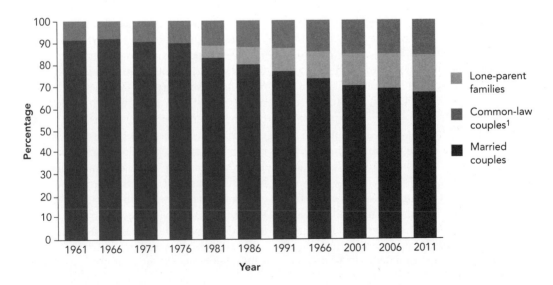

Figure 8.1 The Distribution of Census Families by Family Structure in Canada: 1961 to 2011

Source: Statistics Canada, *Census in Brief—Fifty Years of Families in Canada: 1961 to 2011*, Catalogue no. 98-312-X2011003, p. 2.

HIGHLIGHT

Box 8.1 The Canadian Family Is Slowly Being Reshaped

by Francine Kopun

Sean Slaven cannot imagine his life without the routine of picking up his 11-year-old son Brendan after school, monitoring his homework, making his favourite meal of Indian butter chicken, and then playing ball or watching the season finale of *Canadian Idol* together.

Slaven, 42, is the male head of a single-parent family—one of a growing number of men in Canada who care for their children half or more than half of the time. He shares custody of his son with his former wife, and Brendan is with him as much as 65 per cent of the time. Slaven wouldn't want it any other way.

"If you're an access parent you're a visitor in that child's life. You're always trying to do things that are fun, fun, fun—you don't get involved with their school, you don't get involved with their lives. They're strangers to you," says Slaven, a self-employed sales professional in Burlington.

The Canadian family is slowly being reshaped: Marriage continues to lose ground to common-law relationships, same-sex unions are on the rise and families without children have become more common than families with children as the population ages and fertility rates decline.

"Family has always been a dynamic institution," said Alan Mirabelli, executive associate of the Vanier Institute for the Family. "If you ask people what their ideal of family is, they'll simply describe the family they grew up in, but family goes back 3,000 years. It transforms itself."

Of the 33 census management areas in Canada (population of at least 100,000) Toronto has the second-highest percentage of married couple families at 75.3 per cent. (Abbotsford, B.C., has the highest at 76.2 per cent.) Toronto has the lowest percentage of common-law families at 7.8 per cent.

"It may be that immigrant families are more likely to be married than to live common-law, and certainly the high immigrant population in Toronto may be a contributing factor," said Pamela White, director of the demography division at Statistics Canada.

Christine van Cauwenberghe, a financial planning expert with Investors Group, says many people in common-law relationships often don't realize the implications of their union. They may find that in some ways they are as legally bound to each other as married couples, but there are important exceptions: in Ontario, for example, married and common-law couples are treated differently when it comes to the division of family property and inheritances.

"There is certainly much more shared custody, especially when you're talking about couples in the 35–45 age range, because more women in that age range have careers that are very demanding," said Nicola Savin, a Toronto family law lawyer with 20 years of experience.

"I'm delighted to see this, absolutely delighted, because I was one of those dads," said Danny Guspie, executive director of Fathers' Resources International. "It tells me that finally society is starting to catch up with itself. As our judiciary begins to age, younger people are coming in with more well-suited family ideas, rather than gender-based family ideas."

In a way the increase in single-parent households led by men is not surprising, says the Vanier Institute's Mirabelli. With more dual-income families, the decision about who gets custody is shaped to a certain extent by the job demands of both parents. He said it could also be that older children are choosing dad as opposed to mom and dads are now willing to honour that choice.

Michael Kaufman, 56, a former single dad who shared custody of his son between the ages of 9 and 16 with his former spouse, says he believes the arrangement allowed him to share more quality time with his son.

"I think quality comes out of quantity," said Kaufman, an educator and independent consultant on gender issues. "Those moments happen when you're shopping together or washing the dishes or making a meal or working in the garden or building something. If you're spending time together, if you're doing things together, those conversations will happen, those wonderful moments will happen."

Source: Kopun, Francine. (September 13 2007). "The Canadian Family Is Slowly Being Reshaped: More Men Heading Up Single-Parent Households, Same-Sex and Common-Law Unions on Rise: Census." *The Star*. Reprinted with permission – Torstar Syndication Services.

However, Popenoe's interpretation of these trends may be criticized on at least two counts. First, because he uses a very conservative and limited conceptualization of "family," he underestimates how central families remain for many people in contemporary American and Canadian societies. Second, he ignores the fact that "the family" is a primary site of oppression of and violence against women, children, and the elderly.

Defining Families

Popenoe defines *family* as "a group in which people typically live together in a household and function as a cooperative unit, particularly through the sharing of economic resources in the pursuit of domestic activities" (2005: 20). On the surface there is nothing particularly troubling about that definition. Yet, because he argues that there are fewer families today than in the past and is critical of lone-parent families, his ideal "group of people" is narrowly defined.

Although it is true that the number of **nuclear families** has declined over the years, the majority of Canadians live with someone else. According to the 2011 census, the number of multi-person households (i.e., more than two members) has been declining since the 1960s. Two-person households are now much more common (see Figure 8.2 below). Outside of Canada, family sizes are also shrinking. Box 8.2 discusses China and its "diminished family unit."

According to Figure 8.2, approximately 73 per cent of Canadians lived in a household with two or more people. However, only some of these are considered "families" according to the restrictive census definition. The Canadian census definition of *family* is

a married couple and the children, if any, of either or both spouses; a couple living common law and the children, if any, of either or both partners; or, a lone parent of any marital status with at least one child living in the same dwelling and that child or those children. All

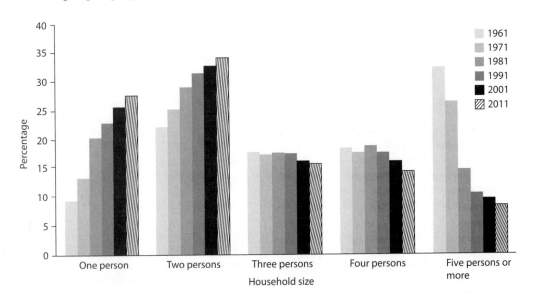

Figure 8.2 Household Size in Canada, 1961–2011

Source: Statistics Canada, *Census in Brief—Fifty Years of Families in Canada: 1961 to 2011*, Catalogue no. 98-312-X2011003, p. 5.

Global perspective

Box 8.2 The Diminished Family Unit: Will China Get Lonely before It Gets Rich?

by Rachel Lu

HONG KONG—"Four Generations under One Roof," a 1940s novel by author Lao She about life in Beijing under Japanese occupation, describes what was then an archetypal Chinese family: large, multigenerational and united. But in modern China, a place of massive internal migration and upheaval, that image is fast becoming quaint.

That's the conclusion reached in an official report released by China's National Health and Family Planning Commission, the agency charged with overseeing the country's demographic policy. The report shows that Chinese families have become grayer and more isolated, with fewer children. The Development Report of Chinese Families is the first official study of Chinese family structure that has been made public, and the picture that emerges from the report is likely to worry some Chinese economists and policymakers.

Chinese families have been getting smaller for decades and not just because of the country's reviled family planning policies. Before the 1950s, the average household in China had more than 5.3 people. But the report shows that number dropping to 3.02 in 2012 from 3.96 in 1990. Since 2000, the decrease in birth rates has not been the primary driver of the shrinking family size, with geographic mobility and changes in social mores playing bigger roles.

Three demographics increasingly stand out: unmarried young workers, couples who have delayed or forgone childbirth, and elderly empty-nesters. One hundred sixty million Chinese households, or 40 percent of the nationwide total, now consist only of one or two people. In the decade between 2000 and 2010, when urbanization was at full throttle, the number of solo households doubled and the number of two-member households increased by 68 percent, according to the report.

In urban areas, 45.4 percent of unmarried residents lived alone, spurning the traditional practice of living with parents until marriage. Millions of young Chinese now work in cities far from home—and even if they live in the same city as their parents, many do not want to move back into a spare bedroom once they start working. Young men and women are delaying marriage to pursue career goals, save up for down payments on cars or houses, fulfill lifestyle choices or wait to find the right mate.

According to the findings, the number of nuclear families, defined as a married couple with children, declined "significantly," but the number of *dingke* families (a Chinese transliteration meaning families with "dual income, no kids"), has been on the rise.

For thousands of years, elderly Chinese had lived with their children and grandchildren, but that is rapidly changing too, as young people leave their hometowns for education and employment opportunities. According to the report, 90 percent of China's elderly live at home instead of assisted living facilities. But their children and grandchildren often choose not to live with them or cannot live with them. The problem is particularly acute in rural areas: Millions of young farmhands have left for factories and construction sites, while rural social security and health care resources are comparatively sparse, leaving many elderly to fend for themselves in squalid conditions.

A nascent social security safety net is being built in rural areas but is not yet particularly sturdy. According to the report, more than 40 percent of senior citizens above the age of 80 live alone. The report cites another study that shows 37.5 million elderly Chinese citizens lacked the ability to care for themselves in 2013. A quarter of all elderly lived below the poverty line. In a survey released by the Health

continued

and Family Planning Commission, 80 percent of Chinese households say they are worried about supporting their elderly relatives.

The report shows anxieties about the expense of caring for children and parents weighing on Chinese families; that, in turn, is likely to reduce their propensity to spend, just as the Chinese economy becomes increasingly reliant on a burgeoning consumer culture to bolster its growth. For Chinese policymakers, this may be the wake-up call they need to continue to reform the country's much-maligned family planning policy. It may get increasingly rare for four Chinese generations to live in one home. But there need not be so many families of one.

Source: Rachel Lu. (May 22, 2014). "The diminished family unit: Will China get lonely before it gets rich?" *The Chicago Tribune.* http://articles.chicagotribune.com/2014-05-22/opinion/ct-china-family-smaller-perspec-0522-20140522_1_family-planning-commission-development-report-chinese

members of a particular census family live in the same dwelling. A couple may be of opposite or same sex. Children may be children by birth, marriage or adoption regardless of their age or marital status as long as they live in the dwelling and do not have their own spouse or child living in the dwelling.

Grandchildren living with their grandparents but with no parents present also constitute a census family. (www.statcan.ca/english/concepts/definitions/cenfamily.htm 2/15/2008)

Hence, siblings who live together or parents who live with their divorced child and his or her children are not families according to the census definition. Indeed, the term *family* is typically a middle-class construct that reproduces white privilege and ideology and neglects racialized families (Dua 1999), older families (Connidis 2009), and working-class families (Gardiner-Barber 2003). Historically, white, middle-class men and women took an especially active role in promoting such ideologies. So too did the Canadian state, which has continued to reproduce white, middle-class views of family through discriminatory immigration and family-welfare policies (see Das Gupta 1995; Mandell and Duffy 2005; chapter 12). Here we see the importance of ideology, as it was discussed in Part I, for understanding social inequality.

Useful and inclusive definitions of families have been elusive in the family-sociology literature. Table 8.1 shows how the definitions of family have evolved. The restrictions in Murdock's definition are obvious, but they resemble the definitions of family proposed by some vocal conservative organizations in Canada, such as Focus on the Family (www.focusonthefamily.ca). Margrit Eichler's discussion of family, which is in reaction to Murdock's and other conservative definitions, concentrates on who constitutes families. Unlike the other definitions, that of the Vanier Institute of the Family concentrates more on what families do (points 1–6) than on who comprises them (e.g., two or more people who are "bound together by ties of mutual consent, birth and/or adoption or placement"). Finally, Fox and Luxton focus exclusively on what families do, equating family with the relations of social reproduction as they are defined in this book (see chapter 3). Hence, a family comprises anyone who is involved in the processes of reproduction, which are contained in the centre of the coalescence framework that was presented in chapter 7. The obvious advantage to this definition is that it includes those who have traditionally been excluded in definitions of family. Fox and Luxton (2001) argue that in all social systems there is a relationship between the processes of production and reproduction. Before industrialization, both productive and reproductive work were organized in the household. These

Table 8.1 Definitions of Family

George Murdock. 1949. *Social Structure*. New York: MacMillan, p. 1.
". . . a social group characterized by a common residence, economic cooperation and reproduction [including adults of both sexes, at least two of whom maintain a socially approved sexual relationship] and one or more children, own or adopted, of the sexually cohabiting adults."

Margrit Eichler. 1988. *Families in Canada Today*. Toronto: Gage, p. 4.
". . . a family is a social group which may or may not include adults of both sexes (i.e., lone-parent families), may or may not include one or more children (i.e., childless couples), who may or may not have been born in wedlock (i.e., adopted children or children by one adult partner of a previous union). The relationship of the adults may or may not have its origin in marriage (i.e., common-law couples), they may or may not share a common residence (i.e., commuting couples). The adults may or may not cohabit sexually, and the relationship may or may not involve such socially patterned feelings as love, attraction, piety and awe."

Vanier Institute. 2008. www.vifamily.ca/about/definition.html.
". . . any combination of two or more persons who are bound together over time by ties of mutual consent, birth and/or adoption or placement and who, together, assume responsibilities for variant combinations of some of the following:

• Physical maintenance and care of group members
• Addition of new members through procreation or adoption
• Socialization of children
• Social control of members
• Production, consumption, distribution of goods and services, and
• Affective nurturance—love"

Statistics Canada. 2008. "Concept: Census Family." www.statcan.gc.ca/concepts/definitions/cfamily-rfamille-eng.htm.
". . . a married couple and the children, if any, of either or both spouses; a couple living common law and the children, if any, of either or both partners; or, a lone parent of any marital status with at least one child living in the same dwelling and that child or those children. All members of a particular census family live in the same dwelling. A couple may be of opposite or same sex. Children may be children by birth, marriage or adoption regardless of their age or marital status as long as they live in the dwelling and do not have their own spouse or child living in the dwelling."
    "Grandchildren living with their grandparents but with no parents present also constitute a census family."

Bonnie Fox and Meg Luxton. 2001. "Conceptualizing Family," p. 26.
The study of family involves "the maintenance of life on a daily and generational basis." Families are "the social relationships that people create to care for children and other dependants daily and to ensure that the needs of the adults responsible for these dependants also are met."

processes were separated by the development of industrial capitalism as more and more men were required to work for a wage so that their families could make ends meet. Processes of reproduction were privatized in a way that they had not been in the past, and the division of labour between men and women became increasingly stringent (Fox and Luxton 2001). Also during this time, ideologies evolved that reinforced the relegation of women to domestic duties and of men's responsibilities for paid labour (Cott 2001; Margolis 2001; May 1993). As the findings from the poverty study discussed above show, these ideologies still exist. The next section of this chapter considers how reproductive processes of care and housework are organized in Canada in ways that create and recreate systems of advantage and disadvantage for various groups of people.

Domestic Labour

There are three main elements of domestic labour, which in turn are all part of the reproductive processes discussed in Part I of this book. These are (1) maintaining the household; (2) caring for adults and children; and (3) the processes involved in consumption or making ends meet (Luxton and Corman 2001). Cleaning, cooking, gardening, shovelling snow, and mowing lawns are examples of the activities required to maintain a household (Luxton 1980). Caring includes both "caring about" and "caring for" others. Hence, *caring* refers to "feelings of affection and responsibility combined with actions that provide responsively for an individual's personal needs or well-being" (Cancian and Oliker 2000: 2). Economic support for caring comes through the processes of distribution (see the coalescence framework, Figure 7.3) in the form of wages, social assistance, retirement pensions, or some combination of these distributive mechanisms. Individuals and families use the money gained through these distributive mechanisms to purchase clothes, food, shelter, and other necessities of life. Low-income families, who usually do not have enough money to buy these things, often use creative and strategic methods to make ends meet.

In Canada, domestic labour is usually organized in families and households, and most research on domestic labour has used the household as the unit of analysis (but see Worts 2005 for an excellent study on the transcendence of domestic labour across households in a co-operative housing community). Yet for those Canadians who live alone (and probably for many others), the processes of domestic labour transcend household boundaries. This is particularly true for people aged 65 and over, who are more likely to live alone as a result of widowhood, and for younger people, who are more likely to be childless and unmarried. Members of other households or paid workers often help older people with household maintenance, while the labour of caring for and about them is often (but not always) undertaken by close relatives

(Connidis and McMullin 1994). Although research tends not to consider how domestic labour is organized among younger, unmarried, and childless Canadians, we can speculate that they either purchase these services or do it on their own. Close family ties likely provide their care, with friends also being instrumental in providing support. However, because most of the research on domestic labour has used the household as the unit of analysis, this chapter must do the same.

Gender is an important structural determinant of who does what for whom in families, regardless of age (Connidis 2009). As Figure 8.3 shows, gender differences in unpaid labour are different across generational groupings in Canada. For those in "Generation Y" (those born roughly from 1980 to the year 2000), women on average do 0.4 hours more of unpaid labour than do men, compared with a 1.2-hour difference for late baby boomers (those born roughly during the years 1946 to 1964) and a 0.9-hour difference for those in "Generation X" (those born roughly during the 1960s and the early 1980s). Women tend to take primary responsibility for meal preparation, dish washing, and cleaning, men for household maintenance (Beaujot 2000). Of course, making meals, cleaning dishes, and general housecleaning are done every day, whereas household maintenance is done much more sporadically. Hence, it is no surprise that compared with men, women spend more time doing housework (Gazso-Windle and McMullin 2003; K. Marshall 1993a, 1993b). This overall pattern in the gendered division of labour in the home intensifies when couples have children, and it remains more or less the same as couples age (McDaniel 2005). But when husbands and wives retire, husbands increase the number of masculine tasks that they perform (Askam 1995).

The amount of household work that men and women do seems to vary according to employment and parental status (K. Marshall 2006). For instance, the amount of housework husbands and wives do increases with the number of hours their partners spend engaged in paid labour

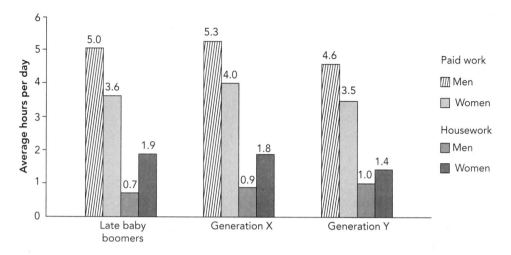

Figure 8.3 Hours of Paid Work and Housework across Generations in Canada

Note: For the population aged 20 to 29 in each generation, daily hours are averaged over 7 days.

Source: Katherine Marshall, *Generational Change in Paid and Unpaid Work* Catalogue No. 11-008-X92-2011002. www.statcan.gc.ca/pub/11-008-x/2011002/article/11520-eng.htm

(Gazso-Windle and McMullin 2003) and when children live in the home (K. Marshall 2006). The more hours women work for pay, the fewer hours they spend doing household labour (Luxton and Corman 2001). Among younger and middle-aged men, married fathers do twice as much unpaid work (including child care and volunteer work) as unmarried, childless men and one and a half times as much unpaid work as married, childless men. Similarly, married mothers do twice as much unpaid work as childless women, regardless of marital status. Women who are employed full-time do less unpaid labour than those who are either not employed or work part-time, regardless of how many children they have living at home. Furthermore, compared with all families, higher proportions of men in two-earner families do half or more of the main household tasks (e.g., cooking and cleaning) and take primary responsibility for them (Beaujot 2000). However, as Box 8.3 discusses, when housework is more equitably distributed, men are more likely than women to feel dissatisfied, believing that they are doing an "unfair" amount.

Caring for family members transcends household boundaries more than housework does. Many of us care for our mothers, fathers, grandchildren, brothers, sisters, aunts, uncles, and so on, even if we do not live with them. Grandparents often care for their grandchildren when parents need help with child care. Similarly, aunts and uncles sometimes care for their siblings' children. Children sometimes care for their older parents, especially if they are ill and unable to care for themselves. Husbands and wives frequently care for one another and, with increasing age and illness, are often required to provide much more physical care for one another.

Class, age, gender, ethnicity, and "race" structure the obligations that family members have to care for and about one another. This is the idea conveyed in the central part of the coalescence framework (Figure 7.3). These obligations are contained within the processes of reproduction and are framed (or structured) by class, age, gender, ethnic, and race relations. The extent and nature of the family care one

Global perspective

Box 8.3 Men More Unsatisfied with Extra Chores in More Gender-Equal Countries

New research finds that household equality is associated with marital dissatisfaction among men.

According to work from Emory University and Umeå University in Sweden, countries where housework is more equitable, married men are more likely to be dissatisfied with their share of household duties, reporting that they take on a greater share of household chores.

This news is surprising because it suggests that in countries where a more egalitarian division of labour is considered the norm (and places with lower-income inequality) men are more likely to feel it's unfair when they tackle a greater share of household chores.

Sabino Kornrich and Maureen Eger analyzed data from nearly 14,000 men and women who were married (or living as married) from 30 countries. When all countries were considered together, women reported doing around 70 per cent of all household duties and men reported doing on average 30 per cent. In other words, on average women were much more likely to report being responsible for most domestic work in this sample of 30 countries,

However, many men in their sample reported doing a much more equitable share of household duties. Roughly 30–38 per cent of men from Poland, the Unites States, Australia, Denmark, Mexico, the United Kingdom, Latvia, and Sweden report handling at least half of all household duties. Surprisingly, men from what are thought of as more gender-egalitarian countries (i.e., the United States, Sweden, and Australia) were the most likely to feel that they were responsible for an unfair amount of housework. Also surprising, men who do more household work in less equitable countries (i.e., where men, on average, do less in countries such as Japan) were less likely to feel that their chore burden was unfair.

These findings seem somewhat paradoxical. Why are men are more dissatisfied with their proportional responsibility for household labour in countries with more gender equality? According to Kornrich, "we presume that living in a more egalitarian society highlights the importance of housework in general, making men more conscious of it and thereby sparking a more negative response the more of it they do. . . . That suggests there's a norm when men and women live in egalitarian countries that housework is an important, shared responsibility," said Kornrich. In other words, men in more equal countries seem to be more aware of housework, unlike men in countries where there is an expectation that women take care of most household duties.

Sources: http://phys.org/news/2015-02-men-unsatisfied-extra-chores-gender.html; Kornrich and Eger (2014).

provides will vary depending on how one is situated within these social structures (Finch 1989). Among the many caring relationships within families, the most widely studied is the relationship between younger parents, especially mothers, and their young children. One of the most consistent findings in the family-sociology literature is that women are primarily responsible for child care and that, compared with men, they spend more time providing care (Rapoport and Lebourdais 2006). This is still the case even though many more women are working in the paid labour force now than in the past (see chapter 9). However, the nature of how children are cared for and by whom has evolved over the past few generations. Compared with past generations of children, more pre-school-aged children are being cared for by babysitters and licensed-care facilities. This is, in large part, because labour-force participation by women has increased substantially. As a result, mothers and fathers make more child-care arrangements with one another, with child-care providers, with their employers, and with other family members than in past generations.

Although fathers have increased the number of hours that they spend with children over recent decades, this has not led to an overall decline in the amount of time mothers spend with their children. In two-parent families, this is probably because, compared with mothers, when fathers spend time with their children it is more often in the context of family activities in which their wives or partners are also involved (Rapoport and LeBourdais 2006).

Parenting and the care involved do not end when children leave home, but the nature of the care relationship changes significantly. Yet, with a few notable exceptions (see Connidis 2009; Eichler and Albanese 2007), family studies rarely consider either how processes of caring evolve throughout the life course or how caring and parenting are experienced in mid-life. Unlike the mainstream family literature, the gerontology literature has paid some attention to issues of lifelong parenting. Early research on mid-life families, for instance, identified a stage in life after children left home that was named the **empty nest**. It was thought that because women in their middle years disengage from their active parenting role, these women would experience the "empty-nest syndrome" and have various social and psychological problems as a result. Later research, however, found that in fact many women enjoyed their lives after their children had left (Black and Hill 1984). More recently the term **cluttered nest**, or the "boomerang generation," has surfaced to refer to families whose children, after having left home and lived elsewhere for a period, return to live with their parents (Mitchell 2000; Mitchell and Gee 1996). Research has shown that parents provide more support to these children, both financially and with respect to domestic services, than they receive from the children (B. Mitchell 2000).

When we consider the links between processes of production and reproduction, it is important to note that most working-age mothers work for pay and most mothers in the labour force work full-time (K.L. Johnson, Lero, and Rooney 2001). Yet the labour-force participation rate among working-age mothers is still much lower than it is for working-age fathers. Barring unemployment or disability, almost all working-age fathers work for pay and almost all fathers in the labour force work full-time. Indeed, compared with fathers, mothers are more likely to have discontinuous paid-work histories and more-tenuous attachments to the labour market, largely because of their family responsibilities. A substantial number of younger mothers forgo a wage to stay at home and raise their children, making them economically dependent on either their partners or the state. Women who work for pay take primary responsibility for the care of their children by making arrangements for child care and taking time off from work when the children are ill or when child care is unavailable (see K. Johnson, Lero, and Rooney 2001). This, however, places women at a labour-market disadvantage because very few workplaces offer child care or dependant care for their employees (Ranson 2005). Because domestic labour is undervalued in Canada, such patterns of paid and unpaid labour result in long-term financial disadvantages for women in relation to men—lower pay, fewer promotional opportunities, and smaller pensions (see chapter 9).

Because gender so deeply structures our taken-for-granted assumptions (see the discussion of Sewell's work in chapter 6) about who does what in families and homes, individual men have little opportunity to take on the role of full-time domestic worker and men are often unable to experience the sometimes fulfilling and gratifying aspects of caring for children.

For instance, the proportion of stay-at-home dads among two-parent families is very low (K. Johnson, Lero, and Rooney 2001: 19), and men are even less likely than women to get support from employers when they request alternative work arrangements. This, according to Lero, Ashbourne, and Whitehead (2006), this is something that must be changed. As they note, researchers and policy-makers in recent years have started to emphasize the changing role of fathers and the desire to support father involvement as a way to enhance their children's well-being. They argue that it is crucial for both parents to be involved, and thus policy-makers and employers must accommodate men's heightened role in the family. Today, men are more likely to take paternity leave from employment following the birth of a child than was true in the past. For example, in the year 2011, 27 per cent of working fathers took paid leave from work to care for their newborn children (however, their leave was only 2.4 weeks long on average). Still, men are much less likely than women to take employment leave after a pregnancy (27 per cent versus 90 per cent), and women spend much more time than men away from employment (on average, 2.4 weeks versus 48 weeks) (Findlay and Kohen 2012).

The story is very different in Quebec, however. Analyzing data from the Survey of Young Canadians (2010), Findlay and Kohen (2012) report that 72 per cent of working fathers in Quebec (almost three-quarters) took **paternity leave** compared with 97 per cent for working mothers. The average length of men's employment leave was also much higher than the national average (5.5 weeks compared with 2.4). Also in Quebec, fathers (14 per cent) were almost equally likely as mothers (21 per cent) to take unpaid leave to care for their children (Findlay and Kohen 2012). As we will discuss in chapter 12, these difference likely reflect provincial variation in policy geared toward families. As we show, Quebec has embraced a more

socially democratic model compared with the rest of Canada, which remains largely conservative in this regard.

In Canada, the Parental Benefits Program (PBP) has been mainly responsible for changes in paid government leave for new parents. It was only in 1990 that legislation was passed to include men: 10 weeks of paid leave was made available for *sharing* by "qualified" new parents. This number increased to 35 weeks in 2001 (K. Marshall 2008). Today, one of the official goals of the PBP is to promote gender equality by encouraging mothers and fathers to share benefits between them. If more fathers use paid parental leave, it would help break down gender stereotypes and the assumption that only mothers should care for children. Also, the exclusive notion of women as caregivers "can fuel employment discrimination against the recruitment and promotion of women" while at the same time making it difficult for fathers to take leave because it "conflicts with workplace cultures and expectations about the appropriate behaviour for men" (Anxo et al. 2007).

Questions regarding what it means to be a mother or a father in a time when fathers are taking more responsibility for parenting have gained considerable research attention of late (Doucet 2006; Fox 2009; Ranson 2013). Andrea Doucet, for instance, discusses in her book *Do Men Mother?* the experiences of 118 fathers who are the primary caregivers of their children—some stay-at-home dads and others single fathers. Mothering, according to Doucet, comprises emotional, community, and moral responsibility. In the emotional realm, the fathers in Doucet's study care for and nurture their children in ways that are quite similar to what we would expect of mothers, although there is sometimes a greater emphasis on playfulness and practicality. These fathers developed community ties and networks that facilitated their parenting and provided avenues for their children's extracurricular activities, but here too the emphasis was on sport and activity. And in the realm of moral responsibility, or the ideology around the "shoulds and oughts of parenting" (Doucet 2006: 209), there are so many structural and ideological expectations about what fathers and mothers are supposed to do that it is extremely difficult for men to mother. Fathers are meant to be earners, mothers are meant to be carers, and because these views are so deeply structured in society, fathers who care are viewed suspiciously and with concern (Doucet 2006).

Notably, the fact that many men are not afforded the opportunity to look after their children should not be interpreted as structural inequality. Recall from Part I that *social inequality* refers to unequal access to resources and privileges in society. Domestic labour is not yet considered a valuable resource or privilege in the same way that paid work is. Hence, the restrictions the gender structure places on men's involvement in housework and child care do not create disadvantage for men in the same way that restricted access to paid work does for women.

Research on caregiving has also considered the difficulties facing adult children, usually daughters, in caring for elderly parents (Aronson 1992). Much of this research emphasizes the stress of combining paid work with care of or support for older parents. Early work in this regard noted that this stress was particularly acute for women because they formed a **sandwich generation** that had to combine work, caring for older parents, and child care. Although subsequent research showed that the proportion of women who are "sandwiched" is actually quite small (Martin-Matthews 2000; Rosenthal, Matthews, and Marshall 1989), the proportion of employees who care for older family members and have children living at home rose from 9.5 per cent in the late 1980s to about 15 per cent in the late 1990s (MacBride-King and Bachmann 1999). Furthermore, a recent study of Canadians showed that more than 90 per cent of employed caregivers experienced emotional strain, ranging from general feelings of anxiety to depression or anger and frustration (Duxbury and Higgins 2013). As is the case with parents' child care, research shows that children who provide support and care to older parents often make alternative work arrangements to facilitate their supportive role. And, compared with sons, daughters are more likely to make such arrangements (see Connidis 2009 for an overview).

Along with gender, indicators of social class also influence housework and family care. Although women do more housework and provide more care than do men regardless of social class, if we use income as a proxy of class, we note that income influences the amount of housework, meal preparation, and child care that Canadians do. On average, high-income Canadians (those with a household income of more than $80,000 a year) do 20 minutes less housework, 12 minutes less meal preparation, and 12 minutes less child care per day than low-income Canadians (household income of less than $30,000 a year) (C. Williams 2002). A more recent study by Heisig (2011) found that this pattern also held in a sample of 33 developed countries. Working-class women often turn to their mothers for help with babysitting and housework (McMullin 2002). Although it is frequently viewed within the context of the love grandmothers feel for both children and grandchildren, we should not lose sight of the labour that is involved. This "labour of love" is grounded in a strong gendered ideology that limits the responsibility fathers and grandfathers have in the care of children and grandchildren (Fox 2001). Alternatively, middle- and upper-class women often pay other women for child care and housework.

This process reproduces white and middle-class privilege because middle-class white women usually hire working-class, racialized, and immigrant women to do this work (Arat-Koc 2001; Glenn 1992).

Both class and gender structure the division of housework and child care among black Canadian families. Black women tend to be responsible for most of the housework, and among the working class, they take responsibility for making ends meet (Calliste 2001). In addition, compared with white women, black women do disproportionately more housework and child care. This is because black families are more likely than white families to be working class and because there are three times as many female, lone-parent families among black Canadians as there are among all other ethnic groups (Calliste 2001).

Intersectional research on families (i.e., research that simultaneously considers class, gender, ethnicity, and race) has been less concerned with the division of domestic labour in families than with how the institution of the nuclear family has reproduced white privilege in Canada (and other countries around the world). As an institution, the **nuclear family** has served to promote the morality of the white middle-class and the colonialization and nation-building projects of the state. As Enakshi Dua (2005: 120) points out,

> White women were racially gendered as mothers of the nation whose participation in the nuclear family was crucial for the (re)production of the nation. In contrast, women of colour were racially gendered as posing a triple threat to the racialized nation as they could not reproduce a white population, allowed for the possibility of interracial sexuality, and challenged, by their presence within the nation state, the very racialized moral order that the nuclear family was to protect.

Such research has also been critical of feminist research on families for concentrating too narrowly on the family experiences of white women. Rather than being oppressive, families, for racialized women, are often seen as a place where they can escape from the oppression they experience in paid work, and they have striven to live in nuclear families, a privilege often denied them (see Dua 1999 for an overview). Further, government policies on immigration (e.g., family sponsorship), pensions, unemployment, and so forth shape ethnic family patterns and experiences because they are framed along hegemonic white, middle-class lines (Albanese 2005).

The transformation of wages into food and other necessities of life is another dimension of domestic labour. Although the work of making ends meet has received relatively little research attention in Canada, Meg Luxton's stands out as exceptional. Luxton's study of domestic labour, which spans three decades, examines the processes of domestic labour in white working-class families in Flin Flon, Manitoba (Luxton 1980), and Hamilton, Ontario (Luxton and Corman 2001). According to Luxton and Corman (2001: 172), transforming wages into the necessities of life involves "allocating the available income to the various needs and choices of household members, from paying the mortgage and buying groceries to purchasing luxury goods and services." Luxton and Corman (2001) find that the shopping involved in making ends meet is done mostly by women in families, but that the paying of bills is evenly divided between men and women. Both studies showed that shopping for the supplies necessary to run a household without breaking one's budget requires considerable skill (Luxton 1980; Luxton and Corman 2001). This involves searching for the best deals, clipping coupons, being frugal if money is tight because of layoffs or unemployment, and coming up with creative ways to make a dollar go farther.

Even though the responsibility for making ends meet usually falls to women, Luxton and Corman's research (2001) shows that it is often men who control the money in the household. Because wages are the legal property of the person who earns them, there are no guarantees that the wage will be redistributed among the members of a family. Hence, most wives are economically dependent upon their husbands because they either do not work for pay or earn significantly less than their spouse.

Unfortunately, there is no Canadian research on the work of making ends meet in middle- and upper-class families or in ethnic and racial minority-group families, on whether this process varies across the life course, or on whether this process transcends household boundaries. Indeed, our understanding of domestic labour in Canada is limited by a focus on households and by our typical understandings about what is meant by "household work." This and other limitations regarding the conceptualization of household work led Eichler and Albanese to redefine household work as the "the sum of all physical, mental, emotional and spiritual tasks that are performed for one's own or someone else's household and that maintain the daily life of those one has responsibility for" (2007: 248). Adopting this kind of definition in studies on domestic labour (although we would change the word "responsibility" to "care") would take us a long way in our understanding of who does what for whom in Canadian families.

Violence in Families

According to the World Health Organization (2007), violence is "the intentional use of physical force or power, threatened or actual, against oneself, another person, or against a group or community, that either results in or has a high likelihood of resulting in injury, death, psychological harm, maldevelopment, or deprivation."

Gender and age structure the likelihood of experiencing violence at the hand of an intimate partner or parent. Hence, women, children, and the elderly are at heightened risk of experiencing violence within families (Krug et al. 2002).

Although strangers most often perpetrate the violence men experience, the most common form of violence against women is intimate partner violence (Krug et al. 2002; Statistics Canada 2002b). *Intimate partner violence* (IPV) refers to intentional, controlling, and systematic behaviour in intimate relationships that causes physical, sexual, or psychological harm (Krug et al. 2002; Middlesex-London Health Unit 2000; Tjaden and Thoennes 2000). Power and control are central dimensions of IPV. Figure 8.4 identifies many of the tactics that (mostly) men use to maintain power and control in intimate relationships. These tactics include physical, sexual, and emotional abuse; isolation; economic deprivation; intimidation; and the use of social status to reinforce power and control within an intimate partnership. All of this makes immigrant women who have become "mail-order brides" particularly vulnerable to IPV.

IPV is a serious public health issue. Even if one considers only abuse of women, IPV is estimated to cost Canadians millions of dollars annually (Greaves, Hankivsky, and Kingston-Riechers 1995). Data from the 1993 Violence against Women Survey show that 29 per cent of Canadian ever-married—that is, divorced, separated, and widowed—women aged 18 and older have experienced some type of violence at the hand of an intimate partner at some point in their lives (H. Johnson 1996; H. Johnson and Sacco 1995). Each year in Canada, 40,000 arrests are made as a result of domestic violence. However, since only about 22 per cent of all incidences are reported to the police, this number is actually much higher than official statistics show (Statistics Canada 2009).

Similar proportions of Canadian men (6 per cent) and women (7 per cent) report that

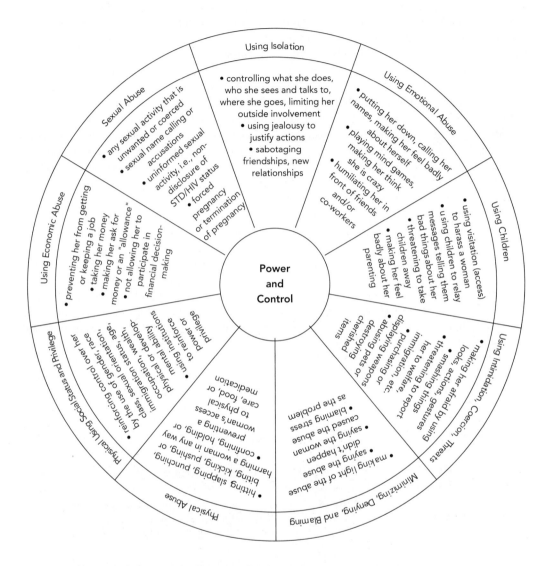

Figure 8.4 Battering in Intimate Relationships "Power and Control Wheel"

Source: Originally developed by the Domestic Abuse Intervention Project, Duluth, MN, further adapted by the London Battered Women's Advocacy Centre, London.

they experienced some form of IPV in the five years preceding the 2004 General Social Survey of Canada (Statistics Canada 2005a). Although these figures indicate that more research needs to be done on intimate violence against men, they may also be misleading because they do not take into account who instigated the violence and whether it was an act of self-defence. Furthermore, the violence inflicted on women is more severe than that inflicted on men.

Compared with male victims, female victims are more likely to have been beaten, choked, or threatened with a gun or knife (Statistics Canada 2005a). Twice the proportion of women victims (44 per cent) were injured as a result of spousal violence than men victims (19 per cent). And although the number of spousal homicides is declining, four times as many wives as husbands are killed each year in Canada (Statistics Canada 2007c).

Age, socio-economic status, ethnicity, and race influence the likelihood of IPV. The rate of spousal violence is higher among those aged 15 to 24 than among other age groups (Statistics Canada 2005a). Wives are more likely to be abused when they live in poor families than in middle- or high-income families. They are also more likely to be abused if their partners have not graduated from high school or are unemployed (H. Johnson 1996). The rate of spousal sexual and physical abuse is three times as high among Aboriginal people as among non-Aboriginal people (Statistics Canada 2005b). Taken together, these findings suggest that women who are involved with men who have relatively little power on the basis of their age, class, race, or ethnicity are more likely to

experience IPV (L. Davies, Ford-Gilboe, and Hammerton 2009). Some commentators argue that men make up for their lack of power in the public sphere by dominating in the private sphere and that this occasionally results in IPV (see H. Johnson 1996 for an overview of the explanations of IPV).

Power imbalances on the basis of age make children vulnerable to abuse in families. Unfortunately, there are no data available on the prevalence of child abuse in Canada. Instead, researchers have relied on a combination of police records and reports of child welfare agencies to assess the extent of child abuse. There is little doubt that this approach underestimates the extent of child abuse and neglect in Canada, especially within families. To assess these shortfalls, the Canadian Incidence Study of Reported Child Abuse and Neglect (CIS) was conducted in 2008. This study examined the cases reported to, and investigated by, child welfare services from 1 October 2008 to 31 December 2008 (CIS 2008). Of course, focusing on "reported and investigated cases" still misses the less severe instances of child abuse and maltreatment that may remain hidden within families. Furthermore, violence in families that

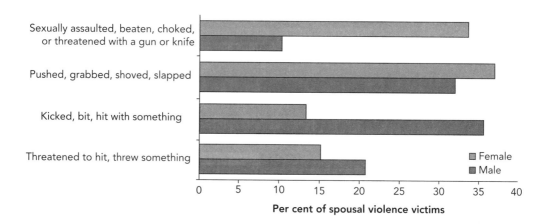

Figure 8.5 Family Violence in Canada: A Statistical Profile

Source: Statistics Canada, 2011. Family Violence in Canada: A Statistical Profile. Catalogue no. 85-224-X.

is defined as "punishment" is not reported as abuse. Although Canadians disagree about whether corporal punishment such as spanking should be defined as abuse, the fact that it is unacceptable to spank adults if they misbehave says a lot about power relations between adults and children. Nonetheless, data from the CIS provide more information about child abuse and neglect in Canada than was previously available. These data suggest that there were an estimated 235,843 (about 39.19/1,000 children) child maltreatment investigations in Canada in 2008 (an increase from 135,573, or 21.47/1,000 children in 1998). Of these investigations in 2008, 36 per cent were substantiated by child welfare workers, 34 per cent were suspicious but unsubstantiated, and in 30 per cent of the cases the investigation revealed that the child was not maltreated. Most of the substantiated cases involved abuse or neglect (77 per cent). In 2010 there were, in Canada, 5,616,700 children between the ages of 0 and 14 years (Statistics Canada 2011). Hence, approximately 0.4 per cent of Canadian children were physically or sexually abused to the point that child welfare agencies intervened. Another 0.4 per cent were neglected, and 0.2 per cent suffered emotional maltreatment. According to these data, girls and boys were equally likely to experience maltreatment in families. Boys were more likely than girls to have been physically abused, and girls were more likely than boys to have been sexually abused in families, a finding that is substantiated by police record data for 2003 (Statistics Canada 2005b). Older boys and girls were more likely to experience abuse than were younger girls and boys. Among girls, the likelihood of sexual assault was highest among those aged 4–7 and 12–15 (Statistics Canada 2001c). Higher incidents of abuse and neglect were found in families that were more likely to be at risk of poverty (e.g., lone-mother families) (Statistics Canada 2001c), and a direct relationship between poverty and child abuse has

been found in other countries around the world (Krug et al. 2002).

The above data took into account only those cases of child abuse that were reported to child welfare agencies, yet the most severe cases of child abuse were usually handled by police. Police records from 2000 show that 23 per cent of victims of physical and sexual assault were children or young people, a figure that corresponds with the percentage of children and young people in the population of Canada at the time. Data from 2003 separated out physical and sexual assault and found that 21 per cent of the victims of physical assault and 61 per cent of the victims of sexual assault were children and youth under 18; children and youth represented 21 per cent of the Canadian population in 2003. The 2000 data showed that the majority of child and youth victims of crime were assaulted by strangers or acquaintances rather than relatives. Family members were the perpetrators in 23 per cent of the cases, and of these family-member perpetrators, parents were the most likely to be the abusers. However, there was some variation on the basis of age. Children aged 5 and under were more likely to be assaulted by relatives, whereas children 6 and older were more likely to be assaulted by someone who was not related to them. In the case of homicide, infants were more likely to be killed by their mothers, and older children and young people by their fathers. With the exception of homicide, the risk of abuse increased with age (Statistics Canada 2002b).

Data taken from police records in 2005 suggest that very little has changed with respect to the physical and sexual abuse of children within families. In 2005 the rates of sexual and physical assaults against children and youth committed by non-family members remained higher than the rate committed by family members (1.5 times higher for sexual assault and 2.6 times higher for physical assault). In 1998 this gap was much higher (2 times higher for sexual assault and 3.6 times higher for physical assault). Thus, over time it has become more common for physical and sexual assault on children to be committed by family members, though more offences are still committed by non-family members (Statistics Canada 2007c).

Elder abuse is defined as an intentional or unintentional act of commission or neglect. It may be physical, psychological, financial, or material (Krug et al. 2002; McDonald et al. 1991; Podnieks 1992). Data from the 2009 General Social Survey (GSS) show that physical or sexual abuse perpetrated by a child, relative, friend, or caregiver over the last five years was reported by only 2 per cent of non-institutionalized Canadians aged 65 and older (Statistics Canada 2012). Although these numbers are too small to allow for subsequent analyses, this 2 per cent figure may represent wife abuse "grown old" (L.R. Phillips 1986: 212).

Police records on violent crime show that adults aged 65 and older experience lower rates of violent crime that do those under 65. However, the rate of violence against older

adults increased by 20 per cent between 1998 and 2005. Although overall rates of violence against seniors are higher for men than for women, older women are more likely to be subjected to violence at the hand of a family member than are older men. Those accused of family violence against seniors (especially mothers; see Figure 8.6 below) are more likely to be children of the abused individual. Yet gender differences emerge here. Among older women, those accused of family violence are more likely to be spouses of the victims, whereas for older men, the accused are more likely to be children of the victims (Statistics Canada 2007c).

Because of the structural intersections between age and gender, Aronson, Thornewell, and Williams (1995) argue that it is important to consider "wife assault in old age" as distinct from either wife assault or elder abuse, and they document the story of Eve, a woman who, at age 75, left an abusive relationship. Indeed, there are continuing debates in the literature about

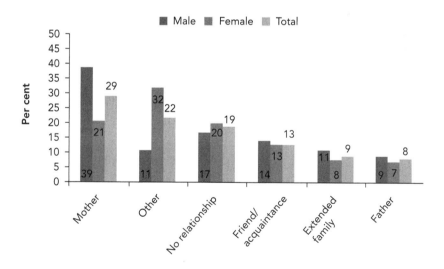

Type of victim–accused relationship

Figure 8.6 Elder Abuse in Canada: Victim/Accused Relationship

Source: Ottawa Police Service, Elder Abuse File Review, 2011. www.justice.gc.ca/eng/rp-pr/cj-jp/fv-vf/rr13_1/p2.html

whether elder abuse is a problem unique to old age or whether it represents a continuation of lifelong family violence (McDonald and Wigdor 1995).

At an individual level, victims of familial abuse have limited agency to deal with violence because of the excessive control and power that husbands, parents, or adult children have over them (L. Davies, Ford-Gilboe, and Hammerton 2009). Nonetheless, agency among the victims of family violence is revealed in the strategies that they use to curtail it or escape from it. In violent families, wives, children, and the elderly pay attention to the things that trigger acts of violence from the abuser and actively seek ways in which they can avoid such things. Wives sometimes flee abusive relationships, often taking their children with them, and teenagers sometimes run away from home. Yet gender, age, race, ethnicity, and class structure the processes of production, reproduction, and distribution in limiting the options that are available to victims of abuse and severely restrict their ability to leave abusive families (see coalescence framework, Figure 7.3). Besides differences in physical strength, women, children, and the elderly are often financially and otherwise dependent on family members.

This structured dependence, combined with ideologies regarding familial love, makes it difficult to leave abusive families (L. Davies, Ford-Gilboe, and Hammerton 2009). For instance, only 43 per cent of abused wives leave their husbands, and three-quarters of those who leave return. Among those who return, a third do so "for the sake of their children," one-quarter want "to give the relationship another chance," 17 per cent feel that their partner will change, and 9 per cent lack the money or housing to live on their own (Rodgers 1994).[1] Although there is no survey evidence that indicates that violence resumes after women return to their partner, the systemic nature of family violence, combined with qualitative data

that demonstrate recurring abuse (L. Davies, McMullin, and Avison 2001), suggests that this is likely. Hence, romanticized ideals of family may perpetuate family violence even among women who have once left the abusive situation. Further, remaining separated from a partner does not guarantee the end of IPV (L. Davies, Ford-Gilboe, and Hammerton 2008). Husbands sometimes find their estranged wives and continue to threaten and abuse them, and sometimes even murder them (D.K. Anderson and Saunders 2003; Statistics Canada 2001g).

Compared with individual agency, collective action has been a much more effective means of dealing with family violence. Indeed, the recognition throughout the 1970s and 1980s of the abuse of women, children, and elderly people as serious social problems was a direct result of the collective lobbying of feminist and other activist groups, such as the National Advisory Council on Aging. Through these efforts, community services have been put in place, especially for women and children, that help victims of family abuse leave abusive relationships and otherwise cope.

Sexuality

Sexuality is a central dimension of the social relations of reproduction. Sexuality has different meanings in different situations. "In some ways it is an expression of human need, of pleasure, and of the social togetherness of lovers. In other ways it is an oppressive and repressive relationship which grinds the tenderness and love out of people, leaving behind the frustration, bitterness, and violence" (Luxton 1980: 55).

Indeed, some argue that heterosexuality itself is a repressive patriarchal institution. For instance, in a seminal article, Adrienne Rich (1980) argues that heterosexuality is not natural but is a mechanism through which men maintain their powerful and privileged status in society. To truly have control over one's sexuality, Rich argues, one needs to be able to choose heterosexuality freely. Yet in contemporary Western societies heterosexuality is not questioned but is taken for granted. According to Rich, the organization of productive relations in capitalism reinforces **compulsory heterosexuality** because (1) women's success at work is often tied to their degree of femininity (which implies acting in an overtly heterosexual manner); (2) women often endure sexual harassment to keep their jobs; and (3) women are economically dependent upon men because they earn less (see also the discussion of the link between processes of production and reproduction in the coalescence framework, Figure 7.3).

In Canada, sexuality is often organized in families and is structured by class, age, gender, ethnicity, and race. Indeed, colonized peoples in North America have had to endure centuries of sexual regulation and abuse by Europeans (Stasiulis 1999). Heterosexual teenage sex, especially for girls, is subjected to excessive moral regulation, and in most nursing homes elderly residents are not permitted to have sexual relations.

Processes of production, reproduction, and distribution are evident in the rules of exchange that frame the dating experience for both teenagers and adults. Even though there has been movement toward more equality in dating, boys and men (who are often older than their dating partners) tend to pay for meals, movies, and other forms of entertainment in exchange for kissing, petting, and intercourse. We do not often think about dating in these terms because our assumptions about love and family suggest that this behaviour is both traditional and normal (Luxton 1980). Yet if a woman does not submit to a man's advances after he has paid for the date, she is at risk of "losing" him (Luxton 1980) or, in more extreme cases, she is at risk of sexual abuse. Although determining the prevalence of sexual abuse among dating couples ("date

rape") is fraught with methodological difficulties, Canadian data from the late 1990s suggest that 28 per cent of women attending college and university were sexually abused within the past year (DeKeseredy and Schwartz 1998). The fact that, on average, men earn more than women (see chapter 9) also reinforces the idea that men "should" pay for entertainment on dates and links inequality in processes of production to sexuality. Indeed, because women are at a disadvantage in the labour market, they are more likely than men to consider the earning potential of their dating partners in making decisions about marriage (Coltrane 2000).

One of the functions that marriage continues to play in Canadian society is the regulation of sexual relations. This remains true regardless of Popenoe's claim that this function is eroding. Indeed, monogamy within marriage is the expectation in Canada. Although most Canadians report that they have never had an extramarital affair, the proportion of men who report such affairs is higher than it is for women. This suggests that there is a power imbalance in the control that men and women have over each other's sexuality within marriage. The fact that men often believe that marriage gives them the right to have sex with their wives on demand and that sex should revolve around a man's pleasures and needs is evidence of this gendered power imbalance in families (Luxton 1980). At the extreme, this gendered power imbalance leads to sexual assault. According to 2004 Canadian GSS data, 16 per cent of women have experienced sexual assault at the hand of a spouse (Statistics Canada 2005a). Wives often feel obligated to fulfill the sexual desires of their husbands either because they fear the physical and emotional response or because they are afraid of losing their husbands to other women. Although the feelings of love and attachment that wives have toward their husbands are related to these fears, the economic insecurity wives face augments such fears.

If their husbands leave, many wives would have economic difficulties. This is because wives are primarily responsible for domestic labour and consequently are connected only tenuously to the labour market (see chapter 9). Hence, sexual relations between husbands and wives are, at some level, economic relations as well (Luxton 1980).

Even though men control women's sexuality both inside and outside of marriage, the regulation of pregnancy and childbirth is usually the woman's responsibility. Furthermore, the consequences of poorly timed pregnancies severely affect women's economic well-being but not men's. Teenage girls who get pregnant reduce the risk of a lifetime of financial struggle if they marry the father of their child. Yet even if a marriage does take place, there is no guarantee that it will last. Furthermore, among women who work for pay and who get pregnant when they are older, careful timing is often also required so that they get the most out of public and private maternity-leave benefits. If, for instance, a woman who is working for pay gets pregnant before she has been employed with a company for six months, she is most often ineligible for either company or government benefits. In such instances, a woman would not even be guaranteed her job if she took a leave. Of course, men tend not to have to deal with these issues, but with recent changes to parental leave policies in Canada, this might change (see chapter 12).

Explaining Inequality in Families

The preceding discussion shows that families are sites of considerable conflict and inequality. Because so many people view families in romanticized ways as places in which love and harmony abound, less emphasis was placed on this topic here. And there is little doubt that many families provide comfort, love, and nurturing for its members; for racialized women, families may also act as protection from oppression in paid work and other social institutions. Moreover, in some families the division of labour is organized in relatively equal ways (Ranson 2013; Risman 1998). Hence, explanations of inequality within families must consider simultaneously both the harmony and the conflict that characterize family life.

Many of the models that have been put forth to explain inequality within families have focused on inequities in the division of household labour and child care. For instance, some researchers have focused on power imbalances within marriage to explain the unequal division of unpaid labour in families (Carrier and Davies 1999). In this literature, marital power is often conceptualized as the relative resources (e.g., income or education) that husbands and wives have within a marriage. For example, one might hypothesize that the more income or education a wife has compared with her husband, the less household work and care she will perform. This hypothesis is generally supported: couples who have relatively equal levels of resources tend to have a more equitable division of household labour than those whose resources are less equal (Gazso-Windle and McMullin 2003; Kamo 1988). Other models have analyzed the views that partners hold about gender equality and correlated these views with the relative time that husbands and wives spend doing household labour. Still other models focus on time availability. A serious problem with all of these models is that the researchers who use them tend not to contextualize them within the structures of gender, class, ethnicity, race, and age. As a result, these analyses tend to place too much emphasis on individual differences to the neglect of social structure. Furthermore, such research usually avoids discussions of the struggle and conflict that often take place as families try to deal with the work of maintaining households and caring for children.

More fruitful approaches to studies of inequality within families would take both structure and agency into account and recognize that through these structures families are often oppressive institutions. In this regard, Ingrid Connidis and I (McMullin) (Connidis and McMullin 2002) have worked to develop a structural concept of sociological ambivalence that characterizes family ties. Our summary of ambivalence is worth repeating here:

> Ambivalence is created by the contradictions and paradoxes that are imbedded in sets of structured social relations (e.g., class, age, race, ethnicity, gender) through which opportunities, rights, and privileges are differentially distributed. Individuals experience ambivalence when social structural arrangements collide with their attempts to exercise agency when negotiating relationships, including those with family members. Managing ambivalence in daily life shapes the very social structures that produce ambivalence in the first place. (Connidis and McMullin 2002: 565)

To explain what is meant by *ambivalence*, I (McMullin) will use a personal example. Gender, class, and race structure my experiences at paid work and as a mother. In a department and university that have traditionally been very conservative, there are rigid expectations about what makes a "good" scholar, and these expectations are classed, gendered, and racialized in the ways that one would expect. One must be articulate, show little emotion, work long hours, and so on. These expectations often clash with the gendered, classed, and racialized expectations of me, particularly of me as a mother. This clash results in a structurally based ambivalence that I must negotiate and try to resolve within my family and at work, which requires that I actively renegotiate the expectations of me as a mother and as a professor.

Beyond Statistics: Agency and Experience within Families

The preceding sections illustrate structured patterns of inequality that persist in Canadian families. Within these structures, individuals negotiate their lives and, in the process, conform or resist these structures of dominance (see chapters 6 and 7). In doing so, individuals are active in the production and reproduction of these social structures. Although concentrating primarily on white middle-class mothers, Bonnie Fox (2001, 2009) has explored how parenthood in heterosexual families socially constructs gender. This study shows that new mothers actively negotiate child care and housework with their partner, but that because mothers must take responsibility for their children and become more dependent upon their partner when they do so, fathers have more "bargaining" power in the negotiations that take place. Using Janet Finch's (1989) terminology, partners and fathers have "legitimate excuses" for not looking after the children. A particularly telling finding from this study is that structures of gender inequality in the division of housework are reproduced through these negotiations. New mothers feel that their partner should be involved in the care of their children and have "prioritized daddy's time with the baby" while they do the housework. As a result, "one product of women's agency in drawing men into active fathering may be a more conventional division of housework" (Fox 2001: 385).

Within the context of class, gender, age, ethnic, and racial structures, even the most structurally disadvantaged individuals make choices about how they should best live their lives. Looking from the outside in, and without hearing the stories, these choices often seem irrational to those who have never experienced extreme disadvantage. Box 8.4 presents an excerpt from the

HIGHLIGHT

Box 8.4 Pam's Family Experiences

From what I remember from about seven, seven up, I don't remember a lot of traumatized stuff. A lot of abuse obviously. Strict, upper hand, you don't talk back, kids are supposed to be seen not heard. There's a lot of violence, 14 years she [Pam's mother] put up with abuse and stuck it. People say you can leave but it's not as easy as said.

I left home at 14, moved here, lived on the streets. Ate out of the garbage bins. I don't know, there was lots of abuse. There was alcohol in my family, left and right. Drugs and, see, my brother he was, started young, he was about 11 when he started drugs. My mom acknowledged it but she was so messed up she really, you know, she didn't do nothing about it. It was rough.

My dad was always in jail so to speak, and she met this guy. This guy was very stiff, upper hand, you know you don't talk back, you do as I say. He used to make us, as kids you know when you run down the stairs and that and you creak the stairs or something, he would think we were banging. So we would have to go up and down the stairs 150 times or more. And if we made one creak, we would have to start all over again. Well to this day I can't walk up stairs properly. Like I can't walk flat, always on the tippy toes. You know, just something like that. There was like dishes, he used to make us do dishes real young. And as kids you don't worry about every little spot on them, and if we had one we had to do them all over again. And we'd do them like five or six times, yeah, in a day. There was little things here and there that he would make us do. School, I wasn't good in school because I was, I had other problems to worry about. You know, more or less taking care of my mom when she was all drunk, and cleaning up the house and doing whatever.

We used to get hung out, we lived in a two-storey house, he'd hang us upside down by our feet out the window. A lot of physical abuse. Later on down the road, when my mom finally did leave this guy, there were two men that raped and molested me, and I told her. She was like, no they wouldn't do that kind of thing, right. So that's when I said that's it, I've had enough. And my brother was the only one who believed me. I just left it.

I lived in the park for the longest time. I cleaned up from the water fountains there. I cleaned up the best I could. Just carried a back pack with me. At night we would have to watch. I met a couple of friends in the park and they would watch for police because at that time they would come through the park and see if anybody was sleeping on the benches and that's where we slept. Then if my friends seen them or whatever, wake me up and we'd just sit there and talk, and then go back to sleep. So it was really rough, I looked like a bag of crap. Not the proper hygiene of it all, I was fairly clean considering some of them, they were really gross. Towards the end of the night we'd just go, like there was a doughnut shop downtown at the time, and we used to go into their dumpsters and get their doughnuts and whatever garbage there was there to eat. We'd go to the Salvation Army, we'd get one meal there, so we'd do that.

And I didn't even panhandle or nothing, so whatever I could get, and it was hard. I did that for about six months and I couldn't take it no more. I was just on the verge of committing suicide and everything. It was all going downhill. I heard about this place that would help so I went there. And they weren't going to take me because I was fifteen and they don't usually, they need a consent and all this. And I explained to them there is no consent, there has never been a consent. I've been my own person for a long time. And I've been feeding myself for a while. Ok the food might have been in the cupboards or whatever, but I'd be making it. So they took that into consideration.

life-history narratives in the poverty study that introduced this chapter. Pam grew up in a poor white family with a physically abusive stepfather and a mother who drank. Poverty combined with gender- and age-based power relations forced Pam onto the streets when

I hated it because people would steal what little stuff I had, and there was like fights. And they would say there is different walks of life and you're going to face that. I didn't agree with that 100 per cent, I said I understand there's different people with different problems, but leave my stuff alone that's all I want. I don't got much. Eventually I got privileges to get my own room, private room. So I enjoyed that. I stayed there for the longest time, I stayed about eight months there. So I was happy about that and when I did finally say ok, I'm out of here, I got my own apartment downtown.

And then I met my husband, well boyfriend at the time. We lived together and stuff like that, my mom was not good about that. First time I ever got a welfare cheque, and it was cool, because I saved money. I didn't really spend nothing because I wasn't in a spending mode, I just wanted to save everything I could get. So every time I'd get my welfare cheque I'd go out and hang around the café, doughnut café and stuff like that, and my mom would say well you can't do that. Well why can't I? I pay my own rent, it's my place. I'm still your mother and you can't do this and you can't do that, I'm going to send you to a girls' home. She used to threaten me with that all the time. And I just lost it, you want to send me, go for it, try it, see what happens. You're not going to get anywhere, they're going to laugh at you because I'm out on my own. You got nothing to do with me. She hated it, we fought for a while there too.

I wouldn't even tell her, because I didn't want to tell her that, my husband now, was living with me. She knew, I knew she knew because she'd seen men's stuff here and there. I just said no, it's just my friend's stuff or whatever. But she knew and I didn't want to hurt her feelings or whatever, you know.

Eventually we, me and my husband, we moved to a bigger place, it wasn't much bigger but it was bigger. We ended up being superintendents cleaning out the garbage. We had to deal with the clientele there so to speak, it was rough. There was a lot of drugs going through there. I didn't like it because I wanted to get away from that situation.

We finally made it. I was sixteen when we moved again over top of a bar and there are nice places there, really, really nice places. I ended up being a superintendent there for like five buildings. They hummed and hawed about it too because I'm 16 being a superintendent, not mature. Well they later on realized that it was a good decision because I got rid of a lot of the drug addicts that were in there. It was hard to deal with because you kind of sleep not knowing if they would break into your apartment and do something to you because you phoned the police on them. So we had lots of difficulties with that but eventually it panned out into a nice place to live.

And then I ended up getting pregnant with my daughter, because we were doing that for a while and I was eighteen when I got pregnant. And I decided to leave [my job]. I gave the landlord proper notice and whatnot and said I can't be bringing my daughter up here in a downtown area, over top of a bar, no. There's no play land or anything for them. He kind of understood but he was disappointed because I had been there for so long. And then we moved over here, like that was a two bedroom, this is a three, and we've been here ever since. It's been not bad, I don't want stay here long because there's so to speak, people call them "lifers" here. Been here 20, 26 years. I've been here six and when I do move it's going to be to a house. I'll stay a long time, length of time you need and I'll never come back again. This is public housing, eh, so and there's different walks of life here. They don't like the fact that my husband works, because a lot of them are on mother's allowance or welfare.

Source: Davies, McMullin, and Avison, unpublished research data.

she was 14. Pam used various survival strategies and made choices within the context of debilitating structures of age, gender, and class to get off the streets. Although she only had a grade 8 education when she left home, when we talked with her, she was 26 years old, was a married mother of two children, had nearly finished high school, was earning a living as a part-time apartment-building superintendent, and was learning a trade. Notably, Pam makes sense of her life by contrasting her life and what she has made of it with her observations of her neighbours' problems. Throughout her teenage years, her mother had tried to enforce middle-class family and gender values upon her and she had resisted. Yet now she struggles to maintain a happy family life with an unfaithful husband so that her children will have what she didn't and so that she does not "become a statistic."

Conclusions

Although Popenoe and other neo-conservative commentators interpret changes in women's lives and families negatively, those interested in eradicating inequality view them positively. Indeed, Anthony Giddens (2002: 65), in speaking about the relationship between families and globalization, goes so far as to suggest that

> the persistence of the traditional family—or aspects of it—in many parts of the world is more worrisome than its decline. For what are the most important forces promoting democracy and economic development in poorer countries? Well, precisely the equality and education of women. And what must be changed to make this possible? Most importantly, the traditional family.

Yet, as Bonnie Fox points out (2001: 388) and as this chapter shows, irrespective of the positive changes that have occurred for women in families, "the division of household work and responsibility in heterosexual couples has stubbornly resisted significant change. This absence of change suggests that gender divisions in intimate relations are deeply embedded in social structures." Added to this is the persistence of physical and sexual violence against women, children, and older adults in families. Clearly, although power imbalances may make families "a haven in a heartless world"[2] for men, for many women, children, and older adults the structure and experience of families may be characterized as much by ambivalence and conflict as by love and harmony.

Compared with gender and age, there has been very little Canadian research on race and ethnic inequality in families and unpaid work. The work of Tania Das Gupta, Enakshi Dua, and Agnes Calliste stands out as exceptions in this regard. Much of this work concerns the role of the state in family formation and the discrimination that racial and ethnic-minority groups face in living in family forms that they choose. As these scholars have noted, more work is needed on the experiences of women and men racialized in families and on the social organization of racialized families.

⚏ Notes

1. Twenty per cent of these women listed other reasons for returning to their husbands. In this survey, women were asked to report the main reason for returning to their husbands, and only one response was allowed. As a result, the data likely underestimate the role that financial dependence plays in women's decisions to return to their husbands.

2. This is the title of a famous sociological book on families written by Christopher Lasch in 1977.

⚏ Questions for Critical Thought

1. Statistics show that the total number of paid and unpaid hours of work that men and women do are similar. Some use these data to argue that there is an even split in the work that men and women do—in other words, that when it comes to "work," the family situations for men and women are equal. Using the material presented in this chapter, develop an argument that would counter this claim.

2. Families are often described as a "haven in a heartless world." Use the information in this chapter to refute this claim.

3. Imagine your life 15 years from now. What do you think is the ideal life for someone of that age? How is this ideal influenced by family ideology? How is this ideal structured by gender, class, age, ethnicity, and race?

4. Write down the decisions that Pam made in her life. How were those decisions informed by ideas about what makes a good family? How were those decisions influenced by intersections of class, age, gender, ethnicity, and race?

5. What is your opinion of "non-traditional" families? Will there be negative social consequences if the traditional family unit continues to decline?

⚏ Glossary

Cluttered nest The situation facing parents when children return to live with them after the parents have experienced an "empty nest" phase.

Compulsory heterosexuality The lack of freedom women have to decide whether they will be heterosexual or homosexual. The phrase also refers to the pressures that confront lesbians when they are forced to act as if they were heterosexual or risk facing discriminatory actions.

Empty nest The life stage in which all children have left their parents' home.

Fertility rate The average number of children born to women of child-bearing age.

Nuclear family A family consisting of a husband and wife who live together with their biological or adopted children.

Paternity leave The time a father takes off work at the birth or adoption of a child. This leave can either be paid or unpaid, depending on one's qualifications.

Sandwich generation The generation in which adult children, usually daughters, are "caught" between caring for their young children and their elderly parents.

⠿ Recommended Reading

Dua, Enakshi. 1999. "Beyond Diversity: Exploring the Ways in Which the Discourse of Race Has Shaped the Institution of the Nuclear Family." In E. Dua and A. Robertson, eds, *Scratching the Surface: Canadian Anti-Racist, Feminist Thought.* Toronto: Women's Press. An excellent article that examines how the institution of the nuclear family has been reinforced through racist state rhetoric and policy.

Duxbury, Linda, and Chris Higgins. 2013. *Balancing Work, Childcare, and Eldercare: A View from the Trenches.* Report for Desjardins Insurance. Retrieved 25 November 2015, from www.desjardinslifeinsurance.com/en/about-us/Documents/RapportDuxbury-ENG-Full-Web.pdf

Fox, Bonnie J., ed. 2001. *Family Patterns, Gender Relations.* 2nd edn. Toronto: Oxford University Press. An excellent collection of essays on how family life is gendered and how family relations and gender relations have changed over time.

Johnson, Holly. 1996. *Dangerous Domains: Violence against Women in Canada.* Toronto: Nelson. Relying heavily on Statistics Canada data, this book provides a comprehensive account of violence against women in Canada.

Luxton, Meg, and June Corman. 2001. *Getting By in Hard Times: Gendered Labour at Home and on the Job.* Toronto: University of Toronto Press. A case study of steelworkers in Hamilton. It examines how these working-class people negotiate the demands of paid and unpaid work.

Lynn, Marion, ed. 2003. *Voices: Essays on Canadian Families.* 2nd edn. Scarborough, ON: Nelson. A collection of essays on family diversity and experiences.

Popenoe, David. 2009. *Families without Fathers: Fathers, Marriage and Children in American Society.* New Brunswick, NJ: Transaction Publishers. An evaluation of the changing nature of families, fatherhood, and child socialization in American society.

⠿ Relevant Websites

The White Ribbon Campaign
www.whiteribbon.ca

**This website provides information and educational tools regarding violence against women. The White Ribbon Campaign is an organization of men who are "working to end men's violence against women."

Canadian Council on Social Development—Families: A Canadian Profile
www.ccsd.ca/factsheets/family

**This webpage is the place to go to for accessible statistics on Canadian families. Graphs and distribution tables for family types, lone-parent families,

marriages and divorces, child-care spaces, mothers in the paid labour force, and costs of raising children are presented. "Families" is just one of the areas covered on the Stats & Facts online service of the Canadian Council on Social Development. Other areas include demographics, health, education, economic security, and the labour market.

Vanier Institute of the Family
www.vifamily.ca

**Established in 1965 under the patronage of Their Excellencies Governor-General Georges P. Vanier and Madame Pauline Vanier, the Vanier Institute of the Family is dedicated to promoting the well-being of Canadian families. The institute aims to create awareness of and to provide leadership on the importance and strengths of families in Canada and the challenges they face in their structural, demographic, economic, cultural, and social diversity.

Long-Term Health Effects of Woman Abuse Research Consortium

www.women-health.ca/publications.htm

**In this consortium, Canadian researchers are brought together by the following goals: to understand the patterns of mental and physical health of women who have left abusive partners, to understand how health is shaped by the conditions of their everyday lives, and to shape the development of services that support women to manage health and social problems they face after leaving. This site lists the various research projects relating to these goals and provides contact information for the investigators and collaborators.

CAGE(s) and Paid Work

Introduction

We begin this chapter by discussing a case study of workplace inequality. In doing so, we show that production processes are structured by class, age, gender, and ethnicity in this particular working-class industry in Canada. In the mid-1990s, I (McMullin) analyzed focus-group data, industry data, key informant interviews, and archival data from the Montreal garment industry. This research confirmed what other research has shown—jobs in the garment industry are bad and garment work is hard (Das Gupta 1995). Managers and owners exploit workers in a quest to maximize productivity and profits, and there is always pressure to produce more. Managers control their workers by restricting the opportunities of those who sign grievances and by eliminating or moving "problem" workers to different departments or jobs (McMullin and Marshall 2001). This is an industry that favours the interest and well-being of the capitalist class at the expense of workers.

In the quest for maximum productivity and profits, bosses may also try to limit the contact that employees have with one another and to supervise their work very closely. As Isabella, one of the focus-group participants put it,

The boss was never far away from us. He was there all day long, you couldn't speak too loudly because you soon saw him coming over. Ah yes and he would say, "That's enough." He was there early in the morning and he stayed with us at all times, all day. If he wanted to shock me, it would be in the morning when I arrived. You had to do a repair, he brought it to you then from the minute you set foot in the office he kept you there and gave you an earful. He ruined my day from the start when he started to tell me off—[when he started to tell me] that I worked badly. (McMullin 1996: 195–6)

Although the exact words that were exchanged between Isabella and her boss in this confrontation are not discussed in detail, the excerpt illustrates how bosses attempt to control their employees by limiting their conversations with other workers and by criticizing their ability to do their job well. All of the above point to how social class shapes the production processes in garment work and how individual owners act as agents in using their power to exploit workers.

The practice of hiring the least expensive workforce in order to maximize profits has a long history in the garment industry. As a result, women and immigrant workers are disproportionately represented in the industry; in the garment industry, women and immigrant workers are paid less. At the industrial level, 82 per cent of the workers in the ladies' clothing industry in Quebec are women. Jobs within the industry are also segregated along gender lines; for instance, women make up between 88 per cent and 96 per cent of the three lowest-paid occupations in the garment industry. Ethnic groups are segregated in particular shops, with higher wages being paid in shops where most of the workers are French Canadian (McMullin 1996; McMullin and Marshall 2001).

One method that employers in the garment industry use to reduce labour expenses is to replace older workers who have been with a company for many years with younger, less expensive workers. Even though union regulations and Quebec law forbid the dismissal of workers on the basis of age, owners circumvent these rules and eliminate older workers by closing their factories and then reopening them later under different names. Bankruptcy laws, too, allow employers to close their plants, thereby terminating their debt and decreasing their labour expenses by eliminating the older workforce and the union. Several months later, many of these companies open up under different names with younger and non-unionized employees. According to Gerald Roy, the Canadian director of the International Ladies' Garment Workers' Union, companies go out of business, move on, and open a new firm in another location all within three or four months. The disgrace that was once attached to bankruptcy has dissipated, states Roy, and now firms have "hot shot" lawyers who tell them exactly how to go out of business; how to not pay their debts to the employees, landlords, machinery rental agencies, and banks; and how and when to open up another shop. Canadian bankruptcy legislation has not been changed to discourage such practices. Roy highlights the seriousness of this problem:

It is too easy to open and close a company in the apparel industry. What is deploring is that the workers are always at the end of the process. They lose conditions of work, they lose their paycheque, they lose vacation pay, they lose their health benefits, they lose their pension benefits, they lose and lose and they are getting older. They are getting fed up, but they would like to go and work some place else maybe, but they do not have the opportunity because there are no jobs. (McMullin and Marshall 2001: 119)

Thus, neo-conservative state policies regarding bankruptcy favour the rights of capital over labour and serve to override legislation and union rules regarding the dismissal of older workers. José, a 53-year-old garment worker, described how difficult such practices are for older workers: "You've been working for 25 years, with all your heart, all your soul. You gave up your health and you fall face to face with nothing . . . we lost part of our early retirement [pension contributions], we lost everything. . . . They [the company] changed the name, they changed the company but it is still there" (McMullin and Marshall 2001: 120).

The preceding discussion shows how production processes are structured by class, age, gender, and ethnicity in a working-class industry. Within these structures of inequality, owners, managers, and workers act with agency in their daily negotiations with one another. For instance, even though garment workers' choices within production processes are constrained by the structures of class, gender, ethnicity, and age relations, garment workers make informed and strategic decisions about their work and retirement within these constraints (McMullin and Marshall 1999).

Class, gender, and racism (see chapter 4) intersect in processes of professionalization as well. Tracey Adams (2000), for instance, argues that dentistry emerged in Ontario during the early part of the 1900s as a profession that was structured as white, middle-class, and male. Students of dentistry were active in this process, as was evident from the opinion pieces submitted to student newspapers, the extracurricular activities they engaged in, their style of dress, and the ways in which some confirmed and others resisted the racial structures of their historical epoch, depending on whether they refused to treat black patients (T.L. Adams 2000).

The production processes described above in relation to garment work highlight three broad issues that may be used to classify jobs as relatively good or bad. First, the physical environments of workplaces vary considerably. People employed in good jobs experience relative comfort at work and a low risk of workplace injuries or illness. Bad jobs, on the other hand, often have physical environments that are uncomfortable and dangerous or unhealthy. Second, jobs vary in the intrinsic rewards that are derived from them. Unlike bad jobs, good jobs tend to be intrinsically rewarding because they are challenging and are characterized by high levels of **autonomy** and low levels of **alienation**. Third, extrinsic rewards, such as high pay, good benefits, job security, and promotion opportunities, are associated with good jobs (Krahn, Lowe, and Hughes 2014; Rinehart 2006).

Within Canada's economic system of advanced **capitalism**, there is a wide continuum of good and bad jobs. The ideology of capitalism suggests that good jobs and bad jobs are distributed on the basis of individual merit, or through a system of **meritocracy** (i.e., the allocation of positions, roles, prestige, power, and economic reward, whereby "excellent" individuals reap disproportionate benefits in relation to others). Good jobs are reserved for highly educated and skilled workers whose contributions to economic activities are considered more valuable than the contributions that others make. With this logic, inequality in the outcomes of paid work seems justified. However, many sociologists are critical of this point of view and instead recognize that if productive processes were organized differently, the inequality associated with paid work might be reduced or eliminated (Rinehart 2006). At the most fundamental level this would require the abolition of capitalism as the predominant mode of production in industrialized societies such as Canada.

In its purest form, capitalism is an economic system that organizes processes of production according to the following characteristics: (1) private ownership and control of the means of production by relatively few people; (2) continuous growth, such that owners of capital continually strive to increase their profits; (3) exploitation, whereby owners of capital profit at the expense of workers; (4) labour-wage exchanges, such that workers act as free agents in selling their labour power to capitalists in exchange for a wage; and (5) commodity exchange that takes place in free markets, subject to supply and demand, which in turn regulates economic activity (Abercrombie, Hill, and Turner 2000; Krahn, Lowe, and Hughes 2014; Rinehart 2006).

Karl Marx was among the first to recognize that capitalism is also a *social* system in which production processes are organized according to the social relations of production. Owners, managers, and workers have various rights, privileges, power, and resources relative to one another. Unequal access to the rights and powers associated with productive resources shapes the social relations of production. According to the coalescence framework discussed in chapter 7, in capitalist systems class, age, gender, and ethnic relations, which are characterized by oppression, power, exploitation, and opportunity hoarding, constitute the social relations of production. The social and economic organization of the processes of production results in a continuum of good and bad jobs. As a result, it is not surprising that access to "good jobs" in capitalist societies, including Canada, is highly restricted by the capitalist class. An example of this restriction is presented in Box 9.1. As this box discusses, elitism is so embedded in British society that one might even call it "social engineering."

Global perspective

Box 9.1 Mobility in Britain Still Strikingly Low, Even "Deeply Elitist"

The United Kingdom may be one of the most "deeply elitist" countries in the world for social-class reproduction and social mobility. According to Lee Elliot Major, chief executive of the Sutton Trust—a think-tank whose agenda focuses on raising awareness about educational inequality and social mobility—the most prestigious employment positions in the UK are awarded to the privately educated elite. As a result, rates of social mobility are starkly low. In order to reverse this trend, access to elite universities—Oxford and Cambridge, for example—should be granted based on intellectual ability rather than income or social class.

In fact, just 10 prestigious private schools produced 12 per cent of professional elites in the United Kingdom. This study found that Eton College, the former school of David Cameron, Boris Johnson, the Duke of Cambridge, and Prince Harry, educated over 330 top earners, a total of 4 per cent of the UK's current elite. According to related research by the Social Mobility and Child Poverty Commission, people educated at public school have created a "closed shop at the top," thereby drastically limiting access to prestigious employment positions in the UK. The commission even went as far as claiming that elitism was so embedded in Britain "that it could be called 'social engineering.'"

In response to this research, Alan Milburn, the Labour former cabinet minister, pointed out that these practices of exclusion lock out "a diversity of talents and experiences [that] makes Britain's leading institutions less informed, less representative and, ultimately, less credible than they should be."

This study analyzed over 4,000 people who filled jobs in elite government, the civil service, the judiciary, the media, business and the creative industries. They analyzed their educational backgrounds, noting that attending a private school is reasonably indicative of a wealthy background.

While only 7 per cent of members of the public attended a private school, the following list percentages of people who attended private schooling and who now occupy positions in the UK elite:

- 71 per cent of senior judges
- 62 per cent of senior officers in the armed forces
- 55 per cent of permanent secretaries in Whitehall
- 53 per cent of senior diplomats
- 50 per cent of members of the House of Lords
- 45 per cent of public body chairs

This new research shows how far the UK must come to improve social mobility and to ensure that young, capable people can achieve their potential regardless of their family's background.

Ironically, public-opinion data show that citizens in the UK want to live in a society where hard work and ability are rewarded. For example, 95 per cent of people believe that in a fair society everyone should have an equal opportunity to get ahead and that people's incomes should reflect their hard work and talent. Unfortunately, as the evidence shows, this desire for an equal society that rewards ability and hard work is far from reality in the UK today (www.gov.uk).

Sources: Andrew Sparrow. (August 28, 2014). "Closed shop at the top in deeply elitist Britain, says study." *The Guardian*; Anon. (Nov. 20, 2012). "Ten private schools produce a tenth of the country's elite." *The Sutton Trust*.

Marx also argued that as capitalism evolved, a proliferation of bad jobs would result from an increasing polarization of workers into two central classes, the proletariat and the bourgeoisie. This polarization would involve at least three things: (1) a reduction in the proportion of small business owners and hence a shrinking of the old middle class; (2) increasing proportions of income going to the owners of large businesses and a reduction in the earnings of middle-class workers; and (3) a continued deskilling of work and corresponding increases in the alienation of workers (Conley 1999). Each of these points, as well as related issues that classify jobs as good or bad, are considered in the sections below. Specifically, this chapter examines how the social organization of production processes and the relationship between production, distribution, and reproduction lead to inequality in the intrinsic and extrinsic rewards of paid work.

Canada's Class and Occupational Structure

In Canada, as in other Western industrialized countries, the processes of production are organized by social class and occupation. Clement and Myles (1994) provide what is perhaps the most comprehensive assessment of the Canadian class structure. As chapter 2 of this book shows, they define social class through a modified, more simplified version of Wright's conceptualization, in which there are four classes. The capitalist-executive class controls both the labour power of others and the means of production. The old middle class—the "petite bourgeoisie" in Marxist terminology—commands the means of production but not the labour power of others. The "new middle" class controls the labour power of others but not the means of production. And, finally, the working class commands neither the labour power of others nor the means of production (see Table 2.1 in chapter 2).

According to this definition of social class, a slight majority of employed Canadians in the early 1980s formed the working class (57.6 per cent). Almost 25 per cent formed the new middle class, 11.3 per cent formed the old middle class, and 6.2 per cent were considered part of the capitalist-executive class (Clement and Myles 1994: 19). Since the early 1900s the proportion of Canada's class structure comprising small business owners declined considerably (Clement and Myles 1994). Between the 1930s and the early 1970s, for instance, the proportion of the workforce comprising small business owners had declined from approximately 25 per cent to between 10 and 12 per cent (Conley 1999). Much of this decline occurred in agriculture, where advances in farm technology made the business of small farming unprofitable (Clement and Myles 1994; Conley 1999).

Nonetheless, for much of the twentieth century it appeared as if Marx's prediction regarding the shrinking middle class was right. Since the mid-1970s, however, this trend has reversed. Indeed, the most significant change in the class structure over the past 20 to 30 years has been the increase in the proportion of the class structure that is held by the old middle class. Clement and Myles (1994) report that non-agricultural self-employment increased from 5.8 per cent in 1975 to 7.4 per cent in 1990. When self-employed owners of incorporated businesses are included, the old middle class made up 14 per cent of the total labour force and 9 per cent of the non-agricultural labour force in the early 1980s. By 2008, 15 per cent of the total labour force was self-employed in both incorporated and unincorporated businesses (Statistics Canada 2008d). Today, the self-employment rate has risen marginally, with the most growth in professional, scientific, and technical services and construction (Statistics Canada 2014c). However, more than 60 per cent of self-employed business owners do not hire paid help (Statistics Canada 2006a), and the majority have fewer than three employees, which classifies them as "small businesses" (Clement and Myles 1994). Information regarding self-employed business owners is difficult to find, but a recent report by Industry Canada notes that 55 per cent of "employer businesses" employ fewer than five people (Industry Canada 2009: Table 3).

Reactions to recent increases in the proportion of employed Canadians in the old middle class have been mixed. On the one hand, some hail these changes as positive. According to this school of thought, small business owners are free of the control of large capitalist enterprises and as a result have more autonomy and other intrinsic rewards associated with their work. Their work is less alienating and this is a positive development of post-industrial capitalism. Others have argued that, far from being a positive occurrence, the rise of small business owners is the result of globalization (see Box 9.2) and workplace restructuring whereby workers lose their jobs and are forced to earn a living without some of the extrinsic rewards (e.g., pensions and benefits) of employment in large companies (see Clement and Myles 1994 for an overview of these views). This suggests that the conditions under which one becomes a small business owner are important considerations in discussions of the social implications of higher proportions of workers belonging to the "old" middle class. Notably, the old middle class is still made up of a relatively small proportion of employed workers. Workers in the new middle class and the working class encompass the overwhelming majority in the Canadian class structure (82.5 per cent according to Clement and Myles [1994]).

One of the most significant social trends of the twentieth century was the dramatic increase in female labour-force participation rates. Although the percentage of women who entered the labour force increased throughout that century, particularly dramatic increases began after 1961. The labour-force participation rates of Canadian women between the ages of 15 and 55 have increased quite significantly since 1961. In 1961, fewer than 30 per cent of women between the ages of 25 and 34 worked for pay. By 1998, that figure was close to 80 per cent, and for all women, the labour-force participation rate in 1998 was about 58 per cent (see Phillips and Phillips 2000 for a detailed discussion). In 2014, 82 per cent of women between the ages of 25 and 44 worked for pay (Krahn, Hughes, and Lowe 2015). But women did not enter the labour force on an equal footing with men. Rather, their social-class positions, as well as the occupations and industries they worked in, were structured by gender.

Canada's class structure is gendered. This means that production processes are shaped by both class relations and gender relations (Hartmann 1981). As a result, the class structure in Canada takes a different form for women and men. Clement and Myles (1994: 129) find that although women constituted 45 per cent of the Canadian labour force in the early 1980s, only 16 per cent of those were part of the executive class. Women were also underrepresented in the new middle class (41 per cent) and overrepresented in the working class (49 per cent). Finally, women were underrepresented in all occupations that involved decision-making and authority, regardless of whether they worked full- or part-time.

Regarding the old middle class, the number of self-employed women almost tripled from 1976 to 2006, yet women still only represented about one-third of all business owners (Statistics Canada 2006a: 46). Yet in 2014, of those who were self-employed, about 61 per cent were men and 39 per cent were women (Statistics Canada 2014c). Most of the gains in self-employment that women have made in relation to men have been as "own account" workers, that is, those who do not have any

HIGHLIGHT

Box 9.2 Globalization and Paid Work in Canada

Globalization is a multi-faceted process in which economic, political, social, and technological transformations have eroded national borders in significant ways (Giddens 2002). One of the most significant ways in which globalization has affected Canadians has been in the gradual reduction in government restrictions on trade and imports. Various trade agreements reflecting the move toward globalization were put into effect during the 1980s and 1990s, including the General Agreement on Tariffs and Trade (GATT), which resulted in a new international body known as the World Trade Organization (WTO); the Free Trade Agreement (FTA), signed in early 1989, which governed trade with the United States (Leach and Winson 1995); and the North American Free Trade Agreement (NAFTA), which came into effect on 1 January 1994, superseding the FTA. These trade agreements, in particular NAFTA, have facilitated economic growth by allowing Canadian companies to restructure their operations and move their production processes to Mexico or the United States. Because the cost of labour is lower in Mexico and some US states, NAFTA has

enabled Canadian companies located there to increase their profitability.

This process of economic globalization has had devastating consequences for many working-class Canadians and particularly for women (Barndt 2002), racialized men and, especially, women (R. Ng 2002), and older workers (Winson and Leach 2002). Manufacturing jobs have been lost, unionized shops have been eliminated, full-time work has been replaced with part-time work, and income has been increasingly polarized (Winston and Leach 2002). In some cases, workers have been forced to make dramatic concessions, such as accepting pay cuts and shorter vacations, to keep production jobs in Canada

Recently, Steven Harper's conservative government negotiated the Trans-Pacific Partnership agreement, which is an extensive and comprehensive free-trade agreement with more than 10 partner countries. With the change of leadership in Canada, it is unclear whether Justin Trudeau's government will support and implement this agreement.

Source: Global Affairs Canada. www.international.gc.ca/trade-agreements-accords-commerciaux/agr-acc/tpp-ptp/index.aspx?lang=eng.

employees. In 2003, for instance, 41 per cent of self-employed men had employees on the payroll compared with only 27 per cent of women (Statistics Canada 2006a; see also Hughes 1999). This pattern continues in Canada today. Hence, although the gains that women have made in self-employment could signify improvements in women's class positions, we must be cautious about such an interpretation because the nature of work among self-employed women is different from that of men. For instance, own-account, self-employed women are more likely than men to be in this employment situation

because of their caregiving responsibilities (Vosko 2007). Further, self-employed women have lower average incomes than self-employed men ($29,000 versus $42,100 in 2003; Statistics Canada 2006a).

Women who work for pay are concentrated in particular occupations and industries. For example, 22.4 per cent of women are employed in administration and clerical positions, 8.6 per cent in retail sales, and 20.1 per cent in other sales and service sectors. These occupations are often called "pink collar" occupations and in 2012 comprised 51.1 per cent of the labour positions women held in Canada. By comparison, men held only 26.8 per cent of these occupational groupings (Krahn, Lowe, and Hughes 2014).

Changes over time to the gender composition in the labour market may—though slowly—be taking place. In 1987, only 7.9 per cent of women were employed in professional and managerial occupations. In 2012, 10.4 per cent of women occupied them (compared with 13.6 per cent of men). Compared with men's jobs, women's jobs are more highly concentrated in health care and social assistance, services-producing, and educational-service industrial sectors of the economy. Men's jobs, on the other hand, are more highly concentrated in the goods-producing and manufacturing sectors (Krahn, Lowe, and Hughes 2014: 81–2).

The coalescence framework presented in chapter 7 suggests that production processes are organized not only according to class and gender relations but by ethnic and race relations as well. Historically, members of British and Jewish English-speaking groups have dominated the professional, managerial, and elite occupations and have been employed in **primary labour markets** (Krahn, Lowe, and Hughes 2014; Nakhaie 1995; Porter 1965). Although this dominance has declined, ethnicity still influences class and occupational structures even when education, age, and place of birth are taken into account (Nakhaie 1995, 2001, 2009).

In general, ethnic- and racial-minority groups (with the exception of those from a Jewish background) are underrepresented among the upper and middle classes and overrepresented in the working class (Nakhaie 1995, 1997). Although members of visible-minority groups are at least as well educated as other Canadians, they are also underrepresented in professional and managerial occupational groups (Adams and Welsh 2008). For instance, although racialized groups constitute about 12.6 per cent of the Canadian population, only 8.2 per cent are senior managers and only 2.0 per cent of senior

managers are women from racialized groups (Adams and Welsh 2008). With the exception of people of Arab and Chinese descent, non-white men and women are overrepresented in working-class jobs (Isajiw 1999; Kelly 2002), and racialized women are overrepresented among domestic workers in Canada (Arat-Koc 1995).

Ethnic and racial employment inequality in Canada becomes even more apparent when we consider the dynamics of labour and income together. Research by Reitz, Curtis, and Elrick (2014) show that university-educated immigrants are more numerous in Canada today, but their access to skilled occupations in the professions and management declined between 1996 and 2006. Surprisingly, the decline in access since 2001 coincided with increased program efforts, including foreign credential assessment and bridge-training, which implies that numerous structural barriers exist that impede immigrant access to "good jobs." Even more discouraging is the fact that when ethnic and racial minorities obtain higher-status jobs, they are rarely (if ever) paid salaries comparable to those of native-born white workers. According to this research, the economic impact measured in total annual earnings lost owing to immigrant skill utilization has grown from about $4.80 billion in 1996 to over $11.37 billion in 2006 (Reitz et al. 2014).

Data on the relationship between self-employment and ethnicity or "race" are rather scarce. However, using 1989 Canadian Social Survey data, Nakhaie (1995) shows that, among men, those from German and Jewish backgrounds are much more likely to be a part of the old middle class while men of French or Italian origin are more likely to be a part of the working class. Finally, Jewish male immigrants are much more likely to be a part of the bourgeoisie than are those from any other ethnic group. Among women and compared with men, higher proportions of each ethnic group are part of the working class. As was the case among the men, women of German and Jewish backgrounds are more likely to be a part of the old middle class, and those who have either French or Italian backgrounds are more likely to be a part of the working class. Peter S. Li (2001a) shows that immigrants often rely on self-employment to supplement their labour-market income and that immigrants with higher educational attainment are more likely to engage in self-employment. Li also shows that immigrants from Asia, Latin America, and Africa are least likely to engage in self-employment. Using more recent data, Hou and Wang (2011) find that more immigrants are consistently self-employed than non-immigrants in Canada. By the late 2000s, nearly 19 per cent of immigrant workers were self-employed compared with 15 per cent of the Canadian-born. These comparisons are displayed in more detail in Figure 9.1.

Along with class, gender, ethnicity, and race, age also structures paid work. Younger workers are disproportionately less well represented among the self-employed (Adams and Welsh 2008: 283). Labour-force participation rates for young adults (aged 15–24) rose throughout the 1970s and 1980s and then declined during the 1990s. In 2012, 63.6 per cent of young adults were working for pay (Krahn, Lowe, and Hughes 2014: 71). Young workers tend to be segregated in low-paid, often part-time service-sector jobs (Allahar and Côté 1998; Krahn, Lowe, and Hughes 2014) even though their educational attainment rates are higher than those of previous cohorts (Lowe 2000).

Older workers are overrepresented among the self-employed (Hou and Wang 2011; Adams and Welsh 2008: 283). The labour-force participation rate for men aged 55–64 declined throughout the 1970s and 1980s from a high of 76 per cent in 1976 to a low of 58 per cent in 1995. By 2014, that rate remained about the same (59.5 per cent), a slight decline from the early 2000s. The labour-force participation rate for same-aged women, on the other hand, steadily increased from 32 per cent in 1976 to 48.3 per cent in 2014 (K. Marshall and Ferrao 2007; Statistics Canada 2015). For women, the rate is a result of overall trends toward retirement before the age of 65 as well as of the contrary trend of increased overall female labour-force participation. Further, statistics on women's retirement are complicated by whether women define themselves through their husband's status or whether they consider that they "retired" 30 years ago when they left the labour market to raise their children (Connidis 1982; Street and Connidis 2001).

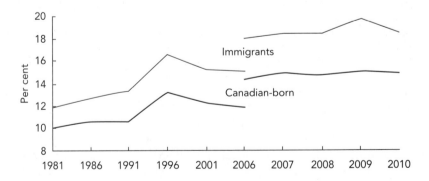

Figure 9.1 Self-employment as a Percentage of Total Employed Individuals by Immigration Status

Source: Statistics Canada, Census of Population, 1981 to 2006; Labour Force Survey, 2006 to 2010. www.statcan.gc.ca/pub/75-001-x/2011003/charts-graphiques/11500/cg00a-eng.htm

The class and occupational position of older workers depends a great deal on the class and occupational positions they have held throughout their working lives. Using life-course research, some scholars have examined the cumulative advantage/disadvantage hypothesis as it pertains to inequality in paid work. According to this hypothesis, the heterogeneity between groups of people increases over time. For the purpose of this discussion, the **cumulative advantage/disadvantage hypothesis** argues that individuals are born with specific class, gender, and racial or ethnic characteristics that provide them with a certain amount of advantage or disadvantage. Initially, there may be little separation between the haves and the have-nots on the basis of these distinctions. However, as time passes, the separation between the advantaged and disadvantaged grows and age groups become increasingly heterogeneous (Dannefer and Sell 1988). This occurs because the economic and social values attached to productive work depend on one's gender, race or ethnicity, class, and age (O'Rand 1996a, 1996b).

Younger and older workers are more likely to be employed in non-standard work. Non-standard employment includes part-time work, multiple jobs, temporary work, and own-account self-employment (Krahn, Lowe, and Hughes 2014: 103). In 2002, non-standard work accounted for one-third of all employment, an increase of about 5 per cent from 1989 (Krahn, Lowe, and Hughes 2014). In 2012, 47 per cent of younger workers (aged 15–24) and nearly 25 per cent of older workers (aged 55–64) worked part-time. Younger workers are much more likely to be employed as temporary workers than are workers in other age groups (Krahn, Lowe, and Hughes 2014). Box 9.3 provides an international example of Taiwanese part-time workers. As this evidence shows, part-time workers in Taiwan are now receiving some of the lowest wages in recent history.

Global perspective

Box 9.3 Income Inequality in Taiwan

New research shows that the income levels of part-time workers in Taiwan have reached the lowest point they have been in years (Huang n.d.). A Ministry of Labor (MOL) survey of 3,005 workers from 2007 and 2014 found that the average part-time Taiwanese worker earned only about NT (New Taiwan Dollar) $12,385 per month (about $485 in Canadian dollars). According to the Ministry of Labor, the incomes of part-time workers have now fallen to their lowest levels since 2004. In 2014, nearly 397,000 people were part-time workers (or, 3.6 per cent of the total population in Taiwan). Unfortunately, part-time work has become a norm for many Taiwanese workers and once people fall into the trap of part-time work, it becomes very difficult to climb out of it. The MOL found that Taiwanese workers had worked on average 2.3 years of part-time work in their lives. However, 11.8 per cent had worked part-time for at least 5 years (Liu 2014). These data show that income inequality for Taiwan's labor force has been steadily rising. For example, in 2006 the Council of Labor Affairs conducted a similar study of 9,000 Taiwanese workers. Those in the service industry in 2006 earned NT$22,747 on average each month (or, 0.62 times the salary of the "average" worker). However, managers (NT$59,960) and professionals such as doctors (NT$91,696) and pilots (NT$152,239) all earn very high salaries—over seven times as high in the case of pilots—compared with service workers.

Source: John Liu. (December 10, 2014). "Part-time workers' earnings the lowest on record: MOL." *China Post.*; Shelley Huang. (August 24, 2014) "Average Taiwanese worker's salary increases slightly." *Taipei Times.*

For women, rates of part-time and other non-standard employment tend to be higher than for men, regardless of age and geographic location. The difference is greatest in the middle years (ages 35–54), probably because of family responsibilities (Krahn, Hughes, and Lowe 2015). This suggests that the specific nature of non-standard work varies throughout the life courses of men and women. Young workers (under the age of 15) are likely to engage in part-time work while they attend school. For older workers, non-standard work could be a choice they have made so that they can retire gradually; some older workers may engage in non-standard employment because they have lost their jobs and are having difficulties finding new ones (see the section on unemployment below).

To understand how age relations influence production processes, we need a life-course approach that documents the age composition of the occupation and class structures with longitudinal data. Unfortunately, this kind of labour market research has not yet been done in North America. Nonetheless, in 1995 Gordon Betcherman and Norman Leckie used 1991 census data to document the age structures of employment in industries and occupations. They showed that the age structures of industries and occupations may be classified in one of five ways: (1) uniform age distribution (age occupational/industrial distribution is the same as it is in the population as a whole); (2) youth overrepresented; (3) "prime age" groups overrepresented; (4) older workers overrepresented; and (5) "prime age" groups underrepresented.

One of the most notable findings from Betcherman and Leckie's (1995) research is that only two industries (construction and wholesale trade) and no occupational groups had a uniform age distribution. Furthermore, young workers and, to a lesser extent, older workers were concentrated in "bad job" industrial sectors and prime-age workers were concentrated in "good job" sectors. Regarding industry, Betcherman and Leckie showed that in 1991 older workers were overrepresented in the resource sector (e.g., agriculture and fishing); parts of the manufacturing sector (e.g., clothing and primary textile); the transportation, communication, and utilities sector; and some parts of retail services (e.g., general retail and furniture and appliances). Young workers were overrepresented in all parts of retail trade, accommodation, food and beverage services, and other services. Prime-age workers were overrepresented in some parts of the manufacturing sector; the finance, insurance, and real estate sector; and the business services sector. Regarding occupation, Betcherman and Leckie found that prime-age workers were overrepresented in most professional and technical occupations, managerial occupations, production occupations, crafts, and trades. Younger workers were overrepresented in clerical, sales, and service occupations, whereas older workers were overrepresented in some service occupations and resource-sector occupations.

Discussions about the "new economy" point to the importance of social time in assessments of inequality in paid work. Tied to globalization (see Box 9.2 above) and the proliferation of information technology, the organization of work in the new knowledge-based economies is quite different from the organization of work in older industrial economies. Work in the new economy is characterized by greater individualism, job insecurity, risk, and instability. Hence, compared with workers in the industrial economy, workers in new economies are much less likely to be employed in the same job for life, and this has implications for how the life courses of individuals are organized (McMullin and Marshall 2010; V.W. Marshall et al. 2001). There is increased pressure on workers to manage their own careers and to engage in lifelong learning to keep pace with technological changes. Workplaces are being restructured, and firms are recruiting employees with more knowledge-based skills (Adams and McQuillan 2000) and placing more emphasis on flexible and non-standard employment.

Like Canada, other countries around the world have struggled to remain competitive in a global market that favours knowledge-based industry. This is true in less developed parts of the world. For example, in recent years Rwanda's economy has rapidly shifted from an agricultural to a knowledge-based economy. Box 9.4 discusses the inability of many Rwandan workers to keep pace with this change.

Global perspective

Box 9.4 Rwanda's Job Crunch

by Honoré Banda

In a landlocked country without natural resources, pushing the service sector and investing in technology is a fine idea. One snag: the strategy has produced too few skilled jobs. Many are now questioning whether the focus should shift to agribusiness and manufacturing.

Agnes Umutoni, 25, wakes up every morning to report to work. By 6.30 am at the latest, she is at the premises of a new hotel on the outskirts of Kigali to prepare the counter for yet another hectic day.

She works at the hotel as a receptionist for six days a week until 10 pm. For the 15 hours a day she works, Umutoni takes home a net salary of RWF100,000 ($145) per month.

"It is better than sitting home all day. For that amount, I pay my rent and afford basic needs but I cannot pay my university tuition yet. I want to go back to school," she says. She already holds a diploma in public administration.

"It is insufficient because the cost of living in Kigali is very high. I'm still looking out for better-paying jobs, but it is very difficult to find a job in Kigali. I know so many people who are unemployed, yet they completed university."

Umutoni is among the thousands of Rwandans employed in the country's much-vaunted service sector who live hand to mouth despite having work.

Stark Choices

When hammering out Rwanda's national business plan, the drafters at the top of the ruling party are faced with stark choices. The country is landlocked and lacks natural resources.

Manufacturing and trade in goods is difficult even with perfect infrastructure.

The government's Vision 2020 strategy is focused on Rwanda transforming itself from an agricultural to a knowledge-based economy.

"Technology is increasingly becoming part of the daily life of every citizen," insisted President Paul Kagame in his December 2014 state of the nation address.

The government wants Kigali to be a regional hub for high-value services in sectors such as technology, finance, tourism and real estate.

But will it work? Can the country gain enough critical mass to displace or complement other regional hubs like Nairobi?

One sceptical airline chief executive who prefers to stay nameless points to the several regional hops that planes take to pick up passengers before heading on intercontinental flights.

"There just aren't enough people transiting in and out of Kigali," he says. It may only be a question of time.

Rwanda's service sector has been among the most dynamic over the 2007–2013 period, with wholesale and retail trade, education, finance and insurance, and transport, storage and communications all growing at average rates in excess of 10% per year since 2007, figures from the UN Economic Commission for Africa (UNECA) show.

continued

The sector now accounts for half of Rwanda's gross domestic product.

"The Rwandan case study shows the difficulties of achieving structural transformation for low-income landlocked countries, even when the country possesses, by all accounts, a fairly efficient government bureaucracy and a policy environment which is generally amenable to private sector development" argues Andrew Mold, a Kigali-based economist with UNECA.

"But with bold policy initiatives, and by adopting a pragmatic, and where necessary heterodox, approach, it is possible to overcome the supply-side constraints," he explains.

International trade has been a key factor in expanding the Rwandan economy far beyond national markets, as exports of goods and services increased from $70m in 1995 to more than $859m in 2011.

Services increased as a share of total exports from 24 to 46% over that period, with a peak at 64% in 2009, according to the UN Conference on Trade and Development.

But Rwanda continues to run a large trade deficit, with the current account deficit expected to deteriorate to $803.2m in 2014 from $537.5m in 2013.

Despite the recent surge in service exports, agricultural commodities—in particular coffee and tea—remain an important source of export growth.

Critics ask if there are enough jobs in services to warrant a focus on the sector. Growth in the sector has been led by wholesale and retail trade businesses, real estate, telecommunications and financial services.

This has largely been driven by rapid urbanisation, though Rwanda remains among the lowest urbanised countries in the world.

Projections indicate that about 35% of the population will be living in cities by 2020.

Few New Positions

New companies in Rwanda's service sector have not delivered many jobs. The East Africa Exchange, a commodities exchange founded in 2012, employs 19 people directly.

Crane Bank Rwanda, a subsidiary of Uganda's fourth-largest bank, began operations in June 2014. It has two branches in Kigali and employs about 30 people.

Given Rwanda's rising population density—416 people/km2—which is among the highest in Africa, creating off-farm jobs is imperative.

The Kigali Conceptual Master Plan lies at the centre of Rwanda's aspiration to reposition itself regionally and globally as a sophisticated service economy.

Kigali's Central Business District includes the neighbourhoods of Muhima, Nyarugenge and Kimicanga.

It is envisaged that these areas be re-developed as the financial, business and entertainment centres for both Rwanda and the region.

The soon-to-be glitzy Kigali Convention Centre by the KG2 roundabout in Kimihurura is currently an inelegant sphere erupting from the ground but should provide the centrepiece for the government's business tourism strategy.

The Rwanda Development Board (RDB) argues that more than 70% of the jobs created in Kigali over the past decade have been in the services sector, particularly in sub-sectors such as telecommunications, finance and tourism.

However, a high proportion of this workforce is employed in low-productivity and poorly paid jobs on a casual basis and without access to the benefits of social security.

"The trend shows that we are heading towards our ambition. The issues of productivity and labour are always very complex in any market," says Francis Gatare, the RDB's chief executive, adding that more productive jobs will be created in the long run with more investment in technology and education.

Others say that quantity rather than quality is the issue.

"We have already made the transition from agriculture to mainly services and industry. There's still a lot that needs to be done," says Yusuf Murangwa, the director general of Rwanda's National Institute of Statistics.

"We still need to see a transition in terms of jobs: though the output is already big in terms of service compared with agriculture and industry, jobs are still less [productive]."

Social Inequality

And should the country be focusing on more job-intensive sectors instead? Some experts argue that as high-tech services demand specialised skills and create few jobs, their contribution to aggregate employment is bound to remain limited.

Manufacturing, on the other hand, can absorb large numbers of workers with moderate skills, providing them with stable jobs and good benefits.

For Dickson Malunda, a senior research fellow at the Institute of Policy Analysis and Research–Rwanda, the government has to do more to attract investment in manufacturing and agro-processing in order to address inequality.

The failure to create decent jobs in the service sector has contributed to the uneven distribution of income and other benefits of growth, making Rwanda one of the most unequal countries in the region.

Statistics from the World Bank for 2011, the most recent year available, show that the top 10% of the population took 43.2% of national income while the bottom 10% took 2.1%.

"In just one decade, most East African economies reduced the share of agriculture in the economy and substantially increased that of the service sector.

"While there is no problem with this, the ability of the service sector to provide decent employment opportunities for rural migrants is weak," observes a 2014 Millennium Development Goals report, pointing out that less than 10% of the working population in most East African countries is formally employed.

That matters in every country. But in a country where the trade-off for curtailed civil liberties is enhanced economic progress, it may matter more.

Source: Honoré Banda. (Feb. 12, 2015) Rwanda's job crunch." *The Africa Report*. www.theafricareport.com/East-Horn-Africa/rwandas-job-crunch.html

In summary, this section shows how classes and occupations are organized according to gender, ethnicity, race, age, and social time. Why does this matter? Because within advanced global capitalism, the intrinsic and extrinsic privileges and rewards that are attached to class position and occupations are different. Hence, the likelihood of being employed in a good job or a bad job—or, for that matter, employed at all—depends not only on one's class, but also on gender, ethnicity, race, and age. The next three sections of this chapter consider three outcomes of inequality—unemployment, levels of income and poverty, and degree of alienation and skill—that are tied to production processes.

Unemployment

Job security has traditionally been one of the most important extrinsic rewards that employment can offer. Individuals who are employed in the primary sector and in unionized occupations have high levels of job security, whereas those who are employed in the secondary sector and in non-unionized environments have low levels of job security. Of course, unions and collective-bargaining processes are gendered and racialized and have served the interests of older, white men at the expense of others (Creese 1996, 1999). Although labour laws exist in Canada to make it illegal to fire employees wrongfully, the extent to which these laws are upheld is questionable, especially for people in jobs that are unstable in the first place.

People who lose their jobs are more liable to experience poverty, homelessness, and distress (Adams and Welsh 2008; Avison, Wade, and Thorpe 1996). In Canada, the rates and duration of unemployment vary on the basis of region, industry, occupation, age, gender, and race. As Map 9.1 shows, unemployment rates in the Atlantic provinces are higher than those in the rest of Canada. This pattern is largely a result of the extent to which a particular region is economically diverse. In the Atlantic provinces, for instance, the heavy reliance on the fishing industry makes for high unemployment. The decline in the manufacturing sector has hit Ontario quite hard and unemployment rates are on the rise as a result. This points to the connection between unemployment and each of occupation and industry. In industries such as manufacturing and construction where there are higher concentrations of working-class jobs, unemployment and layoffs are more likely. Although professional and highly skilled occupations are not as well protected from unemployment as they once were, unemployment is still less likely in professional and highly skilled occupations (Krahn, Lowe, and Hughes 2014).

Although men and women have historically had quite different unemployment rates, their relative disadvantage with unemployment varied until the mid-1980s, when some convergence occurred. During the 1950s and until about 1966, women had lower rates of unemployment than men. From 1966 until about 1990, unemployment rates for men were lower than or similar to the rates for women. Such trends defy simple explanation, but they probably have a lot to do with the types of jobs women were employed in during the 1950s and 1960s as well as with the social stigma that was attached to unemployment during that time. During the 1950s and 1960s, women were usually employed in teaching and service positions, sectors that have always had lower rates of unemployment than blue-collar areas of employment (Krahn, Lowe, and Hughes 2014). Also, some women who were unemployed during this period may not have defined themselves as such but rather as housewives because of the social acceptability of the latter

status. Regardless of why there was such divergence in the unemployment rates for men and women, the important point is that there has been convergence in these rates since 1990. It should be noted, however, that women and other groups more likely to have non-standard work patterns may be undercounted in official unemployment statistics (Pulkingham 1998).

Unemployment rates and employment success vary with ethnicity and race (Reitz 2007). Members of ethnic- and visible-minority groups and recent immigrants have relatively high levels of unemployment. For example, in 2011 in Ontario, the employment rate for the Canadian-born was about 83 per cent compared with only about 75 per cent for immigrants. In Quebec, the employment rate for immigrants was the lowest of the Canadian provinces at only about 70 per cent compared with about 83 per cent among the native-born (Statistics Canada 2011). Among the Aboriginal population in Canada, unemployment is endemic. The rate of unemployment for Aboriginals living on reserves was 37.7 per cent in 2001 (Statistics Canada 2006a: 97). In 1996, almost one in four (24 per cent) of Aboriginal labour-force participants was unemployed, and the rate was even higher for young Aboriginal workers (32 per cent) and for Aboriginal men (35 per cent).

Finally, unemployment varies with age. According to McGregor (2001), in the 1990s the unemployment rate increased more dramatically for older workers (those aged 55–64) than for members of any other age group, and between 1976 and 1998 the increase in unemployment rates for older workers was 30 per cent and 50 per cent for 55- to 59-year-olds and 60- to 64-year-olds respectively. However, older workers fared quite well compared with younger workers (aged 15–24), whose unemployment rate—higher to begin with—doubled during the same period (Krahn and Lowe 2014). In 1996, youth unemployment stood at about 12.6 per cent, whereas the unemployment rate

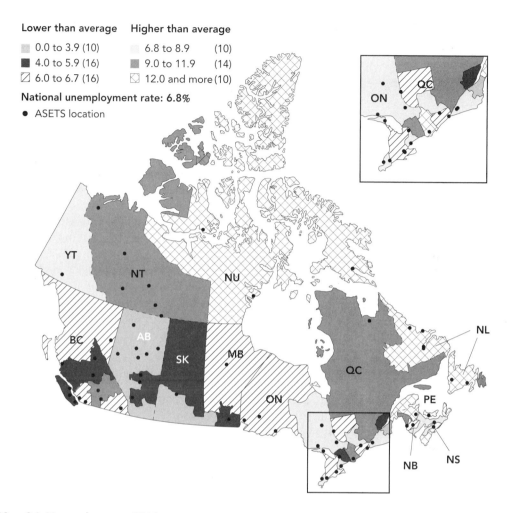

Lower than average
- 0.0 to 3.9 (10)
- 4.0 to 5.9 (16)
- 6.0 to 6.7 (16)

Higher than average
- 6.8 to 8.9 (10)
- 9.0 to 11.9 (14)
- 12.0 and more (10)

National unemployment rate: 6.8%
- ● ASETS location

Map 9.1 Unemployment 2014

Note: Estimates are based on 3-month moving averages; bracketed numbers in the legend represent the breakdown of unemployment levels among Canada's 76 economic regions in January 2014.

Source: Map generated by ESDC Geomatics Services; data from Statistics Canada. 2011 Labour Force Survey.

for adults aged 55–64 was only 7 per cent, somewhat lower than the unemployment rate for the population as a whole. And by 2014 (www.tradingeconomics.com), the youth unemployment rate had hardly changed (12.8 per cent), whereas the unemployment rate for those aged 25–54 and over had dropped to 5.1 per cent (Statistics Canada 2014).

However, we must be cautious in interpreting these statistics. Indeed, it is highly likely that biases in definitions of "unemployment" lead to an underestimation of the problem of unemployment among older people. Compared with younger workers, older workers are unemployed for longer periods of time (Statistics Canada 2004b), and agist stereotypes often work against older workers in finding employment (McMullin and Berger 2006). As McGregor (2001) points out, only 67 per cent of men and 45 per cent of women between the ages of 55 and 59 and 41 per cent of men and 22 per cent of women between the ages of 60 and 64 were employed in 1996. This—combined with overall increases in unemployment rates for older workers, the difficulty distinguishing between involuntary and voluntary retirement, and the rise in non-standard employment among this group—suggests that many older workers are having increasing difficulty in finding work.

Income and Poverty

The wage-exchange relationship is a crucial process of distribution in capitalism (see the centre of the coalescence framework in Figure 7.3 in chapter 7) and one that is intimately linked to production processes. Workers exchange their labour power for a wage that equals less than the market value of what they produce. The **surplus value** that is created in this exchange produces

a profit for the owners of capital. As a result, there is a strong correlation between social class and income. This relationship holds for each of the societies discussed in this book. Working-class jobs pay less than middle-class jobs, and owners of capital tend to have higher incomes than others (Krahn, Lowe, and Hughes 2014). For instance, according to www.payscale.com, average annual earnings in Canada for dentists ($101,343), lawyers ($71,955), and associate professors ($99,098) were much higher than were the average annual earnings for cashiers ($20,343) and hairstylists ($30,003). These earnings stand in stark contrast to the incomes of the chief executive officers (CEOs) of large companies. In 2010, the average compensation package for Canadian CEOs in Canadian companies was $2.5 million. CEO income and compensation is even higher in the United States. As Figure 9.2 shows, the top 100 CEOs earned well over $10 million in the United States (2000 data).

However, a strong correlation between social class and income does not mean that

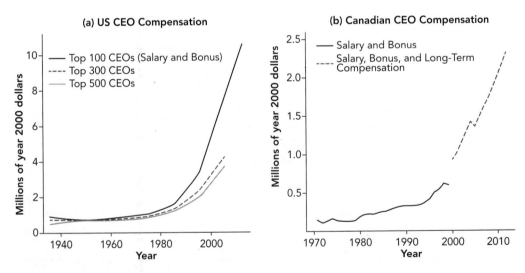

Figure 9.2 US/Canadian CEO Compensation

Source: Andersen, Robert and Mitch McIvor (2014) "Rising Inequality and Its Impact in Canada: The Role of National Debt", In *Changing Inequalities and Societal Impacts in Thirty Rich Countries: Thirty Countries' Experiences*, edited by Brian Nolan, Wiemer Salverda, Daniele Checchi, Ive Marx, Abigail McKnight, István György Tóth and Herman van de Werfhorst. Oxford: Oxford University Press.

it is a perfect correlation. There are certain jobs that, on the basis of the above definitions of social class, would be considered working-class jobs even though they command a relatively high wage. For example, traditionally, assembly-line workers in any of the "big three" auto-manufacturing plants, though part of the working class, were paid a relatively good wage and had good benefits because they were members of a relatively strong union. However, with the rise in globalization, steep economic recessions, free-trade agreements, and the like, such well-paid working-class jobs seem to be on the decline.

From the income figures listed above we can see clearly that owners of capital and executives have much higher incomes than workers. The question that remains is whether there has been an increasing polarization of income over time. One way to answer this question is to divide Canadians into equal groups (either deciles or quintiles) on the basis of their income, calculate the proportion of the total income in Canada that each group receives, and then examine whether that proportion has changed. In 1980, 40.4 per cent of all before-tax income was concentrated in the top quintile of the Canadian population, 23.9 per cent in the fourth quintile, 19.1 per cent in the third (middle) quintile, 11.6 per cent in the second quintile, and only 5 per cent in the lowest quintile. Between 1981 and 2010, the second, third, fourth, and fifth quintiles either remained stable or declined slightly. By 2010, families in the highest income quintile increased their market share by 5.9 per cent (or, 46.3 per cent total). By 2010, the top income quintile increase its average income by $49,400 (from $128,500 in 1980 to $177,900 in 2010). By comparison, the fifth quintile (i.e., the bottom 20 per cent) only gained $1,700 during this 30-year period (Andersen and McIvor 2013). All told, these figures support the idea that there is increasing polarization of income in Canada. Since the 1980s, it is only the top-income quintile that has gained any ground. The earnings

of all other Canadians have remained stable (or stagnant).

What these figures do not tell us is that this stability has been maintained largely through government transfers such as tax credits, social assistance, and unemployment insurance. Indeed, for low-income families, the proportion of their total income that comes from labour-market earnings has declined since the 1970s (Picot and Myles 1995; Statistics Canada 2005c). Hence, income polarization is not as serious as it could be because government policies ensure more-equitable income distributions in Canada (Ross, Shillington, and Lochhead 1994). But how equitable is a system in which the lowest quintile receives only 4.6 per cent of all before-tax income? And how equitable is a system in which the $15-billion gain made in the upper quintile during the 1980s and 1990s is equivalent to the amount of money it would take to eliminate poverty in Canada (Osberg 1992, cited in Urmetzer and Guppy 2004)?

Historically, women's wages have been less than men's. In 1931, the average wage for employed women in Canada was 60 per cent that of an employed man's average wage. By 1997, women, on average, earned 63.8 per cent of the average employed man's salary (Phillips and Phillips 2000). Obviously, some of the variation between women's and men's incomes exists because more women (27.7 per cent) than men (10.2 per cent) work part-time (Beaujot 2000, using 1996 data). Yet even among full-year, full-time workers, women earned only about 68.5 per cent as much as men in 2011 (Cornish 2014). Interesting variations across countries are evident in Figure 9.3. Though Canada has a reputation of being an egalitarian country, it may be surprising that we rank only twentieth when it comes to gender equality. Among all OECD countries, Canada ranks fourth worst for gender wage inequality (ahead of only South Korea, Japan, and Germany).

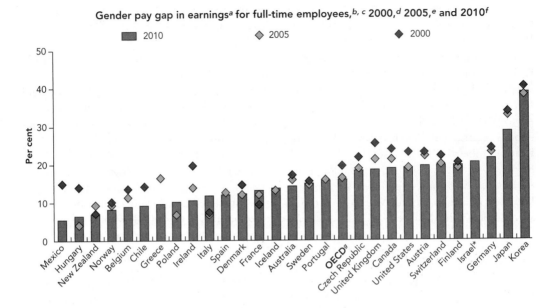

Figure 9.3 The Gender Wage Gap in Cross-National Perspective

Note: Countries are arranged in ascending order or gender gap for median earnings in 2010.

* Information on data for Israel: http://dx.doi.org/10.1787/888932315602

a. The wage gap is defined as the difference between male and female median wages divided by male median wages.

b. Estimates of earnings used in the calculations refer to gross earnings of full-time wage and salary workers. Self-employed women and unpaid family workers are not included in the calculations. However, this definition may slightly vary from one country to another. Further information on the national data sources and earnings concepts used in the calculations can be found at: www.oecd.org/employment/outlook.

c. Data is not adjusted for parity of time worked among full-time employees.

d. Data refer to 1999 (instead of 2000) for the Czech Republic.

e. Data refer to 2004 (instead of 2005) for Italy and Switzerland.

f. Data refer to 2009 (instead of 2010) for Austria, the Czech Republic, Demark, Finland, Germany, Ireland, Israel, Korea, Sweden, and Switzerland; to 2008 for Belgium, France, Greece, Iceland, Italy, Poland, Portugal, and Spain.

g. OECD unweighted average excluding Mexico and Chile.

Source: Metadata from OECD.stat. www.oecd.org/gender/closingthegap.htm

One reason women earn less than men in Canada is that they are disproportionately employed in low-paid occupations and industries and in occupations and industries that are considered to require little **skill**. But even in the 20 most highly paid occupations—occupations that are disproportionately held by men—women earn less than their male counterparts. For instance, in 2010 women made up 39.7 per cent of the total employment among judges, 36.6 per cent of specialist physicians, and 32.4 per cent of dentists. In these occupations (with judges being the exceptions), men earned on average much more than women. Among senior managers in the goods-producing industrial sector, women accounted for 23.0 per cent of the total employment and earned an average of only 77.0 per cent of the average male salary. In fact, more generally, in Ontario new evidence suggests that the average gender pay gap may in fact be rising (Krahn, Lowe, and Hughes 2014).

Wages were also linked to gendered processes of reproduction. Among full-time, full-year workers, parental status influences the personal incomes of both men and women. In 1976, mothers with children ($28,000) had lower incomes than fathers who had children at home ($53,000). By 2008, average earnings for single mothers had risen to $42,300 and to $60,400 for single fathers. Although single mothers made greater net gains than single fathers from 1976 to 2008 (14,300 versus 7,100), it is striking that fathers with children in 1976 still earned more than mothers with children in 2008 ($11,100 more). This speaks to the level of inequality that women still face in Canadian society today (Williams 2010).

Wages and income also vary with ethnicity and race (see Beaujot and Kerr 2003). Statistics Canada (2010a) reports the average incomes of various visible minority groups. For example, Japanese immigrants had the highest average income ($46,222), followed by those of Chinese ethnicity. The lowest visible-minority earners in Canada were Latin Americans ($33,960) (Statistics Canada 2010). Indeed, on average, workers of colour earn 16.3 per cent less than all other workers. Among men, workers of colour earn 17 per cent less than all other workers. The difference is smaller for women, with workers of colour earning 12 per cent less than all other workers (Jackson 2002). And the income disadvantages for racialized persons remain when education and other social variables are taken into account (Lian and Matthews 1998). As is the case for women, occupational and industrial segregation of particular ethnic- and visible-minority groups accounts for much of the ethnic and racial variation in income.

Much of the research on the relationship between income and ethnic- and racial-minority groups has focused on poverty. If individuals have tenuous ties to labour markets or if they are employed in bad jobs, poverty often results.

Poverty is a serious social problem in Canada. The National Council of Welfare (2006a) reports that although poverty rates declined between 1996 and 2001, there was still a higher poverty rate in 2001 (15.5 per cent) than there was in 1989 (14 per cent). Approximately 16 per cent of Canadians were poor in 2003; poverty rates were about 12 per cent for families and about 38 per cent for unattached individuals. Although the NCW provided a rich source for Canadian data on income inequality, government funding for the NCW was eliminated by the Harper government. Even though a new Liberal government is now in power, it remains to be seen whether this program will be reinstated.

As a group, Aboriginal people in Canada suffer extreme financial deprivation and hardship and have higher rates of poverty (43.4 per cent) than non-Aboriginal people in Canada (19.3 per cent) (Ross, Scott, and Smith 2000). According to one study, 54 per cent of Aboriginal Canadians earned less than $10,000 per year, compared with 35 per cent of all Canadians (R. Armstrong 1999). Unfortunately, the "best-off" First Nations communities in Canada are more disadvantaged than the "worst-off" non-Aboriginal areas, which demonstrates that the most advantaged First Nations communities are still significantly disadvantaged when compared with the least advantaged non-Aboriginal communities (R. Armstrong 1999: 17).

Racialized persons are more likely to live in poverty and to have a longer duration of poverty than other Canadians (A. Jackson 2002). Compared with the total Canadian population (29.5 per cent), higher proportions of visible-minority immigrants (42.5 per cent) and Aboriginal persons living off reserves (49.4 per cent) lived in poverty for at least one year between 1993 and 1998. Furthermore, members of visible-minority groups and Aboriginal persons are more liable to be poor for two years or more (A. Jackson 2002; Ross, Scott, and Smith 2000).

There are significant regional variations in poverty rates in Canada. In 2003, British Columbia had the highest poverty rate (20.1 per cent), followed by Newfoundland and Labrador (17.3 per cent) and Manitoba (16.9 per cent). Prince Edward Island had the lowest poverty rate (11.8 per cent). Provincial variations in poverty rates are a result of regional differences in economic structures, provincial inconsistencies in government policies regarding social welfare transfers, and differential access to other social and economic resources (National Council of Welfare 2006b).

Poverty rates also vary on the basis of gender, age, education, and labour-force attachment. For instance, in 2003 the poverty rate for single-parent mothers was 48.9 per cent, more than four times the poverty rate for all families. Unattached women under the age of 65 were more likely to be poor than were their male counterparts (42.8 per cent versus 34.4 per cent respectively) as were unattached women aged 65 and over (40.9 per cent compared with 31.6 per cent). Compared with all Canadians (16 per cent), children were somewhat more likely to be poor (17.6 per cent). Being gainfully employed significantly reduces poverty rates among both unattached individuals and families; yet the poverty rate, which was 6.2 per cent for families with two earners, was higher for families with one earner, at 25.2 per cent. Finally, families in which the major earner was a woman were more likely to be living in poverty than were families in which the major earner was a man. This was true even when education level was held constant (National Council of Welfare 2006b). Evidence also suggests that single mothers, older adults (especially women), young people (aged 15–24), children (especially under age 6), and those with less than a high school education experienced durations of poverty that lasted two years or more (Ross, Scott, and Smith 2000).

The fact that rates of poverty are higher and that poverty lasts longer among young people, children, and older adults suggests that there is a significant relationship between income and age. Table 9.1 shows the average "real" earnings for men and women of "working age" in 2008. The average income difference for men between the ages of 45 and 54 compared with men between the ages of 55 and 64 ($10,300) was only $200 less than it was for same-aged women ($11,500). This suggests that the impact of age on earnings is about the same for men as it is for women. Average earnings are lowest among the 16–24 age group, largely as a result of voluntary part-time work and minimum-wage legislation that allows employers to pay teenagers under the age of 18 less than those over the age of 18 (Williams 2010).

In the 25 to 54 age group, younger men earned on average 76 per cent (ages 25 to 34) and 96 per cent (ages 35 to 44) of the average income of men aged 45 to 54. For women, the experience gradient was not as large. On average younger women (between the ages of 25 and 44) earned between 89 per cent and 101 per cent of the average income among older women (those aged 45 to 54).

Although not shown in Table 9.1, average incomes of both men and women aged 65 and over are lower than they are for working-age Canadians, largely because of retirement. In 2010, adults aged 65 and over had average incomes of about $25,201.

Table 9.1 Average Total Income of Women and Men, by Age Group, 2008

Age Group	Women	Men
	Dollars	
Total age 16 and over	30,100	47,000
16 to 19	7,100	7,800
20 to 24	15,100	21,100
25 to 34	32,500	43,200
35 to 44	36,300	59,900
45 to 54	40,900	63,700
55 to 64	29,400	53,400
65 and over	24,800	38,100

Source: Statistics Canada, CANSIM table 202-0407. www.statcan.gc.ca/pub/89-503-x/2010001/article/11388/tbl/tbl002-eng.htm

This compares with an average income of about $38,589 for persons in the 25 to 34 and 35 to 44 age groups and with an average income of $52,539 for persons 45 to 54, and $48,590 for persons 55 to 64 (Statistics Canada 2011). In the United States, the risk of experiencing poverty in later life is greatest for racialized women, unmarried women, and racialized men (Hardy and Hazelrigg 1995). Although research on the intersection of race and age is limited in Canada, evidence regarding the income disadvantages and poverty faced by older Aboriginal Canadians (Gyimah, White, and Maxim 2004) suggests that similar racial and age trends exist in Canada.

Alienation and Skill

Recall that Marx's third prediction with respect to the polarization of classes was that as capitalism developed, jobs would become increasingly deskilled and alienated. Indeed, skill and alienation are both characteristics of paid work that vary with social class. Generally, working-class jobs are characterized by the low levels of skill required to do the job and often by corresponding high levels of alienation, whereas jobs held by those in the new middle class and the old middle class tend to require more skill and to be more intrinsically rewarding. Therefore, for Marx's prediction to be supported, we must see evidence that middle-class jobs have become increasingly deskilled.

Following Marxist traditions, Harry Braverman's (1974) classic book *Labor and Monopoly Capitalism* depicts the imbalance of power between workers and capitalists, which he argues would ultimately lead to a deskilling of labour. Braverman argues that as capitalists attempted to maximize profit, they would simultaneously seek to gain the maximum amount of control over the "pace and manner" of the labour process in order to gain the most value from workers' labour power. According to Braverman, this was the sole, and the fundamental, prerogative of the capitalist ruling class. The drive for economic gain would lead business owners to systematically centralize both skills and knowledge under the control of management, ultimately casting the "worker" as a "manipulable" element of the production process (Smith 1997).

Taking issue with those who believed that rising white-collar employment was a positive effect of post-industrialism that resulted in an increasingly large middle class, Braverman convincingly argues that most white-collar jobs (e.g., clerical and retail jobs) should be considered working class, not middle class. White-collar jobs, Braverman argues, were increasingly being deskilled and organized according to scientific management techniques that eliminated most of the control and autonomy that workers may have previously had over their work. Advances in new technologies contributed to this process by giving managers sophisticated tools with which they could monitor their employees' work. Before computerized cash registers, for example, cashiers needed to know how to make change. Now cash registers tell the cashier how much change to give the customer. Furthermore, cash registers can now monitor the speed of keystrokes and the number of customers a cashier serves per minute. Managers use this information to evaluate their employees' job performance. Hence, new technology has been used both to deskill the work process and to monitor and control it.

One year before Braverman published his book, Daniel Bell published what was to become an influential text on post-industrial society, *The Coming of Post-Industrial Society*. Unlike Braverman, who argues that occupations were becoming increasingly deskilled, Bell (1973) looked to the future and argued that knowledge, and hence skill, would become a highly valued commodity in post-industrial society. Bell prophesizes that the United States economy would "structurally differentiate" (1973: 173) into a post-industrial service economy that rewarded skill and knowledge over efficiency. Knowledge would be a basis of power much as the ownership of property had traditionally been, and knowledge workers would form a significant class (both in number and in power) in their own right. Bell argues that as the proportion of knowledge workers grew, the historical trend toward the polarization of society into two central classes—the bourgeoisie and the proletariat—would lose speed.

In the 40 years since Bell and Braverman published their books, debates have ensued over which thesis better explains the relationship between skill and class structure in post-industrial society. Although such debates are far from resolved, Clement and Myles are worth quoting at length on the issue:

> We face either a postindustrial Nirvana of knowledge where everyone will be a brain surgeon, artist, or philosopher (Bell) or, alternatively, a post-industrial Hades where we shall be doomed to labour mindlessly in the service of capital (Braverman). When drawn in these terms, the historical debate is now no debate at all. Bell is the clear winner. Although much less than a knowledge revolution the net result of the shift to services has been to increase the requirements for people to think on the job. (Clement and Myles 1994: 72)

Furthermore, Clement and Myles point out that the growth in the services sector has brought both skilled and unskilled jobs, but they underscore the fact that, at least in Canada and the United States, unskilled service jobs are often entry jobs for new and younger workers rather than a basis for working-class formation. This—combined with the fact that these service jobs are now often exit jobs for older workers who have been displaced, discouraged, restructured, or forced to retire early—suggests that age may play a more significant role in labour-market inequality in the years to come. It is no coincidence that during the market restructuring of the 1980s and 1990s we began to see older workers greeting us in department stores or serving us in fast-food chains. As one older worker who lost his job as a computer programmer put it, "I can't find work. But, I'm not destitute yet so I don't need to sell running shoes and make 1/8 of the salary I was making before—like my friend is doing" (personal correspondence, January 2003).

In short, although the conditions of work in contemporary Canadian capitalism are far from ideal, the proletarianization of the labour force as predicted by Braverman has not occurred, even though skilled jobs are concentrated in the new middle and executive classes (Clement and Myles 1994). However, most of the literature on the deskilling debate has focused on class. More work must be done to consider whether and how jobs that are usually held by women or by members of racial- and ethnic-minority groups have been disproportionately deskilled. This requires critically examining the concept of skill itself and recognizing that gendered and racialized perceptions of skill have been driving these debates. Furthermore, when jobs are the unit of analysis (as is the case in this literature), important information regarding the "skill mobility" of individuals over their life courses is often missed.

Explaining Inequality in Paid Work

The preceding discussion shows that class, age, gender, race, and ethnicity structure the outcomes of inequality derived from paid work. And yet we know very little about how all of these structures work together in producing and reproducing market-based inequality. This points to the complexities associated with considering simultaneously all of these intersecting structures in analyses of paid work.

Labour-market segmentation perspectives help to explain many of the relative disadvantages that women, visible minorities, immigrants, ethnic minorities, and younger and older employees experience in paid work. According to these perspectives, good and bad jobs are located in different labour markets; the processes through which people get these jobs are different; there is little movement between these labour markets; and segregation within labour markets occurs on the basis of gender, race, ethnicity, and age. Bad jobs tend to be located in secondary labour markets, and good jobs in primary labour markets.

The dual-economy perspective is one of many models of labour-market segmentation. It posits that there is a core sector and a periphery sector in the economy. The core sector comprises large companies that face little competition for their product. These firms "exert considerable control over suppliers and markets and are also able to manipulate their political environment" (Krahn, Lowe, and Hughes 2014: 145). Examples of such companies are banks, telecommunication companies, automobile manufacturers, and airlines. The periphery sector of the economy, on the other hand, is dominated by smaller firms that are highly competitive with one another, are less profitable than firms in the core sector, have less political and economic power, and have lower rates of unionization. Examples of such companies are small manufacturing companies, retail outlets, and small hospitality firms. Jobs in this sector tend not to require as much skill or education as those in the core sector (Krahn, Lowe, and Hughes 2014: 145–6). According to this perspective, the reason women, people of colour, immigrants, ethnic minorities, and younger and older employees encounter labour-market disadvantages is that they are segregated in the periphery sector of the economy.

Unlike labour-market segmentation theories, which emphasize the structure of labour markets in explaining inequality, human-capital explanations of labour-market–based inequality suggest that individuals are sorted into good jobs and bad jobs on the basis of individual skill, education, and experience. Hence, those who invest more in these

things will reap greater labour-market rewards, especially higher incomes. We cannot dismiss human-capital explanations, for better education does lead to better jobs and better incomes regardless of gender, age (if we consider only prime working ages), ethnicity, and race. And yet a crucial theoretical difficulty with human-capital explanations of labour-market–based inequality is that they assume that there is free and open competition for good jobs and that everyone is on a level playing field when it comes to their ability to invest in or use their education. However, research shows that racialized persons have lower returns on educational investments and that racism exists in labour markets (Kazemipur and Halli 2001; P.S. Li 2001b; P.S. Li and Dong 2007; Nakhaie 2006). A crucial methodological difficulty with human-capital approaches is that the complex multivariate models used in assessing labour-market outcomes control for many variables but do not explain structural disadvantage.

The problem with human-capital explanations is that they often conclude that one factor accounts for more of (to give one example) the variation in income than another factor, all else being equal. The results of these models may suggest that a given bivariate relationship—between, for example, ethnicity and income—can be explained away by human-capital variables such as education, language, and experience. This then leads to the conclusion that human-capital variables account for differences in income and that ethnicity does not. Of course, what is missing in such conclusions is the fact that there are structural barriers that preclude certain ethnic- and visible-minority groups from attaining the human capital required for high incomes. All else is *not* equal, and adequate explanations of inequality must take that into account.

Structural barriers to good jobs and good wages feed on the logic of capitalism and its related assumptions about productive work, and they negatively affect labour-market outcomes for the working class, women, older and younger workers, particular ethnic groups, visible minorities, and Aboriginal people. As a result, all else is not equal for persons over the age of 65, who could be excluded from "productive" life as a result of mandatory or forced retirement. All else is not equal for 16-year-olds, who earn less than 18-year-olds doing the same job because of age-based minimum wages. All else is not equal for racialized persons, who face discrimination and racism in paid work and, before that, substandard education. And all else is not equal for women. Indeed, a second assumption under capitalism (and in human-capital theory) is that productivity increases with experience and that workers with more experience should therefore be paid higher wages. Yet experience is defined narrowly, and the skills and experience that are learned in "non-productive" activities, such as raising children, are not considered transferable to the realm of paid work. Furthermore, as Gillian Ranson's (2003) work on engineers shows, the combination of gender-minority status and lack of seniority makes it difficult for young women to challenge masculinist work cultures and career paths. Such difficulties are especially problematic in light of the fact that, among computer professionals, women earn significantly less than men (Dryburgh 2000; see also Gunderson, Jacobs, and Vaillancourt 2005: 110).

The organization of production processes does not stand in isolation, apart from the organization of distributive and reproductive processes. For instance, some argue that because women "choose" to work part-time, only data that compare income differences between full-year, full-time male and female employees should be considered. Yet for many women, part-time work is involuntary, and for others the choice to work part-time is conditioned by the ways in which class and gender relations structure the intersecting processes of production and reproduction.

Indeed, "choice" is a complex word in sociology. Some women choose not to work for pay because they believe that it is better for their children to have one parent at home when they are young. The one parent who stays at home is usually a mother, in part because mothers are most often employed in jobs that pay less than fathers earn. Furthermore, this is often an easy choice for women because the jobs that they are employed in tend not to be "good" jobs. From a particular family's point of view, this "choice" makes sense. Yet the choice is structured by gendered labour markets that pay women less and that employ them in jobs that are more alienating and less autonomous than the jobs that are more often held by men. Of course, this argument does not hold up well for working-class families. Indeed, family "choices" are structured by both the nature of jobs held by mothers and fathers within families and by gendered ideologies that suggest that women are better caregivers than men.

The most obvious link between distributive and productive processes is through the wage (see "Income and Poverty" earlier in this chapter). For people who have tenuous relationships to labour markets or earn very little, state-based mechanisms of distribution help to alleviate some of the financial strain such individuals face. Welfare policy, employment insurance, maternity and parental leave, Old Age Security, and publicly managed pension schemes are examples of state-based forms of distribution. These policies will be discussed in greater detail in chapter 12 when we discuss the state.

Beyond Statistics: Agency and Experience in Paid Work

It is clear that gender, class, age, ethnicity, and race are structural barriers to securing good, well-paid employment in Canada. But how do the choices that people make intersect with these structures in creating systems of advantage and disadvantage? How do women, the working class, older and younger workers, and racialized people experience the "isms" that infiltrate paid work? Helen Ralston's (1996) study of immigrant women in Atlantic Canada demonstrates how racialized women experience the double-edged sword of diminished labour-market returns on their education combined with public re-employment policies that do not target those who have university educations. In the words of one of Ralston's (1996: 87) informants,

> If you want to go to a programme in Manpower and Immigration, if you have a degree they are not even going to look at you. They say you have a degree. But you take that degree and go for a job and they say, "Oh, we don't know this degree. We won't hire you." They won't say it in so many words, but that's the implication. So I think you lose on both ends.

Once employed, subtle and overt racism, sexism, and agism are often experienced at work (Das Gupta 2002; McMullin and Marshall 2001). Within the structures of class, age, gender, race, and ethnicity, people make choices about the paid work that they will do. In making these choices, people often conform to structural expectations about what kind of work they should do. Women work as nurses; men work as engineers. When people resist social structures and make choices of paid work that go against the grain, they are often required to conform to established structures and to the middle-class white male way of life.

Conclusion

As noted in the introduction to this chapter, some sociologists argue that the elimination of capitalism and a reorganization of work are needed in order to reduce or eliminate the "tyranny of work" (Rinehart 2006). Although theoretically and philosophically this argument makes sense, the practicalities of revolutionizing capitalism in such a way are elusive. Nonetheless, within capitalism there are ways in which work could be organized that would make the experience of it better for many. On the basis of the discussion in this chapter, obvious places to start would be to eliminate systemic, statistical, and other forms of discrimination; to increase wages; and to reorganize work so that it is more meaningful and autonomous. Although such changes would not require the elimination of capitalism, they would require a radical shift in logic and a commitment on the part of members of business communities, governments, and individuals to redistribute wealth and to place less emphasis on capital growth. As it stands, if a company makes a $9-billion profit in one year and an $8-billion profit the next, it suffers on the stock market. Managers are then often forced to restructure and eliminate workers so that the company can show not profitability, but *increased* profitability. If inequality is to be eradicated, this logic must change.

Recall Marx's prediction about polarization. He argued that, with advanced capitalism, work would be increasingly deskilled, the middle class would shrink, and there would be an increasing polarization in the distribution of income and poverty. This chapter has shown that, on the one hand, overall increases in the skill levels associated with many jobs and recent increases in the number of self-employed small business owners suggest that the polarization thesis is incorrect. On the other hand, huge inequities in the distribution of income in Canada cannot be ignored. Furthermore, regardless of where one comes down on the debate about overall class polarization, the fact is that compared with middle-class jobs, working-class jobs are characterized by lower levels of income and other benefits, lower levels of autonomy and control in the work process, poorer working conditions, lower levels of skill, and greater alienation. This chapter has also shown that discussions of polarization are incomplete unless they also consider how gender, age, ethnicity, and race influence outcomes of inequality related to paid work.

⚏ Questions for Critical Thought

1. What is your ideal job after you graduate? Is it a "good job" or a "bad job"? Why or why not? After reading this chapter, has your perspective about your ideal job changed?

2. This chapter argued that paid-work outcomes are mutually shaped by processes of production and distribution. Discuss this in relation to income disadvantages older persons face in retirement.

3. Explain labour-market–based inequality using a human-capital framework. Critique that approach, paying attention to the structures of class, age, gender, ethnicity, and race.

4. Discuss the relationship between technology and skill. Will Marx's prediction about deskilling be realized in the years to come? How do gender, ethnicity, race, and age relations influence the "deskilling" argument?

5. The gender pay gap in Canada is relatively high compared with other OECD countries. Does this surprise you? Based on your understanding of this chapter, why is it so low? Do you think we will see greater equality in the future? Why or why not?

⚏ Glossary

Alienation Marx identified four dimensions of alienation. First, workers are separated from the products of their labour. If people work on a product without knowing its purpose, they are alienated from their product. Second, workers are separated from their labour process; they have little autonomy over how their work is done. Third, because to labour is part of the essence of being human, if workers are alienated from the products and processes of their labour, they are also alienated from themselves. In other words, workers are unable to derive a meaningful existence from their work. The fourth dimension of alienation is the separation of workers from each other. This happens because work processes are set up in such a way as to minimize interaction among workers and because capitalism establishes inherently antagonistic relationships across classes (see Rinehart 2006: 11–13).

Autonomy The ability of workers to make their own decisions about how to do the work, how fast to do it, and what needs to be done. It refers to the control that workers have over their work processes.

Capitalism The economic and social organization of production processes in modern industrialized countries.

Cumulative advantage/disadvantage hypothesis The idea that social and economic advantage and disadvantage cumulate over time. The basic premise of this hypothesis may be captured by the following colloquialism: "The rich get richer and the poor get poorer."

Meritocracy The allocation of positions, roles, prestige, power, and economic reward whereby "excellent" individuals are over-benefited in relation to others.

Primary labour markets A pool of good jobs that are characterized by high pay, good benefits, and job security.

Skill In the sociological literature, the combination of job complexity and autonomy.

Surplus value The value of surplus product that results when workers labour for more hours than would be required for them to achieve their means of subsistence. In capitalist systems of production, workers labour for themselves and for the owners of the means of production. If workers owned the product they produced and were able to sell it, they would need to work for fewer hours than they currently do to make the same wage. The excess time that they work and the surplus product that results from it (surplus value) is appropriated by owners.

Recommended Reading

Adams, Tracey, and Sandy Welsh. 2008. *The Organization and Experience of Work*. Toronto: Thomson Nelson. This book provides the most comprehensive detail on each of class, age, gender, and ethnicity/race in relation to paid work and is particularly good in relation to its treatment of age.

Hughes, Karen D. 1999. *Gender and Self-Employment in Canada: Assessing Trends and Policy Implications*. CPRN Study W104. Changing Relationships Series. Ottawa: Renouf. One of the few comprehensive studies of self-employment in Canada. Although the emphasis is on gender, readers who are interested in all aspects of self-employment would do well to read this paper.

Krahn, Harvey J., Karen D. Hughes, and Graham S. Lowe.2014. *Work, Industry and Canadian Society*, 7th edn. Toronto: Thomson Nelson. A comprehensive text on paid work in Canada. Covering a wide range of topics, including class, age, race, ethnicity, and gender, it is essential reading for students interested in paid work and inequality.

Luxton, Meg, and June Corman. 2001. *Getting By in Hard Times: Gendered Labour at Home and on the Job*. Toronto: University of Toronto Press. This excellent book is a case study of steelworkers in Hamilton, Ontario. It examines how capital restructuring is gendered and classed and how class, gender, and race mutually constitute one another through paid and unpaid labour.

Rinehart, James W. 2006. *The Tyranny of Work: Alienation and the Labour Process*. 5th edn. Toronto: Harcourt Brace. A Marxist account of paid work in Canada that concentrates mainly on social class.

Relevant Websites

Foreign Affairs, Trade, and Development Canada

www.international.gc.ca/trade-agreements-accords-commerciaux/agr-acc/tpp-ptp/index.aspx?lang=eng

**A federal government site for details of trade agreements and accords.

Human Resources and Social Development Canada

www.hrsdc.gc.ca/eng/home.shtml

**A federal government site for issues relating to work and the life course.

Hire Immigrants

www.hireimmigrants.ca/index.php

**This advocacy site out of Toronto identifies challenges and opportunities for businesses to utilize the talents of skilled immigrants.

MySafeWork.com

www.mysafework.com

**Run by the charitable foundation OYAW (Our Youth at Work), the site presents workplace health and wellness issues with a focus on young workers.

Service Canada—Youth Employment Strategy Programs
www1.servicecanada.gc.ca/en/epb/yi/yep/newprog/yesprograms.shtml

**A federal government site for helping young people who face barriers to employment.

Service Canada—Labour Market Information
www.labourmarketinformation.ca/

and

Service Canada—Training, Career and Workplace Information
www.jobsetc.ca/

**More federal government sites for work-related issues.

CAGE(s) and Education

by Tammy Duerden Comeau, Julie McMullin, and Josh Curtis

Introduction

In 1998 the Ontario government began mandatory testing of students in grades 3, 6, and 9. These tests are thought to evaluate students' abilities in reading, writing, and mathematics. They were established to make schools and school boards accountable for the quality of education that they provide and to identify areas that need improving. An office called the Educational Quality and Accountability Office (EQAO) does the testing. Every year, test scores are published for each school and individual students are given their scores so that they, their parents, and their teachers are aware of how they are doing and how they can improve (Bacigalupo 2003).

More than 15 years later, controversy over the measurement and use of these scores continues. Although EQAO and school-board officials stress that these scores should not be used to rank schools, the variation among the schools in their aggregate test scores makes that temptation hard to resist. Indeed, two conservative Canadian think-tanks are in disagreement over how to rank schools and, specifically, over whether and how socio-economic factors should be accounted for in these rankings (Long 2007:

C1). Using different methods from the Fraser Institute, the C.D. Howe Institute argues that 40 per cent of the variation in school test scores is related to socio-economic factors, and it accounts for this in its calculations. Regardless of the statistical methods used, a number of education administrators caution against the use of a single score to evaluate a school and have called such practices "demoralizing" for schools and students (Long 2007: C1). Yet parents with economic means do appear to take these test scores into account, and in some cases move to areas where they believe schools are academically stronger (Alcoba 2008). Ironically, these movements may then exacerbate inequities between schools. Of course, these reports are not a systematic analysis of the relationship between socio-economic status (SES) and education. Nevertheless, a large body of literature does show that people of lower-SES backgrounds tend not to be as highly educated as those from higher-SES backgrounds. It also suggests that "universally" accessible education in Canada may vary considerably in its quality.

The pursuit of higher education is often viewed as an accessible and practical avenue for obtaining upward mobility. In a society that strongly promotes an individualistic ethos of success and failure, education is seen as an opportunity for the talented and motivated individual to move up the social ladder. Canadians would prefer not to believe that the education system is also a place where societal inequalities are reproduced and where privileged groups solidify and maintain their advantages (B. Curtis, Livingstone, and Smaller 1992; Lehmann 2007a). This is not to deny that higher education tends to result in better life opportunities. Usually, highly educated people are employed in well-paid jobs (Chung 2006; D. Little 1995) with relatively high degrees of autonomy and authority (Butlin and Oderkirk 1997). However, the chances of attaining higher education and, more specifically, of obtaining a lucrative degree that will result in substantial labour-market returns are significantly affected by one's class (S. Davies and Guppy 2014; Frenette 2007; Knighton and Mirza 2002), "race" or ethnicity (P.S. Li 2000; Mata 1997; McMullen 2005), gender (S. Davies, Mosher, and O'Grady 1996; Frenette and Zeman 2007; Thiessen and Nickerson 1999), and age (Kapsalis, Morissette, and Picot 1999). The historical period in which we live also significantly shapes our chances for a higher education (Clark 2001). In 2006, for example, 11 per cent of adults aged 25–34 did not have a high school diploma, compared with 23 per cent of adults aged 55–64 (Statistics Canada 2008c: 10). The proportion of individuals who obtain post-secondary education has been steadily increasing over time. This means that older age groups of the future will be more highly educated than those of the past. For example, in 2012, 69.2 per cent of people aged 25 to 44, and 59.2 per cent of people aged 45 to 64, had earned some post-secondary certification. These age groups also had the lowest proportions of people without high school diplomas: 7.9 per cent of people aged 25 to 44 and 13.8 per cent of people aged 45 to 64—both noticeable declines from 2006. Now, societal demands for an educated workforce have made a high school education almost compulsory for sustained labour-force participation. This marks a significant change from the popular educational expectations and

aspirations of previous generations (Bowlby and McMullen 2002; Clark 2001; S. Davies and Guppy 2014).

The chances of obtaining a post-secondary education also differ by province (Krahn and Taylor 2007). Place, or the location or region where we live, matters for educational attainment and opportunities. For example (see Figure 10.1), of the provinces, Newfoundland and Labrador has the lowest proportion of adults aged 25–64 with a university degree (17 per cent) and the highest proportion with less than a high school diploma (21.6 per cent) (Statistics Canada 2011a). It is important to note that migration and mobility also affect the educational attainment of residents—in Alberta, 25 per cent of adults aged 25–64 have a university degree (Statistics Canada 2011a); however, Alberta also had the largest net inflow of post-secondary graduates from other provinces (Statistics Canada 2008c). Provincial educational policies help to shape opportunities and educational trajectories. In some provinces, the courses taken early on in high school can determine educational and occupational directions for years to come. The **streaming** (see Box 10.1 for critique of educational streaming in Germany) of high school students into different educational pathways has often been found to disadvantage or close off career options for students whose parents have lower educational attainment (Krahn and Taylor 2007). Students whose parents have one or two post-secondary degrees are more likely to have their post-secondary options open in grade 10. Interestingly, there are differences between provinces. For example, 86 per cent of grade 10 students in Saskatchewan whose parents have no degrees still have their post-secondary options open, compared to 52 per cent of their counterparts in Alberta (Krahn and Taylor 2007).

Pierre Bourdieu's work on the concepts of social and cultural capital has taken a prominent place in explaining the persistent inequalities (particularly in regard to social class) reproduced in education systems (Wotherspoon 2004). According to Bourdieu, parents with more

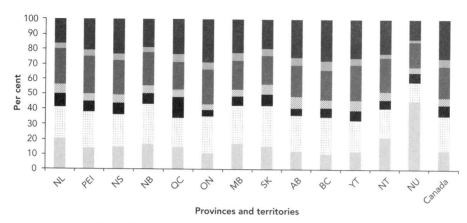

Figure 10.1 Educational Attainment in Canada (2011) by Province (people aged 25–64)

1. Comparisons with other data sources suggest that the category "university certificate or diploma below bachelor level" was over-reported in the National Household Survey. It is recommended that users interpret the results for this category with caution. For detailed explanations on concepts and for information on data quality, please refer to the reference guide on the 2011 National Household Survey (NHS) website.

2. The term "trades certificate other than Registered Apprenticeship certificate" refers to trade certification that was completed through a school-based program as opposed to completing an apprenticeship program or a Certificate of Qualification/Journeyperson's designation.

Source: Statistics Canada, National Household Survey 2011, CANSIM table 202-0407. www12.statcan.gc.ca/nhs-enm/2011/as-sa/99-012-x/2011001/c-g/c-g03-eng.cfm

educational resources have richer reserves of cultural capital. **Cultural capital**, which is derived mostly from education, reflects the middle- and upper-class values, attitudes, and beliefs that people hold about various aspects of social life. Cultural capital can be understood as "institutionalized, *i.e.*, widely shared, high status cultural signals (attitudes, preferences, formal knowledge, behaviors, good and credentials) used for social and cultural exclusion" (Lamont and Lareau 1988: 156). Again, returning to the notion of power, we find that the content of the cultural signals is relatively arbitrary. What is important to understand, however, is the way culture is employed to produce benefits for some while simultaneously excluding others. If education and related activities, such as reading, discussing

politics, and learning about the world and music, are valued in a family and by its members, high levels of educational attainment are more likely.

Working-class families tend not to expose their children to these activities to the extent that middle- and upper-class families do. Therefore, these children are often less prepared and less familiar with the knowledge that is taken for granted and drawn upon in the classroom. As Dimaggio (1982) argues, "[i]t takes more than measured ability to do well in school" (1982: 189). Dimaggio believes that the impact of middle-class students' cultural resources provides significant rewards during their schooling (resources that the lower classes often do not have access to) (DiMaggio 1982; Bourdieu 1977; Kingston 2001).

Global perspective

Box 10.1 School Streaming and the Rise of Educational Inequality in Germany

Germany was once highly regarded, even admired, for its education system. For many generations its elite universities produced Nobel Prize winners and their technical institutions trained highly skilled and successful tradesmen. After four years of primary school, the smartest students go on to *Gymnasien* (top-level high schools for university-bound students) and the average students go to *Realschulen* (a path usually to white-collar or technical trades). Students with the lowest grades go to *Hauptschulen*, schools that prepare students for mid-to lower-level vocational training. At least in theory, this streaming process was intended to nurture the skill sets of students and to prepare them for occupations that match their abilities.

Today, however, the historical success of this program is fading. Almost one-fifth of Germany's 15-year-olds are not able to read proficiently. And, about 29 per cent of young adults have a higher-education degree, below the EU average of about 34 per cent. Some German policy-makers believe that the early-selection system is at the heart of the problem.

The three-track system continues to have strong support, especially among middle-class parents. Middle-class parents are determined to maintain a status quo that favours their children by streaming them into the best schools. Backlash against reform has been strongest in Hamburg, Germany. Parents launched a campaign, "Wir Wollen Lernen" (We Want to Learn), which collected 182,000 votes in order to force a referendum to reconsider changing the current system.

"The idea is that homogenous learning groups are better at helping children perform," says Katharina Spiess, education and family research director at the German Institute for Economic Research, of the early-selection system. The result, according to *The Guardian*, was "a political storm which ejected the Christian Democrats (cdu) from power in the city and forced the cdu mayor, Ole von Beust, who had proposed the reforms in coalition with the Greens, to resign." Politicians are now questioning whether its streaming policy is now untouchable.

It isn't surprising that middle-class families would oppose changing the current system. Children from privileged backgrounds are four times as likely to attend *Gymnasien* as children with similar grades from a working-class family. This disparity is even worse for immigrants. According to the federal education body, children of immigrant families attend the *Hauptschule* (the lowest level of German schooling) twice as often as native-born children, even within the same socio-economic class.

Sources: Andrea Thomas. (June 13, 2014). "German Students Snub Vocational Schools." *The Wall Street Journal*; Alexandra Topping. (March 15, 2011). "Germany's middle class happy with rampant inequality in schools." *The Guardian*.

The related concept of **social capital** concerns the information and social connections that are available to individuals. Social capital usually takes the form of networks, norms, and social trust that facilitate coordination and co-operation for mutual benefit (Putman 2000). For example, the possession of knowledge about the workings of the education system, such as a familiarity with the meanings of terms such as special education, is vital to successfully navigating through that system. The future implications of decisions made now about course offerings and topics of study may also be unfamiliar to those with little experience in the education system.

A quick look at the history of education in Canada makes it clear that achieving societal equality (even equality on the basis of "merit") was not an overriding goal of the education system at the outset (B. Curtis, Livingstone, and Smaller 1992; Wotherspoon 2004). Early educational aims for the Canadian masses included the desire to create agreeable and obedient workers and a contented working class (Baldus and Kassam 1996; B. Curtis, Livingstone, and Smaller 1992). Baldus and Kassam (1996), analyzing the predominant values found in nineteenth-century Ontario schoolbooks, found strong prescriptive statements and moral lessons that recommend accepting one's lot in life and embracing social inequality. This is illustrated in the following excerpt from a nineteenth-century reader:

> Our present lot, my parents say,
> Is better for us, in every way,
> Than one of our own choice could be
> . . .
> So now I am a little child,
> Then let me try to be content;
> My duty let me strive to do,
> And with a thankful heart and true,
> Accept the blessings heaven has sent.
>
> (quoted in Baldus and Kassam 1996: 338)

Children were not encouraged to strive beyond their social roots, and the virtues of leading a simple and hard-working life were extolled in poems and fables (Baldus and Kassam 1996). Historically, then, educational curricula and policies have accepted social inequalities rather than challenged them (B. Curtis, Livingstone, and Smaller 1992; Wotherspoon 2004).

R. Ng (1993) shows how the early educational aims of Canadian missionaries were structured by racist, sexist, and class-based ideologies. Aboriginal men and women were taught different skills in order to reproduce European gendered societal patterns. Only the men were taught how to farm, and the women were schooled in "domestic" duties. The goal was to produce a new and subordinate working class that would benefit the colonizers. A strong theme of Aboriginal inferiority was woven through religious and educational teachings (R. Ng 1993). The delivery of these educational imperatives was later refined and developed in all-encompassing institutional forms (Guppy and Davies 1998; Wotherspoon 2004).

The residential school system to which Aboriginals in Canada were subjected in the nineteenth and twentieth centuries provides a graphic illustration of the extent to which racism and class ideologies can direct "educational" programs (Nicholas 2001; Wotherspoon 2004). Aboriginal children were cut off from their families and taught to be ashamed of their cultural heritage (Nicholas 2001). Indeed, according to Schissel and Wotherspoon (2003: 43), "the expressed intent of residential school policy was to destroy a culture and rebuild Indian children as active participants in the industrial economy, if not remove them as impediments to economic development." Generations of Aboriginal people are still paying the price for the humiliating, alienating, and abusive experiences endured in residential schools (Jaine 1993). Indeed, the last residential school did not close until the 1980s (Nicholas 2001).

This chapter examines the barriers to educational attainment in Canada. In particular, it considers the historical influence of social class, race, ethnicity, gender, and age in educational attainment; how these factors currently affect educational attainment; and the relationship between these factors and the educational returns achieved through labour markets.

Focusing on Class: Historical Notes and Existing Patterns

The class position we are born into has a significant impact on our educational prospects and consequent life trajectory (Bowlby and McMullen 2002; Frenette 2007; Knighton and Mirza 2002). The effect of class on the educational attainment of Canadians has been described by Guppy and Davies (1998: 59) as a particularly "enduring" feature of inequality. The education achieved by our parents and the kind of work that they perform have an undeniable influence on our early school experiences and on our level of educational attainment (Bowlby and McMullen 2002; B. Curtis, Livingstone, and Smaller 1992; S. Davies and Guppy 2014; Nakhaie and Curtis 1998). This is true, not just in Canada, but across the globe as well. Indeed, *streaming*, or filtering, occurs before some children ever enter a school building (B. Curtis, Livingstone, and Smaller 1992). Parents with enough money can choose to send their children to elite private schools, where students are groomed to attend the top universities. Within public schools, students have been classified and "sorted" into various academic avenues or streams in which some children are relegated to learning "basic skills" and others are academically challenged and channelled to go on to higher learning (Davies 1995; Robson et al. 2014).

Curtis and his colleagues (B. Curtis, Livingstone, and Smaller 1992), who have examined the practice of streaming in Ontario schools, have shown that the allocation of students to various ability levels in both elementary and secondary schools is not free of class bias. In other words, children from lower-class and lower-middle-class backgrounds were found to be much more likely to end up in special education or remedial programs at the elementary school level and in basic streams or vocational schools at the secondary school level (B. Curtis, Livingstone, and Smaller 1992). These authors cite studies from the 1970s and 1980s that show that children from families on social assistance were "60 times more likely" to be in special- or remedial-education programs than children from the families of professional workers (B. Curtis, Livingstone, and Smaller 1992: 59). Being in special or remedial education in elementary school tended to be a permanent placement that led to a "basic" stream in

an academic high school or a vocational school. Students who attended these vocational schools were predominantly of working-class or ethnic- or racial-minority backgrounds. These students faced fairly dismal job prospects, as they were not eligible for university or most college programs, and even those who achieved a vocational certificate from their high school were not actually qualified to enter many trade apprenticeship programs (B. Curtis, Livingstone, and Smaller 1992).

Some may argue that these statistics are outdated and that streaming is no longer a predominant teaching practice in the education system. However, more recent studies confirm that white children from higher socio-economic backgrounds often enjoy significant advantages in elementary and secondary schools. Research in Canada using 2006 data shows that lower SES students are disproportionately placed in applied streams in grades 7 and 8 (Robson et al. 2014). While academic achievement gaps have been explained by other factors, such as race/ethnicity and gender, social class is typically the strongest predictor of academic inequality in North America (Davies and Janus 2009; Galindo and Sheldon 2012). Lower SES children are more likely to face academic setbacks in the long term, including an increased likelihood of dropping out of high school (Waxman et al. 2002; Wyner et al 2007), and they have lower chances of attending prestigious post-secondary institutions (Alon 2009; Wiggers and Arnold 2011). Despite the increase in access to higher education, only a minority of high-achieving, low-income students apply to colleges and universities (Hoxby 2009). Early results that were gathered in 1994–5 from the National Longitudinal Survey of Children and Youth showed that children from the highest socio-economic backgrounds were significantly less likely to be receiving remedial education (5 per cent) than those from the lowest socio-economic backgrounds (17 per cent) (Lipps and Frank 1997). Children from the highest socio-economic backgrounds were also significantly more likely to be enrolled in some form of a gifted educational program (9 per cent) than children from the lowest socio-economic backgrounds (5 per cent) (Lipps and Frank 1997: 54). Children from privileged socio-economic backgrounds were also ranked considerably higher in academic-ability assessments by their teachers (Lipps and Frank 1997). In fact, Lipps and Frank (1997: 54) found that students with the highest socio-economic status were "two to three times as likely" to be ranked among the best in the class by their teachers in reading, writing, and math. Using more recent data from the National Longitudinal Survey of Children and Youth (1994–5 to 2000–1), Caro, McDonald, and Willms (2009) explore the relationship between SES, academic achievement, and age. They find that the SES/achievement gap remains fairly

stable from the age of 7 to 11 years, but that it widens at an increasing rate from the age of 11 to the age of 15 years. This increase, they argue, has as much to do with school streaming as it does with the "out of school" context, such as family environments and socialization. This evidence suggests that streaming and other inequalities are limiting capable working-class students from accessing higher education.

It is not surprising, then, that parental expectations and impressions of their children's ability have been shown to affect educational trajectories. Figure 10.2 shows the proportion of children ranked as "very well" by the person most knowledgeable (PMK, often the parent) about the child's academic ability in terms of math, reading, and composition. This figure demonstrates a general increase in "very well"

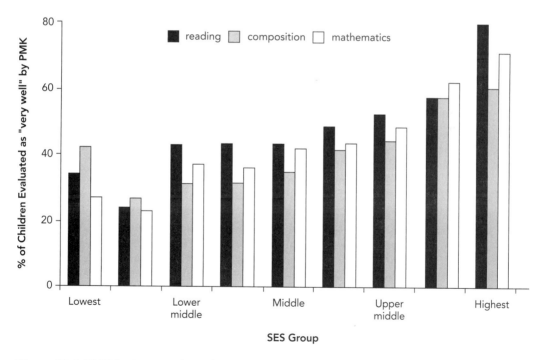

Figure 10.2 PMK Evaluation of Academic Performance by Socio-economic Status (SES)

Note: PMK is the person most knowledgeable (typically a parent or guardian); SES group is composite measure comprising family income, parents' occupation, and parents' education.

Source: Statistics Canada. National Longitudinal Survey of Children and Youth, 1998-99. Catalogue no. 89F0078XPE, no. 3

rankings as the socio-economic status of the child increases, especially in comparison to the academic evaluations of the lowest- and highest-SES children (represented here on a scale of 1 to 9). Here we see that in most cases parents with higher SES are more likely to rank their children highly in terms of academic ability.

At the secondary level, Lehmann's (2007a) study of 105 youth in apprenticeship and academic educational tracks in Germany and Canada provides a strong illustration of the role of habitus and cultural capital in shaping educational pathways. As Lehmann points out, Bourdieu's concepts of cultural capital and **habitus** help in conceptualizing how agency and human action are shaped and constrained by structure in complex ways. Educational choices that students make in selecting which "stream" or educational pathway to take are not random but structured, in part, by what is comfortable, familiar, and perceived as attainable. Cultural capital is one way in which to encompass and assess practices and knowledge that can affect performance and preferences in school such as "reading books versus reading magazines" (Lehmann 2007a: 84). In his measure of cultural capital for students in both countries, Lehmann (2007a: 85) found that those who scored highly on this measure were more likely to be in an academic track (61 per cent) than those in apprenticeships (39 per cent).

Also, in more recent work, Lehmann (2014) again uses Bourdieu's concept of habitus to explain how working-class students achieve academic success at the university level. As Lehmann writes, "we need to gain a better understanding of the different ways in which they consolidate their working-class habitus with the middle-class culture of the academic field" (2014: 1). In doing so, he concludes that socially mobile students gain new knowledge about the world, change their outlooks on life, and grow their repertoire of cultural capital by developing new dispositions and tastes about

a range of issues, including food, politics, and work. However, during this process, many students distance themselves from their working class culture, while at the same time they find themselves in adult situations in which they are perceived as "cultural outsiders" among the middle class.

Nevertheless, in Canada, parental educational backgrounds and parents' educational expectations for their children continue to exert a strong influence on whether youth attend university, and according to Frenette (2007), only 12 per cent of the gap between the attendance of high-income and low-income youth is directly attributable to finances. Indeed, the importance of cultural and social dispositions or "fit" is a compelling component of some students' narratives of their educational trajectories. Lehmann (2007b) found that those students from working-class backgrounds who left university tended to feel alienated in certain post-secondary academic environments and that this was a factor in their departure. Thus, the patterns of educational advantage and disadvantage by class discussed by Curtis, Livingstone, and Smaller (1992) do not appear to have substantially dissipated over time.

SES also drives achievement gaps during the summer months (Davies and Aurini 2013; Entwisle and Alexander 1992). Research on **summer setback**—the loss of numeracy and literacy during the summer months, finds that children from lower SES backgrounds are greatly disadvantaged, while their higher-SES peers continue to gain valuable academic skills (Alexander, Entwisle, and Olson 2007; Allington and McGill-Franzen 2003; Cooper, Nye, Charlton, Lindsay, and Greathouse 1996; Entwisle 1997). Cooper, Lindsay, and Greathouse (1996) conducted a meta-analysis of 11 summer setback studies and found, on average, that the summer months result in a literacy gap of roughly three months between lower and higher SES children. Alexander, Entwisle, and Olson (2007) found that two-thirds of the achievement gap between higher and lower SES students was attributed to gaps that occurred over the summer months. While during the school year these SES gaps decreased, children's lives outside the school from preschool years and during elementary school predict high school grades, drop-out rates, and post-secondary enrollment rates.

Using data from an Ontario-wide population of elementary students, Davies and Aurini (2013) found that SES was the most statistically significant demographic variable, controlling for family practices and academic achievement scores such as previous years' tests. For instance, children from the top SES quartile gained "a month of literacy, while the bottom quartile [lost] nearly the same amount (Davies and Aurini 2013). Moreover, when testing the same students in the fall, "the SES gap has grown to almost three-quarters of a school year." Davies and Aurini (2013) found that 25 per cent of the SES gap was attributed to differences in learning during the previous summer. For instance, a "one standard deviation increase in student SES, holding control and other demographics constant, raised literacy by 0.22 years" (Davies and Aurini 2013).

Educational Attainment

The class background of students (including parental education, income, and occupation) exerts a significant influence on their chances of obtaining a high school diploma and a post-secondary education. By high school, students with university-educated and higher SES parents score notably higher on reading, math, and science tests compared to their peers with less educated and affluent parents (S. Davies and Guppy 2014: 113; see also Frenette 2007; Zeman 2007). Labour markets increasingly require post-secondary education of some form for sustainable employment. According to the Canadian Council on Learning (2007: 8), "in

the decade leading up to 2015, nearly 70 per cent of the projected 1.7 million new jobs in Canada are expected to be in management or in occupations usually requiring post-secondary qualification." In this environment, prospects for people who do not have a high school diploma are not promising (Bowlby and McMullen 2005). Indeed, those who left high school without a diploma have experienced unemployment rates much higher than those of university-degree holders (CCL 2007: 8). For example, in 2012 the unemployment rate for people without a high school diploma was 16.4 per cent, compared to only 5.8 per cent for those with a university degree (Statistics Canada 2014).

Since the early 1990s, the high school dropout rate has decreased quite dramatically, from 17 per cent to 7.8 per cent by 2011–12 (**www.hrsdc.gc.ca**). Still, some youth are more likely to drop out than others. Data on family income show that 11.7 per cent of youth from families in the lowest income quartile dropped out of high school by age 19, compared with 3.6 per cent of youth in the highest income quartile (Zeman 2007). Parental education is important: 25 per cent of youth whose parents did not complete high school also dropped out, compared with only 7 per cent of youth who had at least one parent with a post-secondary degree (Hango and de Broucker 2007: 29). In addition, youth living in large cities were much less likely to drop out of high school than those in small towns and rural areas (CCL 2008: 17). As Figure 10.3 shows, the average dropout rate from 2009 to 2012 was highest in Quebec (10.6 per cent). Newfoundland saw the largest dropout rate decrease, lowering from 19.9 in 1990–3 to 8.7 in 2009–12.

In their detailed study of high school dropouts and graduates, Bowlby and McMullen (2002) found that the mothers of high school graduates were more likely to work in government, health, social science, management, business, finance, art, or culture and recreation,

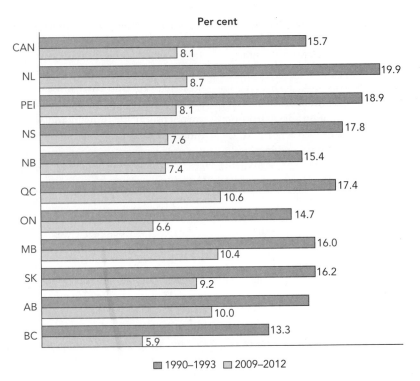

Per cent

CAN 15.7 / 8.1
NL 19.9 / 8.7
PEI 18.9 / 8.1
NS 17.8 / 7.6
NB 15.4 / 7.4
QC 17.4 / 10.6
ON 14.7 / 6.6
MB 16.0 / 10.4
SK 16.2 / 9.2
AB / 10.0
BC 13.3 / 5.9

■ 1990–1993 □ 2009–2012

Figure 10.3 Dropout Rate in Canada by Region, 1990–1993 and 2009–2012 (Percentages)

Source: Statistics Canada. Labour Force Survey 2012, www4.hrsdc.gc.ca/.3ndic.1t.4r @-eng.jsp?iid=32

whereas the mothers of students who dropped out were more concentrated in sales/service and manufacturing/trade occupations. Similarly, the fathers of dropouts were more likely to be employed in trades and manufacturing occupations, while the fathers of graduates were more often in management, finance, and the sciences (Bowlby and McMullen 2002). These findings suggest that it is not just family finances and income that affect high school completion rates; rather, the mechanisms of social and cultural capital in the form of the valuation of education and exposure to educationally enhancing experiences are also having an influence. According to Finnie, Lascelles, and Sweetman (2005), each year of parental post-secondary education increases the likelihood that youth will attend university by as much as 5 percentage points. More highly educated parents and

those who have been "successful" and accomplished in the education system are more easily able to pass down the excitement of learning and to expect a certain level of education on the part of their offspring (S. Davies and Guppy 2014: 113). The completion of high school is a necessary step for entrance to most types of post-secondary education, and it is here that the influence of income is seen more vividly.

More than one-third of youth who have not yet attended post-secondary education report that financial barriers have prevented them (Berger, Motte, and Parkin 2007: 44). Post-secondary education, particularly university education, is becoming more and more expensive (CCL 2007; Finnie 2002). The Canadian Council on Learning (2007: 86) notes that the cost of tuition increased 44 per cent from 1995–6 to 2005–6. As Table 10.1 shows, this trend

Table 10.1 Undergraduate Tuition Fees for Full-Time Canadian Students by Discipline and Province

	2010/11	2011/12	2012/13	2013/14ʳ	2014/15ᵖ
			Average ($)		
Canada	**5,146**	**5,313**	**5,586**	**5,767**	**5,959**
Agriculture, Natural Resources and Conservation	4,803	4,961	5,119	5,251	5,407
Architecture and related technologies	5,179	4,788	5,340	5,495	5,711
Humanities	4,638	4,769	4,941	5,023	5,165
Business Management and Public Administration	5,386	5,673	6,097	6,274	6,525
Education	3,850	3,804	4,273	4,394	4,510
Engineering	5,992	6,155	6,560	6,871	7,151
Law, legal professions and studies	8,657	9,335	9,549	10,039	10,508
Medicine	10,867	11,313	12,012	12,470	12,959
Visual and Performing Arts & Comm. Technologies	4,748	4,591	5,002	5,138	5,287
Physical and Life Sciences and Technologies	5,049	5,247	5,335	5,481	5,640
Math, Computer and Information Sciences	5,526	5,781	6,051	6,245	6,471
Social and Behavioural Sciences	4,586	4,656	4,966	5,116	5,262
Other Health, Parks, Recreation and Fitness	4,698	4,873	5,232	5,529	5,691
Dentistry	15,062	16,037	16,678	17,387	18,187
Nursing	4,662	4,731	4,985	5,140	5,287
Pharmacy	9,014	9,719	10,463	10,691	11,173
Veterinary Medicine	5,612	5,889	6,383	6,680	6,926

p : preliminary.

r : revised.

Notes: Since the distribution of enrolment across the various programs varies from period to period, caution must be exercised in making long-term historical comparisons.
For Nova Scotia and Quebec, both in- and out-of-province students are included in the weighted average calculations.

Source: Statistics Canada, Centre for Education Statistics, www.statcan.gc.ca/tables-tableaux/sum-som/l01/cst01/educ50a-eng.htm

continued from 2010–11 to 2014–15. During this time, the cost of tuition rose by almost 16 per cent, with more significant increases in professional programs such as law, medicine, and dentistry. Indeed, these increases have exceeded the annual inflation rate in Canada. There is a clear relationship between family income levels and the chance or likelihood of continuing to post-secondary and particularly university education. Frenette (2007: 7) found a marked income gradient in university participation based on parental income level: 50 per cent of 19-year-old youth in the top income quartile attended university, compared with 31 per cent of those in the bottom income quartile, controlling for family size.

There is a strong relationship between socio-economic status and university enrolment. While 20 per cent of youth from families earning less than $25,000 a year attend university, more than double that, 46 per cent, of youth from families with incomes of more than $100,000 attend (Berger, Motte, and Parkin 2007). Here we see that the differences in university attendance according to family income are much more pronounced as compared with college attendance. Part of this difference may be attributed to doubts about the value of return on an investment in university education given the cost (Berger, Motte, and Parkin 2007). The class/educational attainment relationship is even more bleak in other parts of the world. In China for example, this relationship is even further aggravated by poor government funding in the rural school system. Box 10.2 discusses this problem in more detail.

In spite of the extension of student aid, many lower-income families are debt averse, and in fact student loan repayments can be long lasting, with nearly one-third of students defaulting in the first three years of repayment and another third continuing to pay off loans 10 years later (Berger, Motte, and Parkin 2007: 89). Finances are a clear factor in the ability to save for and afford educational goals. For instance, families with earnings under $30,000

a year have a 24 per cent participation rate in the Registered Education Savings Plan (RESP), compared with a 56 per cent participation rate for families who earn over $70,000 a year (Berger, Motte, and Parkin 2007: 51). University student debt loads more than doubled between 1990 and 2006, from an average of $11,636 to an average of $24,047 (CCL 2007: 88). In 2010, the amount of student loans owed to the Canadian government reached $15 billion. This figure only accounts for a small portion of student debt, given that it does not include provincial and personal loans, lines of credit, and education credit card debt. Students in Ontario and the Maritimes held the highest debt loads (approximately $28,000), while students in Quebec held the lowest (about $13,000) (Canadian Federation of Students 2013). Research by Andersen and McIvor (2013) shows that debt more adversely affects the lower classes post-graduation. More specifically, students from lower-SES backgrounds with debt are more likely than those from higher-SES backgrounds with debt to take temporary positions with fewer job benefits. This leads to lower earnings over the life course, even for people with the same educational credentials.

Still, past research and more recent reports suggest that parental education is even more influential in whether and how youth participate in post-secondary education (CCL 2007; S. Davies and Guppie 2006; Frenette 2007; Knighton and Mirza 2002). Although most Canadian students (60 per cent) engage in post-secondary education of some sort, higher levels of parental income and higher levels of parental education mean higher post-secondary participation rates (CCL 2007). As Finnie and his colleagues (2005: 22) note, "family background appears to have an enduring effect on the determination of who goes on to post-secondary participation, even among what appear to be equally qualified, and perhaps even equally motivated young people." Table 10.2 illustrates the enduring nature of these relationships by showing how little these odds have changed over time.

Global perspective

Box 10.2 China's Urban/Rural Education Gap

Helen Gao, a master's student in East Asian studies at Harvard University, recently told the story of Chang Qing and Jiand Heng in a *New York Times* op-ed titled "China's Education Gap." In her article, she tells of two polarizing life stories that illustrate perfectly the education divide in China's urban and rural regions:

> Chang Qing, a friend and mother of a 16-year-old girl, has been preparing her daughter, Xiaoshuang, for America since the girl was a toddler. She played her tapes of English lessons made from Disney movies, and later hosted a steady stream of exchange students from America to hone her child's accent. Now, her daughter speaks impeccable English and attends a private academy in Beijing where annual tuition is around $24,000. Ms. Chang believes that nothing short of an Ivy League education will suffice.
>
> On a trip to the countryside in Hunan Province (the home of Mao Zedong), I met Jiang Heng, a skinny 11-year-old whose parents work in a handbag factory in neighboring Guangdong. The boy attends a local elementary school that takes him an hour and half to walk to and, together with his younger brother, is looked after by his grandparents. I asked him what he wanted to do after high school. He looked confused, as if the answer was too obvious. "I want to be a migrant worker," he told me, without blinking.

According to Gao, China's education system hasn't always been so ripe with inequality. Gao's mother attended Peking University in the late 1970s and told stories of being surrounded by students from all walks of life—"from the heirs of party officials and the scions of intellectuals, to workers fresh out of factories and peasants hailing from far-flung provinces." Gao believes that rising income and wealth inequality is largely to blame for rising educational inequality in China today. Sadly, an education system that once served as an equalizer for economic opportunity now seems to reinforce class-based inequality.

This division has become most pronounced for students who live in urban versus rural regions of China, Gao says. A recent survey that sampled people from Beijing, Shanghai, and southern Guangdong Province, reported that only 0.7 per cent of their sample of rural respondents held a university degree, while 13.6 per cent of people living in urban areas held the same credential. In fact, by the time students are ready to take college entrance exams nearly 95 per cent of rural students already dropped out. The 5 per cent of rural students who do write their entrance exams are less likely to be accepted into higher-profile Chinese schools based simply on the fact that they were educated in a rural school system (even if their test scores are competitive with their urban counterparts). For example, elite universities allocate much higher admission quotas to top-tier cities like Beijing and Shanghai. One researcher showed that an applicant from Beijing was over 40 times more likely to be admitted to Peking University (Chinese elite institution) than a comparable student from a poor and largely rural province.

Sources: Helen Gao. (Sept. 4, 2014) "China's Education Gap." *The New York Times*.

Table 10.2 Probability of Having a University Degree in 2009, by Sex, Age Group, and Highest Level of Father's Education

	Highest Level of Father's Education			
	Less than high school graduation	High school graduate	At least some post-secondary	(Weighted) Sample size
Women				
Aged 30–39	.20	.26	.47	1,449
Aged 40–49	.19	.26	.44	1,587
Aged 50–59	.18	.29	.42	1,139
Aged 60+	.11	.24	.29	1,290
Men				
Aged 30–39	.17	.29	.42	1,454
Aged 40–49	.14	.28	.45	1,565
Aged 50–59	.23	.41	.49	1,129
Aged 60+	.16	.34	.40	1,086

Note: Includes only Canadian-born; sample weighted to represent Canadian population.

Source: Davies and Guppy (2006: 100). Reprinted by permission of Oxford University Press.

As Davies and Guppy (2014: 115) point out, those individuals whose parents had at least some post-secondary education are more than twice as likely to have a university degree themselves compared with those whose parents have no university education, and these ratios have changed little over time. Davies and Guppy conclude that educational opportunity has not extended its reach in more recent generations.

The aspirations of students are significantly affected by the aspirations their parents have for them (Looker and Lowe 2001), and the aspirations of those students from more privileged socio-economic backgrounds are usually higher than the aspirations of those from less privileged backgrounds. The benefits of social capital in terms of the depth of information available about post-secondary options and the consequences of early academic decisions thus play a role in the advantages accrued for those from higher-SES backgrounds (CPRN 2002; Childs, Finnie, and Mueller 2010; Chin 2000).

Educational Returns in the Labour Market

The decisions over whether to attend university as opposed to college, which university or college, what program of study, and whether to pursue graduate studies have consequences for students' future earnings potential (Betts, Ferrall, and Finne 2007; Butlin 2001; S. Davies and Guppy 2014; Guppy and Davies 1998). For example, as Figure 10.4 shows, income and education are very highly correlated. Although there are exceptions, the higher the degree students earn the more likely it is that they will fall into higher-income categories.

Expanding on this relationship Betts, Ferrall, and Finnie (2007) show that earnings five years after graduation differed by as much as 60 per cent between fields of undergraduate study. The authors conclude that "what you study" and "where you study" have a large bearing on postgraduate earnings (Betts, Ferrall, and Finnie 2007).

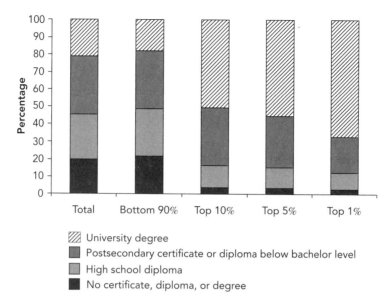

Figure 10.4 The Relationship between Income and Education in Canada, 2011

Source: Statistics Canada. National Household Survey, 2011. Catalogue No. 99-014-X2011003. www5.statcan.gc.ca/access_acces/
alternative_alternatif.action?t=99-014-XWE2011003&l=eng&loc=. www12.statcan.gc.ca/nhs-enm/2011/as-sa/99-014-x/99-014-
x2011003_2-eng.pdf

The choice of what type of post-secondary or university program to enroll in depends on adequate information; however, it also increasingly depends on finances. This is particularly true in professional programs, which tend to have the highest labour-market returns. Interestingly, although there has been a large push for Canadian youth to move into apprenticeships and trades, a study of educational investments show that returns, at least on average, "remain stubbornly low" (Boothby and Drewes 2006: 17). Issues of financing have especially been the case in Ontario, where fees for professional programs rose as much as 241 per cent (for medicine) and 315 per cent (for dentistry) from the mid-1990s to the early 2000s (Frenette 2005). And, fees for professional programs continue to rise disproportionately. For instance, as shown in Table 10.1 above, in 2014–15 annual tuition in dentistry, medicine, and law were $18,187, $12,959, and

$10,952 respectively. Each program's average tuition rose by about $2,000 from the 2010–11 academic calendar year. This table also shows, for example, that the cost of enrolment in the humanities was only $5,165 in 2014–15 (rising only $529 from 2010–11). In the wake of these increases, enrolment levels rose among youth whose parents had a graduate or professional degree as well as among youth whose parents had no post-secondary education (Frenette 2005). Frenette (2005) states that while access for disadvantaged students opened up through bursaries and scholarships, those students in the middle (whose parents had some post-secondary qualification) saw their enrolment levels in professional programs drop dramatically.

Parental education and income also have a significant effect on whether or not students who achieve a bachelor's degree continue on to graduate studies (Finnie and Mueller 2008). Students whose parents had a high school diploma or less were much less likely to enroll in post-secondary programs. The proportion of Canadian-born university graduates for which at least one parent was university educated was almost double (41 per cent) the proportion of college graduates with university-educated parents (22 per cent) (Adamuti-Trache and Hawkey 2009). Higher levels of education tend to lead to more authoritative and higher-paying jobs (Butlin 2001; Butlin and Oderkirk 1997). According to Statistics Canada's National Household Survey (2011a), the richest 10 per cent of Canadians are disproportionately university educated (about 55 per cent) or hold a post-secondary degree (about 20 per cent). This relationship becomes even more pronounced with respect to the top 1 per cent, where about 63 per cent are university educated and about 22 per cent have post-secondary training (Statistics Canada 2013). In other words, it has become nearly impossible in Canada to hold the status of a top income earner without attending university. Therefore, those students who come from more highly educated families maintain their advantage throughout university and into the labour market.

Focusing on Race/Ethnicity: Historical Notes and Existing Patterns

Issues of class and race or ethnicity are closely bound together, and many of the educational disadvantages and difficulties faced by racial and ethnic minorities stem from long-standing economic exploitation and disadvantage (as in the case of Aboriginal Canadians) and from the financial and social struggles of emigrating to a new country (Ali and Grabb 1998; Bernhard and Freire 1999; S. Davies and Guppy 2014). In spite of these barriers, visible minorities in Canada tend to be more highly educated than the general population; they are more likely to have a high school diploma and more likely to be university educated (S. Davies and Guppy 2006: 148–52; Taylor and Krahn 2005). Yet, as Figure 10.5 shows, education does not lead to guaranteed

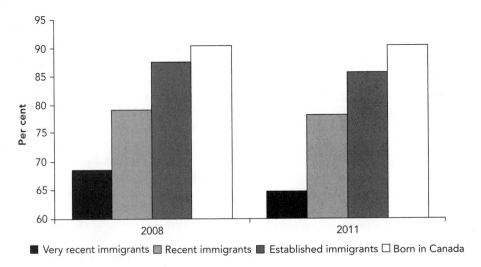

Figure 10.5 Employment Rate for University-Educated Immigrants and Canadian-Born Aged 25 to 54, 2008 and 2011

Source: Statistics Canada. National Household Survey, 2011. Catalogue No. 99-014-X2011003. www5.statcan.gc.ca/access_acces/alternative_alternatif.action?teng=71-606-x2012006-eng.pdf&tfra=71-606-x2012006-fra.pdf&l=eng&loc=/71-606-x2012006-eng.pdf

employment: Canadian-born university-degree holders are much more likely to use their degrees to gain employment than both recent and established immigrants in Canada.

Currently, higher levels of education among visible minorities are due to the high levels of education required to gain entrance to Canada through immigration policy. In 2011, Canadian immigrants between the ages of 25 and 64 represented just under one-quarter of Canada's total adult population but over one-third (about 35 per cent) of Canadian adults with a university degree. About 50 per cent of all STEM (science and technology, engineering, mathematics and computer sciences) degrees were held by immigrants (Statistics Canada 2013). Yet, minority groups in Canada have historically faced barriers and educational obstacles owing to their perceived ethnic and racial background. Individuals from racial and ethnic minority groups have experienced exclusion and racism in Canadian classrooms (Carr and Klassen 1996; Kelly 2002; Knight 1997; Dei 1993, 2006). This is illustrated by the history of classroom segregation and eventual "separate" schooling for black students in Canada West in the nineteenth century, instituted in spite of vigorous protests by black parents (Knight 1997). In Upper Canada, the Common School Act of 1859 provided black students with schools that were distinctly separate from the institutions attended by white children (Knight 1997). By the twentieth century, these schools no longer existed, though the Act remained on the books until 1964. These issues continue today, as the Toronto District School Board has opened a school for black students that some call "segregated" and others call "Afrocentric" (Bradshaw 2008).

These sentiments of exclusion and difference are echoed in the history of educational programs directed at Aboriginals in Canada (Wotherspoon 2004). The residential schools for Aboriginal children that operated from the late nineteenth century until the 1980s effectively stripped these children of their families and their culture (S. Davies and Guppy 2014; Guppy and

Davies 1998). This was entirely intentional. Guppy and Davies (1998: 180) note that "a deliberate and concerted effort was made to remove thousands of Aboriginal children from their families and communities and immerse them in European traditions, thereby assimilating or 'Canadianizing' large portions of the Aboriginal population." These programs have had a devastating and lasting impact on Aboriginal populations (Guppy and Davies 1998). Only as recently as 11 June 2008 did the Canadian government formally apologize to Aboriginal communities for its role in creating and administering these residential schools.

Davies and Guppy (2014: 148–9) point out that the relationship between visible minority status and educational achievement is complex and highly influenced by Canada's changing immigration policy, by its history of colonization, and by socio-economic factors. The high education levels of more recent immigrants are becoming evident in the high educational aspirations and attainments of their children (Krahn and Taylor 2007; Taylor and Krahn 2005). In addition, recent data on reading, vocabulary, and mathematics test scores of the children of immigrant and non-immigrant parents show a convergence over time. In other words, immigrant children whose parents' mother tongue is not English or French catch up to their peers in academic performance (Guppy and Davies 2014: 151). Yet some visible minority groups continue to encounter exclusion and barriers in Canadian educational settings. Bernhard and Freire (1999) give an example of the way in which elementary schools fail students from minority backgrounds. They specifically look at the school experiences of the children of recent Latin American immigrants to Canada and the way in which these parents and teachers interact and communicate (Bernhard and Freire 1999). A primary aim was to find out how the school system could serve these families better and how these parents could be more effective advocates for their children. In

Global perspective

Box 10.3 Female Enrollment in Universities in Rwanda: Looking beyond Affirmative Action

by Nelson Ijumba

Statistics of the initial admissions to the University of Rwanda (UR) for the 2014/2015 academic year showed that only one third of the admitted applicants were female, which is in line with past trend.

This subsequently sparked a media debate on how to increase the proportion of female students in Higher Learning Institutions (HLIs). One of the popularly proposed methods was affirmative action by giving female applicants extra marks.

It is not an option UR Management is considering. Before discussing the merits and demerits of affirmative action as a solution, it is essential to critically examine data on female students' participation in the education sector, from Primary school through to Tertiary.

According to the 2012 Education Statistics Year Book released by the Rwanda Ministry of Education in February 2013, from 2008–2012, the average female enrollment was about 50.8% in Primary schools and 50.2% in Secondary schools.

On the other hand, at the tertiary level and in the same period, the average female enrollment was 33% in Public HLIs and 53.4% in the Private HLIs. For the TVETs, the average female enrollment from 2010–2012 was about 41.8%.

The low female enrollment in the Public HLIs seems to also be the trend in some of the institutions in East Africa where the average female enrollment is about 33%. However, in South Africa about 61% of the enrollment in Public HLIs is female.

The above statistics tend to suggest the existence of a hurdle that constrains the access of female students to TVETs and Public HLIs. The obstacle cannot be their inability to qualify because from the same pool of students that completed secondary schools more female were enrolled in the Private HLIs.

Furthermore, an analysis of the 2013 S6 examination results shows that 46% of the 23,958 candidates who got at least 2 principal passes, and, therefore, eligible for admission into the University, were female. Of those students who completed senior secondary school last year and were qualified to apply, only about 18,962 applied for admission to UR and 30% of them were female.

It means that only 5,759 females out of the possible 11,092 applied for admission to UR. The question is why did the rest (i.e., 5,333) of them not apply and where are they? It is most likely that some of them will be admitted into the Private HLIs. This raises a further question as to why female applicants seem to prefer Private to Public HLIs.

One might tend to argue that Private HLIs offer humanities based programmes which usually attract more female students. However, at UR currently, the College of Arts and Social Sciences (CASS) has the lowest proportion of female students (about 26 per cent).

In conclusion, the low female enrollment at UR is a matter of concern and it needs to be addressed since, based on the preliminary analysis, failure to qualify does not seem to be the issue, and then the proposed affirmative action process of inflating marks or lowering admission levels will not address the problem.

In fact it will make matters worse because the under qualified female students will not perform as well and this could lead to stigmatization and stereotyping of female intellectual capacity.

There is a need for further research to understand why only few females apply for admissions to Public HLIs although many more qualify to apply.

There is also a need to investigate why more female students prefer to enroll in Private HLIs than in Public ones. The solution to the problem is more complex and may require socio-economic interventions or even review of modes of programmes deliveries at Public HLIs to allow the flexibility that might suit female students.

Source: Nelson Ijumba. (August 4, 2014). "Female enrollment in universities: Looking beyond affirmative action." *The New Times.* www.newtimes.co.rw/section/article/2014-08-04/214/

spite of the high educational aspirations and valuation of education found in these Latin American families, the authors found a general pattern of academic underperformance for these children and parental alienation and confusion in the parents' relations with educational personnel (Bernhard and Freire 1999). One of their main findings was that many parents did not understand much of the vocabulary used by the teachers. For instance, the teachers' practice of using "positive" and complimentary descriptors when describing difficulties with a child's progress was seen by parents to indicate a good performance. In addition, educational terms like "special education" and "reading clinics" were not fully understood by or explained to parents. Parents expected a more compassionate and personal approach from their children's teachers and were disappointed with the impersonal and all-business attitude on the part of Canadian teachers (Bernhard and Freire 1999). These findings illustrate that even when parents have high educational goals for their children and want to facilitate their children's education, the structures of the institution itself (e.g., institutional jargon) can pose significant barriers to a positive academic experience and effective parental involvement.

Educational Attainment

Although there is a significant body of research on the educational attainment of Aboriginal people in Canada, much more information is needed on the effect that race or ethnicity and place of birth have on educational attainment (Looker and Lowe 2001). The diversity among groups designated "visible and ethnic minorities" and the factors of nativity, the period of immigration, and the changing effect of immigration policy make these investigations complex (S. Davies and Guppy 2014). Again, the high educational attainments required by current immigration regulations and the younger

age of many immigrants compared with the general population may artificially inflate the educational levels of ethnic and racial minority groups and thus lead to underestimation of the barriers encountered in the Canadian education system (Guppy and Davies 1998). Nonetheless, a number of studies contend that class is a more important predictor than race and ethnicity of educational attainment (Ali and Grabb 1998; S. Davies and Guppy 2014; Guppy and Davies 1998).

In fact, visible minority youth are slightly *more* likely than other youth to have their post-secondary options open in grade 10 (Krahn and Taylor 2007), and the aspirations of visible minority immigrant youth for university are also higher than those of other youth (Taylor and Krahn 2005). Indeed, in the latest results from the Youth in Transition Survey, 62 per cent of visible minority youth aged 24 to 26 had attended university, compared with 49 per cent of same-age youth who were not members of a visible minority (Shaienks and Gluszynski 2007: 9). Davies and Guppy (2014) highlight Frenette's (2005) data that show that in terms of educational attainment, visible minorities as a group are not collectively disadvantaged when compared with non-visible minorities. In terms of university-degree attainment, 29.6 per cent of those aged between 25 and 34 with visible minority status had a university degree in 2001 compared with 23.7 per cent of same-aged whites (S. Davies and Guppy 2006: 118). Of those who reported Asian visible minority status, 41 per cent had a university degree. While university degrees are more common among visible minority adults than among other adults, the educational attainments of racial and ethnic minorities are extremely variable (S. Davies and Guppy 2006). In fact, all recent trends suggest that visible minority groups in Canada today are far more likely to hold a university degree than the average white native-born Canadian (AUCC 2011). This will likely not change given the emphasis placed on education in Canada's immigration and selection policies.

Aboriginal people in Canada have encountered numerous barriers in the education system (CCL 2007; CPRN 2002; S. Davies and Guppy 2006). Though the educational attainment of Aboriginal people in Canada is improving, 8.7 per cent of Aboriginal people aged 25–64 had a university degree in 2011, which is a large gap considering that over 23 per cent of same-aged non-Aboriginal Canadians have a university degree (Statistics Canada 2008c; Statistics Canada 2011a). Some of the obstacles faced in the process of obtaining a post-secondary education reported by on-reserve Aboriginal Canadians are as follows: "53 per cent have inadequate funding, 46 per cent have poor academic preparation, 28 per cent do not feel welcome on campus, 20 per cent consider post-secondary education unnecessary" (CCL 2007: 76). This combination of factors echoes many of those identified in Frenette's study (2005) on the gap in university participation between low-income and high-income youth.

Canada's education system has failed Aboriginal students, and consequently, Aboriginal Canadians have much lower levels of educational attainment than the non-Aboriginal population, though their levels of educational attainment are growing (Statistics Canada 2008c). Despite some improvement—from 1996 to 2011 (see Figure 10.6), the number of Aboriginal people graduating from post-secondary institutions rose by 183,170 (White and Peters 2013)—there continue to be large gaps in the educational attainment of Aboriginal and non-Aboriginal Canadians (Gordon and White 2014). According to 2011 statistics, 39.8 per cent of First Nations adults aged 25–64 had not completed high school, compared with 15 per cent of same-aged adults in Canada (Statistics Canada 2011a). Nonetheless, Aboriginal students are increasingly engaged in post-secondary education, with 44 per cent having some post-secondary certification in 2006 (Statistics Canada 2008c: 19). For those Aboriginal students who do engage in post-secondary education, the attrition rate is extremely high (Gordon and White 2014). Indeed, these attrition rates may not be surprising given that 59 per cent of on-reserve First Nations youth report not engaging in post-secondary education because of the "need to support family" (Berger, Motte, and Parkin 2007: 59). According to Mata's (1997) investigation of the process of socio-economic and educational

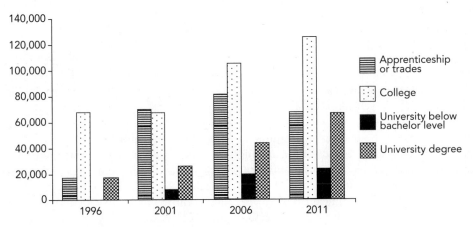

Figure 10.6 Aboriginal Educational Attainment, 1996–2011

Note: University below bachelor level became a category in the 2001 Census; therefore, data are not available for 1996.

Source: Statistics Canada. 1996, 2001, 2006 & 2011. Census of the Population.

"transmission" in Canada, Aboriginal sons and daughters experienced distinct disadvantages when compared with other ethnic and racial minority groups. While the parents in many other ethnic and racial groups were able to successfully "transmit" their level of education to their children, in the case of highly educated Aboriginal parents, there was little success in passing on attained educational levels (Mata 1997). The only other group to face such systemic and enduring obstacles to educational attainment in Mata's study were foreign-born minority daughters.

Educational Returns in the Labour Market

The high educational attainment of many visible minority groups and the educational mobility experienced by some ethnic minority groups in a society that discriminates on the basis of race and ethnicity are testament to the power of individual agents. This trend is shown clearly in Figure 10.7. Here we see the disadvantage that university-educated immigrants face relative to the native-born. From 2008 to 2011 average earnings (compared with those of native-born Canadians) declined for "recent" and "very recent" immigrant groups. During this period, the earnings

of "established immigrants" did not gain any ground.

Unfortunately, as shown in chapter 9, the true impact of racial and ethnic privilege is more starkly evident in the workings of the labour market (Hum and Simpson 2007; Li 2001b; Li 2010; Li, Gervaise, and Duval 2006; Mata 1997; Tran 2004). Hum and Simpson (2007: 104) found that black men in Canada, whether immigrant or native-born, experience a 22 per cent wage penalty in the labour market. They further note, "[T]he evidence is clear that economic disadvantage for blacks in Canada stems from unique structural features of Canadian society and economy, and it is hard to resist the suggestion that racial discrimination is an important factor" (106).

Indeed, higher education is no guarantee of occupational and socio-economic mobility (Reitz, Curtis, and Elrick 2014). All educational credentials are not valued equally, and a number of studies have shown that visible minorities encounter systemic devaluation of their educational credentials, especially when they happen to be among Canada's more highly educated recent immigrants (Li, Gervais, and Duval 2006; Samuel and Basavarajappa 2006). Visible minority professionals who immigrated

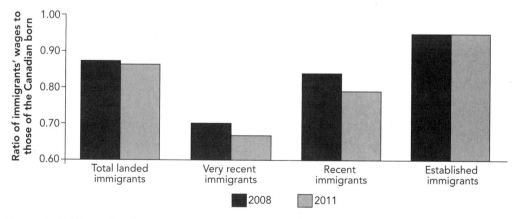

Figure 10.7 Wage Gap for University-Educated Immigrants, 2008 and 2011

Note: Reference group are those born in Canada.

Source: Statistics Canada, 2011 Labour Force Survey. www.statcan.gc.ca/pub/71-606-x/2012006/ct006-eng.htm

to Canada have been found to experience downward mobility compared with their occupational positions in their country of origin (Basran and Zong 1998). Samuel and Basavarajappa (2006: 250) report that for recent immigrants (of whom 70 per cent are visible minorities), the unemployment rate for adults aged 25–44 is twice that of the same-aged Canadian-born population. Kelly (2002) notes that there are significant levels of underemployment among highly educated visible minorities and that, despite their higher educational attainment, they are less likely to obtain employment in professional or managerial occupations when compared with the non-visible minority population.

In addition, Samuel and Basavarajappa (2006: 257) note that among the Canadian-born, although "visible minority men and women had higher proportions with university degrees . . . their shares in the top income quintiles were less than those of the non-visible minority counterparts, indicating that their earnings were not commensurate with their educational attainments." Visible minority immigrants who are not educated in Canada also face significant barriers in obtaining jobs and earnings on par with their education (P.S. Li 2000b). In fact, Picot, Hou, and Coulombe (2008: 416) found that recent immigrants entering under the "skilled economic" classification are more likely to become poor in Canada than those entering as "family class."

P.S. Li (2001b) analyzes the labour-market returns that visible minority immigrants and non-visible minority immigrants can expect in comparison with native-born Canadians. Gender and race and ethnicity were found to have significant effects on the extent to which immigrants encountered underemployment and weak labour-market returns. Visible minority immigrants (both men and women) were penalized much more harshly in the labour market for their foreign credentials than were white immigrants. Visible minority immigrant women with foreign degrees were the most disadvantaged in the labour market. For example, white immigrant women with a foreign degree earned an average of $30,770 annually, while visible minority immigrant women with a foreign degree earned the least of any group—$26,797 (P.S. Li 2001b: 32). C. Li and his colleagues (2006: 9) found that recent immigrants are also twice as likely to be overqualified for their jobs and twice as likely to remain in positions for which they are overqualified. P.S. Li (2010) finds that this is particularly true for Chinese-Canadian immigrants. Between 1998 and 2007 new Chinese immigrants numbered approximately 33,500 annually, most of which came with a university degree. Yet, as Li (2010) estimates, only about 59 per cent integrate into the Canadian labour market, and those who do often work far below their qualifications. Not only is this troubling from an inequality perspective, but it also means that only a portion of this human capital is benefiting the Canadian economy (P.S. Li 2010). These findings also illustrate that the achievement of credentials and educational mobility cannot in and of themselves overcome systemic discrimination for disadvantaged groups.

Focusing on Gender: Historical Notes and Existing Patterns

Historically, women have had to fight for their right to be educated, and educational policies have tended to emphasize women's wifely and motherly roles in processes of reproduction (R. Ng 1993; Wollstonecraft 1792). Yet, in Canada, women's access to education and enrolments at the elementary and secondary levels have been equivalent to men's for some time (S. Davies and Guppy 2014; Wotherspoon 2004). In fact, the educational level of women has surpassed men's since the mid-1980s, except at the doctoral level (Butlin 2001; CCL 2007; Wotherspoon 2004). Figure 10.8 shows the female share of university graduates by field of study in 1992 and 2007. This figure shows that women exceed men in nearly every aggregated bachelor's category.

Although alienation and **silencing** in the classroom are still concerns for girls and women and women continue to be underrepresented in post-secondary technical, mathematical, and engineering programs (see Figure 10.8 below), the gender-equity issue that is gaining attention in the elementary and secondary school systems has been the relative "underperformance" of boys

in comparison to girls (CPRN 2002; Looker and Lowe 2001; McMullen 2004; Wotherspoon 2004).

However, lumping all boys together as "at risk" may confuse the issue, because it is more specifically boys from families with low socio-economic status, Aboriginal boys, boys from visible minority ethnic groups, and boys for whom English is a second language who are systemically disadvantaged in the education system (CPRN 2002: 15). In other words, gender

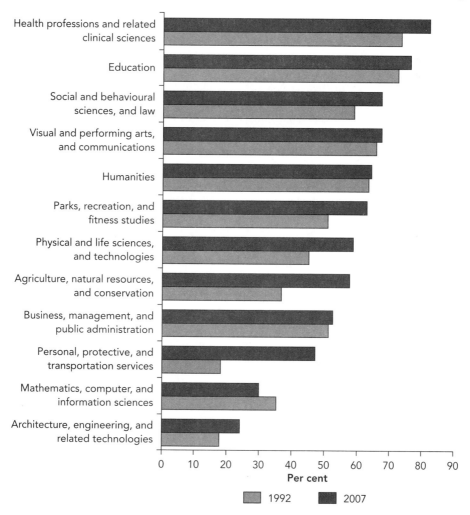

Figure 10.8 Female Share of University Graduates by Field of Study, 1992 and 2007

Source: Anon. (n.d.), "Women in Non-Traditional Occupations and Fields of Study," Statistics Canada. 2006 Census of the Population. www.statcan.gc.ca/pub/81-004-x/2010001/article/11151-eng.htm

is not the most important causal mechanism; social class, ethnicity, and language barriers play an equally strong role, especially for young boys. As with race and ethnicity, where some ethnic minority groups attain very high levels of education and others are at a substantial disadvantage, within the "variable" gender there are significant differences in academic performance and post-secondary participation rates among groups of boys (CPRN 2002). These findings speak to the complexity of identities and to the enmeshment of the social relations of class, age, gender, and race and ethnicity, particularly when it comes to social privilege and disadvantage.

Still, a number of studies illustrate that boys constitute the majority of students "at risk" of educational difficulties (Bohatyretz and Lipps 1999; Bussière, Knighton, and Pennock 2007; CPRN 2002; McMullen 2004; Sokal et al. 2005; Statistics Canada 2008c). Unfortunately, most of these studies do not give us more specific information about the class or race/ethnicity of boys and girls in a synthesized way (i.e., where data are separately tabulated for these factors). Work by Thomas (2006: 48) showed that "readiness to learn" at age five differed between boys and girls, with girls exhibiting stronger communication skills and abilities in symbol use, as well as better independence, self-control, and attention.

Similar to Thomas (2006), earlier studies found that when children were rated by their teachers for various behavioural traits, boys were perceived to be more physically aggressive and more hyperactive and inattentive than girls (Julien and Ertl 1999). In contrast, girls exhibited better work habits and more **pro-social behaviour**, or altruistic behaviour, although they were also perceived to exhibit more indirect aggressive behaviour. Of note, however, was that there were no perceived gender differences in anxiety and emotional disorders, and when all behavioural scores were compared, no substantial behavioural differences were found (Julien and Ertl 1999). Overall, these findings provide few answers as to why boys encounter

disadvantages in the educational process. Guppy and Davies (1998) have suggested that, historically, many men have not required educational credentials to obtain well-paying, stable jobs, whereas the fields of teaching, nursing, and clerical work, in which the majority of women found employment, have required an education. Therefore, this disparity in academic attainment may partially stem from lower educational aspirations on the part of boys and their families as a result of mistaken beliefs about the current demands of the labour market. Young men do tend to have somewhat lower academic aspirations than young women (Looker and Lowe 2001).

Educational "role modelling" by our parents appears to be an important factor. Indeed, Frenette and Zeman's (2007) study found that parental expectations were more important than peer influences in education attainment; however, Frenette and Zeman found that the most critical factors in explaining the differences between boys' and girls' educational attainment were those relating to academic performance. The authors suggest that gender differences in early school performance and study habits may explain much of the differential in later educational trajectories. For example, 70 per cent of young women had parents who expected them to complete a university degree, compared with 60 per cent of young men (Frenette and Zeman 2007). Nancy Mandell (CPRN 2002) outlines several arguments that have been proffered to explain the lower educational performance of boys. These range from an incompatibility between boys' "inherent nature" and classroom imperatives, to a female-biased curriculum, to class and race or ethnic discrimination in the school system (CPRN 2002: 15–16). Mandell concludes that while these factors likely play a role, in order to understand boys' underachievement in school, we have to stop viewing it as a problem of boys versus girls. This may be difficult to do with the data at hand. In the future, more complex and detailed information about students and their families will be required.

Educational Attainment

The gendered trends of educational performance that are evident in elementary school appear to continue into secondary school (Bowlby and McMullen 2002; Frenette and Zeman 2007). Thiessen and Nickerson (1999) found that in the teen years, girls showed stronger academic performance than boys in almost all subjects. Although after the age of 16 boys do score higher on problem-solving, these differences are significantly smaller than the language and reading advantage shown by girls (Thiessen and Nickerson 1999; Fortin, Oreopoulos, and Phipps 2013). Bussière, Knighton, and Pennock (2007) report the recent OECD's Programme for International Student Assessment (PISA) results, which show that while 15-year-old Canadian boys had a 14-point advantage in mathematics, girls were 33 points ahead in reading. Likewise, Frenette and Zeman (2007) report that at age 15 approximately one-third (32 per cent) of boys have overall marks of 80 per cent or higher, compared with 46 per cent of same-aged girls. These differences are partially attributed to boys' greater disengagement and dissatisfaction with the school environment (Thiessen and Nickerson 1999). These conclusions remain consistent with more recent research (McMullen 2004; Statistics Canada 2008c; Fourtin et al. 2013). Young men continue to be significantly less likely than young women to complete high school (Bowlby and McMullen 2002; CCL 2008; Looker and Lowe 2001). In 2011–12, young men dropped out of high school 4.2 per cent more often than young girls (the national average at this time was 7.8 per cent) (Statistics Canada 2012). According to the latest Youth in Transition Survey, young men cited a desire to work and dissatisfaction with school as their main reasons for dropping out of high school (CCL 2008). Related to this point, Fourtin

et al. (2013) found that the desire to work and "plans for the future" (2011: 22) pushed girls in the opposite direction. Measuring "planning for the future" helped account for the 2.3 per cent increase in high school senior girls' receiving "A"-range grades from 1980 to the 2000s.

The relationship between gender and educational achievement is very different in other parts of the world. For example, in China, discrimination is much more prevalent for girls compared with boys in the primary and secondary level. Although improvements were made in urban areas of China, gender inequalities in rural schools remain very high as boys are much more likely to attend post-secondary schooling. Other research suggests that gender inequalities are substantially reduced when controlling for urban/rural differences in education (Zhang and Chen 2014).

Clearly, academic performance in high school and high school completion are significant determinants of whether students go on to post-secondary education. The academic "underperformance" of young men in high school and their higher rate of high school non-completion put them at a disadvantage in the pursuit of post-secondary education (Bowlby and McMullen 2002; CCL 2007; Thiessen and Nickerson 1999). According to many studies, young men are underrepresented among post-secondary graduates and participants (with the exception of doctoral studies) (Bowlby and McMullen 2002; CCL 2007; Frenette and Zeman 2007; Looker and Lowe 2001). The latest figures show that 25- to 34-year-old women make up 59.1 per cent of students in bachelor's degrees and 58.2 per cent in master's degrees (Statistics Canada 2011a). This represents a substantial change in the gendered composition of post-secondary students in a relatively short time. For example, in 1972–3 women made up 43 per cent of university undergraduates, whereas in 1992–3 they constituted 53 per cent of undergraduates, and women's representation in higher educational levels continues to increase

(Thiessen and Nickerson 1999: 27). However, as Box 10.3 shows, access to post-secondary education is very unequal in other parts of the world (Frenette and Zeman 2007). Still, change has tended to be slower in terms of the fields of university study pursued by men and women and in the number of women in full-time doctoral studies (Butlin 2001; S. Davies and Guppy 2014; Looker and Lowe 2001), though women now constitute 47.3 per cent of doctoral candidates (Statistics Canada 2011a).

Despite the fact that almost equal numbers of men and women graduate from university in Canada, the educational tracks that girls and boys and men and women take in high school and university vary markedly. As a result of socialization, the toys that girls and boys play with, and different levels of encouragement for girls and boys, few girls claim to be good at math or science—even with progressive educational programs that try to eliminate gendered messages and regardless of girls' objective test scores. In university, these early trends translate into fewer women enrolling in engineering, science, or math programs. Although there have been significant improvements in the number of women who enter law and medical programs, women tend to pursue the lower-status streams within these programs by specializing in family law or family medicine. Men are discouraged from entering streams of education that are associated with women, such as nursing, but once in these programs, men are often viewed with greater esteem by their peers and professors (C.L. Williams 1995).

Research suggests that the university studies pursued by young men and women continue to adhere to these traditional gendered ideologies, with women largely concentrated in education, health, and the humanities and men in mathematics and engineering (CCL 2007; Looker and Lowe 2001). Women remain clustered in education and health fields, with men dominating in engineering, mathematics, and science. The continued underrepresentation of women in these fields of study is somewhat perplexing, especially given the generally equivalent levels of mathematical performance that are emerging between young men and women. And among women who do choose the non-traditional route of the maths and sciences, attrition rates tend to be high. Erwin and Maurutto (1998) examined the experiences of university women enrolled in science programs and found that the women most likely to leave the program were those who had to engage in significant hours of part-time work, many of them black working-class students. The underrepresentation of women in these well-paying scientific and technical fields and in doctoral studies further disadvantages women in the labour market—where women have tended to need much higher educational levels in order to earn wages comparable to those of men (S. Davies and Guppy 2014; Thiessen and Nickerson 1999).

Educational Returns in the Labour Market

In spite of being more highly educated than men, women continue to earn fewer returns on their **educational investments** than men (S. Davies and Guppy 2014; Frenette and Coulombe 2007; Frenette and Zeman 2007). Indeed, women's earnings remain lower than men's at all levels of education and in spite of women's growing educational attainment (Frenette and Coulombe 2007; Statistics Canada 2006a). Overall, little has changed in terms of the gap between men's and women's earnings, and in fact, in the 1990s the earnings gap between university-educated men and women increased (Frenette and Coulombe 2007). In 2001, women aged 25 to 29 earned 18 per cent less than same-aged men (CCL 2007) and in 2003, data for full-year, full-time employment show that at all educational levels women generally earned 71 per cent of what men earned (Statistics Canada 2006a: 139). Thiessen and Nickerson (1999) suggest that **occupational segregation** and child-care responsibilities help to account for women's lower monetary returns for their educational attainment. However, it is not only monetarily that women are disadvantaged in the labour market (Butlin and Oderkirk 1997). By considering a comparative perspective, we are able to see how much worse gender inequality is in Canada compared with other similar OECD nations. As Figure 10.9 shows, Canada is below average when it comes to earnings parity.

Although educational attainment usually leads to greater control and authority in the workplace, Butlin and Oderkirk (1997) found women to be far less likely than men to obtain significant amounts of autonomy and authority in their workplace even when education and other factors were controlled for. Men were more than twice as likely as women to achieve a top management post, and among male and female supervisors, men had significantly more decision-making power in their supervisory position. These patterns persist; although the proportion of women in managerial positions increased to 37.3 per cent in 2011, it has only risen by about 7 per cent since the late-1980s (TD Economics 2013). Butlin and Oderkirk (1997) attribute these disparities largely to the concentration of women in occupations that differ in marked ways from those of men. The underrepresentation of women

in the fields of engineering and the technical sciences and the concentration of women in the educational fields of teaching and nursing have a significant influence on labour-market returns and career trajectories. Since the mid-1980s, women's representation in engineering and natural science occupations has remained virtually unchanged, from 20 per cent in 1987 to 21 per cent in 2004 (Statistics Canada 2006a: 113). Data from 2011 show that women held only 13.1 per cent of Canadian engineering positions. Gendered discrimination in the labour market appears to be a contributing factor to the difficulty that women encounter in converting their educational credentials into monetary and other labour-market rewards (Butlin and Oderkirk 1997).

Focusing on Age and Life Course

Historical Trends in Canadian Educational Attainment

The times in which we live have a profound effect on our educational opportunities (S. Davies and Guppy 2014; Wanner 1999). Consequently, there are substantial differences in the educational attainment levels of different age cohorts

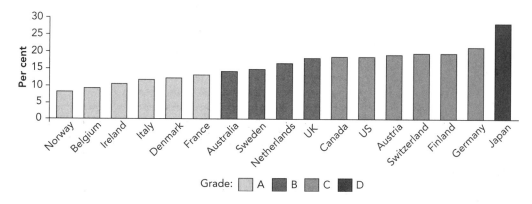

Figure 10.9 Gender Income Gap across Selected OECD Countries

Source: Published in Conference Board of Canada. (2016). *How Canada Performs: A Report Card on Canada*. Data from OECD Employment online database and Statistics Canada.

in Canada. Younger Canadians tend to be more highly educated than older Canadians (Clark 2001; Wanner 1999). For example, in 1951, approximately 2 per cent of the Canadian population 15 years of age and older possessed a university degree, but by 1996 that number had risen to approximately 12 per cent (Clark 2001: 23). In 2011, 64.1 per cent of Canadians aged 25–64 had some post-secondary qualifications (Statistics Canada 2011a). Davies and Guppy (2014) point out that before the 1950s, very few Canadians went on to university and those who did were from a distinctly elite upper class. An even greater generational contrast is evident in the percentage of Canadians with less than a grade 9 education. In 1951, over 50 per cent of Canadians 15 years of age and older had less than a grade 9 education; in 1996, about 11 per cent did (Clark 2001: 23); and by 2014 that figure had fallen to less than 5 per cent (Statistics Canada 2014). By the mid-twentieth century, "schooling" at the elementary and secondary levels had become an expected rite of passage for Canadian children; at the beginning of the twentieth century and before, school had played only a fleeting and sporadic role in many children's lives (Clark 2001).

The post-war baby boom and the subsequent expansion of the education system produced some dramatic changes in the educational attainment levels of Canadians (Clark 2001; Wanner 1999). Clark (2001: 19) notes that in 1901, most children were not regularly in the classroom: only 4 out of 10 children attended elementary and secondary school daily. Even later in the century, many children began school much later than they do now (Clark 2001). In 1921, 48 per cent of 6-year-olds and 17 per cent of 7-year-olds did not attend school (Clark 2001: 19).

Consider, for example, school attendance over the course of the twentieth century. In 1941, fewer than half of 16-year-olds attended school, whereas in 1996 approximately 85 per cent attended (Clark 2001: 20). The school attendance rates of 20- to 24-year-olds give an indication of the differences in post-secondary participation. Post-secondary participation rates in 1911 and 1941 were extremely small for this group, whereas in 1996 close to 50 per cent of 20- to 24-year-olds were attending school (Clark 2001: 20). These changes have continued to evolve.

The historical shifts in educational directives from a focus on issues of citizenship and comportment to a concern with vocational skills and the accumulation of credentials have meant a substantially different educational experience for Canadians of different age groups (Bruno-Jofre and Henley 2000; Osborne 2000; Wotherspoon 2004). Over the course of the twentieth century, some groups also experienced marked gains in their educational attainment as barriers and social norms underwent change (S. Davies and Guppy 2006; Wanner 1999). For instance, whereas women constituted only 17 per cent of university students in 1920, today they make up the majority of those enrolled in university (CCL 2007; Clark 2001; Frenette and Zeman 2007).

Wanner (1999) specifically examines the changes in educational opportunity for Canadians throughout the twentieth century in order to ascertain the effects of the **baby-boom expansion** on the educational opportunities of historically disadvantaged groups (e.g., women, those with a first language other than English, and those from a low socio-economic background). According to Wanner (1999), educational expansion has benefited some groups more than others. Analyzing age cohorts over time, he finds that the educational disadvantages experienced earlier in the century by women and those having English as a second language have largely been eliminated, except when it comes to graduate degrees, where men still have an advantage over women. In contrast, the educational disadvantage of coming from a lower socio-economic background has remained a stubborn feature of the educational landscape (Wanner 1999). In spite of the vast expansion in education, one's socio-economic background continues to operate as a most powerful predictor of educational attainment (CCL 2007; Frenette 2007; Wanner 1999). The growing importance of—and increased time devoted to—education in the lives of Canadians in the form of adult training and educational programs means that the educational disadvantages faced by those from lower socio-economic backgrounds promise to have stronger lifelong economic ramifications than in the past (Clark 2001; Livingstone 2001).

Adult Education and the Changing Face of Education

The profile of students and of those seeking further education has changed from the stereotypical image of the young, supposedly carefree individual (Sales, Drolet, and Bonneau 2001). The imperatives of a changing labour market, along with credential inflation, have meant that a number of older adults are engaged in education and training programs (Livingstone 2001; Statistics Canada 2001f). However, an analysis of results from the 2003 Adult Literacy and Life Skills Survey shows some disturbing trends in Canada (Rubenson, Desjardins, and Yoon 2007). There has been no increase in the participation of Canadian adults in education courses between 1994 and 2003—in fact, Canadian participation rates lag behind those of the United States, Norway, and Switzerland (Rubenson, Desjardins, and Yoon 2007). This is in spite of the fact that some workers see significant gains when they return to post-secondary education (Zhang and Palameta 2006). Among young men and women who return to school and get a post-secondary qualification, wages have increased 8 per cent and 11 per cent respectively (Zhang and Palameta 2006: 20). The same types of gains are not evident for older workers who

obtain a qualification and then switch employers; however, those who remain with their employers see a 13 per cent increase in wages among men and a 7 per cent increase among women (Palameta and Zhang 2006: 9).

Some workers have more difficulty than others in the pursuit of adult education and training. Older workers have lower adult-education participation rates, with 9.9 per cent of men aged 35–59 participating compared with 19 per cent of men aged 17–34 (Palameta and Zhang 2006). Among adults aged 45–54, only 3.4 per cent attended a post-secondary education program in 2002 (Myers and de Broucker 2006: 35). Only 8.2 per cent of men with less than a high school diploma participate in formal adult education, compared with 14 per cent who have a bachelor's degree or more (Palameta and Zhang 2006). Indeed, vulnerable groups in Canada—including those with low literacy levels, those with low socio-economic status, older adults, and less educated adults—are least likely to engage in adult education (Rubenson, Desjardins, and Yoon 2007). In other words, prior levels of educational attainment predict the participation rates of adult learners. As a result, well-educated adults are more likely to maintain and enhance their educational advantage in the workplace.

More immediately connected with the workplace, more than half (51.7 per cent) of Canadians who had an undergraduate degree participated in job-related formal training in 2002 compared with 17.9 per cent of those with high school or less (CCL 2007: 82). Researchers suggest that contrary to their purpose, adult education and training may actually "amplify rather than attenuate social inequalities in labour market outcomes" (Rubenson, Desjardins, and Yoon 2007: 38). Among those with less than a high school education and who would have liked to participate in adult education but did not, the top reasons for not going back to school were cost and family responsibilities (Myers and de Broucker 2006). Much more support was also needed for low-literacy learners in Canada: only 1 in 10 Canadians with low-literacy skills received government support for education and training compared with 1 in 5 in Norway (Rubenson, Desjardins, and Yoon 2007).

Although more adult learners are attending post-secondary institutions now than was true in the past, the age profile at universities is getting younger as more and more youth are enrolling (Myers and de Broucker 2006). Older learners tend to face more challenges in returning to school. Sales and his colleagues (2001) analyzed the academic routes taken by a sample of university students in Quebec and found predominantly non-linear and interrupted paths in the effort to obtain a university degree. These academic disruptions were primarily attributable to financial difficulties, which forced students to leave their studies and seek out means of financing their education. The students most vulnerable to these lengthened academic pathways were those from lower socio-economic backgrounds, master's students without scholarships, and older students (Sales, Drolet, and Bonneau 2001).

And, as Table 10.1 above shows, Canadian tuition costs have continued to rise since 2010–11. Older students typically have to rely on different types of financing than that of younger students and their expenses are generally higher (Myers and de Broucker 2006). For example, 83 per cent of students aged 20 to 21 receive financial support from parents, compared with only 38 per cent of those aged 26 and older (Myers and de Broucker 2006: 41). Researchers have argued that the heavy and growing debt loads of Canadian students place a particular burden on the present generation of students and their families and that this may be especially so for older students, who must borrow more heavily from outside sources (CPRN 2002; Myers and de Broucker 2006; Plager and Chen 1999).

The grant system once in place has been largely replaced by loans, and many graduates have difficulty repaying them (Plager and Chen 1999). One researcher poses the question, "Why [do] we find it acceptable that some young people, purely by an 'accident of birth,' are burdened by student loan debts of $20,000–30,000?" (CPRN 2002: 23). The rising cost of education is making debt an increasing reality for the present generation of post-secondary graduates.

Educational Returns in the Labour Market

Canadians can expect some changes in the labour-market returns from their educational investments (Kapsalis, Morissette, and Picot 1999; Wanner 2001). Some researchers have found that younger workers in Canada experienced a drop in real wages in comparison to older age groups (S. Davies, Mosher, and O'Grady 1996; Kapsalis, Morissette, and Picot 1999). These relative declines in labour-market returns have affected men more dramatically than women (Kapsalis, Morissette, and Picot 1999; Wanner 2001). Before 1960, university graduates with a bachelor's degree, particularly male graduates, could expect much higher labour-market returns on their degree than later graduates could (Wanner 2001). Graduates with a high school diploma in the first half of the twentieth century could also expect better monetary returns in the labour market than those in the latter half of the century (Wanner 2001). However, graduate and advanced degrees brought reliable returns for men and women over the course of the century, with men maintaining their labour-market advantage within this group (Wanner 2001). Wanner (2001) suggests that the drop in the value of undergraduate degrees stems from a lowered demand for them in the labour market and not from credentialism per se, since the returns on advanced degrees have remained relatively high. In fact, Finnie (2000) argues that the concern about poor labour-market returns for younger Canadians may be overblown. He finds that earnings among graduates are only moderately lower than in previous years; however, his comparison is limited to graduates in the 1980s and 1990s. More recent data on earnings and education show that at virtually all levels, higher educational attainment is coupled with higher income (CCL 2007), though it is important to note that 25 per cent of Canadians with a university degree earned less than Canadians with a high school diploma (CCL 2007) and that the earnings of young, less-educated men rose more rapidly than those of other groups between 2000 and 2005 (a rise that came in the wake of previous declines and stagnation) (Chung 2006). In fact, concern over the issue of overqualification in Canada has been growing (Li, Gervais, and Duval 2006). The number of university-educated workers who are overqualified for their jobs is on the rise, having gone up by one-third between 1993 and 2001 (Li, Gervais, and Duval 2006). In 2001, 19 per cent

of university-educated workers were overqualified for their jobs, and while younger workers were more prone to be overqualified for their jobs, once older workers were overqualified, they were more likely than younger workers to stay overqualified (Li, Gervais, and Duval 2006).

Immigrant workers were among the groups most prone to be overqualified for their job. Figure 10.10 shows the extent to which overqualification occurs for recent immigrants compared with Canadian-born workers. Immigrants are twice as likely to work in jobs that they are overqualified for and twice as likely to stay overqualified for the maximum length of time measured (Li, Gervais, and Duval 2006: 9).

In an earlier study, by Frenette (2000), respondents with a master's degree experienced high percentages of overqualification, from 48 per cent to 72 per cent across three age cohorts (Frenette 2000: 10). Even so, those with a master's degree maintained a wage advantage over those with a bachelor's degree. Frenette (2000) suggests that overqualified master's candidates are often hired for jobs that require only

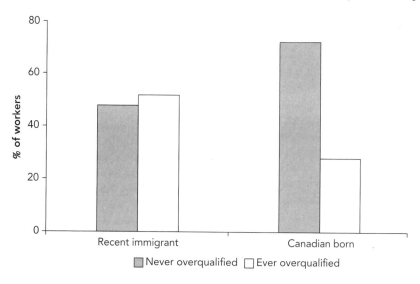

Figure 10.10 Overqualification among Recent Immigrants and Canadian-Born Workers

Source: Adapted from Li, Gervais, and Duval (2006: 9). Data: Statistics Canada, Survey of Labour and Income Dynamics, 1993 to 2001.

a bachelor's degree. This phenomenon may play a role in the lesser economic returns enjoyed by bachelor's-degree graduates in comparison to previous age cohorts.

The educational requirements of the labour market will probably continue to increase, and education continues to serve as an important control on access to monetary rewards and occupational autonomy (Butlin and Oderkirk 1997; Frenette 2000). Although some groups encounter more difficulty than others in reaping commensurable economic gains for their educational investment, the investment in education is now, more than ever, a vital requirement in the competition for jobs and occupational advancement in a global economy (CCL 2007; CPRN 2002).

Beyond the Statistics: Agency and Experience in Education

Although the preceding discussion provides a statistical overview of education in Canada, it does little to show how education is experienced or what choices people make about their education. Furthermore, because statistics rely on averages and typical experiences, variation from the average and the processes involved in varying from the norm are hidden. As we discussed above, Lehmann's (2014) study of the experiences of working-class university graduates speaks well to this point. Although they belong to that statistical category of "university graduate," their sense of belonging compared with that of the average "middle-class" graduate is strikingly different.

In addition, Judith Blackwell (1998) points out that although women are educated at similar or somewhat higher levels than men, women enrolled in universities sometimes experience difficulties because of overt sexism in the classroom, which is often reinforced by other aspects of university life. White privilege is perpetuated in educational institutions (Bedard 2000; Schick 2001), with racialized students feeling that their success depends on their ability to act as if they were white (Aguiar 2001). Indeed, racism runs rampant in Canadian educational institutions: racialized students are taunted and ridiculed by students and discouraged by teachers (Codjoe 2001). Henry Codjoe (2001) describes how the different experience of racism affected students in Alberta. For a minority of students, racism made them strive to be the best students so that they could be labelled exceptional. For most, however, racism was a barrier to success in education. As Kwame, one of Codjoe's (2001: 351) informants put it,

> To this day, it [racism] still affects me. It was a big hindrance. I dropped out twice as a direct result of that and other stuff like problems in high school with security guards and principals, and when one black person does something the whole black population in the school gets to go to the principal's office and stuff like that. You get fed up and want to quit.

Conclusion

The research presented in this chapter shows that a serious obstacle to high levels of education is social class; gender, race, and ethnicity seem to matter less. Yet what is also clear from this chapter is that much more Canadian research on educational attainment needs to be done to explore how class, age, gender, ethnicity, and race simultaneously shape educational pathways. Some of the research discussed above shows how class intersects with each of age, gender, ethnicity, and race, but rarely does research explicitly consider the complexities of all these factors. But the barriers to education probably vary in enigmatic ways. Consider a middle-aged black mother who just lost her job after the factory she was working in closed down and went south. She needs to work to help support her family, but she has few marketable skills. She would like to go to school to upgrade her skills, but colleges, universities, and the like are organized with the life-course stage of a 20-year-old in mind. This hypothetical case illustrates the complex relationships among class, age, gender, ethnicity, and race as they pertain to education and potential barriers to education. It also highlights the links between education, skill, and globalized labour markets.

Policy-makers are quick to point out that Canada needs to be innovative in an era of globalized markets and heightened competitiveness. Yet the traditional education system in Canada lacks the creativity that is needed to break down the barriers to lifelong learning. Although there has been some movement toward distance learning and Internet-based courses, these innovations have been slow to evolve. This is at least partly due to the overly elitist, class-based attitudes among educators in our schools of higher learning, who suggest that traditional methods of learning are superior to others.

The fact that boys are falling behind in elementary and high school also requires immediate policy attention. Again, it is not enough to examine the differences between boys and girls in this regard. The family experiences of class, gender, race, and ethnicity must also be considered. Do boys and girls employ social and cultural capital in the same way? Or do masculinities (as they vary by age, class, race, and ethnicity) influence whether and how social and cultural capital is used to one's advantage (CPRN 2002)? Obviously, the agency of parents and children is important here. Once we have insight into these and similar questions, Canadians will be in a better position to devise policy that will help to make education more readily accessible and useful to all.

⠿ Questions for Critical Thought

1. Does obtaining an educational credential guarantee positive labour-market outcomes? Which groups in society are able to maximize the benefits of their education in the labour market? What implications does this have for agency?

2. Which groups in Canada tend to be the most highly educated? Men? Women? Native-born Canadians? Recent immigrants? What factors lead to their more advantaged academic achievement?

3. What do you think will happen to the Canadian population's educational attainment levels over the twenty-first century? What effect, if any, will tuition increases have on access to post-secondary education? What effect, if any, will educational debts have on future generations?

4. What processes do you think are responsible for the educational underperformance of boys? How does this phenomenon illustrate the enmeshment of the CAGE social relations? What can be done to improve the educational experience and attainment levels of vulnerable populations?

5. What is social and cultural capital? How does it help students in the education system? Which groups are most likely to benefit from these forms of capital?

6. What factors went into your own educational choices and opportunities? Do you think that your educational attainment and

aspirations have been affected by the social relations of CAGE? If so, in what way?

7. What is the gender wage gap? Where does Canada fit relative to other OECD societies in terms of gender wage inequality? Does our position in global society surprise you?

8. How does Canada's education system compare to that of other countries around the world? Are we *more* or *less* educated than people living in other OECD countries?

⧉ Glossary

Baby-boom expansion The growth in the educational sector in response to the high fertility rate following the Second World War.

Cultural capital Bourdieu's concept of the collective dispositions, likes, dislikes, and typical recreational pursuits of the privileged classes in a given society. These activities (reading the newspaper, going to museums, golfing, and so on) are transmitted from one generation to the next through family socialization in a middle- to upper-middle-class milieu. Children from these families achieve higher levels of cultural capital and are therefore at an advantage in the educational process, where many of their activities and world views are taken for granted and are expected forms of knowledge.

Educational investment The monetary and occupational labour-market rewards that groups can expect as a result of their level of educational attainment, their field of study, and their demographic profile (age, race or ethnicity, gender, and class).

Occupational segregation The division of the labour force in such a way that men and women usually perform quite different tasks in their work. Men and women are generally sorted into occupations that are separate and distinct from each other (e.g., construction, transportation, and engineering traditionally employ men, while clerical work, nursing, and child care are traditionally done by women). This separation exists both in the type of work that men and women do and in the career and occupational ladders within an occupational field (e.g., within education, women tend to teach younger children, while men tend to teach older children and teenagers and are more often principals and administrators). These labour divisions also operate along ethnic and racial lines, and they tend to result in occupational advantages for the dominant social group.

Pro-social behaviour Socially altruistic behaviour, including that which results in the inclusion of other children or that involves listening to and showing concern, comfort, or compassion to classmates.

Silencing The practice among some students of remaining silent or not participating in response to a classroom experience that is exclusionary and does not validate their lived experience.

Social capital Bourdieu's concept of the social networks and informational resources upon which individuals are able to draw in their daily lives. The possession of large amounts of social capital presumes high reserves of economic and cultural capital, as it is through monied, educational, and prestigious connections that valuable social networking is accomplished.

Special education A form of educational delivery designed to address educational deficiencies and/or difficulties (e.g., social or behavioural problems, difficulty learning to read). This program may be offered directly in the classroom or it may involve separate classroom or teacher time for the student.

Streaming The educational practice of grouping and teaching children according to different levels of ability, either informally in a classroom or more formally within secondary educational programs (e.g., basic or advanced pathways).

Summer setback The loss of numeracy and literacy among students during the summer months.

⁝⁝ Recommended Reading

Apple, Michael W., Stephen J. Ball, and Luis Armando Gandin. 2010. *The Routledge International Handbook of the Sociology of Education*. New York: Routledge. This handbook synthesizes major advances in the sociology of education from a global perspective.

Berger, Joseph, Anne Motte, and Andrew Parkin. 2007. *The Price of Knowledge: Access and Student Finance in Canada*. 3rd edn. Montreal: Canada Millennium Scholarship Foundation. An excellent resource on access to post-secondary study in Canada and how finances currently affect educational attainment.

Canadian Council on Learning. 2007. *Post-secondary Education in Canada: Strategies for Success, Report on Learning in Canada 2007*. Ottawa: CCL. A comprehensive report on the state of post-secondary education in Canada, with current information on access to education for vulnerable groups.

Canadian Education Statistics Council. 2007. *Education Indicators in Canada: Report of the Pan-Canadian Education Indicators Program, 2007*. Ottawa: Statistics Canada and the Council of Ministers of Education, Canada (CMEC). The Pan-Canadian Education Indicators Program is a joint venture of Statistics Canada and the CMEC. This document, aimed at policy-makers, practitioners, and the general public, contains various statistical measures on education in Canada, with the goal of monitoring the performance of education systems across jurisdictions and over time.

Davies, Scott, and Neil Guppy. 2014. *The Schooled Society: An Introduction to the Sociology of Education*. Don Mills, ON: Oxford University Press. This book draws on sociological research and popular accounts to examine contemporary debates about schooling and the intersections between society, education, and the labour market within a Canadian context. The authors explore the notion of a "schooled society" in which education has become a central institution and document core themes of inequality in the context of education.

Lehmann, Wolfgang. 2007. *Choosing to Labour? School–Work Transitions and Social Class*. Montreal and Kingston: McGill-Queen's University Press. This book provides an in-depth comparative analysis of how social class affects educational trajectories and labour-market pathways.

Wotherspoon, Terry. 2004. *The Sociology of Education in Canada: Critical Perspectives*. 2nd edn. Don Mills, ON: Oxford University Press. This book outlines the main sociological perspectives that have been used to explain educational inequalities and takes a critical approach to the analysis of education in Canada.

⁂ Relevant Websites

Canadian Council on Learning
www.ccl-cca.ca

**This site has comprehensive reports on many aspects of learning, including adult education, literacy, and post-secondary education in Canada.

Council of Ministers of Education, Canada
www.cmec.ca

**This site has current educational indicators and a wealth of information about education in Canada.

Canadian Education Association
www.cea-ace.ca

**The CEA aims to build better links between research, policy, and practice to advance understanding of critical issues in education and learning. The site has information on the CEA's projects, events, and publications.

Canadian Federation of Students
www.cfs-fcee.ca

**The Canadian Federation of Students and the Canadian Federation of Students—Services were formed in 1981 to provide students with an effective and united voice, provincially and nationally, to ensure that students' rights and concerns are fully represented. This site shows how students' lives are affected by provincial and national policies.

11

CAGE(s) and Health

by Tammy Duerden Comeau, Julie Ann McMullin, and Josh Curtis

Introduction

Audre Lorde, who was born in 1934, is well known for her work as a poet and equal-rights activist. Lorde was a black woman, a feminist, and a lesbian who grew up in Harlem in the 1930s and 1940s and came of age during the 1950s. The daughter of recent Grenadian immigrants, she was raised in a working-class household. The substantive cohort in which she was born profoundly shaped her experiences in the processes of production, reproduction, and distribution—experiences that, in turn, had negative consequences for her health.

Unlike generations of black women who were born before her, Lorde did have some opportunities for paid work. This was true in part because of the progress made by equal-rights movements in the United States and in part because of the prosperous economic times that New York was experiencing in the 1950s. Yet her structural positioning as a young, working-class black woman profoundly shaped her employment options. In her search for work, Lorde's employment agency told her, "There's not too much choice of jobs around here for Coloured people, and especially not for Negro girls. . . . [M]ost of our unskilled peoples

find some sort of work in the 'hardware' factories on the other side of town" (Lorde 1982: 125). Lorde chose not to tell the employment service that she could type. In her refusal to type she acted with agency and, in doing so, knew that she would have to work either in a factory or as a maid. Although some would no doubt question this decision, Lorde chose (at the time) to reserve her typing for the self-expression and creativity of her own writing.

Lorde found work in a factory. Her youth meant that the alternative "option" of being a maid was not possible, for, as the employment agency told her, their clients "usually like[d] older women" (Lorde 1982: 125). Lorde's factory wages were somewhat better than they would have been had she been employed as a domestic worker, but the working conditions were deplorable. The following quotation from Lorde's book *Zami: A New Spelling of My Name* (1982: 125–6) documents her harrowing experience of working at Keystone Electronics, a plant that processed the quartz crystals used in radar equipment and radios:

> It was dirty work. . . . The air was heavy and acrid with the sickly fumes of carbon tetrachloride used to clean the crystals.

Entering the plant after 8:00 a.m. was like entering Dante's Inferno. It was offensive to every sense, too cold and too hot, gritty, noisy, ugly, sticky, stinking, and dangerous. . . . Nobody mentioned that carbon tet destroys the liver and causes cancer of the kidneys. Nobody mentioned that the X-ray machines, when used unshielded, delivered doses of constant low radiation far in excess of what was considered safe even in those days. Keystone Electronics hired Black women and didn't fire them after three weeks. We even got to join the union.

Every worker in the Keystone factory was either black or Puerto Rican except for the foreman and forewoman. Jobs were segregated by sex on the basis of traditional gendered ideologies, with the men cutting the crystals and doing the "heavy" work and the women X-raying and washing the crystals.

Before she got the job at Keystone, Lorde had worked nights as a nurse's aide and had gone to school part-time. She was a part of the working poor and was not eligible for social assistance. As an unmarried woman, she did not have access to a "family" wage distributed through an employed husband.[1] Making ends meet was a challenge, and yet Lorde redistributed her wages by providing financial support to a number of men and women who regularly "crashed" at her apartment. Since she could not afford nutritious food, Lorde's meals consisted of canned soup, sardines, and occasionally the treat of chicken-foot stew. Cooking was not easy, as there was no hot water (or heat) in the apartment and the kitchen was mired in years of filth and neglect from previous renters.

Regarding the processes of reproduction, high expectations of caregiving and nurturing placed upon women of colour have been well documented (Collins 1990). Lorde was unexceptional in this regard. She nurtured, fed, and sheltered her friends with what little she had, often to the detriment of her own well-being.

Lorde failed the summer school courses in trigonometry and German that she was taking. She attributed her failure to her own inability and not to friends' mounting demands on her time and money. When she eventually left New York City to find work in Stamford, Connecticut (at Keystone Electronics), she escaped many of the emotional and financial demands in her life only to encounter a physically toxic environment.

Our bodies are potent signifiers of the degree to which we experience inequality throughout our lives. Audre Lorde's exposure to toxic and dangerous working conditions was not a random event; black working-class women were deliberately hired for jobs no one else wanted. Some evidence suggests that this trend continues today and that black workers may be exposed to more serious toxic contaminants than white workers (Briggs et al. 2003; Krieger, Rowley, Herman, Avery, and Phillips 1993). The long-term health effects of exposure to workplace toxins, especially increased risks of cancer, have been well documented (Aragones, Pollan, and Gustavsson 2002; Fincham, Ugnat, Hill, Krieger, and Mao 2000; Pichora and Payne 2007; Richardson, Band, Astrakianakis, and Le 2007). Audre Lorde developed breast cancer in the late 1970s and died, at the age of 58, in 1992.

Although Audre Lorde's health experience centred on her blatant exposure to workplace pathogens and toxic substances, health inequalities can manifest themselves in more insidious ways. Indeed, the World Health Organization (2002) defines *health* broadly as "a state of complete physical, mental, and social well-being and not merely the absence of disease or infirmity." The fact that Lorde's wages were too low to provide her with nutritious meals or a suitable environment for their preparation probably took its toll on her physical, mental, and social health. Furthermore, the struggle to combine emotional and financial nurturing with long working hours in deplorable conditions has been shown to influence all aspects of "health" negatively.

Lorde's life history demonstrates that to understand inequities in health that result from the intersection of CAGEs and agency is a complex task. Yet empirical research has rarely considered these issues simultaneously. With this in mind, in the next sections we review the literature on health inequality in an effort to weave a complex tapestry of the social determinants of health in Canada.

Inequality in Health: Some Current Perspectives and Critiques

Health researchers and epidemiologists have long struggled to discover why there are inequalities in health (Herd, Goesling, and House 2007; Link and Phelan 2000; Phelan, Link, Diez-Roux, Kawachi, and Levin 2004; Phelan et al. 2010; Pearlin et al. 2013), and explanations for inequality in the study of health and illness have gone through numerous paradigm shifts (Adler and Rehkopf 2008). In his review of the literature, House (2001) documents the overwhelming emphasis in the mid-twentieth century on a purely biomedical approach to health and illness. Inequalities in health were analyzed and examined largely through the biology of the individual and the workings of the medical system. An individual's behaviour in the form of "lifestyle" choices (e.g., smoking, alcoholism, obesity, and physical exercise) was also believed to have a significant impact on health (House 2001: 127). Although studies that focused on individual biology, the failings of medical systems, and lifestyle choices added to our understanding of health inequality, none of these studies explained it adequately. Rather, researchers began to recognize that factors such as socio-economic status played a significant role in health experiences and that smoking, exercise, immoderate eating, and so

forth accounted only moderately (10 to 20 per cent) for socio-economic inequalities in health (House 2001: 134; Chen and Miller 2013).

In the 1960s, psychosocial factors came to the forefront of health research, and social epidemiologists began to emphasize the effects of "stress" on the physiology of the body (House 2001: 128). Indeed, the idea that stress may have negative consequences for human health has interested researchers since at least the nineteenth century (Koltai and Schieman, 2015; Seeman et al. 2010). Stress researchers have argued that the connection between SES and physical and mental health largely reflects (1) differential exposure to social stress over the life course based on social status, and (2) status-based differences in the distribution of personal and social resources (i.e., mastery and/or social support) to buffer the effects of these stressors (Pearlin 1989; Turner, Wheaton, and Lloyd 1995; Pearlin 2010; Pearlin and Bierman 2013). This approach aligns closely with what social epidemiologists label the "exposure-resource" framework (Lynch and Kaplan 2000).

This research led to a recognition that health is influenced by a large number of psychosocial factors, including social support, stress, and psychological or personality dispositions (House 2001). Problematic, however, was the fact that these **psychosocial risk factors** had been identified in the absence of an integrating theory; hence, much of the inequality in health remains unexplained (House 2001).

House (2001) draws on Link and Phelan's research (2000) to argue that if we are to understand health inequality, we need an integrated theory revolving around macro-social factors as the fundamental causes of disease risk. This work led to the development of **fundamental cause theory**—the leading social theory on health and inequality. House (2001: 125) suggests that investigators should concentrate on factors such as socio-economic status and "race" or ethnicity because these characteristics "shape individual exposure to and experience of virtually all known psychosocial, as well as many environmental and biomedical risk factors, and these risk factors help to explain the size and persistence of social disparities in health." House's framework is outlined in Figure 11.1. This figure shows that broader societal factors such as race, ethnicity, gender, and socio-economic status are integral to health outcomes and psychosocial risk factors. Because there are complex relationships between these factors, an emphasis on psychosocial aspects alone ignores the influence that social inequities have on health. If the analytic lens is shifted to the effects of race, ethnicity, and socio-economic status on psychosocial risk factors and health outcomes, a fuller picture of health inequality emerges.

Although House's conceptual framework includes class, ethnicity, and gender, his inclusion is additive rather than interactive. A close look at Figure 11.1 reveals that gender and race or ethnicity are not considered to be related and that both race and ethnicity or gender are thought to be mediated by socio-economic status in their relation to health outcomes. Age and the influence of social time are not explicitly accounted for, and the explanatory variables (e.g., social supports and social roles) are thought to be only "minorly" affected by gender and ethnicity. Hence, this conceptualization continues to treat gender, race, ethnicity, and socio-economic status as variables that can in some way be viewed as separate from one another, thus ignoring the importance of intersectionality.

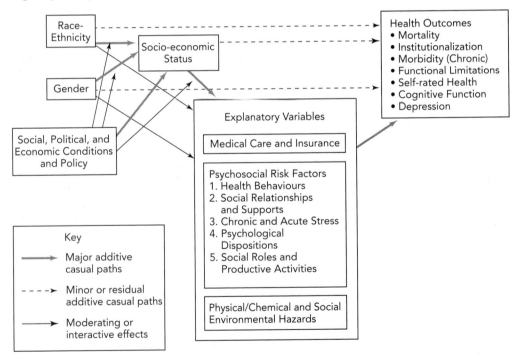

Figure 11.1 A Conceptual Framework for Understanding Social Inequalities in Health and Aging

Source: House (2002). Reprinted by permission of the American Sociological Association and the author. © 2002 American Sociological Association.

The epidemiological literature abounds in studies that document the impact on health of the variables of class or socio-economic status (Adler and Rehkopf 2008; Umberson and Montez 2010; Turner and Turner 2013; Marmot 2005; van Doorslaer, Masseria, and Koolman 2006), age (Ng and Feldman 2013; Parker and Thorslund 2007), sex (Connell 2012 Rieker and Bird 2005; Trovato and Lalu 2007), and race or ethnicity (Montazer and Wheaton 2011; D. Williams 2005), both singly and in various combinations (Cooper 2002; Cruz, Natividad, and Saito 2007; Huguet, Kaplan, and Feeny 2008; O'Loughlin 1999; Prus and Gee 2003). There is no doubt that health is shaped and moulded by these social relations, and many of the studies listed here point out the deficiencies and difficulties inherent in treating social relations as variables. While epidemiologic research is taking note of these elements and critiques, these variables continue most often to signify differences located in "biological" bodies rather than to indicate interrelated social patterns (Frohlich and Potvin 2008; Hatch and Dohrenwend 2007; Krieger 2003; Shim 2002). Given the prominent tendency of health research to treat class, age, gender, and ethnic or race relations as separate variables, the following discussion must do the same.

Mortality, Morbidity, and Mental Health

Social Class and SES

The association between social class and health is now well known (Hankin and Wright 2010; Mirowsky and Ross 2003). Those who possess more resources (e.g., income, education, and social connections) often enjoy longer and healthier (both physical and mental) lives than people lower in the class structure (Health Disparities Task Group 2005; Mao, Hu, Ugnat, Semenciw, and Fincham 2001; Marmot 2005, 2007). Health education

and awareness, access to prevention, and the capacity to avoid risk factors (e.g., toxic neighbourhoods)—resources that are held by members of the middle and upper classes—contribute to health advantage (Phelan and Link 2005; Phelan et al. 2004; Phelan et al. 2010). The latest figures on Canadian health-adjusted life expectancy (a measure that takes current health conditions into account) show that income makes a difference (Statistics Canada 2011; see Figure 11.2). People living in the highest-income neighbourhoods had a higher life expectancy than people in the lowest-income neighbourhoods. While women have a higher life expectancy than men in all income groups, as income rises, the life expectancy gap between men and women life diminishes: from 6.1 years in the lowest-income group to 3.7 years in the highest. People in low-income groups face more constraints on their abilities to "look after their health," and inequitable social conditions in workplaces, neighbourhoods, and regions significantly affect health throughout the life course (Krieger 2007; Statistics Canada 2011; Wight et al. 2008).

Beyond the simple yet strong relationships among individual income, education, occupation, and each of life expectancy and health, there has been a growing focus on these factors in relation to geographic regions or studies of health and place (Bernard et al. 2007; CIHI 2006a, 2006b; Duranceau and McCall 2007). Life-expectancy rates vary across regions of Canada, with those born in the territories (Yukon, the Northwest Territories, and Nunavut) having a life expectancy far lower than those born in Canada's provinces. For example, in Nunavut women live on average 73.9 years, while men live about 68.8. In Ontario, average life expectancy for women and men is 83.9 and 79.8 respectively (Statistics Canada 2013). Still, there are further differences between specific populations in the territories. Although the average life-expectancy rate increased for Canadians

Figure 11.2 Life Expectancy at Birth by Sex and Neighbourhood Income Quintiles, 2005–2007

Source: Lawson Greenberg and Claude Normandin, "Disparities in Life Expectancy at Birth," p. 6, component of Statistics Canada Catalogue no. 82-624-X, www.statcan.gc.ca/pub/82-624-x/2011001/article/11427-01-def-eng.htm#def3/

on the whole between 1991 and 2001, an analysis of life expectancy for the majority of the Inuit population in Canada showed no increase during this time, and life expectancy of Inuit at birth averaged 68 years (R. Wilkins et al. 2008). This marks nearly a 12-year difference in life expectancy between Inuit inhabitants and non-Inuit. Infant mortality in Nunavut was nearly double Canada's national average in 2005, with 10.0 deaths per 1,000 live births compared with the national average of 5.4 per 1,000 (Statistics Canada 2008b).

Health disparities in the average length of life one can expect also vary significantly across cities in Canada. For example, in Vancouver, life expectancy at birth is 81.1 years, while in Greater Sudbury it is only 76.7 years (CIHI 2006b: 13). There are mortality differences as well between rural and urban regions, with the generally higher mortality rates resulting from injuries

and various occupational hazards, particularly for men in rural areas (CIHI 2006a). Health patterns across regional Census Metropolitan Areas show that CMAs in Atlantic Canada each have life expectancies below the Canadian national average (J. Gilmore 2004). Within Ontario, CMAs show variation between the north and the south, with northern Ontario CMAs showing lower life-expectancy rates (J. Gilmore 2004).

The study of low-income or disadvantaged regions and neighbourhoods contextualizes health experiences by highlighting health risks that are beyond the control of people who often have no means of moving to another area (CIHI 2006a, 2006b; Safaei 2007). The presence of manufacturing and industry creates jobs; however, the risk of toxins and pollutions from these sources may also create health risks (Jerrett, Buzzelli, Burnett, and DeLuca 2005; Premji, Bertrand, Smargiassi, and Daniel 2007).

Research on mortality and morbidity shows that health status is correlated with income level (Kim, Kawachi, Vander Hoorn, and Majd Ezzati 2008; Wilkinson and Pickett 2007; Pickett and Wilkinson 2014) and, further, that health status in some contexts deteriorates with incremental declines in income (Gupta and Ross 2007). Indeed, investigations of the socio-economic gradient have shown that in places where incomes are more variable, death rates are higher (Marmot 2005, 2007; Wilkinson and Pickett 2006). Compared with findings in the United States, national socio-economic gradients in health are less evident in Canada. Although much more muted than in the United States, significant relationships between health and income exist in Canada (Wheeler 2007). The extent of the health disparities between high- and low-income populations is stark indeed. Researchers found that low-income populations were 16 times more likely to attempt suicide than high-income populations (Canadian Population Health Initiative

2007: 13). Infant mortality rates are much higher in Canadian territories, likely as a result of greater income inequality. Nunavut (18.53) and the North West Territories (8.03) have the highest infant mortality rates. British Colombia (3.73), PEI (3. 73), and New Brunswick (4.23) sit well below the national average of 4.90 infant deaths per 1,000 live births. As Figure 11.3 shows, Canada fares poorly compared with other OECD countries (Conference Board of Canada 2015).

Indeed, research assessing income and health status has repeatedly shown linkages between high SES levels and better health status (Auger, Raynault, Lessard, and Choiniere 2004; Gupta and Ross 2007). Recent research has shown that the length of time individuals spend in either economic advantage or disadvantage may influence health trajectories over the life course (Buckley, Denton, Robb, and Spencer 2006; Willson, Shuey, and Elder 2007). Using US longitudinal data and measures of income, education, and wealth, Willson and her colleagues

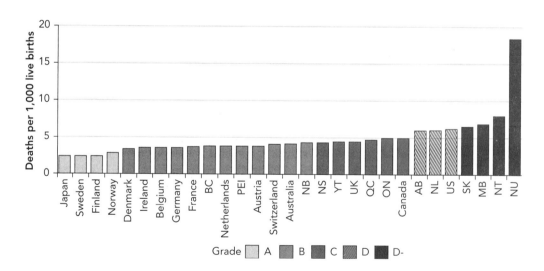

Figure 11.3 Infant Mortality, Provinces, Territories, and International Peers, 2009–2011 (deaths per 1,000 live births)

Source: Conference Board of Canada (2015), data from: Statistics Canada. Table 102-0030; OECD, http://public.tableau. com/views/HPP_Health/Infant_dash?:embed=y&:showVizHome=no&:host_url=https%3A%2F%2Fpublic.tableausoftware. com%2F&:tabs=no&:toolbar=yes&: animate_transition=yes&:display_static_image=yes&:display_spinner=yes&:display_over-lay=yes&:display_count=yes&: showVizHome=no&:loadOrderID=0

(2007) found that the duration of time for which respondents experienced economic advantage or disadvantage made a difference: extended SES disadvantage was related to stronger declines in health, and long-term SES advantage was linked to slower health declines over time. There is considerable debate among health researchers about whether the relationship between health and SES is causal or a result of selectivity. At issue is whether low income, education, and bad jobs result in poor health and an increased risk of death or whether those with poor and declining health consequently experience lower income and education levels (Phelan et al. 2004; Wolfson, Rowe, Gentleman, and Tomiak 1993). No doubt both of these explanations account for some of the SES variation in health. Nonetheless, compelling evidence for the causality argument is evident in work by Phelan and her colleagues (Phelan et al. 2004; Phelan and Link 2005). They argue that higher socio-economic status enables individuals to marshal greater flexible resources in protecting their health (e.g., by moving to healthier neighbourhoods), and they found significantly stronger relationships between preventable causes of mortality and SES compared with less preventable forms of mortality (Phelan et al. 2004). In this way, the authors suggest, those individuals with higher SES are able to better avoid health risks from known causes of disease. In contrast, this relationship is less pronounced for diseases that are less preventable and/or less curable. This means that rather than ill health primarily influencing SES level, the relationship between SES and health is one where SES enables individuals to better avoid and predict health risks (Phelan and Link 2005; Phelan et al. 2004).

At the same time, those who struggle with existing health conditions often do face difficulty in securing stable employment and income (McMullin and Shuey 2006; C. Williams 2006). Although employers in Canada are required to accommodate workers with disabilities, stigma, misconceptions, and stereotypes have resulted in unmet needs for many Canadians (McMullin and Shuey 2006). The tendency to regard disability in older age groups as part of the "natural aging" process is particularly worrisome and may result in older workers' being prematurely excluded from productive employment (McMullin and Shuey 2006). Clearly, this exclusion would also negatively affect their income level and socio-economic status.

Despite evidence of an SES gradient, conditions of poverty and the associated problems of poor health cannot be ignored (Health Disparities Task Group 2005; Trovato 2001). As research shows, the relationship between inequality and health is particularly strong in the United States (see Box 11.1). In Canada (see Box 11.2), those who are poor also face many challenges in maintaining their health over time. For example, new research in Ontario shows that 66 per cent of people who were "working non-poor" reported their health as excellent or very good compared with 49 per cent of the working poor and 35 per cent of people who were non-working poor (Wellesley Institute 2013). The experience of poverty has an indelible and unmistakable effect on the condition and health of the body (Adair 2001). As Adair (2001: 451) points out, "poor children are often marked with bodily signs that cannot be forgotten or erased," and reflecting on her own experience, she says, "In spite of my mother's heroic efforts, at an early age my brothers and sisters and I were stooped, bore scars that never healed properly, and limped with feet mangled by ill-fitting, used Salvation Army shoes" (2001: 456). Adair grew up in the United States, and many might argue that in Canada universal health care modifies or ameliorates many of the relationships between class and health. However, Crompton (2000: 16) finds in her retrospective of 100 years of health in Canada that even after 40 years of universal health care, low-income earners have higher rates of morbidity and lower life expectancies than those with higher incomes. These patterns continue to hold true (Health Canada 2006: 31).

The "poor" are, however, not a homogeneous group, and attempts to treat them as such may mask important health risks (Adler and Rehkopf 2008; Health Disparities Task Group 2005). Everyone's "chances" of being poor are not equal, and one's marital status (Avison and Davies 2005; Curtis and Pennock 2006), gender (Spitzer 2005), age (Bailis, Chipperfield, and Helagson 2008; Prus 2007), and race and ethnicity (Quan, Wang, Schopflocher, and De Coster 2007; Shuey and Willson 2008) are all integrally bound up with one's class and socio-economic status. Krieger (2007) notes that, in biomedical research, it is critically important to take these distinctions and social factors into account. She states that the failure to recognize social determinants of health such as poverty, race, and gender has resulted in less effective and sometimes harmful treatment and research paths. Krieger (2007: 661) argues that by failing to take socio-economic status

Global perspective

Box 11.1 Income Inequality and Health

In a 2014 newspaper article titled "How being poor makes you sick," Olga Khazan told the story of Alan Meyers, a pediatrician in Boston who has implemented a unique approach to caring for his patients. On top of following all standard medical procedures for his patients, Meyers provides all of his patients who suffer from weight issues with a one-year membership to Boston's bike-sharing program. This unorthodox practice, Meyers argues, was meant to promote healthy daily living practices for his patients. As he explains, "What we know is that if we are trying to get some sort of exercise incorporated into their daily routine, [the bike] works better than saying, 'Take x time every day and go do this.'"

Unfortunately, people from low-income brackets are more likely than others to live unhealthy and inactive lifestyles (Burton et al. 1995). Poorer parts of cities often have few parks and recreation centers which limits their accessibility. Moreover, people with more precarious employment contracts also have less time to engage in exercise after work. For these reasons, Meyers's bike system is truly an inventive one.

Income inequality also affects other areas of health. For example, studies continuously show that income inequality and poverty are divisive, socially corrosive, and that they hold serious consequences of mental well-being. Richard Wilkinson and Kate Pickett, two top scholars on income inequality and well-being, found that rates of mental illnesses became much more common in societies where the gap between the rich and the poor becomes more pronounced. In the US, they argue, rates of depression and anxiety are nearly three times higher compared with, for example, Japan and Germany. Other American research finds that within the US, depression was much more common in states with higher levels of income inequality (Wilkinson and Pickett 2011).

Shockingly, other research on inequality and mental health found that living in poverty was a stronger predictor of poor mental health than was being enlisted for *war*.

Sources: Olga Khazan. (May 21, 2014) "Poverty Makes You Sick." *The Atlantic*; L.C. Burton et al. (1995), "The Effect among Older Persons of a General Preventive Visit on Three Health Behaviors: Smoking, Excessive Alcohol Drinking, and Sedentary Lifestyle," *Preventive Medicine* 24, 5: 492–7; Richard Wilkinson and Kate Pickett (2011), *The Spirit Level: Why Greater Equality Makes Societies Stranger* (New York: Bloomsbury Press).

HIGHLIGHT

Box 11.2 Sarnia's Emissions Affecting Health, Study Says

by Martin Mittelstaedt

Sarnia is fabled as Canada's chemical valley because of its many petroleum plants, but a new study says the community's industrial prosperity has a dark side: The area is the most polluted in Ontario when it comes to smokestack emissions.

The study, by Ecojustice Canada, an environmental group, also makes the controversial assertion that pollution is so severe in the city and a nearby Native reserve that the health of the 130,000 people living in the area is being harmed due to exposure to such harmful substances as mercury, dioxins and volatile organic compounds.

"The toll these emissions are taking is dramatic and there is growing evidence that the health of the residents of Sarnia and Aamjiwnaang First Nation and the local environment has been severely compromised," says the study, a copy of which has been obtained by The Globe and Mail.

According to the study, which is being released today, the cluster of plants in and around the Southwestern Ontario city released more dangerous chemicals into the air in 2005 than all the industries in Manitoba or New Brunswick or Saskatchewan, based on federal pollution data.

Among the worrisome health developments it cited were an excessive rate of girls' births compared with boys for native women living on the reserve near the chemical plants; a toll of asbestos-related diseases among Sarnia workers,

considered one of the highest in the world; and an incidence of leukemia among women aged 25 to 44 in the county that is double the provincial rate.

"We're exposing the human population, on almost like a huge clinical trial, to these very high levels of toxic substances," said Jim Brophy, director of Sarnia's Occupational Health Clinic for Ontario Workers, which in recent years has treated hundreds of workers for medical problems related to dangerous chemical exposures.

The clinic, along with several community groups, has been lobbying to have the health of area residents studied to see what effects pollution might be having, but Mr Brophy said no level of government has been willing to commit funding for such a review.

An association representing major chemical companies in the area, the Sarnia-Lambton Environmental Association, declined to comment yesterday on the adverse health claims until the study is publicly released.

Elaine MacDonald, one of the study's authors and senior scientist at Ecojustice, said Sarnia's plants, which represent about 40 per cent of the country's chemical manufacturing, are often located near housing, without much of a buffer zone to separate residents from industry. Ministry of Environment spokesman John Steele said the province plans to place more air-monitoring equipment in the area, and in 2005 it tightened pollution standards.

City	Pollutants (tonnes)
Sarnia	5,669
Sudbury	4,574
Hamilton	3,334
Toronto	2,829
Oshawa	1,939
Windsor	1,308
Kitchener	1,229
Thunder Bay	1,201

Prov., Terr.	Pollutants (tonnes)
Man.	3,966
NB	3,519
Sask.	3,177
NS	2,998
Nfld	1,061
NWT	210
PEI	72
Nun.	33

Source: Ecojustice Canada based on Environment Canada NPRI 2005 Data and pollutionwatch.org.

Source: Mittelstaedt (2007). Copyright © CTVglobemedia Publishing Inc. All Rights Reserved.

into account, research findings advocating hormone treatment to combat cardiovascular risk inadvertently caused a significant jump in the number of breast cancer cases:

> Recommendations for hormone therapy effectively asked these women to increase their short-term and not inconsiderable risk of cancer, with the hope of decreasing their long-term risk of cardiovascular disease. The tradeoff has been costly. Studies conducted between 2002 and 2005 in the United States, United Kingdom, Australia, and Norway suggest that hormone therapy accounts for somewhere between 10 and 25 per cent of observed breast cancer cases. In the United Kingdom, this has been estimated to translate to an extra 20,000 breast cancers among women ages 50–64 in the past decade alone.

By ignoring the impact of the social determinants of health such as the protective effect of socio-economic status, generalized recommendations from biomedical research may increase health risks. Findings such as these illustrate that biomedical research and data collection must be conducted in more complete and complex ways that acknowledge and account for socio-economic status and other social determinants of health (Krieger 2007).

The prevalence of mental illness also varies according to social advantage: "The poor, the young, ethnic minorities, and blacks have higher rates of mental illness than the well-to-do, older persons, ethnic majorities, and whites" (Simon 2000: 72; Simon 2007). Canadian data from 2005 in Toronto shows not only that the poorest Canadians have worse physical and mental health than higher-income groups, but also that overall health follows a clear income gradient: the lower a person's income, the worse their mental health (Leightman et al. 2008). In Canada, we also see clear neighbourhood-level effects between income and mental health. For example, in Ontario, people living in the poorest Canadian neighbourhoods reported lower positive mental health (66 per cent) compared with those living in the "best off" neighbourhoods (78 per cent) (Wellesley Institute 2013).

Accounts of the relationships between social factors, environmental context, and mental health have focused on stress-process and vulnerability explanatory models (Simon 2000). Researchers working within the stress-process paradigm argue that the experience of stress in various forms affects physical and mental health (Avison and Gotlib 1994; H. Turner and Turner 2005). But although stress affects physical health, much of the stress-process research has concentrated on the effects of stress on mental health (Lantz, House, Mero, and Williams 2005; Pearlin et al. 2005; Simon 2007). McLeod and Lively (2007: 277–8) note two main streams in current stress research: one examines the extent to which different societal groups (e.g., varying by income, race/ethnicity, age, or gender) are exposed to chronic strains and stressful events and, in doing so, documents the effect of inequality on population mental health; the other focuses more on individual perceptions of stress and the resources or buffers at hand for maintaining mental health.

Currently, there is some debate over the relative importance of the "neo-material" or structural aspects prone to influence mental health (e.g., substandard housing, environmental toxins, access to health care) and the psychosocial aspects (e.g., perceptions of inequality, health behaviours, cognitive processes) in explaining the persistent associations between socio-economic disadvantage and health (Muntaner, Borrell, and Chung 2007). Adler (2006: 848) notes that researchers pursuing the psychosocial aspects of health inequality still acknowledge the effect of structural inequality on these factors and states that the two approaches are best viewed as "complementary." There is general agreement that people with less power in society are more exposed to ongoing life stresses and strains and often have fewer resources and social supports to help them cope (Pearlin, Schieman, Fazio, and Meersman 2005; Simon 2000, 2007; Turner and Avison 2003; Turner and Lloyd 1999). Pearlin and his colleagues (2005: 206) state this eloquently:

> Salient among the circumstances linking status and health, we submit, is the differential exposure to serious stressors, both those built into the warp and woof of social and economic life and those that are eventful. We refer to the dogged hardships, demands, conflicts, and frustrations that may be instrumental in structuring people's experiences across time and to events that may disrupt the continuities of their lives.

The development of psychosocial resources, such as mastery, self-esteem, and the perception of control over one's environment, is hindered for those who encounter ongoing structural barriers and disadvantages (H.A. Turner and Turner 2005; Pearlin and Bierman 2013). The experience of childhood poverty manifests itself in higher rates of depression and antisocial behaviour throughout the life course (George 2007; McLeod and Shanahan 1996). In their systematic review of the literature, Lemstra and his colleagues (2008) found that youth aged 10–15 from lower socio-economic backgrounds were more than twice as likely (2.49 times) to suffer from depression or anxiety disorders. Psychiatric disorders, including depressed moods, anxiety, and drug and alcohol problems, are generally more prevalent among those from disadvantaged class backgrounds—those with fewer financial assets (Muntaner, Borrell, and Chung 2007; Muntaner, Eaton, Diala, Kessler, and Sorlie 1998). In 2012, 2.8 million Canadians over age 15 (or 10.1 per cent of the population) reported symptoms of mental or substance abuse disorders. Over the life course, nearly 6 million Canadians are affected, many of whom were from lower SES backgrounds (Statistics Canada 2013). Using a national probability sample from the Canadian Community Health Survey of 56,428 adults living in 25 Census Metropolitan Areas, Matheson, Moineddin, and Glazier (2008) found that neighbourhoods with high chronic stressors in the form of material deprivation and residential instability are associated with depression. Indeed, the nature of physical surroundings appears to be an important factor in mental health. Even the development of schizophrenia—a psychiatric condition that is believed to have a strong genetic component—is linked to early work experience of "noisome" occupational conditions (such as noise, temperature extremes and fluctuations, hazards, and fumes), suggesting that **class-linked stress** may be a predisposing factor for the disease (Link, Dohrenwend, and Skodol 1986). Recent data snapshots of homelessness in Canada have found a much higher incidence of schizophrenia in this population as well, though the causal pathways remain uncertain (Canada's Public Policy Forum 2014).

Race and Ethnicity

In Canada, death rates and the incidence and prevalence of physical disease and mental health show variance across measures of race and ethnicity (Kobayashi, Prus, and Lin 2008; E. Ng, Wilkins, Gendron, and Berthelot 2005; Trovato 2001). Aboriginal peoples in Canada face many health challenges, and their rating on a variety of health-status measures is worse than those of non-Aboriginals (CIHI 2004).

Figures 11.4 (kidney disease) and 11.5 (heart disease) present comparative data for Aboriginal and non-Aboriginal groups in Canada. In both cases, Aboriginal populations were nearly twice as likely to be hospitalized and receive treatment for these ailments from 2005 to 2011.

Although Aboriginal peoples are often collectively grouped, it's important to note that there are differences among peoples; the rate of tuberculosis among Inuit, for example, is

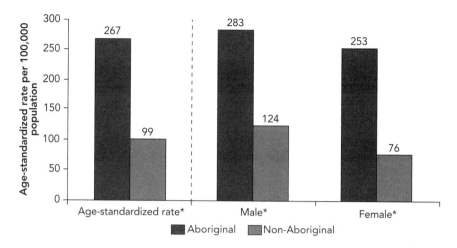

Figure 11.4 Rates of Chronic Kidney Disease by Sex, 2004–2005 to 2010–2011

Note: *Statistically significant

Source: Statistics Canada. Health Reports. Catalogue No. 82-003-X.

Figure 11.5 Heart Attack Hospitalization by Sex, 2004–2005 to 2010–2011

Notes: *Significantly different from low-Aboriginal areas (p<0.05).
Error bars indicate 95% confidence intervals.
Rates have been age-standardized to the population that identified as First Nations in the 2006 Census.
Rates do not include Quebec data due to differences in data collection.

Source: Statistics Canada. Health Reports. Catalogue No. 82-003-X.

92.0 per 100,000/year compared with a rate of 30 among First Nations groups and 1.3 among non-Aboriginals in Canada. As noted, the prevalence of a number of chronic conditions is higher in Aboriginal populations, and particularly among First Nations groups. For example,

22 per cent of First Nations men have high blood pressure compared with 8 per cent of non-Aboriginal men in Canada. In a Canadian study of cardiovascular disease, Aboriginal people were found to be much more likely to have the disease than those of European ancestry (18.5 per cent compared with 7.6 per cent) (Anand et al. 2001). The new data presented above in Figures 11.4 and 11.5 suggest that the same patterns may also be true today. Indeed, there are differences in the primary causes of mortality between Aboriginal and non-Aboriginal people in Canada: for Aboriginal people, the leading cause of death is injury, while injuries sit as the fourth leading cause of death in Canada for other groups (Allard, Wilkins, and Berthelot 2004). Although the Aboriginal population is substantially younger than the non-Aboriginal population in Canada (median age of 27 compared with 40), even when controlling for age, there are significantly more injuries among Aboriginal people (Statistics Canada 2008a; Tjepkema 2005). Again, these health challenges should be viewed in light of the social, cultural, and economic oppression against which Aboriginal groups in Canada have struggled (CIHI 2004).

Given these conditions and our knowledge of the relationships between socio-economic status and health, it is not surprising that Aboriginal peoples have higher mortality rates than the non-Aboriginal population (CIHI 2004: 81), though it is important to note that compared with Aboriginal peoples in the United States and New Zealand, those living in Canada are particularly disadvantaged in terms of mortality rates (Trovato 2001). For Canadian Aboriginals, life expectancy is approximately five to seven years shorter than for the general population in Canada (CIHI 2004) and infant mortality rates are generally twice as high—and are triple among Canada's Inuit populations (CIHI 2004). Future projections by Statistics Canada (2005e) suggest that this gap in life expectancy may grow by 2017 (Figure 11.6).

The high mortality and morbidity rates of Aboriginal populations in Canada are accompanied by high rates of poorer mental health (Beaujot and Kerr 2003; MacMillan et al. 2003). Suicide and self-injury are the leading causes of death among First Nations youth and adults between ages 10 and 44. Compared with the national average, First Nations youth (15–24 years) are nearly 7 times more likely to

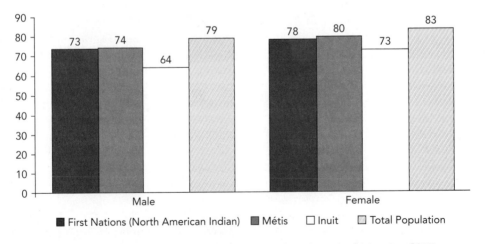

Figure 11.6 Projected Life Expectancy at Birth by Sex, by Aboriginal Identity, 2017

Source: Statistics Canada, Projections of the Aboriginal Populations, Canada, Provinces and Territories, 2001 to 2017. Catalogue No. 91-547-XIE.

commit suicide than non-Aboriginals (Health Canada 2013). Suicide rates for Canada's Inuit populations are even more severe at 11 times higher than the national average. Paradoxically, only 3.1 per cent of Inuit had a major depression in 2001, leaving researchers to speculate that mental health measures may be invalid and/or that depression may manifest itself among Inuit in alternative ways (Public Health Agency of Canada 2006: 164). Depression is also highly prevalent in Aboriginal populations; as many as 30 per cent of First Nations people report feeling depressed for two weeks or more, an indicator of clinical levels of depression (Health Canada 2013). Based on these statistics, it is evident that isolation, poverty, racism, and post-colonial legacies of abuse continue to affect the health of Aboriginal peoples.

Different patterns of health and illness are evident in the study of immigrant populations in Canada, as the study of health and ethnicity is complicated by immigration screening procedures (Newbold 2005; E. Ng et al. 2005). Immigrants to Canada are selected partly on the basis of health, and research has shown that the "healthy-immigrant effect" plays a significant role in studies of health and ethnicity. In other words, immigrant populations, particularly those from non-European countries, exhibit better health and live longer than Canadian-born populations (Ali, McDermott, and Gravel 2004). This is partly because immigration to Canada is dependent upon an applicant's good health. However, the healthy-immigrant effect starts to dissipate after 10 years in Canada (Dunn and Dyck 2000; Halli and Anchan 2005; E. Ng et al. 2005). Although it is difficult to explain, some researchers have attributed the diminishing health advantage of immigrant populations to lifestyle factors such as diet and physical activity (Chen, Ng, and Wilkins 1996; E. Ng et al. 2005) and to social isolation and lack of access to health care (Newbold 2005; Oxman-Martinez, Abdool, and Loiselle-Leonard 2000).

Using data from the Canadian Community Health Survey (2000–1), Kobayashi, Prus, and Lin (2008) found that visible minority groups in Canada rated higher on health measures compared with non-visible minority and Aboriginal peoples. In contrast to prior studies, these authors found that Canadian-born South Asians and Chinese had better health than their foreign-born counterparts (at least within the first decade of immigration), though the authors note that "the health advantages of the Chinese and South Asians, regardless of immigrant status, are explained away by differences in social structural and lifestyle environments" (Kobayashi, Prus, and Lin 2008: 140). Their findings underscore the need to examine social determinants in health research.

Racism and discrimination are important factors to consider when examining the relationships between ethnicity and health (Kobayashi, Prus, and Lin 2008; Krieger et al. 2005; Noh, Kaspar, and Wickrama 2007; D.R. Williams 2005). Karlsen and Nazroo (2002: 15) document the effect that experiences of racism have on the health status of ethnic minorities in Britain. They found a substantial correlation between reporting fair or poor health and having experienced an instance of racial harassment: "Those who reported having experienced racially-motivated verbal abuse were 60 per cent more likely to report having fair or poor health compared with those who said they had experienced no racial harassment." Although immigrants and visible minorities in Canada have rated higher on mental health measures than non-immigrants and non-visible minorities (Public Health Agency of Canada 2006: 34; Patten and Juby 2008), racism and racial harassment constitute a potential risk for psychological distress and depression, as well as for other morbidities (Krieger 2003; Noh, Kaspar, and Wickrama 2007; Noh et al. 1999; Whitbeck et al. 2001). A Canadian study involving 647 Southeast Asian immigrants showed that depression is higher for those who had experienced racial discrimination (Noh et al. 1999). Noh and his colleagues (1999) found that depression was moderated by a forbearing coping style that was characterized by acceptance and avoidance. Kuo et al. (2008) drew similar conclusions in their review of two decades of research on depression and its psychosocial correlates among Asian immigrants in North America. In a more recent study using data from the Korean Mental Health Study in Toronto, Noh, Kaspar, and Wickrama (2007) again found associations between racial discrimination and mental health. The perception of overt discrimination was associated with a decline in positive affect or mood, while the perception of subtle discrimination was associated with depressive symptoms that were strongly mediated by the subjects' appraisals of the situation. According to the authors, ambiguity and uncertainty in deciphering subtle discrimination

may result in considerable stress (Noh, Kaspar, and Wickrama 2007). It is important to note that ethnic identity may also work as a protective factor in mental health. Indeed, Wu, Noh, Kaspar, and Schimmele (2003) suggest that the superior mental health of East Asian, Southeast Asian, Chinese, and South Asian Canadians compared with English Canadians may be explained in part by the presence of a strong, positive ethnic identity that bolsters belonging and esteem for group members.

Gender

One persistent puzzle in the study of mortality rates has been women's persistent advantage over men. Women in industrialized countries

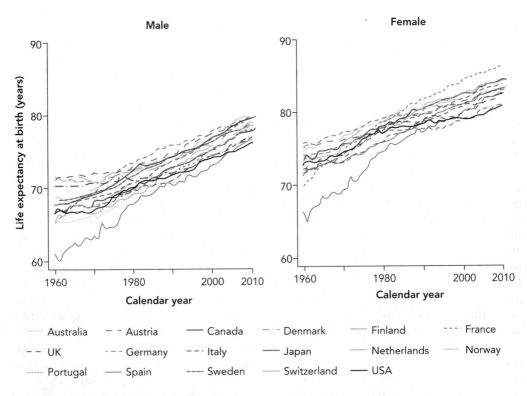

Figure 11.7 Mortality Rate at Birth in 17 OECD Countries, 1960–2010

Source: Mauricio Avendano and Ichiro Kawachi. (2014). "Why Do Americans Have Shorter Life Expectancy and Worse Health Than Do People in Other High-Income Countries?" 35 Annual Review of Public Health 307-325. Modified with Permission from the Annual Review of Public Health, Volume 35 (c) by Annual Reviews, www.annualreviews.org.

(see Figure 11.7) tend to live longer than men of the same racial, ethnic, and SES backgrounds, though in Canada this gap is narrowing (Trovato and Lalu 2007). In 2011, Canadian women (83.6 years) could expect to live 4.3 years longer than Canadian men (79.3 years) (Statistics Canada 2013). In Canada, the leading causes of death for men and women continue to be cancer and cardiovascular disease; and although more men continue to die from both, this disadvantage is closing, particularly with regard to cardiovascular disease (Statistics Canada 2011).

Throughout the life course, men are more likely to die than women, although this difference peaks in early and middle adulthood, owing to the strong influence of external causes on men's death rate (Statistics Canada 2007b). Cancer accounts for more potential years of life lost for women, while accidents typically account for a greater number of potential years of life lost for men (DesMeules, Manuel, and Cho 2003). Age-standardized mortality rates from 2011 show a male mortality rate of 589.9 per 100,000 and a female mortality rate of 406.3 per 100,000 (Statistics Canada 2014). Although most of the causes of death are similar for men and women, suicide is a notable exception. Men's suicide rates are higher than women's in every age group, and the overall suicide rate for men is 16.3 compared with 5.4 for women in 2004 (Statistics Canada 2015). Compared with other age and gender groups, men aged 55 to 64 have the highest overall suicide rate (Statistics Canada 2015). Although gender differences in health behaviour and the impact of gendered identities have been suggested as possible explanations for differences in rates and causes of mortality, the mortality advantage of women over men has not yet been well explained (Rieker and Bird 2005).

Interestingly, measures of societal gender inequity are associated with mortality and morbidity, even after socio-economic deprivation is taken into account (Kawachi and Kennedy 1999). For example, an examination of levels of gender inequality in all 50 American states has shown that in states where women's status (measured by political participation, economic autonomy, employment, earnings, and reproductive rights) is higher, both women *and* men had lower mortality rates. However, when black women and white women were analyzed separately, only one significant correlation is found for black women (that of women in elected office), suggesting that the measures of inequality used in the study may not reflect the experiences of black women (Kawachi and Kennedy 1999).

Historically, women have experienced a higher degree of morbidity than men (Dean 1992; Verbrugge 1989). In Canada, nearly three-quarters of women aged 15 and older reported having a chronic health condition, compared with about 60 per cent of men (private household dwellers) (Statistics Canada 2015). Although Canadian women's life expectancy at birth is longer than men's, women have more disability during their lifetime (Statistics Canada 2009). In Canada, women generally have higher disability rates than men, and these differences increase over the life course, with women over the age of 75 having a disability rate of 57.8 per cent and their male counterparts 54.0 per cent (Statistics Canada 2009). Women are also more likely to experience pain and limitations of mobility and agility. For almost all chronic health conditions (except diabetes), women are more often afflicted than men; that is particularly true of arthritis and rheumatism (Statistics Canada 2014).

New Statistics Canada data from 2007 show that the gap in life expectancy measures narrows between men and women when *quality of life* is taken into account: women have a Health Adjusted Life Expectancy, or HALE (HALE is a relatively new measure that uses the Health Utility Index, taking into account quality of life or the years lived in full health), of 83.0, compared with 78.3 for men (Statistics Canada 2012).

The long-standing finding that women have more illness than men has come under fire because so much morbidity research relies on self-reported health measures (Hunt and Annandale 1999; Walters, McDonough, and Strohschein 2002). Hence, some believe that women's higher reported morbidity rates are due to women "overreporting" their symptoms. Yet, in a comparison of men's and women's reporting on chronic illness, Macintyre and her colleagues (1999) found no gender differences in the initial reporting of a condition. Arber and Cooper (1999), who examined data from over 14,000 men and women over the age of 59, found that older women did experience more functional impairments than older men but considered themselves healthier than men who were less impaired.

Historically, women were thought to suffer worse mental health than men; much of the research in this regard concentrated on depression (Simon 2000). More recently, research has shown that men and women experience similar levels of mental illness but that it manifests itself in different ways in men and women (Simon 2000). Hence, the previous belief in a gendered imbalance in the prevalence of mental illness has now been offset by the inclusion of certain behaviours more common to men as indicators of psychological distress, such as alcohol consumption and drug use (Simon 2000). These patterns are evident in Canadian data that look at the prevalence of any mood or anxiety disorder along with substance dependence. In 2013, 1,364,645 women and 899,998 men reported symptoms of a mood disorder (about a 35 per cent difference). Rates were highest for both men and women between the ages of 45 and 64 (Statistics Canada 2014). The susceptibilities to various types of mental illness varied, with women being 1.5 times more likely to meet the criteria for an anxiety or mood disorder and men being 2.6 times more likely to meet the criteria for substance dependence (Public Health Agency of Canada 2006). McDonough and Walters (2001) outline the hypotheses generated from the stress literature that attempts to explain this imbalance. One explanation, called the **differential exposure hypothesis**, argues that women are subject to more stressors than men on account of their heavier domestic

and caring responsibilities. The other explanation, the **differential vulnerability hypothesis**, argues that women are more affected by stressors than men on account of a "generalized female disadvantage in social roles and coping resources" (McDonough and Walters 2001: 549). McDonough and Walters (2001), who tested both hypotheses with data from the Canadian National Health Population Survey for 1994, found higher distress scores and morbidity among women. However, while women were generally exposed to more stressors than men (specifically, chronic stress and life events), this exposure accounted only for the gender differences in distress (McDonough and Walters 2001). In addition, the differential vulnerability hypothesis did not explain any of the gendered variance in the results. The authors suggest that their results stemmed from the complexity in the relationship between gender and health and the inadequacy of the data to reflect this variability. They point to the impact of age on health and note that their study could not take this into account.

Other research by Denton, Prus, and Walters (2004) explores the complexity of these relationships and finds that structural, behavioural, and psychosocial factors manifest differently for men and women and tend to hold different outcomes for health. Overall, structural and psychosocial factors appear to better predict women's health outcomes than men's, with chronic stress emerging as an important health predictor. Again, women experience stress, anxiety, and depression differently depending on their socio-economic status, ethnicity, family relationships and structure, and labour-market participation (Walters 1993). Avison, Ali, and Walters (2007) find that differential exposure (rather than vulnerability) to stress explains nearly all of the elevated psychological distress experienced by single mothers compared with married mothers in both cross-sectional and longitudinal analyses.

Studies such as these highlight the importance of daily pressures in women's mental health and the necessity to examine the differences in women's lives in relation to their mental health. In a more recent study, using data from 500 families, Offer and Schneider (2011) find that mothers spend 10 more hours each week multi-tasking—mainly time spent on housework and child care—compared with fathers. Women's multi-tasking was associated with an increase in negative emotions, stress, psychological distress, and work–family conflict.

Age and Social Time

The length of time one can expect to live and the diseases one is likely to die from have varied considerably over time, partly because of historical variation in the social factors that influence health. For instance, education level is a strong predictor of health status, and whereas more than 50 per cent of Canadians had less than a grade 9 education in 1951 (Clark 2000), this rate had dropped to approximately 15 per cent by 2006 (Statistics Canada 2008c). In 2011, only 12.7 per cent of Canadians had less than a high school education (Statistics Canada 2011). Furthermore, the life expectancy and the overall health of Canadians increased over the twentieth century (Crompton 2000). Whereas an infant born in the 1920s could expect to live only 59 years, an infant born in 2014 could expect to live about 81 years (www.worldbank.org). This improvement is largely attributable to public health programs, sanitation, and immunization (Crompton 2000). Sadly, the distribution of these amenities remains inequitable. For example, infants born in the territories have a life expectancy of roughly 75 years compared with just over 81.1 years for Canada (Statistics Canada 2012).

Nonetheless, in an era of globalization and "reform" of health care delivery and service, people born today will most likely experience different health care services and delivery than those born before them. They will also be exposed to different and less well understood viruses and in some cases to the resurgence of viruses once stamped out. Indeed, since the 1970s more than 30 new disease-causing agents have been identified, including HIV and the Ebola virus (Lee and Patel 2003). Canadian events since the early 2000s point to the link between economic globalization and the international spread of disease. Several examples stand out. In 2002 the first human cases of West Nile virus (which is carried by mosquitoes) were identified in Ontario. In the early spring of 2003, major cities in the world, including Toronto, were "combating" a new disease called SARS (severe acute respiratory syndrome). In May 2003 a cow infected with mad cow disease was discovered in Alberta, and in February 2004 avian influenza, or "bird flu," was identified in southern British Columbia. Now, in 2016, the Zika virus—most commonly spread through the bite of an infected mosquito—and Ebola— transmitted to people from wild animals—are becoming global health concerns. At the time of writing, these serious diseases have not yet reached Canada.

The global health implications of mad cow disease are worth considering. In 1986 mad cow disease, or BSE (bovine spongiform encephalopathy), was first found in a cow in the United Kingdom. It spread quickly among cattle in Britain, but the effect of BSE on humans who had eaten infected beef was unclear. Nonetheless, by the early 1990s, 15 countries, including Canada, had banned British beef imports, causing a devastating economic blow to the cattle industry in Britain. Concern over the economic impact of these bans led Britain's Ministry of Agriculture, Fisheries, and Food to minimize the potential human health risks of consuming tainted beef. However, in 1996 BSE was linked to 10 human cases of a new form of

Creutzfeldt-Jakob disease (CJD), a disease of the brain that is usually fatal in less than one year. This new form of the disease (vCJD) differed from CJD because it affected young people rather than old people and because the duration of the illness from onset to death was shorter. By July 2002, there were 115 confirmed cases of vCJD in the UK and the disease seems to be spreading more rapidly despite radical measures to control it (Lee and Patel 2003). On 21 May 2003, the headline on the front page of the *Globe and Mail* read "Mad-Cow Hits Canada Hard." After more than a decade of being free of mad cow disease (there had been only one previous case of the disease in Canada), "the discovery of mad-cow disease in Alberta walloped the country's multibillion-dollar cattle industry yesterday as the United States banned imports of Canadian beef and producers braced for fallout at home from frightened consumers" (*Globe and Mail*, 21 May 2003). At the time, Canadian politicians reacted to the mad cow crisis by eating beef in order to show that Canadian beef was safe; however, long-term economic effects were not averted.

Causes of mortality differ over the life course not only because of the aging of the body but also because of changes in socio-economic status, lifestyles, environmental stressors, life events, and surrounding social supports (Statistics Canada 2007d; K. Wilkins 2006). For example, Kathryn Wilkins (2006) found that high levels of psychological distress were a strong predictor of death for women over the age of 65. This is especially worrisome given that, on average, the level of social support available to Canadians over the age of 65 is quite low (Statistics Canada 2015). The influence of persistent poverty, fluctuations in socio-economic status, marital status, and changing conceptualizations of race, ethnicity, and gendered meanings over the life course all contribute to health status, and all have changed historically.

Studies that ignore historical context and social time may present an inaccurate picture of health risks and outcomes. For example, in 1926 Canadians aged 5–64 accounted for more than half of deaths (54 per cent), whereas in 2002 this group accounted for only 21 per cent of deaths (K. Wilkins 2006). Studies show that health in later life may also depend on cumulative experiences and exposures over the life course (Hunt 2002; Willson, Shuey, and Elder 2007). Income and education are protective of health (Buckley et al. 2006; K. Wilkins 2006). For example, according to a study of Canadian Mortality Database data and of data from the National Population Health Survey over an eight-year period, Canadians aged 65 and older who did not graduate from high school were more likely to die than those who had graduated from high school (K. Wilkins 2006). Other childhood experiences and exposures, such as poverty and domestic violence, also influence adult health (E. Chen 2004; Raphael 2006).

Rates of sickness tend to increase as people age physiologically. Many seniors, for instance, suffer from chronic pain. Long-term limitations on mental or physical activity are also prominent among those aged 65 and older. However, these limitations are often not permanent: 60 per cent of those aged 65 and older who reported a limitation in 1994/5 were free of it by 1998/9 (Statistics Canada 2001e: 29). In 2012, about 2.2 million Canadians with a disability, long-term illness, or aging needs required home care. Women held only a slight majority of those requiring care (56 per cent) as a result of longer life expectancies (Statistics Canada 2014). Although the majority of seniors (81 per cent) report at least one chronic health condition (the most common being arthritis/rheumatism) (Gilmour and Park 2006), over a third of seniors rank their health high, with 37 per cent rating their health as "excellent" or "very good" (Turcotte and Schellenberg 2007). Interestingly, the majority of seniors (58 per cent) aged 65–74 who are university graduates rated their health as "excellent" or "very good" compared with 48 per cent of 25- to 64-year-olds who did not graduate from high school (Turcotte and Schellenberg 2006: 46).

Socio-economic status has a significant influence on morbidity as we age, and a number of studies have charted the ways in which health inequities differ over the life course and at older ages (O'Rand and Hamil-Luker 2005; Prus 2007; Willson et al. 2007). The impact of socio-economic status on health over the life course is substantial, and the cumulative effects of poverty and economic hardship have been shown to imprint health over time (Willson et al. 2007). Analyzing data from the US Panel Study of Income Dynamics, Willson and her colleagues found that socio-economic status yielded cumulative effects on health status over time, where those with higher SES saw less dramatic declines in health over time. In addition, their longitudinal data analysis found evidence of bias in the sample population over time, in that those with lower socio-economic status died prematurely. Their data suggested that those individuals most disadvantaged were not present in studies of older-aged individuals and that this bias must therefore be taken into account when interpreting data on mortality, life course, and economic advantage/disadvantage. Peek and Coward (2000) also found that age, education, and poverty status were the most predictive factors for disability in older age, with low educational status and the experience of poverty indicating a greater risk for developing multiple disabilities (see also Samman and Rodriguez-Takeuchi 2013). Poor education and personal resources were also identified as risk factors in a World Health Organization (2003) study using European data.

Mental health varies considerably over the life course. Recently, researchers have been paying more attention to the mental health of adolescents because the emergence of disorders at this time of life is a risk factor for the development of adult mental health disorders (Gore, Aseltine,

and Schilling 2007; Samman and Rodriguez-Takeuchi 2013). In Canada, 70 per cent of young adults with mental health issues report that their symptoms began in childhood (Mental Health Commission of Canada 2012). Indeed, of all age groups, young adults aged 15–24 in Canada have the highest annual prevalence of mood, anxiety, or substance-use disorder (Public Health Agency of Canada 2006). Social determinants are linked to the mental well-being of children, as 46 per cent of children in Canada whose family affluence score is low report low emotional well-being compared with 24 per cent for children whose family affluence score is high (Public Health Agency of Canada 2008). Socio-economic and environmental factors in the mental health of children and youth are significant. Aneshensel and Sucoff (1996) investigated whether neighbourhood racial or ethnic segregation and socio-economic stratification were associated with the mental health of adolescents. Neighbourhoods with a lower socio-economic status were perceived by study participants as the most hazardous and threatening. In neighbourhoods that were perceived as the most hazardous or dangerous, symptoms of depression, anxiety disorders, oppositional defiant disorders, and conduct disorders were more common. These neighbourhood factors were more strongly associated with symptoms of mental health than was family socio-economic status. Gender significantly influenced the type of mental disorder, with girls more commonly exhibiting depression and anxiety disorders and boys more commonly exhibiting conduct and oppositional defiant disorders. A protective effect for depression was found in neighbourhoods with high levels of social cohesion, measured as communities where people knew one another (Aneshensel and Sucoff 1996). These findings suggest that studies of mental health must consider the milieu in which people live their lives (Aneshensel and Sucoff 1996).

Mental health and well-being are increasingly being conceptualized as cumulative effects, with experiences across the life course, particularly early experiences, shaping and determining later health outcomes (Raphael 2007; Wadsworth 1997). For example, Wu et al. (2013) found that childhood socio-economic status was associated with the incidence of stroke in adulthood. Akhtar-Danesh and Landeen (2007) found that low levels of education and other SES characteristics predicted higher levels of depression and that this relationship intensified with age. Education levels, age, and income mutually influence each other, as our age and our cohort influence our chances of obtaining education. In addition, our income is influenced by our age and gender. Social time is also important, as Canadian policy changes have demonstrated. While more than half (57 per cent) of unattached women aged 65 and older were classified as low income in 1980, this number dropped to 19 per cent in 2003 largely on account of changes in distributive processes (Statistics Canada 2006b: 144). In essence, the targeting of social policy has profound implications on the well-being of citizens, especially vulnerable groups like aging populations (see Box 11.3).

Age also influences the extent to which we are exposed to the stressors of work and family demands, the extent to which social support is available (Shields 2004; Statistics Canada 2001e), and our levels of self-esteem (McMullin and Cairney 2004). Women experience higher levels of personal stress than men at every age, but men and women aged 65 and older experience significantly less stress than younger adults. However, younger men and women experience more social support than do men and women aged 65 and older (Statistics Canada 2001e). Nurullan (2010) explored gender differences in stress and distress (self-esteem, negative life events, and childhood/adult trauma) using the National Population Health Survey (NPHS). She found clear gender differences, with women expressing far more distress than men over the life course. Also

using the NPHS, McMullin and Cairney (2004) showed that in their early teens, boys and girls, regardless of family income, have similar levels of self-esteem. However, at each successive age, girls have lower levels of self-esteem than boys do. Once people reach their mid-40s, income levels begin to significantly affect self-esteem. From middle age on, income groups diverge in their levels of self-esteem, such that men and women from the lowest-income groups have the least self-esteem. Although the level of depression in elderly men is quite low, their high rates of suicide suggest that under-diagnosis of psychological distress and disorders may be a problem; in fact, researchers have suggested that as many as "90 per cent of people who commit suicide are suffering from depression or another mental illness, or a substance abuse disorder, which could potentially be diagnosed" (Langlois and Morrison 2001: 17).

Understanding Inequality in Health

Agency and Lifestyle Behaviour

The decisions people make about whether to smoke, how much to drink, how much physical activity to get, whether to engage in risky activities, and whether to take part in preventive health actions are all embraced under the rubric of "lifestyle behaviour." These factors were once thought to account for much of the inequality that manifested itself in mortality and morbidity (House 2001; Robertson 1998). Indeed, in spite of existing research on the social and environmental determinants of health, much Canadian statistical data focuses on individual behaviour in terms of health outcomes and recommendations of how health can be improved (Raphael 2004, 2007). As Raphael (2007: 10) points out, a concentration on health behaviours such as smoking and weight deflects the focus from structural factors even though "behavioural risk factors are rather

Global perspective

Box 11.3 Aging and Mental Health in Cross-National Perspective

Aging populations around the world live very different social and economic lifestyles depending on the country in which they live. Consider the figure to the right. Norway boasts an old age poverty rate—the percentage of people aged 65 and over with an income of less than half the national median—of only 1.8 per cent. Other notable countries include France (3.9 per cent), India (5.1 per cent), and Germany (9.7 per cent). As this figure also shows, lower poverty rates are also associated with greater relative mental well-being—i.e., the proportion of people over the age of 50 who feel that their life has meaning, compared with people aged 35–49 who feel the same. Countries with high levels of old age poverty (such as Japan, South Africa, and Australia) show lower rates of relative mental well-being.

This underscores the importance of keeping levels of poverty low for people once they retire. But how? As we discuss throughout the book, the state plays an important role in reducing inequality throughout the life course—especially for older people who are transitioning out of the labour force. For example, Canada's public pension system has been relatively effective in keeping seniors out of poverty (Myles 2000). Old age poverty rates in Canada are about 7 per cent and are among the lowest compared with other OECD nations, even comparable to Scandinavian countries where levels of government spending on retirement are much higher.

Another solution, according to the WHO, is to promote *active aging*. This strategy emphasizes participation in society, healthy life experiences, and a high quality of life. More specifically, "active" refers to full participation in social, economic, cultural, spiritual, and civic affairs after retirement. In other words, it is premised on the notion that people should remain engaged in society in order to maintain healthy and vibrant social connections that have a positive impact on emotional and mental well-being.

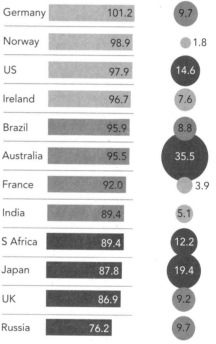

Source: © 2015 Guardian Graphic; data from Global Agewatch Index 2014.

Sources: Helen Davidson et al. (March 3, 2015). Which are the best countries in the world to grow old in?" *The Guardian*; WHO. (2002). *Active Aging: A Policy Framework.* Madrid: United Nations World Assembly on Ageing; John Myles. (2000). "The Maturation of Canada's Retirement Income System: Income Levels, Income Inequality and Low-Income among the Elderly," 19(3) *Canadian Journal on Aging*, 287–316.

weak predictors of health status as compared to socio-economic and demographic measures of which income is a major component." Still, this is not to deny that agency, even when heavily constrained, plays a role in health.

Lower socio-economic status has been associated with less healthy behaviours (Pampel, Krueger, and Denney 2010). For example, low SES individuals are more likely to engage in unhealthy behaviours such as tobacco use, physical inactivity, and poor nutrition. Conversely, Canadians in the highest income groups are more likely to be physically active, to take vitamins, and to eat fruits and vegetables than are those with lower family incomes (Power 2005)—though recent data have shown that nearly 25 per cent of Canadians in the highest income groups get 35 per cent of their dietary intake from fat compared to 15 per cent of those in the lowest income groups (Garriguet 2006). Clearly, rising obesity rates and the associations between income and weight are not explained by diet alone. Canadians living in low-income and impoverished neighbourhoods face significant challenges in obtaining fruits and vegetables and healthy foods (Grenon, Butler, and Adams 2007; Latham and Moffat 2007). Grenon, Butler, and Adams (2007) discuss how the "built environment" can affect health behaviours in terms of the accessibility and availability of food and the space in which to exercise in neighbourhoods and cities. They characterize those areas where there is limited access or choice of supermarkets, along with high social deprivation, as "food deserts." Challenges in terms of obtaining healthy food in deprived neighbourhoods may account in part for the greater rate of childhood obesity in low-income neighbourhoods. Oliver and Hayes (2008) found that children in the poorest neighbourhoods gained the greatest amount of weight over an eight-year period. In their longitudinal analysis of data from the Canadian National Survey of Children and Youth, they found that it was the negative effect of poverty (rather than the protective effect of higher income) that accounted

for weight increases over time. Again, this demonstrates the importance of recognizing the structural context of health behaviours.

Smoking is on the decline in Canada, with 16.1 per cent of Canadians smoking in 2014 compared with almost 30 per cent in the early 1990s (Shields 2007). Smoking accounts for much preventable illness and death. In 2014 about 26,000 Canadians were diagnosed with lung cancer and about 20,000 (27 per cent of all cancer deaths) people died from lung cancer. Today, men are still somewhat more likely to develop lung cancer than women, but this gap is narrowing (Canadian Cancer Statistics 2015). Besides the direct health effects of smoking, there are also confounding effects because smokers tend to eat fewer fruits and vegetables and more fatty foods than non-smokers (Palaniappan, Jacobs, O'Loughlin, and Gray-Donald 2001). Nonetheless, when the number of cigarettes smoked is controlled for, the ill effects of smoking are greater among those from lower socio-economic groups than among those of higher socio-economic status (Mao et al. 2001: 7).

Among Aboriginal populations in Canada, high rates of smoking, obesity, and alcohol consumption have been documented (Anand et al. 2001; CIHI 2004). These health risks are probably due to the poverty and discrimination experienced by Aboriginal people throughout their lives (Whitbeck et al. 2001). In an American study, Chae and his colleagues (2008) found that racial discrimination and unfair treatment were risk factors for smoking among Asian Americans. The marked influence of environment on health behaviour is also evident among immigrants. Healthful behaviour tends to be more common among immigrants than among Canadian-born residents, although over time non-European immigrants are more likely to report a decline in health (Chen, Wilkins, and Ng 1996; E. Ng et al. 2005). Physical activity also tends to be less common among immigrants regardless of their length of time in the country (Gilmour 2007). Again, we should consider the factors of structural elements and built environments when assessing whether and how people are physically active (Grenon, Butler, and Adams 2007). Smoking rates also vary significantly by ethnic group in Canada, with Asian and southern European Canadians being the least likely to smoke (Millar 1992). Immigrants tend to be significantly less likely to smoke than the Canadian-born (Chen, Wilkins, and Ng 1996; Millar 1992; E. Ng et al. 2005). Data from previous years show that whereas three-quarters of recent non-European immigrants had never smoked, only 34 per cent of the Canadian-born population had never smoked (Chen, Wilkins, and Ng 1996: 41). However, after 10 years in Canada, the percentage of non-European immigrants who had never smoked dropped to 61.7, and among recent European immigrants this percentage dropped after 10 years from 55.7 to 37.6 (Chen, Wilkins, and Ng 1996: 43). Generally, researchers believe that immigrants adopt less healthful behaviours as they adapt over time; however, little is known about the mechanisms and pathways of these changes (Halli and Anchan 2005).

Men and women exhibit significantly different kinds of health behaviour even within the same socio-economic groups (Statistics Canada 2013). Although men are more likely to be physically active than women (Statistics Canada 2001i: 14), the fact that women are less likely than men to engage in binge drinking (Statistics Canada 2013), to smoke (Lung Cancer Statistics 2015), or to be overweight contributes to the higher risk of premature death from heart diseases among men. Men engage in riskier activities than women and are more likely to die as a result of suicide and motor vehicle accidents (Statistics Canada 2014). Men are less likely than women to visit a physician and more likely than women to have emergency-room visits (Kazanjian, Morettin, and Cho 2003), while women tend to survive longer than men with the same chronic conditions (e.g., heart disease, lung cancer) (Rieker and Bird 2005).

Lifestyle behaviour varies significantly over the life course. Smoking is much less common among seniors, 12.2 per cent of whom are daily smokers compared with 21.8 per cent of those aged 20–34, and physical activity levels appear to drop substantially after the age of 19 (Reid et al. 2014). Other kinds of behaviour, such as eating fruit and vegetables, have been found to increase with age: seniors report eating more fruits and vegetables than those aged 18–64 (Shields and Martel 2006). Aging and generational ideologies have an effect on the health behaviour that people engage in or ignore (Gillis and Hirdes 1996; Spitzer 2005). Graham, Carver, and Brett (1995: 769) found that women aged 65 and older drink less alcohol, smoke less, and use illicit drugs less than any other age or gender group. These trends have continued: in 2003 only 3 per cent of women aged 64–75 were heavy drinkers compared with 11 per cent of women aged 25–54 (Turcotte and Schellenberg 2007). Researchers have noted that changing attitudes toward women's drinking and smoking may result in an increased risk for future age cohorts (Graham, Carver, and Brett 1995).

Alcohol consumption varies by gender, ethnicity, and changing social roles over the life course (F.W. Johnson, Gruenewald, Treno, and Taff 1998). In their American study, F.W. Johnson and his colleagues (1998) found that whites drink more alcohol over the course of their lives than blacks or Hispanics; however, blacks and Hispanics drink more in later life per occasion than do whites. Men were found to drink more than women, and people who had many children or were regular churchgoers were found to drink less (F.W. Johnson et al. 1998). Recent Canadian data show that using alcohol and illicit drugs is much more common for male young adults (Health Canada 2012).

Although lifestyle choices highlight the agency that people have in their lives, the simplicity of classifying behaviour as either healthful or unhealthful masks the complexity of social relations and related ideologies that mediate and constrain the lifestyle choices that people make in their daily lives. For example, the increase in the number of young women smokers in the late 1990s has been thought to stem from changes in gender ideologies (Hunt 2002).

Health Care Access and Utilization

Access to health care, even within the "equal access" Canadian system, varies on the basis of class, gender, ethnicity, race, and age. Poverty, for example, can impede access to health care in concrete ways. Roos and Mustard (1997) found that although prenatal visits made for the first-born child were not significantly different for women from the lowest and the highest income groups, the number of visits decreased for women from the lower-income groups with the second birth and on; it is not hard to imagine the difficulties in arranging child care, coping with children on public transportation, and facing other problems that would make it more difficult for the low-income mothers with several children to keep appointments than for a woman with greater socio-economic support (N.P. Roos and Mustard 1997: 105). Spitzer (2005) points out that current early-discharge policies for newborns have increased the hospital readmission rate for low-income families.

Reported unmet health care needs are correlated with household income: people in low-income households are 10 times more likely to report unmet health care needs than are people in middle- to high-income households (Chen and Hou 2002). Of particular concern for low-income households are the expense of drugs and transportation difficulties (Chen and Hou 2002). Curtis and MacMinn (2008) found significant inequities in the Canadian health care system in terms of initial contact with medical care and accessing specialist services. In their study of health care utilization patterns from 1978 to 2003, they found a trend toward more outpatient care for higher-SES groups over time, and until the first physician contact had been made, higher-SES groups were more likely to visit a physician than were lower-SES groups. Using more recent data from 7,049 men and 8,353 women aged 45–64, McCartney, Hart, and Watt (2012) found that the SES variations had converged relative to earlier studies. Although some aspects of health care (e.g., preventive care) are underused by low-income Canadians, other health services, such as hospital admissions (Glazier et al.

2000; Nabalamba and Millar 2007), are used by them more often. Higher rates of morbidity in lower-income neighbourhoods are thought to explain the higher levels of hospital utilization (Glazier, Badley, Gilbert, and Rothman 2000). A recent Canadian study of hospitalization rates for ambulatory care sensitive conditions (ACSC) or chronic conditions considered manageable through appropriate primary care (e.g., various heart conditions, diabetes, asthma, chronic obstructive pulmonary disease, epilepsy, and hypertension) found significant differences in hospitalizations by neighbourhood income levels (CIHI 2008). Indeed, the hospitalization rate for these conditions for those in the lowest-income quintile was more than twice that for those in the highest-income quintile). As Curtis and MacMinn (2008) point out, the higher rate of hospitalizations for those with lower SES may well indicate gaps in primary care and access. Although the majority of Canadians do have regular medical doctors (in 2005, 17 per cent of Canadians reported not having a regular doctor; Asanin and Wilson 2008), there is geographic variation in the likelihood of having a doctor.

Paradoxically, even though people from lower-income and poorer neighbourhoods use hospitals more often than people from higher-income neighbourhoods, they undergo less surgery (N. Roos and Mustard 1997). Roos and Mustard (1997) argue that this is due to the underuse of specialist services by lower-income individuals, possibly owing to better access and a stronger communicative relationship on the part of individuals with higher socio-economic status. Specialists and surgeons offer more treatment to people with higher socio-economic status (N. Roos and Mustard 1997), perhaps as a result of referral decisions from a treating physician. Using data from the 2005 Canadian Community Health Survey, Nabalamba and Millar (2007) found that specialist visits were significantly less likely for those living in low-income households, visible minorities, Aboriginal people, and those over the age of 75.

These gaps in care may affect mortality. Cancer survival rates vary by community income (Boyd, Zhang-Salomons, Groome, and Mackillop 1999), and access to preventive treatments is a crucial factor in the cancer survival advantage that low-income Canadians have over low-income Americans (Gorey et al. 2000). Singh and his colleagues (2004) found that Ontario patients with higher SES were more likely to receive screening for colorectal cancer. The time it takes to wait for diagnostic tests and other procedures constitutes another barrier to quality care and is the number-one health care barrier reported by First Nations adults living on-reserve (33 per cent) (Health Canada 2006: 43).

Access to health care is also determined by the extent to which people feel comfortable making use of the available resources (Benoit and Carroll 2001; Newbold 1998; Oxman-Martinez, Abdool, and Loiselle-Leonard 2000). Benoit and Carroll (2001), who interviewed urban Aboriginal women from Vancouver, found that the most important public health issues were those of access and availability of health care. Aboriginal women underuse preventive health care services, and their access to prenatal care is limited (National Collaborating Centre for Aboriginal Health 2012). Accessibility meant encountering "a non-judgmental, encouraging, informal environment ... [which included] a more central service focus on Aboriginal women's health concerns" (Benoit and Carroll 2001: 6). Also, Aboriginal Canadians living on reserves have very little access to physicians and hospitals; in the territories only 31 per cent of off-reserve Aboriginals reported having a regular doctor compared with 67 per cent of non-Aboriginals in the region (Tjepkema 2002: 10). More recent research by Tait (2008) found that 52 communities across Inuit Nunaat did not have year-round access to doctors and that only a few communities had hospitals. Geographic isolation plays a large role in the difficulty of obtaining health services; however, education and greater self-governance over community issues are viewed by health care professionals as more vital to addressing health needs (Newbold 1998).

Immigrant status does not appear to lead to differences in physician visits. In fact, for both Canadian-born and immigrant populations with low incomes, the number of physician contacts is higher than for similar high-income Canadians (Chen, Wilkins, and Ng 1996), though Quan and his colleagues (2006) found that cancer screening and hospital services were less utilized by visible minorities. In other research, Wu, Penning, and Schimmele (2005) found that unmet health care needs were not more likely among immigrants; however, among those who reported unmet needs, immigrants were more likely to report that the care would not be adequate, that there were language barriers, and that they were not sure where to access health care. A recent Statistics Canada report also found that accessing health care services was the activity in which the second-largest number (31,300 or 20 per cent) of immigrants reported as a barrier following immigration (Statistics Canada 2011). A focus group study with immigrants in Mississauga, Ontario, found that the three main issues for accessibility were geographic, socio-cultural, and economic (Asanin and Wilson 2008).

In fact, the actions and decisions of health care providers have been shown to be influenced by the racial or ethnic backgrounds of their patients (Dunlop, Coyte, and McIsaac 2000; Krieger et al. 1993; N. Roos and Mustard 1997). In their review of instances of racial discrimination in health care, Krieger and her colleagues (1993) discuss several studies that document preferential treatment regimes for white patients. Geiger (2001: 1699) notes that "disparaging racial stereotyping, not clinical data, was predictive of refusal to recommend bypass surgery for many African-American patients in one large series of cases." These findings suggest that once a person is in the medical system, the services that are made available to them vary on the basis of race.

Although physicians are trained to be "neutral" and to shed or ignore their own socio-demographic characteristics and those of their patients, studies indicate that in practice this is not done (Beagan 2000; van Ryn and Burke 2000). African-American patients and patients from lower-income groups are perceived in a variety of more negative ways than white patients and patients from higher-income groups. Furthermore, physicians believe that African-American and low-income patients are less compliant and less intelligent, and physicians felt less "affiliated" with patients from minority backgrounds (van Ryn and Burke 2000). These perceptions affect the health care that racial or ethnic minorities and people of lower socio-economic status are likely to obtain (van Ryn, Burgess, Malat, and Griffin 2006). Patients sense and respond to the perceptions of the physician, so that "when patients perceive that physicians like them, care about them, and are interested in them as a person, they are likely to volunteer more information and be more active in the encounter, more satisfied, and more compliant with medical regimens" (van Ryn and Burke 2000: 823). Patients are less likely to ask questions and be active health care consumers when they are aware of hostility or negativity on the part of their physician; furthermore, disadvantaged groups believe that self-presentation is particularly important in the medical treatment they receive (Malat, van Ryn, and Purcell 2006; van Ryn and Burke 2000).

In fact, being an active consumer of health care may be more vital than ever. Provincial differences between the types of medicines available and whether they are funded by the government are giving rise to new inequities in the treatment of disease and increased requirements for patients to self-advocate.

The extent to which health care is used is strongly related to gender, with women using many more health preventive and health care services than men do (Statistics Canada 2006b). Although some of this use is explained by visits for reproductive and prenatal care (Statistics Canada 2001i), women's greater use of health care has been documented independently of these types of visits (Kazanjian, Morettin, and Cho 2003). Men are much less likely to visit physicians or consult a specialist (Statistics Canada 2006b). In fact, in 2010 almost 20 per cent of men reported that they did not have a regular medical doctor (Statistics Canada 2011). Unlike relationships

between health care access and each of class and race or ethnicity, however, explanations for the underuse of health care services by men emphasize masculine ideologies that promote unhealthy, risk-taking behaviour (Courtenay 2000; Mahalik, Burns, and Syzdek 2007; Statistics Canada 2001i; Trovato and Lalu 1995).

In an insightful study, Courtenay (2000), who examines the relationships between conceptualizations of masculinity and their consequences for men's health, suggests that different health care utilization rates for men and women are manifestations of the gender structure. According to Courtenay (2000), masculine imperatives to be "strong" and self-sufficient inhibit men from attending to their health and encourage the medical establishment to under-analyze the effect of gendered beliefs on men's health behaviour. He argues that the attributes of "masculinity" are in contradiction to healthy behaviour and that the way in which these attributes manifest themselves is shaped by class and ethnicity. For example, men from different social classes may take risks in varying ways: "Demonstrating masculinities with fearless, high-risk behaviours may entail skydiving for an upper-class man, mountain climbing for a middle-class man, racing hot rods for a working-class man and street fighting for a poor urban man" (Courtenay 2000: 1390).

According to the constructs of masculinity, health-conscious behaviour fails to connote a "strong" persona and is considered to be "feminine" (Courtenay 2000). This is an instance where gender structures work against both men and women. On the one hand, physicians provide less information to men than to women and spend less time with men, and this may jeopardize men's health (Courtenay 2000). On the other hand, the fact that physicians spend more time with women may also be the reason for the overmedicalization and pathologization of women's bodies. Hence, although women's use of the medical system is thought to be due to their greater tendency to be ill and their overuse of health services, men's utilization of health care is considered a sign that they are healthier than women. According to Courtenay (2000: 1395), the broader societal view of women as "overusers" of medical services and of men as "naturally" healthy should be reversed:

> Given that women are unquestionably less susceptible to serious illness and live longer than men, it would seem that women should provide the standard against which men's health and men's health behaviour are measured. . . . If this were the case, we would be compelled instead to confront . . . men's underutilization of health care.

The actions and decisions of health care providers are influenced by the gender and age of patients. The medical establishment has played a critical role in defining and enforcing gendered behaviour norms on women (Mitchinson 1991; Offman and Kleinplatz 2004). Women's bodies have been viewed as problematic, and natural processes (e.g., menstruation) have been considered to be illnesses in need of medical treatment (Lorber 1997). The construction of "premenstrual syndrome" as a disease is a telling example of how societal imperatives are translated into medical problems. Lorber (1997: 60) argues that "stereotypically, women suffering from PMS are said to be cranky, irritable, angry, violent and out of control. . . . These characteristics assume some kind of comparison—with the same woman at other times of the month or with the way women are supposed to be." She notes that there are no control groups in this research, either with men or with women cross-culturally or by ethnicity (Lorber 1997). When women voice dissatisfaction or anger about their life circumstances, physicians have tended to see the problem as an internal one requiring a medical solution (e.g., psychotropic drugs) rather than as a symptom of societal inequality requiring a societal solution. For example, medical responses to menopause have typically involved medication such as hormone replacement therapy as opposed to challenging society's negative and stereotypical views of women aging (Calasanti and Slevin 2001, 2006; Morris and Symonds 2004). Box 11.4 shows how **medicalization** can in fact lead to illness and increased risks of disease.

Sadly, the overmonitoring of women's bodies seems to pertain largely to conditions that are believed to be "female." Some conditions that are common in women are undertreated or ignored despite women's greater contact with the medical profession. Adams and her colleagues (2008) found that physicians (regardless of their gender) are more likely to consider age-related conditions when diagnosing men for coronary heart disease. They note that attention to age in diagnosing men "may, in part, reflect the historical male bias in medical knowledge, arising out of women's under-representation in CHD-related medical research" (Adams et al. 2008: 10). These biases have been well documented by McKinlay (1996) in his review of the underdetection of coronary heart disease in women. He notes that gender has been a primary determinant in treatment decisions on the part of physicians:

> When confronted with exactly the same presenting symptoms, vital signs, and test results depicted in a professionally acted colour videotaped patient-doctor encounter, 192 randomly sampled male internists were much less likely to arrive at a cardiac diagnosis in younger women, treat women medically, believe treatment was necessary or, for the younger women especially, to make health education and lifestyle change recommendation. (McKinlay 1996: 17)

Similarly, when older adults present physicians with their symptoms, physicians sometimes dismiss these symptoms as signs of old age and not as indicators of illness or disease.

HIGHLIGHT

Box 11.4 Mad? No, but They Deserve to Be; Post-menopausal Women Show Drop in Diseases after Giving Up HRT

by Judy Gerstel

We're mad as hell and we're not going to take it any more.

The last part, at least, is true.

Most women past menopause aren't going to take hormone replacement drugs any more.

They realize any superficial benefits of HRT—estrogen combined with progestin—are outweighed by the increased risk of breast cancer, heart disease, stroke, blood clots, ovarian cancer and dementia.

In the five years since the Women's Health Initiative (WHI) suddenly called a halt to its landmark HRT study in the summer of 2002 because it was too risky to continue, a stream of research has confirmed the havoc the drugs can wreak.

Starting that same summer, the use of hormone replacement therapy plummeted.

But what happened the very next year was unpredictable, unprecedented and stunning: a plunge in breast cancer rates—significantly, cancers fuelled by estrogen in women over 50.

"The largest single drop in breast cancer incidence within a single year I am aware of," declared Dr Peter Ravdin, a biostatistics professor and researcher at M.D. Anderson Cancer Center in Texas, after results were announced at the San Antonio Breast Cancer Symposium last December.

"Hormones are the most logical explanation," University of California professor Karla Kerlikowske told reporters when her study, the latest to link the abandonment of HRT with the drop in breast cancer, appeared this summer in the *Journal of the National Cancer Institute*.

US researchers say 14,000 cases of breast cancer were prevented in 2003, compared to 2002, after millions of women dumped their HRT.

Canadian estimates range from about 600 to 700 fewer cases of breast cancer in 2003 than in 2002 because of the drop in HRT.

"The WHI findings have probably prevented tens of thousands of strokes, heart attacks, blood clots, and breast cancers in the US population alone," Dr Jacques Roussow, National Heart, Lung, and Blood Institute project officer of the WHI, has said. In April, the respected Million Women Study in the UK reported in the *Lancet* that HRT was responsible for 1,000 deaths from ovarian cancer between 1991 and 2005.

So the question is not whether HRT after menopause can fuel breast cancer and other illnesses (it can), not whether it's a dangerous drug that should be used only sparingly when absolutely necessary (it is), not whether abandoning HRT prevents life-threatening illness and death (it does).

The question isn't even why, during all these years of running for the cure and raising money for research and "awareness," and wearing and promoting pink, women have at the very same time been swallowing HRT propaganda and pills that were causing breast cancer.

The question is, Why aren't we mad as hell?

"It's a very good question," says Kathleen O'Grady, with the Winnipeg-based national Women's Health Network. "With Vioxx, there was a huge outcry and court cases right away. It's not clear why the same hasn't happened with HRT."

British Columbia family physician Dr Warren Bell agrees there's been a disconnect between women taking an activist role in fighting breast cancer while ingesting hormones that fuel it—and then giving up hormones but not getting angry about the way the drugs were prescribed and promoted, without evidence of their safety.

Visits to physicians are common among people aged 65 and older, with 86.8 per cent of male seniors and 89.2 per cent of female seniors reporting they had visited a general practitioner in the last year (Rotermann 2006: 35). The gender imbalances in the use of health care services,

"Older women are still the generation conditioned and socialized to be compliant and not to ask questions and not to get angry at the imposition of something that was inappropriate," he says. "And there's still a belief in the probity and scientific acumen of physicians. The combination is one that is very hard to subvert."

(Women also know their anger is not well tolerated. For example, in his blog, medpundit.blogspot.com, a physician referred to a 2002 column I wrote post-WHI about the dangers of HRT, as "a hormonal hissy fit.")

Breast cancer activist Sharon Batt thinks "women should be really angry" but "most of the reports in the media have reported it as a finding that wasn't that clear cut. And maybe people don't understand the statistics well enough to recognize what an enormous finding this is."

Other observers believe much of the confusion has been perpetrated by what Dr Deborah Grady, head of the Women's Health Clinical Research Center, at the University of California, calls "the hormone-industrial complex"—Big Pharma and the constellation of businesses that feed off them.

"The industry is probably doing its best to ensure that it's considered a grey area," says BC physician Bell. He likens the obfuscation to the tobacco industry's initial strategy. "Create an impression of uncertainty and lack of unanimity. It's a lesson learned by the corporate sector across the board.

"If you want to keep on selling a product, actively foment the illusion of a lack of consensus."

Dr Adriane Fugh-Berman, a professor at Washington's Georgetown University School of Medicine, and principal investigator of a project to educate physicians about the influence that pharmaceutical companies have on prescribing, published a paper last year in *Perspectives in Biology and Medicines* titled "Gynecologists and Estrogen."

"It is mysterious why gynecologists seem to be so much more susceptible to drug company influence," she told the *Guardian*. "About 10 to 20 years ago, HRT was really promoted as a panacea like snake oil, it cured and prevents everything—dementia, incontinence, wrinkles. It made you look better and feel better.

"But whenever you see something promoted as a panacea, it is a fake."

Yet far from being mad as hell about the promotion and widespread prescribing of HRT and choosing to not take it, some women still cling to their panacea and damn the consequences.

"They were very angry at the WHI for bursting their balloon," says American author and women's health activist Barbara Seaman. "There was a refusal to really accept it for a while. A lot of women are very devoted to their products."

Seaman, who warned against the use of hormones in the late '60s, has described "the medical establishment's reckless prescription of estrogen" as "the greatest experiment ever performed on women."

She is especially scornful about some earlier observational studies, including one by US healthcare provider Kaiser Permanente, suggesting that HRT protected women from memory loss.

Sought after in the US by lawyers representing women who are suing drug companies, Seaman says it's very difficult to prove HRT is responsible for any particular case of breast cancer, although she believes women who have been taking HRT and have suffered strokes may have a better case.

Sadly, the confluence of genuine hope, greed and vanity has cost the lives of millions of women.

But very little anger.

Source: Gerstel, Judy. (September 4 2007). 'Mad? No, But They Deserve to Be; Post-menopausal Women Show Drop in Diseases after Giving Up HRT'. *The Star*. Reprinted with permission - Torstar Syndication Services.

with women having significantly more physician visits and hospitalization stays, largely disappears among Canadians aged 65 and older.

This shows the impact of child-bearing and reproductive concerns on health care utilization for women in early and middle adulthood (Chen and Hou 2002). Women are more likely than men to receive home care (17.6 per cent compared with 11.7 per cent for men), and home care use rises over time, with 42 per cent of seniors aged 85 and older receiving home care compared with 8 per cent of those aged 65–75 (Rotermann 2006). Unmet health care needs in the form of accessibility and acceptability are more common for people under the age of 45 (Chen and Hou 2002). Therefore, older age as such does not appear to impede access to health care in Canada (Turcotte and Schellenberg 2007).

In fact, the process of aging has led to a number of interventions that medicalize this natural process (Dinnerstein and Weitz 1998; Krieger et al. 1993; K.P. Morgan 1998). The medicalization of menopause and the advent of hormone replacement therapy epitomize the quest to freeze women in a youthful mode (Lorber 1997). Vertinsky (1998: 90) notes that "menopausal women are prime targets of medical experts, pharmaceutical companies and the media who bombard women with the message that hormones are required to cope with the 'death of their ovaries.'" Moreover, cosmetic surgery is becoming more of an imperative than a choice for many women in response to society's valorization of youth (Hurd Clarke, Repta, and Griffin 2007). Historically, women's bodies and functions have been medicalized, though scholars have noted the increasing tendency to medicalize men's aging bodies (e.g., erectile dysfunction, andropause) (Conrad 2007; B.L. Marshall and Katz 2006).

CAGE(s) and the Processes of Production, Reproduction, and Distribution

Clearly, different lifestyle choices (reflecting agency) and limited access to health care do not fully explain health inequality in Canada.

To understand better why some Canadians are healthier than others, we must consider structural interpretations of the intersections among class, age, gender, ethnicity, and race alongside lifestyle and access factors. For instance, variations in levels of physical activity illustrate how class, age, gender, ethnicity, and race structure health behaviour. Gendered ideologies inhibit women from engaging in physical-fitness activities, and despite attempts to increase women's involvement in sport and exercise, fewer women than men are physically active in all age groups (Gilmour 2007; Vertinsky 1998). As Vertinsky (1998: 82) says, "Healthy exercise is closely entwined with the social and economic status of women, disempowering stereotypes of the female body, and the issue of control over women's bodies." Vertinsky (1998) has identified four structural factors that contribute to the limited physical activity of women: (1) the authoritative role played by medical discourse in discouraging strenuous exercise for both younger and older women; (2) the impact of media and beauty standards that see physical fitness only as a means to reach unattainable standards, along with the perception that women are naturally weaker and less physically able; (3) agist assumptions about the physical abilities of older women, along with the reliance on drug therapies; and (4) racial and ethnic bias in accounts of physical activity, with young white women idealized in sport. Further, women's positioning within the processes of production, reproduction, and distribution means that women of various ages and racial and ethnic backgrounds tend not to have as much money or time to spend on physical activity as men do. This suggests that ideological structures combine with material structures to influence lifestyle "choices."

The ways in which processes of production, reproduction, and distribution are organized contribute to health inequalities. The nature of the productive labour that people perform may involve exposure to toxins, a lack of control over the work process, and discriminatory or oppressive treatment, all of which make an imprint on the physical and mental health of bodies. Similarly, individuals with higher degrees of control in productive processes and positive work experiences likely enjoy better health.

Of course, our place in the productive realm and the related health consequences are not randomly assigned but are strongly influenced by our class, age, gender, and race or ethnicity (Jackson and Williams 2006). Even when men and women share the same occupation in paid work, they often experience differing work realities that manifest themselves in differing health consequences (Messing 1997, 1998). For example, Messing says, in her review of the literature on women's occupational health (1997: 3), "Women and men with the same job titles can have very different exposures—male cleaners mop and female cleaners dust." Furthermore, women's occupational illnesses are likely underrepresented because waitresses, supermarket clerks, and cleaners (female-dominated jobs) are under-studied in the occupational literature (Messing 1997). Although employment is associated with better overall health for women (Rose et al. 2004; Walters, McDonough, and Strohschein 2002), some researchers have observed that the combination of caregiving and paid employment can take a toll (Pavalko and Woodbury 2000), suggesting that processes of production and reproduction must be considered simultaneously. Indeed, the increased likelihood for women to be in precarious and less stable forms of employment constitutes yet another health risk stemming from production processes (Menendez et al. 2007).

Similarly, the organization of reproductive processes leads to variations in health. Social ties and contacts are not always health protective and may in fact be stressful. Thus, to the extent that women's primary responsibility for reproductive processes engages them in vast social networks, there may be a "cost of caring" that produces poor health effects. Moreover, marriage is health protective for many men, but the effect of marriage for women on health is more complex: "Marriage may at once improve economic and social support opportunities, while diminishing control over paid and unpaid work—potentially increasing as well as compromising the health status of women" (Ballantyne 1999: 27).

Unpaid work includes domestic work in the form of meal preparation, cleaning, clothing care, repairs and maintenance, child care, adult care, financial management, shopping, transportation, and volunteer work (C. Jackson 1996). Among dual-earner families, women continue to spend more time in housework and domestic labour, with 90 per cent of women doing housework daily compared with 74 per cent of men (K. Marshall 2006). In spite of the importance of domestic work for women's health, Walters and her colleagues (Walters, McDonough, and Strohschein 2002: 687) note that the 1994 Canadian National Population Health Survey still contains no information on the domestic conditions in the home—"a striking omission." Dean (1992) argues that a more equitable division of caregiving and child-raising in the family would benefit the health of both men and women.

According to Katherine Marshall (2006), women, especially those balancing long work hours and child care, are more "time-stressed" than men in similar circumstances. Walters (2003) points out that examining the social context in which lives are lived is critical to disentangling how gender, race, class, and health are intertwined. Walters and her colleagues (1996) looked at the health of 2,285 male and female registered nurses in Ontario through a proportional random sample and compared their health in relation to paid work, unpaid work, and social support; they found that unpaid work substantially affected health, particularly for women. Women were much more affected by caregiver burdens and time constraints and had to contend with "having to divide themselves up in pieces and juggle things" (Walters et al. 1996: 1633). Walters and her colleagues viewed this as indicative of the burden of the "double day" for women who must contend with additional responsibilities in the home. Among the men in the sample, the only significant unpaid-work variable was "disliking housework." The occupational concerns of "overload" and "hazard exposure" were relevant to both male and female nurses, and the authors did not find discrimination or harassment in the workplace to be significant. However, male nurses were much more likely than their female counterparts to be concerned with issues of sexual harassment (Walters et al. 1996). This may indicate the importance of context and the experience of being in the minority in a male- or female-dominated profession.

The preceding discussion of the processes of production, distribution, and reproduction illustrates the tendency in the health literature to treat race, ethnicity, gender, social class, and age as separate entities. Yet the intersections of race and ethnicity, gender, class, and age influence health in a particular historical context and over time (Krieger et al. 1993). The confusion and contradictions in the study of gendered patterns of morbidity discussed in the preceding sections attest to the need for integrating class, ethnicity, and age into these investigations (Cooper 2002; S. Curtis and Lawson 2000). For instance, some research has shown that, in early adulthood, few socio-economic health inequalities are found for men and women. However, over time the impact of reproductive processes and the "cost of caring" appear to have greater health consequences for women, while occupational concerns seem to have greater health consequences for men (Matthews, Manor, and Power 1999). Yet, as Walters (2003) notes, gender relations are complex, changing, and bound

up with other social relations such that using an indicator of sex or gender in research is unlikely to capture the complexity of health effects over time. Instead, it is important to research and assess the social determinants of health and the nature in which vulnerability and advantage cluster within social relations to affect health pathways and outcomes (Raphael 2006, 2007).

The health status and length of life of Aboriginal people can often be attributed to poverty and geographic isolation (CIHI 2004; Public Health Agency of Canada 2006; Trovato 2001: 81), adding further support to the idea that multiple bases of inequality must be considered simultaneously if we are to understand disparities in health. Housing has been shown to be a key determinant of health (Bryant 2004; Raphael 2007), and yet there is an intensifying housing crisis in Canada, where as many as 47 per cent of Aboriginal lone parents are in need of core housing (Campaign 2000, 2007). Indeed, research in the United States has revealed substantial racial differences in health that can be largely attributed to socio-economic factors (Jackson and Williams 2006); however, even within socio-economic groups there are disadvantages stemming from the effects of discrimination. Anderson and Armstead (1995: 217) have found that poor whites and poor blacks in the United States experience different levels of deprivation and therefore are exposed to different health risks. Shuey and Willson (2008) also found that health disadvantages and differential outcomes between black and white Americans remained even after accounting for socio-economic status. The **hypersegregation** or "housing discrimination that blacks face at every level of socio-economic status but especially at the low end . . . may partially explain the disparity in health outcomes between poor blacks and poor whites" (Anderson and Armstead 1995: 217). This hypersegregation means that more poor blacks live in more-impoverished neighbourhoods than do poor whites (Anderson and Armstead 1995), and this leads to increased health risks, as these neighbourhoods are more often used as toxic waste dump sites (Jackson and Williams 2006; Krieger et al. 1993; Maher 1998). In fact, mortality rates are higher for black Americans at nearly every SES level (Anderson and Armstead 1995; Shuey and Willson 2008). Krieger and her colleagues (1993: 87) suggest that these disparities may be due to the fact that socio-economic class is experienced differently by blacks and whites. They point to studies that show that the "economic return for the same level of education is lower for blacks than whites (and also for women than men within each racial group)." In Canada, the clustering of diverse groups of immigrants and visible minorities in neighbourhoods that are impoverished and transient has been shown to negatively affect the mental health of visible minority youth (Abada, Hou, and Ram 2007). Scholars in Canada suggest that there is a need for further research on racism, health, and the effects of social exclusion (Abada, Hou, and Ram 2007; Galabuzi 2004). In summary, although we know much about how gender, class, age, ethnicity, and race influence health separately, the mutual structural coalescence of class, age, gender, race, and ethnicity found in only a handful of studies suggests that this issue should be further explored in health research (Krieger et al. 1993; Mullings and Schulz 2006).

Conclusion

Our experience of health is located squarely in the body, and this embodiment permeates every aspect of our lives. Health is not a haphazard phenomenon. As Audre Lorde's life history and the various sections of this chapter demonstrate, our experiences and opportunities within productive, reproductive, and distributive processes, as they are shaped by structural CAGEs, influence our physical and mental health. Our

class, age, gender, ethnicity, and race may work to constrain or facilitate our experiences in the processes of production, reproduction, and distribution. These processes, in turn, significantly shape both the degree of health we enjoy over the life course and the very length of our lives. Of course, biology, genetics, and physiological aging processes also play a part in determining health outcomes. So, too, does agency. People often make informed and conscious decisions about their health. They decide whether to exercise or whether a symptom warrants a visit to the physician, or they decide what type of treatment is best suited for them, including something as simple as deciding whether they need to take a pill for a headache. The extent to which people are informed or financially able to seek a physician's advice or take a pill are, however, also influenced by structural CAGE(s).

Yet health research rarely considers how the structures of class, age, gender, ethnicity, and race mutually constitute inequality in health outcomes. Furthermore, the focus in the health literature on individual causes of disease outcomes precludes adequate consideration of how the processes of reproduction, distribution, and production, as they are structured by class, age, gender, ethnicity, and race, influence health. Even in the literature on occupational health, which is located squarely in production processes, the emphasis is on occupations that are more commonly held by men than by women. We are still learning about the health effects of waitressing or of being a secretary or a teacher (Messing 1998). And, with the possible exception of mental health, we know very little about how gendered processes of reproduction influence inequality in health. We also know very little about how the processes of distribution within families influence health. In poor families, for instance, do mothers or fathers go without medicine so that they can afford to buy it for their children? When parents sacrifice good nutrition so that their children can eat well, does their health suffer?

Health care is a social-policy issue that the majority of Canadians are passionate about. In the fall of 2002, Roy Romanow, a former NDP premier of Saskatchewan, was commissioned by the federal government to write a report on the health care system in Canada. Romanow talked with Canadians from across the country and examined the provincial health care systems to assess what changes and improvements were needed. One strong message he received from Canadians was that we valued our publicly funded health care system and that most of us wanted to keep it. Romanow recommended that the federal government direct more money to health services and that reform of health services be focused in three areas: home care, primary patient care, and "catastrophic" drug care, such as the treatment necessary for people with HIV/AIDS.

Although these recommendations are commendable, health care access is still not universal in Canada. Numerous Canadian studies show, for example, that disadvantaged groups—for example, lower-income Canadians—do not access health-related services at the same rate as higher-income Canadians (Williamson et al. 2006). Furthermore, new research shows that the three recommendations contained in the Romanow report still require more resources and attention. For example, 10 years after Romanow's report, the Broadbent Institute (2012) argued that the taxpayer-funded health care model needed to be aggressively restructured to cover home care, long-term care, and prescription drugs so that the basic health care needs of Canadians are finally met.

⁑ Note

1. Lorde was married for eight years in the 1960s.

⁑ Questions for Critical Thought

1. In what ways could an individual's psychosocial resources (mastery, self-esteem, social support, and so on) be shaped by his or her class, age, gender, race, and ethnicity?
2. How can we explain persistent health inequality in spite of a system of "universal health care access" in Canada?
3. How do class, age, gender, and ethnicity or race contribute to the development of a healthy or unhealthy lifestyle?
4. Describe how societal ideologies of gender, race, ethnicity, age, and class affect patterns of health care utilization and delivery.
5. In what ways does the historical period in which we live influence our health? What do you think the major health problems will be in the future?

⁑ Glossary

Class-linked stress Stress exposures that are largely dependent on social status. For example, working-class and lower-income individuals are more frequently employed in physically stressful jobs (e.g., where there are extreme temperatures, high noise levels, shift work, or noxious fumes, or where the worker has to work on an assembly-line pace).

Differential exposure hypothesis The argument that women experience more morbidity because they are exposed to more chronic and daily stressors in their lives.

Differential vulnerability hypothesis The argument that women experience more morbidity because their caregiving role makes them more susceptible to emotional stress; this may also involve vulnerabilities due to women's internalized coping styles when dealing with stress.

Fundamental cause theory This theory proclaims that an ongoing association exists between socio-economic status and health status (SES) because SES "embodies an array of resources, such as money, knowledge, prestige, power, and beneficial social connections that protect health no matter what mechanisms are relevant at any given time." In other words, despite medical advances,

the underlying fact is that those from low SES communities lack resources to protect and/or improve their health status.

Hypersegregation The situation in which disproportionate numbers of minority-group members are located in impoverished, dangerous, and environmentally polluted neighbourhoods. Poor African-Americans more often live in extremely disadvantaged neighbourhoods than do poor non-Hispanic whites.

Medicalization The defining of a natural biological event or progression as a form of illness requiring medical intervention and treatment (e.g., menopause has been treated with hormone replacement therapy).

Psychosocial risk factors A system of exposures, resources, and situational variables believed to have an impact on health; they include mastery or sense of control, self-esteem, ease or availability of social supports, negative life events, and daily exposure to stress or exposure to traumatic events.

⠿ Recommended Reading

Aneshensel, Carol S., Jo C. Phelan, and Alex Bierman. 2013. *The Handbook of the Sociology of Mental Health,* 2nd edn. New York: Kluwer Academic. This book features empirical and theory-driven reviews of research on the ways in which society shapes the mental health and the lives of those who have been diagnosed with a mental illness.

Courtenay, Will H. 2000. "Constructions of Masculinity and Their Influence on Men's Well-Being: A Theory of Gender and Health." *Social Science and Medicine* 50, 10: 1385–401. The author examines how socially constructed forms of masculinity (shaped by ethnicity, social class, sexuality, and so on) influence men's health behaviour and men's consequent health risks.

House, James S. 2001. "Understanding Social Factors and Inequalities in Health: 20th Century Progress and 21st Century Prospects." *Journal of Health and Social Behavior* 43 (June): 125–42. An important article that chronicles the main ways in which health inequalities have been explained and outlines the current state of research with future directions.

Inhorn, Marcia C., and K. Lisa Whittle. 2001. "Feminism Meets the 'New' Epidemiologies: Toward an Appraisal of Antifeminist Biases in Epidemiological Research on Women's Health." *Social Science and Medicine* 53, 5: 553–67. The authors examine gender biases in current epidemiologic approaches to women's health research (e.g., biological essentialism) and suggest more feminist-friendly research directions.

Krieger, N., D.L. Rowley, A.A. Herman, B. Avery, and M.T. Phillips. 1993. "Racism, Sexism, and Social Class: Implications for Studies of Health, Disease, and Well-Being." *American Journal of Preventive Medicine* 9, 6: 82–122. The authors provide a comprehensive critical review of US epidemiologic literature, including detailed recommendations on how to overcome racism, sexism, and class biases in future health studies.

Link, Bruce G., and Jo Phelan. 1995. "Social Conditions as Fundamental Causes of Disease." *Journal of Health and Social Behavior* 35: 80–94. An important article in which the authors argue that health policy and research must shift from the focus on individual risk factors to more fundamental causes of disease (e.g., SES).

Lynch, J.W., G.A. Kaplan, and J.T. Salonen. 1997. "Why Do Poor People Behave Poorly? Variation in Adult Health Behaviours and Psychosocial Characteristics by Stages of the Socioeconomic Lifecourse." *Social Science and Medicine* 44, 6: 809–19. A population-based study of Finnish men who found that socio-economic conditions in childhood were significantly associated with adult health behaviours. This life-course approach illustrates how health or "lifestyle" behaviour is influenced by socio-structural factors.

Raphael, Dennis. 2004. *Social Determinants of Health: Canadian Perspectives.* Toronto: Canadian Scholars' Press. An outstanding work on the social determinants of health in Canada, including the effects of food security, housing, education, and income along with a large section on the impact of social policy.

Raphael, Dennis. 2007. *Poverty and Policy in Canada: Implications for Health and Quality of Life.* Toronto: Canadian Scholars' Press. An excellent interdisciplinary text that examines the devastating and long-lasting health effects of poverty in this country and what can be done about it.

Simon, Robin. 2000. "The Importance of Culture in Sociological Theory and Research on Stress and Mental Health: A Missing Link?" Chapter 5 in Chloe E. Bird, Peter Conrad, and Allen M. Fremont, eds, *Handbook of Medical Sociology*, 5th edn. Englewood Cliffs, NJ: Prentice-Hall. This chapter outlines the three main approaches to explaining the relationship between stress and mental health; it argues that cultural context (norms, values, and so on) and meanings deserve a more prominent place in sociological theories of stress and mental health.

Wadsworth, M.E.J. 1997. "Health Inequalities in the Life Course Perspective." *Social Science and Medicine* 44, 6: 859–69. The author outlines the value of a life-history approach to research by explaining how social factors (particularly those associated with poverty) may affect an individual's health trajectory. For example, nutrition in childhood may influence adult blood pressure levels, height, and so on.

⸬ Relevant Websites

Health-evidence.ca
www.health-evidence.ca/

**This website sponsored by a group of Canadian health agencies, including the Canadian Institute for Health Information, provides an excellent search engine for health-related articles and reviews.

Health Council of Canada
www.healthcouncilcanada.ca/

Funded by the Government of Canada, the **Health Council of Canada fosters accountability and transparency by assessing progress in improving the quality, effectiveness, and sustainability of the health care system. Publications, videos, news, and events, as well as external links, are all posted on the site.

World Health Organization—Commission on Social Determinants of Health
www.who.int/social_determinants/en/

**The Commission on Social Determinants of Health (CSDH) supports countries and global health partners to address the social factors leading to ill health and inequities. This site has links to strategy documents, essays, and articles on health equity and social determinants of health, as well as summary reports from associated collaborations or projects and people's stories about health inequities.

SexualityandU.ca
www.sexualityandu.com

**A comprehensive site about all aspects of sexuality over the life course administered by the Society of Obstetricians and Gynaecologists of Canada.

The Politics of Population Health
http://msl.stream.yorku.ca/mediasite/viewer/?peid=ac604170-9ccc-4268-a1af-9a9e04b28e1d

**A lecture by Dr Dennis Raphael, York University.

Health Disparities: From Genetics to Health Policy
http://video.google.com/videoplay?docid=-4129139685624192201&hl=en

A presentation by Dr Dennis Raphael on politics and health at the Centre for Health Disparities in Cleveland, Ohio.

12

CAGE(s) and the State

by Tammy Duerden Comeau, Julie Ann McMullin, and Josh Curtis

Introduction

In January 2003, André Le Corre, a retired medical lab technician, was in court presenting a $3-billion class-action suit against the Government of Canada for not informing him and 380,000 other seniors that they were eligible for the Guaranteed Income Supplement (GIS). The GIS is a federal social assistance program that tops up Old Age Security (OAS) benefits for seniors who earn less than $12,648 a year. This figure does not include OAS benefits that were approximately $5,000 a year in 2003 (and, more recently, about $6,600 in 2014). This is a point of confusion for many seniors. Mr Le Corre, who was 76 years old, had thought he was ineligible for the top-up because his pension income and OAS combined were greater than $12,648 a year. In fact, he had been eligible for the GIS benefits since 1994 but had never made a claim. Mr Le Corre's court case argued that Ottawa was negligent in not informing seniors who were eligible for benefits, as it could have used Revenue Canada data banks to identify these people. For Mr Le Corre, the GIS benefits would have made a big difference in the quality of his life, including "the awful events that could have been prevented, the rent that could have been paid, the medications that could have been bought." But for Mr Le Corre, the "lawsuit is a matter of principle. It's more about the sadness I feel for the poorer people" (Thuanh Ha 2003: A7).

This tiny glimpse into Mr Le Corre's life tells us a lot about the role the **state** plays in processes of distribution and in distributive outcomes of inequality for older adults. Without social assistance, Mr Le Corre's income would be less than $12,648 per year, well below official poverty lines. If he had claimed all the benefits for which he was eligible, the quality of his life would have been greatly enhanced. But in acknowledging the "poorer people," Mr Le Corre recognizes that, while he is poor, there are many older Canadians who are worse off than he is. In fact, research (Luong 2009) has shown that many seniors who are eligible for the GIS do not apply (see Table 12.1), and in the oldest senior age group, only 24 per cent of those eligible to receive a benefit of $2,000 or more applied (Poon 2005). According to recent research, the OAS and the GIS accounted for only 37.6 per cent of the total income of the senior population (Statistics Canada 2013a). Although significant gains have been made in eradicating poverty among older Canadians, 14.9 per cent of unattached Canadians aged 65

Table 12.1 GIS Recipients and Eligible Non-recipients

	LAD		SLID
Total seniors	4,122.7	'000	4,006.8
OAS recipients	4,010.3		3,861.4
GIS recipients and eligible non-recipients	1,710.6		1,577.5
Recipients	1,565.1		1,418.1
Non-recipients	145.5		159.4

Source: Statistics Canada. 2000 & 2006. Longitudinal Administrative Database and Survey of Labour and Income Dynamics. www.statcan.gc.ca/pub/75-001-x/2009107/article/10906-eng.htm

and older still live in poverty (Statistics Canada 2013a). The incidence of low income is greatest for senior women (16.1 per cent) living alone compared to men (12.2 per cent) in 2011 (Statistics Canada 2013a).

Hence, the ways in which gender relations shape the interrelated processes of production, reproduction, and distribution (see chapters 8 and 9) intersect with age relations in determining income inequality in later life. Of course, class, ethnicity, and "race" matter too. If Mr Le Corre were a member of the capitalist executive class, he would not likely have to worry about GIS. If he were a recent immigrant to Canada, he would be ineligible for OAS or GIS even if he became a Canadian citizen. Box 12.1 explores this issue.

Indeed, the state encompasses a vast range of institutions, policies, and programs that have a profound effect on the individuals living in a society. The workings of the state provide a strong example of the overlapping and intertwining nature of the processes of production, reproduction, and distribution. For instance, the Canadian state's influence on the processes of production and the labour market, as discussed in chapter 9, is evident in the management of immigration policy, anti-strike legislation, pay-equity policies, maternity benefits,

child care, and unemployment insurance (see also Pupo 2001). The processes of reproduction and the work of caring discussed in chapter 8 are directly shaped and affected by maternity benefits, pensions, and immigration policy, particularly in the realm of paid reproductive work (Stasiulis and Bakan 1995, 2005). Governments dictate education and health policies, which influence the outcomes of education and health inequality that we discussed in chapters 10 and 11. Indeed, education and health policies have come under intense scrutiny in recent years as conservative policies have led to significant service cutbacks. All of these policies concern largely distributive processes, and the form in which wages and benefits are distributed in the family constitutes another process through which inequality is manifested. While the state can act to ameliorate or mend unequal relations and while agents have used the state for retribution, the state's actions are often ambiguous and contradictory (Armstrong and Connelly 1999). One recent example is found in Harper's 2015 family tax cut policy, which allows couples with children to split their incomes for tax purposes. In this new policy, higher-earner spouses are allowed to transfer up to $50,000 of income to their lower-earner spouse, thus becoming eligible to be taxed in a lower bracket (Geddes 2015). Critics of this new policy suggest that the new family tax cut is a step backward for women in the workforce—it encourages women (usually) to stay at home to look after children. Justin Trudeau's Liberal government made an election promise to eliminate the family tax cut policy, but at the time of writing (February 2015) a formal announcement had not yet been made.

Armstrong and Connelly (1999) provide another example. They point out that the beneficiaries of state actions, such as women whose incomes are increased by pay equity, are often the most privileged in the first place and there is considerable difficulty in predicting the effects

HIGHLIGHT

Box 12.1 OAS Benefits Denied to Canadian Immigrant Citizens

Nicholas Keung—a writer for the *Toronto Star*—recently told the story of Yvonne Gardner, a retired registered nurse who gave medical care to Canadians for 40 years since immigrating from England in the 1970s. Despite being eligible, Yvonne has been struggling to prove her eligibility for monthly Old Age Security (OAS) pension benefits since retiring at 65.

The Old Age Security pension is a monthly payment available to Canadians age 65 and older who apply and meet certain requirements—namely, having a work history in Canada. OAS is available to Canadian citizens and legal residents living in the country who have spent at least 10 years in Canada after age 18. Yvonne clearly meets the government's criteria for eligibility, yet has somehow fallen through the cracks.

According to Keung, Yvonne was asked for copies of plane tickets for all of her travels in and out of Canada since moving from England in 1975—clearly, an impossible task—as proof she has lived here for the 10-year minimum.

Yvonne understands the importance of having safeguards to prevent abuse of the pension system, but feels—and for good reason—that the government's insistence on plane tickets is ludicrous. Other documents, such as easily accessible tax returns should be sufficient.

"It just doesn't make any sense. All they have to do is to check and see when I paid my taxes," said Yvonne, who has delivered over 300 babies and cared for tens of thousands for patients in hospital emergency rooms and intensive care units since her permanent employment in the 1970s.

"I've looked after millions of people in my life and paid all the taxes. I need some help now. They can't use these rules and regulations to beat me over the head."

Unfortunately, Yvonne is not alone. Thousands of eligible Canadian immigrants are denied pension benefits each year, even though they have paid taxes for decades and have invested in the Canadian pension system.

According to Service Canada, as of June 2012, 5 million Canadians were receiving OAS, at a cost of more than $28 billion a year. Some feel that the Canadian government is looking to save by trying to deny applicants the benefits they are entitled to. Around 385,000 people applied for OAS in 2012 and about 3 per cent (11,550 people) were rejected for failing to qualify under the 10-year residence requirement.

Currently, Yvonne lives on $486 from the Canadian Pension Plan and $431 government assistance a month. This income doesn't even cover her monthly rent of about $1,000.

Sources: Nicholas Keung. (July 30, 2012) "OAS benefits denied: Immigrants told to produce residency proofs." *The Toronto Star*; anon. (Feb. 1, 2012). "Canada Pension Plan vs. Old Age Security—the differences explained." *CBC News*.

of even well-intentioned policies. Pupo (2001: 136) argues that the state's policy of treating men and women as the "same" in divorce and child-custody legislation disadvantages women by discounting their care work in the family. The state's undervaluation of caregiving and nurturing puts women in a losing position even though the policy is ostensibly equitable.

According to Pupo (2001: 129), the state's main tasks are those of "accumulation, legitimation, and coercion or social control," and these tasks are played out in the economy, the labour market, and among individuals and families. To carry out these tasks involves the establishment of a citizenship regime consisting of boundaries, rules, definitions, and geographic boarders

(Dobrowolsky and Jenson 2004; Jenson and Papillon 2000: 246). Citizenship rights are defined, and avenues for obtaining access to these rights are made clear. A complex bureaucracy establishes the "democratic rules of the game" and determines things such as acceptable ways in which to make claims. Nations are defined on the basis of historical claims and conceptualizations of nationality. Finally, states establish "the geographical borders of the political community" as an exclusionary principle of citizenship (Jenson and Papillon 2000: 246).

One way to examine the reach of the state on groups and individuals is to look at the state's role in denoting who are deemed **citizens** and what are their entitlements. T.H. Marshall's concept of citizenship organizes the rights and responsibilities of citizens into three groups: **civil citizenship**, which includes basic human rights, such as the right to individual freedom and legal justice; **political citizenship**, which includes the right to participate in the political process; and **social citizenship** (perhaps the broadest concept), which includes financial well-being, social heritage, and access to social services (T.H. Marshall 1950). Marshall's typology has been criticized for its generalization of the experience of white European men to represent the process of citizenship in general (Walby 1997). In fact, Walby (1997) notes that the means by which white European men achieved citizenship do not represent the experience of most other groups. Box 12.2 elaborates on this theme by showing that women and children face difficulties when trying to obtain full citizenship in some parts of Northern Africa and the Middle East.

However, in Walby's (1997: 168) analysis, there are "degrees" of citizenry, and she argues that Marshall's conceptualization is useful in the study of how portions of citizenship were meted out to different groups at different historical times. It is important to note that although the state has a substantial amount of power with which to structure and constrain the lives of its citizens, state institutions have also been successfully mobilized by agents for the purposes of social justice (Pupo 2001; Walby 2004, 2011). Individuals and groups can use state institutions (e.g., the legal system) and programs to their own ends (e.g., to seek redress or to monopolize resources).

In this chapter, "social citizenship" will be a main point of discussion, because the state programs of unemployment insurance, parental benefits or maternity leave, social welfare, pensions, and old age security in many ways reproduce the existing inequalities and shore up long-standing advantages among the privileged. Although aid and assistance for the disadvantaged groups in Canadian society are desperately needed, the form that this aid has frequently taken has had mixed and often negative results. Furthermore, Canadian citizens are experiencing more and more infringements on their civil liberties with advances in surveillance technology and security measures (Brodie 1999; Crocker et al. 2007; Tator and Henry 2006).

This chapter will take a critical view of the role of the state, focusing on the part played by the state in social regulation and the social reproduction of the relations of class, gender, race, ethnicity, and age. The division of the chapter into separate sections on class, age, gender, and race and ethnicity is in some ways arbitrary and is done largely for the purposes of organization. The state's conceptualization of these social relations is integral to the way in which policies are conceived and developed and to the effects that they have on groups and individuals. Notions of who is counted as a citizen shape the penalties, constraints, and privileges meted out to Canadians. In order to situate Canada within the global context, we discuss the state and citizenship from a cross-national perspective.

Global perspective

Box 12.2 Sexist Laws and Citizenship in Middle East

Several countries in the Arab world have denied women the ability to transfer their citizenship to their children if they were born to foreign fathers. This means that their children would not have access to crucial social benefits—including health care and education—and would be unable to own and inherit their mother's property. The same laws do *not* apply to men who have children with foreign women.

This practice is particularly common in Lebanon. On the one hand, the Lebanese constitution promotes gender equality. Article 7 of the Lebanese Constitution states that "all Lebanese are equal under the law, they enjoy equality in civil and political rights and they assume duties and responsibilities without any difference between them." On the other hand, this article is contradicted by Article 1 of the Lebanese Nationality Code: only a "person born to a Lebanese father" can be considered an official Lebanese citizen. This contradiction has allowed politicians in Lebanon to exclude citizenship to all children born into mixed families. Even if these children have lived in Lebanon for decades, they are still not recognized as official citizens.

A 2004 report by the Beirut Collective for Research and Training on Development-Action (CRTD.A) drew attention to this contradiction. Its authors argued that the "current nationality laws in the countries under study contradict with the notion of equality between all citizens as enshrined in their respective constitutions" (CRTD.A 2004: 10). However, politicians in Arab countries responded that they were simply following the international trend in defining citizenship by generics (Joseph, Charafeddine, Al-Labadi, and Mahdawi 2010).

To raise political attention to the issue, the CRTD.A made a film titled *My Child the Foreigner* to tell the stories of women and children who have been affected by citizenship laws in the Middle East.

Sources: Angie Zambarakji. (March 29, 2012). "Sexist laws deprive families of citizenship in Middle East." The Bureau of Investigative Journalism; Neil Singh and Sawsan Abdulrahim. (June 7, 2015). "Salma Hayek and the Sexist Lebanese Citizenship Law." Jadaliyya; Joseph, Charafeddine, Al-Labadi, and Mahdawi (2010); Collective for Research and Training on Development-Action (CRTD.A). (2004), "Denial of Nationality: The Case of Arab Women: Gender, Citizenship, and Nationality Program. Summary of regional research."

Focusing on Class: Making Citizens, Making "Class"

Poverty

The face of poverty and social class is deeply gendered, racialized, and age-based. Canadians living in poverty and low-income situations are more often women, particularly lone women raising children, who in 2011 represented the largest group living below the low-income cut-off of any other group, at 23 per cent (Statistics Canada 2013a). Women and men who have recently immigrated, particularly visible-minority immigrants and Aboriginal men and women are also at increased risk of being poor and of having low incomes (Palameta 2004; Reitz, Curtis, and Elrick 2014). Aboriginal peoples in Canada (whose poverty rate in 2010 was 15.2 per cent compared with the national average of 9.0 per cent) have been described as "colonized" peoples, existing as a reserve labour army and kept dependent on the economic imperatives of the Canadian state (Frideres 1988; Frideres and Gadacz 2008). Immigration policies in Canada have historically favoured workers who could be more easily exploited, both by the manufactured vulnerability of their citizenship status and through overtly racist practices (Bolaria and Li 1988; Calliste 1996; Trumper and Wong 2007). Immigrants were allowed entry to Canada specifically to fill the need for cheap labour (e.g., Chinese workers were paid less than European workers in the construction of the Canadian Pacific Railway) and to toil at jobs that no one else wanted (e.g., Caribbean black women were brought in to perform domestic labour) (Calliste 1996; Li 1988). Thus, because immigrants were desired largely for their labour, immigration practices constructed classes. Furthermore, strict limitations have often accompanied the entry of immigrants into the country (Calliste 1996). This is illustrated for Calliste (1996: 73) by the exclusion "in July 1911, [of] eight Guadeloupean domestics when it was judged that they were likely to become a public charge because they were single parents. . . . The immigration officer surmised that they were likely to become pregnant again and would probably become a drain on the public purse." Calliste (1996: 72) argues that these actions show the Canadian state's racialization of Caribbean women as "immoral" because of the belief that they are "likely to become single parents." Assumptions about who was likely to be "poor" and who would be supported in such a circumstance are evident in Canadian social assistance policy.

The Canadian state has a long history of policies designed to aid those who are poor, but the state's conceptualization of the "deserving" poor has largely incorporated the image of the "white, working-class breadwinner" who is temporarily out of work (Scott 1996). The poor of Canadian society are not all viewed as entitled to the rights of economic well-being and social security. They are sorted and classified on the basis of their age, race and ethnicity, and gender in order to determine their measure of entitlement (CPJ 2010). Traditionally, the white, working-class breadwinner has been seen as the "real" citizen, deserving of the guarantee of the

rights of social citizenship. The conflation of the "deserving worker-citizen" with the white, male, working-class worker engaged in paid work has long shaped policy-making (Brodie and Bakker 2007; Evans 1997; Scott 1996).

Tracing the history of social assistance, Scott (1996) analyzes how the assistance for single mothers originated from the notion of entitlement owed to the "worker," ostensibly the "white, male, middle-aged, family supporter." Thus, the "deserving" mother-recipient of social citizenship was fundamentally racialized, since "racial" homogeneity in families (in particular the quest to reproduce a "sanitized" white, northern citizen) was strongly encouraged (Mackey 1999; McLaren 1991; Valverde 1991). Consider the moral panics over the "corruption" of young white women by Chinese men (Valverde 1991), the exclusion of current and "potential" Caribbean black mothers (Calliste 1996), and the effect that the Indian Act had on unions between Aboriginal people and white settlers (Aboriginal women who married a non-Aboriginal were stripped of their Indian status) (Nelson 2002). The very possibility of existing in a family was itself also strongly controlled and racialized. For example, Chinese men who emigrated were not allowed to bring their families with them. This policy deliberately limited the number of non-white families in Canada (Das Gupta 1995; Li 1998).

Mother's Allowance (which evolved into Family Benefits) was introduced in 1920 and was restricted to First World War widows, who were eligible for support from the government because they were not to blame for their own widowhood (Scott 1996: 17). Evans (1997: 99) calls this the "breadwinner/dependent model of the family." In this case, the "mother-citizen" was owed a stake in social citizenship (only because of her association to her deceased "citizen" husband); however, she had to adhere to the prevailing gender norms and strict behavioural guidelines (Scott 1996: 18; see also

M. Little 1999). The gendering of social policy is noted by Scott (1996), who argues that women were not granted state support for their role as paid workers or even for their reproductive labour but only as a proxy for their relationship to a bona fide and entitled "worker." Scott (1996: 18) points to the "man about the house" rule, which prohibits any woman living with a man from collecting government support. This prohibition is imbued with assumptions about men's presumed support of women. Though it is now called the "spouse about the house" rule, heavy monitoring and policing of single women on welfare continues, with the assumption that a "man" in the house means that he is contributing to finances (Mirchandani and Chan 2007). The family-class immigration status is yet another example of the state's construction of women as dependent on a male provider, for women are more likely than men to enter under this status, which effectively denies them the language training and social programs that are available to their "independent"-class immigrant sponsor (Ighodaro 2006). The notion of the "deserving" recipient and the moral regulation and monitoring of those receiving state support illustrate the state's role in constructing gendered and racialized ideologies and in perpetuating class inequalities.

Poverty statistics in Canada show that lone-parent families headed by women are much more likely to be in poverty (36.8 per cent) than those headed by men (9.1 per cent). Poverty rates have risen for women since the early 2000s, but have generally improved for men (Statistics Canada 2013a). The penalization of women for existing as single heads of families is evident in Kilkey and Bradshaw's international comparative analysis (1999) of mothers in lone- and two-parent families. The countries studied were the Nordic countries as well as France, Germany, Austria, the United States, the United Kingdom, Ireland, the Netherlands, Australia, and Canada. In this comparison,

Canada is grouped with the UK and Australia as a country where lone mothers have "an above average rate of poverty whether in paid work or not" (Kilkey and Bradshaw 1999: 176). These findings are reproduced in a later study that confirms that lone mothers are disproportionately employed in low-wage employment (see Figure 12.1). There are few incentives or legitimate opportunities for women in these circumstances to engage in paid work, and, the authors argue, in most cases the policies designed to support lone mothers do not make it possible to escape poverty, even if those women do join the labour force (Kilkey and Bradshaw 1999). For lone mothers on social assistance, there is little consideration for the difficulties of balancing work and child care (Gazso 2007; Lessa 2006; Stephensen and Emery 2003). Furthermore, in Ontario, the imperative to reduce government spending on social assistance means that some lone mothers who work full-time are left "worse-off" financially than lone mothers who work less than half-time and qualify for an Ontario Works supplement (Evans 2007).

Single mothers have simply joined the leagues of the working poor. In fact, many of the lone mothers in the UK, Australia, and Canada in Kilkey and Bradshaw's study (1999) were found to live in multi-generational households. Kilkey and Bradshaw (1999) suggest that the poverty rate (as measured by household income) may underestimate the extent of poverty and that those lone mothers who have paid jobs may be able to hold them only because of support from their families. The lack of support from the state fuels the perpetuation of poverty for lone mothers and creates an "underclass" in Canadian society out of these women and their families. Politics and policy play an important role in reducing the inequalities that lone parents face. As Box 12.3 shows, political systems that cater to families (e.g., in Sweden) are able to successfully reduce economic disparities through progressive social policy.

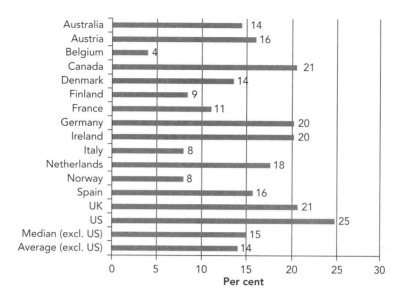

Figure 12.1 Single Parents in Low-Wage Employment

Source: Timothy Casey and Laurie Maldonado, "Worst Off—Single-Parent Families in the United States: A Cross-National Comparison of Single Parenthood in the U.S. and Sixteen Other High-Income Countries." The Women's Legal Defense Action Fund. www. legalmomentum.org/sites/default/files/reports/worst-off-single-parent.pdf

Re-manufacturing Class: Workfare

Some observers suggest that the rights of Canadian citizens are in jeopardy (Fuller, Kershaw, and Pulkingham 2008; Mooers 1999). Mooers (1999: 288) argues that as with the idea of "lean production" in the global workplace, there has been a shift in the notion of citizenship, such that social citizenship rights are being pared down and citizens are increasingly being required to "earn" their right to social benefits. This ideology stands in stark contrast to the notion of **decommodification**, where social rights are viewed as entitlements rather than commodities to be earned. The requirement that Canadians perform labour for the right to economic survival can be seen as one example of the move to "lean citizenship." Similarly, Fuller, Kershaw, and Pulkingham (2008: 157) state that there has been a move from "rights-based

concepts of citizenship to obligation-centred notions," where employment acts as the key signifier of "active citizenship." The obligation to contribute to society through paid employment is best illustrated through the ushering in of "work-for-welfare" programs. Yet, in other parts of the world, social citizenship is much more exclusive. For example, in China, entitlement to income security and welfare provisions is only granted to those who live in urban centres, thus exposing the most disadvantaged workers to even greater risk (Liu 2007).

Workfare has been described by some as a harking back to the era of the workhouses for the poor, who were required to "pay" in one way or another for a minimal amount of aid (Shragge 1997). Indeed, this aid is truly minimal, as social assistance amounts continue to shrink and payments generally leave recipients living far below Statistic Canada's low income cut-off

Global perspective

Box 12.3 Single Mothers, Poverty, and Social Policy

A recent Pew Research Center poll on family structures reported that nearly 69 per cent of Americans—almost 7 of 10 people—believe that single-mother families are "bad for society." And, about 60 per cent believe that a child needs both a mother and father "to grow up happily."

In an op-ed *New York Times* piece, Katie Roiphe spoke on behalf of single mothers. Roiphe has two children. And they were born by different fathers, with neither of whom Roiphe currently lives. Despite only having one income she is financially stable, which was earned because she obtained a higher-level education. Roiphe knows she is not a "typical" single mother. In today's society, however, one wonders whether such a label actually exists anyhow.

According to Roiphe, "Conservatives obsess over moral decline, and liberals worry extravagantly—and one could argue condescendingly—about children, but all exhibit a fundamental lack of imagination about what family can be—and perhaps more pressingly—what family is." In reality, 53 per cent of American women under 30 are born to unmarried mothers. In other words, it seems that public opinion has not kept up with demographic changes over the past several decades.

Americans seem to be concerned that there is causal link between single family households, poverty, and social ills. Research does find that conditions like poverty and instability—which frequently accompany single mothers—increase the chances that the children will experience alcoholism, mental illness, academic failure and other troubles. However, there is no academic evidence that single motherhood alone leads to these problems.

This interpretation is threatening to policymakers in the US because it implies that national poverty, not single motherhood, is the problem. Given that poverty is not inevitable—i.e., through government programs, redistribution, and social spending—it puts the onus for poverty reduction on the state rather than the individual.

For example, the proportion of single mothers in Sweden is even higher than in the United States. However, rates of single-mother poverty are very low. Sweden has policies that fully support caring for children, universal health care, paid parental and family leave, and education subsidies for parents. These programs do not exist in the United States, and the economic burden of raising young children has become a major cause of poverty in US families, especially for single mothers.

Sources: Media Inquiries (Jan 6, 2011), "Disapprove of Single Mothers," *Pew Research Center*; Katie Roiphe. (Aug. 11, 2012). "In Defense of Single Motherhood," *The New York Times*; Riane Esler & Shereen Mitchell. (August 31, 2012). "Single Mothers in Poverty: A Symptom of Failed Economic Policies," *Huffington Post*.

(Snyder 2006: 311). Shragge (1997: 26) notes that the Canadian government's endorsement and development of workfare reflect the view that "able-bodied individuals" who are collecting welfare do so simply because of their own lack of skills and lack of initiative. These recipients are now required to work or take training in order to receive government aid. The wider societal shifts in the labour market and the difficulty in finding work are discounted as explanations for receiving welfare. The assumption is that if workers are sufficiently qualified, they will be able to find a job that adequately supports themselves and, by extension, their family. Yet, in a study of the Ontario Works program in Toronto, those who left welfare for employment were found to be far worse off in all categories compared with the rest of the Canadian labour market (Lightman, Mitchell, and Herd 2005). For example, 30 per cent of welfare leavers were in non-permanent positions compared with 7 per cent of the labour force, and welfare leavers earned two-thirds (64 per cent) less than the adult labour force on average (Lightman, Mitchell, and Herd 2005: 71). In fact, Shragge (1997) argues that workfare is calculated to make use of the unemployed and the vulnerable who would perform work for less than a job would normally pay. Workfare is a "coercive" method of government control over the most underprivileged in society (deRouche 2001: 329). Interestingly, although the significant decline in welfare caseloads in Ontario is commonly attributed to the Ontario Works workfare program, researchers have found that stricter eligibility requirements for collecting social assistance are likely behind the decrease (Snyder 2006: 319). In either case, the right to social citizenship is being eroded in the face of demands that citizens must demonstrate that they deserve support.

In British Columbia, changes in eligibility requirements for welfare in 2002 and extensions in work and employment requirements have had devastating consequences (Klein and Pulkingham 2008). Indeed, in 2010 poverty rates were higher in British Columbia than in any other province and the rate of poverty for BC lone-parent families the highest by far, at 45.6 per cent (CPJ 2010; CCSD 2007: 7). Klein and Pulkingham (2008) examined the impact of social assistance policies on 62 British Columbian longer-term welfare recipients over a span of two years (2004–6). They note that welfare is by no means "generous" and document that during their study period "a single person considered employable received $510 per month—$325 for shelter and $185 (or about $6 per day) for all other needs, including food, clothing, transportation, telephone, etc." (Klein and Pulkingham 2008: 2). For their participants, living on welfare was a matter of survival, and food, shelter, and basic necessities were difficult to obtain. The majority of their participants (77 per cent) frequented food banks, and 46 per cent had suffered from hunger in the past month (Klein and Pulkingham 2008).

Finding work and employment under these circumstances was clearly a great challenge, especially considering that at the start of the study 39 per cent of participants had not had a fixed address in the previous six months and half did not have a phone number (Klein and Pulkingham 2008). The investigators found that a key problem was the misclassification of many of their participants into the "expected to work" category when physical, mental, and other health difficulties clearly made employment unobtainable. In fact, most were reclassified over the course of the study period, but Klein and Pulkingham (2008) argue that this took far too long and the need for reclassification should have been evident much earlier to government officials. The expectation that valid societal contributions should take the form of work in productive processes—while reproductive labour and contributions in voluntary capacities are ignored—continues to penalize citizens in a number of ways (Fuller, Kershaw, and Pulkingham 2008).

Workfare programs also illustrate inconsistency and contradictions inherent in state policies (Breitkreuz 2005; deRouche 2001; Evans 2007). For instance, despite the fact that historically some women have been able to obtain social assistance on the basis of their rights as mothers, the advent of workfare programs has largely ignored gender and "mother status" (Evans 1997, 2007). In this case, the class status of individuals as "welfare recipient" appears to take precedence. According to Breitkreuz (2005: 154),

The most striking contradiction is that although some welfare states encourage middle-class women to be "stay at home" moms and dependent on their husbands for financial sustenance, they simultaneously require low-income lone mothers to work for wages and pay someone else to care for their children. Thus, while "stay at home" mothers with male breadwinners are saluted for their outstanding "family values," poor women who wish to raise their children full-time are declared lazy and psychologically dependent on the state.

Similarly, in Alberta's social assistance program, single mothers are considered "employable once the youngest child is six months old," and in the expansion of Ontario's workfare program, single mothers with children over the age of three are required to participate (Evans 1997: 100; Evans 2007). Therefore, Evans (1997: 100; 2007) argues, in the area of social assistance there has been a move to define "mothers" as "workers" simultaneously with the increasing inaccessibility of child care.

Indeed, the type of work that lone-mother welfare recipients most often obtain is inflexible, precarious, and unfriendly to the demands and requirements of raising a child (Breitkreuz 2005; Evans 2007). Training and education for those on welfare is minimal unless it seems likely to steer people as quickly as possible into work of any kind. Evans (2007: 35–6) points out that the motto "any job is a good job" is made explicit in the Ontario Works policy guidelines, and education and training have been reduced and their access limited in recent years. For recipients of social assistance and employment insurance who are unskilled, workfare programs are unlikely to significantly improve their skills or even—for extended periods—their income; however, with tightening requirements and workfare programs, the social assistance payments required of the province have been reduced, thus benefiting the state (deRouche 2001).

Agents in Action: Dissent and Co-optation

Although the preceding sections have emphasized the significant reach of the state into people's lives, this does not mean that individuals and groups in Canadian society do not exercise agency with regard to the state. Mooers (1999) uses Gramsci's idea of hegemony to discuss the co-optation of workers in the state's renewed emphasis on "self-reliance" and "active citizenship" (e.g., workfare). Certainly, these programs have had both widespread public support and strident opposition (as during the Days of Action), thus illustrating the contradictory and complex nature of hegemony (Mooers 1999). Mooers claims that the state's recruitment of public support and community input for government privatization projects was a tactic in the attempt to minimize opposition. Still, citizens have continued to mobilize against the state's welfare reforms and attempts to privatize various public enterprises (e.g., health care). Mr Le Corre's decision to sue the federal government for not making people aware of their eligibility for GIS is another case in point.

Indeed, class actions against governments are quite common. In the last few years, gay- and lesbian-rights activists have challenged provincial and federal governments on various human rights and family issues and gained significant ground. There has been somewhat less success for those contesting workfare programs. Louise Gosselin brought a class action against the Quebec government for its "coercive" welfare policies. These policies substantially reduced payments to able-bodied welfare recipients under the age of 30 who do not participate in "schooling, job training, or community work" (Seeman 2001). Gosselin contends that the welfare reforms are unconstitutional and that they violate basic citizenship rights. However, Neil Seeman, a journalist with the *Globe and Mail*, trivialized and condemned Gosselin's lawsuit, claiming that granting "protected 'rights' . . . would spiral the country into debt . . . [and] would also reverse political priorities established by voters at the ballot box" (2001). Seeman's response and portrayal of Gosselin and workfare is an apt example of the hegemonic control of the state. Citizen protest and dissent exist, but they are often harshly challenged by those who support the ideologies of the ruling regime.

Focusing on Race: Making Citizens, Making "Race"

The often oppressive nature of government policy and state action is evident in the history of policies concerning Aboriginal peoples in Canada. The outright denial of basic citizenship rights and the intricate and totalitarian declaration of the Indian Act (1876) have wreaked havoc on Aboriginal communities and crafted a perpetual cycle of poverty and dysfunction for many (R. Armstrong 1999; Dickason 2006; Frideres and Gadacz 2008). Political citizenship has been historically denied to Aboriginal groups by the Canadian government (Borrows 2001).

The civil and social citizenship rights of Aboriginal peoples have also been strongly curtailed by the Indian Act and its legacy. If social citizenship includes the right to one's social heritage, then this entitlement has been severely compromised for Aboriginal Canadians. Heritage and social relations were ignored because Indian status was defined by the government on the basis of where one lived (e.g., on a reserve) and with which band one was registered (Boyko 1995; D.G. Smith 1975). The Indian Act effectively denied people their social heritage,

for Aboriginal women who married a non-Indian were stripped of their Indian status, as were their children (Boyko 1995; Dickason 2006). These women were forced to leave the reserve and live apart from their families. This aspect of the policy illustrates that the Indian Act was both a racial and a gender project. Although Aboriginal women who married a non-Indian were subsumed under their husband's status, this stipulation did not apply to Aboriginal men who married a non-Indian. The policy is dehumanizing because it treats a person's identity and social heritage like a set of clothes that can be taken on and off (at will or by force).

This approach is also evident in the government's location tickets scheme, by which Aboriginals were granted a plot of reserve land in exchange for their right to Indian status, as well as in the government's attempt to strip Aboriginal people of their culture and heritage through residential schools (Boyko 1995; Wotherspoon 2004). Of course, these government acts and initiatives have been strongly resisted by the Aboriginal peoples in Canada (Borrows 2001). Aboriginal groups have made citizenship claims and have demanded that the Canadian government honour the historical land treaties and pacts (Dickason 2006). Jenson and Papillon (2000), who have traced the citizenship claims and mobilization of the James Bay Cree, argue that they have mounted challenges to the Canadian "citizenship regime" in all of its four dimensions. These challenges will be discussed in more depth in the sections that follow.

Re-manufacturing "Race"/Ethnicity: Immigration

Citizenship in Canada has long been a racial project (see chapter 4). Race affects who is allowed to enter Canada, what work people are allowed to perform, what "class" of citizenship they are granted, and whether this citizenship can be revoked (Ighodaro 2006; Li 2003). The experience of Chinese Canadians is a poignant example of the extent to which citizenship rights can be denied and diluted. The history of immigration policies concerning Chinese immigrants also illustrates how policy is shaped by class-based and capitalistic imperatives, and the way in which gendering and racialization are built into these objectives. Bolaria and Li (1988: 106) contend that "from the outset, the whole Chinese question in Canada was in essence a question of labour exploitation." In the late nineteenth and early twentieth centuries, Chinese immigrants did the labour-intensive work that "white" Canadians would not do, and they did so for a lesser wage. They worked on the railway, in salmon canneries, and, until they were barred from doing so, in mines (Bolaria and Li 1988; Li 1998). As soon as the exigencies of labour passed, citizenship infringements were imposed on Chinese immigrants. Head taxes were imposed as early as 1885, and by 1903 they were as high as $500 per person (Bolaria and Li 1988). The federal government required all Chinese in Canada to be registered and to have a certificate (Bolaria and Li 1988). The province of British Columbia barred the Chinese from voting in provincial and municipal elections, and they were legally excluded from numerous professions (including law, pharmacy, public works, and skilled jobs in coal mines). The second-class citizenship status of Chinese Canadians (both naturalized and immigrant) was upheld by the Supreme Court of Canada in 1903 despite the fact that the court conceded that the prohibitions enacted by the province "were in truth devised to deprive the Chinese, naturalized or not, of the ordinary rights of the inhabitant of British Columbia" (Bolaria and Li 1988: 109).

The government's immigration policy significantly shaped social relations within Chinese communities, as women were effectively excluded from entering Canada for many years (Abu-Laban 1998; Li 1998). Although the vast majority of Chinese men who emigrated were married and had families, the head tax intentionally prevented most of them from bringing their families to Canada (Li 1998). Table 12.2 shows the impact of government immigration policies on the subsequent sex ratios of Chinese immigrants over the course of the twentieth century.

Chinese men were treated pre-eminently as "last-resort" and expendable workers who were not entitled to the rights of white workers. Abu-Laban (1998: 17) notes that "racialized immigrant minorities" were "active[ly] discouraged from permanent settlement." Chinese women were largely excluded from Canadian society, and those who were in Canada were also treated as second-class citizens in the gendering of legislation. Like the Indian Act, the 1914 Naturalization Act made certain that a woman's status was that of her husband's; therefore, any Chinese woman with Canadian citizenship lost it if she married a man who was not a Canadian citizen (Li 1998). Racism against the Chinese in Canada has become more "covert" in recent years (Zong 2007). Although China is now the country from which the majority of immigrants to Canada come (with 33,908 entering in 2013), Chinese-Canadian immigrants continue to face discrimination, encountering work opportunities that do not match their high skills and education (Reitz et al. 2014; Zong 2007: 111). Overqualification, downward mobility, and devaluation of foreign qualifications are some of the consequences of institutionalized racism experienced by Chinese immigrants (Zong 2007). By undervaluing the education of highly skilled immigrants, skilled labour at "cheaper" rates continues to be provided.

It has not only been men who have been targeted as "cheap" labour through Canadian immigration policy. Domestic labour has a long history of being done by the most vulnerable members of any society (Glenn 1992).

Table 12.2 Number and Sex Ratio of Chinese Immigrants Admitted to Canada,[a] and Major Immigration Legislation Affecting Chinese Immigration, 1906–1976

Period	Total # of Chinese Immigrants Admitted to Canada	Males per 100 Females	Major Immigration Legislation	Impact on Chinese Immigrants
1906–24[b]	43,470	3,578	Chinese Immigration Act, 1903	Head tax raised
1924–46[c]	7	–	Chinese Immigration Act, 1923	Exclusion of Chinese
1947–62[d]	21,877	98	Repeal of 1923 Act, 1947; Immigration Act, 1952	Repeal of exclusion, limited sponsored immigrants permitted
1963–67	18,716	72	Immigration Act, 1962	Independent and sponsored immigrants permitted
1968–76	91,490	98	Immigration Act, 1967	Universal point system applied

[a] Data Source: Annual Reports of the Department of the Interior (1906–17); Department of Immigration and Colonization (1918–36); Department of Mines and Resources(1936–49); Department of Citizenship and Immigration (1950–65); Department of Manpower and Immigration (1966–76). Figures from 1907–25 are based on reported nationality (China); 1926–8, racial origin (Chinese); 1929, nationality (China); 1930–1, racial origin (Chinese); 1932, nationality (China); 1933-49, racial origin (Chinese); 1950–1, nationality (China); 1952–4, racial origin (Chinese); 1956–61, ethnic origin (Chinese); 1962–6, country of last permanent residence (China, Hong Kong, Taiwan); 1967–71, country of former residence (China, Hong Kong, Taiwan); and 1972–6, country of last permanent residence (China, Hong Kong, Taiwan). Figures for 1905–55 are computed on fiscal year ending 31 March; for 1956–76, on calendar year ending 31 December.

[b] The Canada Yearbook, 1931 (Table 15, p. 184), provides somewhat different figures of Chinese immigration to Canada, which add up to 44,911 for the period of 1906–24. The sex ratio for this period is estimated from the sex distribution of the adult population, based on figures from the reports indicated in note a (approximate years). The figures for 1907 are based on a nine-month period.

[c] Six of the seven immigrants were male.

[d] Figures for the entire year of 1955 were not available, due to a change in reporting on calendar-year statistics from fiscal-year statistics in 1955.

Source: Abridged from Bolaria and Li (1988: 112). Reprinted with the permission of Garamond Press.

Immigrant women have historically been used to fill the need for domestic labour and child care in Canada (Stasiulis and Bakan 2005). In the first half of the twentieth century, young, white, single women were targeted both for domestic labour and for "nation-building" imperatives and were regarded as needed permanent propagators of a "white, Canadian nation" (Abu-Laban 1998). Significant restrictions were placed upon the entry of women from non-European countries (Bolaria and Li 1988; Calliste 1996). In the early twentieth century, Caribbean black women were recruited for Canadian domestic work only in the face of severe labour shortages, and their arrival was often opposed owing to racist perceptions of their "unfitness" and "undeservedness" for motherhood (Calliste 1996: 80). Unlike the view of white European women as future "mothers of the nation," black Caribbean women were wanted not for their biological reproductive capabilities but for their reproductive labour. The classification of minority women as "workers" and not as "mothers" has a long history, and the desire to separate migrant domestic workers from a motherhood role continues to be evident in contemporary immigration policies (Glenn 1992; Stasiulis and Bakan 2005).

One of Canada's main immigration policies concerning domestic labour—crafted in 1992—is the **Live-In Caregiver Program** (Jakubowski 1997; Stasiulis and Bakan 1997). The overt discrimination in immigration policies has been replaced by more insidious forms of differentiation and preference. Jakubowski (1997) argues that the Live-In Caregiver Program has been "deracialized" by removing specified "race" preferences of caregivers in exchange for specified "educational requirements" that are generally available more readily in First World countries. In this way, applicants from developed countries can be given preferential treatment. Still, the majority of live-in domestic workers in Canada are women from Third World countries, and these workers are classified as temporary workers and are required to live in their employer's home for two years of a three-year period (Stasiulis and Bakan 2005). Their status as temporary residents and their employment within a private household leave them vulnerable to exploitation and abuse with little recourse (Stasiulis and Bakan 1997, 2005). Arat-Koc (1997: 431; 2006) notes the irony in immigrant women being effectively denied their right to "motherhood" and femininity and being classified as "individual workers" similar to the male conceptualization of "worker" and yet they are still excluded from citizenship.

According to Arat-Koc (1997: 432), there is a sharp difference between the nature of the domestic work expected and the classification of caregivers from the "First World" and the "Third World." Domestic workers from Western Europe are conceptualized as "deserving immigrants." Arat-Koc argues that they are "generally employed as 'nannies,' expected to be involved only in childcare.... They are likely to get higher pay, better treatment, and recognition for their work" (1997: 432). In contrast, caregivers from the Philippines or the Caribbean are seen as "undeserving immigrants," are required to do more for less, and are expected to be grateful

for the "opportunity" to do so (Arat-Koc 1997: 432). The poor working conditions and non-citizenship status of migrant domestic workers in Canada are considered justified on the basis of "where they've come from" (see also Taylor and Foster 2014). Thus, a complex of intersections of social relations dictates the rights and privileges that people are thought to deserve. In this sense, the possession of a "devalued social identity" is used as a justification for exclusion from basic citizenship rights and infringements.

Social Regulation: "Race"/Ethnicity and the Law

Systemic discrimination in the Canadian justice system is evident in the disproportionate number of Aboriginal Canadians in the penal system, in the disproportionate targeting of racial minorities by police, and in the use of "racial profiling" by government officials (Brzozowski, Taylor-Butts, and Johnson 2006; Tanovich 2006; Tator and Henry 2006). According to Tanovich (2006: 13),

> racial profiling occurs when law enforcement or security officials, consciously or unconsciously, subject individuals at any location to heightened scrutiny based solely or in part on race, ethnicity, Aboriginality, place of origin, ancestry, or religion or on stereotypes associated with any of these factors rather than on objectively reasonable grounds to suspect that the individual is implicated in criminal activity.

Racial profiling sees "race" first and then seeks out a crime (Tanovich 2006). Although the term *racial profiling* is relatively new, the practice is not, and C.C. Smith (2006) compiles a large amount of data to show the extent to which racial minorities, and particularly African-Canadians, have been and continue to be targeted by the law. He reports data from the *Toronto Star*'s study of 480,000 incidents of criminal charges and ticketing offences, showing that 34 per cent of African-Canadians were charged with traffic violations, though they are only 8.1 per cent of Toronto's population—an overrepresentation of 4.2 times (C.C. Smith 2006: 90). Other data suggest that once in the system, African-Canadians are treated more punitively (C.C. Smith 2006). Indeed, Perreault (2008) found that 14 per cent of visible minorities felt that they had experienced discrimination from the police or courts as compared with 8 per cent of non-visible minorities. In 2002, as Maher Arar found out, citizenship is no guarantee of protection or fair treatment by the law. This Canadian citizen, IT worker, and father of two was detained on his way back from a family vacation and then sent to Syria, where he was tortured and held for a year before the efforts and lobbying of his wife resulted in his return (www.maherarar.ca). The Canadian government has now apologized and offered compensation, though this cannot undo the damage done. Arar continues to fight for justice (see Box 12.4).

Agents in Action: Citizenship Claims

In 2013, 23.2 per cent of those admitted to federal correctional services were Aboriginal (First Nation, Métis, or Inuit), although Aboriginal people make up only around 2.6 per cent of the population of Canada. The overrepresentation of Aboriginals in Canadian prisons has risen by 56.2 per cent since 2000–1, and Aboriginal women are even more overrepresented than Aboriginal men, making up 33.6 per cent of all federally sentenced women in Canada (Statistics Canada 2013e). Aboriginal people have been targeted, monitored, and regulated by the legal system as a potential disruptive force, and many miscarriages of justice have resulted (Boyko 1995; C.C. Smith 2006). Schissel (1997: 83) documents the significantly

higher arrest rate for Aboriginal street youth than for youth from other backgrounds. He found that 77 per cent of Aboriginal street youth have been arrested in comparison to 44.2 per cent of non-Aboriginal street youth. He also notes that in Saskatchewan 76 per cent of young offenders in custody are Aboriginal (Schissel 2006: 114). This treatment of Aboriginal youth may also lead to subsequently harsher sentences for any future offences, since they would now have a record and any prior offences would affect future sentences.

At the same time that Aboriginal people are targeted for surveillance, crimes against Aboriginal people have historically been treated lightly and many have gone unsolved (Amnesty International 2004; Boyko 1995). In fact, Aboriginal people in Canada are three times more likely to be victims of violent crime than non-Aboriginals, and for Aboriginal women this rate rises to three and a half times (Brzozowski, Taylor-Butts, and Johnson 2006). Canada's record on investigating and prosecuting crimes against Aboriginal women is abysmal and is the cause of international concern and outcry (Amnesty International 2004). In a 2013 RCMP report it was indicated that there were 1,017 homicides and 164 incidences of missing Aboriginal women, of which there were 225 unsolved cases in a time period from 1980–2012 (RCMP 2014). Other estimates suggest that as many as 500 Aboriginal women have gone missing in the past two decades in Canada and officials have done little about it (Amnesty International 2004; Monture 2007). Yet, as Monture (2007: 209) points out, "the violent deaths of Aboriginal women in Canada are not a recent phenomenon and should not be viewed as an emerging problem." There is a long history of violence against Aboriginal men and women in Canada that has been condoned and overlooked in white communities and white courtrooms (Monture 2007). Boyko (1995: 202) recounts the case of Helen Betty Osborne,

HIGHLIGHT

Box 12.4 With Persistence, the Truth Will Come Out

by Maher Arar

On my way home to Canada from a family vacation in September of 2002, I was stopped and interrogated at John F. Kennedy Airport in New York. Within two weeks, against my will, the US government sent me to Syria, where I was tortured and detained for a year before being released back to Canada without any charge being filed against me.

Following a request by a US congressman shortly after my release, the inspector-general of the Homeland Security Department launched an investigation. Early this month, Richard Skinner released a much-anticipated report on the actions of US immigration officials surrounding the decision to send me to Syria.

Despite the limited scope of the investigation and the refusal by key decision-makers to be interviewed, the heavily redacted public version of the report points to the important fact that the decision to send me to Syria was made at the highest levels of President George W. Bush's administration. The report found that the decision to send me to Syria was made before, and without regard for, the Immigration and Naturalization Service's assessment that I would likely be tortured there.

Mr Skinner's report clearly establishes that what happened to me was a rendition in disguise. Mr Skinner found that on Sunday, Oct. 6, 2002, the government prepared the "operations order" to remove me and sent flight clearances to Rome and Amman, so the United States could fly me on a private jet. These actions were taken before my six-hour interview with the INS concerning my fears of being tortured in Syria, before the INS concluded it was likely I would be tortured there and before the

INS received supposed ambiguous "assurances" that I would be protected.

In other words, my fate had already been decided—the "immigration process" meant to safeguard me from torture was a sham.

So far, these high-level officials have evaded accountability and public scrutiny of their own wrongdoing by keeping me on their watch list, thereby attempting to keep the focus on me. The US government claims to rely on classified information to keep me on the watch list—information that New York Congressman Jerrold Nadler has seen and called "nonsense," and that Canadian Public Safety Minister Stockwell Day has seen and confirmed that it does not justify keeping me on a watch list.

The Canadian government has already apologized and launched a full public inquiry. It is only my hope that the US government follows Ottawa's example and rights its wrongs by at least conducting an independent investigation examining the actions of all officials who shipped me off to Syria like a parcel without regard for my basic human rights, international law or the US Constitution.

I would like to commend the efforts of the US House of Representatives foreign affairs and judiciary subcommittees trying to get to the bottom of what happened to me. I appreciate their courage in standing up for justice and reminding Mr Bush's administration that America is a country of the rule of law. It is my hope that through their persistence and good work, the full truth will eventually come out.

Source: Arar, Maher. (June 17, 2008). "With Persistence, the Truth Will Come Out." *The Globe and Mail*.

a Cree teenager who was brutally raped and murdered in 1971 in The Pas, Manitoba. Betty Osborne's desire to become a teacher meant that she was required to move from the reserve to a school where upper grades were available, and this meant a move to "white" space in the town of The Pas (Monture 2007: 209). The white men who had raped and murdered her bragged about their crime and "whispers around town indicated that everyone seemed to know who the four were" (Boyko 1995: 202). In spite of this, the police did little to investigate and the crime went unpunished for nearly 16 years (Monture 2007). Still, Osborne's family did not give up, and eventually one of the four murderers was convicted. The Osborne case was specifically investigated in 1991 in a study examining the treatment of Aboriginal people in the Manitoba justice system, the conclusion being that Helen Betty Osborne was attacked and her case was allowed to languish because she was Aboriginal (Boyko 1995; Monture 2007). Clearly, the identity of the victim, as well as her attackers, structured the response of the police and the justice system.

Agents in Action: Citizenship Claims

Aboriginal people have faced violence from the state through both its action and its inaction. After years of struggle, Aboriginal communities in Canada have gained compensation and an apology from the government for the creation and operation of residential schools. The intent of the residential schools and the devastating impact of their operation still resonate today. As part of the settlement, the Aboriginal Truth and Reconciliation Commission worked to compile a comprehensive record of the trauma inflicted by residential schools in order to better understand their impact and to aid in the healing process. The length of time Aboriginal peoples had to wait for the government's apology and admission to the horror of Aboriginal schools and the theft of Aboriginal children from their families reveals a complicit public acceptance of racist and colonial policies. At long last the government publicly admitted that what it had done was wrong, and its apology validated the Aboriginal communities' pain and need for justice. Indeed, Aboriginal communities have long sought out justice in regard to land

claims and their right to citizenship (Dickason 2006). The Aboriginal Truth and Reconciliation Commission concluded in June 2015 with a report that included a call for action. Ninety-four recommendations were made in areas such as child welfare, education, language and culture, health, justice, and reconciliation (see www.trc.ca/websites/trcinstitution/File/2015/Findings/Calls_to_Action_English2.pdf).

The James Bay Cree have had success in the courts and in mobilizing and using **transnational action** through human-rights and environmental organizations to make citizenship claims. Jenson and Papillon (2000) document the success of the James Bay Cree in contesting the infringements on their territories and asserting their citizenship rights on the basis of "nationhood" rather than as individual citizens. The Cree have fought the attempts of the Quebec government to subsume them into questions of sovereignty through the Quebec referendum, arguing that they already exist as a sovereign nation (Jenson and Papillon 2000). Their first success came in 1971 when they opposed the attempts of the Quebec government to build an enormous hydroelectric project on the Cree's traditional hunting grounds. The James Bay Cree won their court challenge, which contended that they had title and rights to the land, and the Quebec government was required to engage in negotiations. Jenson and Papillon (2000: 251) state that "this was the first, and until very recently the only, comprehensive land claim settlement in Canada. . . . Beyond that, it was the first time in modern history that Canadian governments, in this case both federal and provincial, recognized that Canadian citizenship included collective rights for aboriginal peoples." The rarity of success in the courts for Aboriginal rights is a reason why Aboriginal groups need to seek international support for the validity of their citizenship claims. The James Bay Cree have found widespread international support for their opposition to the

Quebec government's plans for hydroelectric projects and have had considerable success in staving off encroachments and in defending their rights (Jenson and Papillon 2000).

Focusing on Gender: Engendering Citizens

In Canada, women's access to the rights of citizenship have been (and continue to be) compromised by the state's adoption of the "breadwinner" policy scheme with all of its racialized and gendered implications (Fuller, Kershaw, and Pulkingham 2008; Townson and Hayes 2007). Women who do not have access to **breadwinner wages**, either because their "breadwinners" are low-income earners or because they themselves are unmarried or lesbians, are disadvantaged in this policy system. The state's ideal family type consists of a husband engaged

in paid productive labour and a wife engaged in unpaid reproductive labour and dependent on the distribution of the "family wage." Again, it is important to note the ideology wrapped up in the package of the "family." Historically, the Canadian government's policies toward Aboriginal families, immigrant families, and visible-minority families (policies such as residential schools and "family"-class immigration limitations and prohibitions) belie the valuation of the "family" as specifically the white families who are Canadianized (Das Gupta 1995). Thus, the privileges of the breadwinner wage are largely limited to racial and ethnic majorities. Although the breadwinner formula is a familiar one, it is not the only way in which to distribute the rights of social citizenship.

Sainsbury (1999: 78) compares three different gendered approaches to policy in democratic welfare states, as shown in Table 12.3. We can see in the table that caring work is given a

Table 12.3 Three Gender Policy Regimes

Regime Attributes	Male Breadwinner	Separate Gender Roles	Individual Earner-Carer
Ideology	Strict division of labour Husband = earner Wife = carer	Strict division of labour Husband = earner Wife = carer	Shared tasks Father = earner-carer Mother = earner-carer
Entitlement	Unequal among spouses	Differentiated by gender role	Equal
Basis of entitlement	The principle of maintenance	Family responsibilities	Citizenship or residence
Recipient of benefits	Head of household Supplements for dependants	Men as family providers Women as caregivers	Individual
Taxation	Joint taxation Deductions for dependants	Joint taxation Deductions for dependants for both spouses	Separate taxation Equal tax relief
Employment and wage policies	Priority to men	Priority to men	Aimed at both sexes
Sphere of care	Primarily private	Primarily private	Strong state involvement
Caring work	Unpaid	Paid component to caregivers in the home	Paid component to caregivers in- and outside the home

Source: Sainsbury (1999: 78). Reprinted by permission of Oxford University Press.

monetary valuation from the state in the separate gender roles regime; however, women and men are explicitly divided and viewed as either productive or reproductive workers (Sainsbury 1999). The "individual earner-carer" is a more equitable option, as women and men are viewed equally as potential earners and/or carers and carework is valued on par with "productive" labour. In contrast, the characteristics of the typical "male breadwinner policy regime" are considered to be predicated upon gender inequality and differential responsibilities (Sainsbury 1999: 78). Social citizenship and benefits in the form of income security are designed and distributed with the ideology of the patriarchal family in mind. In this schema, caring work in the household is unpaid, it is predominantly performed by and expected of women, and these responsibilities penalize women in a citizenship regime that preferentially rewards paid work (particularly work that does not involve caring) (Fuller, Kershaw, and Pulkingham 2008).

Historically, the imperatives of the breadwinner policy have worked to exclude and limit the participation of women (especially married women) in the labour force (Townson and Hayes 2007). Pulkingham (1998) charts the evolution of unemployment insurance in Canada to illustrate the ways in which social policy was gendered and the extent to which women were encouraged and expected to be dependent on a male breadwinner. From its beginnings in 1940, unemployment insurance was intended for the male breadwinner; married women could not receive direct compensation on the basis of their own work history. Instead, they were eligible for state support only through their status as a dependant of their husband. In 1950, the impact of gendered ideologies on policy inequality became even more apparent, as a woman who married was rendered ineligible to claim unemployment insurance benefits for a period of two years following her marriage (Pulkingham 1998). This effectively barred "12,000 to 14,000 women each year" from collecting unemployment insurance until this stipulation was withdrawn in 1957 (Evans 1997: 102). In fact, in order to obtain unemployment insurance a woman was required to "prove her attachment to the labour force" in a number of ways (Pulkingham 1998: 15). Women who refused to take low-paying jobs for which they were overqualified were also denied benefits, unlike men in similar circumstances (Pulkingham 1998). Thus, women's access to the "first-track" citizenship benefits of unemployment insurance (as opposed to the "second-track" benefits of social assistance) was made exceptionally difficult (Pulkingham 1998: 10). Here we see that "claims made through social assistance on the basis of 'citizen-mother' were accorded neither the degree of legitimacy nor the level of benefits that accompanies 'worker' claims through social insurance" (Evans 1997: 98).

Changes to Canada's unemployment insurance policy in 1996 that were intended to help women qualify for the program in fact had the opposite effect, such that unemployed women were less eligible than men to get benefits (Townson and Hayes 2007). Not surprisingly, then, Canadian men disproportionately claimed unemployment benefits, now called "employment insurance" (EI). Women accounted for 40.0 per cent of total regular claims in 2012–13 and received 35.2 per cent of regular benefits, while men accounted for nearly 60.0 per cent of total regular claims in 2012–13 and 64.8 per cent of the EI regular benefits. Men also received notably higher weekly benefits than women (Government of Canada 2014).

Where eligibility once rested on the number of weeks worked, the new system required 420–700 hours (in most locales) in the preceding 12 months in order to qualify for EI (Townson and Hayes 2007). This requirement meant that many part-time workers (who were disproportionately women) were not eligible to qualify for benefits. Many women were therefore contributing to a program that they were unlikely to benefit from should the need arise (Townson and Hayes 2007).

Women were also disadvantaged in their access to social insurance on the basis of their paid productive and reproductive labour. Child-bearing and caring responsibilities meant that women had more frequent departures and absences from the formal labour force than men did (Evans 1997, 2007; Townson and Hayes 2007). A parental leave policy was introduced in 1990 and extended in 2001, but the vast majority of claimants continued to be women, and in fact, the gender gap increased in the usage of parental leave (Evans 2007). Further, a greater number of women in paid employment worked in non-standard (e.g., part-time) employment than men (40 per cent vs 30 per cent) and their employment tended to be more precarious (Evans 2007; Townson and Hayes 2007). In addition, men on average worked more hours and more paid overtime hours, both of which benefited them in EI calculations (Townson and Hayes 2007). Even when women worked full-time and year-round (as the majority of employed women do) and "conformed" to the "male" worker formula, they did not receive equal pay for their efforts, and this too affected the level of compensation they were eligible to receive (Pulkingham 1998; Statistics Canada 2006f).

As chapter 9 shows, there is considerable occupational segregation by sex, and the work that women have disproportionately performed has been devalued and paid less than the work done by men (Armstrong 1997). The job-evaluation schemes that determine levels of pay under Ontario's Pay Equity Act have tended to reinforce traditional gender ideologies of "valued" work (Busby 2006). For instance, "garbage removal is considered more onerous than cleaning dirty diapers; police work more dangerous than dressing the wounds of patients

with contagious diseases. . . . The stress created by working outdoors or in excessive heat is often counted, but the stress of working with dying patients or demanding children does not get counted" (Armstrong 1997: 261). Thus, the combination of domestic responsibilities, devalued work, and lower wages all work to make EI a predominantly "male" benefit (Evans 1997; Townson and Hayes 2007).

Social Regulation: Reproductive Rights

There are ironic contradictions in the state's regulation and control of aspects of women's lives. Historically, women's reproductive potential has been closely watched by the state, while in the areas of sexual assault and "domestic" violence the state has been less willing to intervene on women's behalf (Walby 1997, 2004). For instance, women's sexuality and reproductive potential have been controlled in varying degrees by the state, from the outlawing of birth control until 1969 to the practice of sterilization for reproducers deemed "unfit" (Findlay and Miller 2002). While some women have been financially and ideologically supported for their reproductive potential (e.g., with baby bonuses and nationalistic rhetoric), other women have been penalized and degraded for it (Comacchio 1993; Valverde 1991). The right to have control over one's own body has not been a guaranteed right for women in general, especially for women of colour and working-class women (Egan and Gardner 1999). Greschner (1990, 1998) points to the case of Chantal Daigle in Quebec as an example of the extent to which fetal and paternal rights take precedence over a woman's right to autonomy. Daigle was forced to carry on with a pregnancy against her will by an abusive ex-boyfriend who obtained a court injunction to halt her attempt to end the pregnancy (Greschner 1990). Only in the Supreme Court was this injunction overturned.

The discourse of fetal and paternal rights frequently emerges without an examination of the threats that they entail for women's personhood (Greschner 1990, 1998).

In fact, there was a renewed push for fetal rights that had the potential to further impinge upon women's rights (Sandstad 2008). Bill C-484, the Unborn Victims of Crime Act, was brought forward as a private member's bill and passed a second reading in Parliament on 5 March 2008. While this bill did not ultimately pass (https://openparliament.ca/bills/39-2/C-484/), it was intended to criminalize any act to "injure, cause the death of or attempt to cause the death of a child before or during its birth while committing or attempting to commit an offense against the mother. Voluntary abortion or any act or omission by the mother are exempted in the legislation" (Canadian Federation for Sexual Health 2008). A number of social-justice and women's-rights groups have taken action to oppose the bill, stating there is no evidence that the bill will prevent violence against women, and in fact, in the United States similar legislation has resulted in increased policing and regulation of pregnant women (Abortion Rights Coalition of Canada 2008). In its opposition statement, the Canadian Federation for Sexual Health (2008) states its concern that "the bill's underlying intention is to create a separate legal status for a fetus . . . . legal separation of individual rights is the premise on which woman's right to choose is built, and to dissolve this separation of rights strategically chips away at a woman's right to an abortion." Indeed, Greschner (1990) argues that the notion of "fetal rights" represents a concerted effort to enforce traditional gender roles. The most disadvantaged women in society tend to be disproportionately targeted and prosecuted under these types of legislation. This tendency is illustrated in an American study of court-ordered Caesarean sections done in a teaching hospital where close to 90 per cent of the women involved were visible minorities, nearly half were unmarried, and all were welfare recipients (Martin and Coleman 1995).

Agents in Action: Violence against Women

As discussed in chapter 8, sexual assault is a weapon by which the relations of power and domination are reproduced and reinforced. McIntyre and Scott (2000) note that the act of sexual assault is strongly gendered, being predominantly committed by men against women. While men are more likely to be physically assaulted, women are more likely to be sexually assaulted, and the number of sexual assaults is likely underestimated, as they are the type of violent assault least likely to be reported to police.

Some women are more vulnerable than others to the threat of violence. According to a 2009 government survey, Aboriginal women were nearly three times more likely than non-Aboriginal women to report victimization from a spouse (Brennan 2011). Feminist groups and grassroots organizations have lobbied provincial and federal governments to take action against the violence in women's lives (Sheehy 2005). Sheehy (2005) outlines some of the difficulties inherent in Canadian laws covering violent domestic assault, one being the use of gender-neutral language and policies. For example, "zero tolerance" policies whereby charges are laid for any domestic complaint have in some cases resulted in the criminalization of women who try to defend themselves from abuse (Sheehy 2005). Although some women may have been helped through zero-tolerance policies, the indiscriminate and inconsistent enforcement of such policies have had mixed results (Sheehy 2005).

Still, feminist action has had an impact on how the state deals with domestic violence. Ursel (1998) notes that policy changes in Manitoba resulted in the establishment of a specialized court for domestic cases. In 1990, the Family Violence Court (FVC) was instituted to handle all cases of spouse, child, and elder abuse. In the past, domestic violence cases were shuffled off to the least experienced prosecutors because they were regarded as "messy, low-profile case[s] with a minimal chance of conviction" (Ursel 1998: 147). In the new system, these cases were redefined as requiring the legal experts who were adept at handling complex cases. The "battered women's movement" has led to effective and more compassionate reforms in the legal system for victims of violence (Ursel 1998). Still, the problem is far from solved, and the serious consequences and wide reach of violence in Canada are still very apparent today. Here we can see that although there has been government action, there are still not enough resources to meet the demands. On a one-day survey snapshot in 2006 of Canada's shelters for abused women, 306 women and 203 children could not be accommodated and had to leave (Taylor-Butts 2007). On an average day as many as 200 women are turned away from shelters (Statistics Canada 2006d). Still, between 1 April 2009 and 31 March 2010 there were about 64,500 admissions of women to shelters across Canada—a rate of 452 admissions per 100,000 women (Burczycka and Cotter, 2011). Although the incidence of spousal assault against men has gained attention in recent years, it is important to note that the degree and severity of assault for men and women differ significantly. For example, in 2009 women were three times more likely than men to report that they had been sexually assaulted, beaten, choked, or threatened with a knife or a gun (Statistics Canada 2011a). Still, the under-reporting of spousal assault remains an issue, with only 34 per cent of woman spousal-assault victims reporting to police in 2009 (and a mere 10 per cent of male spousal-assault victims reporting) (Statistics Canada 2011a).

Focusing on Age: Citizenship over the Life Course

The examination of citizenship shows how the historical period and the socio-historical circumstances in which we live have a powerful impact on the structures of inequality (McDaniel 2001, 2004). Citizenship, in all its forms, has historically been denied to various groups on the basis of race, ethnicity, and gender. Consider that in the 1960s employers in Canada had the legal right to fire women if they married or became pregnant (Sangster 1995). Individuals and groups have struggled and triumphed over inequality throughout history; however, in some ways we are fated to grapple with the socio-historical milieu into which we are born. Over time, this milieu has changed, especially in regard to citizenship in Canada.

Still, the expectation that women will perform most of the tasks involved in reproductive labour has remained fairly stable. As we have seen throughout this chapter, women's involvement in caring work over the life course puts them at a disadvantage in their ability to gain the rights of citizenship. And the life chances of women and men of different ethnic and racial groups and of different ages are shaped by the substantive birth cohort into which they were born. In this regard, McDaniel (2001, 2004) discusses "gendered generations," pointing out, among other things, that state benefits are influenced by the historical time of one's birth. These benefits must also be considered within the context of changes in gender relations that have occurred over the last three generations. McDaniel cautions, however, that we should not be overly optimistic about the opportunities for the youngest generation of women. Post–baby-boom women (born between 1965 and 1975), according to McDaniel (2001: 204), "although benefitting from the legacies of previous generations of women in struggling for rights and job equity, are finding jobs difficult to find and family formation/dissolution economically challenging."

Women's contributions to society go largely unrecognized and unrewarded. In spite of the devaluation of caring work and the artificial separation of the home from the "productive" realm, unpaid caring work is vital to the workings of the state. McDaniel (2002: 136) argues that "caring is central to welfare states, not because they are inherently caring (abundant evidence calls this into question), but because care (for the young, old, sick and infirm, and those who cannot work) leads to more productive, less discontented, workers and consumers for capitalist economies." Indeed, according to McDaniel (2004: 37), one of many "new normativities" or requirements of citizenship for women involves the increased downloading of care expected from the state, demonstrated in day surgeries and more intense forms of home care. As was outlined earlier, the weight of this imbalance in caring-work intensity penalizes women through increased work absences, more departures from and entries into the labour force, and, consequently, lower lifetime wages (Denton and Boos 2007; Morissette and Ostrovsky 2006; Pyper 2006; Statistics Canada 2006f). For example, in 2011, 79.5 per cent of income-tax filers in the highest income category (the top 1 per cent) were men, even though men constituted less than 50 per cent of those who filed (Statistics Canada 2015f). This disparity exists in part because women make up the majority of minimum-wage workers. Moreover, income is distributed unequally over the life course: people aged 15–24 (0.1 per cent), 25–34 (3.4 per cent), and 65+ (12 per cent) are much less likely to be top income earners in Canada.

The successive effects of wage inequality, marginalized work status, and interrupted or unstable work histories exact a specific toll for women in older age, though women's labour-force participation and pension contributions have been increasing (Gough 2001; Marshall and Ferrao 2007). Women aged 45–64 have seen a steady increase in their labour-force participation, from around 32 per cent in 1976 to 48.3 per cent in 2014, and while same-aged men's labour-force participation remains higher (at 59.5 per cent in 2014), it has been more unstable, having declined overall from 76 per cent in 1976 (Marshall and Ferrao 2007). Still, older men (aged 55–64) earn substantially more than same-aged women, on average $300 more per week (Marshall and Ferrao 2007). Men also have higher average retirement incomes from employment earnings and private pensions than women. All of the inequalities and discriminatory practices experienced in the labour force (e.g., the creation of "reserve armies of labour" and the exclusion of groups through racism and sexism) have consequences for the class status of aging adults.

In the mid-twentieth century, the poverty of Canadian seniors sparked the enactment of a number of distributive policies designed to ameliorate this situation (Gazso 2005; Myles 2000). The Canadian government instituted a network of financial support for elderly citizens, including Old Age Security (OAS), the Guaranteed Income Supplement (GIS), the Canada/Quebec Pension Plan (C/QPP), and incentives for retirement savings in the form of Registered Retirement Savings Plans (B.L. Marshall 2000). Although the financial coverage of the Canada/Quebec Pension Plan (C/QPP) is dependent upon labour-force earnings, and although RRSPs require individual contributions, the other policies were intended to improve the situation of low-income seniors (B.L. Marshall 2000). All seniors receive OAS regardless of their employment history, while the GIS and a spouse's allowance are intended to improve the financial situation of those seniors with low or no pre-retirement income (B.L. Marshall 2000). These policies have had success in alleviating extreme poverty among seniors (Myles 2000; Turcotte and Schellenberg 2007). For instance, less than 15 per cent of seniors were below the low-income cut-off before tax in 2011 (Curtis and McMullin 2016) compared to 34.1 per cent in 1980 (Myles 2000; Turcotte and Schellenberg 2007: 68). Poverty among unattached female seniors was also reduced over this period, dropping from 70 per cent in the lowest income quintile in 1980 to 42 per cent by 1995 (Myles 2000: 18). In 2011, 16.1 per cent of unattached women aged 65 and older were living in poverty—a dramatic reduction from 1980; yet it is still high compared with the 7.8 per cent of Canadian families living in poverty in 2011 (Novak 2013).

This and the fact that widows (in comparison to widowers) are highly vulnerable to experiencing significant income losses and low income in the years after their spouse's death suggest that "safety nets" continue to be inadequate (Bernard and Li 2006). So too, does the fact that Aboriginal Canadians living on reserves were not allowed to contribute to the C/QPP until 1988 (Myles 2000). Thus, Canadians are differentially protected from the vulnerabilities of old age.

Older Canadians who have immigrated recently are especially vulnerable because they are ineligible for social security benefits (Morissette 2002). And evidence from Britain indicates that all ethnic minorities may have smaller pensions in later life. Ginn and Arber (2001), who documented the extent of pension inequality in Britain by gender and ethnicity, found significant disadvantages for visible minorities in comparison to whites. After controlling for a number of other factors, they found that both minority men and minority women were significantly less likely to have private pensions. Discriminatory labour-market practices, shorter employment histories, and gendered ideologies are among the variables that disadvantage ethnic-minority groups in

the accumulation of private pensions (Ginn and Arber 2001). Hence, the likelihood of having a significant pension and financial stability in older age is not determined by chance. In Canada, 90 per cent of families with an after-tax income of $85,000 or more had RRSPs, while 35 per cent of families with an income of $36,500 or less had them (Pyper 2008: 10). The experience of inequality throughout the life course casts a long shadow in old age.

Although secure and stable employment has long been denied to many groups, researchers have emphasized the lack of employment opportunities and citizenship participation for today's youth (Allahar and Côté 1994; Côté and Allahar 2006; Kapsalis, Morissette, and Picot 1999; Wanner 2001). Although this crisis may be somewhat overestimated, young men have seen some losses in their labour-market returns from educational investments, while women have seen somewhat higher returns (Bourbeau et al. 2012). In general, today's youth are experiencing "negative mobility compared to their parents and grandparents," and this means that the parents of these young people will encounter longer periods when they will be supporting their children financially (McDaniel 2002: 141; 2004). This has as much to do with a tough labour market as it does with prolonged periods of educational attainment (Bourbeau et al. 2012). For today's youth, pension prospects and life-course earnings appear to be less promising than for previous generations. In a recent *Globe and Mail* article, Grant and McFarland (2012) comment on the bleak future of 20-somethings in Canada. Many of today's youth face "crippling debt to buy credentials no one wants. Low-paying, short-term jobs that put middle-class prosperity out of reach. And, for good measure, the prospect of a penurious retirement." By all accounts, young people in today's labour force are far less likely to retire with a reasonable company pension than their parents' generation. Furthermore, the Canadian state's retreat from the tasks of caring has resulted in further "intergenerational inequities" between women, as women responsible for children and for elderly parents face additional burdens. The intensification of private caring responsibilities means that youth and elderly people from the middle and upper classes will be protected and sheltered against the contingencies of market imperatives, while those from lower-income groups will be further disadvantaged (Bookman and Kimbrel 2011; McDaniel 2002, 2004).

Social Regulation: Child Welfare Legislation

The state's intervention in the lives of its citizens starts in childhood (Ferguson 2007). Although the protection of children and young people would appear to be desirable, Ursel (1990) shows that the roots of the Canadian child welfare laws established in the late nineteenth and early twentieth centuries were paternalistic and punitive rather than supportive. The welfare agencies strongly favoured the regulation of reproductive processes, and rather than work with parents to improve the family situation, they were quick to remove children and make them wards of the state (Ursel 1990). Kline (1993, 2005) shows how this legacy continues to affect present-day child welfare practices. She examines how the ideology of motherhood, with its attendant racialized and bourgeois meanings, is applied in legal discourse to Aboriginal women, who are then found to be "lacking." Kline (1993) argues that Aboriginal women have been construed by child welfare agencies as inadequate and unco-operative mothers who violate the dominant definitions of "good" mothering. According to Kline (1993), the moralizing dictates of the "good mother" ideology include an ethic of selflessness whereby a mother is ready and able to provide her children with a stable and enriched environment. All of the expectations of "good mothering" are judged without any consideration of the impact of the broader socio-structural factors of inequality (Kline 1993, 2005).

Kline (1993, 2005) points to several cases involving Aboriginal women and child welfare agencies to show that the courts individualized and personalized the societal inequalities stemming from colonization and racism that were present in the lives of Aboriginal women. For instance, Aboriginal women who were being abused have had their children taken from them, the rationale being that these women made unstable "choices" (Kline 1993). This was a classic case of blaming the victim and reducing social issues to individual problems. In this sense, the reduction of violent abuse to a "lifestyle" carried strong elements of blame for the mothers involved (Kline 1993). The difficulties inherent in providing basic sustenance and adequate living conditions while living in poverty were subsequently ignored in assessments by the courts. In fact, Aboriginal women are much more likely to experience spousal violence, having a three and a half times greater risk than non-Aboriginal women in the same time period (Brzozowski, Taylor-Butts, and Johnson 2006: 6). Investigators have noted that colonialism and government policies concerning Aboriginal groups have constructed a system in which Aboriginal women live disproportionately in poverty, with all of its disadvantages and hardships, and this leaves many Aboriginal women (like other poor women) much more vulnerable to state intervention and the potential dissolution of their families (Kline 1993; Waterfall 2006).

Agents in Action: Mandatory Retirement

The regulative force of the state stretches and intertwines through the life course and into the domains of reproduction, production, and distribution. At the end of the life course, the inequalities that have manifested themselves throughout these processes do not disappear, but rather crystallize and extend their reach. Privileged adults who have weathered little in the way of inequality or disadvantage are often introduced at this point to the experience of age discrimination in the processes of production. The virtual exclusion of aging adults from the world of productive labour by the mechanism of mandatory retirement has been challenged and overturned in Canada (Ibbott, Kerr, and Beaujot 2006). As of July 2009, provincial legislation was enacted across Canada to abolish mandatory restrictions that forced older workers to retire (Berger 2012). Yet, the rights to remain active in the labour force and to re-enter the labour force have both been points of contention for the growing numbers of older workers. This is because the state of the economy no longer guarantees financial security later in life. Working past retirement age is a necessity for many people over the age of 65 in Canada today (Berger 2012). However, as Berger (2012) notes, eliminating mandatory retirement "theoretically" allows older workers the ability to work, yet employer agism prevents many workers from obtaining well-paying employment (2012: 1–2).

Conclusion

The meanings of the term *citizen* have a significant effect on the development and delivery of policy, and these meanings are intimately structured by the social relations of class, gender, race, ethnicity, and age. Jenson (1997: 632) argues that there are a number of different citizenship "identities," including the "model citizen," the "second-class citizen," and the "non-citizen." A "model citizen" can expect to receive the full entitlements of citizenship, whereas those groups and individuals that are considered "second-class" or "non-citizens" are offered few, if any, of the benefits of citizenship. This chapter has shown that the fragility of citizenship is produced and reproduced through state policy and legislation that are shaped by the intersections of

class, age, gender, ethnic, and race relations. We have provided examples of how Canadian policies have failed to assist marginalized groups—including children, the elderly, single parents, women, and visible minorities.

Regarding social welfare, for instance, there are clear distinctions between model citizens and second-class citizens or those who are deemed deserving or undeserving of social assistance. Consider the extremely high rates of poverty among lone mothers. Because welfare policies are often based on narrow ideas of "productive" citizenship, the work that women do in the processes of reproduction are often unacknowledged in social welfare policy. This leads to state distributive processes that reproduce the gendered structures of inequality. In old age, when many adults are not working for pay, pension schemes are established on the basis of a "typical" labour-force career, or a secure and stable relationship with someone who has had such a career. Yet, even if an Aboriginal Canadian has had a stable career, he or she will have a very small pension after retirement because of pre-existing biases in pension-contribution rules. Hence, state distributive processes are not only gendered, but are also structured by age and race relations. And as shown in the preceding sections of this chapter, race, ethnicity, and class are implicated in state distributive processes as well. Indeed, views of morality and idealized traditional families still frame much of the political rhetoric around poverty. Governments are committed to reducing child poverty, not poverty among single mothers—but of course that is part of the same thing.

To alleviate social inequality in Canada, state policy and legislation must evolve so that the complexities of inequality that result from coalescent CAGE(s) are its heart. This requires radical social change, and the process will be slow even if policy-makers have the best intentions. The value of "neutral" social policy (discussed in chapter 13) must be challenged if such change is to take place.

▦ Note

1. Scott (1996).

▦ Questions for Critical Thought

1. What do you see as the advantages and disadvantages of Sainsbury's (1999: 78) "three gender policy regimes"? What implications do these various regimes have for class, age, gender, and ethnic or race relations?
2. How have immigration policies affected the processes of production, reproduction, and distribution in various families and communities? What type of compensation or redress, if any, should governments offer to individuals and groups that have been discriminated against and that have been denied citizenship rights in the past?
3. How would you characterize the role of the state? Does the state primarily ameliorate or exacerbate societal inequities? Give examples to make your case.
4. How have the social relations of class, age, race or ethnicity, and gender affected the achievement of citizenship rights in Canada? What rights do you think should be included in the notion of full citizenship? Explain why.
5. How has the state's intervention in and regulation of the processes of reproduction changed over time (e.g., reproductive rights, child welfare, and social welfare)? Do you support more intervention or less on the part of the state? What implications would this have for different groups in society?

▦ Glossary

Breadwinner wages The "family supporting" wages to which some men (especially white European men) were considered to be entitled during the twentieth century. State laws and support systems reinforced and sustained this gendered division of labour in the family, thereby reproducing an ideology of female economic dependence for some groups of women.

Citizen Often considered a neutral term, *citizens* are members of nations or societies. Citizens are entitled to all the benefits of being a member of a particular society (e.g., rights, political voice, social welfare); however, many individuals and groups within societies are denied the full rights of citizenship and are treated as second-class citizens (perhaps granted some rights but denied others; e.g., granted welfare benefits but not allowed to vote) (Jenson 1997). Those who are treated as "non-citizens" are denied virtually all of the benefits of citizenship and are left extremely vulnerable to exploitation with little recourse.

Civil citizenship T.H. Marshall's citizenship conceptualization of an individual's basic human rights. These include the right to sign a legal contract, the right to freedom of person and freedom of speech, and the right to seek redress in the courts for any violation of property or person.

Decommodification The strength of social entitlements and the degree to which people are protected from market dependency. It is the process of viewing social rights as an entitlement rather than as a commodity that must be paid for.

Live-In Caregiver Program An immigration policy that gives temporary work permits to women coming to fill the Canadian need for live-in caregivers (e.g., nannies). This policy aims to fill a demand for child care, while at the same time severely restricting the activities and the duration of stay of the women involved in the program.

Political citizenship T.H. Marshall's conceptualization of an individual's right to political involvement in society. This guarantees a political voice for citizens in the form of voting and/or seeking political office.

Social citizenship T.H. Marshall's conceptualization of an individual's right to full social inclusion in a society's wealth. Citizens should be guaranteed economic well-being, educational and health services, and participation or inclusion in the culture and heritage of their society.

State A complex array of governing institutions in a society. The state includes national-security, parliamentary, judicial, and bureaucratic institutions, to name just a few. For this reason, the state itself cannot be said to act either consciously or uniformly; however, agents (both internal and external) can use the tools of the state to acquire, monopolize, or distribute resources and services and to maintain social order. This diversity of institutions means that dissent and conflict within and between institutions are a feature of democratic states. Clearly, some individuals and groups in a society are more vulnerable to punitive action on the part of state institutions, whereas individuals and groups with more power are better equipped to attempt to use the state to their advantage.

Transnational action The mobilization of international agencies and non-governmental organizations (e.g., environmental or human-rights groups) to generate support for the protection of Aboriginal lands and land claims.

Workfare A type of social assistance program that requires the recipients to take certain paid work or enroll in educational or training courses as a condition for receiving welfare benefits. Although some recipients, notably mothers of young children, have been exempt from this requirement, some of these exemptions are being revised or abolished.

▓ Recommended Reading

Armstrong, Pat, and M. Patricia Connelly. 1999. *Feminism, Political Economy and the State: Contested Terrain*. Toronto: Canadian Scholar's Press. This anthology looks at how welfare, health, and education policies have been shaped by feminist struggles, and examines how women's lives have been affected by the state. The countries examined include Canada and Latin American and European countries.

Brooks, Clem, and Jeff Manza. 2007. *Why Welfare States Persist*. Chicago: University of Chicago Press. This study explores how public opinion influences government spending and welfare state development in the modern world. Brooks and Manza find that the preferences of citizens profoundly influence the welfare policies of their governments.

Esping-Andersen, G. 1990. *Three Worlds of Welfare Capitalism*. Princeton: Princeton University Press. This work provides a rigorous analysis of the character and role of the welfare state in contemporary advanced Western societies. Esping-Andersen identifies three types of welfare states—socially democratic, conservative, and liberal—and connects them with variations in the economic and political development of different Western societies.

Hier, Sean P., and B. Singh Bolaria, eds. 2007. *Race and Racism in 21st Century Canada: Continuity, Complexity and Change.* Peterborough, ON: Broadview Press. An excellent volume of analyses on race and racism in Canada.

Pupo, Norene. 2001. "The Role of the State in a Restructured Economy." Chapter 4 in Dan Glenday and Ann Duffy, eds, *Canadian Society: Meeting the Challenges of the Twenty-First Century.* Toronto: Oxford University Press. In her chapter, the author succinctly reviews theories of the state and explains the influence of the Canadian state in the economy, the labour market, and the lives of individuals and families.

Sainsbury, Diane, ed. 1999. *Gender and Welfare State Regimes.* New York: Oxford University Press. A valuable collection that provides international comparisons of welfare policies in a broad range of areas (including child care, taxation, the labour market, and employment equality), with an emphasis on gender issues.

Stasiulis, Davia K., and Abigail B. Bakan. 2005. *Negotiating Citizenship: Migrant Women in Canada and the Global System.* Toronto: University of Toronto Press. The authors challenge predominant conceptualizations of "citizenship," arguing that citizenship is a "negotiated relationship" that is shaped by numerous societal axes of inequality. They illustrate this negotiation through the experience of foreign domestic workers in Canada.

Westhues, Anne, ed. 2006. *Canadian Social Policy: Issues and Perspectives.* 4th edn. Waterloo, ON: Wilfrid Laurier University Press. A comprehensive collection of analyses on contemporary Canadian social policies.

▒ Relevant Websites

Canadian Council on Social Development
www.ccsd.ca

**A non-governmental, non-profit website that promotes social equity and equitable policies in Canada.

www.trc.ca

***The Truth and Reconciliation Commission of Canada site that provides its report as well as resources for educators, exhibitions, and oral history versions of the TRC report.

Native Women's Association of Canada
www.nwac-hq.org/en/index.html

**The Native Women's Association of Canada (NWAC) is an aggregate of 13 Native women's organizations from across Canada. The organization aims to enhance, promote, and foster the social, economic, cultural, and political well-being of First Nations and Métis women within First Nations, Métis, and Canadian societies.

Canadian Race Relations Foundation
www.crr.ca

**The Canadian Race Relations Foundation is committed to building a national framework for eliminating racism in Canadian society. It explores the causes and manifestations of racism, provides independent national leadership, and acts as a resource and facilitator in the pursuit of equity, fairness, and social justice.

Citizenship and Immigration Canada
www.cic.gc.ca

**Citizenship and Immigration Canada provides information and services regarding issues relating to immigration, citizenship, and multiculturalism.

13

Conclusion: Equality, Politics, Platforms, and Policy Issues

Part I of this book discussed influential theoretical contributions to the study of class, gender, ethnicity, "race," and age. After outlining the strengths and weaknesses of these theories, each of the chapters concluded with a working definition of the concept in question. These working definitions incorporated many elements of the theories previously assessed. Yet a crucial reason for formulating these concepts was to ensure that they would be compatible with one another in a conceptual framework that combined them all. Thus it was important to identify a nucleus around which class, age, gender, ethnicity, and race could be grouped. Three elements of this nucleus were identified: *processes of production, processes of distribution*, and *processes of reproduction* (see chapter 2 for definitions). These processes were chosen because they are essential for the survival of individuals and societies. Class, age, gender, ethnicity, and race are structured sets of social relations that organize the interrelated processes of production, distribution, and reproduction in Canada. Hence, class, age, gender, ethnicity, and race are characterized by power, oppression, opportunity hoarding, and exploitation.

Whereas chapters 2 to 5 discussed the structural dimensions of inequality, chapter 6

considered the idea that individuals are agents in the social construction of class, age, gender, ethnic, and race relations. Chapter 7 introduced a conceptual framework of social inequality that brought together many of the ideas discussed in the previous chapters into a cohesive whole. Besides organizing concepts that have traditionally been studied in research on social inequality, this framework contributes to our understanding of social inequality by explicitly considering social time, agency, and place.

Part II of this book examined various outcomes of inequality in five social domains. Chapters 8 and 9 considered outcomes of inequality that arise through families and paid work, such as differences in the division of household labour, caregiving, violence, occupations, and income. Chapters 10 and 11 discussed inequalities in education and health, and chapter 12 examined the role the Canadian state plays in producing and reproducing various forms of inequality through its ideas of what it is that constitutes citizenship and social rights. Each chapter considered global examples or case studies that demonstrated the relevance of inequality in the social domain in question. These chapters also provided an overview of the Canadian literature on social inequality, exploring Canada's advantage in this regard by situating it in relation to other countries.

The purpose of Part II was twofold. In the first place, the chapters showed how outcomes of inequality in Canada are shaped by class, age, gender, and ethnicity and race. In doing so, the chapters demonstrated how certain groups of Canadians are disadvantaged in relation to others in various domains of social life. These chapters also identified issues that require further research. The ideas presented in the conceptual framework of the book were often captured most explicitly through the examples and case studies presented in the chapters. Although our goal was to organize the chapters in Part II with these ideas in mind, much of the available research is deficient in three important ways. First, very little of it has considered whether and how class, age, gender, and ethnicity and race work together simultaneously in creating systems of advantage and disadvantage. Second, and related to the first, there is a dearth of research on inequality that considers whether and how age and social time influence outcomes of inequality. Third, more research is needed on the strategies that agents use in conforming to or resisting the social-structural influences in their lives. Although a picture of inequality in Canada has evolved from the material presented, it remains incomplete.

Many aspects of social life need to change if inequality is to be eradicated in Canada and elsewhere around the world. Widely held ideologies about gender, class, ethnicity, race, and age need to be challenged, and the processes through which the activities of production, distribution, and reproduction are organized need to change. Another avenue through which such changes might begin to take place is the reform of social policy. Although it would take another book to outline the specific policies needed to address all of the issues identified here, some general ideas about how such policies should evolve are worth considering. First and

foremost, given what we know about how class, age, gender, ethnicity, and race work together in structuring inequality, it is useful to consider how policy-makers might better integrate these structures of inequality into their programs. They will need to give up the idea that gender, class, age, ethnic, or racial "neutrality" is desirable in social policy and, instead, recognize that such neutrality actually reproduces systems of inequality.

The goal of "neutral" social policy is to treat everyone the same way. Neutral social policy emerged in response to policies that explicitly treated certain groups of people unfairly. For example, in the early part of the twentieth century, laws and policies changed so that women were entitled to own property. Before that, women had to relinquish control of anything that was theirs—land, money, furniture, and so on—to their husbands when they married. The law became neutral so that both men and women were eligible to control their own possessions. Why then is neutral social policy that assumes formal equality problematic? Because "strict adherence to the principle of formal equality in the absence of substantive equality leads to inequality; treating unalikes in the same way simply perpetuates differences" (Chunn 2000: 242). As an example, consider Canadian family law. Under the guise of equality, Canadian family law assumes that mothers and fathers are both able to contribute to the financial support of their children. Technically, of course, this is true. As a result, spousal support payment schemes are generally short-term and work on the assumption that individuals will and should be able to support themselves economically after a short time. The "substantive" problem with such assumptions is that women are at a disadvantage in labour markets and are unlikely to be able to support themselves financially to the same extent as men (Chunn 2000). Clearly, such policy leads to the reproduction of inequality.

Equality means different things to different people. Consider, for instance, the version of equality that is presented by the Conservative Party of Canada. Equality is one of the basic political principles that guided the Canadian Alliance and the Progressive Conservative Party of Canada, the two parties that merged to form the Conservative Party of Canada in 2003. Indeed, "a belief in the equality of all Canadians" is listed as the sixth founding principle of the Conservative Party of Canada. In Box 13.1 we compare the views of the Conservative Party of Canada, the Liberal Party of Canada, and the New Democratic Party of Canada on families and households—i.e., women, family planning, and seniors/pensions—in their policy and issue documents and in their 2011 election platforms. Here we see differences among the parties in their views of equality. The Liberal Party of Canada identified women, Aboriginal peoples, and seniors as disadvantaged groups and outlined what it had done or was trying to do in order to improve the quality of life for these groups. The NDP did the same but offered more broad-reaching support for these disadvantaged groups. The Conservative Party of Canada, on the other hand, did not mention women, and with respect to Aboriginal peoples and seniors, the implication was that their policies would treat these groups equally under Canadian law and encourage their individualism in ensuring their well-being. While this language may have seemed innocuous, the fact that groups were not treated equally under Canadian law and policy in the first place went unacknowledged (see chapter 12). Furthermore, and as noted above, treating everyone as "equal" under policy and law reinforced substantive inequality. Clearly, the Conservative Party of Canada's understanding of equality was different from that of the Liberal Party or NDP and from the ideas of equality that are adopted in this book.

HIGHLIGHT

Box 13.1 Comparison of Conservative Party of Canada, Liberal Party of Canada, and New Democratic Party of Canada Views on Seniors, Child Care, and Health

Conservative Party

Seniors

- Home Accessibility Tax Credit of 15 per cent of costs up to $10,000 per year.
- Lower the mandatory withdrawal amount for Registered Retirement Income Funds (RRIF).

Child Care

- The Conservative Party has already implemented the Universal Child Care Benefit. This benefit provides $160 monthly per child up to age 6 and $60 monthly per child aged 6 to 17.

- To extend parental leave for federal workers from 12 to 18 months.
- To implement a two-year pilot project that allows parents to continue to receive their parental leave benefits if they must return to work early.

Health

- The Conservatives will not renew the 10-year, $41-billion Canada Health Accord that expired in 2014.
- $31.5 million in funding for a plan to fight dementia.

Liberal Party

Seniors

- Restore 65 years as the age of eligibility for receipt of Old Age Security.
- Increase the Guaranteed Income Supplement (GIS) by 10 per cent for single, low-income seniors.
- Introduce a new Seniors Price Index to ensure financing of Old Age Security and the Guaranteed Income Supplement.
- Propose to keep the Home Accessibility Tax Credit and pension splitting.

Child Care

- To replace the Universal Child Care Benefit, the Child Tax Credit, and the National Child Benefit Supplement with a complete Canada Child Benefit. This would base payments by household income: the lowest incomes would receive $6,400 per year per child under 6 and $5,400 for children 6 to 17.
- To extend Employment Insurance (EI) benefits up to 18 months at lower benefit levels.

Health

- $3 billion in funding over four years to the national health care system, targeting home care, high cost of drugs, and mental health care facilities.
- Negotiate better prices for prescription drugs.

New Democratic Party

Seniors

- Restore 65 years as age of eligibility for receipt of the Old Age Security.
- $400 million annually to the Guaranteed Income Supplement.
- Extend the CPP and the Quebec Pension Plan.
- Universal drug coverage.
- 5,000 nursing home beds.
- More home care funding for 41,000 seniors.
- $40 million to create a national Alzheimer's and Dementia Strategy.

Child Care

- One million new day care spaces—specifically, 164,000 spaces in the Greater Toronto Area and 110,000 in British Columbia.
- Keep the Universal Child Care Benefit and increase the National Child Benefit Supplement.

Health

- $1.8 billion over four years to ensure universal access to prescriptions.
- $40 million over four years to develop a nationwide Alzheimer's and Dementia Strategy.
- $500 million to expand smaller-scale health care clinics and to hire more health care providers.

Source: www.cbc.ca/news/politics/compare-federal-party-platforms-and-election-promises-1.3271149

The brief illustration of the policies and electoral platforms of the Conservative Party, Liberal Party, and NDP in Box 13.1 shows three different understandings of equality. For the Conservative Party, equality reflects both the ontological view that all people are created equal and the idea that all people have equal opportunities. This assumes that individuals, regardless of their class, age, gender, ethnicity, or race are on a level playing field and that with similar levels of intelligence and ambition, they will have equal chances of success. The Liberal Party takes the idea of equality one step further. Along with an ontological view of equality, the Liberal Party promotes equality through social-policy attempts to make the playing field more level. Equal opportunities are not assumed, and social programs are established to help produce situations that treat groups equally. Such views of equality have led to equal-opportunity policies and legislation that have helped to open doors to paid work for women and members of ethnic- and visible-minority groups in Canada and the United States.

Neither the Conservative Party's nor the Liberal Party's views of equality go far enough, however. For social policy to eradicate social inequality, it must rely on a definition of equality that also considers the outcomes of inequality discussed in this book (e.g., income, occupation, and health). In other words, social policy must be established with the goal of equality of outcomes in mind. The NDP policy statements come closest to this view of equality.

But still more is needed. To adequately lead to equality in outcomes, policy must simultaneously consider the intersecting structures of inequality and not simply consider one particular disadvantaged group at a time. An example of how such policy might be formulated is reproduced here in Box 13.2. On the basis of their research on gender inequality and poverty, Davies, McMullin, and Avison (2001) make policy recommendations that are informed by gender, class, and age. The guiding assumption in this work is that public policy must be situated within a life-course framework (see also V.W. Marshall and Mueller 2002) and must be developed in a way that does not penalize individuals for their responsibilities in processes of reproduction. Another assumption is that men and women should divide equally the work involved in production, reproduction, and distribution. The problem with the policies described in Box 13.2 is that it will be a long time before that is done in Canadian society (see chapter 8). Indeed, to achieve equality of outcomes, changes to social policy will not suffice. Rather, Canadians will need to challenge both the ways in which the processes of production, distribution, and reproduction are organized and the dominant ideologies that shape such organization.

HIGHLIGHT

Box 13.2 Sensitizing Policies to Gender, Class, and Age

The introduction of the Canada Health and Social Transfer (CHST) in 1995 resulted in sweeping changes to the administration and funding of social programs across Canada. These changes jeopardized income security by providing provinces with greater autonomy over spending decisions (thereby reducing national standards for social assistance) and by limiting the availability of funds. The consequences of these changes affect women's economic circumstances in ways that are distinct from those of men. . . . [In] order to reduce low income among women, social policy changes are needed that target individuals at various points in the life cycle, beginning in childhood. The underlying goal of these policy changes should be to make it easier for women to acquire the education and job training that would ensure their economic independence *regardless of their marital and parental status*. In outlining the policy implications of our findings, we address the following questions:

- How can children's needs be better met to ensure greater opportunities to become economically independent adults?
- How can the frequency of unplanned teenage pregnancies be reduced? And how can we ensure that young mothers continue with their schooling and/or acquire life and job skills?
- What changes need to be implemented to social assistance programs to improve economic security and economic independence?

- What do our results reveal about the importance of maternity benefits and employment insurance for the economic security of low income women?
- What other changes should be made to social policies to enhance the economic security of women?

These questions reflect the life course perspective of the study and we address them below in turn.

5.2 Childhood

Although our quantitative results do not reveal a significant relationship between early adversities and low income in adulthood, other research does find that exposure to adversities in childhood and adolescence increases the likelihood of single parenthood. Given that economic disadvantages of single motherhood are widely documented both here and elsewhere, there is additional support for our qualitative findings that family background characteristics portend economic difficulties in adulthood. Specifically, our qualitative results suggest that parental absence is an adversity that makes it very difficult for children to acquire the social capital necessary to obtain life skills and human capital. Thus, within our community are children who, for example, witness and experience violence within their homes, and/or who have alcohol or drug dependent parents; in short, children whose parents for these or various other reasons are unwilling or unable to provide the time and effort necessary to build trusting relationships with their children.

Consequences for children include poor school performance, dropping out of school, running away from home, drug or alcohol dependency, and teenage pregnancy, each of which reduces educational attainment. And as our quantitative results underscore, lack of education increases the risk of low income. Thus, interventions that compensate for parental absence in childhood may significantly reduce economic insecurity in adulthood.

5.2.1 Recommendations

a. Increase the visibility of and access to organizations with a non-punitive mandate that will fill gaps left by parental absence (e.g., respite centres for families and/or Big Sisters, Big Brothers).

- the creation of family respite care centres that would also serve as a sounding board for families experiencing economic and social stress, and would provide a place where parents could temporarily leave children, and obtain information about other available resources within their community to deal with their particular circumstances
- organizations such as Big Sisters foster a mentoring relationship between adult and child, thereby providing important support that may be absent in her home.

b. Incorporate education about family violence, sex education, birth control, drug and alcohol abuse within public and high school curriculums.

- educators must be trained to break down resistance to discussing these topics and to encourage open communication among students and teachers
- students must be made aware of agencies and community groups that can provide information and assistance to those who need it

c. Increase government funding to shelters and second stage housing for abused women and children and improve awareness of these options.

- ensure that women and children who experience violence have a place to go and assistance to start a new life

Contrary to the common view of families as private refuges, economic and social conditions affect family relationships, and, in particular, the well-being of children. Investing in children has long-term implications for the health of a community. Thus, as we recommend above, it is important for government to support communities so that they can assume greater responsibility for the health of their children.

continued

5.3 Young Adulthood

When faced with pregnancy (regardless of whether or not it is accompanied by marriage) the typical response of women is to leave school. While this is risky at any age, it is particularly consequential for young women because they have accumulated fewer years of schooling by the time of their pregnancy. Yet, pregnancy outside of marriage or a cohabiting union is rarely planned. Nonetheless, young girls grow up believing that marriage and motherhood should take precedence over education and careers. Social programs that dismantle the relationship among motherhood, education, and low income promise to improve women's economic security.

The Ontario government has clearly recognized the economic benefits that young mothers would accrue if they stayed in school. In March of this year, the Community and Social Services Minister revealed the details of a new mandatory program, Learning, Earning, and Parenting (LEAP), whose goal is to encourage teen mothers to stay in school. It falls under OntarioWorks and makes enrolment in school mandatory for mothers between the ages of 16 and 17 in order to receive welfare, and provides for transportation costs and offers child care subsidies. An additional requirement is participation in parenting workshops. The program also provides opportunities to develop employment skills and/or transitions to education beyond high school. The government should be commended for its efforts to improve the education of young mothers. Based on the results of our qualitative study, however, we recommend the following changes to this program, and propose an additional intervention that would increase accessibility of education to mothers generally.

5.3.1 Recommendations

1. Inject flexibility into the program by not tying eligibility for General Welfare Assistance to participation in LEAP.

   Teen mothers will vary with respect to their readiness to combine schooling and parenting. There is evidence to suggest that teen mothers are selected into this status because of adverse family

backgrounds. For those who had trouble managing school before they became pregnant, combining courses and a baby is unlikely to enhance human capital. Thus, LEAP delivery agents should be trained to evaluate the readiness of teen mothers to continue with their schooling, rather than enforce legislation that makes going to school a requirement of General Welfare Assistance.

2. Eliminate day care costs for all teen mothers rather than providing subsidies.
   - make more fully subsidized daycare spots available
   - provide additional funds to accommodate extra caregiving costs when children are sick, when schools are not operating etc. (i.e., professional development days, spring break)

   Current LEAP child care subsidies fall short of need and are problematic because any child care costs reduce the income available for food and shelter.

3. Provide on-site daycare facilities at all adult learning centres, colleges and universities
   - provide services to parents of infants as well as toddlers and preschool children

   This will increase accessibility of education by reducing time, cost and stress of taking children first to daycare before going to school, and provide greater contact between children and parents during the day. We view the above recommendations as changes that would eventually be encompassed within a national childcare system.

5.4 Adulthood

5.4.1 Social Assistance

As others have noted and predicted our qualitative data confirm that changes to Ontario General Welfare Assistance since the introduction of the CHST have undermined the economic security of women. Two examples are the cuts to rates and the repeal of the three-year cohabitation rule. As a consequence of the 21.6 percent reduction in welfare rates, many women in our study report moving to less adequate housing, an increase in food bank use, as well as greater personal debt. For example, Carrie (#15) was a single mother with a 5-year-old and a 3-year-old when her cheque was reduced because of the cuts to General Welfare Assistance. As she explains,

> When they took that $300 off me, it was just brutal, absolutely brutal. . . . I couldn't make ends meet. There was no way, I was not going to not have food in my kids mouths. So bills suffered a great deal. I got into financial trouble. I had bill collectors coming after me. I moved out of that apartment because I couldn't afford it. It was a cheap place anyway but I had to move out of there.

The intense stress involved in trying to manage on an inadequate income reduces mothers' real and perceived control over their lives, contributing to a state of helplessness rather than empowerment.

Another example of how changes to Ontario General Welfare Assistance jeopardize women's economic security is the decision to revoke the three-year cohabitation rule. On the one hand, marriage or cohabitation is an obvious pathway off of social assistance. On the other hand, marriage or cohabitation guarantees neither safety nor economic security. Understandably, many women have serious reservations about entering into a marital or cohabiting relationship again. Furthermore, equitable distribution of financial resources does not characterize all relationships. In describing a live-in relationship with a man during the period when the three-year cohabitation rule was in place, Martha (#35) says, "The thing that made me mad . . . was that he got a really good job and he didn't give me rent. Because he figured he was on the road a lot that he didn't need to give me rent. And I kept asking for money." The relationship did not last beyond three years and her social assistance was not compromised. Having a period where one can "try out" relationships and still continue to receive assistance gives women more control over their ability to find a stable, equitable long-term relationship.

5.4.1.1 Recommendations

1. The Federal government should reinstate an open-ended federal–provincial cost-sharing arrangement like the Canada Assistance Plan and, in response, the Ontario government should revoke the changes it has made to General Welfare Assistance since 1995.

While this would be a start, our data underscore the importance of providing mothers on assistance with financial support that better reflects their expenses. Raising the standard of living for low income families would improve their health and well-being, reduce their stress, and therefore improve their ability to parent their children. In essence, governments need to recognize and value the work that mothers do; for example:

2. The Federal government should require that all low income families receive the Canada Child Tax Benefit and encourage provinces to allow those receiving social assistance benefits to keep the full amount.
3. The financial costs of post-secondary education should be reduced for mothers on social assistance by allowing them to receive student assistance in addition to their benefits.

This will ensure that the student loans cover only their educational costs and thus minimize their debt accumulation.

4. Childcare should be free to all parents receiving social assistance or those with comparable incomes.

This would enable women to better their lives by giving them the freedom to explore work and educational opportunities.

While decreasing financial constraints is critical, it must be accompanied by a social support system that recognizes and effectively confronts the disadvantages mothers face as they venture to improve their economic situation. Two problems with the current and previous social assistance systems is that first, they do not recognize the heterogeneity that exists among recipients, and mothers are no exception to this. Second, they do not understand

continued

that most women do not need incentives to be independent of assistance, they need opportunities. By emphasizing "incentives" they grossly underestimate the barriers that exist between incentive and welfare independence and therefore maintain or even undermine the economic insecurity of women.

Many of the barriers facing mothers on social assistance are linked directly to their limited knowledge of available options and resources that would facilitate their entry into the labour force or educational system. Our qualitative results confirm previous research that finds "information support . . . [to be] the type of support mothers are least likely to receive and with which they are least satisfied." Limited knowledge of community supports and resources restrict women's ability to help themselves. For example, without up-to-date information, women who have been removed from the workforce for a significant period of time will be unaware of recent changes in the job search process; therefore, they will be less competitive in the job market. Additionally, women are often not aware of the opportunities for upgrading that are available to them. The ability of current social assistance case workers to help clients is limited because of their enormous caseloads and administrative duties. As such, they are unable to offer the individual support, disseminate information or provide the individualized assistance that would more effectively increase opportunities to become employment reliant.

5. Specialized workers are needed to give individualized help to women attempting to become self-sufficient.

Communication among these workers, and then between workers and government officials, would convey information about programs that are not achieving their goals, would alert policy makers to program restrictions that limit accessibility and effectiveness, and would identify needs for other services that would enhance exit strategies and simultaneously improve economic security.

5.4.2 Employment Insurance and Maternity Benefits

It is revealing that only three of the women in this sample had ever received employment benefits, and in each instance receiving EI was followed by the receipt of social assistance. This reflects a national pattern whereby men are more likely than women to collect EI benefits, and points to the inapplicability and inaccessibility of EI for women. One of ways in which EI inadvertently excludes women is illustrated by a recent change to the policy that makes employees ineligible if they quit their jobs. This stipulation assumes that there is no valid reason for leaving one's employment. Yet, women in our sample described "quitting" jobs because of sexual harassment and problems with childcare—situations that reflect broader disadvantages of women in society.

Further, EI is virtually inaccessible to low income mothers. As a monitoring report for Human Resources Development Canada finds, women are disproportionately represented in non-standard jobs and as such often do not accumulate enough hours to qualify for benefits. Further, because EI benefits only replace 55 percent of earnings, they do not offer enough assistance to support a family.

5.4.2.1 Recommendations

1. Consideration should be given to the reasons for quitting a job making allowances for exceptional circumstances.
2. Low income employees should receive 100 per cent of their earnings in employment benefits.
3. Lower the number of hours one has to work in a year to qualify for benefits.
4. Make allowances for repeat users who have family care responsibilities, thereby increasing the value of unpaid labour.

All of the preceding points regarding EI apply to maternity benefits as well because curiously, this program is tied to Employment insurance. Consequently, only those mothers who are strongly attached to the labour market (excluding self-employed women) qualify for benefits. In addition to the above recommendations we argue that:

5. Maternity benefits should be replaced by parental benefits and should be available to everyone, regardless of their labour force attachment. This would require disassociating maternity and paternity benefits from the EI system.

This would compensate women for the economic costs of child-bearing while encouraging a more equitable division of labour among couples. This would also reduce the barriers that prevent men from taking an employment leave to care for their infants, ultimately increasing gender equality and the value of unpaid work.

5.5 General Recommendations

In addition to the recommendations made above, we have also addressed divorce laws and policies related to workplace flexibility that would further benefit women's economic security. The data from our study led us to conclude that a concerted effort must be made on various fronts to make women economically independent. All of our suggested changes reflect this view. However, if we had to identify the change that is most necessary, it would be the implementation of a universal childcare system.

There has been a great deal of political rhetoric over the issue of providing stay-at-home mothers with tax relief. This is simply not an issue for low income mothers and such tax-relief would not have an impact on their lives. Further, this proposal is problematic for middle-class women because of the individual nature of the tax filing system. Tax credits would more directly benefit fathers because it is they who have the taxable earnings. Regardless of social class, married mothers who are not economically independent are at risk for low income if their marriages end. Consequently, any policies aimed at implementing tax credits should be critically reviewed.

More important, in our view, is the necessity for a universal child care system. In addition to the child care system recommendations we have made earlier, we suggest the following:

1. After parental leave, quality child care should be available and affordable to all parents.
2. Transportation of children should be provided by child care centres.
3. Workplaces and educational institutions should receive incentives to implement on-site child care centres.
4. Recognize and support a diversity of child care arrangements to provide parents with as much choice and flexibility as possible concerning their children's needs.

In closing, Canadians should not underestimate the negative consequences of reducing social spending in favour of tax cuts. By undermining the economic security of women, these cuts put all families at risk of experiencing social, economic, mental and physical health hardships. The effects of these hardships on children are particularly worrisome because they will resonate throughout their lives, impairing their potential to be productive citizens of Canadian society.

Source: Davies, McMullin, and Avison (2001: 73–80).

References

Abada, Teresa, Feng Hou, and Bali Ram. 2007. "Racially Mixed Neighborhoods, Perceived Neighborhood Social Cohesion, and Adolescent Health in Canada." *Social Science and Medicine* 65: 2004–17.

Abercrombie, Nicholas, Stephen Hill, and Bryan S. Turner. 2000. *The Penguin Dictionary of Sociology*, 4th edn. London: Penguin.

Abortion Rights Coalition of Canada. 2008. "Oppose Bill C-484, 'Unborn Victims of Crime Act.'" http://www.arcc-cdac.ca/c484.htm

Abu-Laban, Yasmeen. 1998. "Keeping 'Em Out: Gender, Race, and Class Biases in Canadian Immigration Policy." Pp. 69–82 in Veronica Strong-Boag, Sherrill Grace, Avigail Eisenberg, and Joan Anderson, eds, *Painting the Maple: Essays on Race, Gender, and the Construction of Canada*. Vancouver: UBC Press.

Acker, Joan. 1988. "Class, Gender and the Relations of Distribution." *Signs* 13: 473–97.

———. 1989. "The Problem with Patriarchy." *Sociology* 23, 2: 235–40.

———. 2000. "Rewriting Class, Race, and Gender: Problems in Feminist Rethinking." Chapter 2 in Myra Marx Ferree, Judith Lorber, and Beth Hess, eds, *Revisioning Gender*. New York: Altamira Press.

———. 2006a. *Class Questions, Feminist Answers*. Lanham, MD: Rowman & Littlefield.

———. 2006b. "Inequality Regimes: Gender, Class, and Race in Organizations." *Gender and Society* 20: 441–64.

Adair, Vivyan C. 2001. "Branded with Infamy: Inscriptions of Poverty and Class in the United States." *Signs* 27, 2: 451–71.

Adams, Ann, Christopher D. Buckingham, Anje Lindenmeyer, John B. McKinlay, Carol Link, Lisa Marceau, and Sara Arber. 2008. "The Influence of Patient and Doctor Gender on Diagnosing Coronary Heart Disease." *Sociology of Health & Illness* 30, 1: 1–18.

Adams, Tracy L. 2000. *A Dentist and a Gentleman: Gender and the Rise of Dentistry in Ontario*. Toronto: University of Toronto Press.

Adams, Tracy L., and Kevin McQuillan. 2000. "New Jobs, New Workers? Organizations, Restructuring, and Management Hiring Decisions." *Relations Industrielles/Industrial Relations* 55, 3: 391–412.

Adams, Tracy L., and Sandy Welsh. 2008. *The Organization and Experience of Work*. Toronto: Thomson Nelson.

Adamuti-Trache, M., and C. Hawkey. 2009. *Canadian Post-Secondary Graduates and Further Education: Who Continues and Why?* Ottawa: Canadian Council on Learning.

Adler, Nancy E. 2006. "When One's Main Effect Is Another's Error: Material vs Psychosocial Explanations of Health Disparities: A Commentary on Macleod et al., 'Is Subjective Social Status a More Important Determinant of Health Than Objective Social Status? Evidence from a Prospective Observational Study of Scottish Men.'" *Social Science and Medicine* 63, 4: 846–50.

Adler, Nancy E., and David H. Rehkopf. 2008. "U.S. Disparities in Health: Descriptions, Causes, and Mechanisms." *Annual Review of Public Health* 29: 235–52.

Agrell, Siri. 2007. "Unmarried and Unabashed." *Globe and Mail*, 13 September.

Aguiar, Luis M. 2001. "Whiteness in White Academia." Pp. 177–92 in Carl E. James and Adrienne Shadd, eds, *Talking about Identity: Encounters in Race, Ethnicity, and Language*. Toronto: Between the Lines.

Akhtar-Danesh, Noori, and Janet Landeen. 2007. "Relation between Depression and Sociodemographic Factors." *International Journal of Mental Health* 1, 4: 1–9.

Albanese, Patrizia. 2005. "Ethnic Families." Chapter 6 in Maureen Baker, ed., *Families: Changing Trends in Canada*. Toronto: McGraw-Hill Ryerson.

Albrecht, Don E. 2007. "Income Inequality: The Implications of Economic Structure and Social Conditions." *Sociological Spectrum* 27: 165–81.

Alcoba, Natalie. 2008. "Making the Grade; Parents Going to Great Lengths to Buy Homes in Hot School Districts." *National Post*, 17 May.

Alexander, K.L., D.R Entwisle, and L.S. Olson. 2007. "Lasting Consequences of the Summer Learning Gap." *American Sociological Review* 72, 2: 167–80.

Ali, Jennifer, and Edward Grabb. 1998. "Ethnic Origin, Class Origin and Educational Attainment in Canada: Further Evidence on the Mosaic Thesis." *Journal of Canadian Studies* 33, 1: 3–21.

Ali, Jennifer, Sarah McDermott, and Ronald G. Gravel. 2004. "Recent Research on Immigrant Health from Statistics Canada's Population Surveys." *Canadian Journal of Public Health* 95, 3: I-9–13.

Allahar, Anton. 1995. *Sociology and the Periphery: Theories and Issues*, 2nd edn. Toronto: Garamond Press.

Allahar, Anton, and James E. Côté. 1994. *Generation on Hold: Coming of Age in the Late Twentieth Century*. Toronto: Stoddart.

———. 1998. *Richer and Poorer: Social Inequality in Canada*. Toronto: Lorimer.

Allard, Yvon E., Russell Wilkins, and Jean-Marie Berthelot. 2004. "Premature Mortality in Health Regions with High Aboriginal Populations." *Health Reports* 15, 1: 51–60. Statistics Canada Catalogue no. 82-003.

Allington, R.L., and A. McGill-Franzen. 2003. "The Impact of Summer Reading Setback on the Reading Achievement Gap." *Phi Delta Kappan* 85, 1: 68–75.

Alon, S. 2009. "The Evolution of Class Inequality in Higher Education Competition, Exclusion, and Adaptation." *American Sociological Review* 74, 5: 731–55.

Amnesty International. 2004. *Stolen Sisters: Discrimination and Violence against Indigenous Women in Canada*. London: Amnesty International.

Anand, Sonia S., Salim Yusuf, Ruby Jacobs, A. Darlene Davis, Quilong Yi, Hertzel Gerstein, Patricia A. Montague, and Eva Lonn. 2001. "Risk Factors, Atherosclerosis, and Cardiovascular Disease among Aboriginal People in Canada: The Study of Health Assessment and Risk Evaluation in Aboriginal Peoples (*SHARE-AP*)." *The Lancet* 358: 1147–53.

Andersen, Robert, and Josh Curtis. 2012. "The Polarizing Effect of Economic Inequality on Class Identification: Evidence from 44 Countries." *Research in Social Stratification and Mobility* 30: 129–41.

Andersen, Robert and Josh Curtis. 2015. "Social Class, Economic Inequality and the Convergence of Policy Preferences: Evidence from 24 Modern Democracies." *Canadian Review of Sociology*, 52: 266–288.

Andersen, Robert, and Tina Fetner. 2008. "Economic Inequality and Intolerance: Attitudes toward Homosexuality in 35 Democracies." *American Journal of Political Science* 52, 4: 942–58.

Andersen, Robert, and Mitch McIvor. 2013. *Growing Inequality and Its Impacts in Canada: Report to the European Commission, Brussels January 2013*. GINI (Growing Inequalities' Impacts international research project). 7th Framework Programme.

———. 2014. "Rising Inequality and Its Impact in Canada: The Role of National Debt." In Brian Nolan, Wiemer Salverda, Daniele Checchi, Ive Marx, Abigail McKnight, István György Tóth, and Herman van de Werfhorst, eds, *Changing Inequalities and Societal Impacts in Thirty Rich Countries: Thirty Countries' Experiences*. Oxford: Oxford University Press.

Anderson, Alan. 1992. "Policing Native People: Native Militancy and Canadian Militarianism." Chapter 19 in Vic Satzewich, ed., *Deconstructing a Nation: Immigration, Multiculturalism and Racism in '90s Canada*. Halifax: Fernwood/ Saskatoon: Social Research Unit, Department of Sociology, University of Saskatchewan.

Anderson, D.K., and D.G. Saunders. 2003. "Leaving an Abusive Partner: An Empirical Review of Predictors, the Process of Leaving, and Psychological Well-Being." *Trauma, Violence, and Abuse* 4, 2: 163–91.

Anderson, Norman B., and Cheryl A. Armstead. 1995. "Toward Understanding the Association of Socioeconomic Status and Health: A New Challenge for the Biopsychosocial Approach." *Psychosomatic Medicine* 57: 213–25.

Aneshensel, Carol S., and Clea A. Sucoff. 1996. "The Neighborhood Context of Adolescent Mental Health." *Journal of Health and Social Behavior* 37, 4: 293–310.

Anthias, Floya. 1992. "Connecting 'Race' and Ethnic Phenomena." *Sociology* 26, 3: 421–38.

Anxo, D., C. Fagan, M. Letablier, C. Perraudin, and K. Smith. 2007. *Parental Leave in European*

Companies—Establishment Survey on Working Time and Work-Life Balance Arrangements 2005–2005. Report for the European Foundation for the Improvement of Living and Working Conditions. Office for Official Publications of the European Communities. Luxembourg, Belgium. Retrieved 21 May 2008, http://www.eurofound.europa.eu/pubdocs/2006/87/en/1/ef0687en.pdf

Aragones, N., M. Pollan, and P. Gustavsson. 2002. "Stomach Cancer and Occupation in Sweden: 1971–89." *Occupational and Environmental Medicine* 59, 5: 329–37.

Arar, Maher. 2008. "With Persistence, the Truth Will Come Out." *Globe and Mail*, 17 June.

Arat-Koc, Sedef. 1995. "The Politics of Family and Immigration in the Subordination of Domestic Workers in Canada." In E.D. Nelson and B.W. Robinson, eds, *Gender in the 1990s: Images, Realities and Issues*. Toronto: Nelson.

———. 1997. "Immigration Policies, Migrant Domestic Workers, and the Definition of Citizenship in Canada." Pp. 224–36 in Veronica Strong-Boag and Anita Clair Fellman, eds, *Rethinking Canada: The Promise of Women's History*, 3rd edn. Toronto: Oxford University Press.

———. 2001. "The Politics of Family and Immigration in the Subordination of Domestic Workers in Canada." Chapter 23 in Bonnie J. Fox, ed., *Family Patterns, Gender Relations*. Toronto: Oxford University Press.

———. 2006. "Whose Social Reproduction? Transnational Motherhood and Challenges to Feminist Political Economy." Chapter 3 in K. Bezanson and M. Luxton, eds, *Social Reproduction: Feminist Political Economy Challenges Neo-Liberalism*. Montreal and Kingston: McGill-Queen's University Press.

Arber, Sara, and Helen Cooper. 1999. "Gender Differences in Health in Later Life: The New Paradox?" *Social Science and Medicine* 48, 1: 61–76.

Archer, Margaret. 1995. *Realist Social Theory: The Morphogenetic Approach*. Cambridge: Cambridge University Press.

———. 2000. *Being Human: The Problem of Agency*. Cambridge: Cambridge University Press.

———. 2007. *Making Our Way through the World: Human Reflexivity and Social Mobility*. Cambridge: Cambridge University Press.

Armstrong, Pat. 1997. "The State and Pay Equity: Juggling Similarity and Difference, Meaning, and Structures." Chapter 10 in Patricia M. Evans and Gerda R. Wekerle, eds, *Women and the Canadian Welfare State: Challenges and Change*. Toronto: University of Toronto Press.

Armstrong, Pat, and M. Patricia Connelly. 1999. "Introduction: Feminism, Political Economy and the State: Contested Terrain." Chapter 1 in Pat Armstrong and M. Patricia Connelly, eds, *Feminism, Political Economy and the State: Contested Terrain*. Toronto: Canadian Scholars' Press.

Armstrong, Robin. 1999. "Mapping the Conditions of First Nations Communities." *Canadian Social Trends*, no. 55: 14–18.

Aronson, Jane. 1992. "Women's Sense of Responsibility for the Care of Old People: But Who Else Is Going to Do It?" *Gender and Society* 6: 8–29.

Aronson, Jane, Cindy Thornewell, and Karen Williams. 1995. "Wife Assault in Old Age: Coming out of Obscurity." *Canadian Journal on Aging* 14, suppl. 2: 72–88.

Asanin, Jennifer, and Kathi Wilson. 2008. "'I Spent Nine Years Looking for a Doctor': Exploring Access to Health Care among Immigrants in Mississauga, Ontario, Canada." *Social Science and Medicine* 66: 1271–83.

Askam, Janet. 1995. "The Married Lives of Older People." Pp. 86–97 in Sara Arber and Jay Ginn, eds, *Connecting Gender and Ageing: A Sociological Approach*. Buckingham, UK: Open University Press.

Association of University and Colleges of Canada (AUCC). 2011. *Trends in Higher Education*. Vol. 1: *Enrolment*. Ottawa. http://www.cais.ca/uploaded/trends-2011-vol1-enrolment-e.pdf

AUCC. *See* Association of University and Colleges of Canada

Auger, Nathalie, Marie-France Raynault, Richard Lessard, and Robert Choiniere. 2004. "Income and Health in Canada." Chapter 3 in Dennis Raphael, ed., *Social Determinants of Health: Canadian Perspectives*, 2nd edn. Toronto: Canadian Scholars' Press.

Avison, William R., Jennifer Ali, and David Walters. 2007. "Family Structure, Stress, and Psychological Distress: A Demonstration of the

Impact of Differential Exposure." *Journal of Health and Social Behavior* 48, 3: 301–17.

Avison, William R., and Lorraine Davies. 2005. "Family Structure, Gender, and Health in the Context of the Life Course." *Journals of Gerontology* 60B, spec. iss. 2: 113–16.

Avison, William R., and Ian H. Gotlib. 1994. "Introduction and Overview." Chapter 1 in William R. Avison and Ian H. Gotlib, eds, *Stress and Mental Health: Contemporary Issues and Prospects for the Future.* New York: Plenum Press.

Avison, William R., Terrance J. Wade, and Cathy F. Thorpe. 1996. "Families' Experiences of Unemployment: Mental Health Consequences for Husbands and Wives." Paper presented to the American Sociological Association, New York.

Bacigalupo, Mardy. 2003. "How Did Your School Do? Overall Tests Results Show Improvement for City." *The Londoner,* 30 January.

Bailis, Daniel S., Judith G. Chipperfield, and Tiffany R. Helgason. 2008. "Collective Self-Esteem and the Onset of Chronic Conditions and Reduced Activity in a Longitudinal Study of Aging." *Social Science and Medicine* 66: 1818–27.

Baldus, Bernhard, and Meenaz Kassam. 1996. "'Make Me Truthful, Good and Mild': Values in Nineteenth-Century Ontario Schoolbooks." *Canadian Journal of Sociology* 21, 3: 327–57.

Baliunas, Dolly, Jayadeep Patra, Jürgen Rehm, Svetlana Popova, Murry Kaiserman, and Benjamin Taylor. 2007. "Smoking-Attributable Mortality and Expected Years of Life Lost in Canada 2002: Conclusions for Prevention and Policy." *Chronic Diseases in Canada* 27, 4: 154–62.

Ballantyne, Peri J. 1999. "The Social Determinants of Health: A Contribution to the Analysis of Gender Differences in Health and Illness." *Scandinavian Journal of Public Health* 27: 290–5.

Banting, K., and J. Myles. 2014. *Inequality and the Fading of Redistributive Politics.* Vancouver: UBC Press.

Barndt, Deborah. 2002. "Fruits of Injustice: Women in the Post-NAFTA Food System." *Canadian Woman Studies* 21/22, 4/1: 82–8.

Barnes, Barry. 2000. *Understanding Agency: Social Theory and Responsible Action.* London: Sage.

Basran, Gurcharn S., and Li Zong. 1998. "Devaluation of Foreign Credentials as Perceived by Visible Minority Professional Immigrants." *Canadian Ethnic Studies* 30, 3: 6–23.

Beagan, Brenda L. 2000. "Neutralizing Differences: Producing Neutral Doctors for (Almost) Neutral Patients." *Social Science and Medicine* 51, 8: 1253–65.

Beaujot, Roderic. 2000. *Earning and Caring in Canadian Families.* Toronto: Broadview Press.

Beaujot, Roderic, and Robert Andersen. 2007. "Time-Crunch: Impact of Time Spent in Paid and Unpaid Work, and Its Division." *Canadian Journal of Sociology* 32, 3: 295–315.

Beaujot, Roderic, and Don Kerr. 2003. *Population Change in Canada.* Toronto: Oxford University Press.

Beaujot, Roderic, Kevin McQuillan, and Zenaida Ravanera. 2007. "Population Change in Canada to 2017 and Beyond: The Challenges of Policy Adaptation." *Horizons* 9, 4: 3–12.

Beck, Urlich. 1992. *Risk Society.* London: Sage.

———. 1999. *World Risk Society.* Cambridge: Polity Press.

———. 2000. *The Brave New World of Work.* Translated by Patrick Camiller. New York: Polity Press.

Beck, Urlich, and Elizabeth Beck-Gernshcim. 2002. *Individualization.* London: Sage.

Beck, Urlich, Wolfgang Bonss, and Christoph Lau. 2003. "The Theory of Reflexive Modernization: Problematic, Hypotheses and Research Programme." *Theory, Culture & Society* 20, 2: 1–33.

Bedard, Gabriel. 2000. "Deconstructing Whiteness: Pedagogical Implications for Anti-racism Education." Chapter 2 in George J. Sefa Dei and Agnes Calliste, eds, *Power, Knowledge, and Anti-racism Education: A Critical Reader.* Halifax: Fernwood.

Bell, Daniel. 1973. *The Coming of Post-industrial Society.* New York: Basic Books.

Bengtson, V.L., T.M. Parrott, and E.O. Burgess. 1994. "The Third Generation of Theories in Social Gerontology." Paper presented to the Annual Scientific Meeting of the Gerontological Society of America, 18–22 November, Atlanta.

Benoit, Cecilia, and Dena Carroll. 2001. "Margin-alized Voices from Vancouver's Downtown Eastside:

Aboriginal Women Speak about Their Health Care Experiences." Centres of Excellence for Women's Health, *Research Bulletin* 1, 2: 6–7.

Berger, Ellie. 2012. "Age Discrimination and Paid Work." *Population Change and Life Course Strategic Knowledge Cluster.* Policy Brief No. 7. Retrieved 1 March 2016 from http://sociology. uwo.ca/cluster/en/publications/docs/policy_ briefs/PolicyBrief7.pdf

Berger, Joseph, Anne Motte, and Andrew Parkin. 2007. *The Price of Knowledge: Access and Student Finance in Canada*, 3rd edn. Montreal: Canada Millennium Scholarship Foundation.

Berger, Peter L., and Thomas Luckmann. 1967. *The Social Construction of Reality.* New York: Doubleday.

Bernard, Andre, and Chris Li. 2006. *Death of a Spouse: The Impact on Income for Senior Men and Women.* Analysis in Brief. Statistics Canada Catalogue no. 11-621-MIE200604.

Bernard, Paul, Rana Charafeddine, Katherine L. Frohlich, Mark Daniela, Yan Kestensa, and Louise Potvin. 2007. "Health Inequalities and Place: A Theoretical Conception of Neighbourhood." *Social Science and Medicine* 65: 1839–62.

Bernhard, Judith K., and Marlinda Freire. 1999. "What Is My Child Learning at Elementary School? Culturally Contested Issues between Teachers and Latin American Families." *Canadian Ethnic Studies* 31, 3: 72–94.

Betcherman, Gordon, and Norman Leckie. 1995. "Age Structure of Employment in Industries and Occupations." Ottawa: Applied Research Branch, Human Resources Development Canada (R-96-7E).

Betts, Julian, Christopher Ferrall, and Ross Finnie. 2007. *The Role of University Characteristics in Determining Post-graduation Outcomes: Panel Evidence from Three Recent Canadian Cohorts.* Analytical Studies Branch Research Paper Series. Statistics Canada Catalogue no. 11F0019MIE, no. 292.

Bhorat, Haroon. 2013. "The Future of South Africa." *New York Times.* Retrieved 20 May 2015 from http://www.nytimes.com/ roomfordebate/2013/07/28/the-future-of-south-africa/economic-inequality-is-a-major-obstacle-to-growth-in-south-africa

Biggs, Simon. 2005. "Beyond Appearances: Perspectives on Identity in Later Life and Some Implications for Method." *Journal of Gerontology* 60B, 3: S118–S128.

———. 2007. "Thinking about Generations: Conceptual Positions and Policy Implications." *Journal of Social Issues* 63, 4: 695–711.

Bittle, Steven, and Laureen Snider. 2006. "From Manslaughter to Preventable Accident: Shaping Corporate Criminal Liability." *Law & Policy* 28, 4: 470–96.

Black, S.M., and C.E. Hill. 1984. "The Psychological Well-Being of Women in Their Middle Years." *Psychology of Women Quarterly* 8: 282–91.

Blackwell, Judith. 1998. "Making the Grade against the Odds: Women as University Undergraduates." Pp. 60–71 in Jackie Stalker and Susan Prentice, eds, *Illusion of Inclusion: Women in Post-secondary Education.* Halifax: Fernwood.

Blakemore, Kenneth, and Margaret Boneham. 1994. *Age, Race, and Ethnicity: A Comparative Approach.* Open University Press.

Bloch, Gary. 2007. "Poverty Takes Huge Toll on Health." *Toronto Star*, 10 September.

Block, Sheila. 2013. "Rising Inequality, Declining Health: Health Outcomes and the Working Poor." Wellesley Institute: http://www.wellesleyinstitute. com/wp-content/uploads/2013/07/Rising-Inequality-Declining-Health.pdf

Bohatyretz, Sandra, and Garth Lipps. 1999. "Diversity in the Classroom: Characteristics of Elementary Students Receiving Special Education." *Education Quarterly Review* 6, 2: 7–19. Statistics Canada Catalogue no. 81-003.

Bolaria, B. Singh, and Peter Li. 1988. "Capitalist Expansion and Immigrant Labour: Chinese in Canada." Chapter 5 in B. Singh Bolaria and Peter S. Li, eds, *Racial Oppression in Canada*, 2nd edn. Toronto: Garamond Press.

Bonilla-Silva, Eduardo. 1997. "Rethinking Racism: Toward a Structural Interpretation." *American Sociological Review* 62: 465–80.

———. 1999. "The Essential Social Fact of Race." *American Sociological Review* 64: 899–906.

Bookman, A., and D. Kimbrel. 2011. "Families and Elder Care in the Twenty-First Century." *The Future of Children/Center for the Future of Children, the David and Lucile Packard Foundation* 21, 2: 117–40.

Boothby, Daniel, and Torben Drewes. 2006. "Postsecondary Education in Canada: Returns to University, College and Trades Education." *Canadian Public Policy/Analyse de Politiques* 32, 1: 1–21.

Borrows, John. 2001. "Domesticating Doctrines: Aboriginal Peoples after the Royal Commission." *McGill Law Journal* 46: 615–61.

Bourbeau, Emmanuelle, Pierre Lefebvre, and Philip Merrigan. 2012. "The Evolution of the Returns to Education for 21- to 35- Year-Olds in Canada and across Provinces: Results from the 1991–2006 Analytical Census Files." *Canadian Public Policy* 38, 4: 1–19.

Bourdieu, Pierre. 1977. *Outline of a Theory of Practice*. Cambridge: Cambridge University Press.

———. 1985. "The Forms of Capital." Pp. 241–58 in J. C. Richardson, ed., *Handbook of Theory and Research for the Sociology of Education*. New York: Greenwood Press.

———. 1998. *Practical Reason: On the Theory of Action*. Stanford, CA: Stanford University Press.

Bowlby, Jeffrey W., and Kathryn McMullen. 2002. *At a Crossroads: First Results for the 18 to 20-Year-Old Cohort of the Youth in Transition Survey*. Catalogue no. RH64-12/2002E. Ottawa: Human Resources and Development Canada.

———. 2005. "Provincial Drop-out Rates: Trends and Consequences." *Education Matters: Insights on Education, Learning and Training in Canada* 2, 4. Statistics Canada Catalogue no. 81-004-XIE.

Boyd, Chris, Jina Y. Zhang-Salomons, Patti A. Groome, and William J. Mackillop. 1999. "Associations between Community Income and Cancer Survival in Ontario, Canada, and the United States." *Journal of Clinical Oncology* 17, 7: 2244–55.

Boyko, John. 1995. *Last Steps to Freedom: The Evolution of Canadian Racism*. Winnipeg: Watson and Dwyer.

Bradshaw, James. 2008. "Afrocentric Schools Not about Segregation, Advocates Argue." *Globe and Mail*, 8 February.

Brady, D. 2005. "The Welfare State and Relative Poverty in Rich Western Democracies, 1967–1997." *Social Forces* 83: 1329–64.

Braverman, Harry. 1974. *Labor and Monopoly Capital: The Degradation of Work in the Twentieth Century*. New York: Monthly Review Press.

Breen, Richard, and Jan O. Jonsson. 2005. "Inequality of Opportunity in Comparative Perspective: Recent Research on Educational Attainment and Social Mobility." *Annual Review of Sociology* 31: 223–43.

Breitkreuz, Rhonda S. 2005. "Engendering Citizenship? A Critical Feminist Analysis of Canadian Welfare-to-Work Policies and the Employment Experiences of Lone Mothers." *Journal of Sociology and Social Welfare* 32, 2: 147–65.

Brennan, Shannon. 2011. "Violent Victimization of Aboriginal Women in the Canadian Provinces, 2009." Statistics Canada Catalogue no. 85-002-X. http://www.statcan.gc.ca/pub/85-002-x/2011001/article/11439-eng.pdf

Briggs, N.C, R.S. Levine, H.I. Hall, O. Cosby, E.A., Brann, and C.H. Hennekens. 2003. "Occupational Risk Factors for Selected Cancers among African American and White Men in the United States." *American Journal of Public Health* 93, 10: 1748–52.

Broadbent Institute. 2012. *Toward a More Equal Canada: A Report on Canada's Economic and Social Inequality*. Retrieved 29 February 2016 from http://ywcacanada.ca/data/research_docs/00000292.pdf

Brodie, Janine. 1999. "Neo-liberalism and the Rise of the Citizen as Consumer." Chapter 2 in Dave Broad and Wayne Antony, eds, *Citizens or Consumers? Social Policy in a Market Society*. Halifax: Fernwood.

Brodie, Janine, and Isabella Bakker. 2007. *Canada's Social Policy Regime and Women: An Assessment of the Last Decade*. Ottawa: Status of Women.

Bruno-Jofre, Rosa, and Dick Henley. 2000. "Public Schooling in English Canada: Addressing Difference in the Context of Globalization." *Canadian Ethnic Studies* 32, 1: 38–54.

Bryant, Toba. 2004. "Housing and Health." Pp. 217–32 in Dennis Raphael, ed., *Social Determinants of Health: Canadian Perspectives*. Toronto: Canadian Scholars' Press.

Brzozowski, Jodi-Anne, Andrea Taylor-Butts, and Sara Johnson. 2006. "Victimization and Offending among the Aboriginal Population in Canada." *Juristat* 26, 3: 14. Statistics Canada Catalogue no. 85-002-XIE.

Buckley, Neil J., Frank T. Denton, A. Leslie Robb, and Byron G. Spencer. 2006. "Socio-economic

Influences on the Health of Older Canadians: Estimates Based on Two Longitudinal Surveys." *Canadian Public Policy* 32, 1: 59–83.

Burczycka, Marta, and Adam Cotter, 2011. "Shelters for Abused Women in Canada, 2010." Statistics Canada. Retrieved 22 April 2015 from http://www.statcan.gc.ca/pub/85-002-x/2011001/article/11495-eng.htm

Burton, Clare. 1985. *Subordination: Feminism and Social Theory.* Sydney, Australia: Allen and Unwin.

Burton, L.C., et al. 1995. "The Effect among Older Persons of a General Preventive Visit on Three Health Behaviors: Smoking, Excessive Alcohol Drinking, and Sedentary Lifestyle." *Preventive Medicine* 24, 5: 492–7.

Busby, Nicole. 2006. "Affirmative Action in Women's Employment: Lessons from Canada." *Journal of Law and Society* 33, 1: 42–58.

Bussière, Patrick, Tamara Knighton, and Dianne Pennock. 2007. *Measuring Up: Canadian Results of the OECD PISA Study: The Performance of Canada's Youth in Science, Reading and Mathematics.* Statistics Canada Catalogue no. 81-590-XPE, no. 3.

Butlin, George. 2001. "Bachelor's Graduates Who Pursue Further Postsecondary Education." *Education Quarterly Review* 7, 2: 22–42. Statistics Canada Catalogue no. 81-003.

Butlin, George, and Jillian Oderkirk. 1997. "Educational Attainment: A Key to Autonomy and Authority in the Workplace." *Education Quarterly Review* 4, 1: 32–52. Statistics Canada Catalogue no. 81-003.

Cairney, John, and Robert Arnold. 1996. "Social Class, Health and Aging: Socioeconomic Determinants of Self-Reported Morbidity among the Non-institutionalized Elderly in Canada." *Canadian Journal of Public Health* 87, 3: 199–203.

Calasanti, Toni M. 1996. "Incorporating Diversity: Meaning, Levels of Research, and Implications for Theory." *The Gerontologist* 36: 147–56.

———. 2004. "Feminist Gerontology and Old Men." *Journals of Gerontology, Social Sciences* 59B, 6: S305–14.

Calasanti, Toni M., and Kathleen E. Slevin. 2001. *Gender, Social Inequalities, and Aging.* Walnut Creek, CA: Altamira Press.

———. 2006. *Age Matters: Realigning Feminist Thinking.* New York: Routledge.

Calliste, Agnes. 1996. "Race, Gender and Canadian Immigration Policy: Blacks from the Caribbean, 1900–1932." Pp. 80–98 in Joy Parr and Mark Rosenfeld, eds, *Gender and History in Canada.* Toronto: Copp Clark.

———. 2001. "Black Families in Canada: Exploring the Interconnections of Race, Class, and Gender." Chapter 26 in Bonnie J. Fox, ed., *Family Patterns, Gender Relations.* Toronto: Oxford University Press.

Campaign 2000. 2007. *2007 Report Card on Child and Family Poverty in Canada.* Toronto: Family Service Association of Toronto. www.campaign2000.ca

Canada's Public Policy Forum. 2014. "Schizophrenia in Canada: The Social and Economic Case for a Collaborative Model of Care." *Canada's Public Policy Forum*, Retrieved 29 February 2016 from https://www.ppforum.ca/sites/default/files/Schizophrenia%20in%20Canada%20-%20Final%20report.pdf

Canadian Cancer Statistics. 2015. *Special Topics: Predictions of the Future Burden of Cancer in Canada.* Retrieved 29 February 2016 from https://www.cancer.ca/~/media/cancer.ca/CW/cancer%20information/cancer%20101/Canadian%20cancer%20statistics/Canadian-Cancer-Statistics-2015-EN.pdf

Canadian Council on Learning (CCL). 2007. *Postsecondary Education in Canada: Strategies for Success: Report on Learning in Canada 2007.* Ottawa: CCL.

———. 2008. "High School Drop-out Rate." *Learning to Know CLI Indicator Fact Sheets.* Ottawa: Canadian Council on Learning. www.ccl-cca.ca.

Canadian Council on Social Development. 2007a. *Age, Gender and Family: Urban Poverty in Canada, 2000.* Ottawa: CCSD. http://www.ccsd.ca/pubs/2007/upp/age_gender_family.pdf.

———. 2007b. "Economic Security Fact Sheet #2: Poverty." Ottawa: CCSD. Retrieved January 2008 from http://www.ccsd.ca/factsheets/economic_security/poverty/index.htm

Canadian Federation for Sexual Health. 2008. "Bill C484 'Unborn Victims of Crime Act' Position Statement." http://www.cfsh.ca/About_CFSH/Positions-Statements/C-484.html

Canadian Federation of Students. 2013. *Student Debt in Canada: Education Shouldn't Be a Debt*

Sentence. Retrieved 24 February 2015 from http://cfs-fcee.ca/wp-content/uploads/sites/2/2013/11/Factsheet-2013-11-Student-Debt-EN.pdf

Canadian Incidence Study (CIS) of Reported Child Abuse and Neglect. 2008. Major. Retrieved 23 February 2016 from http://cwrp.ca/sites/default/files/publications/en/CIS-2008-rprt-eng.pdf

Canadian Institute for Health Information (CIHI). 2004. *Improving the Health of Canadians.* Ottawa: CIHI.

———. 2006a. *How Healthy Are Rural Canadians: An Assessment of Their Health Status and Health Determinants.* Ottawa: CIHI.

———. 2006b. *Improving the Health of Canadians: An Introduction to Health in Urban Places.* Ottawa: CIHI.

———. 2007. *Improving the Health of Canadians: Mental Health and Homelessness.* Ottawa: CIHI.

———. 2008. *Health Indicators 2008.* Ottawa: CIHI.

Canadian Policy Research Networks (CPRN). 2002. *Access to Postsecondary Education in Canada: Fact and Gaps.* Prepared by Sussex Circle Inc. Ottawa: CPRN. http://www.cprn.org/doc.cfm?doc=59&l=en

Canadian Population Health Initiative. 2007. *Proceedings Report: Reducing Gaps in Health: Knowledge Synthesis, Translation and Exchange.* Ottawa: Canadian Institute for Health Information.

Cancian, Francesca M., and Stacey Oliker. 2000. *Caring and Gender.* Walnut Creek, CA: Altamira Press.

Caro, Daniel H., James Ted McDonald, and J. Douglas Willms. 2009. "Socio-economic Status and Academic Trajectories from Childhood to Adolescence." *Canadian Journal of Education* 32, 3: 558–90.

Carr, Paul R., and Thomas R. Klassen. 1996. "The Role of Racial Minority Teachers in Anti-racist Education." *Canadian Ethnic Studies* 28, 2: 126–38.

Carrier, Patricia Anne, and Lorraine Davies. 1999. "The Importance of Power Relations for the Division of Household Labour." *Canadian Journal of Sociology* 24, 1: 35–51.

Casper, Lynne M., Sara S. McLanahan, and Irwin Garfinkel. 1994. "The Gender-Poverty Gap: What We Can Learn from Other Countries." *American Sociological Review* 59: 594–605.

Casper, Monica J. 1998. *The Making of the Unborn Patient: A Social Anatomy of Fetal Surgery.* New Brunswick, NJ: Rutgers University Press.

Cassell, Philip, ed. 1993. *The Giddens Reader.* Stanford, CA: Stanford University Press.

CCL. *See* Canadian Council on Learning.

CCSD. *See* Canadian Council on Social Development.

Chae, David H., David T. Takeuchi, Elizabeth M. Barbeau, Gary G. Bennett, Jane Lindsey, and Nancy Krieger. 2008. "Unfair Treatment, Racial/Ethnic Discrimination, Ethnic Identification, and Smoking among Asian Americans in the National Latino and Asian American Study." *American Journal of Public Health* 98, 3: 485–92.

Chafetz, Janet Saltzman. 1990. *Gender Equity: An Integrated Theory of Stability and Change.* Newbury Park, NJ: Sage.

Charness, N., K. Dykstra, and C. Philips. 1995. "Luminance and Legibility in the Workplace." Paper presented to the Canadian Aging Research Network 5th Annual Colloquium, Toronto.

Chen, Edith. 2004. "Why Socioeconomic Status Affects the Health of Children: A Psychosocial Perspective." *Current Directions in Psychological Science* 13, 3: 112–15.

Chen, Edith, and Gregory E. Miller. 2013. "Socioeconomic Status and Health: Mediating and Moderating Factors." *Annual Review of Clinical Psychology* 9, 1: 723–49.

Chen, Jiajian, and Feng Hou. 2002. "Unmet Needs for Health Care." *Health Reports* 13, 2: 23–33. Statistics Canada Catalogue no. 82-003.

Chen, Jiajian, Edward Ng, and Russell Wilkins. 1996. "The Health of Canada's Immigrants in 1994–95." *Health Reports* 7, 4: 33–45. Statistics Canada Catalogue no. 82-003.

Chen, Jiajian, Russell Wilkins, and Edward Ng. 1996. "Health Expectancy by Immigrant Status, 1986 and 1991." *Health Reports* 8, 3: 29–37. Statistics Canada Catalogue no. 82-003.

Childs, S., R. Finnie, and R. E. Mueller. 2010. "Family Environment, Family Habits, and Children's Cultural Experiences: Is There a Link to Participation in Post-secondary Education?" Pp. 243–65 in *Pursuing Higher Education in Canada: Economic, Social, and Policy Dimensions.* Montreal and Kingston: McGill-Queen's University Press.

Chin, T. 2000. "'Sixth Grade Madness': Parental Emotion Work in the Private High School Application Process." *Journal of Contemporary Ethnography* 29, 2: 124–63.

Chung, Lucy. 2006. "Education and Earnings." *Perspectives on Labour and Income.* Statistics Canada Catalogue no. 75-001-XIE.

Chunn, D.E. 2000. "'Politicizing the Personal': Feminism, Law, and Public Policy." Pp. 225–59 in Nancy Mandell and Ann Duffy, eds, *Canadian Families: Diversity, Conflict and Change,* 2nd edn. Toronto: Harcourt, Brace.

Church, Elizabeth. 2000. "Balancing Work and Family: Firms Still Struggling with How to Help Workers Who Care for Others." *Globe and Mail,* 28 June.

CIHI. *See* Canadian Institute for Health Information.

CIS. *See* Canadian Incidence Study.

Citizens for Public Justice (CPJ). 2010. "Bearing the Brunt: How the 2008–2009 Recession Created Poverty for Canadian Families." http://www.cpj.ca/files/docs/Bearing_the_Brunt.pdf

———. 2012. "Poverty Trends Scorecard." Accessed 10 February 2016 from http://www.cpj.ca/files/docs/poverty-trends-scorecard.pdf

———. 2013. "Poverty Trends Highlights: Canada 2013." Accessed 1 March 2016 from http://www.cpj.ca/files/docs/Poverty-Trends-Highlights-2013.pdf

Citizenship and Immigration Canada. 2011. "Portrait of an Integration Process." Retrieved 7 May 2015 from http://www.cic.gc.ca/english/resources/research/integration/6-health-care.asp

———. 2014. "2014 Annual Report to Parliament on Immigration." Retrieved 22 April 2015 from http://www.cic.gc.ca/english/resources/publications/annual-report-2014/index.asp

Clark, Warren. 2000. "'Education' in 100 Years of. . . ." *Canadian Social Trends* 58: 3–6. Statistics Canada Catalogue no. 11-008.

———. 2001. "100 Years of Education." *Education Quarterly Review* 7, 3: 18–24. Statistics Canada Catalogue no. 81-003.

———. 2014. "Canadian Social Trends: Delayed Transitions of Young Adults." Retrieved 28 May 2015 from http://www.statcan.gc.ca/pub/11-008-x/2007004/10311-eng.htm

Clarke, T.N., and S.M. Lipset. 1991. "Are Social Classes Dying?" *International Sociology* 6: 397–410.

CLC. *See* Canadian Labour Congress.

Clement, Wallace, and John Myles. 1994. *Relations of Ruling: Class and Gender in Postindustrial Societies.* Montreal and Kingston: McGill-Queen's University Press.

Coates, K.S., and B. Morrison. 2013. *Campus Confidential: 100 Startling Things You Don't Know about Canadian Universities.* Toronto: Lorimer.

Codjoe, Henry M. 2001. "Fighting a 'Public Enemy' of Black Academic Achievement: The Persistence of Racism and the Schooling Experiences of Black Students in Canada." *Race, Ethnicity, and Education* 4: 343–75.

Collective for Research and Training on Development–Action (CRTD.A). 2004. *Denial of Nationality: The Case of Arab Women.* Gender, Citizenship, and Nationality Programme. Summary of regional research. Retrieved 28 February 2016 from http://www.pogar.org/publications/gender/nationality/crtdesum.pdf

Collins, Patricia Hill. 1990. *Black Feminist Thought: Knowledge, Consciousness, and the Politics of Empowerment.* Boston: Unwin Hyman.

———. 2000. *Black Feminist Thought: Knowledge, Consciousness, and the Politics of Empowerment,* 2nd edn. New York: Routledge.

Coltrane, Scott. 2000. *Gender and Families.* Walnut Creek, CA: Altamira Press.

Comacchio, Cynthia. 1993. *Nations Are Built of Babies: Saving Ontario's Mothers and Children, 1900–1940.* Montreal and Kingston: McGill-Queen's University Press.

Conference Board of Canada. 2015. "HPP_Health." *Tableau Software.* Retrieved 5 May 2015 from http://public.tableau.com/views/HPP_Health/Infant_dash?:embed=y&:showVizHome=no&:host_url=https%3A%2F%2Fpublic.tableausoftware.com%2F&:tabs=no&:toolbar=yes&:animate_transition=yes&:display_static_image=yes&:display_spinner=yes&:display_overlay=yes&:display_count=yes&:showVizHome=no&:loadOrderID=0

Conley, James. 1999. "Working-Class Formation in Twentieth-Century Canada." Chapter 3 in James E. Curtis, Edward G. Grabb, and Neil L. Guppy, eds, *Social Inequality in Canada: Patterns, Problems, and Policies*. Scarborough, ON: Prentice Hall Allyn and Bacon Canada.

Connell, Raewyn. 2012. "Gender, Health and Theory: Conceptualizing the Issue, in Local and World Perspective." *Social Science & Medicine* 74, 11: 1675–83.

Connidis, Ingrid Arnet. 1982. "Women and Retirement: The Effect of Multiple Careers on Retirement Adjustment." *Canadian Journal on Aging* 1, 3/4: 17–27.

———. 2009. *Family Ties and Aging*, 2nd edn. Thousand Oaks, CA: Sage.

Connidis, Ingrid Arnet, and Julie Ann McMullin. 1994. "Social Support in Older Age: Assessing the Impact of Marital and Parent Status." *Canadian Journal on Aging* 13, 4: 510–27.

———. 2002. "Sociological Ambivalence and Family Ties: A Critical Perspective." *Journal of Marriage and Family* 64, 3: 558–67.

Conrad, Peter. 2007. *The Medicalization of Society: On the Transformation of Human Conditions into Treatable Disorders*. Baltimore, MD: Johns Hopkins University Press.

Cooke, M. 2005. "Trajectories through Lone Motherhood, Social Assistance, and Work." Paper presented to the annual meeting of the Canadian Anthropology and Sociology Association, 31 May–3 June, London, ON.

Cooper, Helen. 2002. "Investigating Socio-economic Explanations for Gender and Ethnic Inequalities in Health." *Social Science and Medicine* 54, 5: 693–706.

Cooper, H., B. Nye, K. Charlton, J. Lindsay, and S. Greathouse. 1996. "The Effects of Summer Vacation on Achievement Test Scores: A Narrative and Meta-Analytic Review." *Review of Educational Research* 66, 3: 227–68.

Corak, Miles. 2006. "Do Poor Children Become Poor Adults? Lessons from a Cross Country Comparison of Generational Earnings Mobility." *Research on Economic Inequality* 13, 1: 143–88.

Cornish, Mary. 2014. *A Growing Concern: Ontario's Gender Pay Gap*. Retrieved 23 February 2016 from https://www.policyalternatives.ca/sites/default/files/uploads/publications/National%20Office,%20Ontario%20Office/2014/04/Ont_Equal_Pay_Day.pdf

Côté, James E. 2000. *Arrested Adulthood: The Changing Nature of Maturity and Identity*. New York: New York University Press.

Côté, James E., and Anton L. Allahar. 1994. *Generation on Hold: Coming of Age in the Late Twentieth Century*. Toronto: Stoddart.

———. 2006. *Critical Youth Studies: A Canadian Focus*. Toronto: Pearson Prentice Hall.

Cott, Nancy F. 2001. "Domesticity." Chapter 9 in Bonnie J. Fox, ed., *Family Patterns, Gender Relations*. Toronto: Oxford University Press.

Courtenay, Will H. 2000. "Constructions of Masculinity and Their Influence on Men's Well-Being: A Theory of Gender and Health." *Social Science and Medicine* 50, 10: 1385–401.

CPJ. *See* Citizens for Public Justice.

CPRN. *See* Canadian Policy Research Networks.

Craig, Gerald. 1968. *Upper Canada: The Formative Years—1784–1841*. Toronto: McClelland & Stewart.

Crane, David. 2008. "A Painful Time for Canada's Industrial Sector." *Toronto Star*, 17 February.

Creese, Gillian. 1996. "Gendering Collective Bargaining: From Men's Rights to Women's Issues." *Canadian Review of Sociology and Anthropology* 33, 4: 437–56.

———. 1999. *Contracting Masculinity: Gender, Class, and Race in a White-Collar Union, 1944–1994*. Toronto: Oxford University Press.

Crocker, D., A. Dobrowolsky, E. Keeble, C.C. Moncayo, and E. Tastsoglou. 2007. *Security and Immigration, Changes and Challenges: Immigrant and Ethnic Communities in Atlantic Canada, Presumed Guilty?* Ottawa: Status of Women.

Crompton, Susan. 2000. "'Health' in 100 Years of . . ." *Canadian Social Trends*, Winter: 12–17. Statistics Canada Catalogue no. 11-008.

CRTD.A. *See* Collective for Research and Training on Development–Action.

Cruz, Grace T., Josefina N. Natividad, and Yashuiko Saito. 2007. "Active Life Expectancy and Functional Health Transition among Filipino Older People." *Canadian Studies in Population* 34, 1: 29–47.

Curtis, Bruce, D.W. Livingstone, and David Smaller. 1992. *Stacking the Deck: The Streaming of Working-Class Kids in Ontario Schools*. Toronto: Our Schools/Our Selves Education Foundation.

Curtis, James E., Edward G. Grabb, and Neil L. Guppy, eds. 2003. *Social Inequality in Canada: Patterns, Problems, and Policies*, 4th edn. Scarborough, ON: Pearson Education Canada.

Curtis, Josh. 2013. "Middle Class Identification in the Modern World: How Politics and Economics Matter." *Canadian Review of Sociology* 50: 203–26.

Curtis, Josh, and Julie McMullin. 2016. "Income Inequality and the Privatization of Retirement Income, 1991–2011." Working Paper.

Curtis, Lori J., and William J. MacMinn. 2008. "Health Care Utilization in Canada: Twenty-Five Years of Evidence." *Canadian Public Policy* 34, 1: 65–87.

Curtis, Lori J., and Michael Pennock. 2006. "Social Assistance, Lone Parents and Health: What Do We Know, Where Do We Go?" *Canadian Journal of Public Health* 97, suppl. 3: 4–10.

Curtis, Sarah, and Kim Lawson. 2000. "Gender, Ethnicity and Self-Reported Health: The Case of African-Caribbean Populations in London." *Social Science and Medicine* 50, 3: 365–85.

Dannefer, D. 1984. "Adult Development and Social Theory: A Paradigmatic Reappraisal." *American Sociological Review* 49: 100–16.

Dannefer, D., and R.R. Sell. 1988. "Age Structure, the Life Course, and Aged Heterogeneity: Prospects for Research and Theory." *Comprehensive Gerontology* B2: 1–10.

Das Gupta, Tania. 1995. "Families of Native Peoples, Immigrants, and People of Colour." Pp. 141–74 in Nancy Mandell and Ann Duffy, eds, *Canadian Families: Diversity, Conflict and Change*. Toronto: Harcourt, Brace.

———. 1996. *Racism and Paid Work*. Toronto: Garamond Press.

———. 2000. "Families of Native Peoples, Immigrants and People of Colour." Pp. 215–30 in Barbara A. Crow and Lise Gotell, eds, *Open Boundaries: A Canadian Women's Studies Reader*. Toronto: Prentice Hall.

———. 2002. "Racism in Nursing." Chapter 5 in Merle Jacobs, ed., *Is Anyone Listening? Women, Work, and Society*. Toronto: Women's Press.

Davies, Lorraine, Marilyn Ford-Gilboe, and Joanne Hammerton. 2009. "Gender Inequality and Patterns of Abuse Post Leaving." *Journal of Family Violence* 24, 1: 27–39.

Davies, Lorraine, and Donna D. McAlpine. 1998. "Gendered Work and Family Relations: The Impact of Unemployment." Paper presented to Restructuring Work and the Life Course: An International Symposium, Toronto, May.

Davies, Lorraine, Julie Ann McMullin, and William R. Avison. 2001. *Social Policy, Gender Inequality and Poverty*. Ottawa: Status of Women Canada.

Davies, Scott. 1995. "Leaps of Faith: Shifting Currents in Critical Sociology of Education." *American Journal of Sociology* 100, 6: 1448–78.

Davies, S., and J. Aurini. 2013. "Summer Learning Inequality in Ontario." *Canadian Public Policy* 39, 2: 287–307.

Davies, Scott, and Neil Guppy. 1997. "Fields of Study, College Selectivity, and Student Inequalities." *Social Forces* 73, 4: 131–51.

———. 2006. *The Schooled Society: An Introduction to the Sociology of Education*. Don Mills, ON: Oxford University Press.

———. 2014. *The Schooled Society: An Introduction to the Sociology of Education*, 3rd edn. Don Mills, ON: Oxford University Press.

Davies, Scott, and Magdalena Janus. 2009. *A Systematic Review of the Longitudinal Impact of Family SES on Child Cognition and Social Emotional Well Being*. Report to Human Resources and Social Development Canada (HRSDC). Ottawa.

Davies, Scott, Clayton Mosher, and Bill O'Grady. 1996. "Educating Women: Gender Inequalities among Canadian University Graduates." *Canadian Review of Sociology and Anthropology* 33, 2: 127–43.

Davis, Kingsley, and Wilbert E. Moore. 1945. "Some Principles of Stratification." *American Sociological Review* 10: 242–9.

Dean, Kathryn. 1992. "Double Burdens of Work: The Female Work and Health Paradox." *Health Promotion International* 7, 1: 17–25.

Dei, George J. Sefa. 1993. "The Challenges of Anti-racist Education in Canada." *Canadian Ethnic Studies* 25, 2: 36–51.

———. 1996. *Anti-racism Education: Theory and Practice*. Halifax: Fernwood.

———. 2006. "Black-Focused Schools: A Call for Re-visioning." *Education Canada* 46, 3: 27–31.

DeKeseredy, W.S., and M.D. Schwartz. 1998. *Women Abuse on Campus: Results from the Canadian National Survey.* Thousand Oaks, CA: Sage.

Dekkers, Midas. 2000. *The Way of All Flesh: A Celebration of Decay.* Translated by Sherry Marx-Macdonald. New York: Farrar, Straus, and Giroux.

Denton, F.T., Steven Prus, and Vivienne Walters. 2004. "Gender Differences in Health: A Canadian Study of the Psychosocial, Behavioural and Structural Determinants of Health." *Social Science and Medicine* 58: 2585–600.

Denton, Margaret, and Linda Boos. 2007. "The Gender Wealth Gap: Structural and Material Constraints and Implications for Later Life." *Journal of Women & Aging* 19, 3–4: 105–20.

deRouche, Constance P. 2001. "Workfare's Cousin: Exploring a Labour-Force Enhancement Experiment in Cape Breton." *Canadian Review of Sociology and Anthropology* 38, 3: 309–35.

DesMeules, Marie, Douglas Manuel, and Robert Cho. 2003. "Mortality: Life and Health Expectancy of Canadian Women." Chapter 8 in *Women's Health Surveillance Report: A Multidimensional Look at the Health of Canadian Women.* Ottawa: Canadian Institute for Health Information.

Dickason, Olive Patricia. 2006. *A Concise History of Canada's First Nations.* Toronto: Oxford University Press.

DiMaggio, P. 1982. "Cultural Capital and School Success: The Impact of Status Culture Participation on the Grades of US High School Students." *American Sociological Review* 47, 2: 189–201.

Dinnerstein, Myra, and Rose Weitz. 1998. "Jane Fonda, Barbara Bush, and Other Aging Bodies: Femininity and the Limits of Resistance." Chapter 14 in Rose Weitz, ed., *The Politics of Women's Bodies: Sexuality, Appearance, and Behavior.* New York: Oxford University Press.

Dobrowolsky, Alexandra, and Jane Jenson. 2004. "Shifting Representations of Citizenship: Canadian Politics of 'Women' and 'Children.'" *Social Politics* 11, 2: 154–80.

Doucet, Andrea. 2006. *Do Men Mother? Fathering, Care, and Domestic Responsibility.* Toronto: University of Toronto Press.

Dowd, J.J. 1980. *Stratification among the Aged.* Monterey, CA: Brooks/Cole.

———. 1987. "The Reification of Age: Age Stratification and the Passing of the Autonomous Subject." *Journal of Aging Studies* 1: 317–35.

Drolet, Marie. 2005. "Participation in Post-secondary Education in Canada: Has the Role of Parental Income and Education Changed over the 1990s?" Ottawa: Statistics Canada.

Dryburgh, H. 2000. "Women and Computer Science: Alternative Routes to Computing Careers." PhD dissertation, McMaster University.

Dua, Enakshi. 1999. "Beyond Diversity: Exploring the Ways in Which the Discourse of Race Has Shaped the Institution of the Nuclear Family." Chapter 10 in E. Dua and A. Robertson, eds, *Scratching the Surface: Canadian, Anti-racist, Feminist Thought.* Toronto: Women's Press.

———. 2005. "Beyond Diversity: Exploring the Ways in Which the Discourse of Race Has Shaped the Institution of the Nuclear Family." In V. Zawilski and C. Levine-Rasky, eds, *Inequality in Canada: A Reader on the Intersections of Gender, Race, and Class.* Toronto: Oxford University Press.

Dunlop, Sheryl, Peter C. Coyte, and Warren McIsaac. 2000. "Socio-economic Status and the Utilization of Physician's Services: Results from the Canadian National Population Health Survey." *Social Science and Medicine* 51, 1: 123–33.

Dunn, James R., and Isabel Dyck. 2000. "Social Determinants of Health in Canada's Immigrant Population: Results from the National Population Health Survey." *Social Science and Medicine* 51, 11: 1573–93.

Duranceau, Richard, and Derek McCall. 2007. "Setting the Stage: The Influence of Place on Health." *Health Policy Research Bulletin* 14: 6–9.

Duxbury, Linda, and Chris Higgins. 2013. *Balancing Work, Childcare, and Eldercare: A View from the Trenches.* Report for Desjardins Insurance. Retrieved 25 November 2015 from https://www.desjardinslifeinsurance.com/en/about-us/Documents/RapportDuxbury-ENG-Full-Web.pdf

Easterlin, R.A. 1987. *Birth and Fortune: The Impact of Numbers on Personal Welfare,* 2nd edn. Chicago: University of Chicago Press.

Economic and Social Research Council. 2013. "Poverty and Social Exclusion in the UK." Retrieved 18 February 2016 from http://www.poverty.ac.uk/sites/default/files/attachments/WP%20Methods%20No%2023%20-%20Disabled%20People%20%28Heslop%202013%29.pdf

Edgell, Stephen. 1993. *Class: Key Ideas*. London: Routledge.

Egan, Carolyn, and Linda Gardner. 1999. "Racism, Women's Health, and Reproductive Freedom." Chapter 25 in E. Dua and A. Robertson, eds, *Scratching the Surface: Canadian, Anti-racist, Feminist Thought*. Toronto: Women's Press.

Ehrenreich, Barbara, and John Ehrenreich. 1979. "The Professional Managerial Class." In *Between Labor and Capital*, edited by Pat Walker, 5–45. Boston: South End.

Eichler, Margrit. 1988. *Families in Canada Today: Recent Changes and Their Policy Consequences*, 2nd edn. Toronto: Gage.

Eichler, Margrit, and Patrizia Albanese. 2007. "What Is Household Work? A Critique of Assumptions Underlying Empirical Studies of Housework and an Alternative Approach." *Canadian Journal of Sociology/Cahiers canadiens de sociologie* 32, 2: 227–58.

Elder, Glenn H., Jr. 1974. *Children of the Great Depression: Social Change in Life Experience*. Chicago: University of Chicago Press.

———. 1985. *Life Course Dynamics: Trajectories and Transitions, 1968–80*. Ithaca, NY: Cornell University Press.

———. 1994. "Time, Human Agency, and Social Change: Perspectives on the Life Course." *Social Psychology Quarterly* 57: 4–15.

———. 1995. "The Life Course Paradigm: Social Change and Individual Development." Chapter 4 in Phyllis Moen, Glenn H. Elder, Jr, and Kurt Luscher, eds, *Examining Lives in Context: Perspectives on the Ecology of Human Development*. Washington, DC: American Psychological Association Press.

Elder, Glenn H., Jr, and Angela M. O'Rand. 1995. "Adult Lives in a Changing Society." Pp. 452–75 in Karen Cook, Gary Fine, and James S. House, eds, *Sociological Perspectives on Social Psychology*. New York: Allyn and Bacon.

Elder, G.H., Jr, and R.C. Rockwell. 1976. "Marital Age in Life Patterns." *Journal of Family History* 1: 34–53.

Ellwood, Wayne. 2001. *The No-Nonsense Guide to Globalization*. Toronto: New Internationalist Publications/Between the Lines.

Elstad, Jon Ivar. 1995. "Employment Status and Women's Health: Exploring the Dynamics." *Acta Sociologica* 38: 231–49.

Employment and Social Development Canada. 2014. "II. Assisting Canadians during Unemployment: EI Regular Benefits." Retrieved 22 April 2015 from http://www.esdc.gc.ca/en/reports/ei/monitoring2013/chapter2_2.page#h3-1.4

Entwisle, D.R. 1997. *Children, Schools, and Inequality*. Social Inequality Series: ERIC.

Entwisle, D.R., and K.L. Alexander. 1992. "Summer Setback: Race, Poverty, School Composition, and Mathematics Achievement in the First Two Years of School." *American Sociological Review* 57, 1: 72–84.

Erickson, Robert, and John Goldthorpe. 1992. *The Constant Flux: A Study of Class Mobility in Industrial Societies*. Oxford, UK: Clarendon Press.

Erickson, Robert, John Goldthorpe, and Lucien Portocarrero. 1979. "Intergenerational Mobility in Three Western European Societies: England, France, and Sweden." *British Journal of Sociology* 33: 1–34.

Erwin, Lorna, and Paula Maurutto. 1998. "Beyond Access: Considering Gender Deficits in Science Education." *Gender and Education* 10, 1: 51–69.

ESRC. *See* Economic and Social Research Council.

Essed, Philomena. 1991. *Understanding Everyday Racism: An Interdisciplinary Theory*. Newbury Park, CA: Sage.

Estes, C.L. 1979. *The Aging Enterprise*. San Francisco: Jossey-Bass.

———. 1991. "The New Political Economy of Aging: Introduction and Critique." Chapter 2 in M. Minkler and C. Estes, eds, *Critical Perspectives on Aging: The Political and Moral Economy of Growing Old*. Amityville, NY: Baywood.

———. 1999. "The New Political Economy of Aging: Introduction and Critique." Chapter 1 in M. Minkler and C. Estes, eds, *Critical Gerontology*. Amityville, NY: Baywood.

Estes, C.L., K.W. Linkins, and E.A. Binney. 1996. "The Political Economy of Aging." Chapter 18 in R.H. Binstock and L.K. George, eds, *Handbook of Aging and the Social Sciences*, 4th edn. San Diego, CA: Academic Press.

Estes, C.L., J.H. Swan, and L.E. Gerard. 1982. "Dominant and Competing Paradigms in Gerontology: Towards a Political Economy of Ageing." *Aging and Society* 12: 151–64.

Evans, Patricia M. 1997. "Divided Citizenship? Gender, Income Security, and the Welfare State." Chapter 4 in Patricia M. Evans and Gerda R. Wekerle, eds, *Women and the Canadian Welfare State: Challenges and Change*. Toronto: University of Toronto Press.

———. 2007. "(Not) Taking Account of Precarious Employment: Workfare Policies and Lone Mothers in Ontario and the UK." *Social Policy & Administration* 41, 1: 29–49.

Fallo-Mitchell, L., and C.D. Ryff. 1982. "Preferred Timing of Female Life Events: Cohort Differences." *Research on Aging* 4: 249–67.

Farran, Sandy. 2006. "The Average Student: SWF, 22, Some Debt, Seeks Degree, Job." *Maclean's*, 26 June.

Ferguson, Lucinda. 2007. "Uncertainty and Indecision in the Legal Regulation of Children: The Albertan Experience." *Canadian Journal of Family Law* 23, 2: 159–214.

Fillion, Kate. 2007. "Housework Doesn't Pay: Leslie Bennet, Author of *The Feminine Mistake*, Talks to Kate Fillion about Women's Risks, Assets and Delusions." *Maclean's*, 7 May.

Finch, Janet. 1989. *Family Obligations and Social Change*. Cambridge, UK: Basil Blackwell.

Fincham, S.M., A.M. Ugnat, G.B. Hill, N. Krieger, and Y. Mao. 2000. "Is Occupation a Risk Factor for Thyroid Cancer?" *Journal of Occupational and Environmental Medicine* 42, 3: 318–22.

Findlay, Leanne C., and Dafna E. Kohen. 2012. "Leave Practices of Parents after the Birth or Adoption of Young Children." Retrieved 23 February 2016 from http://www.statcan.gc.ca/pub/11-008-x/2012002/article/11697-eng.pdf

Findlay, Deborah A., and Leslie J. Miller. 2002. "Through Medical Eyes: The Medicalization of Women's Bodies and Women's Lives." Chapter 13 in B. Singh Bolaria and H. Dickinson, eds, *Health, Illness, and Health Care in Canada*. Toronto: Nelson.

Finnie, Ross. 2000. "Holding Their Own: Employment and Earnings of Postsecondary Graduates." *Education Quarterly Review* 7, 1: 21–37. Statistics Canada Catalogue no. 81-003.

———. 2002. "Student Loans: Borrowing and Burden." *Education Quarterly Review* 8, 4: 28–42. Statistics Canada Catalogue no. 81-003.

Finnie, Ross, Eric Lascelles, and Arthur Sweetman. 2005. *Who Goes? The Direct and Indirect Effects of Family Background on Access to Post-secondary Education*. Analytical Studies Branch Research Paper Series. Statistics Canada Catalogue no. 11F0019MIE2005237.

Finnie, Ross, and Richard E. Mueller, 2008. "The Effects of Family Income, Parental Education and Other Background Factors on Access to Post-Secondary Education in Canada." In *Measuring the Effectiveness of Student Aid* (MESA). Educational Policy Institute: Queen's University.

Firestone, Shulamith. 1971. *The Dialectic of Sex*. New York: Bantam Books.

Fleras, Augie, and Jean Leonard Elliott. 2007. *Unequal Relations: An Introduction to Race, Ethnic, and Aboriginal Dynamics in Canada*. Toronto: Pearson, Prentice Hall.

Foner, Anne. 1974. "Age Stratification and Age Conflict in Political Life." *American Journal of Sociology* 83: 1081–104.

———. 1986. *Aging and Old Age: New Perspectives*. Englewood Cliffs, NJ: Prentice Hall.

Foner, Anne, and Karen Schwab. 1981. *Aging and Retirement*. Monterey, CA: Brooks/Cole.

Fortin, Nicole, Philip Oreopoulos, and Shelley Phipps. 2013. "Leaving Boys Behind: Gender Disparities in High Academic Achievement." Working Paper. http://faculty.arts.ubc.ca/nfortin/LeavingBoysBehind.pdf

Fortner, Brian. 2007. "Raise Kids Like a Man." *Men's Health*, June.

Fox, Bonnie J. 1988. "Conceptualizing 'Patriarchy.'" *Canadian Review of Sociology and Anthropology* 25: 163–81.

———. 1989. "The Feminist Challenge: A Reconsideration of Social Inequality and Economic Development." Chapter 5 in R.J. Brym and B.J. Fox, eds, *From Culture to Power: The Sociology of English Canada*. Toronto: Oxford University Press.

———. 2001. "The Formative Years: How Parenthood Creates Gender." *Canadian Review of Sociology and Anthropology* 38, 4: 373–90.

———, ed. 2001. *Family Patterns, Gender Relations*, 2nd edn. Toronto: Oxford University Press.

———. 2009. *When Couples Become Parents: The Creation of Gender in the Transition to Parenthood*. Toronto: University of Toronto Press.

Fox, Bonnie, and Meg Luxton. 2001. "Conceptualizing Family." Chapter 3 in Bonnie Fox, ed., *Family Patterns, Gender Relations*, 2nd edn. Toronto: Oxford University Press.

Frenette, Marc. 2000. "Overqualified? Recent Graduates and the Needs of Their Employers." *Education Quarterly Review* 7, 1: 6–20. Statistics Canada Catalogue no. 81-003.

———. 2005. *The Impact of Tuition Fees on University Access: Evidence from a Large-Scale Price Deregulation in Professional Programs*. Analytical Studies Branch Research Paper Series. Statistics Canada Catalogue no. 11F0019, no. 263.

———. 2007. *Why Are Youth from Lower-Income Families Less Likely to Attend University? Evidence from Academic Abilities, Parental Abilities, and Financial Constraints*. Analytical Studies Branch Research Paper Series. Statistics Canada Catalogue no. 11F0019MIE2007295.

Frenette, Marc, and Simon Coulombe. 2007. *Has Higher Education among Young Women Substantially Reduced the Gender Gap in Employment and Earnings?* Analytical Studies Branch Research Paper Series. Statistics Canada Catalogue no. 11F0019MIE2007301.

Frenette, Marc, and Klarka Zeman. 2007. *Why Are Most University Students Women? Evidence Based on Academic Performance, Study Habits and Parental Influences*. Analytical Studies Branch Research Paper Series. Statistics Canada Catalogue no. 11F0019MIE, no. 303.

Frideres, James S. 1988. "Institutional Structures and Economic Deprivation: Native People in Canada." Chapter 4 in B. Singh Bolaria and Peter S. Li, eds, *Racial Oppression in Canada*, 2nd edn. Toronto: Garamond Press.

Frideres, James S., and René R. Gadacz. 2008. *Aboriginal Peoples in Canada: Contemporary Conflicts*, 8th edn. Toronto: Pearson Education Canada.

Frohlich, Katherine L., and Louise Potvin. 2008. "The Inequality Paradox: The Population Approach and Vulnerable Populations." *American Journal of Public Health* 98, 2: 216–21.

Fry, Christine L. 1976. "The Ages of Adulthood: A Question of Numbers." *Journal of Gerontology* 3: 199–217.

———. 1980. "Cultural Dimensions of Age: A Multidimensional Scaling Analysis." Pp. 42–64 in C.L. Fry, ed., *Aging in Culture and Society: Comparative Viewpoints and Strategies*. New York: Praeger.

———. 1985. "Culture, Behavior, and Aging in the Comparative in Perspective." Pp. 216–44 in V.E. Birren and V.W. Schaie, eds, *Handbook on the Psychology of Aging*. New York: Van Nostrand-Reinhold.

———. 1986. "Emics and Age: Age Differentiation and Cognitive Anthropological Strategies." Pp. 105–30 in C.L Fry and J. Keith, eds, *New Methods for Old Age Research*. South Hadley, MA: Bergin and Garvey.

Frye, Marilyn. 1983. *The Politics of Reality: Essays in Feminist Theory*. Freedom, CA: Crossing Press.

Fuller, Sylvia, Paul Kershaw, and Jane Pulkingham. 2008. "Constructing 'Active Citizenship': Single Mothers, Welfare, and the Logics of Voluntarism." *Citizenship Studies* 12, 2: 157–76.

Gaetz, Stephen, Tanya Gulliver, and Tim Richter. 2014. *The State of Homelessness in Canada: 2014*. Toronto: Homeless Hub Press.

Galabuzi, Grace-Edward. 2004. "Social Exclusion." Pp. 235–52 in Dennis Raphael, ed., *Social Determinants of Health: Canadian Perspectives*. Toronto: Canadian Scholars' Press.

Galindo, Claudia, and Steven B. Sheldon. 2012. "School and Home Connections and Children's Kindergarten Achievement Gains: The Mediating Role of Family Involvement." *Early Childhood Research Quarterly* 27, 1: 90–103.

Gannon, M., and K. Mihorean. 2006. "Criminal Victimization in Canada, 2004." *Juristat* 25, 7. Statistics Canada Catalogue no. 5-002-XIE.

Gardiner-Barber, Pauline T. 2003. "The 'Culture of Making Do': Gender, Work, and Family in Cape Breton Working Class Life." Chapter 14 in M. Lynn, ed., *Voices: Essays on Canadian Families*, 2nd edn. Scarborough, ON: Thomson Nelson.

Garriguet, Didier. 2006. "Nutrition: Findings from the Canadian Community Health Survey, Overview of Canadians' Eating Habits 2004." Statistics Canada Catalogue no. 82-620-MIE.

Gazso, Amber. 2005. "The Poverty of Unattached Senior Women and the Canadian Retirement Income System: A Matter of Blame or Contradiction?" *Journal of Sociology and Social Welfare* 32, 2: 41–6.

———. 2007. "Balancing Expectations for Employability and Family Responsibilities While on Social Assistance: Low-Income Mothers' Experiences in Three Canadian Provinces." *Family Relations* 56: 454–66.

Gazso-Windle, Amber, and Julie McMullin. 2003. "Doing Domestic Labour: Strategising in a Gendered Domain." *Canadian Journal of Sociology* 28, 3: 341–66.

Geddes, John. 2015. "The Surprising Spoils of Income-Splitting: We've Got New Numbers on Who Gets How Much." *Macleans.ca*. Retrieved 13 May 2015 from http://www.macleans.ca/politics/ottawa/new-numbers-on-who-wins-from-income-splitting/

Gee, Ellen. 2000a. "Contemporary Diversities." Chapter 3 in Nancy Mandell and Ann Duffy, eds, *Canadian Families: Diversity, Conflict, and Change*, 2nd edn. Toronto: Harcourt Brace.

———. 2000b. "Population and Politics: Voodoo Demography, Population Ageing, and Social Policy." Chapter 1 in Ellen Gee and G.M. Gutman, eds, *The Overselling of Population Aging: Apocalyptic Demography, Intergenerational Challenges, and Social Policy*. Toronto: Oxford University Press.

Geiger, H. Jack. 2001. "Racial Stereotyping and Medicine: The Need for Cultural Competence." *Canadian Medical Association Journal* 164, 12: 1699–704.

George, Linda K. 2007. "Life Course Perspectives on Social Factors and Mental Illness." Chapter 9 in William Avison, Jane McLeod, and Bernice Pescosilido, eds, *Mental Health, Social Mirror*. New York: Springer.

Gerson, Judith M., and Kathy Peiss. 1985. "Boundaries, Negotiation, Consciousness: Reconceptualizing Gender Relations." *Social Problems* 32, 4: 317–31.

Gerstel, Judy. 2007. "Mad? No, but They Deserve to Be; Post-menopausal Women Show Drop in Diseases after Giving Up HRT." *Toronto Star*, 4 September.

Giddens, Anthony. 1971. *Capitalism and Modern Social Theory: An Analysis of the Writings of Marx, Durkheim, and Max Weber*. Cambridge: Cambridge University Press.

———. 1979. *Central Problems in Social Theory*. London: Macmillan.

———. 1984. *The Constitution of Society: Outline of the Theory of Structuration*. Berkeley: University of California Press.

———. 1993. *New Rules of Sociological Method: A Positive Critique of Interpretative Sociologies*, 2nd edn. Stanford, CA: Stanford University Press.

———. 2002. *Runaway World: How Globalisation Is Reshaping Our Lives*. London: Profile Books.

Giddens, Anthony, and Christopher Pierson. 1998. *Conversations with Anthony Giddens: Making Sense of Modernity*. Cambridge, UK: Polity Press.

Gillis, Kelly J., and John P. Hirdes. 1996. "The Quality of Life Implications of Health Practices among Older Adults: Evidence from the 1991 Canadian General Social Survey." *Canadian Journal on Aging* 15, 2: 299–314.

Gilmore, Jason. 2004. *Health of Canadians Living in Census Metropolitan Areas*. Ottawa: Minister of Industry.

Gilmour, Heather. 2007. "Physically Active Canadians." *Health Reports* 18, 3: 45–65. Statistics Canada Catalogue no. 82-003.

Gilmour, Heather, and Jungwee Park. 2006. "Dependency, Chronic Conditions and Pain in Seniors." *Health Reports* 16, suppl.: 21–32. Statistics Canada Catalogue no. 82-003-SPE.

Ginn, Jay, and Sara Arber. 2001. "Pension Prospects of Minority Ethnic Groups: Inequalities by Gender and Ethnicity." *British Journal of Sociology* 52, 3: 519–39.

Glazier, Richard H., Elizabeth M. Badley, Julie E. Gilbert, and Lorne Rothman. 2000. "The Nature of Increased Hospital Use in Poor Neighbourhoods: Findings from a Canadian Inner City." *Canadian Journal of Public Health* 91, 4: 268–73.

Glenn, Evelyn Nakano. 1992. "From Servitude to Service Work: Historical Continuities in the Racial Division of Paid Reproductive Labour." *Signs* 18, 1: 1–43.

———. 2000. "The Social Construction and Institutionalization of Gender and Race: An Integrative Framework." Chapter 1 in Myra Marx Feree, Judith Lorber, and Beth B. Hess, eds, *Revisioning Gender*. New York: Altamira Press.

Goffman, Erving. 1983. "The Interaction Order." *American Sociological Review* 48, February: 1–17.

Goldthorpe, John. 1980. *Social Mobility and Class Structure in Modern Britain*. Oxford: Oxford University Press.

———. 2002. "Globalisation and Social Class." *Western European Politics* 25, July: 1–28.

Goodman, Marcene. 1996. "Culture, Cohort, and Cosmetic Surgery." *Journal of Women and Aging* 8, 2: 55–73.

Gordon, C.E., J.P. White. 2014. "Indigenous Educational Attainment in Canada." *International Indigenous Policy Journal*, 5, 3.

Gore, Susan, Robert H. Aseltine Jr, and Elizabeth A. Schilling. 2007. "Transition to Adulthood, Mental Health, and Inequality." Chapter 10 in William Avison, Jane McLeod, and Bernice Pescosilido, eds, *Mental Health, Social Mirror*. New York: Springer.

Gorey, Kevin M., Eric J. Holowaty, Gordon Fehringer, Ethan Laukkanen, Nancy L. Richter, and Cynthia M. Meyer. 2000. "An International Comparison of Cancer Survival: Relatively Poor Areas of Toronto, Ontario and Three US Metropolitan Areas." *Journal of Public Health Medicine* 22, 3: 343–9.

Gough, Orla. 2001. "The Impact of the Gender Pay Gap on Post-retirement Earnings." *Critical Social Policy* 21, 3: 311–34.

Grabb, Edward. 2007. *Theories of Social Inequality*, 5th edn. Toronto: Thomson Nelson.

Graham, Jennifer. 2007. "U.S. Border Set to Reopen to Older Canadian Cattle." *Globe and Mail*, 19 November.

Graham, Kathryn, Virginia Carver, and Pamela J. Brett. 1995. "Alcohol and Drug Use by Older Women: Results of a National Survey." *Canadian Journal on Aging* 14, 4: 769–91.

Gramsci, Antonio. 1971. *Selections from the Prison Notebooks*. Edited and translated by Quintin Hoare and Geoffrey Nowell Smith. New York: International.

Grant, Tavia. 2007. "Immigrant Unemployment Most Acute in Quebec." *Globe and Mail*, 11 September.

Grant, Tavia, and Janet McFarland. 2012. "Generation Nixed: Why Canada's Youth Are Losing Hope for the Future." *Globe and Mail*, 27 October. Retrieved 13 May 2015 from http://www.theglobeandmail.com/report-on-business/economy/jobs/generation-nixed-why-canadas-youth-are-losing-hope-for-the-future/article4705553/

Greaves, L., O. Hankivsky, and J. Kingston-Riechers. 1995. *Selected Estimates of the Costs of Violence against Women*. London, ON: Centre for Research on Violence against Women and Children.

Green, Carla A., and Clyde R. Pope. 1999. "Gender, Psychosocial Factors and the Use of Medical Services: A Longitudinal Analysis." *Social Science and Medicine* 48, 10: 1363–72.

Grenon, Joanna, Greg Butler, and Randy Adams. 2007. "Exploring the Intersection between the Built Environment and Health Behaviours." *Health Policy Research Bulletin* 14: 29–32.

Greschner, Donna. 1990. "Abortion and Democracy for Women: A Critique of Tremblay v. Daigle." *McGill Law Journal* 35: 633–69.

———. 1998. "Pregnant with Meaning: Discourse, Democracy, and the Daigle Decision." Chapter 8 in Les Samuelson and Wayne Antony, eds, *Power and Resistance: Critical Thinking about Canadian Social Issues*, 2nd edn. Halifax: Fernwood.

Grimes, Michael, D. 1991. *Class in Twentieth-Century American Sociology: An Analysis of Theories and Measurement Strategies*. New York: Praeger.

Guerra, R.O., B.E. Alvarado, and M.V. Zunzunegui. 2008. "Life Course, Gender and Ethnic Inequalities in Functional Disability in a Brazilian Urban Elderly Population." *Aging Clinical and Experimental Research* 20, 1: 53–61.

Guillemard, A. 1982. "Old Age, Retirement, and the Social Class Structure: Toward an Analysis of the Structural Dynamics of the Later Stage of Life." Chapter 9 in T.K. Hareven and K. Adams, eds, *Aging and the Life Course Transition: An Interdisciplinary Perspective*. New York: Guildford Press.

———. 1983. "The Making of Old Age Policy in France." Pp. 75–99 in A.M. Guillemard, ed., *Old Age and the Welfare State*. Beverly Hills, CA: Sage.

Gunderson, Morley, Lee Jacobs, and François Vaillancourt. 2005. *The Information Technology (IT) Labour Market in Canada: Results from the National Survey of IT Occupations*. Prepared for the Software Human Resource Council (SHRC). Ottawa: Government of Canada, Sector Council Program.

Guppy, Neil, and Scott Davies. 1998. *Education in Canada: Recent Trends and Future Challenges*. Ottawa: Statistics Canada Catalogue no. 96-321.

Gupta, Shamali, and Nancy A. Ross. 2007. "Under the Microscope: Health Disparities within Canadian Cities." *Health Policy Research Bulletin* 14: 23–8.

Gyimah, Stephen Obeng, Jerry White, and Paul Maxim. 2004. "Income and First Nations Elderly: Policies for a Better Future." Chapter 4 in Jerry P. White, Paul Maxim, and Dan Beavon, eds, *Aboriginal Policy Research: Setting the Agenda for Change*. Toronto: Thompson Educational.

Habermas, Jürgen. 1984. *The Theory of Communicative Action*. Vol. 1: *Reason and the Rationalization of Society*. Boston: Beacon Press.

———. 1987. *The Theory of Communicative Action*. Vol. 2: *Lifeworld and System: A Functionalist Critique*. Cambridge, UK: Polity Press.

Hagestad, Gunhild. 1990. "Social Perspectives on the Life Course." Pp. 151–68 in R.H. Binstock and L.K. George, eds, *Handbook of Aging and the Social Sciences*, 3rd edn. Toronto: Harcourt Brace Jovanovich.

Hagestad, Gunhild, and Bernice Neugarten. 1985. "Age and the Life Course." Pp. 36–61 in E. Shanas and R. Binstock, eds, *Handbook of Aging and the Social Sciences*, 2nd edn. New York: Van Nostrand-Reinhold.

Hainsworth, Jeremy. 2006. "Mail-Order Bride Industry Rife with Abuse, Study Says." *Globe and Mail*, 9 October.

Halli, Shiva S., and John P. Anchan. 2005. "Structural and Behavioural Determinants of Immigrant and Non-immigrant Health Status: Results from the Canadian Community Health Survey." *Journal of International Migration and Integration* 6, 1: 93–122.

Hampson, Sarah. 2007. "The New Class Wars." *Globe and Mail*, 5 July.

Hango, Darcy, and Patrice de Broucker. 2007. *Education-to-Labour Market Pathways of Canadian Youth: Findings from the Youth in Transition Survey*. Culture, Tourism and the Centre for Education Statistics Research Papers. Statistics Canada Catalogue no. 81-595-MIE2007054.

Hankin, Janet R., and Eric R. Wright. 2010. "Reflections on Fifty Years of Medical Sociology." *Journal of Health and Social Behavior* 51 (1 suppl): S10–S14.

Hardy, Melissa, and Lawrence E. Hazelrigg. 1995. "Gender, Race/Ethnicity, and Poverty in Later Life." *Journal of Aging Studies* 9, 1: 43–63.

Hartmann, Heidi. 1981. "The Unhappy Marriage of Marxism and Feminism: Towards a More Progressive Union." Pp. 1–42 in L. Sargent, ed., *The Unhappy Marriage of Marxism and Feminism: A Debate on Class and Patriarchy*. London: Pluto Press.

Hatch, Stephani L., and Bruce P. Dohrenwend. 2007. "Distribution of Traumatic and Other Stressful Life Events by Race/Ethnicity, Gender, SES and Age: A Review of the Research." *American Journal of Community Psychology* 40: 313–32.

Health Canada. 2002. "Income Inequality as a Determinant of Health." Presentation summary, Social Determinants of Health across the Life-Span Conference, Toronto, November. http://www.phac-aspc.gc.ca/phsp/phdd/overview_implications/02_income.htm

———. 2006. *Healthy Canadians: A Federal Report on Comparable Health Indicators 2006*. Ottawa: Minister of Health Canada.

———. 2012. "Canadian Alcohol and Drug Use Monitoring Survey: Summary of Results for 2011—Health Canada." Retrieved 7 May 2015 from http://www.hc-sc.gc.ca/hc-ps/drugs-drogues/stat/_2011/summary-sommaire-eng.php#a2

————. 2013. "First Nations and Inuit Mental Health and Addictions—Cluster Evaluation 2005/06-2009/10." Retrieved 5 May 2015 from http://www.hc-sc.gc.ca/ahc-asc/performance/eval/2012/fni-addiction-evaluation-pni-eng.php

Health Disparities Task Group of the Federal/Provincial/Territorial Advisory Committee on Population Health and Health Security. 2005. *Reducing Health Disparities—Roles of the Health Sector: Discussion Paper.* Ottawa: Minister of Health.

Heinz, Walter. 2001. "Work and the Life Course: A Cosmopolitan-Local Perspective." Chapter 1 in V.W. Marshall, W.R. Heinz, H. Krueger, and A. Verma, eds, *Restructuring Work and the Life Course.* Toronto: University of Toronto Press.

Heisig, Jan Paul. 2011. "Who Does More Housework: Rich or Poor? A Comparison of 33 Countries." *American Sociological Review* 7, 1: 74–99.

Herd, Pamela, Brian Goesling, and James S. House. 2007. "Socioeconomic Position and Health: The Differential Effects of Education versus Income on the Onset versus Progression of Health Problems." *Journal of Health and Social Behavior* 48, 3: 223–39.

Hier, Sean P., and B. Singh Bolaria, eds. 2007. *Race and Racism in 21st Century Canada: Continuity, Complexity, and Change.* Peterborough, ON: Broadview Press.

Hou, Feng, and Shunji Wang. 2011. *Immigrants in Self-Employment.* Statistics Canada Catalogue no. 75-001-X Perspectives on Labour and Income.

House, James S. 2001. "Understanding Social Factors and Inequalities in Health: 20th Century Progress and 21st Century Prospects." *Journal of Health and Social Behavior* 43, 2: 125–42.

House, James S., James M. Lepkowski, Ann M. Kinney, Richard P. Mero, Ronald C. Kessler, and A. Regula Herzog. 1994. "The Social Stratification of Aging and Health." *Journal of Health and Social Behavior* 35, 3: 213–34.

Hoxby, C.M. 2009. "The Changing Selectivity of American Colleges." National Bureau of Economic Research, Working Paper.

Huang, Shelly. 2009. "Average Taiwanese Worker's Salary Increases Slightly." Retrieved 1 March 2016 from http://www.taipeitimes.com/News/taiwan/archives/2009/08/24/2003451881

Hugenberg, Kurt, and Galen V. Bodenhausen. 2004. "Ambiguity in Social Categorization: The Role of Prejudice and Facial Affect in Race Categorization." *Psychological Science* 15, 5: 342–5.

Hughes, Karen D. 1999. *Gender and Self-Employment in Canada: Assessing Trends and Policy Implications.* CPRN Study no. W104. Changing Relationships Series. Ottawa: Renouf.

Huguet, Nathalie, Mark S. Kaplan, and David Feeny. 2008. "Socioeconomic Status and Health-Related Quality of Life among Elderly People: Results from the Joint Canada/United States Survey of Health." *Social Science and Medicine* 66, 4: 803–10.

Hum, Derek, and Wayne Simpson. 2007. "Revisiting Equity and Labour: Immigration, Gender, Minority Status, and Income Differentials in Canada." Pp. 89–110 in Sean P. Hier and B. Singh Bolaria, eds, *Race and Racism in 21st Century Canada: Continuity, Complexity, and Change.* Peterborough, ON: Broadview Press.

Humphries, Karin H., and Eddy van Doorslaer. 2000. "Income-Related Health Inequality in Canada." *Social Science and Medicine* 50, 5: 663–71.

Hunt, Kate. 2002. "A Generation Apart? Gender-Related Experiences and Health in Women in Early and Late Mid-life." *Social Science and Medicine* 54, 1: 663–76.

Hunt, Kate, and Ellen Annandale. 1999. "Relocating Gender and Morbidity: Examining Men's and Women's Health in Contemporary Western Societies." *Social Science and Medicine* 48: 1–5.

Hunter, Alfred A. 1981. *Class Tells: On Social Inequality in Canada.* Toronto: Butterworths.

Hurd Clarke, Laura. 2001. "Older Women's Bodies and the Self: The Construction of Identity in Later Life." *Canadian Review of Sociology and Anthropology* 38, 4: 441–64.

Hurd Clarke, Laura, Robin Repta, and Meridith Griffin. 2007. "Non-surgical Cosmetic Procedures: Older Women's Perceptions and Experiences." *Journal of Women and Aging* 19, 3/4: 69–87.

Ibbitson, John. 2007. "Is Globalization Killing the American Middle Class?" *Globe and Mail*, 17 October.

Ibbott, Peter, Don Kerr, and Roderic Beaujot. 2006. "Probing the Future of Mandatory Retirement in Canada." *Canadian Journal on Aging* 25, 2: 161–78.

Ighodaro, MacDonald E. 2006. *Living the Experience: Migration, Exclusion, and Anti-racist Practice.* Halifax: Fernwood.

Immen, Wallace, and James Rusk. 2002. "Toronto's Tent City Sealed Off, Squatters Ejected." *Globe and Mail*, 25 September.

Industry Canada. 2009. "Key Small Business Statistics—July 2008: How Many Businesses Are There in Canada?" Ottawa: Industry Canada. Retrieved 23 July 2015 from http://www.ic.gc.ca/eic/site/sbrp-rppe.nsf/eng/rd02300.html

Inglehart, R. 1987. "Value Change in Industrial Societies." *American Political Science Review* 81: 1289–1303.

———. 1990. *Culture Shift in Advanced Industrial Society.* Princeton, NJ: Princeton University Press.

Inhorn, Marcia C., and K. Lisa Whittle. 2001. "Feminism Meets the 'New' Epidemiologies: Toward an Appraisal of Antifeminist Biases in Epidemiological Research on Women's Health." *Social Science and Medicine* 53, 5: 553–67.

Isajiw, Wsevolod W. 1999. *Understanding Diversity: Ethnicity and Race in the Canadian Context.* Toronto: Thompson Educational.

Jackson, Andrew. 2002. *Is Work Working for Workers of Colour?* Research paper no. 18. Ottawa: Canadian Labour Congress. http://canadianlabour.ca/en/Is_Work_Working_colour

Jackson, Chris. 1996. "Measuring and Valuing: Households' Unpaid Work." *Canadian Social Trends*, Autumn: 25–9. Statistics Canada Catalogue no. 11-008.

Jackson, Pamela Braboy, and David R. Williams. 2006. "The Intersection of Race, Gender and SES: Health Paradoxes." Chapter 5 in Amy J. Schultz and Leith Mullings, eds, *Gender, Race, Class and Health: Intersectional Approaches.* San Francisco: Jossey-Bass.

Jaine, Linda. 1993. *Residential Schools: The Stolen Years.* Saskatoon: University Extension Press.

Jakubowski, Lisa Marie. 1997. *Immigration and the Legalization of Racism.* Halifax: Fernwood.

Jenkins, Stephen P., and John A. Rigg, 2003. "Disability and Disadvantage: Selection, Onset, and Duration Effects." ISER Working Paper Series 2003-18, Institute for Social and Economic Research.

Jenson, Jane. 1997. "Fated to Live in Interesting Times: Canada's Changing Citizenship Regimes." *Canadian Journal of Political Science* 30, 4: 627–44.

Jenson, Jane, and Martin Papillon. 2000. "Challenging the Citizenship Regime: The James Bay Cree and Transnational Action." *Politics and Society* 28, 2: 245–64.

Jerrett, Michael, Michael Buzzelli, Richard T. Burnett, and Patrick F. DeLuca. 2005. "Particulate Air Pollution, Social Confounders, and Mortality in Small Areas of an Industrial City." *Social Science and Medicine* 60: 2845–63.

Johnson, Fred W., Paul J. Gruenewald, Andrew J. Treno, and Gail Armstrong Taff. 1998. "Drinking over the Life Course within Gender and Ethnic Groups: A Hyperparametric Analysis." *Journal of Studies on Alcohol* 59: 568–80.

Johnson, Holly. 1996. *Dangerous Domains: Violence against Women in Canada.* Toronto: Nelson.

Johnson, Holly, and Vincent Sacco. 1995. "Researching Violence against Women: Statistics Canada's National Survey." *Canadian Journal of Criminology* 37, 3: 281–304.

Johnson, Karen L., Donna Lero, and Jennifer Rooney. 2001. *Work-Life Compendium 2001: 150 Canadian Statistics on Work, Family, and Well-Being.* Guelph, ON: Centre for Families, Work, and Well-being/Human Resources Development Canada.

Jones, Vanessa E. 2007. "Black and Not-So-Beautiful Stereotypes." *Globe and Mail*, 12 October. Originally published in the *New York Times*.

Joseph, Suad, Fahmia Charafeddine, Fadwa Al-Labadi, and Dalila Mahdawi. 2010. "Citizenship and Gender in the Arab World." *The Pioneer*, no. 129–30.

Julien, Ann-Marie, and Heidi Ertl. 1999. "Children's School Experiences in the NLSCY, 1994–1995." *Education Quarterly Review* 6, 2: 20–34. Statistics Canada Catalogue no. 81-003.

Kalbach, Madeline A., and Warren E. Kalbach, eds. 2000. *Perspectives on Ethnicity in Canada.* Toronto: Harcourt Canada.

Kamo, Y. 1988. "Determinants of Household Division of Labour." *Journal of Family Issues* 9: 177–200.

Kapsalis, Costa, René Morissette, and Garnett Picot. 1999. *The Returns to Education and the Increasing Wage Gap between Younger and Older Workers.* Statistics Canada Catalogue no. 11F0019MPE No. 131.

Karlsen, Saffron, and James Y. Nazroo. 2002. "Relation between Racial Discrimination, Social Class, and Health among Ethnic Minority Groups." *American Journal of Public Health* 92: 624–31.

Katz, Stephen. 1996. *Disciplining Old Age: The Formation of Gerontological Knowledge.* Charlottesville: University Press of Virginia.

Katz, Stephen, and Barbara Marshall. 2003. "New Sex for Old: Lifestyle, Consumerism, and the Ethics of Aging Well." *Journal of Aging Studies* 17, 1: 3–16.

Kawachi, Ichiro, and Bruce P. Kennedy. 1999. "The Relationship of Income Inequality to Mortality." Chapter 13 in Ichiro Kawachi, Bruce P. Kennedy, and Richard G. Wilkinson, eds, *The Society and Population Health Reader: Income Inequality and Health.* New York: New Press.

Kazanjian, Arminée, Denise Morettin, and Robert Cho. 2003. "Health Care Utilization by Canadian Women." In *Women's Health Surveillance Report: A Multidimensional Look at the Health of Canadian Women.* Ottawa: Canadian Institute for Health Information.

Kazemipur, Abdolmohammad, and Shiva S. Halli. 2001. "The Changing Colour of Poverty in Canada." *Canadian Sociological and Anthropological Review* 38, 2: 217–38.

Kelly, Karen. 2002. *Visible Minorities: A Diverse Population.* Statistics Canada Catalogue no. 1-008-XIE. Retrieved December 2002 from http://statcan.ca/english/ads/11-008-XIE/vismin.html

Khazan, Olga. 2014. "How Being Poor Makes You Sick." Retrieved March 2016 from http://www.theatlantic.com/health/archive/2014/05/poverty-makes-you-sick/371241/?utm_content=buffer0fba7&utm_medium=social&utm_source=twitter.com&utm_campaign=buffer

Kilkey, Majella, and Jonathan Bradshaw. 1999. "Lone Mothers, Economic Well-Being, and Policies." Chapter 5 in Diane Sainsbury, ed., *Gender and Welfare State Regimes.* New York: Oxford University Press.

Kim, Daniel, Ichiro Kawachi, Stephen Vander Hoorn, and Majid Ezzati. 2008. "Is Inequality at the Heart of It? Cross-country Associations of Income Inequality with Cardiovascular Diseases and Risk Factors." *Social Science and Medicine* 66: 1719–32.

Kingston, P. 2001. *The Classless Society.* Stanford: Stanford University Press.

Klein, Naomi. 2007. "Democracy Born in Chains: South Africa's Constricted Freedom." Retrieved 1 March 2016 from http://www.commondreams.org/views/2011/02/14/democracy-born-chains-south-africas-constricted-freedom

Klein, Seth, and Jane Pulkingham. 2008. *Living on Welfare in BC: Experiences of Longer-Term 'Expected to Work' Recipients.* Ottawa: Canadian Centre for Policy Alternatives.

Kline, Marlee. 1993. "Complicating the Ideology of Motherhood: Child Welfare Law and First Nation Women." *Queen's Law Journal* 18: 310–19.

———. 2005. "Complicating the Ideology of Motherhood: Child Welfare Law and First Nation Women." Pp. 189–99 in B.A. Crow and L. Gotell, eds, *Open Boundaries: A Canadian Women's Studies Reader*, 2nd edn. Toronto: Pearson Prentice Hall.

Knight, Claudette. 1997. "Black Parents Speak: Education in Mid-Nineteenth-Century Canada West." *Ontario History* 89, 4: 269–84.

Knighton, Karen, and Sheba Mirza. 2002. "Postsecondary Participation: The Effects of Parent Education and Income." *Education Quarterly Review* 18, 3: 25–32. Statistics Canada Catalogue no. 81-003.

Knowles, Valerie. 1992. *Strangers at Our Gates: Canadian Immigration and Immigration Policy, 1540–1990.* Toronto: Dundurn Press.

Kobayashi, Karen M., Steven Prus, and Zhiqiu Lin. 2008. "Ethnic Differences in Self-Rated and Functional Health: Does Immigrant Status Matter?" *Ethnicity and Health* 13, 2: 129–47.

Kohen, Dafna, Sharanjit Uppal, Anne Guevremont, and Fernando Cartwright. 2006. "Children with Disabilities and the Educational System—a Provincial Perspective." Retrieved 18 February 2016 from http://www.statcan.gc.ca/pub/81-004-x/2007001/9631-eng.htm

Kohli, Martin. 1988. "Ageing as a Challenge for Sociological Theory." *Ageing and Society* 8: 367–94.

Koltai, Jonathan, and Scott Schieman. 2015. "Job Pressure and SES-Contingent Buffering: Resource Reinforcement, Substitution, or the Stress of Higher Status?" *Journal of Health and Social Behavior* 56, 2: 180–98.

Kopec, Jacek A., Ivan Williams, Teresa To, and Peter C. Austin. 2001. "Cross-Cultural Comparisons of Health Status in Canada Using the Health Utilities Index." *Ethnicity and Health* 6, 1: 41–50.

Kopun, Francine. 2007. "The Canadian Family Is Slowly Being Reshaped: More Men Heading Up Single-Parent Households, Same-Sex and Common-Law Unions on Rise: Census." *Toronto Star*, 13 September.

Koretz, Gene. 2001. "Why Married Men Earn More." *Business Week*, 17 September.

Kornrich, Sabino, and Maureen A. Eger. 2014. "Family Life in Context: Men and Women's Perceptions of Fairness and Satisfaction across Thirty Countries." *Social Politics: International Studies in Gender, State & Society*, DOI: 10.1093/sp/jxu030.

Korpi, Walter. 1983. *The Democratic Class Struggle*. Routledge & Kegan Paul.

Krahn, Harvey, J., and Graham S. Lowe. 1998. *Work, Industry, and Canadian Society*, 3rd edn. Toronto: ITP Nelson.

Krahn, Harvey J., Karen D. Hughes, and Graham S. Lowe. 2007. *Work, Industry and Canadian Society*, 5th edn. Toronto: Thomson Nelson.

———. 2014. *Work, Industry and Canadian Society*, 7th edn. Toronto: Thomson Nelson.

Krahn, H., and A. Taylor. 2007 (19 June). "'Streaming' in the 10th Grade in Four Canadian Provinces in 2000." *Education Matters*. www.statcan.ca

———. 2007. "Streaming in the 10th Grade in Four Canadian Provinces in 2000." *Education Matters: Insights on Education, Learning and Training in Canada* 4, 2. Statistics Canada Catalogue no. 81-004-XIE. http://www.statcan.gc.ca/pub/81-004-x/2007002/9994-eng.htm

Krieger, Nancy. 2003. "Genders, Sexes and Health: What Are the Connections—and Why Does It Matter?" *International Journal of Epidemiology* 32: 652–7.

———. 2007. "Why Epidemiologists Cannot Afford to Ignore Poverty." *Epidemiology* 18, 6: 658–63.

Krieger, Nancy, Charles Quesenberry, Tiffany Peng, Pamela Horn-Ross, Susan Stewart, Susan Brown, Karen Swallen, Tessie Guillermo, Dong Suh, Luz Alvarez Martinez, and Felicia Ward. 1999. "Social Class, Race/Ethnicity, and Incidence of Breast, Cervix, Colon, Lung, and Prostate Cancer among Asian, Black, Hispanic, and White Residents of the San Francisco Bay Area, 1988–92 (United States)." *Cancer Causes and Control* 10: 525–37.

Krieger, Nancy, D.L. Rowley, A.A. Herman, B. Avery, and M.T. Phillips. 1993. "Racism, Sexism, and Social Class: Implications for Studies of Health, Disease, and Well-Being." *American Journal of Preventive Medicine* 9, 6: 82–122.

Krieger, Nancy, Kevin Smith, Deepa Naishadham, Cathy Hartman, and Elizabeth M. Barbeau. 2005. "Experiences of Discrimination: Validity and Reliability of a Self-Report Measure for Population Health Research on Racism and Health." *Social Science and Medicine* 61: 1576–96.

Krug, Etienne G., Linda L. Dahlberg, James A. Mercy, Anthony B. Zwi, and Rafel Lozano, eds. 2002. *World Report on Violence and Health*. Geneva: World Health Organization.

Kuo, B.C.H, Vanessa Chong, and Justine Joseph. 2008. "Depression and Its Psychosocial Correlates among Older Asian Immigrants in North America: A Critical Review of Two Decades' Research." *Journal of Aging and Health* 20, 6: 615–52.

Lamont, M., and A. Lareau. 1988. "Cultural Capital: Allusions, Gaps and Glissandos in Recent Theoretical Developments." *Sociological Theory* 6: 153–68.

Langlois, Stephanie, and Peter Morrison. 2001. "Suicide Deaths and Suicide Attempts." *Health Reports* 13, 2: 9–21. Statistics Canada Catalogue no. 11-008.

Langton, Nancy, and Jeffrey Pfeffer. 1994. "Paying the Professor: Sources of Salary Variation in Academic Labor Markets." *American Sociological Review* 59: 236–56.

Lantz, Paula M., James S. House, Richard P. Mero, and David R. Williams. 2005. "Stress, Life Events, and Socio-economic Disparities in Health: Results from the Americans' Changing Lives Study." *Journal of Health and Social Behaviour* 46: 274–88.

Lasch, Christopher. 1977. *Haven in a Heartless World: The Family Besieged*. New York: Basic Books.

Laslett, B., and J. Brenner. 1987. "Gender and Social Reproduction: Historical Perspectives." *Annual Review of Sociology* 15: 381–404.

Latham, Jim, and Tina Moffat. 2007. "Determinants of Variation in Food Cost and Availability in Two Socioeconomically Contrasting Neighbourhoods of Hamilton, Ontario, Canada." *Health and Place* 13: 273–87.

Laurence, Margaret. 1964. *The Stone Angel*. Toronto: McClelland & Stewart.

Layder, Derek. 1994. *Understanding Social Theory*. Thousand Oaks, CA: Sage.

Leach, Belinda, and Anthony Winson. 1995. "Bringing 'Globalization' Down to Earth: Restructuring and Labour in Rural Communities." *Canadian Review of Sociology and Anthropology* 32: 341–64.

Leclere, Felicia B., Richard G. Rogers, and Kimberley D. Peters. 1997. "Ethnicity and Mortality in the United States: Individual and Community Correlates." *Social Forces* 76, 1: 169–98.

Lee, K., and P. Patel. 2003. "Far from the Maddening Cows: The Global Dimensions of BSE and vCJD." Chapter 4 in K. Lee, ed., *Health Impacts of Globalization: Towards Global Governance*. New York: Palgrave.

Lehmann, Wolfgang. 2007a. *Choosing to Labour? School–Work Transitions and Social Class*. Montreal and Kingston: McGill-Queen's University Press.

———. 2007b. "'I Just Didn't Feel Like I Fit In': The Role of Habitus in University Dropout Decisions." *Canadian Journal of Higher Education* 37, 2: 89–110.

———. 2014. "Habitus Transformation and Hidden Injuries: Successful Working Class University Students." *Sociology of Education* 87, 1: 1–15.

Leisering, Lutz, and Stephan Leibfried. 1999. *Time and Poverty in Western Welfare Studies*. Cambridge: Cambridge University Press.

Lemstra, Mark, Cory Neudorf, Carl D'arcy, Anton Kunst, Lynne M. Warren, and Norman R. Bennett. 2008. "A Systematic Review of Depressed Mood and Anxiety by SES in Youth Aged 10–15 Years." *Canadian Journal of Public Health* 99, 2: 125–9.

Lero, Donna S., Lynda M. Ashbourne, and Denise L. Whitehead. 2006. "Inventory of Policies and Policy Areas Influencing Father Involvement." *Father Involvement Research Alliance (FIRA)*. Centre for Families, Work and Well-Being: University of Guelph. www.fira.uoguelph.ca/pdf/executive_summary/FIRA-Policy-Doc-Aug2006-FINAL.pdf

Lessa, Iara. 2006. "Single Motherhood in the Canadian Landscape: Postcards from a Subject." Pp. 291–308 in Anne Westhues, ed., *Canadian Social Policy: Issues and Perspectives*, 4th edn. Waterloo, ON: Wilfrid Laurier University Press.

Lero, D.S., L.M. Ashbourne, and D.L. Whitehead. 2006 (April). *Inventory of Policies and Policy Areas Influencing Father Involvement*. www.fira.uoguelph.ca/pdf/executive_summary/FIRA-Policy-Doc-Aug2006-FINAL.pdf

Li, Chris, Ginette Gervais, and Aurelie Duval. 2006. "The Dynamics of Overqualification: Canada's Underemployed University Graduates." Retrieved 25 February 2016 from http://publications.gc.ca/collections/Collection/Statcan/11-621-M/11-621-MIE2006039.pdf

Li, Peter S. 1988. *Ethnic Inequality in a Class Society*. Toronto: Wall and Thompson.

———. 1998. "The Market Value and Social Value of Race." Chapter 5 in Vic Satzewich, ed., *Racism and Social Inequality in Canada*. Toronto: Thompson Educational.

———. 2000. "Earning Disparities between Immigrants and Native-Born Canadians." *Canadian Review of Sociology and Anthropology* 37, 3: 289–311.

———. 2001a. "Immigrants' Propensity to Self-Employment: Evidence from Canada." *International Migration Review* 35, 4: 1106–28.

———. 2001b. "The Market Worth of Immigrants' Educational Credentials." *Canadian Public Policy* 27, 1: 23–38.

———. 2003. *Destination Canada: Immigration Debates and Issues*. Don Mills, ON: Oxford University Press.

———. 2010. "Immigrants from China to Canada: Issues of Supply and Demand of Human Capital." In L. Suryadinata, ed., *Migration, Indigenization, and Interaction: Chinese Overseas and Globalization*. New Jersey: World Scientific Publishing.

Li, Peter S., and Chunhong Dong. 2007. "Earnings of Chinese Immigrants in the Enclave and

Mainstream Economy." *Canadian Review of Sociology and Anthropology* 44, 1: 65–99.

Lian, Jason Z., and David Ralph Matthews. 1998. "Does the Vertical Mosaic Still Exist? Ethnicity and Income in Canada, 1991." *Canadian Review of Sociology and Anthropology* 35, 4: 461.

Lightman, Ernie, Andrew Mitchell, and Dean Herd. 2005. "Workfare in Toronto: More of the Same?" *Journal of Sociology and Social Welfare* 32, 4: 65–75.

Lightman, E., A. Mitchell, and B. Wilson. 2008. "Poverty Is Making Us Sick: A Comprehensive Survey of Income and Health in Canada." Retrieved 1 March 2016 from http://www.wellesleyinstitute.com/publications/poverty_is_making_us_sick__a_comprehensive_survey_of_income_and_health_in_canada/

Link, Bruce G., Bruce P. Dohrenwend, and Andrew E. Skodol. 1986. "Socio-economic Status and Schizophrenia: Noisome Occupational Characteristics as a Risk Factor." *American Sociological Review* 51: 242–58.

Link, Bruce G., and Jo Phelan. 1995. "Social Conditions as Fundamental Causes of Disease." *Journal of Health and Social Behavior* 35: 80–94.

———. 2000. "Evaluating the Fundamental Cause Explanation for Social Disparities in Health." Chapter 3 in Chloe E. Bird, Peter Conrad, and Allen M. Fremont, eds, *Handbook of Medical Sociology*, 5th edn. Englewood Cliffs, NJ: Prentice Hall.

Lipps, Garth, and Jeffrey Frank. 1997. "The National Longitudinal Survey of Children and Youth, 1994–95: Initial Results from the School Component." *Education Quarterly Review* 4, 2: 43–57. Statistics Canada Catalogue no. 81-003-XPB.

Little, Don. 1995. "Earnings and Labour Force Status of 1990 Graduates." *Education Quarterly Review* 2, 3: 10–20. Statistics Canada Catalogue no. 81-003.

Little, Margaret. 1999. "The Blurring of Boundaries: Private and Public Welfare for Single Mothers in Ontario." Chapter 6 in Pat Armstrong and M. Patricia Connelly, eds, *Feminism, Political Economy and the State: Contested Terrain*. Toronto: Canadian Scholars' Press.

Liu, John. 2014. "Part-Time Workers' Earnings the Lowest on Record: MOL." Retrieved 25 February 2016 from http://www.chinapost.com.tw/taiwan/national/national-news/2014/12/10/423716/Part-time-workers.htm

Liu, Serena. 2007. "Social Citizenship in China: Continuity and Change." *Citizenship Studies* 11, 5: 465–79.

Livingstone, David W. 2001. "Public Education at the Crossroads: Confronting Underemployment in a Knowledge Society." Chapter 5 in Dan Glenday and Ann Duffy, eds, *Canadian Society: Meeting the Challenges of the Twenty-First Century*. Toronto: Oxford University Press Canada.

Lobao, Linda M., Gregory Hooks, and Ann R. Tickamyer. 2007. *The Sociology of Spatial Inequality*. Albany: State University of New York Press.

Long, Cindy. 2007. "Institutes at Odds over Methodology: C.D. Howe Says Fraser Disregarded Socioeconomic Factors." *Ottawa Citizen*, 1 March.

Looker, E. Diane, and Graham S. Lowe. 2001. *Postsecondary Access and Student Financial Aid in Canada: Current Knowledge and Research Gaps*. Ottawa: Canadian Policy Research Networks/Canadian Millennium Scholarship Foundation. http://www.millenniumscholarships.ca/images/Publications/cprn-bkgnd.pdf

Lorber, Judith. 1994. *Paradoxes of Gender*. New Haven, CT: Yale University Press.

———. 1997. *Gender and the Social Construction of Illness*. Thousand Oaks, CA: Sage Publications.

———. 2000. "Believing Is Seeing: Biology as Ideology." Chapter 1 in Maxime Baca Zinn, Pierrette Hondagneu-Sotelo, and Michael A. Messner, eds, *Through the Prism of Difference*, 2nd edn. Needham Heights, MA: Allyn and Bacon.

———. 2006. "Shifting Paradigms and Challenging Categories." *Social Problems* 53, 4: 448–53.

Lorde, Audre. 1982. *Zami: A New Spelling of My Name*. Freedom, CA: Crossing Press.

Loveman, Mara. 1999. "Is 'Race' Essential?" *American Sociological Review* 64: 891–8.

Lowe, Graham S. 2000. *The Quality of Work: A People-Centred Agenda*. Toronto: Oxford University Press.

Lukes, Steven. 1974. *Power: A Radical View*. London: Macmillan.

Lundberg, Olle. 1997. "Childhood Conditions, Sense of Coherence, Social Class and Adult Ill Health: Exploring Their Theoretical and Empirical Relations." *Social Science and Medicine* 44, 6: 821–31.

Luong, May. 2009. "GIS Update." Statistics Canada Catalogue no. 75-001-X. http://www.statcan.gc.ca/pub/75-001-x/2009107/pdf/10906-eng.pdf

Luxton, Meg. 1980. *More Than a Labour of Love: Three Generations of Women's Work in the Home.* Toronto: Women's Press.

Luxton, Meg, and June Corman. 2001. *Getting By in Hard Times: Gendered Labour at Home and on the Job.* Toronto: University of Toronto Press.

Lynch, John, and George Kaplan. 2000. "Socioeconomic Position." Pp. 13–35 in L.F. Berkman and I. Kawachi, eds, *Social Epidemiology.* New York: Oxford University Press.

Lynch, J.W., G.A. Kaplan, and J.T. Salonen. 1997. "Why Do Poor People Behave Poorly? Variation in Adult Health Behaviours and Psychosocial Characteristics by Stages of the Socio-economic Lifecourse." *Social Science and Medicine* 44, 6: 809–19.

Lynn, Marion, ed. 2003. *Voices: Essays on Canadian Families*, 2nd edn. Scarborough, ON: Nelson.

McAll, Christopher. 1990. *Class, Ethnicity and Social Inequality.* Montreal and Kingston: McGill-Queen's University Press.

MacBride-King, Judith, and Kimberley Bachmann. 1999. *Is Work-Life Balance Still an Issue for Canadians and Their Employers? You Bet It Is.* Ottawa: Conference Board of Canada.

McCall, L. 2001. "Sources of Racial Wage Inequality in Metropolitan Labor Markets: Racial, Ethnic, and Gender Differences." *American Sociological Review* 66: 520–42.

McCartney, Gerry, Carole Hart, and Graham Watt. 2013. "How Can Socioeconomic Inequalities in Hospital Admissions Be Explained? A Cohort Study." *BMJ OPEN* 3, 8: e002433.

McCourt, Frank. 1996. *Angela's Ashes: A Memoir.* New York: Touchstone.

McDaniel, Susan A. 2001. "Born at the Right Time? Gendered Generations and Webs of Entitlement and Responsibility." *Canadian Journal of Sociology* 26, 2: 193–214.

———. 2002. "Women's Changing Relations to the State and Citizenship: Caring and Intergenerational Relations in Globalizing Western Democracies." *Canadian Review of Sociology and Anthropology* 39, 2: 125–50.

———. 2004. "Generationing Gender: Justice and the Division of Welfare." *Journal of Aging Studies* 18, 1: 27–44.

———. 2005. "The Family Lives of the Middle-Aged and Elderly in Canada." Chapter 9 in M. Baker, ed., *Families: Changing Trends in Canada.* Toronto: McGraw-Hill Ryerson.

McDonald, L., J. Hornick, G. Robertson, and J. Wallace. 1991. *Elder Abuse and Neglect in Canada.* Toronto: Butterworths.

McDonald, L., and B. Wigdor. 1995. "Taking Stock: Elder Abuse Research in Canada." *Canadian Journal on Aging* 14, suppl. 2: 1–6.

McDonough, Peggy, and Vivienne Walters. 2001. "Gender and Health: Reassessing Patterns and Explanations." *Social Science and Medicine* 52, 4: 547–59.

McDonough, Peggy, David R. Williams, James S. House, and Greg J. Duncan. 1999. "Gender and the Socioeconomic Gradient in Mortality." *Journal of Health and Social Behavior* 40, 1: 17–31.

McGregor, Gaile. 2001. *A Fact Sheet on the Economics of Aging in Canada.* London, ON: Terraconnaissance.

Macintyre, Sally, Graeme Ford, and Kate Hunt. 1999. "Do Women 'Over-report' Morbidity? Men's and Women's Responses to Structured Prompting on a Standard Question on Long Standing Illness." *Social Science and Medicine* 48, 1: 89–98.

McIntyre, Sheila, and Jennifer Scott. 2000. "Submissions to the Committee on Justice and Legal Affairs Review of Bill C-46." Pp. 348–56 in Barbara A. Crow and Lise Gotell, eds, *Open Boundaries: A Canadian Women's Studies Reader.* Toronto: Prentice Hall.

Mackey, Eva. 1999. *The House of Difference: Cultural Politics and National Identity in Canada.* London: Routledge.

McKinlay, John B. 1996. "Some Contributions from the Social System to Gender Inequalities in Heart Disease." *Journal of Health and Social Behavior* 37, 1: 1–26.

McLaren, Angus. 1991. *Our Own Master Race: Eugenics in Canada, 1885–1945.* Toronto: McClelland & Stewart.

McLaren, Angus, and Arlene Tigar McLaren. 1997. *The Bedroom and the State: The Changing Practices and Politics of Contraception and Abortion in Canada, 1880–1997,* 2nd edn. Toronto: Oxford University Press.

McLeod, Jane D., and Kathryn J. Lively. 2007. "Social Psychology and Stress Research." Chapter 12 in William Avison, Jane McLeod, and Bernice Pescosilido, eds, *Mental Health, Social Mirror.* New York: Springer.

McLeod, Jane D., and Michael J. Shanahan. 1996. "Trajectories of Poverty and Children's Mental Health." *Journal of Health and Social Behavior* 37, 3: 207–20.

McMahon, Martha. 1995. *Engendering Motherhood: Identity and Self-Transformation in Women's Lives.* New York: Guilford Press.

MacMillan, Harriet L., Christine A. Walsh, Ellen Jamieson, Maria Y-Y. Wong, Emily J. Faries, Harvey McCue, Angus B. MacMillan, David (Dan) R. Offord, and the Technical Advisory Committee of the Chiefs of Ontario. 2003. "The Health of Ontario First Nations People: Results from the Ontario First Nations Regional Health Survey." *Canadian Journal of Public Health* 94, 3: 168–72.

McMullan, John L. 2006. "News, Truth and the Recognition of Corporate Crime." *Canadian Journal of Criminology and Criminal Justice* 48, 6: 905–39.

McMullen, Kathryn. 2004. "The Gap in Achievement between Boys and Girls." *Education Matters: Insights on Education, Learning and Training in Canada* 1, 4. Statistics Canada Catalogue no. 81-004-XIE.

———. 2005. "Aboriginal Peoples in Canada's Urban Area: Narrowing the Education Gap." *Education Matters: Insights on Education, Learning and Training in Canada* 2, 3. Statistics Canada Catalogue no. 81-004-XIE.

McMullin, Julie Ann. 1995. "Theorizing Age and Gender Relations." Chapter 3 in Sara Arber and Jay Ginn, eds, *Connecting Gender and Ageing: A Sociological Approach.* Buckingham, UK: Open University Press.

———. 1996. "Connecting Age, Gender, Class, and Ethnicity: A Case Study of the Garment Industry in Montreal." PhD dissertation, University of Toronto.

———. 2000. "Diversity and the State of Sociological Aging Theory." *The Gerontologist* 40: 517–30.

———. 2002. "Negotiating Mothering and Caring in an Inflexible Paid Work Environment: A Case Study of Older Garment Workers." *Hallym International Journal on Aging* 4, 2: 141–60.

McMullin, Julie Ann, and Peri Ballantyne. 1995. "Employment Characteristics and Income: Assessing Gender and Age Group Effects for Canadians Aged 45 Years and Over." *Canadian Journal of Sociology* 20, 4: 529–55.

McMullin, Julie Ann, and Ellie Berger. 2006. "Gendered Ageism/Age(ed) Sexism: The Case of Unemployed Older Workers." Chapter 9 in Toni Calasanti and Kate Slevin, eds, *Age Matters: Realigning Feminist Thinking.* New York: Routledge.

McMullin, Julie Ann, and John Cairney. 2004. "Self-Esteem and the Intersection of Age, Class, and Gender." *Journal of Aging Studies* 18: 75–90.

McMullin, Julie Ann, and Victor W. Marshall. 1999. "Structure and Agency in the Retirement Process: A Case Study of Montreal Garment Workers." Chapter 11 in C.D. Ryff and V.W. Marshall, eds, *The Self and Society in Aging Processes.* New York: Springer.

———. 2001. "Ageism, Age Relations and Garment Industry Work in Montreal." *The Gerontologist* 41: 111–22.

———, eds. 2010. *Ageing and Working in the New Economy: Careers and Changing Structures in Small and Medium Size Information Technology Firms.* Camberley, UK: Edward Elgar Publishing.

McMullin, Julie Ann, and Kim M. Shuey. 2006. "Ageing, Disability and Workplace Accommodations." *Aging & Society* 26: 831–47.

McMullin, Julie Ann, and Stephen Smith. 1997. "Toxic Steel: State-Corporate Crime and the Contamination of the Environment." Chapter 3 in John McMullan, David Perrier, Stephen Smith, and Peter Swan, eds, *Crimes, Laws and Communities.* Halifax: Fernwood.

Mahalik, James R., Shaun M. Burns, and Matthew Syzdek. 2007. "Masculinity and Perceived Normative Health Behaviors as Predictors of Men's Health Behaviors." *Social Science and Medicine* 64: 2201–9.

Maher, Timothy. 1998. "Environmental Oppression: Who Is Targeted for Toxic Exposure?" *Journal of Black Studies* 28, 3: 357–67.

Makarenko, Jay. 2008. "2008 Election Campaign Political Party Platforms." *Mapleleafweb*, 3 October. http://www.mapleleafweb.com/features/2008-election-campaign-political-party-platforms

Malat, Jennifer R., Michelle van Ryn, and David Purcell. 2006. "Race, Socioeconomic Status, and the Perceived Importance of Positive Self-Presentation in Health Care." *Social Science and Medicine* 62: 2479–88.

Mandell, Nancy, and Ann Duffy. 2005. "Explaining Family Lives." Chapter 1 in Nancy Mandell and Ann Duffy, eds, *Canadian Families: Race, Class, Gender, and Sexuality*, 3rd edn. Toronto: Thomson Nelson.

Mannheim, Karl. [1928] 1952. "The Problem of Generations." Part 7 in Karl Mannheim, *Essays on the Sociology of Knowledge*, edited by P. Kecskemeti. London: Routledge & Kegan Paul.

Mao, Yang, Jinfu Hu, Anne-Marie Ugnat, Robert Semenciw, and Shirley Fincham. 2001. "Socioeconomic Status and Lung Cancer Risk in Canada." *International Journal of Epidemiology* 30: 809–17.

Mao, Y., J. Hu, A.M. Ugnat, and K. White. 2000. "Non-Hodgkin's Lymphoma and Occupational Exposure to Chemicals in Canada." *Annals of Oncology* 11, suppl. 1: 69–73.

Margolis, Maxine, 2001. "Putting Mothers on the Pedestal." Chapter 10 in Bonnie J. Fox, ed., *Family Patterns, Gender Relations*. Toronto: Oxford University Press.

Marmot, M.G. 2005. "Social Determinants of Health Inequalities." *The Lancet* 365: 1099–104.

———. 2006. "Status Syndrome: A Challenge to Medicine." *JAMA* 295, 11: 1304–7.

———. 2007. "Achieving Health Equity: From Root Causes to Fair Outcomes." *The Lancet* 370: 1153–63.

Marshall, Barbara L. 2000. *Configuring Gender: Explorations in Theory and Politics*. Peterborough, ON: Broadview Press.

Marshall, Barbara L., and Stephen Katz. 2002. "Forever Functional: Sexual Fitness and the Ageing Male Body." *Body and Society* 8, 4: 3–70.

Marshall, Katherine. 1993a. "Dual Earners: Who's Responsible for Housework?" *Canadian Social Trends* 31: 11–14.

———. 1993b. "Employed Parents and the Division of Housework." *Perspectives on Labour and Income* 5, 3: 23–30.

———. 2000. "Incomes of Younger Retired Women: The Past 30 Years." *Perspectives on Labour and Income* 12, 4: 9–17. Statistics Canada Catalogue no. 75-001-XPE.

———. 2006. "Converging Gender Roles." *Perspectives on Labour and Income* 7, 7. Statistics Canada Catalogue no. 75-001-XIE.

———. 2008. "Fathers' Use of Paid Parental Leave." Retrieved 23 February 2016 from http://www.statcan.gc.ca/pub/75-001-x/2008106/pdf/10639-eng.pdf

Marshall, Katherine, and Vincent Ferrao. 2007. "Participation of Older Workers." *Perspectives*, August. Statistics Canada Catalogue no. 75-001-XE.

Marshall, T.H. 1950. *Citizenship and Social Class*. Cambridge: Cambridge University Press.

Marshall, Victor W. 1983. "Generations, Age Groups, and Cohorts: Conceptual Distinctions." *Canadian Journal on Aging* 2: 51–61.

———. 1995. "The Micro-Macro Link in the Sociology of Aging." Pp. 337–71 in C. Hummel and C. Lalive D'Epinay, eds, *Images of Aging in Western Societies*. Proceedings of the 2nd Images of Aging conference. Geneva: Centre for Interdisciplinary Gerontology, University of Geneva.

Marshall, Victor W., Walter Heinz, Helga Krueger, and Anil Verma, eds. 2001. *Restructuring Work and the Life Course*. Toronto: University of Toronto Press.

Marshall, Victor W., Fay Lomax Cook, and Joanne Gard Marshall. 1993. "Conflict over Intergenerational Equity: Rhetoric and Reality in a Comparative Context." Pp. 119–40 in Vern

L. Bengtson and W.A. Achenbaum, eds, *The Changing Contract across Generations*. New York: Aldine de Gruyter.

Marshall, Victor W., and Margaret Mueller. 2002. *Rethinking Social Policy for an Aging Workforce and Society: Insights from the Life Course Perspective*. Ottawa: Canadian Policy Research Networks. Document no. 11849.

Marshall, Victor W., and J. Tindale. 1978. "Notes for a Radical Gerontology." *International Journal of Aging and Human Development* 9: 163–75.

Martin, Sheilah, and Murray Coleman. 1995. "Judicial Intervention in Pregnancy." *McGill Law Journal* 40: 947–91.

Martin, Steven P., and John Robinson. 2007. "The Income Digital Divide: Trends and Predictions for Levels of Internet Use." *Social Problems* 54: 1–22.

Martin-Matthews, Anne. 2000. "Intergenerational Caregiving: How Apocalyptic and Dominant Demographies Form the Questions and Shape the Answers." Pp. 80–79 in Ellen M. Gee and Glori M. Guttman, eds, *The Overselling of Population Aging: Apocalyptic Demography, Intergenerational Challenges, and Social Policy*. Don Mills, ON: Oxford University Press.

Marx, Karl. [1893–94] 1956. "Capital, Vol. III." Pp. 178–9 in Karl Marx, *Selected Writings in Sociology and Social Philosophy*. Translated by T.B. Bottomore, edited by T.B. Bottomore and Maximilien Rubel. New York: McGraw-Hill.

———. [1852] 1963. *The 18th Brumaire of Louis Bonaparte*. New York: International Publishers.

———. 1969. *Selected Works*. Vol. I. Moscow: Progress Publishers.

———. [1848] 1983. "The Communist Manifesto." In *The Portable Karl Marx*. New York: Penguin.

Marx, Karl, and Friedrich Engels. [1848] 1970. *The Communist Manifesto*. New York: Washington Square Press.

Mata, Fernando. 1997. *Intergenerational Transmission of Education and Socio-economic Status: A Look at Immigrants, Visible Minorities and Aboriginals*. Income and Labour Dynamics Working Paper Series. Statistics Canada Catalogue no. 97-077-5F0002M.

Matheson, Flora I., Rahim Moineddin, and Richard H. Glazier. 2008. "The Weight of Place: A Multilevel Analysis of Gender, Neighborhood Material Deprivation, and Body Mass Index among Canadian Adults." *Social Science and Medicine* 66, 3: 675–90.

Matthews, Sharon, Orly Manor, and Chris Power. 1999. "Social Inequalities in Health: Are There Gender Differences?" *Social Science and Medicine* 48, 1: 49–60.

Maxwell, Judith. 2008. "Bridging the Access Gap: It Starts with First-Generation Students." *Globe and Mail*, 19 May.

May, Martha. 1993. "Bread before Roses: American Workingmen, Labour Unions and the Family Wage." Chapter 11 in Bonnie J. Fox, ed., *Family Patterns, Gender Relations*. Toronto: Oxford University Press.

Mayer, L.U., and W. Muller. 1986. "The State and the Structure of the Life Course." Chapter 10 in A.B. Sorensen, F.E. Weinert, and L.R. Sherrod, eds, *Human Development and the Life Course: Multidisciplinary Perspectives*. Hillsdale, NJ: Lawrence Erlbaum Associates.

Menaghan, Elizabeth G. 1990. "Social Stress and Individual Distress." *Research in Community and Mental Health* 6: 107–41.

Menec, Verena H., Lisa Lix, and Leonard Mac-William. 2005. "Trends in the Status of Older Manitobans, 1985 to 1999." *Canadian Journal on Aging* 24, suppl. 1: 5–14.

Menendez, Maria, Joan Benach, Carles Muntaner, Marcelo Amable, and Patricia O'Campo. 2007. "Is Precarious Employment More Damaging to Women's Health Than Men's?" *Social Science and Medicine* 64: 776–81.

Mental Health Commission of Canada. 2012. "Changing Directions Changing Lives: The Mental Health Strategy for Canada." *Mental Health Commission of Canada*. http://strategy.mental-healthcommission.ca/pdf/strategy-images-en.pdf

Messing, Karen. 1997. "Women's Occupational Health: A Critical Review and Discussion of Current Issues." *Women and Health* 25, 4: 39–68.

———. 1998. *One-Eyed Science: Occupational Health and Women Workers*. Philadelphia: Temple University Press.

Metcalfe, Chris, George Davey Smith, Jonathan A. C. Sterne, Pauline Heslop, John Macleod, and

Carole L. Hart. 2005. "Cause-Specific Hospital Admission and Mortality among Working Men: Association with Socioeconomic Circumstances in Childhood and Adult Life, and the Mediating Role of Daily Stress." *European Journal of Public Health* 15, 3: 238–44.

Middlesex-London Health Unit. 2000. *Final Report of the Task Force on the Health Effects of Women Abuse*. London, ON: Middlesex-London Health Unit.

Miech, Richard Allen, and Michael J. Shanahan. 2000. "Socioeconomic Status and Depression over the Life Course." *Journal of Health and Social Behavior* 41, 2: 162–76.

Miles, Robert. 1989. *Racism*. London: Routledge.

Miles, Robert, and Rudy Torres. 2000. "Does Race Matter? Transatlantic Perspectives on Racism after 'Race Relations.'" Chapter 2 in Madeline A. Kalbach and Warren E. Kalbach, eds, *Perspectives on Ethnicity in Canada*. Toronto: Harcourt Canada.

Millar, Wayne. 1992. "Place of Birth and Ethnic Status: Factors Associated with Smoking Prevalence among Canadians." *Health Reports* 4, 1: 7–24. Statistics Canada Catalogue no. 82-003.

Millett, Kate. 1969. *Sexual Politics*. New York: Avon Books.

Mirchandani, Kiran, and Wendy Chan. 2007. *Criminalizing Race, Criminalizing Poverty: Welfare Fraud Enforcement in Canada*. Halifax: Fernwood.

Mirowsky, John, and Catherine E. Ross. 2003. *Social Causes of Psychological Distress*. New York: Transaction Publishers.

Mitchell, B. 2000. "The Refilled 'Nest': Debunking the Myth of Families in Crisis." Pp. 80–99 in E.M. Gee and G.M. Guttman, eds, *The Overselling of Population Aging: Apocalyptic Demography, Intergenerational Challenges, and Social Policy*. Don Mills, ON: Oxford University Press.

Mitchell, B., and E.M. Gee. 1996. "Boomerang Kids and Midlife Parental Marital Satisfaction." *Family Relations* 45: 442–8.

Mitchinson, Wendy. 1991. *The Nature of Their Bodies: Women and Their Doctors in Victorian Canada*. Toronto: University of Toronto Press.

Mittelstaedt, Martin. 2007. "Sarnia's Emissions Affecting Health, Study Says." *Globe and Mail*, 4 October.

Monsebraaten, Laurie. 2008. "Having a Job, but Losing Ground; Report Shows Ontario Child Poverty Rate Still Rising; System Penalizes Working Poor." *Toronto Star*, 2 April.

Montazer, S., and B. Wheaton. 2011. "The Impact of Generation and Country of Origin on the Mental Health of Children of Immigrants." *Journal of Health and Social Behavior* 52, 1: 23–42.

Monture, Patricia A. 2007. "Racing and Erasing: Law and Gender in White Settler Societies." Pp. 197–216 in Sean P. Hier and B. Singh Bolaria, eds, *Race and Racism in 21st Century Canada: Continuity, Complexity, and Change*. Peterborough, ON: Broadview Press.

Mooers, Colin. 1999. "Can We Still Resist? Globalization, Citizenship Rights and Class Formation." Chapter 20 in Dave Broad and Wayne Antony, eds, *Citizens or Consumers? Social Policy in a Market Society*. Halifax: Fernwood.

Morgan, D.H.J. 1985. *The Family, Politics, and Social Theory*. London: Routledge & Kegan Paul.

Morgan, Kathryn Pauly. 1998. "Women and the Knife: Cosmetic Surgery and the Colonization of Women's Bodies." Chapter 11 in Rose Weitz, ed., *The Politics of Women's Bodies: Sexuality, Appearance, and Behavior*. New York: Oxford University Press.

Morissette, René. 2002. "Pensions: Immigrants and Visible Minorities." *Perspectives on Labour and Income* 3, 6: 5–11. Statistics Canada Catalogue no. 75-001-XIE.

Morissette, René, and Yuri Ostrovsky. 2006. "Earnings Instability." *Perspectives on Labour and Income* 18, 4: 5–16. Statistics Canada Catalogue no. 75-001-XIE.

Morris, Margaret E., and Anthea Symonds. 2004. "'We've Been Trained to Put Up with It': Real Women and the Menopause." *Critical Public Health* 14, 3: 311–23.

Morris, Martina, Annette D. Bernhardt, and Mark S. Handcock. 1994. "Economic Inequality: New Methods for New Trends." *American Sociological Review* 59, 2: 205–19.

Mullings, Leith, and Amy J. Schultz. 2006. "Intersectionality and Health: An Introduction." Chapter 1 in Amy J. Schultz and Leith Mullings, eds, *Gender, Race, Class and Health: Intersectional Approaches*. San Francisco: Jossey-Bass.

Muntaner, C., W.W. Eaton, C. Diala, R.C. Kessler, and P.D. Sorlie. 1998. "Social Class, Assets, Organizational Control and the Prevalence of Common Groups of Common Groups of Psychiatric Disorders." *Social Science and Medicine* 47, 12: 2043–53.

Muntaner, Carles, Carme Borrell, and Haejoo Chung. 2007. "Class Relations, Economic Inequality and Mental Health: Why Social Class Matters to the Sociology of Mental Health." Chapter 6 in William Avison, Jane McLeod, and Bernice Pescosilido, eds, *Mental Health, Social Mirror*. New York: Springer.

Murdock, George. 1949. *Social Structure*. New York: Macmillan.

Murphy, Brian, Paul Roberts, and Michael Wolfe. 2007. "High-Income Canadians." *Perspectives on Labour and Income* 19, 4: 5–17. Statistics Canada Catalogue no. 75-001-XIE.

Mustard, Cameron A., Shelley Derkson, Jean-Marie Berthelot, Michael Wolfson, and Leslie L. Roos. 1997. "Age-Specific Education and Income Gradients in Morbidity and Mortality in a Canadian Province." *Social Science and Medicine* 45, 3: 383–97.

Myers, Karen, and Patrice de Broucker. 2006. *Too Many Left Behind: Canada's Adult Education and Training System*. Research Report 34, Work Network. Ottawa: Canadian Policy Research Networks. www.cprn.org/documents/43977_en.pdf

Myles, John F. 1980. "The Aged, the State, and the Structure of Inequality." Pp. 317–42 in J. Harp and J. Hofley, eds, *Structural Inequality in Canada*. Toronto: Prentice Hall.

———. 1981. "Income Inequality and Status Maintenance." *Research on Aging* 3: 123–41.

———. 1984. *The Political Economy of Public Pensions*. Boston: Little, Brown.

———. 1989. *Old Age in the Welfare State: The Political Economy of Public Pensions*, rev. edn. Lawrence: University Press of Kansas.

———. 1995. "The Market's Revenge: Old Age Security and Social Rights." Wilson Abernathy Distinguished Lecture, University of Toronto, April.

———. 2000. *The Maturation of Canada's Retirement Income System: Income Levels, Income Inequality and Low-Income among the Elderly*. Statistics Canada Catalogue no. 11F0019MPE, no. 147. Ottawa: Statistics Canada/Tallahassee: Florida State University.

Myles, John F., and Debra Street. 1995. "Should the Economic Life Course Be Redesigned? Old Age Security in a Time of Transition." *Canadian Journal on Aging* 14: 335–59.

Nabalamba, Alice, and Wayne J. Millar. 2007. "Going to the Doctor." *Health Reports* 18, 1: 23–35. Statistics Canada Catalogue no. 82-003.

Nakhaie, Reza. 1995. "Ownership and Management Positions of Canadian Ethnic Groups in 1973 and 1989." *Canadian Journal of Sociology* 20, 2: 167–92.

———. 1997. "Vertical Mosaic among the Elites: The New Imagery Revisited." *Canadian Review of Sociology and Anthropology* 34, 1: 1–24.

———. 2001. "Ethnic and Gender Distribution of Sociologists and Anthropologists in Canada, 1972–1996." *Canadian Journal of Sociology* 26, 2: 215–32.

———. 2006. "A Comparison of the Earnings of the Canadian Native-Born and Immigrants, 2001." *Canadian Ethnic Studies* 38, 2: 19–46.

———. 2007. "Ethno-racial Origins, Social Capital and Income Inequality." *Journal of International Migration and Integration* 8: 307 25.

———. 2009. "Immigrants, Visible Minorities and Self-employment: Does Social Capital Make a Difference?" *Business Review* 13, 1: 80–6.

Nakhaie, Reza, and James Curtis. 1998. "Effects of Class Positions of Parents on Educational Attainment of Daughters and Sons." *Canadian Review of Sociology and Anthropology* 35, 4: 483–515.

National Collaborating Centre for Aboriginal Health. 2012. "Art and Wellness: The Importance of Art for Aboriginal Peoples' Health and Healing." *Emerging Priorities*. Retrieved 29 February 2016 from http://www.nccah-ccnsa.ca/Publications/Lists/Publications/Attachments/26/art_wellness_EN_web.pdf

National Council of Welfare. 2000. *Poverty Profile: A Report*. Ottawa: Minister of Public Works and Government Services Canada.

———. 2006a. "Persistence of Poverty." http://www.ncwcnbes.net/en/research/povertstats/related-factsheets.html

———. 2006b. *Poverty Profile 2002–2003*. Ottawa: Minister of Public Works and Government Services.

———. 2007. *Poverty Statistics 2004*. Ottawa: Minister of Public Works and Government Services.

———. 2008. "Factsheet 1: Statistics Canada's before-Tax Low Income Cutoffs (1992 Base) for 2006." http://www.ncwcnbes.net/ documents/researchpublications/OtherFactSheets/PovertyLines/2006ENG.pdf

Nelson, Jay. 2002. "'A Strange Revolution in the Manners of the Country': Aboriginal-Settler Intermarriage in Nineteenth-Century British Columbia." Chapter 1 in John McLaren, Robert Menzies, and Dorothy E. Chunn, eds, *Regulating Lives: Historical Essays on the State, Society, the Individual and the Law*. Vancouver: UBC Press.

Neugarten, B.L. 1970. "The Old and the Young in Modern Societies." *American Behavioral Scientist* 4: 13–24.

Neugarten, B.L., and G.O. Hagestad. 1976. "Age and the Life Course." In R.H. Binstock and E. Shanas, eds, *Handbook of Aging and the Social Sciences*. New York: Van Nostrand-Reinhold.

Neugarten, B.L., J.W. Moore, and J.C. Lowe. 1965. "Age Norms, Age Constraints, and Adult Socialization." *American Journal of Sociology* 70: 710–17.

Newbold, Bruce. 1998. "Problems in Search of Solutions: Health and Canadian Aboriginals." *Journal of Community Health* 23, 1: 59–73.

———. 2005. "Health Status and Health Care of Immigrants in Canada: A Longitudinal Analysis." *Journal of Health Services Research & Policy* 10, 2: 77–83.

Ng, Edward, Russell Wilkins, François Gendron, and Jean-Marie Berthelot. 2005. "Dynamics of Immigrants' Health in Canada: Evidence from the National Population Health Survey." *Healthy Today, Healthy Tomorrow? Findings from the National Population Health Survey* 1, 2: 1–11. Statistics Canada Catalogue no. 82-618.

Ng, Roxanna. 1993. "Racism, Sexism and Nation-Building in Canada." Pp. 50–9 in Cameron McCarthy and Warren Crichlow, eds, *Race, Identity and Representation in Education*. New York: Routledge.

———. 2002. "Freedom for Whom? Globalization and Trade from the Standpoint of Garment Workers." *Canadian Women's Studies* 4: 74–81.

Ng, Thomas W.H., and Daniel C. Feldman. 2013. "Employee Age and Health." *Journal of Vocational Behavior* 8, 3: 336–45.

Nicholas, Andrea Bear. 2001. "Canada's Colonial Mission: The Great White Bird." Chapter 1 in K.P. Binda, ed., with Sharilyn Calliou, *Aboriginal Education in Canada: A Study in Decolonization*. Mississauga, ON: Canadian Educators' Press.

Nichols, Michael "Nick." 2001. "Gallery: Ndoki: Last Place on Earth." http://www.michaelnicknichols.com/works/ndoki-last-place-on-earth/

Nicholson, Linda. 1994. "Interpreting Gender." *Signs* 20, 1: 79–105.

Noh, Samuel, Morton Beiser, Violet Kaspar, Feng Hou, and Joanna Rummens. 1999. "Perceived Racial Discrimination, Depression, and Coping: A Study of Southeast Asian Refugees in Canada." *Journal of Health and Social Behavior* 40, 3: 193–207.

Noh, Samuel, Violet Kaspar, and K.A.S. Wickrama. 2007. "Overt and Subtle Racial Discrimination and Mental Health: Preliminary Findings for Korean Immigrants." *American Journal of Public Health* 97, 7: 1269–74.

Novak, M. 2013. *Aging and Society*, 7th edn. Toronto: Nelson Education.

Nurullan, Abu Sadat. 2010. "Gender Differences in Distress: The Mediating Influence of Life Stressors and Psychological Resources." *Asian Social Science* 6, 5: 27–35.

O'Brien, Mary. 1981. *The Politics of Reproduction*. Boston: Routledge & Kegan Paul.

OECD. *See* Organization for Economic Co-operation and Development.

Offe, C., and V. Ronge. 1982. "Thesis on the Theory of the State." Pp. 249–56 in A. Giddens and D. Held, eds, *Classes, Power and Conflict*. Berkeley: University of California Press.

Offer, Shira, and Barbara Schneider. 2011. "Revisiting the Gender Gap in Time-Use Patterns: Multitasking and Well-Being among Mothers and Fathers in Dual-Earner Families." *American Sociological Review* 76, 6: 809–33.

Offman, Alia, and Peggy J. Kleinplatz. 2004. "Does PMDD Belong in the DSM? Challenging the Medicalization of Women's Bodies." *Canadian Journal of Human Sexuality* 13, 1: 17–27.

Oliver, Lisa N., and Michael V. Hayes. 2008. "Effects of Neighbourhood Income on Reported Body Mass Index: An Eight-Year Longitudinal Study of Canadian Children." BMC *Public Health* 8: 16.

Oliver, M. 2013. "The Social Model of Disability: Thirty Years On." *Disability and Society* 28, 7: 1024–6.

O'Loughlin, Jennifer. 1999. "Understanding the Role of Ethnicity in Chronic Disease: A Challenge for the New Millennium." *Canadian Medical Association Journal* 161, 2: 152–5.

Omi, Michael, and Howard Winant. 1994. *Racial Formation in the United States from the 1960s to the 1990s*, 2nd edn. New York: Routledge.

O'Neill, Katherine. 2008. "Graphic List of Abuse to Settle Claims: Complex System of Determining Payment Seen as Necessary to Manage Huge Numbers of Complaints by Former Residential-School Students." *Globe and Mail*, 25 February.

Ontario Health Quality Council. 2008. *Qmonitor: 2008 Report on Ontario's Health System*. Toronto: Ontario Health Quality Council.

O'Rand, Angela. 1996a. "The Cumulative Stratification of the Life Course." Pp. 188–207 in R.H. Binstock and L.K. George, eds, *Handbook of Aging and the Social Sciences*, 4th edn. New York: Academic Press.

———. 1996b. "The Precious and the Precocious: Understanding Cumulative Disadvantage and Cumulative Advantage over the Life Course." *The Gerontologist* 36: 230–8.

O'Rand, Angela, and Jennifer Hamil-Luker. 2005. "Processes of Cumulative Adversity: Childhood Disadvantage and Increased Risk of Heart Attack across the Life Course." *Journals of Gerontology* 60B, spec. iss. 2: 117–24.

Organization for Economic Co-operation and Development. 2009. *Sickness, Disability and Work: Keeping on Track in the Economic Downturn*. Paris: OECD.

———. 2011. *Divided We Stand: Why Inequality Keeps Rising*. Paris: OECD.

———. 2015. "Income Inequality-Sweden." Retrieved 1 March 2016 from http://www.oecd.org/els/soc/ OECD-Income-Inequality-Sweden.pdf

Osberg, Lars. 1992. "Canada's Economic Performance: Inequality, Poverty, and Growth." Pp. 39–52 in Robert Allen and Gideon Rosenbluth, eds, *False Promises: The Failure of Conservative Economics*. Vancouver: New Star Books.

Osborne, Ken. 2000. "Public Schooling and Citizenship Education in Canada." *Canadian Ethnic Studies* 32, 1: 8–37.

Oxman-Martinez, Jacqueline, Shelly N. Abdool, and Margot Loiselle-Leonard. 2000. "Immigration, Women and Health in Canada." *Canadian Journal of Public Health* 91, 5: 394–5.

Pakulski, Jan, and Malcolm Waters. 1996a. "The Reshaping and Dissolution of Social Class in Advanced Society." *Theory and Society* 25: 667–91.

———. 1996b. *The Death of Class*. London: Sage.

Palameta, Boris. 2004. "Low Income among Immigrants and Visible Minorities." *Perspectives on Labour and Income* 5, 4. Statistics Canada Catalogue no. 75-001-XIE.

Palameta, Boris, and Xuelin Zhang. 2006. "Does It Pay to Go Back to School?" *Perspectives on Labour and Income* 7, 3: 5–11. Statistics Canada Catalogue no. 75-001-XIE.

Palaniappan, U., L. Starkey Jacobs, J. O'Loughlin, and K. Gray-Donald. 2001. "Fruit and Vegetable Consumption Is Lower and Saturated Fat Intake Is Higher among Canadians Reporting Smoking." *Journal of Nutrition* 131, 7: 1952–8.

Pampel, Fred C. 1998. *Aging, Social Inequality, and Public Policy*. Thousand Oaks, CA: Pine Forge Press.

Pampel, Fred C., Patrick M. Krueger, and Justin T. Denney. 2010. "Socioeconomic Disparities in Health Behaviors." *Annual Review of Sociology* 36: 349–70.

Parker, Marti G., and Mats Thorslund. 2007. "Health Trends in the Elderly Population: Getting Better and Getting Worse." *The Gerontologist* 47, 2: 50–8.

Parkin, Frank. 1979. *Marxism and Class Theory: A Bourgeois Critique*. London: Tavistock.

Parsons, Talcott. 1929. "Capitalism in Recent German Literature: Sombart and Weber—Concluded." *Journal of Political Economy* 37: 31–51.

———. 1942. "Age and Sex in the Social Structure of the United States." *American Sociological Review* 7: 604–16.

———. 1949. *The Structure of Social Action: A Study in Social Theory with Reference to a Group of Recent European Writers*. Glencoe, IL: Free Press.

———. 1951. *The Social System*. Glencoe, IL: Free Press.

Passuth, P.M., and V.L. Bengtson. 1988. "Sociological Theories of Aging: Current Perspectives and Future Directions." Pp. 335–55 in J.E. Birren and V.L. Bengtson, eds, *Emergent Theories of Aging*. New York: Springer.

Patten, Scott, and Heather Juby. 2008. *A Profile of Clinical Depression in Canada*. Research Data Centre Network, Research Synthesis Series no. 1. Calgary: Department of Community Health Science and Psychiatry, Faculty of Medicine, University of Calgary. http://hdl.handle.net/1880/46327

Pavalko, Eliza K., and Shari Woodbury. 2000. "Social Roles as Process: Caregiving Careers and Women's Health." *Journal of Health and Social Behavior* 41, 1: 91–105.

Pearce, Tralee. 2007. "Adolescence Is Obsolete." *Globe and Mail*, 25 August.

Pearlin, L.I. 1989. "The Sociological Study of Stress." *Journal of Health and Social Behavior* 30, 3: 241–56. http://doi.org/10.2307/2136956

———. 2010. "The Life Course and the Stress Process: Some Conceptual Comparisons." *Journals of Gerontology Series B: Psychological Sciences and Social Sciences* 65B, 2: 207–15. http://doi.org/10.1093/geronb/gbp106

Pearlin, Leonard I., and Alex Bierman. 2013. "Current Issues and Future Directions in Research into the Stress Process." Pp. 325–40 in *Handbook of the Sociology of Mental Health*. Springer.

Pearlin, Leonard I., Scott Schieman, Elena M. Fazio, and Stephen C. Meersman. 2005. "Stress, Health, and the Life Course: Some Conceptual Perspectives." *Journal of Health and Social Behavior* 46, 2: 205–19.

Peek, M. Kristen, and Raymond T. Coward. 2000. "Antecedents of Disability for Older Adults with Multiple Chronic Health Conditions." *Research on Aging* 22, 4: 422–44.

Peppin, Patricia. 1995. "Feminism, Law, and the Pharmaceutical Industry." Chapter 5 in Frank Pearce and Laureen Snider, eds, *Corporate Crime: Contemporary Debates*. Toronto: University of Toronto Press.

Perkel, Colin. 2000. "Ontario's Black Guards Want Probe into Workplace Racism." *Globe and Mail*, 7 April.

Perreault, Samuel. 2008. *Visible Minorities and Victimization*. 2004. Canadian Centre for Justice Statistics Profile Series. Statistics Canada Catalogue no. 85F0033MIE, no. 15.

Pheasant, Valerie Bedassigae. 2001. "My Mother Used to Dance." Pp. 38–43 in Carl E. James and Adrienne Shadd, *Talking about Identity: Encounters in Race, Ethnicity, and Language*. Toronto: Between the Lines.

Phelan, Jo C., and Bruce G. Link. 2005. "Controlling Disease and Creating Disparities: A Fundamental Cause Perspective." *Journals of Gerontology* 60B, spec. iss. 2: 27–33.

Phelan, Jo C., Bruce G. Link, Ana Diez-Roux, Ichiro Kawachi, and Bruce Levin. 2004. "'Fundamental Causes' of Social Inequalities in Mortality: A Test of the Theory." *Journal of Health and Social Behavior* 45, 3: 265–85.

Phelan, Jo C., Bruce G. Link, and Parisa Tehranifar. 2010. "Social Conditions as Fundamental Causes of Health Inequalities Theory, Evidence, and Policy Implications." *Journal of Health and Social Behavior* 51, suppl. 1: S28–S40.

Phillips, L.R. 1986. "Theoretical Explanations of Elder Abuse: Competing Hypotheses and Unresolved Issues." Pp. 197–217 in K.A. Pillemer and R.S. Wold, eds, *Elder Abuse: Conflict in the Family*. Dover, MA: Auburn House.

Phillips, Paul, and Erin Phillips. 2000. *Women and Work: Inequality in the Canadian Labour Market*. Toronto: Lorimer.

Phillipson, C. 1982. *Capitalism and the Construction of Old Age*. London: Macmillan.

Pichora, E.C., and J.I. Payne. 2007. "Trends and Characteristics of Compensated Occupational Cancer in Ontario, Canada, 1937–2003." *American Journal of Industrial Medicine* 50, 12: 980–91.

Pickett, Kate E., and Richard G. Wilkinson. 2015. *Income Inequality and Health: A Causal Review.* Agency for Healthcare Research & Quality. Retrieved 26 February 2016 from http://www.ahrq. gov/professionals/education/curriculumtools/ population-health/pickett.html

Picot, Garnett, Feng Hou, and Simon Coulombe. 2008. "Poverty Dynamics among Recent Immigrants to Canada." *International Migration Review* 42, 2: 393–424.

Picot, Garnett, and John Myles. 1995. *Social Transfers, Changing Family Structure, and Low Income among Children.* Statistics Canada Catalogue no. 11F0019MPE, no. 82.

Pilat, Dirk, Agnès Cimper, Karsten Olsen, and Colin Webb. 2006. *The Changing Nature of Manufacturing in OECD Countries.* STI Working Paper 2006/9. OECD.

Pinto, Laura. 2006. "The Streaming of Working Class and Minority Students in Ontario." *Our Schools, Our Selves* 15, 2: 79.

Plager, Laurie, and Edward Chen. 1999. "Student Debt from 1990–91 to 1995–96: An Analysis of Canada Student Loans Data." *Education Quarterly Review* 5, 4: 10–35. Statistics Canada Catalogue no. 81-003.

Podnieks, Elizabeth. 1992. "National Survey on Abuse of the Elderly in Canada." *Journal of Elder Abuse and Neglect* 4: 5–58.

Pollan, M., and P. Gustavsson. 1999. "High-Risk Occupations for Breast Cancer in the Swedish Female Working Population." *American Journal of Public Health* 89, 6: 875–81.

Pomerleau, Joceline, Linda L. Pederson, Truls Ostbye, Mark Speechley, and Kathy N. Speechley. 1997. "Health Behaviours and Socio-economic Status in Ontario, Canada." *European Journal of Epidemiology* 13: 613–22.

Poon, Preston. 2005. "Who's Missing Out on the GIS?" *Perspectives on Labour and Income* 6, 10. Statistics Canada Catalogue no. 75-001-XIE.

Popenoe, David. 1993. "American Family Decline, 1960–1990: A Review and Appraisal." *Journal of Marriage and the Family* 55: 527–55.

———. 2005. *War over the Family.* New Brunswick, NJ: Transaction Publishers.

———. 2009. *Families without Fathers: Fathers, Marriage and Children in American Society.* New Jersey: Transaction Publishers.

Porter, John. 1965. *The Vertical Mosaic: An Analysis of Social Class and Power in Canada.* Toronto: University of Toronto Press.

Poulantzas, Nicos. 1975. *Classes in Contemporary Capitalism.* London: New Left Books.

Power, Elaine M. 2005. "Determinants of Healthy Eating among Low Income Canadians." *Canadian Journal of Public Health* 96, S3: 37–42.

Premji, Stéphanie, Frédéric Bertrand, Audrey Smargiassi, and Mark Daniel. 2007. "Socio-economic Correlates of Municipal-Level Pollution Emissions on Montreal." *Canadian Journal of Public Health* 98, 2: 138–42.

Prus, Steven G. 2007. "Age, SES, and Health: A Population Level Analysis of Health Inequalities over the Lifecourse." *Sociology of Health & Illness* 29, 2: 275–96.

Prus, Steven G., and Ellen Gee. 2003. "Gender Differences in the Influence of Economic, Lifestyle, and Psychosocial Factors on Later Life Health." *Canadian Journal of Public Health* 94, 4: 306–9.

Public Health Agency of Canada. 2006. *The Human Face of Mental Health and Mental Illness in Canada.* Ottawa: Public Health Agency of Canada.

———. 2008. *Healthy Settings for Young People in Canada.* Catalogue no. HP35-6/2007E-PDF. Ottawa: Minister of Health Canada.

Public Safety Canada. 2013. "Backgrounder—Aboriginal Offenders—A Critical Situation." Retrieved 13 May 2015 from http://www.oci-bec. gc.ca/cnt/rpt/oth-aut/oth-aut20121022info-eng. aspx

Pulkingham, Jane. 1998. "Remaking the Social Divisions of Welfare: Gender, 'Dependency,' and UI Reform." *Studies in Political Economy* 56, Summer: 7–48.

Pupo, Norene. 2001. "The Role of the State in a Restructured Economy." Chapter 4 in Dan Glenday and Ann Duffy, eds, *Canadian Society: Meeting the Challenges of the Twenty-First Century.* Toronto: Oxford University Press.

Putnam, R. 2000. *Bowling Alone.* New York: Simon and Schuster.

Putnam, M. 2002. "Linking Aging Theory and Disability Models: Increasing the Potential to Explore Aging with Physical Impairment." *Gerontologist* 42, 6: 799–806.

Pyper, Wendy. 2006. "Aging, Health, and Work." *Perspectives on Labour and Income* 18, 1: 5–15. Statistics Canada Catalogue no. 75-001-XIE.

———. 2008. "RRSP Investments." *Perspectives on Labour and Income* 9, 2: 5–11. Statistics Canada Catalogue no. 75-001-XIE.

Quan, Hude, Andrew Fong, Carolyn De Coster, Jianli Wang, Richard Musto, Tom W. Noseworthy, and William A. Ghali. 2006. "Variation in Health Services Utilization among Ethnic Populations." *Canadian Medical Association Journal* 174, 6: 787–91.

Quan, Hude, Fu-Lin Wang, Donald Schopflocher, and Carolyn De Coster. 2007. "Mortality, Cause of Death and Life Expectancy of Chinese Canadians in Alberta." *Canadian Journal of Public Health* 98, 6: 500–5.

Ralston, Helen. 1996. *The Lived Experience of South Asian Immigrant Women in Atlantic Canada: The Interconnections of Race, Class, and Gender.* New York: Edwin Mellen Press.

Ramsay, S., S. Ebrahim, P. Whincup, O. Papacosta, et al. 2008. "Social Engagement and the Risk of Cardiovascular Disease Mortality: Results of a Prospective Population-Based Study of Older Men." *Annals of Epidemiology* 18, 6: 476–83.

Ranson, Gillian. 2003. "Beyond Gender Differences: A Canadian Study of Women's and Men's Careers in Engineering." *Gender, Work, and Organization* 10, 1: 22–41.

———. 2005. "Paid and Unpaid Work: How Do Families Divide Their Labour?" Chapter 5 in M. Baker, ed., *Families: Changing Trends in Canada.* Toronto: McGraw-Hill Ryerson.

———. 2013. *Fathering, Masculinity and the Embodiment of Care.* Palgrave Macmillan: New York.

———. 2010. *Against the Grain.* Toronto: University of Toronto Press.

———. 2013. *Fathering, Masculinity and the Embodiment of Care.* New York: Palgrave Macmillan.

Raphael, Dennis, ed. 2004. *Social Determinants of Health: Canadian Perspectives.* Toronto: Canadian Scholars' Press.

———. 2006. "Social Determinants of Health: An Overview of Concepts and Issues." Chapter 5 in Dennis Raphael, Toba Bryant, and Marcia Rioux, eds, *Staying Alive: Critical Perspectives on Health, Illness, and Health Care.* Toronto: Canadian Scholars' Press.

———. 2007. *Poverty and Policy in Canada: Implications for Health and Quality of Life.* Toronto: Canadian Scholars' Press.

Rapoport, B., and C. Le Bourdais. 2006. "Parental Time, Work Schedules, and Changing Gender Roles." Chapter 4 in K. McQuillan and Z.R. Ravanera, eds, *Canada's Changing Families: Implications for Individuals and Society.* Toronto: University of Toronto Press.

Ray, Raka. 2006. "Is the Revolution Missing or Are We Looking in the Wrong Places?" *Social Problems* 53, 4: 459–65.

Reid J.L., D. Hammond, V.L. Rynard, and R. Burkhalter. 2014. *Tobacco Use in Canada: Patterns and Trends.* Waterloo, ON: Propel Centre for Population Health Impact, University of Waterloo.

Reiter, Ester. 1996. *Making Fast Food: From the Frying Pan into the Fire.* Montreal and Kingston: McGill-Queen's University Press.

Reitz, Jeffrey G. 2007. "Immigrant Employment Success in Canada, Part I: Individual and Contextual Causes." *Journal of International Migration and Integration* 8, 1: 11–36.

Reitz, Jeffrey G., and Rupa Banerjee. 2007. *Racial Inequality, Social Cohesion and Policy Issues in Canada.* Montreal: Institute for Research on Public Policy. www.irpp.org

Reitz, Jeffrey, Josh Curtis, and Jennifer Elrick. 2014. "Immigrant Skill Utilization: Trends and Policy Issues." *Journal of International Migration and Integration* 15: 1–26.

Remington, Robert. 2007. "The Shocking Toll of Domestic Violence; Thousands of Women Feel Trapped." *Calgary Herald*, 2 December.

Reynolds, L.T. 1992. "A Retrospective on 'Race': The Career of a Concept." *Sociological Focus* 25, 1: 1–14.

Rich, Adrienne. 1980. "Compulsory Heterosexuality and Lesbian Existence." *Signs* 5: 631–60.

Richardson, K., P.R. Band, G. Astrakianakis, and N.D. Le. 2007. "Male Bladder Cancer Risk and Occupational Exposure According to a Job-Exposure Matrix: A Case-Control Study in British Columbia, Canada." *Scandinavian Journal of Work and Environmental Health* 33, 6: 454–64.

Rieker, Patricia P., and Chloe E. Bird. 2000. "Sociological Explanations of Gender Differences in Mental and Physical Health." Chapter 7 in Chloe E. Bird, Peter Conrad, and Allen M. Fremont, eds, *Handbook of Medical Sociology*, 5th edn. Englewood Cliffs, NJ: Prentice Hall.

———. 2005. "Rethinking Gender Differences in Health: Why We Need to Integrate Social and Biological Perspectives." *Journals of Gerontology* 60B, spec.iss. 2: 40–7.

Riley, Matilda White. 1971. "Social Gerontology and the Age Stratification of Society." *The Gerontologist* 11: 79–87.

———. 1985. "Age Strata in Social Systems." Pp. 369–411 in R.H. Binstock and E. Shanas, eds, *Handbook of Aging and the Social Sciences*. New York: Van Nostrand-Reinhold.

———. 1988. "On the Significance of Age in Sociology." Pp. 24–45 in M.W. Riley with B.J. Huber and B.B. Hess, *Social Structures and Human Lives*. Newbury Park, CA: Sage.

———. 1994. "Aging and Society: Past, Present and Future." *The Gerontologist* 34: 436–46.

Riley, Matilda White, Anne Foner, and Joan Waring. 1988. "Sociology of Age." Pp. 243–90 in N.J. Smelser, ed., *Handbook of Sociology*. Newbury Park, CA: Sage.

Riley, Matilda White, Marilyn Johnson, and Anne Foner. 1972. *Aging and Society*. Vol. 3: *A Sociology of Age Stratification*. New York: Russell Sage Foundation.

Riley, Matilda White, and John W. Riley, Jr. 1994a. "Age Integration and the Lives of Older People." *The Gerontologist* 34: 110–15.

———. 1994b. "Structural Lag: Past and Future." Chapter 1 in M.W. Riley, R.L. Kahn, and A. Foner, eds, *Age and Structural Lag: Society's Failure to Provide Meaningful Opportunities in Work, Family, and Leisure*. New York: John Wiley.

Rinehart, James W. 2006. *The Tyranny of Work: Alienation and the Labour Process*, 5th edn. Toronto: Harcourt Brace.

Risman, Barbara J. 1998. *Gender Vertigo: American Families in Transition*. New Haven, CT: Yale University Press.

Robertson, Ann. 1998. "Shifting Discourses on Health in Canada: From Health Promotion to Population Health." *Health Promotion International* 13, 2: 155–66.

Robson, K.L., P. Anisef, R.S. Brown, and G. Parekh. 2014. "The Intersectionality of Postsecondary Pathways: The Case of High School Students with Special Education Needs." *Canadian Review of Sociology/Revue Canadienne de Sociologie* 51, 3: 193–215. http://doi.org/10.1111/cars.12044

Rodgers, Karen. 1994. "Wife Assault in Canada." *Canadian Social Trends*, Autumn: 2–8. Ottawa: Statistics Canada.

Roos, Leslie L., Jennifer Magoon, Sumit Gupta, Dan Chateau, and Paul J. Veugelers. 2004. "Socioeconomic Determinants of Mortality in Two Canadian Provinces: Multilevel Modelling and Neighborhood Context." *Social Science & Medicine* 59, 76: 1435–47.

Roos, Noralou P., and Cameron A. Mustard. 1997. "Variation in Health and Health Care Use by Socioeconomic Status in Winnipeg, Canada: Does the System Work Well? Yes and No." *Milbank Quarterly* 75, 1: 89–111.

Rose, Kathryn M., April P. Carson, Diane Catellier, Ana Diez Roux, Carles Muntaner, Herman A. Tyroler, and Sharon B. Wyatt. 2004. "Women's Employment Status and Mortality: The Atherosclerosis Risk in Communities Study." *Journal of Women's Health* 13, 10: 1108–18.

Rosenberg, T., and S. Martel. 1998. "Cancer Trends from 1972–1991 for Registered Indians Living on Manitoba Reserves." *International Journal of Circumpolar Health* 57, suppl. 1: 391–8.

Rosenthal, C.J., S.H. Matthews, and V.W. Marshall. 1989. "Is Parent Care Normative? The Experiences of a Sample of Middle-Aged Women." *Research on Aging* 11, 2: 244–60.

Ross, David P., Katherine J. Scott, and Peter J. Smith. 2000. *The Canadian Fact Book on Poverty*. Ottawa: Canadian Council on Social Development.

Ross, David P., E. Richard Shillington, and Clarence Lochhead. 1994. *The Canadian Fact Book on Poverty*. Ottawa: Canadian Council on Social Development.

Ross, Nancy. 2004. *What Have We Learned Studying Income Inequality and Population Health?* Ottawa: Canadian Institute for Health Information.

Rotermann, Michele. 2006. "Seniors' Health Care Use." *Health Reports* 16, suppl.: 33–46. Statistics Canada Catalogue no. 82-003-SPE.

Rowntree, J., and Rowntree, M. 1968. "The Political Economy of Youth." *Our Generation* 6, 1–2: 155–90.

Rubenson, Kjell, Richard Desjardins, and Ee-Seul Yoon. 2007. *Adult Learning in Canada: A Comparative Perspective: Results from the Adult Literacy and Life Skills Survey.* Statistics Canada Catalogue no. 89-552, no. 17.

Ryder, N. 1965. "The Cohort as a Concept in the Study of Social Change." *American Sociological Review* 30: 834–61.

Sabourin, Sharon. 2003. "My Story—A Narrative: Refusing Mediocrity: Barriers to Higher Education for Sole Support Parents." Unpublished manuscript.

Safaei, Jalil. 2007. "Income and Health Inequality across Canadian Provinces." *Health and Place* 13: 629–38.

Sainsbury, Diane. 1999. "Gender and Social-Democratic Welfare States." Chapter 3 in Diane Sainsbury, ed., *Gender and Welfare State Regimes.* New York: Oxford University Press.

Sales, Arnaud, Rejean Drolet, and Isabelle Bonneau. 2001. "Academic Paths, Ageing, and the Living Conditions of Students in the Late 20th Century." *Canadian Review of Sociology and Anthropology* 38, 2: 167–88.

Samman, Emma, and Rodriquez-Takeuchi, Laura K. 2003. "Old Age, Disability and Mental Health." *Overseas Development Institute.* http://www.odi.org/sites/odi.org.uk/files/odi-assets/publications-opinion-files/8415.pdf

Samuel, John, and Kogalur Basavarajappa. 2006. "The Visible Minority Population in Canada: A Review of Numbers, Growth and Labour Force Issues." *Canadian Studies in Population* 33, 2: 241–69.

Sandstad, Nora Christie. 2008. "Pregnant Women and the Fourteenth Amendment: A Feminist Examination of the Trend to Eliminate Women's Rights during Pregnancy." *Law & Equality* 26, 1: 171–202.

Sangster, Joan. 1995. "Doing Two Jobs: The Wage-Earning Mother, 1945–70." Pp. 98–134 in Joy Parr, ed., *A Diversity of Women: Ontario, 1945–1980.* Toronto: University of Toronto Press.

Satzewich, Vic. 1998. "Race, Racism and Racialization: Contested Concepts." Chapter 1 in Vic Satzewich, ed., *Racism and Social Inequality in Canada.* Toronto: Thompson Educational.

Schick, Carol. 2001. "Keeping the Ivory Tower White: Discourse of Racial Domination." Pp. 99–119 in S.H. Razack, ed., *Race, Space and the Law: Unmapping a White Settler Society.* Toronto: Between the Lines.

Schissel, Bernard. 1997. *Blaming Children: Youth Crime, Moral Panics and the Politics of Hate.* Halifax: Fernwood.

———. 2006. *Still Blaming Children: Youth Conduct and the Politics of Child Hating.* Black Point, NS: Fernwood.

Schissel, Bernard, and Terry Wotherspoon. 2003. *The Legacy of School for Aboriginal People: Education, Oppression and Emancipation.* Don Mills, ON: Oxford University Press.

Scott, Katherine. 1996. "The Dilemma of Liberal Citizenship: Women and Social Assistance Reform in the 1990s." *Studies in Political Economy* 50, Summer: 7–36.

Seeman, Neil. 2001. "A Right to Welfare Is a Loss of Democracy." *Globe and Mail*, 31 October.

Seeman, Teresa, Elissa Epel, Tara Gruenewald, Arun Karlamangla, and Bruce S. McEwen. 2010. "Socio-Economic Differentials in Peripheral Biology: Cumulative Allostatic Load." *Annals of the New York Academy of Sciences* 1186, 1: 223–39.

Sewell, William H.J., Jr. 1992. "A Theory of Structure: Duality, Agency, and Transformation." *American Journal of Sociology* 98: 1–29.

———. 2005. *Logics of History: Social Theory and Social Transformation.* Chicago: University of Chicago Press.

Shaienks, Danielle, and Tomasz Gluszynski. 2007. *Participation in Postsecondary Education: Graduates, Continuers and Drop Outs, Results from YITS Cycle 4.* Culture, Tourism and the Centre for Education Statistics Research Papers. Statistics Canada Catalogue no. 81-595-MIE2007059.

Sharpe, Andrew, and Jill Hardt. 2006. *Five Deaths a Day: Workplace Fatalities in Canada, 1993–2005.* CSLS Research Paper 2006-04. Ottawa: Centre for the Study of Living Standards.

Sheehy, Elizabeth A. 2005. "Legal Responses to Violence against Women in Canada." Pp. 256–65 in B.A. Crow and L. Gotell, eds, *Open Boundaries:*

A Canadian Women's Studies Reader, 2nd edn. Toronto: Pearson, Prentice Hall.

Shellenbarger, Sue. 2001. "Anger over Age Discrimination Grows as Baby Boomers Hit 55." *Globe and Mail,* 4 June.

Shields, Margot. 2004. "Stress, Health and the Benefit of Social Support." *Health Reports* 15, 1: 9–38. Statistics Canada Catalogue no. 82-003.

———. 2007. "Smoking Bans: Influence on Smoking Prevalence." *Health Reports* 18, 3 (August). Statistics Canada Catalogue no. 82-003, pp. 9–24. Retrieved 11 May 2010 from http://www.statcan.gc.ca/pub/82-003x/2006008/article/smoking-tabac/10306-eng.pdf

Shields, Margot, and Laurent Martel. 2006. "Healthy Living among Seniors." *Health Reports* 16, suppl.: 7–20. Statistics Canada Catalogue no. 82-003.

Shields, Margot, and Stéphane Tremblay. 2002. "The Health of Canada's Communities." *Health Reports* 13, suppl.: 1–24. Statistics Canada Catalogue no. 82-003.

Shim, Janet K. 2002. "Understanding the Routinised Inclusion of Race, Socioeconomic Status and Sex in Epidemiology: The Utility of Concepts from Technoscience Studies." *Sociology of Health & Illness* 24, 2: 129–50.

Shragge, Eric. 1997. "Workfare: An Overview." Chapter 1 in Eric Shragge, ed., *Workfare: Ideology for a New Underclass.* Toronto: Garamond Press.

Shuey, Kim M., and Andrea E. Willson. 2008. "Cumulative Disadvantage and Black-White Disparities in Life-Course Health Trajectories." *Research on Aging* 30, 2: 200–25.

Simmons, Alan B., and Dwaine E. Plaza. 1998. "Breaking through the Glass Ceiling: The Pursuit of University Training among African-Caribbean Migrants and Their Children in Toronto." *Canadian Ethnic Studies* 30, 3: 99–120.

Simon, Robin. 2000. "The Importance of Culture in Sociological Theory and Research on Stress and Mental Health: A Missing Link?" Chapter 5 in Chloe E. Bird, Peter Conrad, and Allen M. Fremont, eds, *Handbook of Medical Sociology,* 5th edn. Englewood Cliffs, NJ: Prentice Hall.

———. 2007. "Contributions of the Sociology of Mental Health for Understanding the Social Antecedents, Social Regulation, and Social Distribution of Emotion." Chapter 11 in William Avison, Jane McLeod, and Bernice Pescosilido, eds, *Mental Health, Social Mirror.* New York: Springer.

Singh, Sheldon M., Lawrence F. Paszat, Cindy Li, Jingsong He, Chris Vinden, and Linda Rabeneck. 2004. "Association of Socioeconomic Status and Receipt of Colorectal Cancer Investigations: A Population-Based Retrospective Cohort Study." *Canadian Medical Association Journal* 171, 5: 461–5.

Smith, Charles C. 2006. "Racial Profiling in Canada, the United States, and the United Kingdom." Chapter 3 in Frances Henry and Carol Tator, eds, *Racial Profiling in Canada: Challenging the Myth of 'A Few Bad Apples.'* Toronto: University of Toronto Press.

Smith, Derek G. 1975. *Canadian Indians and the Law: Selected Documents, 1663–1972.* Toronto: McClelland & Stewart.

Smith, Dorothy E. 1987. *The Everyday World as Problematic: A Feminist Sociology.* Toronto: University of Toronto Press.

Smith, Vikki. 1997. "New Forms of Work Organization." *Annual Review of Sociology* 23: 315–39.

Snider, Laureen. 1993. *Bad Business: Corporate Crime in Canada.* Toronto: Nelson Canada.

Snyder, Linda. 2006. "Workfare: Ten Years of Pickin' on the Poor." Pp. 309–30 in Anne Westhues, ed., *Canadian Social Policy: Issues and Perspectives,* 4th edn. Waterloo, ON: Wilfrid Laurier University Press.

Social Development Canada, 2006. "Learning—School Drop-Out/Indicators of Well-Being in Canada." Retrieved 23 February 2015 from http://www4.hrsdc.gc.ca/.3ndic.1t.4r@-eng.jsp?iid=32

Sokal, Laura, Herb Katz, Matthew Adkins, Tannis Grills, Crystal Stewart, Greg Priddle, Anastasa Sych-Yereniuk, and Lori Chochinov-Harder. 2005. "Factors Affecting Inner-City Boys' Reading: Are Male Teachers the Answer?" *Canadian Journal of Urban Research* 14, 1: 107–30.

Spitzer, Denise L. 2005. "Engendering Health Disparities." *Canadian Journal of Public Health* 96, suppl. 2: S78–96.

Stackhouse, John. 2001. "Canada's Apartheid, Part 2, Crystal's Choice: The Best of Both Worlds." *Globe and Mail,* 5 November.

Stasiulis, Davia. 1999. "Feminist Intersectional Theorizing." Chapter 12 in Peter Li, ed., *Race and Ethnic Relations in Canada*, 2nd edn. Toronto: Oxford University Press.

Stasiulis, Davia, and Abigail B. Bakan. 1995. "Making the Match: Domestic Placement Agencies and the Racialization of Women's Household Work." *Signs* 20, 2: 303–35.

——. 1997. "Negotiating Citizenship: The Case of Foreign Domestic Workers in Canada." *Feminist Review* 57, 1: 112–39.

——. 2005. *Negotiating Citizenship: Migrant Women in Canada and the Global System*. Toronto: University of Toronto Press.

Statistics Canada. 2001a. *Annual Demographic Statistics*. Statistics Canada Catalogue no. 91-213XPB.

——. 2001b. "Death-Shifting Trends." *Health Reports* 12, 3: 41–6. Statistics Canada Catalogue no. 82-003.

——. 2001c. *Family Violence in Canada: A Statistical Profile, 2001*. Statistics Canada Catalogue no. 85-224.

——. 2001d. "Health Care/Self-Care." *Health Reports* 12, 3: 33–40. Statistics Canada Catalogue no. 82-003.

——. 2001e. "The Health Divide: How the Sexes Differ." *The Daily*, 26 April. Ottawa: Statistics Canada.

——. 2001f. *A Report on Adult Education and Training in Canada: Learning a Living*. Statistics Canada Catalogue no. 81-586-XPE.

——. 2001g. *Spousal Violence after Marital Separation*. Statistics Canada Catalogue no. 85-002-XIE.

——. 2001h. "Stress and Well-Being." *Health Reports* 12, 3: 21–32. Statistics Canada Catalogue no. 82-003.

——. 2001i. "Taking Risks/Taking Care." *Health Reports* 12, 3: 11–20. Statistics Canada Catalogue no. 82-003.

——. 2002a. CANSIM II, Table 282-0008. www.statcan.ca.

——. 2002b. *Family Violence in Canada: A Statistical Profile, 2002*. Statistics Canada Catalogue no. 85-224.

——. 2003a. *Ethnic Diversity Survey 2002*. Ottawa: Statistics Canada.

——. 2003b. *Women and Men in Canada: A Statistical Glance*. Ottawa: Statistics Canada. http://dsp-psd.pwgsc.gc.ca/Collection/SW21-50-2003E.pdf

——. 2004a. *Health Indicators*, no. 1. Statistics Canada Catalogue no. 82-221-XIE.

——. 2004b. "Long-Term Unemployment." *The Daily*, 21 April. Ottawa: Statistics Canada.

——. 2005a. "Family Violence in Canada: A Statistical Profile." *The Daily*, 14 July. Ottawa: Statistics Canada.

——. 2005b. *Family Violence in Canada: A Statistical Profile*. Statistics Canada Catalogue no. 85-224-XIE.

——. 2005c. *Income in Canada*. Statistics Canada Catalogue no. 75-202-XIE.

——. 2005d. *Survey of Earned Doctorates*. Statistics Canada Catalogue no. 81-595-MIE2005032.

——. 2005e. "Projections of the Aboriginal Populations, Canada, Provinces and Territories." Retrieved 5 May 2015 from http://www5.statcan.gc.ca/olc-cel/olc.action?objId=91-547-X&objType=2&lang=en&limit=0

——. 2006a. *The Canadian Labour Market at a Glance, 2005*. Ottawa: Statistics Canada, Labour Statistics Division.

——. 2006b. "Health-Adjusted Life Expectancy, at Birth and at Age 65, by Sex and Income Group, Canada and Provinces, Occasional (years)." CANSIM Table 102-0121. Ottawa: Statistics Canada.

——. 2006c. *Health Indicators*, no. 1. Statistics Canada Catalogue no. 82-221-XIE.

——. 2006d. *Measuring Violence against Women: Statistical Trends 2006*. Statistics Canada Catalogue no. 85-570-XIE.

——. 2006e. "Minimum Wage." *Perspectives on Labour and Income* 7, 9: 12–17. Statistics Canada Catalogue no. 75-001-XIE.

——. 2006f. *Women in Canada: A Gender-Based Statistical Report*. Statistics Canada Catalogue no. 89-503-XIE.

——. 2007a. "Deaths, by Selected Grouped Causes, Age Group and Sex, Canada, Provinces and Territories, Annual." CANSIM Table 102-0551. Ottawa: Minister of Industry.

——. 2007b. "Deaths, by Selected Grouped Causes and Sex, Canada, Provinces and Territories,

Annual." CANSIM Table 102-0552. Ottawa: Minister of Industry.

———. 2007c. *Family Violence in Canada: A Statistical Profile, 2007*. Statistics Canada Catalogue no. 85-224-XIE.

———. 2007d. *Mortality, Summary List of Causes 2004*. Statistics Canada Catalogue no. 84F0209XIE.

———. 2007e. *Navigating Family Transitions: Evidence from the General Social Survey, 2006*. Statistics Canada Catalogue no. 89-625-XIE, no. 2.

———. 2007f. *Participation and Activity Limitation Survey 2006: Analytical Report*. Statistics Canada Catalogue no. 89-628-XIE, no. 002.

———. 2008a. *Aboriginal Peoples in Canada in 2006: Inuit, Métis and First Nations, 2006 Census*. Statistics Canada Catalogue no. 97-558-XIE.

———. 2008b. *Deaths 2005*. Statistics Canada Catalogue no. 84F0211X.

———. 2008c. *Educational Portrait of Canada, 2006 Census*. Statistics Canada Catalogue no. 97-560-X.

———. 2008d. *Labour Force Survey, Monthly Statistics*. Tables 282-0087 and 282-0089. Ottawa: Statistics Canada. http://www40.statcan.ca/l01/cst01/labor66a.htm

———. 2008e. *Labour Force Characteristics by Age and Sex*. CANSIM Table 282-002. Ottawa: Statistics Canada. http://www40.statcan.ca/l01/cst01/labor20b.htm

———. 2008f. *2006 Census of Population*. Statistics Canada Catalogue no. 97-562-XCB2006017. http://www12.statcan.ca/english/census06/data/topics/Print.cfm

———. 2009. Government of Canada, Statistics Canada. 2009. "Persons with Disabilities, by Age Group and Sex (2006)." Retrieved 5 May 2015 from http://www.statcan.gc.ca/tables-tableaux/sum-som/l01/cst01/health71a-eng.htm

———. 2010a. "Archiving." Retrieved 19 February 2015 from http://www5.statcan.gc.ca/access_acces/alternative_alternatif.action?t=98-312-XWE2011003&k=425&l=eng&loc=http://www12.statcan.gc.ca/census-recensement/2011/as-sa/98-312-x/98-312-x2011003_1-eng.pdf

———. 2010b. "Archiving." Retrieved 23 February 2015 from http://www5.statcan.gc.ca/access_acces/alternative_alternatif.action?t=99-014-XWE2011003&l=eng&loc=http://www12.statcan.gc.ca/nhs-enm/2011/as-sa/99-014-x/99-014-x2011003_2-eng.pdf

———. 2010c. "Archiving." Retrieved 23 February 2015 from http://www5.statcan.gc.ca/access_acces/alternative_alternatif.action?teng=71-606-x2012006-eng.pdf&tfra=71-606-x2012006-fra.pdf&l=eng&loc=../71-606-x2012006-eng.pdf

———. 2010d. *Projections of the Diversity of the Canadian Population, 2006 to 2031*. Retrieved 23 February 2015 from http://www.statcan.gc.ca/pub/91-551-x/91-551-x2010001-eng.htm

———. 2011a. "Unknown." http://www12.statcan.gc.ca/nhs-enm/2011/dp-pd/dt-td/Rp-eng.cfm?LANG=E&APATH=3&DEAIL=0&DIM=0&FL=A&FREE=0&GC=0&GID=0&GK=0&GRP=0&PID=106671&PRID=0&PTYPE=105277&S=0&SHOWALL=0&SUB=0&Temporal=2013&THEME=98&VID=0&VNAMEE=&VNAMEF.

———. 2011b. "Mortalist: Overview, 2010 and 2011." http://www.statcan.gc.ca/pub/82-624-x/2011001/article/11427-eng.htm

———. 2011c. *National Household Survey*. Statistics Canada Catalogue no. 99-014-X2011037.

———. 2011d. "Family Violence in Canada: A Statistical Profile." http://www.statcan.gc.ca/pub/85-224-x/85-224-x2010000-eng.pdf

———. 2012a. "Health-Adjusted Life Expectancy, by Sex." Retrieved 5 May 2015 from http://www.statcan.gc.ca/tables-tableaux/sum-som/l01/cst01/hlth67-eng.htm

———. 2012b. "Income in Canada." CANSIM table 202-0802 and Catalogue no. 75-202-X. Last modified 27 June 2013.

———. 2013a. CANSIM table 202-0802 and Catalogue no. 75-202-X. Last modified 27 June 2013. http://www.statcan.gc.ca.myaccess.library.utoronto.ca/tables-tableaux/sum-som/l01/cst01/famil19-eng.htm?sdi=low%20income

———. 2013b. *Life Tables, Canada, Provinces and Territories: 2009 to 2011*. Statistics Canada Catalogue no. 84-537.

———. 2013c. "Mortality: Overview, 2010 and 2011." Retrieved 5 May 2015 from http://www.statcan.gc.ca/pub/91-209-x/2013001/article/11867-eng.htm

———. 2013d. "Mental and Substance Use Disorders in Canada" by Caryn Pearson, Teresa Janz, and Jennifer Ali, Health Statistics Division. http://

www.statcan.gc.ca/pub/82-624-x/2013001/article/11855-eng.pdf

———. 2013e. "Backgrounder—Aboriginal Offenders—A Critical Situation." Retrieved 1 March 2016 from http://www.oci-bec.gc.ca/cnt/rpt/oth-aut/oth-aut20121022info-eng.aspx

———. 2014a. "Adjusting the Scales: Obesity in the Canadian Population after Correcting for Respondent Bias." Retrieved 7 May 2015 from http://www.statcan.gc.ca/pub/82-624-x/2014001/article/11922-eng.htm

———. 2014b. "Age-Standardized Mortality Rates for the 10 Leading Causes of Death, Canada, 2000, 2010 and 2011." Retrieved 5 May 2015 from http://www.statcan.gc.ca/daily-quotidien/140128/t140128b002-eng.htm

———. 2014c. "The Daily—Labour Force Survey, August 2014." Retrieved 19 February 2015 from http://www.statcan.gc.ca/daily-quotidien/140905/dq140905a-eng.htm

———. 2014d. "The Daily—Labour Force Survey, October 2014." Retrieved 18 February 2015 from http://www.statcan.gc.ca.myaccess.library.utoronto.ca/daily-quotidien/141107/dq141107a-eng.htm

———. 2014e. "Heavy Drinking, 2013." Retrieved 7 May 2015 from http://www.statcan.gc.ca/pub/82-625-x/2014001/article/14019-eng.htm

———. 2014f. "Mood Disorders, by Age Group and Sex (Number)." Retrieved 5 May 2015 from http://www.statcan.gc.ca/tables-tableaux/sum-som/l01/cst01/health113a-eng.htm

———. 2014g. "Undergraduate Tuition Fees for Full Time Canadian Students, by Discipline, by Province (Canada)." Retrieved 3 December 2015 from http://www.statcan.gc.ca/tables-tableaux/sum-som/l01/cst01/educ50a-eng.htm

———. 2015a. "CANSIM—102-0551—Deaths and Mortality Rate, by Selected Grouped Causes, Age Group and Sex, Canada." Retrieved 7 May 2015 from http://www5.statcan.gc.ca/cansim/a26

———. 2015b. "CANSIM—102-0561—Leading Causes of Death, Total Population, by Age Group and Sex, Canada (Year-to-Date [averages])." Retrieved 5 May 2015 from http://www5.statcan.gc.ca/cansim/a47

———. 2015c. "Education Indicators in Canada: Report of the Pan-Canadian Education Indicators Program." 81-582-X. http://www5.statcan.

gc.ca/olc-cel/olc.action?ObjId=81-582-x&-ObjType=2&lang=en&limit=0

———. 2015d. "Labour Force Characteristics by Sex and Age Group." Retrieved 19 February 2015 from http://www.statcan.gc.ca/tables-tableaux/sum-som/l01/cst01/labor05-eng.htm

———. 2015e. "Self-Employment, Historical Summary." Retrieved 19 February 2015 from http://www.statcan.gc.ca/tables-tableaux/sum-som/l01/cst01/labor64-eng.htm

———. 2015f. "Education and Occupation of High Income Canadians." Retrieved 1 March 2016 from https://www12.statcan.gc.ca/nhs-enm/2011/as-sa/99-014-x/99-014-x2011003_2-eng.cfm

Statistics Canada and the Canadian Institute for Health Information. 2008. *Health Indicators 2008*. Ottawa: Canadian Institute for Health Information.

Stephensen, Marylee, and Ruth Emery. 2003. *Living beyond the Edge: The Impact of Trends in Nonstandard Work on Single/Lone-Parent Mothers*. Ottawa: Status of Women.

Street, Debra, and Ingrid Connidis. 2001. "Creeping Selectivity in Canadian Women's Pensions." Pp. 158–78 in Jay Ginn, Debra Street, and Sara Arber, eds, *Women, Work and Pensions*. Buckingham, UK: Open University Press.

Su, Fubing. 2006. "Gender Inequality in Chinese Politics: An Empirical Analysis of Provincial Elites. *Politics and Gender* 2, 143–63. http://www.theatlantic.com/china/archive/2013/06/chinas-glass-ceiling-women-still-excluded-from-high-level-politics/276589/

Tait, Heather. 2008. "Aboriginal People's Survey, 2006: Inuit Health and Social Conditions." Statistics Canada, Catalogue no. 89-637-X—no. 001.

Tanovich, David M. 2006. *The Colour of Justice: Policing Race in Canada*. Toronto: Irwin Law.

Tator, Carol, and Frances Henry. 2006. *Racial Profiling in Canada: Challenging the Myth of "A Few Bad Apples."* Toronto: University of Toronto Press.

Taylor, Alison, and Jason Foster. 2014. "Migrant Workers and the Problem of Social Cohesion in Canada." *Journal of International Migration and Integration* 16, 1:153–72.

Taylor, Alison, and Harvey Krahn. 2005. "Aiming High: Educational Aspirations of Visible Minority Immigrant Youth." *Canadian Social Trends* 79, Winter. Statistics Canada Catalogue no. 11-008.

Taylor-Butts, Andrea. 2007. "Canada's Shelters for Abused Women, 2005/2006." *Juristat* 27, 4. Statistics Canada Catalogue no. 85.

TD Economics. 2013. "Overview of Canada's Labour Market." Retrieved 25 February 2016 from https://www.td.com/document/PDF/economics/special/OverviewOfCanadasLabourMarket.pdf

Tett, Gillian. 2014. "Social Mobility: A Family Affair." *Financial Times*, 7 March. Retrieved 27 July 2016 from www.ft.com/cms/s/2/d939bfd0-a4c3-11e3-9313-00144feab7de.html.

Thiessen, Victor, and Christy Nickerson. 1999. *Canadian Gender Trends in Education and Work*. Catalogue no. MP32-30/00-4E. Ottawa: Applied Research Branch, Strategic Policy, Human Resources Development Canada (T-00-4E).

Thomas, E.M. 2006. *Readiness to Learn at School among Five-Year-Old Children in Canada*. Children and Youth Research Paper Series. Statistics Canada Catalogue no. 89-599-MIE2006004.

Thompson, E.P. 1963. *The Making of the English Working Class*. New York: Vintage.

Thuanh Ha, Tu. 2003. "Senior Seeks to Sue Ottawa over Unpaid Supplement." *Globe and Mail*, 31 January.

Tickamyer, Ann R. 2000. "Space Matters! Spatial Inequality in Future Sociology." *Contemporary Sociology* 29: 805–13.

Tilly, Charles. 1998. *Durable Inequality*. Berkeley: University of California Press.

Tindale, J., and V.W. Marshall. 1980. "A Generational-Conflict Perspective for Gerontology." Pp. 43–50 in V.W. Marshall, ed., *Aging in Canada: Social Perspectives*. Toronto: Fitzhenry and Whiteside.

Tjaden, P., and N. Thoennes. 2000. *Extent, Nature and Consequences of Intimate Partner Violence: Findings from the National Violence against Women Survey*. Ottawa: National Institute of Justice and the Centre for Disease Control Prevention.

Tjepkema, Michael. 2002. "The Health of the Off-Reserve Aboriginal Population." *Health Reports* 13, suppl.: 1–16. Statistics Canada Catalogue no. 82-003.

———. 2004. "Alcohol and Illicit Drug Dependence." *Health Reports* 15, suppl.: 9–19. Statistics Canada Catalogue no. 82-003.

———. 2005. "Non-fatal Injuries among Aboriginal Canadians." *Health Reports* 16, 2: 9–22. Statistics Canada Catalogue no. 82-003.

Tomiak, Monica, Jane F. Gentleman, and Maurice Jette. 1997. "Health and Gender Differences between Middle and Senior Managers in the Canadian Public Service." *Social Science and Medicine* 45, 10: 1589–96.

Tomic, Patricia, and Ricardo Trumper. 1992. "Canada and the Streaming of Immigrants: A Personal Account of the Chilean Case." Chapter 7 in Vic Satzewich, ed., *Deconstructing a Nation: Immigration, Multiculturalism and Racism in '90s Canada*. Halifax, NS: Fernwood Publishing and Social Research Unit, Department of Sociology, University of Saskatchewan.

Tope, D., and D. Jacobs. 2009. "The Politics of Union Decline: The Contingent Determinants of Union Recognition Elections and Victories." *American Sociological Review* 74: 842–64.

Townsend, P. 1981. "The Structured Dependency of the Elderly: A Creation of Social Policy in the Twentieth Century." *Ageing and Society* 1: 5–28.

Townson, Monica, and Kevin Hayes. 2007. *Women and the Employment Insurance Program: The Gender Impact of Current Rules on Eligibility and Earnings Replacement*. Ottawa: Status of Women Canada.

Tran, Kelly. 2004. "Visible Minorities in the Labour Force: 20 Years of Change." *Canadian Social Trends* 73, Summer: 7–11. Statistics Canada Catalogue no. 11-008.

Trovato, Frank. 2001. "Aboriginal Mortality in Canada, the United States and New Zealand." *Journal of Biosocial Science* 33: 67–86.

Trovato, Frank, and N.M. Lalu. 1995. "The Narrowing Sex Differential in Mortality in Canada since 1971." *Canadian Studies in Population* 22, 2: 145–67.

———. 2007. "From Divergence to Convergence: The Sex Differential in Life Expectancy in Canada, 1971–2000." *Canadian Review of Sociology and Anthropology* 44, 1: 101–22.

Trumper, Ricardo, and Lloyd L. Wong. 2007. "Canada's Guest Workers: Racialized, Gendered and Flexible." Pp. 151–74 in Sean P. Hier and B. Singh Bolaria, eds, *Race and Racism in 21st Century Canada: Continuity, Complexity, and Change*. Peterborough, ON: Broadview Press.

Tumin, Melvin. 1953. "Some Principles of Stratification: A Critical Analysis." *American Sociological Review* 18: 387–93.

Turcotte, Martin. 2013. "Family Caregiving: What Are the Consequences?" Catalogue no. 75-006-X. http://www.statcan.gc.ca/pub/75-006-x/2013001/article/11858-eng.pdf

Turcotte, Martin, and Grant Schellenberg. 2007. *A Portrait of Seniors in Canada, 2006*. Statistics Canada Catalogue no. 89-519-XIE.

Turner, Heather A., and R. Jay Turner. 2005. "Understanding Variations in Exposure to Social Stress." *Health: An Interdisciplinary Journal for the Social Study of Health, Illness & Medicine* 9, 2: 209–40.

Turner, J. Blake, and R. Jay Turner. 2013. "Social Relations, Social Integration, and Social Support." Pp. 341–56 in *Handbook of the Sociology of Mental Health*. Springer.

Turner, Jonathan H. 1988. *A Theory of Social Interaction*. Stanford, CA: Stanford University Press.

Turner, Jonathan H., and Leonard Beeghley. 1981. *The Emergence of Sociological Theory*. Homewood, IL: Dorsey Press.

Turner, R. Jay, and William R. Avison. 2003. "Status Variations in Stress Exposure: Implications for the Interpretation of Research on Race, Socioeconomic Status, and Gender." *Journal of Health and Social Behavior* 44, 4: 488–505.

Turner, R. Jay, and Donald A. Lloyd. 1999. "The Stress Process and the Social Distribution of Depression." *Journal of Health and Social Behavior* 40, 4: 374–404.

Turner, R. Jay, Blair Wheaton, and Donald A. Lloyd. 1995. "The Epidemiology of Social Stress." *American Sociological Review* 60: 104–25.

Ujimoto, Victor K. 1994. "Aging, Ethnicity and Health." Pp. 220–43 in B.S. Bolaria and H.D. Dickinson, eds, *Health, Illness and Health Care in Canada*, 2nd edn. Toronto: Harcourt Brace.

Umberson, Debra, and Jennifer Karas Montez. 2010. "Social Relationships and Health a Flashpoint for Health Policy." *Journal of Health and Social Behavior* 51, suppl. 1: S54–S66.

Urmetzer, Peter, and Neil Guppy. 2004. "Changing Income Inequality in Canada." Chapter 5 in James E. Curtis, Edward G. Grabb, and Neil L. Guppy, eds, *Social Inequality in Canada: Patterns, Problems, and Policies*, 2nd edn. Scarborough, ON: Prentice Hall Allyn and Bacon.

Ursel, Jane. 1990. "The State and the Maintenance of Patriarchy: A Case Study of Family, Labour, and Welfare Legislation in Canada." Pp. 108–45 in Arlene Tigar McLaren, ed., *Gender and Society: Creating a Canadian Women's Sociology*. Toronto: Copp Clark Pitman.

———. 1998. "Eliminating Violence against Women: Reform or Co-optation in State Institutions?" Chapter 7 in Les Samuelson and Wayne Antony, eds, *Power and Resistance: Critical Thinking about Canadian Social Issues*, 2nd edn. Halifax: Fernwood.

Valverde, Mariana. 1991. *The Age of Light, Soap, and Water: Moral Reform in English Canada, 1885–1925*. Toronto: McClelland & Stewart.

van Doorslaer, Eddy, Cristina Masseria, and Xander Koolman. 2006. "Inequalities in Access to Medical Care by Income in Developed Countries." *Canadian Medical Association Journal* 174, 2: 177–83.

Van Praet, Nicolas. 2008. "Manufacturing Slump Deepens: Auto Sector May Merely Be Canary in Mine to Troubled Economy in Ontario." *National Post*, 16 February.

van Ryn, Michelle, Diana Burgess, Jennifer Malat, and Joan Griffin. 2006. "Physicians' Perceptions of Patients' Social and Behavioral Characteristics and Race Disparities in Treatment Recommendations for Men with Coronary Artery Disease." *American Journal of Public Health* 96, 2: 351–7.

van Ryn, Michelle, and Jane Burke. 2000. "The Effect of Patient Race and Socio-economic Status on Physicians' Perceptions of Patients." *Social Science and Medicine* 50, 6: 813–28.

Verbrugge, Lois M. 1989. "The Twain Meet: Empirical Explanations of Sex Differences in Health and Mortality." *Journal of Health and Social Behavior* 30, 3: 282–304.

Vertinsky, Patricia. 1998. "'Run, Jane, Run': Central Tensions in the Current Debate about Enhancing Women's Health through Exercise." *Women and Health* 27, 4: 81–115.

Villarreal, M. Angeles, and Ian F. Fergusson. 2014. *NAFTA at 20: Overview and Trade Effects*. (CRS Report No. R42965). Washington, DC: Office of Congressional Information and Publishing.

Vinograd, Julia. 1997. *Dead People Laughing*. Berkeley, CA: Zeitgeist.

Vosko, Leah F. 2007. "Gendered Labour Market Insecurities: Manifestations of Precarious Employment in Different Locations." Chapter 3 in Vivian Shalla and Wallace Clement, eds, *Work in Tumultuous Times: Critical Perspectives.* Montreal and Kingston: McGill-Queen's University Press.

Wadsworth, M.E.J. 1997. "Health Inequalities in the Life Course Perspective." *Social Science and Medicine* 44, 6: 859–69.

Walby, Sylvia. 1989. "Theorizing Patriarchy." *Sociology* 23: 213–34.

———. 1990. *Theorizing Patriarchy.* Oxford: Basil Blackwell.

———. 1997. *Gender Transformations.* London: Routledge.

———. 2004. "The European Union and Gender Equality: Emergent Varieties of Gender Regime." *Social Politics* 11, 1: 4–29.

———. 2011. *The Future of Feminism.* Cambridge: Polity Press.

Walby, Sylvia, Jo Armstrong, and Sofia Strid. 2012. "Intersectionality and the Quality of the Gender Equality Architecture." *Social Politics* 19, 4: 446–81.

Walker, Alan. 1981. "Towards a Political Economy of Old Age." *Ageing and Society* 1: 74–94.

Walters, Vivienne. 1993. "Stress, Anxiety and Depression: Women's Accounts of Their Health Problems." *Social Science and Medicine* 36, 4: 393–402.

———. 2003. "The Social Context of Women's Health." Chapter 1 in *Women's Health Surveillance Report: A Multidimensional Look at the Health of Canadian Women.* Ottawa: Canadian Institute for Health Information.

Walters, Vivienne, Rhonda Lenton, Susan French, John Eyles, Janet Mayr, and Bruce Newbold. 1996. "Paid Work, Unpaid Work and Social Support: A Study of the Health of Women and Men Nurses." *Social Science and Medicine* 43, 11: 1627–36.

Walters, Vivienne, Peggy McDonough, and Lisa Strohschein. 2002. "The Influence of Work, Household Structure, and Social, Personal and Material Resources on Gender Differences in Health: An Analysis of the 1994 Canadian National Population Health Survey." *Social Science and Medicine* 54, 5: 677–92.

Wanner, Richard A. 1999. "Expansion and Ascription: Trends in Educational Opportunity in Canada, 1920–1994." *Canadian Review of Sociology and Anthropology* 36, 3: 409–42.

Wanner, Richard. 2001. "Diagnosing and Preventing 'Brain Waste' in Canada's Immigrant Population: A Synthesis of Comments on Reitz." *Journal of International Migration and Integration* 3 (2): 386–91.

Waterfall, Barbara. 2006. "Native Peoples and Child Welfare Practices: Implicating Social Work Education." Pp. 223–44 in Anne Westhues, ed., *Canadian Social Policy: Issues and Perspectives,* 4th edn. Waterloo, ON: Wilfrid Laurier University Press.

Waxman, H.C., J.P. Gray, and Y.N. Padrón. 2002. "Resiliency among Students at Risk of Academic Failure." *Yearbook of the National Society for the Study of Education* 101, 2: 29–48.

Weber, Max. [1922] 1978. *Economy and Society: An Outline of Interpretive Sociology.* Vol. 1. Edited by Guenther Roth and Claus Wittich. Berkeley: University of California Press.

Wellesley Institute 2013. "Poverty Is a Health Issue." Wellesley Institute Submission on the Ontario Poverty Reduction Strategy. Retrieved 29 February 2016 from http://www.wellesleyinstitute.com/wp-content/uploads/2013/09/Poverty-Reduction-Strategy-2013.pdf

Welsh, Sandy. 1999. "Gender and Sexual Harassment." *Annual Review of Sociology* 25: 169–90.

Welsh, Sandy, Jacquie Carr, Barbara MacQuarrie, and Audrey Huntley. 2006. "'I'm Not Thinking of It as Sexual Harassment': Understanding Harassment across Race and Citizenship." *Gender and Society* 20, 1: 87–107.

Wente, Margaret. 2006. "Cancer Care at the Grocer's." *Globe and Mail*, 16 November.

West, Candace, and Don Zimmerman. 1987. "Doing Gender." *Gender and Society* 1: 125–51.

Westhues, Anne, ed. 2006. *Canadian Social Policy: Issues and Perspectives,* 4th edn. Waterloo, ON: Wilfrid Laurier University Press.

Wheeler, Mark. 2007. "Being Strategic with Our Interventions." *Health Policy Research Bulletin* 14: 3–5.

Whitbeck, Les B., Dan R. Hoyt, Barbara J. McMorris, Xiaojin Chen, and Jerry D. Stubben. 2001. "Perceived Discrimination and Early Substance

Abuse among American Indian Children." *Journal of Health and Social Behavior* 42, 4: 405–24.

White, J.P., and J. Peters. 2013. "Editors' Commentary: The Challenges in Improving Indigenous Educational Attainment." *International Indigenous Policy Journal* 4, 4: 3.

Wiggers, R., and C.H. Arnold. 2011. *Defining, Measuring and Achieving "Student Success" in Ontario Colleges and Universities.* Higher Education Quality Council of Ontario.

Wight, Richard G., Amanda L. Botticello, and Carol S. Aneshensel. 2006. "Socioeconomic Context, Social Support, and Adolescent Mental Health: A Multilevel Investigation." *Journal of Youth and Adolescence* 35, 1: 115–26.

Wight, Richard G., Janet R. Cummings, Dana Miller-Martinez, Arun S. Karlamangla, Teresa E. Seeman, and Carol S. Aneshensel. 2008. "A Multilevel Analysis of Urban Neighborhood Socioeconomic Disadvantage and Health in Late Life." *Social Science and Medicine* 66, 4: 862–72.

Wilkins, Kathryn. 2006. "Predictors of Death in Seniors." *Health Reports* 16, suppl.: 57–67. Statistics Canada Catalogue no. 82-003.

Wilkins, Russell, Jean-Marie Berthelot, and Edward Ng. 2002. "Trends in Mortality by Neighbourhood Income in Urban Canada from 1971 to 1996." *Health Reports* 13, suppl.: 1–27. Statistics Canada Catalogue no. 82-003.

Wilkins, Russell, Sharanjit Uppal, Philippe Finès, Sacha Senécal, Éric Guimond, and Rene Dion. 2008. "Life Expectancy in the Inuit-Inhabited Areas of Canada, 1989 to 2003." *Health Reports* 19, 1: 1–14. Retrieved 26 February 2016 from http://search.proquest.com/openview/c8892d325d126a79f1a02e1a5360659b/1?pq-orig-site=gscholar

Wilkinson, Richard G., and Kate E. Pickett. 2006. "Income Inequality and Population Health: A Review and Explanation of the Evidence." *Social Science and Medicine* 62: 1768–84.

———. 2007. "The Problems of Relative Deprivation: Why Some Societies Do Better Than Others." *Social Science and Medicine* 65: 1965–78.

Wilkinson, Richard, Kate Pickett, and Robert B. Reich. 2011. *The Spirit Level: Why Greater Equality Makes Societies Stronger.* New York: Bloomsbury Press.

Williams, Cara. 2002. "Time or Money? How High and Low Income Canadians Spend Their Time." *Canadian Social Trends*, Summer: 7–11.

———. 2006. "Disability in the Workplace." *Perspectives on Labour and Income* 7, 2. Statistics Canada Catalogue no. 75-001-XIE.

———. 2010. "Women in Canada: A Gender-Based Statistical Report." *Economic Well-Being*, 6th edn. Component of Statistics Canada Catalogue no. 89-503-X.

Williams, Christine L. 1992. "The Glass Escalator: Hidden Advantages for Men in the 'Female' Professions." *Social Problems* 39, 3: 253–67.

———. 1995. *Still a Man's World: Men Who Do "Women's Work."* Berkeley: University of California Press.

Williams, David R. 2005. "The Health of U.S. Racial and Ethnic Populations." *Journals of Gerontology* 60B, spec. iss. 2: 53–62.

Williams, David R., and Chiquita Collins. 2004. "Reparations: A Viable Strategy to Address the Enigma of African American Health." *American Behavioral Scientist* 47, 7: 977–1000.

Williamson, Deanna L., et al. 2006. *Low-Income Canadians' Experiences with Health-Related Services: Implications for Health Care Reform.* Retrieved 29 February 2016 from http://homelesshub.ca/sites/default/files/LOW-IN~1.pdf

Willis, Paul. 1977. *Learning to Labour.* Farnborough, UK: Saxon House.

Willson, Andrea E., Kim M. Shuey, and Glen H. Elder. 2007. "Cumulative Advantage Processes as Mechanisms of Inequality in Life Course Health." *American Journal of Sociology* 112, 6: 1886–924.

Winson, Anthony, and Belinda Leach. 2002. *Contingent Work, Disrupted Lives: Labour and Community in the New Rural Economy.* Toronto: University of Toronto Press.

Wolfson, Michael, Geoff Rowe, Jane F. Gentleman, and Monica Tomiak. 1993. "Career Earnings and Death: A Longitudinal Analysis of Older Canadian Men." *Journal of Gerontology* 48, 4: S167–79.

Wollstonecraft, Mary. 1792. *A Vindication of the Rights of Woman: With Strictures on Political and Moral Subjects.* London.

World Bank. 2015. "Poverty Overview." Retrieved 10 February from http://www.worldbank.org/en/topic/poverty/overview/

World Health Organization. 2002. Preamble to the Constitution of the World Health Organization. Retrieved September 2002 from http://www.who.int/about/definition/en

———. 2003. "What Are the Main Risk Factors for Disability in Old Age and How Can Disability Be Prevented?" http://www.euro.who.int/__data/assets/pdf_file/0008/74708/E82970.pdf

———. 2007. *Third Milestones of a Global Campaign for Violence Prevention Report*. Geneva: World Health Organization. Retrieved February 2008. http://www.who.int/violence_injury prevention/violence/en/

World Health Organization. 2011. *World Health Report on Disability*. Retrieved February 2016 from http://www.who.int/disabilities/world_report/2011/report.pdf

Worts, D. 2005. "'It Just Doesn't Feel Like You're Obviously In': Housing Policy, Family Privacy, and the Reproduction of Social Inequality." *Canadian Review of Sociology and Anthropology* 42, 4: 445–65.

Wotherspoon, Terry. 2004. *The Sociology of Education in Canada: Critical Perspectives*, 2nd edn. Don Mills, ON: Oxford University Press.

Wright, E.O. 1985. *Classes*. London: Verso.

———. 1997. *Class Counts: Comparative Studies in Class Analysis*. Cambridge: Cambridge University Press.

———. 1999. "Foundations of Class Analysis: A Marxist Perspective." Paper presented to the annual meeting of the American Sociological Association, Chicago.

———. 2005. *Approaches to Class Analysis*. Cambridge: Cambridge University Press.

Wu, Sheng Hui, Jean Woo, and Xin-Hua Zhang. 2013. "Worldwide Socioeconomic Status and Stroke Mortality: An Ecological Study." *International Journal for Equity in Health* 12: 42.

Wu, Zheng, Samuel Noh, Violet Kaspar, and Christoph M. Schimmele. 2003. "Race, Ethnicity, and Depression in Canadian Society." *Journal of Health and Social Behavior* 44, 3: 426–41.

Wu, Zheng, Margaret J. Penning, and Christoph M. Schimmele. 2005. "Immigrant Status and Unmet Health Care Needs." *Canadian Journal of Public Health* 96, 5: 369–73.

http://www.ciaworldfactbook.com

http://www.indexmundi.com/canada/age_structure.html

http://www.tradingeconomics.com/canada/youth-unemployment-rate

Wyner, J., J. Bridgeland, and J. Diiulio. 2007. *The Achievement Trap: How America is Failing Millions of High-Achieving Students from Lower-Income Families*. Jack Kent Cooke Foundation.

Yezierska, Anzia. 1979. "A Window Full of Sky." In Anzia Yezierska, *The Open Cage*. New York: Persea Books.

Young, Iris. 1981. "Beyond the Unhappy Marriage: A Critique of the Dual Systems Theory." Pp. 43–69 in Lydia Sargent, ed., *The Unhappy Marriage of Marxism and Feminism: A Debate on Class and Patriarchy*. London: Pluto Press.

Zeitlin, I.M. 1990. *Ideology and the Development of Sociological Theory*, 4th edn. Englewood Cliffs, NJ: Prentice Hall.

Zeman, Klarka. 2007. "A First Look at Provincial Differences in Educational Pathways from High School to College and University." *Education Matters: Insights on Education, Learning and Training in Canada* 4, 2. Statistics Canada Catalogue no. 81-004-XIE. http://www.statcan.gc.ca/pub/81-004-x/2007002/9989-eng.htm

Zeng, Junxia, Xiaopeng Pang, Linxiu Zhang, Alexis Medina, and Scott Rozelle. 2014. "Gender Inequality in Education in China: A Meta-Regression Analysis." *Contemporary Economic Policy* 32, 2: 474–91.

Zhang, Xuelin, and Boris Palameta. 2006. *Participation in Adult Schooling and Its Earnings Impact in Canada*. Analytical Studies Branch Research Paper Series. Statistics Canada Catalogue no. 11F0019MIE, no. 276.

Zhang, Zhaoshu, and Qi Chen. 2014. "The Expansion of Higher Education Admissions and the Gender Equalization of Higher Education Opportunity: An Empirical Study Based on Chinese General Social Survey (CGSS2008) Data." *Journal of Chinese Sociology* 1: 1–19.

Zong, Li. 2007. "Recent Mainland Chinese Immigrants and Covert Racism in Canada." Pp. 111–30 in Sean P. Hier and B. Singh Bolaria, eds, *Race and Racism in 21st Century Canada: Continuity, Complexity, and Change*. Peterborough, ON: Broadview Press.

Index

Caribbean women: and immigration policies, 297, 305–6

caring and caring work, 166, 293, 310–11, 311–12, 312; and citizenship, 314; impact on paid work, 315

Caro, D.H., J.D. Willms, and J.T. McDonald, 223

categorically bounded network, 64

census, Canadian: definition of family, 162, 164

Chae, D.H., 276

charismatic authority, 32

chief executive officers (CEOs), 204

child abuse, 175–7; gender of victim, 176; relationship of victim to accused, 176–7

child care: and Conservative Party of Canada policies/platforms, 324; gendered division of responsibility for, 166–73, 242, 312; and Liberal Party policies/platforms, 325; and NDP policies/platforms, 325

children: and poverty, 208; reforming social policies on, 327; socialization of, 160

child welfare legislation, 317

Chinese Canadians, 304; discrimination, 304; second-class citizenship status, 304

Chinese workers, 297

chronic health conditions, 270; Aboriginal incidence of, 265; by gender, 269; hospitalization rates, 278; of older people, 272

citizen: definition of, 319

citizens: state support for elderly, 315–16

citizens and class, 296–303

citizenship: different identities, 318; in the Middle East, 296; over the life course, 314–18; rights of, 295

citizenship regime, 294

civil citizenship, 295; definition of, 319

civil rights: and Aboriginal peoples, 303

class: difficulty in defining, 22–4; and educational attainment, 221–2, 225–6, 228, 230; Goldthorpe's analysis of, 34–6; Marx's analysis of, 22–3; Wright's analysis of, 24–8; see also social class

class actions against governments, 302–3

class and education: historical notes and existing patterns, 221–32

class and occupational structure, 192–201

class-linked stress, 264; definition of, 288

class relations, 10; and globalization, 38–9; of older people, 112; in production processes, 193

class reproduction: definition of, 136

class situation, 31

class typologies and schema: Clement and Miles's, 28; Goldthorpe's, 34–6; Grabb's, 37; Wright's, 27

Clement, Wallace, 28, 192, 193, 210

cluttered nest, 169; definition of, 185

Coates, Ken, 146

Codjoe, Henry, 248

cohort: Ryder's definition of, 103

cohort centrism, 101

cohort flow, 99, 103

cohorts, 101; definition of, 116

Collins, Patricia Hill, 60

Coming of Post-Industrial Society, The (Bell), 209–10

common-law families, 160, 161

Common School Act, 233

communicative action, 123

Communist Manifesto (Marx), 22

compulsory heterosexuality, 179; definition of, 185

conformation: definition of, 151, 155

Connelly, M.P., 293

Connidis, I.A., and J.A. McMullin, 138

Conservative Party of Canada: policies and platforms, 324

Constant Flux, The (Goldthorpe), 34

Cooper, H., 270

Cooper, H., J. Lindsay, and S. Greathouse, 224

core sector, 211

Corman, J., 172

corporate agents, 133

correctional services, federal, 307

Côté, J.E., 71, 109

Coulombe, S., 238

Courtenay, W.H., 280

Coward, R.T., 273

credentialism, 33

Creutzfeldt-Jakob disease (CJD): new strain (VCJD), 272

critical theory, 9, 18; assumptions, 138

Crompton, S., 260

cultural capital, 219; definition of, 250; and education, 224

cumulative advantage/disadvantage hypothesis, 197; definition of, 214

Curtis, B., 222

Curtis, B., D.W. Livingston, and D. Smaller, 224

Curtis, J., 195

Curtis, L.J., and W.J. MacMinn, 278

Daigle, Chantal, 312

Das Gupta, Tania, 184

date rape, 179